N

I

8

M:

The

HOUSE *of* LABOR

Internal Operations of
American Unions

The

HOUSE *of* LABOR

Internal Operations of American Unions

Edited by

J. B. S. Hardman

Maurice F. Neufeld

Professor, N. Y. State School of
Industrial and Labor Relations, Cornell University

PREPARED UNDER THE AUSPICES OF THE

Inter-Union Institute, Inc.

PRENTICE-HALL, INC.   New York

1951

PRENTICE-HALL INDUSTRIAL RELATIONS AND PERSONNEL SERIES

DALE YODER, *EDITOR*

PRINTED IN THE UNITED STATES OF AMERICA

Foreword

THIS VOLUME GREW OUT OF A STUDY INITIATED SEVERAL YEARS AGO BY THE Inter-Union Institute, Inc. The aim was two-fold: (1) to acquaint persons outside of organized labor with the "inside" of the fifteen-million-strong American labor movement, its performance, and motivation; and (2) to present to the participants in union activity an over-all view of their group activities in the promotion of union objectives.

While books and the press keep the interested public reasonably well informed on the major lines of union activity—labor-management negotiations, contractual relations, and strikes—relatively little is known on the outside of the vast, continually expanding, and largely intra-mural activities within the union edifice. Confined in earlier years to carrying on educational activities of rather limited content, and to developing press-publicity that might prove helpful to the union's negotiations, the internal union activities have since developed in both scope and variety, and are now concerned with: politics, research, press, public relations, education, community and welfare action, health and life insurance, retirement pensions, international activity, and the complicated problems of modern union administration. This volume seeks to do justice to this aspect of American unionism.

The title of the book, *The House of Labor*, derives from the term which Mr. William Green, President of the American Federation of Labor, frequently uses when he speaks of the oneness of labor—this despite some very sizeable quarrels among the dwellers on the common lot, but under separate roofs.

Most of the writing for this book was done by leading staff members of a number of national unions, in charge of important union activities and working in close cooperation with the union heads. They write out of intimate and extensive familiarity with the subjects they cover, each writer dealing with the realities of his respective functional engagement and presenting the problems which he encounters in the discharge of his task. The contributors to this volume have not sought publicity for their

v

particular union or phase of union activity; their aim has been to inform and to analyze, to point up the general logic of specialized endeavors.

The House of Labor is the first full-sized, privately-produced book in which the "union staff" dominates the writing. Union staff members, although not policy determinators, are nonetheless close to the process of policy shaping and, barring lack of willingness to try, they cannot help exercising influence. So they have a significant story to tell. In the closing section of the book—Part Eight—members of the staff hold a "bull session," telling what they think of their functions, responsibilities, and opportunities. To their statements are added the views of a national labor leader of the "younger set," and of several "academicians" who have been closely linked with the labor field in their day-to-day and extra-curricular activities, or who have observed it at close range for a considerable length of time.

As the study expanded to include practically all phases of vital internal union action, it appeared logical to precede it with a general, coordinated view of the movement as a whole; this was done in the introductory Part One.

The initial planning of the volume and the execution of the project: gathering and organization of material, and editing, were carried on by the Editorial Board of the Inter-Union Institute, Inc.: Messrs. Solomon Barkin, Henry David, J. B. S. Hardman, C. Wright Mills, Broadus Mitchell, Larry Rogin, Mark Starr, and the Executive Secretary, Pauline W. Fox. In the second, expanded stage of the work, Professor Maurice F. Neufeld joined the Chairman, as co-editor of the book, in completing the editorial tasks.

The Inter-Union Institute, Inc.
J. B. S. Hardman, Chairman

Who's Who of Contributors

Thelma E. Anderson, b. 1921; B.A., Brooklyn College; graduate study in sociology at Columbia University. Formerly Research Assistant, Bureau of Applied Social Research, Columbia; currently Research Analyst at International Public Opinion Research, Inc.

Solomon Barkin, b. 1907; B.S., College of the City of New York; M.A., Columbia University. Instructor, City College (1928-31); later, Assistant Director of Research, N. Y. State Commission on Old Age Security; Assistant Director, Labor Advisory Board, NRA Chief, Labor Section, Division of Industrial Economics, Department of Commerce. Since 1937, Director of Research, Textile Workers Union of America (CIO). U.S. Delegate to Inter-American Statistical Institute, 1948; Textile Consultant, United Kingdom Mission, ECA, 1948.

Alfred Braunthal, b. 1897; Ph.D., University of Vienna. Formerly Research Director, United Hatters, Cap and Millinery Workers International Union (AFL). At present, head of Economic and Social Department, International Confederation of Free Trade Unions.

John M. Brumm, b. 1910; B.A., University of Michigan (1930); M.A., Harvard (1931). Has been an economist for the Industrial Relations Branch, Bureau of Labor Statistics; Research Director, Dyers Federation, TWUA, and a sociology and economics teacher. Currently, Professor of Labor and Industrial Relations at the University of Illinois Institute of Labor and Industrial Relations.

James B. Carey, b. 1911; First full-time job was with a radio laboratory, testing, trouble-shooting, balancing and inspection work; active in organization of union. Vice-President, Philadelphia Central Labor Union; General Organizer, AFL (1934); President, United Electrical, Radio and Machine Workers (CIO), 1936-1941. Secretary of the CIO from 1938 to 1942, Secretary-Treasurer in 1942. He has headed the International Union of Electrical, Radio and Machine Workers since its inception in 1949. CIO's representative at establishment of International Confederation of Free Trade Unions.

Lewis Carliner, b. 1909; B.A., George Washington University. At one time, Editor, *Consumers Guide*, Department of Agriculture; now Managing Editor of *Ammunition*, official publication of the Education Department, United Automobile Workers (CIO).

Gordon H. Cole, b. 1912; B.A., Syracuse University; Editor, *The Machinist*, official weekly of the International Association of Machinists. Was labor reporter, for fifteen years, for *United States News*, the newspaper *PM*, and the *Wall Street Journal*. Past president of the Washington Newspaper Guild.

John D. Connors, b. 1903; Boston University, College of Business Administration; graduate work at Boston University and Harvard. Director, Workers Education Bureau, AFL, since 1943; Vice-President, American Federation of Teachers (1937-47).

Henry David, b. 1907; B.A., College of the City of New York; M.A. and Ph.D., Columbia. Taught history at C.C.N.Y., 1932-38; Professor of History, Queens College, since 1938. On leave during the war to serve as Director of Research for British Broadcasting Corporation, and its adviser on American affairs until 1947. Author, *The History of the Haymarket Affair;* co-author, *Labor Problems in America; History of Western Civilization.* Co-editor, two series of volumes: *Labor in Twentieth Century America; Economic History of the U.S.*

Helen S. Dinerman, b. 1920; graduate study in sociology, Columbia University (M.A., 1948). Formerly, Research Analyst for Bureau of Applied Social Research at Columbia; Research Associate, Scientific Department, American Jewish Committee. At present, study director for International Public Opinion Research, Inc.

Agnes M. Douty, b. 1910; B.A., Hunter College; M.A., Teachers College, Columbia University. Formerly on education staff, Amalgamated Clothing Workers (CIO); Assistant Director, Georgia Workers Education Service; Workers' Education Specialist, U.S. Office of Education; Director of Workers' Education Training Course for School for Workers, University of Wisconsin.

Warren F. Draper, b. 1883; B.A., Amherst College; M.D., Harvard Medical School. Dr. Draper has been Executive Medical Officer for the United Mine Workers' Welfare and Retirement Fund since 1948. Medical Officer, U.S. Public Health Service, 1910-1947; Assistant Surgeon General, 1922-39, and Deputy Surgeon General, 1939 to 1947.

Katherine P. Ellickson, b. 1905; B.A., Vassar College; graduate work, Columbia University. Assistant Director of Research, CIO. At one time, Instructor, Bryn Mawr Summer School, and Brookwood Labor College; economic researchist for NLRB, and editor of Statistical Reports, Social Security Board.

Eleanor Finger, b. 1919; B.A. and M.A., Wellesley College. Is at present Labor Specialist for the Economic Cooperation Administration. Formerly, Assistant Professor of Economics, Champlain College; Labor Specialist for Department of Labor and Social Security Administration.

Henry C. Fleisher, b. 1912; B.A., Amherst College, 1934. With the CIO Publicity Department since 1937; at present Assistant Publicity Director. Served with the U.S. Army 1943 to 1945; assigned to OSS in Italy and Austria.

Joseph Glazer, b. 1919; B.A., Brooklyn College; graduate work, University of Wisconsin and New York University. Education Director, United Rubber Workers (CIO); formerly in Education Department, TWUA-CIO (1944-50).

Ruth Glazer, b. 1922; B.A., Queens College. Recently on staff of *Labor and Nation;* formerly with Education Department, Amalgamated Clothing Workers (CIO).

William Gomberg, b. 1911; B.S., C.C.N.Y.; M.A., New York University; Ph.D., Columbia. Director, Management Engineering Department, International Ladies' Garment Workers' Union (AFL). Toured Europe in 1950 as special consultant to ECA.

J. B. S. Hardman, b. 1882; studied law at University of St. Petersburg, Russia. Exiled from Russia in 1908, by Order-in-Council of Imperial Government for participation in social-democratic and labor union activities. Graduate work, Columbia University School of Political and Social Sciences (1910-1913). Education Director, Amalgamated Clothing Workers (CIO), and Editor of the union's publication, *The Advance* (1920-44). Currently, Editor, *Labor and Nation;* Chairman, Inter-Union Institute, Inc. Co-author and Editor, *American Labor Dynamics;* author, *Rendezous with Destiny.*

Marion H. Hedges, b. 1888; B.A., DePauw University; M.A., Harvard. Special Assistant to the Labor Advisers, Economic Cooperation Administration. He has been Research Director for the International Brotherhood of Electrical Workers (AFL); deputy delegate and labor adviser to the first International Labor Conference (1935); and member of Planning Committee of War Production Board.

William C. Hushing, b. 1883. Chairman, National Legislative Committee, American Federation of Labor. Worked as molder and patternmaker, and later foreman patternmaker; was Secretary-Treasurer, St. Louis Patternmakers Association; legislative representative, Canal Zone Central Labor Union (1922-26), and general organizer and legislative representative for the AFL (1928-40).

Herbert B. Jackman, b. 1919; Antioch College and Ohio State University; Ph.B., University of Chicago. Director of Film Division, United Automobile Workers (CIO).

A. E. Kazan, b. 1888; started union career as clerk for the ILGWU-AFL, rose to position of secretary of one of its larger locals. Later joined the staff of the Amalgamated Clothing Workers. As President of the Amalgamated Housing Corporation, Mr. Kazan has, for the past twenty-five years, managed the large and successful ACWA cooperative housing enterprises.

Joseph D. Keenan, b. 1896; Director, Labor's League for Political Education, American Federation of Labor. Secretary of the International Brotherhood of Electrical Workers (AFL) in Chicago for fifteen years; later, Secretary, Chicago Federation of Labor. Has served as Chief of the Manpower Division, Allied Control Commission for Germany, and Vice-Chairman, Labor Production, WPB.

W. P. Kennedy, b. 1892; President, Brotherhood of Railroad Trainmen since August 1949. His first train service job was as a freight brakeman at 17; active member of the BRT, he became successively local union chairman, general chairman, and lodge delegate to the national union conventions; elected member of the Board of Trustees in 1928, and named a vice-president in 1935.

Joseph Kovner, b. 1909; B.A., Yale College; LL.B., Yale Law School. Assistant General Counsel, CIO (1937-1942); counsel to WPB labor vice-chairmen (1942-44); Research Associate, Johns Hopkins Labor Organization Study (1944-47); Special Counsel, American Federation of Musicians and International Typographical Union (1947-49). Since 1949, attorney on staff of Department of Justice.

Jack Kroll, b. 1885; Vice-President, Amalgamated Clothing Workers and manager of the union's Cincinnati Joint Board. Director since 1946, of CIO Political Action Committee. President, Ohio State CIO Council.

William M. Leiserson, b. 1883; B.A., University of Wisconsin; Ph.D., Columbia; LL.D., Oberlin. Professor of Economics, Antioch College (1925-34); Chairman, National Mediation Board (1934-39); member, National Labor Relations Board (1939-43); visiting professor, Johns Hopkins University (1944-47); member, President's Commission on Migratory Labor (1950).

Lawrence Levin, b. 1912; studied at University of Chicago and American Institute of Banking. Formerly, Assistant Director, Education Department, Amalgamated Clothing Workers; assistant to Secretary-Treasurer, ACWA; lecturer in finance, Roosevelt College. Currently, Assistant Cashier, Amalgamated Trust & Savings Bank, Chicago.

Val R. Lorwin is at present engaged in a study of the French trade union movement, under the auspices of Harvard University. He has taught history at Cornell University and Brooklyn College; has worked in the Department of Labor, and for the Division of International Labor Affairs, Department of State. Served as adviser on various United States delegations to UN meetings.

Robert S. Lynd, b. 1892; B.A., Princeton University; Ph.D., Columbia. Professor of Sociology, Columbia University. Co-author, with Helen Merrell Lynd, of *Middletown* and *Middletown in Transition.*

C. Wright Mills, b. 1916; B.A. and M.A., University of Texas; Ph.D., University of Wisconsin. Associate Professor, University of Maryland (1940-45). Now Associate Professor, Department of Sociology, Columbia University. Author, *New Men of Power;* editor and translator, with H. H. Gerth, *Max Weber: Essays in Sociology;* co-author, with Clarence Senior and Rose K. Goldsen, *The Puerto Rican Journey.*

Broadus Mitchell, b. 1892; B.A., University of South Carolina; Ph.D., Johns Hopkins University. Professor of Economics, Rutgers University. Formerly, Acting Director of Research, ILGWU-AFL; member of faculty, Johns Hopkins and New York University. Author, *Depression Decade;* co-author with Louise P. Mitchell, *American Economic History.*

Emanuel Muravchik, b. 1916; B.S., Columbia University; graduate work, New School for Social Research. National Field Director, Jewish Labor Committee. Formerly, Executive Director, Veterans League of America; organizer, ILGWU-AFL.

Maurice F. Neufeld, b. 1910; B.A. and M.A., University of Wisconsin, 1932; Ph.D., University of Wisconsin, 1935. Professor of Industrial and Labor Relations, School of Industrial and Labor Relations, Cornell University. Past activities include: Executive Officer, Sicily, Naples, Rome, and Milan Regions, American Military Government; Deputy Commissioner of Commerce, New York State; Chairman, Governor's Committee on Postwar Employment; Education Director, Trenton local, ILGWU; organizer, ACWA.

Morris S. Novik, b. 1903; Formerly, Director, Municipal Broadcasting System, City of New York; radio consultant to the AFL, ILGWU, and UAW. Currently, Executive Secretary, National Association of Educational Broadcasters.

Leo Perlis, b. 1912; National Director, CIO Community Services Committee since 1943. Has worked in textile mills, garment center, and retail shops; helped to organize laundry workers, teachers, textile workers, rubber workers, newspapermen. Edited *Paterson Press* (1936); *New Jersey LNPL News* (1938); *American Labor Party News* (1940).

Eric Peterson, b. 1894; General Secretary-Treasurer, International Association of Machinists (Ind.) Mr. Peterson has been with the IAM since 1913 and has served as Local Lodge Officer, District Lodge Officer, Grand Lodge Representative, and General Vice-President.

Esther Peterson, b. 1906; A.B., Brigham Young University; M.A., Teachers College, Columbia University. Taught at Bryn Mawr Summer School for Women Workers in Industry; Assistant Director, Department of Cultural Activities, ACWA-CIO (1939-44). More recently, she served as ACWA legislative representative in Washington.

Nora Piore, b. 1912; B.A. and M.A., University of Wisconsin. Mrs. Piore is at present a free-lance writer. Past activities include: Program Consultant, USO Division, YWCA; Education Director, New York Women's Trade Union League; Education Director, Philadelphia Joint Board, ACWA.

Victor Reuther, b. 1912; studied at University of West Virginia and Wayne University. Director of Education, United Automobile Workers (CIO). Has served as Director, War Policy Division, UAW; and as local union officer, international representative, and organizer for the union.

Lawrence Rogin, b. 1909; B.A. and M.A., Columbia University. Instructor, Columbia University Extension Division (1932-33) and Brookwood Labor College (1935-37). Education Director, American Federation of Hosiery Workers (1937-41). Education Director, Textile Workers Union of America (CIO), since 1941.

Morris Sackman, b. 1921; B.A., Brooklyn College; M.S. in industrial and labor relations, Cornell University. Supervisor, Sick Benefit Department, Dressmakers' Union, ILGWU-AFL, since 1948. Formerly on research staff, Industrial Union of Marine & Shipbuilding Workers (CIO); Research Assistant, School of Industrial and Labor Relations at Cornell.

Sidney S. Shulman, b. 1916; B.S., Temple University. Partner in firm of Roy E. Williams and Company, Accountants and Analysts. Member, American Arbitration Association; American Institute of Accountants. Formerly, international representative, Industrial Union of Marine & Shipbuilding Workers.

Arthur Stark, b. 1919; B.A. and M.A., University of Chicago. Assistant Executive Secretary, New York State Board of Mediation, since 1947. Education Director, Chicago Joint Board, ACWA (1940-42); principal field examiner, National Labor Relations Board (1942-47).

Mark Starr, b. 1894; Education Director, International Ladies' Garment Workers' Union since 1935. Worked in the mines of South Wales before coming to the U. S. in 1928 to teach British Labor History at Brookwood Labor College; also taught at Bryn Mawr Summer School. Was Vice-President, American Federation of Teachers (1940-42). His books include: *Trade Unionism: Past and Future, Lies and Hate in Education*, and *Labor Looks at Education*.

George H. Wartenberg, b. 1918; Editor, *Cincinnati Sun*, a CIO labor publication. Member, CIO-PAC public relations staff in Washington. Formerly, research analyst and investigator for U. S. Treasury Department and American Military Government in Germany. Member, State Department "Safe Haven" team in Germany, 1946.

Abraham Weiss, b. 1913; B. A., Brooklyn College; M. A., Georgetown University. Mr. Weiss is a labor economist for the Division of Industrial Relations of the U. S. Department of Labor's Bureau of Labor Statistics.

Matthew Woll, b. 1880; studied at Kent College of Law and Lake Forest University. Vice-President, American Federation of Labor. Editor, *The American Photo-Engraver*, monthly publication of the International Photo-Engravers Union which Mr. Woll formerly headed. President, AFL Union Label Trades Department, and Union Labor Life Insurance Company.

Contents

PART SEVEN: UNION EDUCATION ACTIVITY

PART EIGHT: THE UNION STAFF—FUNCTION AND AIM

APPENDICES

PART ONE

The American Labor Movement

Introduction

The American labor movement

FULL-SCALE UNION OPERATION IN-
cludes a wide variety of activities.
Central and most publicized are those
that are involved in the process of
union organization and collective bargaining. Less known are the many
collateral and auxiliary union activities
that aim at facilitating and making
ever more effective the main objective of unionism: an advantageous
and satisfying labor-management relationship. These manifold collateral
endeavors of American unions are the
subject matter of this book: legislative pressuring and political cam-
paigning; economic research; public
relations; problems of union government; communication; industrial engineering plans; public and member
education; health and welfare programs; participation in community
activities; recreational and cultural
pursuits; and international labor relations.

However, labor unionism does not
function in a vacuum nor in an isolation ward. It is an integral part of the
evolving American community, affected by it and in turn influencing
the play of forces within the community. Consequently, all union activities, whether collateral or central,
tend to be progressively significant in
the measure that they reflect and bear

upon the environing circumstances of
national economic and political reality. Indeed, the notable expansion of
American unions in recent years followed closely upon the insistent and
consistent activation of union interest
in national issues, broadly political as
well as economic.

In this first, introductory, part of
the book the several writers aim at relating the whole of unionism to the
national and international socio-economic and political milieu in which
the movement operates and which affects the orientation and course of
union action. To that end the several
chapters of Part One have the following objectives:

(a) to depict the broad, over-all
sense or motivation of unionism,
which prompts the activities in which
its leaders and members engage, and
consequently determines the place the
union movement occupies in the
American community;

(b) to familiarize readers with the
organizational anatomy of unionism,
the origins of and the relations between the two major federations—the
American Federation of Labor and
the Congress of Industrial Organizations, and to acquaint readers with
the several non-affiliated national
unions, as well as the working inter-

relation of parts within each of the national centers;

(c) to present a collective portraiture of the leadership of labor unionism, of the background influence and intellectual endowment which the leaders bring to the performance of their task, and whatever information is obtainable about the members of the unions.

There is no final word on the "theory" of the union movement. By its very nature, union action is experimental and pragmatic. And, more specifically, under the circumstances which attended the earlier period of union development, the leadership and the practices of American unionism in the first several decades of this century leaned more heavily upon an individualist orientation than upon a broad labor mutualism; as a result there was an active antagonism toward any attempt to generalize specific experiences into a general behavior pattern. The first quarter of the century was particularly the age of "the theory of no theory," and labor appeared to be—as its authori-

tative spokesmen would have it—a loosely associated multitude of organizations, sentimentally linked by the fact of sharing a common economic lot, rather than a cohesive movement with an appreciable common intellectual denominator and shared sense of direction. But a striking change in orientation took place with the deepening of the Great Depression in the early thirties, the pace accelerated by the oncoming World War II and the developments in its wake. A growing number of unions have since recognized that they are a movement. Nonetheless, the period of reorientation has been relatively brief, and the students of the process are not of one mind as to the full significance of what has been taking place. Judgment expressed in the chapters of this part of *The House of Labor,* in so far as it relates to the state of the movement, represents individual interpretations. Indeed, each writer in this volume bears the responsibility for the views he entertains wherever he touches on matters beyond ascertainable facts.

J. B. S. HARDMAN

Chapter I

State of the unions

UP TO THE CLOSE OF THE NINETEENTH CENTURY, AMERICAN DEVELOPMENT, as interpreted by Frederick Jackson Turner and his followers, was to a large degree the history of the colonization of the Great West. Accordingly, the existence of an area of free land open to settlement created the most signal influence upon our national life up to 1900. Since that date, a force of comparable magnitude in the evolution of American democracy may well prove to be the ascendance of organized labor to a position of national and world prestige. If this hypothesis should be confirmed by the course of our history after 1950, then we shall need to re-examine our immediate past. We shall have to look back upon the existence of large unorganized segments in American industry and their slow unionization during the run of five tumultuous decades as the most significant influence upon American economic, political, and social development in the first half of the twentieth century.

The conquest of the West by the bearers of civilization and the humanizing of industry by organized labor parallel each other, as historical phenomena, at yet another point: the orbit of popular understanding. The heroic aspects of the frontier process still stir the popular imagination to the exclusion of other facets that are equally vital. Even up to the present day, mass attention has centered in the banded struggles of our hardy pioneering ancestors against the inimical forces of nature and the furious attacks of the Red Men. In contrast, the rise of cities in the wilderness, the beginnings of trade, the planting of industries, and the founding of transportation systems have not attracted wide appeal. Repeating this pattern, the popular mind has grasped at the more colorful and bold episodes in the American labor movement as its distinguishing features: violent strikes and lockouts, embattled picket lines, and bitter court struggles. The creation by "the unlettered statesmen of labor" of wholly novel institutions, the unions, and of a new form of industrial democracy, the collective agreement, has eluded common notice. Moreover, the emergence of highly significant administrative and governmental

5

arrangements within the unions has failed to receive the close attention of even the scholars.

In the next half century, therefore, as the labor movement in the United States moves across the historical horizon silhouetted as grandly as the figures of government and management, the internal life of the unions will necessarily assume full stature and compel national interest. This book, in which labor experts of the present time describe the various administrative functions they perform, looks out toward the future when labor unions will be more generally recognized as administrative, institutional, and political entities as well as economic organizations. Perhaps, too, the nonbargaining responsibilities of unions, which contribute so notably to the welfare of their membership, might even replace the strike as the popular concept associated with the American labor movement.

This labor movement, claiming a membership of 15,600,000 adherents, does not constitute a single administrative entity that can establish economic, political, and social policy for all American unions. Organized workers belong to 209 national and international unions, which cover the trades and industries of the country and actually control the destiny of the movement. Since November 1935, the loyalties of most organized workers, with the enduring, important exception of the railroad brotherhoods, have been divided between the two great houses of labor, the AFL and the CIO. Although they are federations possessing considerable moral force, they have not as yet attempted to exert fundamental controls (except in the two instances of the AFL in 1937 and the CIO in 1949) over the internationals affiliated with them.

The labor movement, therefore, must be thought of as many-dimensional. During periods of crises, like those of the Taft-Hartley controversy, there ensues a drawing together of the internationals and of the two houses of labor against the world. The labor movement then takes on a semblance of unity. (In 1950, this semblance brightened into hope as statements endorsing unity came from Philip Murray, William Green, John L. Lewis, and Al Hayes of the Machinists). It is this aspect of American unionism upon which friends of labor prefer to dwell and which, in a real sense, represents the enduring qualities of the labor movement. But two houses of labor, made up of largely independent internationals, do exist at the moment, and labor's friends cannot ignore the implications of this reality on the labor landscape.

1. THE AMERICAN FEDERATION OF LABOR

The older house, the American Federation of Labor, is proud of its 8,000,000 sons and daughters. Most of them are now grown and do not reside in the parental home at 901 Massachusetts Avenue, N. W., in Washington, D. C. They have smaller homes of their own scattered throughout the country: the headquarters of the 107 national and inter-national unions federated with the AFL. But some of the children still live at home. They are the five councils (similar to the "organizing com-mittees" of the CIO), which are progressing from adolescence to full-fledged international-union adulthood. They continue to function under the direct surveillance of the parent body. There are also 1,204 federal labor unions that, for varying reasons, do not adhere to any one of the 107 international unions. The national AFL charters these federal locals directly. The national parental bonds also stretch forth from Washington to embrace 50 state and territorial (Alaska and Puerto Rico) federations and 811 city central organizations.

In Washington, the head of the household, President William Green, carries out his responsibilities with the aid of Secretary-Treasurer George Meany. They occupy the front row of what might be considered a family portrait. Ranged behind them stand the 13 vice-presidents, for the most part the stronger older brothers of the 107 international unions. They are chosen at large to guide the destiny of the entire family.

This circle comprises the powerful Executive Council of the Federa-tion. Although the whole family assembles in convention, through repre-sentatives, once a year, in addition to these annual gatherings, William Green and the other members of the Executive Council convene in various parts of the country every three months. At these Council meetings, matters of urgent policy are fought out and the press is then informed of the decisions.

The staff that aids in the work of the household is generally expert and devoted. Its responsibilities center around a counsel, a director of organization, permanent representatives in Europe with offices in Brussels and Frankfort, participants in the work of the ILO, the ECA, and the UN, a full-time representative cooperating in the activities of the Inter-American Confederation of Workers, a research director, a committee of legislative agents, a director of publicity, and the editors of the chief publications: *AFL Weekly News Service*, *The Federationist*, and *Labor's Monthly Survey*. The Workers' Education Bureau was adopted by the AFL in 1923 and since then has been close to the family's public life. In October 1947, the family decided to welcome another foster child—Labor's League for Political Education. In 1950, the Workers' Education Bureau finally became an official department of the AFL. There is, of course, a close connection between this development and the AFL's reinforced interest in large-scale political action.

What purpose, then, does this top family group and its staff serve? One of the chief activities of the AFL centers around a preoccupation with the molding of labor opinion. Selig Perlman and Philip Taft in their *History of Labor in the United States, 1896-1932* have stated that the officers and leaders of the Federation attempt to develop a unified labor will by nourishing the art of persuasion. Mention of the necessity for entreaty within a family brings the mind to attention. Cannot President Green and the older Executive Council brothers, who together speak so authoritatively in labor's name, issue orders that are obeyed? The history of American labor in the nineteenth and twentieth centuries illuminates this necessary weakness of the AFL (as well as of the CIO) structure. At the same time it also brings to light the strongest characteristic of the family: its continued existence through moral suasion rather than force.

The strong internationals that banded together in 1886 and decided to call themselves brothers, and then proceeded to choose a father, antedated the family in time and eclipsed it in power and funds. They insisted then, and still insist, upon real independence. International unions, be they AFL or CIO, are jealous of their own firesides and will fight any brother or sister foolhardy enough to try to partake of their warmth. In the AFL, particularly, because it accommodates over 100 internationals whose fundamental structure rests upon fine craft and multicraft distinctions (as contrasted to the CIO's 33 industrially based internationals), jurisdictional disputes have been rampant since the earliest days of federation. The craft principle of organization has been zealously guarded by declaration even when concessions were made to occasional structural modifications. The parent organization, therefore, in addition to molding labor opinion, is called upon to serve as a family council of last resort when its children take to squabbling among themselves. At certain grave times, after wayward offspring refuse to abide by parental suggestions and, finally, orders, the dark power of disownment is employed. They can henceforth never again seek shelter within the AFL (or CIO) until they make amends. Sometimes a union like the International Association of Machinists persists in being stubborn and prospers, nonetheless, away from home, to the tune of 1,800 locals with 624,000 members.

Since the walls of the AFL are not completely solid, since outright fighting within may topple them, and since upraised voices and public expulsion always result in scandal and a show of weakness, the AFL has sought to smother its quarrels under a blanket of administrative padding. Four departments have been created to accomplish unity through persuasion and compromise wherever possible. The Building and Construction Trades are covered in one department. In 1948, to improve its chances at peace-making, the department consented to the creation of a National Joint Board for the Settlement of Jurisdictional Disputes in the Building and Construction Industry, a device that includes representatives of the employers as well as an impartial chairman. The other three departments handle the jurisdictional and collective bargaining problems of the Metal Trades, Maritime Trades, and Railway Employees. These departments also have progeny of their own: 1,200 state and local councils.

A fifth department promotes union standards of workmanship through the use of the label and has no connection with the problem of jurisdictional disputes. Another unofficial department is the Government Employes Council. It performs functions for government employees in AFL unions similar to those undertaken by the trades departments. For this reason, although it is not listed as a department, it is mentioned here. The Government Employes Council is composed of 22 unions.

The test of a home lies in the perpetual hope that it will be moderately happy, relatively stable, and reasonably prolific and well-fed. Although complete unity and harmony are not the perfect adjectives with which to describe the parent body of AFL unions, yet it can be said without straining the facts that the home on Massachusetts Avenue still stands solidly. Even after the defection of some of its stronger sons in 1935, it has become sturdier and not weaker. Its large influence on our national and international life cannot be questioned. And contrary to the criers of doom in 1935, its leaders still display an amazing and biblical virility of purpose and accomplishment.

2. THE CONGRESS OF INDUSTRIAL ORGANIZATIONS

Before the CIO purge of November 1949, the 40 (now 33) international and national unions affiliated with the second house of labor had carved out for themselves an equal number of jurisdictions, which recognized no union-made craft boundaries, but stretched across the far reaches of entire industries. The 6,000,000 (prepurge) vigorous offspring, despite their radical reputation in some circles, claim a highly fashionable national address at 718 Jackson Place, N. W., in Washington, D. C. And if any of these CIO members should care to visit the Capital City, they could easily view from their modern offices, within less distance than the stretch of a good picket line, the White House on Pennsylvania Avenue.

The house of the CIO was founded upon the curious bedrock of dissension, first, and then civil war; the unsatisfied ambitions of vigorous and able leaders chafing within the AFL; and a simple idea about the obvious efficacy of organizing industrially. This notion, which rested upon the economic, social, and political realities of the decade, grew, through unbending opposition by the AFL, into a first principle of the CIO.

At the October 1935 Convention of the AFL in Atlantic City, the CIO was not only conceived, but its later birth was also assured by the hostility of certain international union leaders to the idea of industrial unionism. While several leaders of the older AFL unions struggled for the right of industrial workers to organize into unions unhampered by jurisdictional jealousies, the industrial union resolution they sponsored was lost.

When later in November 1935, the presidents of eight AFL internationals formed the Committee for Industrial Organization, they laid the cornerstone for an enduring new home without quite realizing it. So, too, the AFL Executive Council unwittingly raised up an abiding wall of enmity, as well as a strengthened wall of organizational permanence for their adversaries, once they suspended the CIO affiliates in 1936. Early in this same year, the success of industrial unionism in rubber, in radio and electrical appliance plants, in steel mills, and in the automobile industry caused the framework of an independent organization to tower still higher.

In November 1938, after two years of phenomenal and continuous organizing triumphs, a constitutional convention in Pittsburgh dubbed the Committee for Industrial Organization the Congress of Industrial Organizations. The initials, CIO, were thus preserved and the cornice of a modern home for a new union family was completed.

The founders of the CIO paid filial homage to the old homestead, outdated as they proclaimed it to be, by displaying, in the administrative layout of their own abode, a consistent talent for duplicating its structure. The constitutional floor-plan of the CIO was simple, and except for the permeating influence of the important industrial union principle, like that of the AFL.

John L. Lewis, the first president of the CIO, reflected the self-confidence, righteousness, and militancy of the youthful clans he headed. Not until 1940 was his successor, Philip Murray, to lend the office that melancholy air of religious patience, slow to anger, which it continued to possess until the summer and autumn of 1949.

John L. Lewis placed in a conspicuous seat in the family portrait— the post of secretary (later, secretary-treasurer)—James B. Carey, who still continues in that office. Carey embodied in his person the ascendancy of youth in the CIO, as contrasted to the patriarchy of the AFL. With a single paternal gesture by Lewis, the aged in the youthful house bowed to the spirit of the Age. After 1941, Carey's job was transformed into a full-time one.

Nine vice-presidents (at the beginning, only two), chosen at large in regular annual convention, might have rounded out the picture of the Executive Board had it not been for the fears of unrepresentative control inherited from the days of repression and stress within the old house on Massachusetts Avenue. In addition, therefore, to the president, secretary-treasurer, and the nine vice-presidents, the Executive Board is composed of "a duly qualified officer" from each of the international and national unions. Sessions of this unwieldy and until 1950, politically divided board are scheduled at least twice a year, but they are also subject to additional calls of the president or a majority vote of the Board. The vice-presidents also meet during the course of the year.

The imprint of the AFL heritage extends to the existence of two organizing committees, not yet mature enough to become international unions, and 41 State councils and 245 city and county councils. Some 200 local industrial unions are directly affiliated with the national parent body. The absence of narrow craft demarcations within the CIO has made unnecessary the creation of multiunion departments for the settlement of jurisdictional disputes.

The staff of experts employed by the CIO is assigned to eight fields into which the work of the national office distributes itself. They are similar to the specialized activities of the AFL. An organization department employs 36 regional directors, 5 subregional directors, 68 field representatives, 6 national representatives, and an additional 42 field representatives paid by the department, but assigned to affiliated internationals. A second office devotes its attention solely to the southern organizing drive. The six other departments include a division on legislation, the legal department, a central office to coordinate and service the industrial union councils, a department assigned to research and education, a seventh one that supervises the multiple obligations of the CIO in international affairs, and a department of press and public relations, which publishes *The CIO News* and the *CIO Economic Outlook*.

The CIO Committees, appointed by the president, often employ full-time staffs of their own. Their names suggest the variety of activities to which organized labor must devote its attention if it wishes to meet its democratic responsibilities in our complex society: political action, abolition of discrimination, housing, community services, social security, Missouri Valley, health, safety, and welfare, Latin America, full employment, union label, and women's auxiliary.

The administrative arrangements of the CIO and the staff of experts it hired to accomplish the industrial and civic goals it had in mind reflected, like those of the AFL, the basic health of the organization. With the capitulation of "Little Steel" and Ford in 1941, even those conservative criers of doom, who had hoped that Lewis' withdrawal in 1940 would be the beginning of the end, had to admit that the CIO was not a short-lived sport in the development of American labor.

But life within the CIO proved no more peaceful than it was within the house of the AFL. To those who had found the AFL's stern consciousness of jurisdictional rights illogical and an open invitation to bickering, the absence of this particular kind of squabble in the CIO blinded them to the potentially more serious menace of political dissension. Nevertheless, political warfare sprang into the open in 1949 after smoldering for some years.

Labor journalists, who reported the darkness of discord and expulsion that hovered over the CIO convention of 1949, sought for the events in the past that are said to cast their shadows before. Some went back to the 1946 convention when Philip Murray's special committee of six international presidents drew up a resolution that stated that the delegates in assembly "resent and reject efforts of the Communist Party or other political parties and their adherents to interfere in the affairs of the CIO." Murray indicated that he wanted a unanimous rising vote. He got it after two dissenters changed their minds. Communists and non-Communists joined in approval of this declaration.

This move received its impetus from the earlier months of Allied disenchantment, which soured the end of the war years and witnessed the beginnings of cold battles and iron curtains. Public opinion turned against Russia and its domestic allies; left-wing intransigency within the unions led to the final disillusion of those who had steadily believed that they could count on compartmentalized Communist cooperation for trade union purposes. The process that world peace initiated eventually ended in the defeat of the Communists within the National Maritime Union, the United Automobile Workers, the Newspaper Guild, the United Shoe Workers, the Gas, Coke, and Chemical Workers, the Woodworkers, and the Transport Workers.

Other observers, more knowing, took Philip Murray at less than his word in the 1949 Convention: "During much of its history, the CIO has been a united organization. Its members and the leaders of all our unions have had a unified approach toward the problems that beset us." They retreated for genealogy to the German-Russian nonaggression pact and its puppet jerkings in the United States during the blatantly provoked strikes of fellow-traveling locals from 1939 to 1941. These onlookers were equally scornful of the golden age of CIO unity after the invasion of Russia by Hitler. They considered the ensuing fervor of the Communist-led unions as too zealous to be permanent.

Still other commentators traveled, in basic fashion, back to the early days of the CIO and arrived directly in front of John L. Lewis himself. They argued that in his eagerness to organize fast and capably, he allowed Communists and fellow-travelers to infiltrate into key positions within the various organizing committees that later grew into internationals. They disinterred unpleasant truths. By 1938, the Communists and their friends had already gained administrative control of 18 unions within the CIO.

Perhaps, these observers conceded, in addition to the obvious necessities of the period, a subtle psychological certainty played Lewis and his close advisors false. Like Sidney Hillman in the Amalgamated Clothing Workers of America, Mr. Lewis had whipped the Communists in the UMW, along with all other dissidents, to a jobless standstill. Because of this accomplishment, both he and Hillman were sure that they could use Communists for their own purposes and not be used, instead, by them. This was the time of Mr. Lewis' famous remark: "Who gets the bird, the hunter or the dog?" But the hatchet work of elimination,

relatively simple in the UMW and the ACWA, proved impossibly difficult in the CIO unions already under the control of Communist enthusiasm, sagacity, ability, parliamentary skill, hard work, and ruthless
mechanical domination.

These same observers also offered an explanation for Philip Murray's
paradoxical patience with the Communist and fellow-traveling sons and
daughters he inherited from Mr. Lewis in 1940. Until 1946, Philip Murray
was publicly engaged in keeping the peace by extending his hand of
friendship to the far left. From then until 1949, he patiently bided his
time. The victory of Walter Reuther in 1946, but especially the subsequent consolidation of his position in the UAW executive board in the
fall of 1947, finally encouraged the anti-Communists within the CIO to
prepare for a clean break. By convention time in 1949, developments
within the United Electrical Workers also indicated that a new, non-
communist international would have a fair chance of success.

The defeated Communists, like the aggrieved craft unionists of the
AFL in 1936, were loudly pious in their condemnation of dual unionism
and civil war in labor's ranks. A unity that they never practiced, except
on their own terms, replaced opposition to the Marshall Plan and all
its works as the most glistening plank in their refurbished program.

A second plank, only a scintilla less shining, declared the inviolability
of an international's autonomy. Their protest was ironic and pitiful.
They were declaiming in the wrong convention. If they had been members of the AFL instead of the CIO, their pleas for autonomy could have
fallen upon tradition-attuned ears. In the CIO, however, the autonomy
of internationals had never had a prolonged opportunity for sinking
roots. It had never become a real, as opposed to an oratorical, principle.
Most of the CIO internationals owed their beginnings, as well as their
later survival, to the financial and moral support of the parent body.
Lewis is credited with having contributed $4,000,000 to the organizing
drives of the CIO. He loaned the Steelworkers $1,080,000. Other unions
received over $2,000,000 in loans. For more than two years, the miners
contributed $30,000 a month to keep the national office going. As late
as 1949, 42 field representatives were still paid by the CIO, but assigned to various internationals that needed aid.

Such economic ties produced a sense of psychological dependency,
even a species of loyalty, which was felt, if only dimly, by the Communist-led international unions themselves. Concretely, financial aid by
the parent body resulted in its unhesitating interference with affairs of
international unions (especially when they were young and weak, or
older but ineffective) undreamed of in the AFL. In the future, it hardly
seems likely that newly chartered CIO internationals will quibble about
their independence so long as the drives they hope to launch are to be
fed out of national CIO coffers. Within the AFL, the internationals, be-

cause of their priority in time and superiority in strength and money, remained independent. Within the CIO, where most internationals started as sucklings, they never quite managed to free themselves of the silver cord, even when grown.

This possibly disputable fact of CIO life may have the effect of establishing even tighter controls over unions in the second house of labor. All of the internationals that will replace the banished Communist unions will be dependent upon Philip Murray and his Executive Board. True, such dominance will have to be exercised shrewdly and with some caution. Yet in the eyes of the impoverished and young, the wealthy and powerful often are endowed with wisdom and qualities of leadership even to the point of control itself.

The CIO home on Jackson Pl   was unquestionably shaken by the storm of the 1949 convention. Large chinks appeared in the walls. But Philip Murray and his associates rushed to brick them up and they were not confused by their anxiety. Today, even during the period of rebuilding, the CIO house of labor is actually stronger than before. It stands not upon the cleft rock of a united front, but rests its weight, in modern structural design, upon the shock-absorbing substratum of American political reality.

3. The International Union

Power and the unity it compels have never resided at the AFL and CIO homes on Massachusetts Avenue and Jackson Place in Washington, D. C. They are the attributes of the autonomous international unions that dominate their own locals and are largely independent of their parent bodies. The industrial exigencies and administrative logic that compelled this development among the internationals must be surveyed carefully because the entire labor movement rests upon the well-being and wisdom of the internationals.

It is true that for a time, 60 years ago, power sometimes accrued to city centrals that then showed a zeal for organizing, cooperative strike action, and political expression. Even later, John Fitzpatrick, anachronistically, transformed the Chicago and Illinois Federations of Labor into a working-class movement. However, as early as the 1890's, effective control and mandated unity began to concentrate more and more in the various international and national union houses of labor. Subsequently, the State Federations were transformed into merely lobbying agencies. They can now threaten the legislatures only with the power of the internationals. The city centrals and industrial councils, with few exceptions, have also been stripped by the internationals of their former flair for organizing and striking. And not since the nineteenth century, again with few exceptions, have the locals of unions commanded the independence of judgment and action with which New England town-meeting democrats would like to endow them. Therefore, it must be acknowledged that economic, industrial, social, political, administrative, and institutional forces in the twentieth century have created at least 209 complex, independent, changing, inconsistent labor movements, composed of very human American citizens who work for a living.

Of the 209 internationals in the United States, some 69 independent spirits have preferred to forego the ties of home life. They are affiliated with neither the CIO nor the AFL. The most notable of these mavericks are the four operating railroad brotherhoods, the International Association of Machinists, the United Mine Workers, the American Federation of Hosiery Workers, and various unions in the field of government and the retail and wholesale trades. Most of the other independent unions are small in size and limited to certain geographical areas. For the moment, until they form a third house of labor of their own, the homeless Communist-controlled international unions are included in this fraternity of independents.

Although the independent railroad brotherhoods have never yearned for home, they have been willing to establish an encampment and pitch a tent for themselves and the railroad unions affiliated with the AFL and CIO. The Railway Labor Executives Association, formed after the passage of the Railway Labor Act in 1926, accommodates 21 unions and encourages cooperative action on matters of general wage increases and particular pieces of legislation. As its name implies, this council under canvas includes only the chief executives or presidents of the participating unions.

As for the affiliated internationals, their individual autonomy was openly declared from the very beginning in 1886. This tune has never altered since then. Yet despite the persistence of autonomy as a principle and practice, the affiliation of internationals with highly articulate parent houses has tended to obscure the actual locus of labor power in the eyes of the public. This illusion has been possible in a country that often confuses nationally heralded utterances with authority itself. In addition, the evolution of the hegemony of the internationals over their locals was historically slow, purposefully unproclaimed, and usually undramatic. But the form of its development rested firmly upon a power-giving, although commonplace, tripod: higher wages, shorter hours, and constantly improving working conditions. Moreover, a new species of labor leader was created: the pure and simple variety who esteemed the signed collective agreement above all of the utopian and political lares and penates that had encumbered the constantly collapsing cabins of labor during the nineteenth century. Most important of all, it was (and still is) this labor leader, and not the head of a federation, who negotiated contracts with employers and brought back the benefits of the agreement to his membership. It was this leader who learned the necessity of group responsibility and finally secured the authority to approve or disapprove of local strikes. And it was he who turned the incoherent mass of workers, who expressed their resentment against degradation in sporadic, dishevelled strikes, into an organized, purposeful, expert, and efficient instrument for wresting dignity and security out of the chaos of the industrial revolution.

Samuel Gompers and Adolph Strasser, after the complete failure of the Cigarmakers' strike in 1877 against the tenement house system, rebuilt their organization upon a triangular pattern that still serves as the model of unionism in America today. First, the elected officers of the international union received complete power over the locals. Second, membership dues were increased in order to build up a large international union fund. Third, an elaborate system of welfare benefits was established with the purpose in mind of assuring stability among the membership through the tangible attractions of the payments. This benevolent device, in turn, gradually created a more tractible membership that would think twice before antagonizing the leaders and running the risk of losing benefits accumulated over the years. This system of government was adopted by the other international trade unions in the country. In 1950, within this three-cornered system, lay the chief features of AFL as well as of CIO international union administration.

The Cigarmakers responded, administratively, to the economic proposition that uncoordinated local bargains and strikes, devoid of long-range, planned strategy, were self-defeating in a country that had evolved a continental system of production and distribution. During the course of the twentieth century, as front-office centralization became a commonplace of industrial management, the internationals that had followed the Cigarmakers' model of union government tightened their own controls even more. John L. Lewis, as late as the 1920's, had to improvise means to deprive the districts within the UMW of their autonomy in order to cleanse the industry of the economic anarchy under which it struggled. Finally, with the emergence of the CIO after 1935, the mass-production unions in the United States faced the most stringently administered of all American industries. If they were to survive, their own efficiency, tactics, speed of operation, unity, and ability had to match the excellence of their adversaries. Administrative inexperience might have impelled the early industrial unionists toward constitutional provisions for the widest exercise of democracy within the new movement. But it was not in the stars of the economic and institutional firmament that such notions could persist for long. Certainly by mid-century, the managerial revolution has already engulfed labor organizations as well as those of industry and government.

The constitutions of internationals, their basic legislation, uniformly declare the primacy of the parent organizations over their locals, as well as Robert Michels' "iron law" of oligarchy. But clear as the language is, even this lucidity conceals the actual heights to which centralization of authority has inescapably been pushed by the drive of industrial and corporate events.

The General Executive Board of an international exercises the firmest authority over its union between conventions. Although varying provisions are obviously found in a search through 209 constitutions, in general the Executive Board has the authority to grant and withdraw local charters, repeal nonconforming by-laws of any local, remove any officer for sufficient reasons, fill vacancies, direct the affairs of a local when it has been agreed that this would be salutary, hear appeals on claims and grievances from locals and other subordinate bodies, countermand actions of any international officer, choose auditors for the preparation of the financial report to the convention, supervise the publication of the official journal, and levy assessments in conformity with the provisions of the constitution.

When these duties and responsibilities are added to the authority of the President and Executive Board with respect to the control of strike action and collective negotiations, the full nature of administrative power within an international can be gauged. But effective control, contrasted with constitutional power, is even more narrowly channeled in the day-to-day operations of a complex operating agency. Even more than business and industrial concerns, a union must be prepared to deal immediately and expertly with almost perpetual crises. It is true that most Executive Boards are composed of the international president and secretary-treasurer, along with a specified number of vice-presidents; but one vital administrative fact is often overlooked: the vice-presidents are not necessarily full-time, paid officers, who are present at headquarters. Most frequently they are chosen to represent a region or a branch of the industry and they hold office in that area of jurisdiction. Perforce, the president and secretary-treasurer, as the only full-time officers in headquarters, have assumed, not necessarily unwillingly, the responsibilities for the governing of men. This development, also common to industry and government, has, in turn, tended to increase the number of expert staff members in labor unions, particularly in the newer organizations.

The president of the UAW, for example, could never fulfill his narrowest concept of duty without the use of a trained staff. Within this union of almost 1,000,000 members, administrative departments, service departments, and organizing and bargaining departments and councils have burgeoned from year to year in a desperate effort to keep pace with the turn of automotive and aeronautical affairs. The very names of the administrative departments mark the distance that separates present-day managerial unionism from past eras of haphazard bookkeeping, tobacco-stained offices, and absence of trained competency and skill: auditing, accounting, clerical center, purchasing and supply, and personnel. The scope and variety of the service departments indicate the good will and strength of a modern international in filling the needs of its members: education (cooperative stores and credit unions, films, radio, and book stores); research, time study, and job evaluation; social security (unemployment compensation, workmen's compensation, union counseling, medical diagnostic and health education center, insurance, and pensions); fair practices (women's department, equal pay for equal work); political action; Washington office; recreation; veterans; housing; legal; publicity; and public relations. The types of organizing and bargaining departments and councils illustrate the administrative flexibility and detailed understanding which a daring, forearmed union must possess today. There are 17 corporation departments, each with full-time staffs, each with specialized knowledge not only of the affairs of the individual corporation, but also of the needs and aspirations of the workers within that corporation. There are also 13 departments organized on an industrial, rather than a corporate, basis. Among the most important of these departments are aircraft; tool, die, and maintenance; tractor and agricultural; and body and trim. In addition, there are councils that devote their attention to the skilled trades, the competitive shops, and office workers within the automobile and aircraft industry.

A government with this degree of responsibility and complexity is ill adapted to rule by committee, as though it were still merely the executive head of a nineteenth century fraternal order. Nevertheless, under most constitutions, the policies and affairs of the various administrative divisions within an international like the UAW, especially the departments, have to be directed and authorized by the Executive Board. Before Walter Reuther consolidated his position fully, the greatest factional battles within the union occurred at this point of the governing process. The energies of the UAW, consequently, were less expended in contesting corporate action than in fratricidal maneuvering within the Board itself. The futility and waste of membership resources in performances of this kind have always led the realistic leader to strive for as much consolidation of power as possible. With his success the Executive Board becomes, through whatever price he is willing to pay for unity, his own creature.

The successful president-administrator must also dominate the General Convention of the international. Theoretically, a purer form of democracy might be supposed to survive in the convention of local delegates that, constitutionally, serves as the final arbiter of union matters and the only legislative authority. But the constant downpour of economic and institutional pressures upon this backwater of nineteenth century democratic action has also brought it into the managerial mainstream.

International union conventions are as unsuited in size and composition to town-meeting equalitarianism as the national assemblies of political parties or the annual meetings of corporation stockholders. Most of the delegates to union conventions prefer the color, the release from daily routine, and the entertainment provided there to the humdrum governing tasks that, in their opinion, can be better performed by the men whom they have elected precisely for that purpose. Just as the stockholders of a notable corporation are attracted by the luncheon they are served in New Jersey and leave the determination of policy to their betters (given the continuing flow of dividends), so union delegates have learned to surrender the privilege of hard thinking to those who are chosen by their president and Executive Board to fill the hotel rooms where authority is shaped. The rank-and-file delegates retire, instead, to various amusements, secure in the knowledge, like stockholders, that their interests will be guarded.

And, truly, so long as elected officials provide union delegates and their followers at home with higher wages, shorter hours, better working conditions, and pension and welfare plans, they need not be too concerned about rank-and-file fears of the dangers inherent in concentration of administrative power. So long as they deliver dividends often enough to halt wagging tongues, international union officers are re-elected annually, are seldom opposed, and serve for many years in their posts. Philip Taft, in "Understanding Union Administration" (*Harvard Business Review*, XXIV, No. 2) and "Opposition to Union Officers in Elections" (*The Quarterly Journal of Economics*, LVIII, No. 2), has pointed out that whether the election is by referendum vote of the entire membership or by delegates at convention, the same longevity of official life results. This law of tenure holds especially for the old AFL internationals. However, the newer CIO unions have not established a reverse drift thus far. Harry Bridges, Benjamin Gold, Joseph Curran, Michael Quill, and Philip Murray have served as presidents virtually since the founding of their unions.

If satisfying the economic wants of the membership is a trying and increasingly complex business, once it is in hand, the administrative tools employed for controlling conventions are simplicity itself. Mirroring Congress, union officials parcel out the work of the convention to committees. These committees are usually selected by the president, sometimes with and sometimes without the approval of the Executive Board, depending on the provisions of the constitution. The committees obviously bear the imprint and carry the voice of their sponsors. Opposition, to be sure, has not ceased to exist within international conventions, except in unions like the United Mine Workers where Mr. Lewis is impatient of democratic pretense and finds his own unchallenged authority savory. However, to be effective, either within committee or on the floor of the convention, the opposition must resort to the same administrative and political devices as those of the ruling group. Deals must be made and caucuses organized and held fast to compel victory. Occasionally, such organized rank-and-file revolts take place, but they are rare enough to become noteworthy. Nor are the principles of the managerial revolution impaired by citing these infrequent instances. On the contrary, they are confirmed by them. As the maturing CIO unions have demonstrated, even those who once revolted learn the easy lessons of administrative centralization rather quickly.

4. THE LOCAL UNION

With logic's finality, the course of labor's family empire leads to the last good place of hope: the humble dwellings that the estimated 60,000 to 70,000 local unions in the United States call home.

Many of the locals have less than 100 members. Perhaps 10 per cent number over 1,000 members, and they tend to take on the characteristics of miniature internationals, including the attributes of power and efficiency. But the overwhelming majority of locals claim less than 200 or 300 members.

In these smaller locals resides the possibility of constantly revivifying health for organized labor. Within those spheres of responsibility left to them—the vital tasks implicit in the day-to-day re-creation of a living relationship among the workers—the freedom of their membership is still apparent enough to be recognizable.

The officers of these modest units are not professional administrators and they conduct their affairs in the easier manner of bygone days. The pattern of international officialdom prevails: president, secretary, treasurer, sergeant-at-arms, trustees, and members of the executive board. Members of this group approve local policy and administer the affairs of their union. Some local officers, where controls by the international are still loose or where the nature of the industry precludes central direction, negotiate their own bargains and apply their own judgment to strike decisions. But for the most part, especially in larger, situation-influencing locals, these privileges have been removed.

Another group of local union representatives, not considered officers in the strictest sense, are the shop committeemen, or stewards. They act as the representatives of the local in the plant, mill, or mine. They perform tasks of the utmost importance with respect to daily grievances and other problems arising out of the collective agreement. But they are generally without voice, except as members, in the shaping of policy and administrative decisions in the local.

The frequency of turnover among local union officials—a limited index of grassroots health—contrasts sharply with the persistence of tenure among officers in the international unions. Local officers are, of course, closer to their membership and their every move can be easily followed and appraised by an awakened opposition. Within small-membership groups, moreover, enemies of the *status quo* can with less difficulty rise to prominence and position. Perhaps more telling is the circumstance that Philip Taft, in the first of the articles already cited, has revealed: less than half of 350 local constitutions surveyed by him showed full-time paid officers. Therefore it seems likely that an officer of a small local who aspires to long tenure would have to be a person completely satisfied by the thin broth of honor. The thicker soup of power and influence is the fare of only the larger locals. Whatever combination of factors may account for the phenomenon of frequent official change, so long as the process does not degenerate (as it easily may) into institutional irresponsibility, it points toward the persistence of democratic vitality among local unions.

Withal, the shadow of the professional manager has also lengthened over the locals of the nation as they increased in size or as industry-wide or multi-employer bargaining replaced the individual agreement. The larger locals and those still in the earlier stages of growth, contemplating the burdens placed upon part-time, largely unsalaried officers, found it necessary to hire paid organizers, better known as business agents. In the older AFL unions, the organizers are still elected by the membership. In the newer CIO unions that have grown from the top downward, business agents are often appointed by the international officers and sometimes paid by them as well. These full-time staff aides, ostensibly hired to recruit new members and to supervise the terms of the collective agreement, become, in good time, a managerial class. The part-time elected officials, naturally, leave the details of work to them. Then, gradually, these minutiae of operations are metamorphosed into the trivia that influence policy decisions. Wise business agents can easily become the most influential individuals in a local. If they are also shrewd, they conceal their power behind the frame of the president's bulk. From that vantage point, their tenure may continue indefinitely, or until the moment when they are summoned by the international to receive the promotion that their skill deserves.

A deeper change in the life of the local occurred when multi-employer bargaining through associations became an economic necessity were the chaos and misery of unbridled competition to be eradicated. Until rational procedures were forced upon employers, the ineptitude of locals acting individually well nigh destroyed the patient organizing work of decades. Out of this desperate situation came an administrative invention of the ablest kind: the trade council and joint board. First, groups of locals in a single international were set up to secure uniform action in collective bargaining and working conditions from employers in the same geographical area. Moving one step farther, locals in the building, printing, and metal trades crossed the jurisdictions established by each of the several internationals in their respective trades and joined together in local, state, and district building trades, printing trades, and metal trades councils.

This form of union government was as rational as it was imperative, but it created another managerial class: the joint board manager and the president of the trade council. In the joint boards especially, the individual locals have been constrained to surrender much of their former initiative and prestige to the managers who combine political sagacity with deep knowledge of the complexities of the industry in which they operate. The result is written on the roster of the international officers of the garment trades. A vice-presidency is usually but the reflection of a joint-board manager's strength.

In the CIO industrial unions, another ingenious type of coordinating process, necessarily over a wider geographical area, has evolved. The opinions and consent of locals are secured on major union policies and contract terms. The UAW's General Motors Department, for example, consults regularly with its legislative body, the GM Council. It is composed of representatives from the nine regional GM subcouncils (about 250 delegates) and meets three times a year, or more frequently during crises. Out in the GM subcouncils, each GM local is represented by its president, the chairman of the shop committee, and one delegate for each 5,000 workers. The subcouncils, on their own, discuss mutual problems and pass their decisions on to higher headquarters. In addition, for streamlined collective bargaining purposes, each subcouncil elects a chairman who serves on the national GM Negotiating Committee. These purposeful techniques limit, to some extent, the powers of de-partmental managers by frequent exposure to the blasts of rank-and-file thinking. Unless they, too, become formalized and rigid, or are circum-scribed by edicts from above, they may well serve as examples to all the houses of labor that are seeking a thread of escape from the full im-plications of managerial control.

Along with the danger of professionalization at the local level runs the obtruding fact of declining membership participation. If current trends continue, they can result only in more intense managerial controls created by the vacuum of indifference. When a general meeting in most locals attracts 25 per cent of the membership, the officers are jubilant, for the percentage usually freezes at a figure anywhere from five to fifteen. The members seem to respond only to those rallies where strike action is voted or collective agreements are approved. Except for these moments of obvious bread-and-butter importance, the average worker, like his other fellow-Americans, is content to receive his union dividends and leave civic duty to Charlie, whoever he may be.

Whether the causes of disinterest lie in outmoded, dull meeting procedures carried over from a gas-lit era, or in the absence of an obvious community of interests among industrial workers in the larger locals, or in the attractions of the radio, movies, and bowling to fatigued factory workers, the resultant sapping of union strength at its base is frightening. Perhaps ingrained notions about the mechanisms of meaningful democracy will have to be completely removed, and fresh ideas substituted, especially in the cases of giant locals with more than a thousand members. Already some of them have instituted a delegate system in place of the full membership meeting. The delegates are elected from representative units of the plant or plants in the local. They can bring to the smaller meeting, which is more suited to discussion, the problems of their divisions or sections and the canvassed opinions of their constituents. The system itself places a sense of responsibility upon the chosen delegates, a feeling wholly lacking among those who attend full membership conclaves where the prevailing anonymity, born of size, conquers any latent feelings about the democratic duty to participate in the process of making decisions.

The managers of unions, whatever their titles, will be forced, in the future, to turn their energies and abilities (if good will is also theirs) toward salvaging the local meeting from atrophy. Otherwise, the prospect offends. And with offense, public opinion sours and threatens.

At this point, the labor expert enters, bearing his skills, his democratic interests, his social vision, and his love for the labor movement. If given the opportunity, he can humbly contribute his gifts toward the solution of the most challenging problem today on the American labor scene as it shifts into the last half of the century.

MAURICE F. NEUFELD

Chapter 2

Leaders of the unions

As THE LABOR UNIONS HAVE GROWN, SO HAS THE POWER OF THE LABOR leaders. In 1948, 34 per cent of the wage-and-salaried workers of the nation were in the unions. It is no small thing to be among the leaders of these 14 or 15 million organized men and women. And it is no wonder that loud spokesmen for both Right and Left, using their most colorful adjectives, sometimes seem quite preoccupied with "slapping the labor leader."

But nobody really knows much about him. There have been only three or four studies of labor leaders; none of them, including the present essay, is really definitive. We probably know more about the business executive and the small businessman than about the labor leaders in the large and small unions. We also understand more of the factors that enter into business decisions than we do those that enter into labor decisions. Nobody knows in a systematic fashion how various types of labor leaders make up their minds about a strike situation or about whether or not to push for a labor party. Indeed, nobody has ever worked out an adequate typology of labor leaders. Nor do we know the areas of strictly personal decisions as against democratic formulations of will that are open to labor leaders, nor how wide or narrow are the ranges of their opportunities in given situations. We don't even know, over a period of years, what the leaders as a group think about current political and economic topics. But our ignorance in this area of labor leadership goes even deeper: we don't know how many there are.

How many individuals should be included in the bracket "labor leaders" is a matter of definition and counting. In this report we are concerned with the leaders of the *national* AFL and CIO unions—the presidents and secretary-treasurers; the presidents and secretaries of the AFL and CIO *state* organizations; and the leaders of the *city* centrals (AFL) and *city* industrial councils (CIO). Among these men are found virtually all of the Big Names of Labor, as well as hundreds who are not at all nationally known. However little is known about labor leaders as a total group, there is little doubt that the power of decision in the world of unions resides with these leaders, and especially with the heads of the national unions. Our report is based on a sample drawn from the AFL and the CIO on national, state, and city levels.[1]

Age and Education

The first and outstanding fact about the world of the labor leader in America today is that it is divided into two great spheres of organization and influence: the AFL and the CIO. This split is not only a division of organizations having different policies; it is also a division of types of men. We begin to grasp this fact by examining two simple differences between the leaders of the two organizations: their ages and their educational levels.

In Table 1, the age distributions of the leaders of AFL and CIO are presented. The outstanding point of this table is that the CIO leaders are noticeably younger: only 35 per cent of the AFL leaders are under 45 years, whereas 73 per cent of the CIO men are in this younger group. This fact, of course, is in large part explained by the youth of the CIO as an organization. When we realize that one of the recognized ways of becoming a top labor leader is to create an organization, we begin to understand these age differences; and perhaps our understanding is made more complete when we realize that an organization built by young men, and still in its early stages, will probably select younger leaders.

TABLE 1

AGES OF AFL AND CIO LEADERS

Age Group	AFL	CIO
Under 35	4%	20%
35-44	31	53
45-54	33	17
55 and over	32	10
Total (100%)	(219)	(169)

When we examine the levels of leadership in each of the union blocs, we find that on each level the CIO leader is younger. Among the presidents and secretaries of the national unions, for instance, 80 per cent of the AFL men are 45 years or over, as compared with 39 per cent of the CIO national leaders. On the city level, 56 per cent of the AFL leaders are 45 or over, as compared with 25 per cent in the CIO.

[1] See Appendix: "The Sample," pp. 546-549, for an explicit discussion of the leaders selected for study.

TABLE 2

PROPORTION OF LEADERS WHO ARE 45 YEARS OF AGE
OR OVER, BY LEVEL OF LEADERSHIP

Level of Leadership	AFL	CIO
National	80%	39%
State	73%	24%
City	56%	25%
Total	65%	27%

Within the AFL, there is an almost perfect age hierarchy: starting with the national level, on which 80 per cent of the leaders are 45 or over; the state level, 73 per cent; and the city level, 56 per cent; we see that this age hierarchy parallels the organizational hierarchy with almost bureaucratic precision. There is also a tendency in the CIO for an age hierarchy to develop, but the gap between the national and the city leader is not nearly so great as it is in the AFL. And furthermore, the CIO age picture is a somewhat mixed situation: 39 per cent of the national heads are 45 or over; 24 per cent of the state, and 25 per cent of the city leaders, respectively, are 45 or over.

As we would expect from these facts of age, the CIO leaders are more highly educated than are those of the AFL. The over-all picture reveals that 56 per cent of the CIO men have graduated from high school or have gone on to college, whereas only 39 per cent of the AFL men are in this category. Of course, in a crude comparison with the population of the United States as a whole, both groups are more highly educated than the adult rank and file at large: only 24 per cent of the U. S. population over 25 years have completed high school, and only 22 per cent of the adult males.

TABLE 3

EDUCATION OF AFL AND CIO LEADERS AND 1940 U. S. POPULATION OVER 25 YEARS

Education	1940 U. S. Pop. over 25	AFL	CIO
College	10%	25%	33%
High school graduate	14	14	23
Some high school	15	26	24
Grammar school	57	34	20
None	4	1	—
Total (100%)	(73.7 million)	(227)	(172)

Within each of the organizations, on each level of leadership, the CIO leader is better educated than his opposite number in the AFL. When we consider each organizational hierarchy separately, however, we find this difference: in the CIO the hierarchy of leadership is paralleled by an educational level; thus, 68 per cent of the national leaders, 61 per cent of the state, and 50 per cent of the city have graduated from high school. In the AFL, however, the city men are better educated than the state or the national: 43 per cent of them are in the higher educated grade. Of course, this distribution within the AFL is due in large part to the tremendous age gap between the local and the national leaders; but the CIO educational hierarchy appears to be somewhat more "professionalized," in that higher positions require higher education. In the AFL, there appears to be something of a statistical tension between age and education, whereas in the CIO, with its flatter age composition, education and age are both graded by organizational structure.

TABLE 4

EDUCATION OF AFL AND CIO LEADERS BY LEVEL OF LEADERSHIP

Education	AFL			CIO		
	National	State	City	National	State	City
College	24%	16%	29%	47%	35%	28%
High school graduate	12	17	14	21	26	22
Some high school	21	31	27	23	23	24
Grammar school	43	36	30	9	16	26
Total (100%)	(61)	(42)	(124)	(34)	(43)	(95)

We must look at education and age together. Unfortunately, we do not have enough cases to do this for each organizational level; but for the leaders as a whole, we can get a picture from Table 5.

TABLE 5

EDUCATION OF AFL AND CIO LEADERS BY AGE

Age	Proportion Who are High School Graduates or More	
	AFL	CIO
Under 45	49%	62%
45 and over	36%	38%
Total	39%	56%

The younger men are better educated in both the AFL and CIO. But the educational level is higher in the CIO in both age groups.

Where They Were Born

One of the most frequent cries raised against labor leaders, especially among people who have reason not to appreciate their more practical activities, is that "they are all a bunch of foreign-born agitators." Their agitating abilities will have to be examined elsewhere, but Table 6 presents some objective evidence on their national origins.

TABLE 6

NATIVITY OF AFL AND CIO LEADERS

Birthplace	AFL	CIO
Born in U. S.	89%	89%
Foreign-born	11	11
Total (100%)	(228)	(174)

It appears that only one in ten of the labor leaders was not born in the United States. Furthermore, the national origins of the CIO leadership are just like the national origins of the AFL leadership. Labor leaders do not deviate appreciably in this respect from the population at large: the 1940 census found that 84 per cent of the U. S. population are native-born.

We can, however, go one step further back and ask how many of the labor leaders had parents who were foreign-born. The answer to this question is given in Table 7. The majority of these leaders represent family residence of at least two generations in America. The fathers of approximately 38 per cent were born abroad. Six out of ten were born of native American fathers.

TABLE 7

NATIVITY OF THE FATHERS OF AFL AND CIO LEADERS

Birthplace of Father	AFL	CIO
Born in U. S.	61%	62%
Foreign-born	39	38
Total (100%)	(227)	(173)

We are curious again about how this compares with the United States population. The census does not give us comparable data, but it tells us that of the white male population in 1940: 66 per cent were native of native parents; 21 per cent were native of foreign or mixed parentage; 13 per cent were foreign born. That is, for 66 per cent of the white male population it is true that both their mothers and their fathers were born in the United States. This is a more rigorous definition than we have used in our study of labor leaders. About 60 per cent of the labor leaders are native white of native fathers, but perhaps somewhat fewer than 60 per cent would meet the test of also having native mothers. On the other hand, it is true that the labor leader population is slightly less likely than the general white male population to be foreign-born. Sixteen per cent of the population, but only 11 per cent of the labor leaders, were born outside this country. The labor leader group contains more people who can be described by this census rubric: "native white of foreign or mixed parentage."

It is well known that the objections raised against foreign-born leaders in high American places are linked with the part of the world from which the leaders come. In the present case of labor leaders, out of the 11 per cent of the AFL who were foreign-born, over half came from Great Britain and Northwestern Europe; the rest came from Central and Southern Europe, very few having been born in Eastern Europe. Of the 11 per cent foreign-born in the CIO, about half are also from Great Britain and Northwestern Europe, and the remaining are more likely to have come from Eastern Europe than Central or Southern. This Eastern European contingent in the CIO is, of course, connected with the industrial composition of the CIO unions: certain of their memberships are predominantly Eastern European in origin.

TABLE 8

NATIONAL ORIGINS OF THE FATHERS OF AFL AND CIO LEADERS

Birthplace of Fathers		AFL		CIO
Total foreign-born		39%		38%
Great Britain	19		12	
Northwestern Europe	6		3	
Central and Southern Europe	12		13	
Russia and Eastern Europe	2		10	
Total native-born		61		62
Total (100%)		(227)		(173)

When we examine the place of origin of the fathers who were foreign-born, we find that 25 per cent of the AFL fathers are from Northwestern Europe or Great Britain; the corresponding figure in the CIO is 15 per cent. In the AFL and CIO, 12 per cent and 13 per cent, respectively, of the fathers came from Central and Southern Europe. In the AFL, 2 per cent of the fathers are from Eastern Europe, and in the CIO, 10 per cent. Table 8 shows in full the places of origin of the foreign-born fathers.

Levels of Origin

Another item in the backgrounds of the labor leaders that is of interest is the occupation pursued by their fathers. This is a good general indicator of the level of origin of an individual. The question we asked the labor leaders in this connection was carefully worded: "What was the main occupation of your father when you were ten or twelve years old?" We specified this age because we felt that pre-adolescence is the period in an individual's life at which his life chances are most crucially set by the economic level of the parent. In Table 9 we present the AFL-CIO breakdown in this connection.

TABLE 9

OCCUPATIONS OF THE FATHERS OF AFL AND CIO LEADERS

Occupation of Fathers	AFL	CIO
Free Enterprisers	33%	32%
Farmers	16	14
Businessmen	17	16
Free professionals	*	2
New Middle Class	8	7
Managers	5	4
Salaried professionals	1	2
Office workers and salespeople	2	1
Wage Workers	59	61
Foremen and skilled	37	34
Semi- and unskilled	14	18
Rural Workers	8	9
Total (100%)	(198)	(158)

* Less than 1 per cent.

The first thing that strikes us about the table is that there is very little difference between the AFL and the CIO. This is rather remarkable in view of the great age and educational differences we found between the two union blocs. But perhaps the key fact about the occupational origin of labor leaders is that they are predominantly from labor itself. Approximately six out of ten come from laboring homes, mainly from the foremen and skilled labor levels. About one out of ten comes from the new middle class of salaried professional and white collar workers; and three come from the free enterprise class of farm owners, large and small business owners and free professionals.

When we compare the occupational origins of the leaders on each of the leadership levels, we do not find any great difference between the

AFL and the CIO. Nor do we find very strong differences between the leadership levels within each of the union blocs. There is a slight tendency for the state leaders in the AFL bloc to come more from labor than is true of the national and city leaders. In the CIO, more national leaders tend to come from the new middle class and slightly fewer from wage workers than is the case on the city or state levels of leadership.

The amount of education an individual receives is normally linked with the occupational level of his parents; the labor leaders whose fathers were wage workers have had less education than those originating from the higher occupational levels.

A comparison of the rural and urban character of the occupational origin of the AFL and CIO leaders reveals no difference between the two groups: 24 per cent of the AFL and 23 per cent of the CIO leaders come from farming families. Nor does a comparison by level of leadership reveal any marked differences. Labor leaders are overwhelmingly urban in origin compared with the U. S. population as a whole.

TABLE 10

RURAL AND URBAN CHARACTER OF OCCUPATIONAL ORIGIN
OF AFL AND CIO LEADERS

Origin	1910 U. S. Population	AFL	CIO
Rural	35%	24%	23%
Urban	65	76	77
Total (100%)	(29,926,007)	(198)	(158)

Before the Union

In our attempt to trace the career of the labor leaders in as much detail as possible, we asked them: "What was your main occupation before you became a trade union official?" [2] About three-fourths of the leaders of American labor worked in wage worker jobs before getting into their union careers. However, this over-all figure hides a difference between the AFL and the CIO. It appears that more of the AFL men worked as foremen or skilled labor than did the CIO men.

This finding probably reflects the age differences between the AFL and the CIO leaders, as well as changes in the composition of the U. S.

[2] There is a possibility that the answers to this question are biased, not in the answering of the questions so much as in the fact that most unions require that an individual be employed at the work being organized before he can take a union position. It may be, therefore, that the labor jobs claimed by the leaders are reflections of this administrative fact. However, in view of the occupations of the fathers reported, we do not feel that this is a very serious bias in the figures we have presented.

wage working class: since the AFL men are older and have been in trade union work a much longer time, their pre-union careers occurred during a period when there was a higher proportion of skilled labor at work, and when trade unions were more likely to be composed of skilled laborers than of the lower grades of wage workers. The finding further reflects the composition of the two union blocs, with more semi-skilled mass industry workers in the CIO.

TABLE 11

PRE-UNION OCCUPATION OF AFL AND CIO LEADERS

Job Before Union Post	AFL		CIO	
Free Enterprisers		9%		4%
New Middle Class		18		18
Wage Workers		73		78
Foremen and skilled	60		47	
Semi- and unskilled	13		28	
Rural workers	—		3	
Total (100%)		(213)		(161)

Union Careers

There are in general three ways in which a man may become a labor leader of considerable rank. He may create a union himself; he may be appointed to the job of organizer or to some other strategic job and climb from there through a series of elections; or he may begin on the local level of leadership and gradually be elevated to the top.

In our efforts to get at the union career-lines of the leaders, we asked the question: "What was your first job in any trade union organization?" The results of this question, cross classified with the present level of the leader, are contained in Table 12.

On the national level of leadership, 14 per cent of the AFL and 9 per cent of the CIO leaders started out as national leaders. On the state level, the corresponding figures are 16 per cent and 17 per cent for AFL and CIO, respectively; and on the city level, 17 per cent and 5 per cent. It is clear from the table that the great bulk of the men now on each of the three levels began as heads of locals or as local committee men. On the national, state, and city levels, over half of the AFL and CIO leaders began in this way. The second largest route is by appointment to the national union as an organizer. On the national level, 23 per cent of the AFL men began as organizers, and 33 per cent of the CIO, a difference reflecting the differences in the recent history of the organizations.

The big fact, however, is in line with our finding about the level of social origin: labor leaders come from the lower occupational circles,

and they began their union careers at the bottom of the union world—
—in the local unions.

TABLE 12

FIRST LABOR UNION POSITION HELD BY AFL AND CIO LEADERS
BY PRESENT POSITION

First Position	AFL			CIO		
	National	State	City	National	State	City
National	14%	1%	1%	9%	—	1%
State	—	16	2	1	17%	—
City	—	1	17	1	1	5
Up from the Local	61	57	68	52	51	78
Up from Organizer	23	22	8	33	27	11
Other	2	3	4	4	4	5
Total (100%)	(51)	(37)	(98)	(33)	(41)	(84)

It is interesting to realize, as we may do by means of the figures in
Table 13, how great the differences between the AFL and the CIO
really are in terms of the careers of their present leaders. In this table
we display the median year in which the leaders in both blocs on each
of the three levels first took a job with a union.

TABLE 13

MEDIAN YEAR OF ENTERING LABOR UNION WORK OF AFL AND CIO
LEADERS BY LEVEL OF LEADERSHIP

Level of Leadership	AFL	CIO
National	1918	1935
President	1919	1933
Secretary	1914	1936
State	1929	1939
President	1919	1938
Secretary	1932	1939
City	1933	1939
Total	1929	1937

On the national level, there is a difference of 17 years of trade union
experience between the average AFL and the average CIO leader.
On the state level, there is a difference of ten years, and even on the
city level, where we would expect a rather rapid turnover to occur
even in older organizations, there is a difference of six years. These
figures reflect, of course, the difference in the ages of the two union
blocs, and the age differences already noted between their leaders.

It is clear, however, that in both union blocs the labor leader has worked his way up from the bottom, either by being appointed as an organizer and later being elected to office, by creating a union himself, or—and this is by far the most typical way—by being elected to a local office and climbing up from that position. The men who are now in the higher echelons of the labor world are the end products of a long process of selection. They are the ones who have persisted in union work, occupying one position after the other, and thus climbing to reach the top, and staying there.

The Big Split

How much chance is there that "organic unity" between the AFL and CIO will be achieved? We asked the leaders of each bloc: "Regardless of what you would like to see happen, how much chance do you see for the AFL and the CIO to become one unified organization within the next few years?" The answers to this question reveal strong differences between the AFL and the CIO.

TABLE 14

VIEWS OF AFL AND CIO LEADERS ON THE CHANCES OF LABOR UNITY

Chances for Unity	AFL	CIO
Good	10%	3%
Fair	30	13
Slight	43	54
None	17	30
Total (100%)	(231)	(176)

Forty per cent of the AFL leaders see either a good or a fair chance for the unification of the two union blocs, as against only 16 per cent of the CIO. There are no real differences between the different levels of leaders with respect to optimism about unification.

Leaving the question of practical realities aside, what is the will of labor leaders as a group? Do they believe a merger is desirable or not? We asked: "From the standpoint of value to labor people as a whole, do you think the AFL and the CIO as nationwide organizations should within the next few years try to: (1) get together as a unified organization; (2) remain separate organizations but engage in all the joint public activities and policies they can; (3) remain separate organizations and have little or nothing to do with each other; (4) fight it out until one or the other loses as an organization?"

More leaders in both the AFL and the CIO feel unity is desirable than believe it can be achieved. Almost no leader is willing to say that

TABLE 15

OPINIONS OF AFL AND CIO LEADERS ON WHETHER OR NOT THE
TWO ORGANIZATIONS SHOULD UNITE

Preferred Action	AFL	CIO
Get together as organizations	83%	56%
Remain separate but cooperate	11	42
Remain completely separate	3	1
Fight it out	3	1
Total (100%)	(230)	(178)

the organizations should remain completely separate or that they should
fight it out, but there is a definite difference between the AFL and the
CIO answers as between getting together as an organization and cooperating as separate organizations: 83 per cent of the AFL leaders
want to unite organizationally, as against 56 per cent of the CIO. Forty-
two per cent of the CIO men think they should cooperate as separate
organizations, as against 11 per cent of the AFL. And on this question,
too, leaders on each power level follow the "party line" of their own
affiliated body. City leaders are as likely as the key men at the head of
national unions to want organic unity.

Just how is this attitude of wishfulness integrated with the practical
estimates? Table 16 combines these two attitudes and classifies labor
leaders on the basis of the four groups they form. In the first row of
the table, we have those who believe that the CIO and AFL should get
together and that there is a good or a fair chance that they will do so;
these might be called optimists. Forty per cent of the AFL as against 13
per cent of the CIO can be classified in this way.

TABLE 16

OUTLOOK ON UNITY QUESTION OF AFL AND CIO LEADERS

Opinion	AFL	CIO
Should get together and there is a *good or fair* chance	40%	13%
Should get together but there is only a *slight or no* chance	43	44
Should not get together and there is only a *slight or no* chance	16	40
Should not get together but there is a *good or fair* chance	1	3
Total (100%)	(229)	(176)

On the second line of the table we have those leaders who say that the organizations should get together, but that there is a slight or no chance of their doing so. These are morally willing but practically pessimistic. About 44 per cent of each organization is in this position. On the third line we have those who say that the organizations should not get together, but should cooperate, and who think, at the same time, that there is only a slight or no chance of their getting together; these are satisfied with two independent labor blocs. Sixteen per cent of the AFL as against 40 per cent of the CIO fall into this bracket.

In a general way, we might say that more of the AFL leaders appear to be all-around optimists on the question of unity, whereas the CIO leaders are less likely to desire unity. There are at least two reasons that are probably reflected in these figures. In the first place, the power of a labor leader often depends primarily upon the number of members in his union. Since the AFL is a larger organization, there is a vested interest factor involved in the differences in outlook. The leaders see the issue as one of "absorbing" or being "absorbed," rather than of "unity" or "disunity." Second, this poll was taken after John Lewis had led the coal miners back into the AFL, and probably some of the speculation and maneuvers that went on in the union world after this event are reflected in the AFL opinion.

Programs and Expediencies

One way in which we might expect a unification of the labor organizations would be a common program of action. Very often from the standpoint of short-run expediencies no cooperation is possible, whereas if a broader view is taken, the parties concerned might see a way of cooperation open to them. Also, many people who are well wishers of American labor unions have criticized the unions about their lack of any large political or even economic program. For these two reasons we asked the leaders the following question: "Over and above the basic concern with such problems as wages, hours, and union security, do you believe that most U. S. unions have or have not any long-range economic and political program?" Their answers are contained in Table 17.

TABLE 17

PROPORTIONS WHO BELIEVE UNIONS DO HAVE A LONG-RANGE PROGRAM

Level of Leadership	AFL	CIO
National	34%	62%
State	41%	77%
City	56%	80%
Total	49%	79%

Definitely more of the CIO leaders believe that there is such a long-term program: 79 per cent of them hold such a view as compared with a rather even split among the AFL leadership.

On each level of leadership, the CIO leaders believe there is a long-range policy more frequently than do the AFL leaders, and in each organization there is a correlation between this belief and the level of leadership: 80 per cent of the city leaders in the CIO believe that there is such a program as compared with only 62 per cent of the national leaders. In the AFL, 56 per cent of the city leaders hold the view as compared with 34 per cent of the national leaders.

Since this is a question that seeks not only attitude but fact as well, one must be guided by the answers of those more likely to possess the objective information one is after. The leaders most likely to know labor's program—the heads of nationals—are least likely to acknowledge that there is such a long-range program. We may assume then that the greater optimism of leaders on the lower levels springs to some extent from "wishful thinking." However, even among the national leaders, the group that takes the most sober view of labor policies, 34 per cent of the AFL and 62 per cent of the CIO men claim there *is* such a long-range program.

But what is the character of this program? We asked those leaders who thought there was such a program: "What are the main points in the unions' long-range program?" We have classified their answers in two ways: first, in terms of the people it would benefit, and second in terms of the types of goals or benefit it would bring them.

TABLE 18

LONG-RANGE PROGRAMS OF THE UNIONS AS SEEN BY THE AFL AND CIO LEADERS

Opinion	AFL	CIO		AFL	CIO
Believe Unions Have a Program	49%	79%		49%	79%
Groups to be Benefitted *			Type of Goal *		
Union Members	15	10	Economic	24	31
Wage Workers	9	12	Social	20	39
Nation	16	43	Political	16	45
World	2	7	No Answer	8	11
No Answer	9	12			
Do not believe unions have a program	51%	21%		51%	21%
Total (100%)	(225)	(172)		(225)	(172)

* Some respondents named more than one group to be benefited or type of goal.

In Table 18 we see that the CIO leaders conceive of union programs having a more expanded range of attention than do the AFL leaders. Thus, 15 per cent of the AFL and 10 per cent of the CIO leaders aim their program at the union members; but only 16 per cent of the AFL leaders, as against 43 per cent of the CIO leaders, have their eye on the national community when they speak of programs. We see also that the CIO leaders think in terms of broader objectives for union programs. AFL leaders are more likely to specify economic or social goals. The CIO leaders also have these in mind, but many more specify political objectives.

Which is Stronger—Business or Labor?

The idea which a labor leader has of the comparative strength of business organizations and labor organizations obviously affects the way in which he will calculate his chances and determine his policies. In an effort to find out whether labor leaders thought business or labor organizations were the stronger, and whether there were any differences in this respect between the CIO and AFL leaders, we asked the following question: "Do you think that such business organizations as the National Association of Manufacturers and the Chamber of Commerce have more influence or less influence over national affairs than trade union organizations such as the AFL and the CIO?" The answers given to this question by the union leaders are presented in Table 19.

TABLE 19

ARE BUSINESS OR LABOR ORGANIZATIONS THE STRONGER IN NATIONAL AFFAIRS?

Opinion	AFL	CIO
Business stronger	65%	81%
Same	24	14
Labor stronger	11	5
Total (100%)	(221)	(175)

Overwhelmingly, the AFL and the CIO leaders believe that business is stronger than labor. Thus, almost two-thirds of the AFL and four-fifths of the CIO leaders impute a greater strength to business organizations. More CIO leaders than AFL leaders think business is stronger than labor; yet even among AFL leadership, only 11 per cent believe that labor is stronger. No different appraisals are made by leaders on different steps of the hierarchy: city, state, and national officials think alike on this matter.

What is Business Up To?

Labor leaders generally agree with one another that business is more powerful than labor. Are they also afraid of the uses to which business may put this power? What do they think business' attitude is vis-à-vis organized labor? We asked: "Do you believe that on the whole the larger businesses in the United States: (1) accept the principle of collective bargaining and deal with unions in good faith; (2) tolerate unions and deal with them as far as they have to and no further; (3) are trying to 'break' the unions?"

Very few leaders believe business deals with unions in good faith. AFL leaders more often than CIO leaders hold this view: 14 per cent of the AFL and 6 per cent of the CIO leaders believe that business accepts the principle of collective bargaining and deals with the unions in good faith.

TABLE 20

OPINIONS OF AFL AND CIO LEADERS CONCERNING THE INTENTION
OF BUSINESS TOWARD UNIONS

Opinion	AFL	CIO
Business:		
Accepts unions	14%	6%
Tolerates them	57	53
Is out to break them	29	41
Total (100%)	(225)	(177)

Many more endorse the opinion that business' intentions are to crush labor unions. We have evidence that the 29 per cent of the AFL and 41 per cent of the CIO who checked this last alternative are only minimum estimates. In all likelihood, many of these now classified as thinking business "tolerates" unions really believe business tolerates them only because it is forced to—that business really hopes to destroy trade unionism.

TABLE 21

OPINIONS OF AFL AND CIO LEADERS CONCERNING THE INTENTION OF BUSINESS
TOWARD UNIONS BY LEVEL OF LEADERSHIP

Opinion	AFL			CIO		
	National	State	City	National	State	City
Business:						
Accepts unions	13%	17%	14%	8%	9%	4%
Tolerates them	66	66	49	65	52	48
Is out to break them	21	17	37	27	39	48
Total (100%)	(61)	(41)	(123)	(37)	(44)	(96)

In both the CIO and the AFL, city leaders are more suspicious of business than are leaders higher in the order.

Among these city leaders, about a third of the AFL men and nearly half of the CIO men believe business is out to crush the labor movement. Among national leaders, there is very little difference in terms of CIO and AFL affiliation on this question.

Political Party Affiliation

American labor leaders are not concentrated in any one political party. There are, a number of third parties available to them, but these are, in the main, New York City affairs. In Table 22 we have the labor leaders' answers to the question of political affiliation.

TABLE 22

PARTY AFFILIATION OF AFL AND CIO LEADERS

Party	AFL	CIO
Republican	19%	7%
Democrat	51	65
Third-Party	4	9
Bipartisan	26	19
Total (100%)	(222)	(175)

Only 4 per cent of the AFL leaders admit affiliation with any of the third parties, and only 9 per cent of the CIO. In a general way, it appears that about half of the AFL leadership is Democratic, one-fourth bipartisan in the tradition of Samuel Gompers, one-fifth Republican, and a few scattered among the third parties. Two-thirds of the CIO, on the other hand, claim to be Democratic and only 7 per cent Republican, whereas 9 per cent admit third-party affiliation; but even in the CIO, 19 per cent of the leaders are bi-partisan. The breakdown of party affiliation by level of leadership, as in Table 23, reveals some interesting variations.

The general patterns of the AFL and the CIO are the same on each level of leadership; on each level there are more Republicans in the AFL than in the CIO; there are more Democrats and more third-party members on each level in the CIO than in the AFL. There are either more or about the same number of bipartisans in the AFL as in the CIO on each level.

Within the AFL, however, the viewpoint of Samuel Gompers is strongest among the national leaders, whereas the Democratic, and to a lesser extent, the Republican affiliation is stronger among the state and city leaders. Within the CIO, more of the national leaders are either bipartisan or belong to third parties than do the city and state CIO men.

TABLE 23

PARTY AFFILIATION OF AFL AND CIO LEADERS BY LEVEL OF LEADERSHIP

Party	AFL			CIO		
	National	State	City	National	State	City
Republican	16%	26%	19%	6%	7%	8%
Democrat	36	55	56	54	70	67
Third-Party	7	2	2	20	5	6
Bipartisan	41	17	23	20	18	19
Total (100%)	(56)	(42)	(124)	(35)	(44)	(96)

Old Parties and New Parties

Among the labor leaders, party affiliation is not necessarily a stable thing. It is true that there is a certain amount of persistent party loyalty among the leaders, just as in the general population; but there is no reason to suppose, in the absence of definitive knowledge, that it involves as large a proportion of people. We know, for instance, that whenever discussion of third parties of any sort comes about, the labor leaders are in one way or another involved in it.

The question of a third party has to be distinguished by level of action: the idea of a new *national* party is quite a different thing from a new *local* party. Therefore, we first asked the question: "As far as *national* politics are concerned, would you during the next two or three years prefer to work for labor's viewpoint within one or both of the major parties, or would you prefer to set up a new labor party entirely separate from either of them?" We then asked: "How about in local (state and city) politics?"

The answers given to both of these questions are presented in Table 24, which shows the percentages of those who favor setting up a new labor party.

We might expect that there would be some over-all differences between the proportion who want a local labor party, as against a national one; but this is not significantly so. In both cases, of course, a minority group of the leaders is interested in such a party at the present time, and in both cases the *CIO city leaders* are the most interested: almost one-third of them are for a labor party.

The CIO as a whole is, of course, more interested than the AFL. However, this difference does not appear at the top level. National leaders in the CIO feel the same way about a labor party as do the national leaders of the AFL.

TABLE 24

PROPORTION OF AFL AND CIO LEADERS WHO WANT A NATIONAL OR
LOCAL LABOR PARTY *Now* BY LEVEL OF LEADERSHIP

Level of Leadership	National Labor Party		Local Labor Party	
	AFL	CIO	AFL	CIO
National	8%	8%	10%	10%
State	5%	19%	6%	11%
City	18%	31%	20%	29%
Total	13%	23%	15%	21%

The answers to such questions as these may depend upon contingencies that are often of the moment or of the month. In an attempt to get a more stable attitude on the matter, we asked: "Do you think that eventually (say, within the next ten years) gains for labor will best be made by working within one or both of the major parties, *or* through a new labor party entirely separate from either of them?"

Many more labor leaders are interested in the possibility of a new labor party in the next ten years than in plugging for one now: 52 per cent of the CIO leaders and 23 per cent of the AFL leaders answer "yes" to the question when the later time period is specified. Within the AFL, we find that the city leaders are more interested than the national or state leaders. In the CIO, however, the national leaders are just as interested in a labor party within ten years as are the city leaders; and both of them are more interested than the state leaders.

TABLE 25

PROPORTION OF AFL AND CIO LEADERS WHO WANT A LABOR PARTY
WITHIN *Next Ten Years* BY LEVEL OF LEADERSHIP

Level of Leadership	AFL	CIO
National	18%	65%
State	15%	33%
City	28%	56%
Total	23%	52%

Function of Government

One of the long-run questions of a general political and economic nature, on which labor leaders presumably have taken stands, concerns the function of government in the maintenance of full employment.

Our question on this topic ran as follows: "Do you think that it should or that it should not be the function of government today to see to it that full employment is maintained?" On all levels of leadership in either the AFL or the CIO, the overwhelming majority of labor leaders answer the question in the affirmative. However, even on this question, there are rather strong differences between the AFL and the CIO: 92 per cent of the CIO leaders believe that government should take on this function, as compared with 72 per cent of the AFL leaders. The CIO leadership is rather uniform in its opinion, with perhaps slightly fewer of the city leaders believing that government should maintain full employment. On the other hand, in the AFL the situation is rather mixed, for the state and then the city leaders favor the proposition more than those on the national level.

TABLE 26

PROPORTION OF AFL AND CIO LEADERS WHO BELIEVE THAT FULL EMPLOYMENT
IS GOVERNMENT'S FUNCTION BY LEVEL OF LEADERSHIP

Level of Leadership	AFL	CIO
National	67%	95%
State	83%	98%
City	72%	85%
Total	72%	92%

The Threat of Fascism

The term "fascism" has many different meanings and it may not be presumed that, even among a group as homogeneous as labor leaders, the meaning they attach to the term is consistent. It is more or less a symbol of economic and political doom. And when we ask questions about it, we are simply fishing in the "doom market." We asked the labor leaders: "Do you think that there is a threat to American democracy by a 'Fascist' totalitarian movement in this country within the next five years?"; and we allowed them four possible answers to check: "(1) there is a definite and serious threat; (2) there is some threat and it is likely to become more serious; (3) there is some threat but it is not likely to become serious; (4) there is no threat at all." See Table 27, page 44.

The CIO is more alarmed about the possibility of totalitarianism than is the AFL. Sixty-nine percent of them think either that it is serious or that it is likely to become more serious, as against 55 per cent of the AFL leaders.

TABLE 27

OPINIONS OF AFL AND CIO LEADERS ON THE THREAT OF FASCISM

Opinion	AFL	CIO
Serious	20%	30%
Somewhat serious, and will be more so	35	39
Some threat, but won't be serious	35	25
No threat at all	10	6
Total (100%)	(225)	(172)

But this difference between AFL and CIO is almost completely accounted for at the national leader level. Within the AFL, the leaders in the lower ranks—the state and city men—are more alarmed at the possibility than the national leaders. Forty per cent of the national leaders think that there is or will be a serious threat of fascism, as against 60 per cent of the state and 59 per cent of the city leaders. In the CIO, however, there is a slightly greater proportion on the national level who believe that fascism is or is likely to become a serious threat than is the case among the leaders on the lower levels.

TABLE 28

PROPORTIONS OF AFL AND CIO LEADERS WHO BELIEVE THE THREAT OF FASCISM IS OR WILL BECOME SERIOUS, BY LEVEL OF LEADERSHIP

Level of Leadership	AFL	CIO
National	40%	78%
State	60%	66%
City	59%	67%
Total	55%	69%

Characteristics of AFL vs. CIO Leader

If we add together the national, state, and city leaderships of each of the two union blocs, we can construct an image of the typical labor leader in each bloc.

The AFL leader is a man fifty years of age who has completed the tenth grade of school. He began labor union work around 1929. The CIO leader is ten years younger than the AFL man: he is forty years old. He is also better educated than the AFL leader, having completed twelve or thirteen years of school. Since he is younger, it is natural to find that he did not begin trade union work as early as the AFL individual: he began, as a matter of fact, during the big organization wave of the late thirties—specifically, in the year 1937.

The typical AFL leadership is about one-half Democratic, one-fourth bipartisan, one-fifth Republican. The CIO leadership, on the other hand, is overwhelmingly Democratic, about two-thirds. One-fifth is not affiliated and the remainder is divided about equally between third party and Republican.

All but one out of ten of the labor union leaders in the United States today were born in the United States, about as high a proportion as is found in the population at large. Yet, four out of ten are of foreign parentage, and there is a slight tendency for a larger proportion of the fathers of the trade union leaders to be foreign-born than is true of the general population.

Overwhelmingly urban in origin, the leaders of the AFL and CIO are also similar in occupational origin. A large majority from both union blocs came from the lower occupational level, specifically, the wage-worker stratum. Their fathers were mostly foremen or skilled laborers, and most union leaders in both of the major union blocs occupied a wage worker position before they got into trade union work. There is a slight difference between the type of wage worker the AFL and CIO leaders had been: the AFL man tends to have been a foreman or skilled laborer, and the CIO man is a little more likely to have come from semi- or unskilled labor groups. In both cases, however, they began their union careers at the bottom of the union world—in the local unions, as committeemen or as presidents of local unions. A good many, of course, were appointed as organizers and worked their way up to the elected positions.

Opinions of AFL vs. CIO Leader

When we come to consider the opinions and the general outlook of the AFL and the CIO leaders, we find that on no question we asked is there uniformity of opinion between the two union blocs. We find, as a matter of fact, that age, education, and position in the union do not substantially affect the social and political and economic opinions that are held. What does affect all opinions is the union bloc to which an individual belongs. As the career of the trade union leader is union-made, so it appears that his opinions are union-made. The AFL leader is quite optimistic about the chances for labor unity, whereas the CIO leader thinks there is only a slight chance, if any. The AFL leader is also more inclined to believe that the organizations should unite, that it would be a good thing for the wage workers of the country. The CIO leader is not convinced of this proposition.

The majority of the CIO leaders believe that the trade unions now have a long-range program. The AFL leader is less likely to think this;

nor does the AFL leader think of a program in terms of such broad objectives as the CIO leader who more often feels that the union program helps the nation attain political goals.

The CIO leadership also believes that business is stronger than labor to a much greater extent than is true of the AFL leadership. However, the leaders in both blocs believe that large business as a whole merely tolerates unions and deals with them as far as it must and no farther. Both leaderships are also inclined to believe that business is out to break the unions, although the CIO is more emphatic about this than the AFL. In line with this opinion, the CIO leaders are more inclined to believe that there is a fascist or totalitarian threat to the United States. They believe that it is either a serious threat or that it may very well within a short time become serious. Despite this fact, however, the majority still feel that they should work for labor's viewpoint within one or both of the two standard parties. They believe this just as the AFL does, and both of them think in these terms for both national and for local politics. However, more of the CIO men believe that eventually, say within ten years, the labor unions will have to start their own labor party if they are going to get anywhere.

The Independent Union Leaders

We have some information on the presidents and secretaries of the independent unions. Responses were received from 34 such leaders. This information is not reliable enough to permit statistical treatment, for we do not attempt to justify such small numbers as a sample. Nevertheless, we can make certain broad statements, and in a crude way, compare the independent leaders with the national leaders of the AFL and CIO.

The most general fact about the leaders of the independent unions is that they are very similar to the national leaders of the AFL. In age, the independents have a median of 50 years, between the AFL median age of 57 and the CIO of 43. But the independent leaders are similar to the AFL in educational level: the median grade of schooling among independent leaders is 9.4 years; that of AFL national leaders is 9.3; and of CIO leaders, 12.5. There is no difference in the nativity between the independent leaders and the leaders of the two union blocs. About nine out of ten of all of them were born in the United States. In occupational origin, the independents come from wage-worker fathers, as do the AFL and CIO leaders; half from foremen or skilled laborers. The independents were, in the main, wage workers before entering trade union work. Six out of ten were foremen or skilled workers, which makes them more like AFL than CIO leaders.

One might suppose that the independent men would have quite a different view of the chances and the moral rightness of unity between the AFL and the CIO, but this is not the case: about the same proportion as among the AFL believe that the chances for the two big blocs to become one unified organization are good, or at least fair. If anything, they are more pessimistic: more of them than in the two big wings think there is no chance at all for labor unity. On the moral side of the question they tend, however, to stand between the AFL and CIO opinion, coming closer to AFL opinion.

As a matter of fact, it is a fairly safe assumption that if our sample were large enough for exact comparison, the backgrounds, careers, and opinions of the independent leaders would be quite similar to those we have found true for the AFL national leadership. Both on background characteristics and in their opinions, the independent leaders stand somewhere between the AFL and CIO national leaders, but they resemble much more closely the AFL leader than the CIO leader.

C. WRIGHT MILLS
HELEN S. DINERMAN

Chapter 3

People in the unions

DURING THE EARLY FALL OF 1945, THE NATIONAL OPINION RESEARCH Center of the University of Denver made a survey that included one direct question on labor union membership. We borrowed the records of this investigation in order to work out a preliminary analysis of this one question. Needless to say, NORC is not responsible for any errors that may have occurred; and we wish to thank that organization for allowing us to analyze and present these materials.

The survey included a 2,533 cross section of people from all sections of the country, over 21 years of age and on all occupational levels. The question was: "Are you, or is anybody in your family, a member of a labor union?" The answers were coded into four categories: "respondent a member"; "husband or wife of respondent a member"; "other family members belong"; "nobody in the family a member."

TABLE 1

INVOLVEMENT OF THE POPULATION IN UNIONS

Respondent	13.1%
Husband or wife	11.4
Other family	6.8
Total involved in unions	31.3%
Total not involved	68.7
Total U. S. population over 21 years	100.0%

Thus in the fall of 1945, almost one-third of all the adults of the country were members of trade unions or had close relatives who were. This over-all figure indicates the extent to which the people of the United States are connected with the trade unions.

In 1945, the year this poll was taken, there were around 92 million people in the population 20 years old and over. Since 13.1 per cent of the respondents in the poll claimed to belong, we can make the crude estimate that something like 12 million people over 20 years of age were union members. This is not an entirely accurate estimate of total union membership, for obviously there were union members under 21 years of age, but it is as close as we can come to an over-all estimate with this adult sample.

We must narrow down the sample in order to get a more accurate picture of the *working* population that belongs, for the over-all figure of involvement includes people who are not employed at all, as well as those who are self-employed. Let us, therefore, take the men only, and among them only those who are the main earners of families: 25 per cent of those in this category belong to trade unions. But again, this base includes independent farmers and all others who work and are the main contributor to a family, and there are no unions available for many such people. Hence it is necessary to eliminate them in order to arrive at a closer figure.

Let us take all the men who live in cities (places over 2,500 population) who are the main earners of families in *wage-working* and *white-collar* employments: these are the two main categories of "wage and salary workers" in the U. S. labor force. *All the rest of our figures will be about these men.* We find that 33 per cent of them are members of some labor union.

Some 22 per cent of the white-collar men and 50 per cent of all the wage working men in the sample are unionized. The categories "wage worker" and "white collar" are naturally quite broad: the former includes highly skilled people as well as day laborers; the latter includes managerial employees and musicians as well as office employees. We can break these down conveniently in terms of what is known as socio-economic status (SES). This is a judgment about each respondent in a survey, made by the interviewers on the basis of the type of house lived in, the condition of the furniture, the appearance of the person, etc. Within each of our two broad occupational strata, we can break the groups into "high" and "low" SES level; this operation yields the data in Table 2.

TABLE 2

PERCENTAGE OF UNION MEMBERS IN EACH OCCUPATION AND STATUS LEVEL

	(SES Level)	
Occupation	High	Low
White-collar workers	21%	30%
Wage workers	57%	40%
All workers	34%	37%

The wage workers in the higher SES level are more likely to be union members than those of lower SES; whereas white-collar workers are more unionized in the lower SES level. The unionization of both occupational strata thus come together, as it were, in the lower middle status group. These are the trade unionists of the country.

It is of interest to inquire as to the regional distribution of trade union membership. Table 3 shows the proportion of urban male breadwinners who belong to the unions in each region by occupational level.

TABLE 3

PERCENTAGE OF UNION MEMBERS IN EACH OCCUPATIONAL LEVEL
AND REGION OF THE COUNTRY

	West	Midwest	Northeast	South
White-collar workers	28%	15%	27%	19%
Wage workers	68%	55%	45%	41%
All workers	43%	34%	34%	27%

The size of the city also influences the extent of unionization. The sample can be divided into "large cities" (those having over 50,000 residents) and "small cities" (those under 50,000). The resulting Table 4 indicates that unions are a "large city" proposition.

TABLE 4

PERCENTAGE OF UNION MEMBERS IN EACH OCCUPATIONAL LEVEL
AND CITY-SIZE GROUP

	Large Cities	Small Cities
White-collar workers	29%	6%
Wage workers	60%	39%
All workers	41%	22%

Among the wage workers, it is the better educated who belong to unions. Of those wage workers who have *not* gone beyond grammar school, 44 per cent are union members; whereas of the wage workers who *have* gone to high school or beyond, 58 per cent are union members.

TABLE 5

PERCENTAGE OF UNION MEMBERS AMONG WAGE WORKERS BY AGE AND EDUCATION

	Under 40		40 and Over	
	High School	Grade School	High School	Grade School
Union members	63%	34%	54%	47%
Not members	37	66	46	53
Totals	100%	100%	100%	100%

But perhaps this apparent difference is due to the fact of age rather than education. The younger people have had more education than the older ones, and perhaps the younger ones join the unions. Accordingly the factor of age must be considered, in order to see whether education really makes a difference.

Table 5 shows that in each age group, the more educated are more likely to be union members than those with less education. This tendency is especially marked among the younger age groups.

The small results given here have had to be pieced together from a poll designed for other purposes. They do not indicate very much of what *could* be obtained from this sort of research if a poll were designed to answer the more precise questions we would like to have answered.

C. WRIGHT MILLS
THELMA E. ANDERSON

Chapter 4

State of the movement

1. THE "UPSURGE OF LABOR"

*A*MERICAN LABOR LIVED FAST IN THE YEARS SINCE 1933, OFTEN CROWDING A decade into a year, vastly enlarging organization and membership; accumulating substantial funds and investing great resources of men and matériel in further "expansion of plant"; building up and utilizing social power; rapidly developing a labor institutionalism—making unionism a recognized constituent part of American democratic society; in brief, making with gusto, although most of the time without "plan," the transition from organization to movement, from a static force to a dynamic power. But, while labor's rise to a position of distinction was in the United States only yesterday's burst of speed, nearly everywhere else labor had gained recognition many years earlier and was in power, for considerable lengths of time, in a number of countries—in some governing in coalition with other groups, in others fully in control of power.

Professor Arthur M. Schlesinger of Harvard, co-editor of the 13-volume *History of American Life*, records the "upsurge of labor" as the third on a list of ten events and developments "that most profoundly shaped and shook history" in the first half of the twentieth century.

"All around the globe," wrote Professor Schlesinger in *The Washington Post*, January 1, 1950, "the half-century witnessed attempts of the labor movement not only to buttress and extend labor unions but to dominate government."

The "world-shaking ten," singled out by the historian, do not include such developments as "the mighty advances in medicine, the greatly expanded life span, an epochal scientific theory like Einstein's relativity, and such revolutionary inventions as the motor car, airplane, movie and radio" because, he thinks, "on balance it would be difficult to substitute for the events selected any others that have so vitally affected mankind's life, liberty and pursuit of happiness. . . . However much science and technology have dominated our time, politics and economics have continued to provide the great turning points in men's fortunes."

Labor shares a position on the record of the ten outstanding developments with the two world wars, the emancipation of women, the Great Depression, the harnessing of atomic energy, the demise of colonial imperialism (excepting the evolving new Russian variety), the successive although thus far unsuccessful efforts toward creating a workable international association of nations, Russia's emergence as a dominant world power, and America's rise to world leadership. The part of labor in the stormy career of the first half of this century, outstanding among other half-centuries for the "sheer multiplicity and magnitude of changes" that it caused and experienced, was most pronounced on the European continent, in the British Isles, in Australia, and in New Zealand long before American union labor had "firmly entrenched itself in law, industry and political life" in the wake of the Roosevelt Revolution of the 'thirties.

The progress of American labor was late but well nigh phenomenal for the speedy headway it made.

Indeed, it was only yesterday, in the early 'thirties, that American labor unions were in a most precarious position. Unions were recognized in only a few industries, and at that, nowhere fully. Union members were mostly apathetic and doubtful or distrustful of their unions' ability, even willingness in some instances, to drive for full, real status. The law was none too friendly to unions when not clearly antagonistic. And the community was at best tolerant, and in most instances indifferent when not altogether opposed to all and any of the unions' work. And then came the change, during the 'thirties, with the result that today, only a decade and a half later—

1. The open antiunion shop is no longer among the recognized virtues of prudent business; and although management will seek to exact the most or yield as little as possible in collective bargaining, and quite often will be ready to countenance strikes rather than consent to certain union terms, the prevailing attitude by and large is that of union recognition.

2. Unions operate under a generally labor-friendly legal and administrative dispensation even though they must cope with difficulties of one kind or another in a number of states and must face the consequences of the basically restrictive orientation in the Taft-Hartley Act (Labor-Management Relations Act of 1947).

3. The prevailing economic thinking of the nation has rejected the time-honored paralyzing restraints of a scarcity economy and is proceeding upon the recognition of the principles and the policies of full employment, social security, and wage improvements as the foundation for continuously expanding high-level economy, which in turn opens vistas of a fairer and greater share for labor even as the community as a whole benefits from economic growth.

4. Labor's own thinking, alongside national orientation, has broken

through the limitations of the traditional isolationist outlook and made possible the joining of the United States with the other free and progressive nations in efforts to develop international economic cooperation.

5. Nearly all segments of the American national community—exceptions here and there but confirming the generality of the fact—have come to recognize the dignity of the "man in overalls" and his right to a fair share in all that a free democratic society brings to its members.

No other nation's labor has a record of achievement of so much good in so short a period of time. It was not all sweetness and light, however. For a good part of the time, the land was agog with struggle. "Unions of their own choosing" were not easily won. They were resisted, openly or in disguise, whether in the wearing apparel industries, in the automotive or steel industries, in the rubber-making plants, or in the manufacture of textiles—indeed everywhere. And labor fought in a great variety of ways: sitdown strikes in General Motors plants, pitched battles at the Ford gates, all but civil war in Akron, Ohio's rubber mills; war of attrition between union and "Little Steel"; diplomatic penetration and "encirclement" forcefully resisted by Big Steel; strikes for what they were worth on the waterfronts of the East, the Gulf, the West; five-and-ten-cent-store girls "sitting down," walking out; Wall Street clerks lying down on the pavement in front of the Stock Exchange and the brokerage offices, and in most instances, the less spectacular, traditional bickering and trading: collective bargaining.

Labor's growth was also accompanied by major upsets within the union movement. The efforts of the more farsighted and audacious leaders to accelerate labor's pace in keeping with what was happening to the country and to the world were stubbornly fought back by those who failed to see the need for a change in methods and policies. There followed the split of the AFL, rivalry among unions, topping and further complicating the old jurisdictional squabbles and leadership feuds.

However, the unions grew, many not only in strength but also in stature and in consciousness of their social responsibility. And, on the other hand, most of the country's men of business, emerging stronger and richer out of the war, made peace with the fact that the unions had come to stay. There were exceptions in both groups, to be sure. Some unions failed to recognize or at least failed to bear in mind at all times that the public had the right to a measure of consideration in cases where community health or safety were at stake. And some employers just wouldn't forget the "good old days"—so good for the few, whereas the new age is so distinctly concerned with the interests of the many.

The spread of collective bargaining—"cumbersome and crude as is that excessively praised process of fumbling, bluffing, and bulldozing toward an adjustment which should be made with hairbreadth precision," to quote Mr. Dexter M. Keezer, economist, War Labor Board member, and onetime college president—has brought an impressive measure of constitutional government into American industrial relations; it has given American labor great power and it has implanted in the minds of many business leaders a greater than hitherto awareness of the public's stake in the social aspects of industry. Conflicts have continued, of course, but they cannot overshadow the fact of growing order—and who would want all conflict to cease? In the words of the always deliberative William H. Davis, former Chairman of the War Labor Board, "creative progress does not come from the absence of conflict, but from conflicts resolved by reasonable agreement."

And so in a matter of only a few years, American labor unionism emerged organized, invigorated, capable of facing and seeing through undertakings of major importance and complexity. Without getting itself immersed in Socialist, Communist, and in-between ideologies and parties, it mustered enough stamina to join in the generation's two campaigns of defense and advance, against the two most powerful physical and intellectual onslaughts upon freedom and humanity: nazism and Stalinist bolshevism.

2. BEYOND "BREAD 'N' BUTTER"

What's Hecuba to him, or he to Hecuba,
That he should weep for her

Watching the unprecedented ascent of American labor to status and power, and wondering what the impact of the development may be, Mr. John Q. American might, indeed, paraphrase Hamlet, not so much puzzled as concerned: what is labor to him or he to labor?

The word "labor" in American English, unlike the term's connotation on the European continent, means the unions; and labor, in this sense, is rapidly becoming most significant in the American scene and in the American way of life. A conscious orientation on the "labor issue" is becoming essential to any citizen's intellectual equipment, but it cannot be said that there is a clear and wide realization of that need.

Indeed, not long ago, a highly qualified candidate for a city-wide adult education post in the largest American city was turned down by that city's Board of Education because, in the words of the Board Chairman, the candidate was known to be a *labor protagonist*. Since it could not be assumed that a *labor antagonist* was wanted for the post, the Board's action in the case could mean only that a *labor neutral* would best qualify. But the Board could hardly count on a long waiting list of candidates thus qualified at this stage of our economic and political civilization. For labor, using the term in its broad, inclusive sense, is right in the explosive thick of contemporary social dynamics, and a position of neutrality toward labor is politically impossible. Many, no doubt, are honestly neutral on specific labor issues, but no such out-of-the-world disposition can for long survive contact with the broad social-economic and cultural realities of our nation and time: one is irretrievably either "for" labor or "against" it.

What is unionism, its nature, its function, its place?

The statement recently made by "an expert of industrial management" that the union is that which "drives a wedge between management and the working force" is about as revealing as a certain young woman's description of a bridge as "that which keeps the two banks of a river apart." But even though our expert's definition is too dated to be considered intelligent opinion, much of what generally passes for an understanding of unionism is altogether unreal. It surely shouldn't be. American unionism has maintained a century-and-a-half long continuity, there is an enormous literature on the subject, and most colleges carry numerous labor courses on their programs. There is a vast union press reaching many millions of Americans, in addition to expanding labor reporting in the daily press. Yet nearly always the same questions are asked as soon as discussion hits upon labor matters, and there is distinct concern and an uncomprehending fear that what is known about unions is not quite the whole story. The substance of these questions, whatever the form, is:

What are the unions, what do they stand for? Is "bread 'n' butter" all that there is to it?

Are these numerous unions an associated movement, and if so how close is that association and what are its ends? Or does each union go its own way in pursuit of particular aims, and what are these aims?

Are the members and the leaders of the unions a democratic team seeking to realize common aims or is there no such unity of purpose? What, then, do workers want of their unions, and what is the leaders' game in unionism? What manner of people are these union leaders? One hears so much bad about them; why do the members tolerate them?

Finally, how does unionism affect the whole of American democracy?

Mr. John Q. American wants to *know*, which is all to the good, but somehow he does not get all the facts right, or they do not seem to add up to a coherent whole.

Yet it is important that Mr. J.Q.A. should know what labor is to him and what he is to labor: he is to live with labor more closely than ever before in this production-geared U.S.A. of mid-twentieth century.

And it is important to labor that it be understood right by Mr. J.Q.A.: integrated, interdependent living in the atomic age and this war-affected civilization calls for a community that is not divided against itself, but united and whole.

Mr. J.Q.A. is, of course, you and I, indeed nearly every one of us who have become tried and true constituents of Mr. Elmo Roper, Mr.

George Gallup, Mr. Archibald M. Crossley, and the other luminaries of that most recent of art forms, catching our thinking as we run. Like most other human arts, this one, too, is less than infallible; but it is the one that exists for the purpose it seeks to achieve.

What is Mr. John Q. American's thinking on labor in the postwar era?

On the testimony of Mr. Roper we have it as, on the whole, labor-friendly. But in an analytical study published in *Labor and Nation* (October, 1945), Mr. Roper wrote:

If there is any one lesson from the results of the public opinion polls we have taken in the last ten or eleven years, in asking about labor unions, it would be this: that the public is getting a little fed up hearing labor union people just talk about their *rights*. The public would like to hear a little talk about the *responsibilities* of labor unions. If labor could judiciously mix a little talk about the responsibilities of labor unions in with continued talk about the rights of labor, it would have a more receptive hearing on the part of the public. Fundamentally, the public is "pro-worker." It just happens to be a little bit suspicious of the contention that at this time the best way to help the worker is through the union labor movement, as now run. Despite that, the public would not do away with unions. It just wants to "fix them up."

In the years since this commentary was written, Mr. Roper's judgment has been substantially confirmed. J.Q.A. has continued friendly right along. Yet he has been even more concerned about the what's whats and whys of labor. He has often been given elaborate, eruditely presented explanations to the effect that labor is a bread-and-butter proposition. The application of this intellectual yardstick should have returned all the right answers and served as a never-failing test of the behavior of labor in a given situation. But it has not worked too well. In fact, J.Q.A. finds it difficult to hold on to a stationary who's who in labor, to fix a clear image of leadership, let alone a what's what. As to that who's who, at one time he thought he had it: it was the lately sainted Samuel Gompers. The man, on the record, at times talked big, but he moved slowly. "A fair day's pay for a fair day's work" was a rather evasive statement of what labor wanted, but he was not persistent on demands. His labor seemed to know its place and no applecarts were in danger of being overturned.

To be sure, there was the violent Bill Haywood, the crusading Gene Debs, the earlier days' John L. Lewis, and the smoothly aggressive Sidney Hillman, all upsetting influences and diversionist practitioners. However, it seemed possible to relegate these men to the category of exceptions whose job was to confirm, if by indirection, the standard and the rule. One knew unionism and had no cause for disquietude.

But then it all changed, went askew. There arose a John L. Lewis, totally different from the one that had been known, and no one knew what was coming next. And as Lewis outlasted his metamorphosis, new and ever so different men were thrown up in rapid succession: Philip Murray, David Dubinsky, Walter P. Reuther, Dave Beck, Al Hayes, A. F. Whitney, Harvey W. Brown, and still other older men in new roles, younger men in still newer roles, a kaleidoscopic variety of leaders in pursuit of new, different, and differing aims. Mr. J.Q.A. has been trying to make sense of it: are all of them, so vastly dissimilar in outlook and ways of action and statement, in the self-same quest for that slice of "bread 'n' butter," nothing more and nothing else? Is that really the case?

The overemphasis on the "bread 'n' butter" idea of unionism, as a guide to the understanding of labor, is of but limited meaning and is on balance misleading: it leaves the questions unresolved and the questioners unconvinced. If "bread 'n' butter" is all that there is to unionism, why do not the opponents dispose of the disturbing movement by offering better bread and richer butter and more of both to the workers? Of course, by "bread alone," even if buttered, unionism could not survive, still less achieve its phenomenal growth and enhanced status in American society. Nor could any other social contingent similarly progress on that restricted diet. "Bread 'n' butter" in a general sense underlay all social movements in recorded history, yet it would be a meager and fruitless reading of the history of man's advance upon this earth that would reduce all conflict and adjustment to mere rearrangement of the distribution of basic foodstuffs.

Unions are the instrumentality that millions of American workers have been becoming accustomed to use ever more eagerly, for the attainment of what they want. Bread and butter are of the things they need and want. At union meetings, at collective bargaining conferences, in court litigations, at sessions of Congressional bodies probing labor, in colleges where labor courses are offered, unions are invariably spoken of as a "bread-'n'-butter proposition." Unions surely are economic organizations. However, to the extent that the definition aims at asserting that wages, hours, and other work conditions constitute the only proper business of unionism, and that nothing else, no "pursuit of visionary goals" is in order, it falls wide of the mark, and no unionist worthy of his salt takes it seriously. Unions are no longer that "pure and simple," if they ever were. They cannot be, and endure.

A great deal more than bakery and dairy service is involved in the procurement of bread and butter. A good deal more than scales of wages and shop regulations are at issue before the relevant labor-management problems are resolved. The "market economy," the operational base of all bread-'n'-butter business, isn't miles distant from the Congress but right in the lobbies; the union is not outside the community, but an integral part of it; the trade agreement is not the philosophers' "thing in itself," but part and parcel of the nation's way of life. Labor and management are more than terms of the industrial relations vocabulary, they are people; and to them as to the Romans of antiquity "nothing human is alien."

If the political parties represent the college level of political practice, unionism of this period in contemporary history is the arena of graduate political work. It should benefit all concerned, and it would considerably relieve the jam in Mr. J.Q.A.'s reasoning if those who tell and teach would make a point of the fact that the "bread-'n'-butter proposition" is greatly enriched with all sorts of political vitamins, and that politics is more than button-holing a legislator and placing a cross in the square on the ballot, or pulling the lever of the voting machine. Twentieth century politics is the art of bringing multitudes into coherent purposive motion. Unions do just that.

Speaking to his organization's annual Convention in 1941, at Detroit, CIO President Philip Murray sketched with moving simplicity the meaning that workers read into their union action:

Organization fundamentally means but one thing. That is: clothing, and bread and butter, and pictures on the wall, and carpets on the floor, and music in the home, and enlarged opportunities for children to receive the benefits of better education. The work of organizing rises so far above triviality that men interested in kids, men whose souls, hearts and minds beat in unison with the aspirations of little children and toiling men and women, will loan their bodies and their souls and their brains and their minds and everything that God has given them in this work of organizing.

To be sure, the form of the statement was that of convention oratory, and it would not stand up too well in a class in biology or anatomy; but millions of workers throughout the land and over the years have responded to the essence of this and similar statements. Again, on a different level, Professor Carroll R. Daugherty, of Northwestern University, Chairman of the President's Steel Fact-Finding Board of 1949, wrote: [1]

The fact that the individual worker regards the union as the instrument of his self-fulfillment, and that groups of workers regard it as their common bond, means that the union, although operating in an economic context and seeking economic ends, is more than an economic institution—more than a cooperative association for marketing their labor.

Essentially, it is two other things. First, a union is a part of a *movement*. Second, it is internally a *political* organization.

The unions' quest for "bread 'n' butter" takes organized labor from shop economics to local, state, and national politics and legislation, and brings education, public relations, mass psychology, community prob-

---

[1] "Organized Labor and the Public Interest," *Yale Review*. Spring 1950.

lems and social engineering, and matters of foreign relations and policies as well within the purview and concern of members and leaders.

The ramifications of its sphere of interest induce a widening expansion of labor's mental processes and intellectual growth. Against the background of industrial, political, and social complexity, the union movement is obliged to puzzle out the problems of democracy and leadership, government and statecraft; to steer through the intellectual maze of the involved relationships between labor and other organized groups and that of the authority of the state in a democratic republic; to battle for group rights under the law without making the law-making organs of democracy the playball of never-ending group contests. To be sure, the 15,600,000 unionized wage earners are not profound students of the social sciences nor, in the majority, even readers of books. They are obliged to "dope it all out" by no more delicate tool than "horse sense," depending upon a sort of "feel" for what is wrong or right, for what makes or doesn't make labor sense. Their wisdom is empirical, their vocabulary none too precise, but they generally know what they want.

The telephone operator and the teamster, the tailor and the carpenter, the electrician and the domestic servant, the hired farm hand, the miner, and the school teacher seek, as citizens of their nation and neighbors in their communities, to apply their knowledge of the "score" to the task of equating their particular functional relation to society with what they consider to be the communal interests and obligations.

Upon how well they perform depends the progress of unionism and of the nation, too. The unions comprise a large part of America's adult active humanity.

If he freed himself of the restrictive "bread 'n' butter" stigmatization of unionism, Mr. J.Q.A. would be certain to secure a grasp of the complex realities of unionism and build a leadership image that would hold despite the constant and conflicting changes upon the stage. J.Q.A. would have no difficulty finding out why labor behaves the way it does if he at all times remembered that labor is not an isolated ghetto, or a charmed circle somewhere in America, but that it is the American people who for a number of hours a day don overalls, aprons, or whatever other working garb.

3. From Union Strength to Labor Power

The degree to which unions succeed in unionizing the workers in their respective trades, industries, or services, is a fair measure, but by no means the full measure, of union strength in the respective area. Nor is the relative labor power in the nation determined solely by the relative strength of the union contingent in the nation's labor force. One hundred per cent unionization does not necessarily spell one hundred per cent union power in the nation. The other elements that enter the power equation include intra- and interunion cohesiveness, the state of the national economy, the mind and the moods of the owner and managerial sides of industry, the political climate in the nation, and lately in an ever-increasing measure, the state of international affairs and relations and their bearing upon the nation and upon labor. There is no fixed yardstick for the measurement of labor power, nor is it to be determined by majority-minority computations. Even though autonomy and a grass-roots pragmatism are cardinal features of the structure and the operational practices of American unionism, and each union, particularly the stronger ones, pretty much runs its own show, it often happens that but a few unions, not necessarily representing a majority of all the unionists, actually determine the direction and the orientation of the movement as a whole. Activism and leadership rather than numerical preponderance are at times the stepping stones to nationwide dominance.

This is not to say that numbers do not count, but only that numerical strength, however important, is only one factor in the determination of the extent to which unionism bears upon the labor force and thus, eventually, upon the nation itself.

What is, to begin with, the arithmetic of American unionism in relation to the labor force in the nation?

The total number of persons in the labor force, as estimated by the Bureau of the Census of the U. S. Department of Commerce, was 64,108,000 as of May 1950. Of that number, 1,320,000 served in the armed forces, leaving the civilian labor force at 62,788,000. As against that number, there were, as of the same date, about 51,000,000 persons "not in the labor force," including civilians, 14 years old and over, engaged in housework in their own homes; students; those permanently unable to work, and all persons without jobs and not looking for any. Again, as of the same date, the estimated total of wage and salaried workers in the labor force of 62,788,000 was 43,000,000. The latter figure, then, is the potential union area.

With union membership accounting for better than 15,000,000, actual unionization is somewhat above 36 per cent. The percentage may appear more impressive, however, if allowance is made for certain labor segments considered, for the present time at least, not easily organizable. Thus, 8,062,000 workers in agricultural employment as of May 1950 are not readily union timber. Nor do unions expect to make much headway with those in domestic service, or at the other end of the line, with the largely middle-class-minded white collar workers. Of the close to 15 million in that category, including salespeople, only about two and a half million or 16 per cent are unionized, as estimated by Professor C. Wright Mills.[2]

---

[2] "White Collar Unionism," *Labor and Nation*, March–April, May–June 1949.

The degree of member activization is another vital point in assaying union strength. How many unionists, and to what extent, are interested in their unions beyond holding membership?

Not all members of unions take an active part in the business of their organizations. An estimate of union activism by a source of fair competence places the number of interested member-participants in union affairs at well over two million, or about one out of every seven unionists. These workers attend local union meetings, participate in voting on policy matters or themselves initiate policy decisions, elect officers, and constitute, in every way, the core of the union organization. Some of them serve as local presidents or secretaries, or on executive boards and committees, or as shop stewards and carry out various assigned duties. Their work is volunteer, but some receive compensation for loss of working time due to such assignments. They are usually reimbursed for incidental expenses incurred while performing their tasks. These people carry a good deal of influence in their local organizations.

The directive and day-to-day administrative responsibilities of the unions, with their 15 million members and some 50 thousand union contracts and other affairs, are vested in elected or appointed local, regional, and national officers employed full time by the organizations. These officers number some 15 thousand, not counting technical and routine help employed by the national and local organization.

The over-all picture of the union force is about as follows:

1. The membership of approximately 15 million comes from the 64 million Americans in the nation's labor force, of whom 43 million or about two-thirds are wage earners; union strength is about 36 per cent of that number.

2. Union membership is assembled in some 200 national and some 60 to 70 thousand local unions, and in well over 1,000 state and city central federated bodies and in a great variety of special-function associations, such as district councils, joint boards, regional conferences, etc., as detailed in Maurice F. Neufeld's "State of the Unions," Chapter 1.

3. Between two and three million, or one in about every seven union members, appear to be actively concerned with the work of the union movement, and in most instances take a more or less assertive part in the promotion of the unions' interests.

4. Of the two to three million actively interested unionists, probably about a half million members hold office in their respective unions, serve on committees, and perform specified functions and assignments for which some of them sometimes receive compensation for loss of working time and refund of expenses incurred through such assignments.

5. Not less than 15 thousand workers are engaged, mostly by the national unions, through appointment or election, to give all of their

time to the continuing organizing, administrative, and directional work of the unions, and are paid accordingly. The local unions and auxiliary organizations employ many thousands more.

Such is the arithmetic of union strength in relation to the nation's labor force. What is the power-potential of the union force in the nation?

Our sensitive social order is readily disturbed by the operation of union power in certain areas. Particularly "touchy" are the industries and services vital to the economy or such as affect the nation's security. The fate of democracy itself may be jeopardized by a labor leadership unwilling or unable to equate union outlook with the nation's interest, domestic or international, or both. From that point of view the high or low percentage of membership in the total labor force is not so important as are union strength and influence in the strategic services or industries affected by the national interest.

Labor is 80 to 100 per cent unionized in all branches of transportation, of coal and metal mining, of manufacturing in basic steel, automobile and aircraft, meatpacking, the apparel industries, shipbuilding, building construction, rubber products, and in the telegraph, newspaper printing, and publishing branches of the communication industries; and about 50 per cent or better unionized in telephone, radio, and motion pictures. These are important and some of them are strategically vital industries and services; unions entrenched in these fields can wield very considerable power if they are keen and alert to their opportunities and inclined to make their power felt. However that may have happened, some of the most alert leaders are in the unions of teamsters, miners, machinists, auto workers, steel workers, electrical machine workers—to mention but six organizations of which five account for over 500,000 members each, three of them close to or over the 1,000,000 mark, and who together represent about four to five million out of the country's 15 million unionists.

The "locus" of labor's power potential is in these unions and in their leaders. They can make unionism a "power-in-being." It is virtually unavoidable that the policies of groups so strong and so strategically placed, whether they act in accord or singly, tend to determine the course and behavior of the majority of organized labor. The "tail wags the dog" within union organization, even as organized labor as a whole performs the same "trick" within the wage-earning majority of the total labor force. The phenomenon of the decisive influence of smaller numbers, when organized and cohered, over larger but not sufficiently assertive or poorly cohered groups, is not unknown in other fields of power exercise: in business and industry, in the professions, in politics.

It is well to note the new phenomenon of union strength growing into labor power. The first is one of industrial and economic order, the other clearly political and social. *American labor unions have become a social power in the nation and are conscious of their new import.*

There were strong unions in the United States in the years before the great depression, and many of them commanded recognition and favorable terms in their respective areas, but labor as a socially significant element in the national power structure did not figure, certainly not clearly, in the thinking of many union leaders. There were strong unions here and there, but the labor group as a whole was not viewed as one of the power groups that either ran or wanted to run the national show. The public, except in rare emergent situations, did not bother much about unions or care to know very much about them or their place in the nation. Unionism, to the people generally, was a term used to represent the annoying but none too important labor-management scraps over wages, hours, featherbedding, rackets, contracts, pickets, seniority rules, and the rest of the dull jargon of labor economics and industrial relations. Unions, it was generally thought, were primarily the concern of personnel managers whose business it was to see that production continued uninterrupted, and of the police authorities who must guard against disorderly conduct in the open. Public reaction to unionism today is vastly different and more intelligent. The amazingly rapid growth of unionism and of its power potential since the mid-'thirties is clearly the consequence of the far-reaching and spectacular expansion of the national economy. However, while the phenomenon of union growth under economic upheaval is not anything novel, the great growth of labor power in the present situation goes beyond anything ever known.

American unionism had experienced great numerical enlargement and an almost automatic, virtually effortless, accumulation of strength in the course of the economic expansion which attended World War I and in the years immediately after. Union membership leaped to a five million height from barely one-half that number a few years earlier. Yet the membership growth and the gain in economic standing did not correspondingly advance labor's social and political status in American life. The consequence of the failure to achieve appreciable entrenchment in the national setup was inability to resist effectively the frontal attacks on the unions that antagonistic employers launched as soon as the war emergency was over and long before the postwar boom began to taper off. A comparison between the behavior of the public authorities, labor, and management in the steel organizing movement and strike of 1919 and the railroad shopmen's strike of 1922, on the one hand, and of the same groups in the conflicts in the steel and auto industries in 1945 and 1946, on the other, points up the difference under consideration. One was determined and ruthless, the other circumspect and mindful of a kind of "protocol" of civilized behavior.

Labor in the 'twenties was not, it would seem, of a mind or in a mood to do what labor, since the early 'forties, has made its primary concern: constantly to build power reserves such as would enable it to cushion off possible economic deterioration, both by way of developing an internal labor and labor-management protective institutionalism and by legislative and political pressuring for remedial measures by the national government that would mitigate the consequences of unemployment and make employer antagonisms less detrimental to unions and union work terms.

With rare, isolated exceptions, the leadership of labor in the 'twenties was satisfied to garner in the harvest, but indisposed to deploy its power potential, and actively and militantly to seek a place and part in the nation's power structure. It was not willing to stake efforts and funds on the "expansion gamble." It was at best defensive-minded, and when the national economy took the course to violent contraction, the time-honored labor Maginot Line collapsed. The late Oscar Ameringer, no red-star gazer among labor men, may have stated the period's facts of labor life too colorfully. He was an imaginative man, but he was true to reality when he cried in anguish, out of the lower depths of the 1931 breakdown, in his *A Message and a Confession of Faith:*

> Oh, I'm not blaming anybody for the bloody mess. But I am tired of fighting tanks with tin cans; I am tired of combatting a united, nigh almighty, plutocracy with such inanities as "Join the Union of Your Craft," "Please Recognize the Label of the Amalgamated Brotherhood of Doughnut Hole Punchers." I am tired of stuffed shirts, phrase-mongers, windbag-politicians, bluffs, heavy-weight leaders with feather-weight brains, whose only qualification for leadership is an unlimited vocabulary hitched up to unlimited gall.

Economic expansion is the answer to the union organizer's prayer, but the translation of union opportunity into consequential labor power taking root in the nation's subsoil cannot be expected as a gift of the economy: it is the job to be done by labor leadership possessive of competence, ambition, imagination and outlook. That has been happening in the decades of "the upsurge of labor" in the United States: economic expansion found a labor leadership willing to utilize helpful circumstances.

In assaying the spurt of labor's social power in recent years, sight need not be lost of the vast change that developed in American public policy with regard to labor since 1933, in some measure even earlier, as manifested in the passing of the Norris-La Guardia Act of 1932, which outlawed "yellow dog" contracts, and among other valuable provisions, closely limited the powers of the courts to issue injunctions.

The "Roosevelt Revolution" and what followed in its wake facilitated the task of labor leadership, but it was no small merit that leadership was quick to make the most of a favorable turn of events.

4. MEMBERS AND LEADERS

"It is a paradox," wrote James Bryce half a century ago, "that the most individualistic of peoples are now the people among whom the art of combination has reached its maximum." Americans have been great "joiners." The 1950 Department of Commerce Directory lists about 50 million Americans holding membership in some 10,000 trade associations, 4,000 Chambers of Commerce, 1,500 civic service groups, 100,000 women's clubs, 70,000 labor union locals, and 10,000 farmers' groups. These groupings, in turn, are affiliated to 1,500 trade associations, some 2,500 farm, labor, professional, and other groups organized on a national basis. The 15 million workers in the 70,000 local unions, no doubt, figure also as members in a considerable number of other organizations.

The activities of no other mass organizations are so frequently discussed and their internal procedures so much probed as those of labor unions. Attention is most often drawn to the internal functioning of unionism, to its democracy or lack of democracy. There is nothing wrong about that, to be sure, but the searchers might profitably look in more than one direction: surely labor is not the only group whose behavior bears significantly upon democracy's destinies. Be that as it may, the "most individualistic of peoples" have woven the "art of combination" into a way of life; but have their numerous organizations leveled them down to a state of numbers? Have these individualistic people permitted the "art of combination" to exact from them a surrender of individual judgment, or do they hold firmly to the "right to dissent" and practice it?

Organizations with which men affiliate tend to influence the thinking and behavior of the members—more particularly of those who take a conspicuous part in organization affairs and act in a representative capacity. "Men are what they function as." [3] This statement applies with a good deal of force to unions, which activize their members to a greater degree than do many of the other groupings with which Americans so widely associate.

The behavior of 15 million adult, economically and politically assertive citizens is of crucial significance to the democratic fate of the other 90 million adults. And, in turn, the fate of the labor movement itself is in jeopardy if democratic practice grows into dry rot, whether centrally or in the union periphery. The logic of healthy unionism calls for a leadership that carries on in cooperation with a supporting membership, giving due consideration to contending members. The subversion of that logic is a holding setup, a powerful bureaucracy. Conceivably,

---

[3] T. V. Smith, *The American Philosophy of Equality* (Chicago: University of Chicago Press), 1927.

such a subverted *modus operandi* may, for a time, appear to be profitable, render good service, and "pay its way." But there is no long pull for an organization in bureaucratic receivership: with internal life ceasing in the union, encompassing death is around the corner. In the final count, organization *is* always cooperation, and it does not thrive on oppression, whether in labor, in the army, in teaching, or in industrial management.

Mr. John Q. American asks: *Do unions function as cooperative teams and are union members a full-scale part of the setup, or is there within the unions a cleavage between leaders and "dues-payers"?*

Teamwork does not presuppose absence of disagreement. Division and even quarreling, however undesirable and harmful they may be at certain times, are "in the day's work" of human organizations, and occur to a greater or lesser extent everywhere. The point of the question is whether there exists in the logic of unionism an institutional, as it were, basic cleavage between union members and "the union," the latter being the officers and leaders and possibly a coterie of member henchmen.

The presumption of such separation of interests between members and leaders was the inspiration of the Taft-Hartley Labor-Management Relations Act of 1947, which sought as its proponents have persistently claimed to protect the former against the latter. Those who see such cleavage in unionism really assume the coexistence of the three parties in the industrial relationship: the employer, the union, the workers; the first two waging war over, or making a bargain regarding control of the work terms of the third. Lloyd H. Fisher, of the California Institute of Industrial Relations, has put it most explicitly:

A modern union is not identical with the membership any more than a corporation is the simple sum of its stockholders and it is not unreasonable that the trade union should have requirements which are distinct and separate from those of its membership.[4]

The supporting reason for Mr. Fisher's views of the members-"union" contrast of interests is that:

in a period of ten years the membership of a trade union will have turned over several times. Its membership is fugitive but the institution has survival needs for which it requires continuity, security and a time perspective in which to plan.

The argument based upon the turnover of union membership "several times in ten years," is considerably less than convincing. If union membership, which now means nearly all workers in most of the major industrial plants, is so "fugitive," management was peculiarly inept when for so long a period of time it powerfully resisted pension coverage of

---

[4] "The Price of Union Responsibility" (*New York Times Magazine*), August 31, 1947.

employees, usually coming after about 25 years of work in the same plant. Don't businessmen read the magazines?

More valid is the reference to the fact that at times the particular and immediate, sometimes the purely local or craft considerations and interests of some union members are at variance with the terms or conditions the union would consider beneficial to the majority of union members in the plant or in the industry as a whole. Such conflict might arise out of a number of cogent and meritorious considerations, which a part of the members may not know about or not care to consider, but which the union, representing the broader interest of the wider membership must heed. Such, for instance, would be insistence on demands that would result in upsetting the competitive position of union-friendly management as against antiunion employers, and thus threaten continuity of employment; or such demands as would raise production costs indiscriminately and thus tend to cause a shift in the market position of the industrial product or service; or the seeking of advantages that would either reflect adversely on an essential public interest or affect public opinion unfavorably, and thus undermine union strength. Finally, disagreement between local and area or national leadership on the merits of an issue or the wisdom of a particular course of action at a given time may be the cause of a conflict within the union. None of this disagreement, however, has "institutional" quality, and in no way does it represent a member-vs.-"union" conflict of interests, or a "philosophic" dichotomy or basic cleavage between the "union" and its "institutional survival needs" as against the members. The "institution" minus the members is a fairly hollow affair.

All officers, even those most mindful of the institution's "survival needs"—and, not unnaturally, identifying themselves with the institution—above all need for their own survival complete support by the members, their willingness to keep the union safe and strong. Members cannot be expected to live up to obligations, unless they can see their interest as one with that of the union, and appreciate its "survival needs" as also their own. And for what valid reasons would union officers cut themselves loose and away from their safest anchorage, the union members? They could not bank on the support of employers to bail them out if they lost the support of the members. Management has no use for union leaders who do not carry their members' allegiance.

The cleavage presumed to exist between the union's and the members' interest may conceivably exist in the lately dwindling number of "captive" unions, those run either by a racketeering, underworld-controlled power, or by a Communist-party-directed group. The party wishes to control the members for the political value of such control, and the members' immediate union interest is not of much concern to the party. The racketeer outfit is interested in the "take," and neither the union as such nor the members are of any interest to this group. However, even union officers in these categories are obliged to appear to represent the members' interest or they will not be certain of long continuance. In the final count, all power must seek recourse to acceptance by consent. But since there are many ways in which consent can be secured some of the people can be held in illegitimate control some of the time.

The vital matter of the democratic operation of unionism is a problem that grows in complexity as the essence of unionism is undergoing the transformation discussed earlier. Neither the two-fisted propensities of early-day combat, nor the town-meeting of early-day democratic union procedures go too well with mid-twentieth century union operation. It is quite likely that union forms of organization, methods of action, and possibly the whole intellectual and emotional content of the movement will not for very long keep out of a far-reaching overhauling, a prospect our entire democratic form of living on all public levels is certainly facing. It is not likely, however, that unions could carry on as mere labor-selling and delivery agencies with aims and interests "distinct and separate" from the interests of the members—not, that is, in a free democracy. That has "worked" only in Soviet Russia, Fascist Italy, and Nazi Germany.

What, then, is the state of democracy in American unions: how is the power of decision-making distributed, and how well are civil rights, including the right to dissent, protected in union practice?

It is currently accepted that in most unions, or at least in a good many, actual power of both decision and enforcement is exercised by but few persons, the national leaders and their "machine" associates. Several widely known national unions and their leaders are readily mentioned in discussions of the issue as examples of especially heavy-handed central control. But it is not necessary to invoke examples of particularly domineering union leaders. There is no doubt that top union officers in nearly all American unions exercise very great authority, and except in but rare instances, also great personal power. What's more, there is widespread acceptance by most union members of the top control as something that is "good for the union." Nonetheless, it would be erroneous to conclude that acceptance of high-powered officaldom indicates surrender of democracy and individual rights by union members. The phenomenon must be viewed in the light of its environing reality.

Pragmatic acquiescence is a native American mode of behavior in workshops and union halls as it is in political assemblies and in halls of learning. Where leaders can prove to members that, because of the leaders' "policies," the boys get the bacon delivered in as sizeable chunks as anybody gets, and maybe even bigger and fatter chunks, there is a disposition to overlook the absence of democratic procedure attending delivery. The ineradicable fact that unionists are human, it must be assumed, is at least in part responsible for the sad fact that they react to certain realities no more wisely nor more nobly than do most other people; *i.e.*, statesmen, professors, clergymen, scientists, politicians. Yet upon the judgment and the exercise of democracy, as it is practiced by all these groups, depends our faith in the survival of this socio-political species. Union democracy obviously can be judged fairly only in the light of the state of the art everywhere. And as to that, perfection is rarer than compromise. Franklin D. Roosevelt had to cope with the Hagues, the Kelleys, the Pendergasts, even as Woodrow Wilson had to take political cognizance of the pork-barrel legislation processors of his time. So perhaps it is too exacting a demand that Tom, Dick, and Harry should be more unsparing toward the malefactors of union democracy than Messrs. Thomas, Richard, and Harris are toward the big-scale national democratic offenders.

There is a distinct difference between two phases of democracy in unions: that of individual assertiveness involving the rights of dissent and open criticism, and that of participating in policy determination.

Internal union practice with regard to individual or member rights differs quite considerably from union to union. There are unions where, except in altogether trivial matters, democracy is nonexistent; and there are unions where the practice is as good as can be expected in economic organizations, with the structural absence of separation between executive, legislative, and judicial powers, and with no press to voice or support dissent, except the official journals controlled by the administrative authorities. By and large, there is not too much on this score for most unions to boast about. (The issue is discussed in somewhat greater detail in Chapter 18, The Labor Press—An Evaluation.)

The situation is better with regard to power of policy decision making insofar as it relates to the hard economic core of unionism. This power is generally shared, if not necessarily so in every union and on every level, by large numbers of persons, although nearly everywhere the formal power exercise as well as the making of emergency decisions is to a very great extent centered in relatively few individuals. The mode of power distribution and concentration varies from union to union. Predominantly, the procedure is not very democratic, and there is less than open discussion of greatly differing proposals: it is more in the nature of a communication or statement "for discussion and adoption." Nonetheless, it offers opportunity for criticism and amendment, and thus there is a modicum of power sharing. Both facts, that there is relatively wide participation and that the method is rather short of what democracy might desire, are rooted in the still continuing contradictory nature of the union, which operates at once as a democratic mass organization, a diplomatic corps, and a combat unit, all in one.

Initial formulation of policy and its subsequent application and implementation are the prerogative and the function of the national union heads.

The presidents in the numerically strong or otherwise important unions are not only administrators but also determinators of policy. But between the initiation of a matter of basic policy and its being set in motion there lies an area in which discussion, amendment, and ratification are processed with substantial participation by considerable numbers of members.

It is an almost inescapable consequence of the ever-widening consolidations of business and industrial controls that counterpart union action should tend to a similar course: local union strength can not cope with major industrial combines. If, in the circumstances, the democratic process is none too complete, it is well to bear in mind that unions elect not legislatures and legislators but executives and administrators expected to act promptly and effectively when facing, or seeking to avert emergencies. The unions' conventions, presumed to be legislative assemblies, are really, in most instances, setups for the election of national officers.

Perhaps we ought to remember a famous High Court Justice's utterance, and assume in this instance that "democracy is what the people think it is." Indeed, the fact is that the coal-diggers won't sell Mr. John L. Lewis short. Nor would many other groups of wage earners sell their own union heads below par. Clearly, most unionists appear not to feel deprived by their union affiliation of anything they particularly value, if judgment is to be based upon the votes workers have been casting on the union shop issue in NLRB elections. Thus, in 2,960 shop elections held in 1948, out of a total of 3,200,000 eligible workers, only 156,830, or not quite 5 per cent, voted against the union shop. The corresponding figures for 1949 were: in 4,971 elections and 693,413 eligibles, only 52,150 or under 7½ per cent voted against the union shop.

More than one conclusion can be drawn from these observations. One might be that unionists generally do not care about democracy if the pay the union secures for them is good enough. Another might be that union leaders have their members so well "sewed up," that no one kicks, and if one does, nobody else knows about it. Still another conclusion might be that there is enough democracy in unions where the members want it badly enough, and that if in some instances there is no smoke of dissension, there is perhaps no fire of contention—which is about what might be said of the operation of the democratic process in the wider areas of city, state, and national politics. And, as suggested earlier, cognizance might be taken of the wide difference between union organizations and the institution of popular politics as to their respective objectives, means, modes of action, and operational procedures. The call is indeed for a thoughtful approach to the problem of union democracy before summary generalizations are evolved. One thing would seem to be certain: that some union editions of democracy's book of rules either abound in typographical errors or have been adjusted to meet particular needs. If "editorial" re-examination be in order, the editors' qualifications must include both familiarity with the text and good knowledge of the score.

5. THE UNION AND THE PUBLIC INTEREST

In Labor-Management Relations. "Collective bargaining is," in the apt expression of Professor John M. Clark, "the worker's alternative to serfdom." Attainment of the positive content of this alternative involves continuous redistribution of the respective shares of labor and of ownership in the products of industry as production and standards of living advance. That is largely what bargaining is about.

There is also bargaining about conditions under which work is to be done and about certain rights, whether of workers on the job or of management, in ordering things in the productive process; about rights and duties as among the workers themselves while on and in relation to their jobs. When the issue is not wages, it is rights, one form of equity or another. Labor, through the union, and ownership represented by management, are the contending interests around the bargaining table. Their undertaking is to compose differences of interests and to prevent strikes, the cessation of production or of services.

However, behind the special interests of the two sides lies a basic public interest. The structure of and the relations within our social order depend upon the progress of the effort. If in the end peace is achieved, and the respective interests of labor, management, and the public are brought into working and enduring agreement, we have the economic elements of a decent social order in the making.

Thus collective bargaining is more than exchange of arguments, presentation of charts and graphs of production costs, marketing problems, calculations of living costs, prices, profits, wages, and like matters of interest only to labor and management. The heart of the matter is work continuity upon a basis that will keep the social equilibrium secure. At stake is a power contest that must not be permitted to proceed to its "logical" conclusion: one side completely overpowering the other side. For regardless of the special form of ownership the unobstructed functioning of both labor and management is crucial to the production process, and consequently to social progress and stability. Yet the achievement of that end must not interfere with the essential rights and freedoms upon which democratic society rests. Labor's right to strike, the safeguard against involuntary servitude, is one such right. The other right involved is that of management's competence to develop effective progressive enterprise allowing for a return on capital and risk, for research and expansion.

Some of these essential rights are so fundamental to the continuance of the relationship in the process of industry and to the freedom of both sides that they will be observed regardless of whether there is law or formal agreement. As Professor John M. Clark illuminatingly points out in his *Guideposts In Time of Change* (Harper and Brothers, 1949), there are unwritten *de facto* conditions to prevent violation of these rights. Thus, if workers are made to "work under a constant sense of inequity, the morale of the force suffers, and production suffers as a consequence." And, on the other end, "it is impossible to coerce the employer into being spontaneously enterprising and vigorous in venturesome investment," if labor drives its "take" past the point where it makes business sense for management to carry on beyond routine limits. This is true regardless of the particular form in which ownership equity is vested. Economic progressivism and the sense of enterprise are equally essential to the operation of a public corporation such as the TVA, an individual's business venture, a stock corporation, or a state-owned industry.

Whether the limits upon the demands of labor and upon management policies are permitted to "seek their own levels" or whether they are regulated by collective bargaining agreement, the public concern, in all instances, is that the arrangement *work;* that is, that it work progressively and in observance of the relevant basic democratic rights. The more complex, sensitive, and interdependent the nation's production and service machinery becomes, the greater is the public stake in the process of collective bargaining. But the "public interest," on the face of it, has no direct representation in the proceeding. The government has no standing in it, except in comparatively few and isolated cases when, in emergency, it temporarily takes over an industry and operates it; or when, as in war, the exigencies of national defense and security make the government the major customer and hence virtually the controlling factor in every wage-profit-price dispute.

In normal times, in theory at least, the government is considered to be the policeman who intervenes only when traffic gets snarled or when a smashup occurs or when a fight starts, and his job is to keep the parties at arm's length and protect the innocent bystander. This notion is widespread and cherished by many as dependable protection of free enterprise. In practice, although physically absent from the bargaining conference and even more absent, if that were possible, from the day-to-day relationship between labor and management on the plant level, government is an ever-participating, influential factor in virtually all phases of the entire proceeding. This influence is accomplished, in the normal course of events, *in absentia*, as it were, through the body of effective industrial law, as represented in the LMRA and its *fair labor practices* provisions, in a great and ever-increasing number of court decisions, which in effect constitute a body of steadily evolving common law of labor-management relations. The recurrent nostalgic wishing, on all sides, that government "stay out" or "be kept out of it," neither hurts nor helps anybody: it merely satisfies a yearning for the good old days, gone without a return ticket. The part of government in industry, as in nearly all other departures of American life, is one of active intervention, under rules, but no longer avoidable. However, in the not-out-of-the-ordinary labor-industry conflicts the government is not physically present in the proceeding, and thus there is no formal representation of the public interest. And it is in this instance that labor, one of the two sides, occupies the vacuum, and assumes the role of spokesman for the "third party," the public interest—in effect, not of course by formal credential.

The union is in fact a dual personality as it enters the performance of the collective bargaining task. The broad two-way outlook derives neither from thoughtful consideration for the public good, nor from unionism's constitutional generosity; rather, it develops as a matter of common sense and self-protection.

The union has to live with the public. It needs the public's good will and it cannot, in safety and with impunity, go counter to what may be ascertained as the mind of the public on a certain matter. If the issue is wages, the union cannot be unmindful of the effect a wage hike will have on prices. If the issue is a strike, the union will endeavor to determine—in its own interest—the point at which public sympathy for the underdog may begin to weaken in the face of inconvenience and even hardship caused by the strike. If the issue is recognition of the closed shop, the union will consider with the utmost care when and what kind of compromise proposal it would be wise to accept. With the nation's wage-earning labor force about one-half of the total adult population, and one-third of it in unions, the lines of public interest and of labor interest are pretty much entangled. The union, as was pointed out earlier, generally brings to its members, involved in a particular conflict, a broader view than they are themselves likely to take of their rights and duties. The union seeks to reconcile their interest both as workers and as citizens.

The union not only has to live with the public—it also has to live with the employer, or more accurately, with his business. The progress of the business enterprise is the condition of the workers' employment, and is essential to a continuous improvement of working terms and conditions. This fact is true, regardless of whether an enterprise is "free and private," monopolistic, or operated by the state or any other public authority. The labor interest coincides with the public interest in that productive processes should continue uninterrupted and be carried on effectively. The workers immediately involved may, in the heat of the contest, overlook the general and the ultimate, but their union, if it is worth its salt, will not. Therein lies a great measure of the union movement's stature as a force in the nation's social dynamics. The union is capable of being, to a large and ever-growing degree, the security agent for the public interest even while it is one of the two contenders in the industrial relationship. It is a quasi-public institution.

Not all unions, of course, are clearly mindful of the complex interrelationship. But a rapidly growing number of unions are. Many unions perform this double role because it is the result of their reasoned philosophy of labor-industry relations. Others function in this manner not because of any "theory" but because it seems to them to be the sensible course to pursue. This is the developing trend, which like many other things in American life acquires accelerating momentum once it gets going and seems to make sense.

The union performs a socially significant function in industry: it guards, to a considerable extent, the public interest.

In the Community and in the Nation. Collective bargaining is the central operational domain of unionism, but union concern goes beyond it. Politics, education, the many civic and cultural activities of the communities where union members live and work, the battle of ideas at home and abroad, all enter the life of unionism. Interest in these "side" matters is not indicative of a shift in the basic outlook of unionism, or of a basically new orientation of labor strategy; it is merely the consequence of the wider content that collective bargaining has acquired and of the greater integration of unionism with the life of the nation in present-day United States: the unions play a part in these new areas of community life, even as they do in their immediate area of collective bargaining. That is not because unionists are necessarily more social-minded than all other people, or because unions are mysteriously endowed with any progressive quality. It is merely that they bring to the activities of individual citizens a measure of cohesive purposefulness, which they carry over from their experience in union life. Unionists' participation in community matters, semirepresentative in a way, even when they act as individuals, gives body to the democratic concept that underlies community action, enriches it because it diversifies it, and brings into play a variety of interests jointly seeking peaceful, cooperative solutions of differences.

Unions have at all times in the past been interested in legislation and hence in politics—as reviewed by Professor Henry David in this volume. The formation of the CIO's Political Action Committee, the AFL's Labor League for Political Education, and similar setups in the major independent unions, signifies not a novel departure in unionism but a rising determination to make effective use of the franchise, and a disposition to streamline the older ways of doing things politically. But there is more to it: with the expanding activity go a great diffusion and wide scope of interest.

The activity in the new form seeks to engage the whole union membership, and is clearly set on continuity; it is not something with which only union "top brass" is concerned, nor a matter of a bit of political horse-trading to reward a deserving, superannuated union head or hand.

A revealing statement of the depth and breadth of the newer labor approach to political activity and of the pragmatic way in which labor proceeds from issue to issue and ever deeper into broad community and national affairs is made in the "Foreword" to *Foundation of Prosperity*, the Program of the CIO Committee on Regional Development and Conservation, first published in 1949. The authors, John Brophy and Anthony Wayne Smith, report:

The CIO became interested in regional development and resource conservation partly because of the Tennessee Valley Authority and partly because the International Woodworkers of America, CIO, our union in the logging camps and sawmills, was deeply concerned about stabilizing timber production and jobs in the timber industries.

The TVA idea, of course, meant employment for labor in construction, and in the material and equipment industries. It also meant cheap electricity, new industries, and hence more new jobs. But it forced on our attention all the other great resource problems, forests, soil, waters, minerals, wildlife, recreation, and scenery; and the difficult human problems behind them: the people displaced from farms and towns by reservoirs; the people crowded beyond endurance in congested, noisy, dirty cities.

We soon learned that enormous operations were afoot for engineering works in great river valleys like the Missouri and the Columbia. They were being planned (by the Army Engineers and the Reclamation Bureau) on a partial and fragmentary basis: for *mere* flood control, *mere* navigation, *mere* reclamation, or even *mere* hydroelectric power. Sufficient regard was not being paid to the damage which was often being done to human settlements, industries, farm land, timberland, wildlife, historical and archaelogical remains of great scientific importance, and scenic and recreational resources of high value to the average man, who is now, by virtue of his trade unions, getting more and more leisure to enjoy such things.

The concern of labor with a variety of matters not strictly "labor" is treated in this volume by AFL Vice-President Matthew Woll and CIO Community Services Director, Leo Perlis. A reference to this growing interest appears in the AFL Executive Council Report to the 1949 Convention (p. 183). It is believed, the Report indicates, that the AFL public relations program had "succeeded in identifying the labor movement with causes and programs which the American people favor . . . succeeded to a degree in making the public understand that the reactionary forces in this country most active in promoting repressive anti-labor legislation like the Taft Hartley Act are the same forces which had obstructed and prevented adoption of effective human welfare legislation."

Labor's concern with the grass-roots community, originating in the civilian defense and other home-front activities of the war years, signified a break-away from an inbred, socially isolated, doghouse psychology that had taken hold of the thinking of most unionists in the last decade of the nineteenth century and carried over into the early 1930's. The new orientation soon broadened out into a democratic development of importance in these trying years of democracy's most taxing strain and stress. Union members learned to work with others in their communities, thus strengthening the local base of democracy. But they did not remain intellectually passive. They soon found themselves involved in a contest with the hitherto dominant and unchallenged non- or antidemocratic forces for a place in the community thinking. The appearance, and above all, the activization of tens of thousands of labor men and women in local committees concerned with all manner of civil affairs gave democracy a new meaning, and a new proving ground. Labor's stock rose appreciably in the esteem of democracy's grass roots when union members, workers in shops and plants, not only union treasuries, started to make sizeable contributions to Community Chests; when labor men and women, in large numbers, took to participating in all kinds of community enterprises, from painting an old school house or church to setting a welfare project in motion; when labor men began to live with the community on a full-time basis, not merely doing "labor's share" in and being concerned solely with the "labor aspect" of the particular business at hand. Labor has profited by this experience even as the community has.

6. Labor and the Nation

"It takes years of analysis to achieve a moment of synthesis." The difficulty expressed in these words of French historian Fustel de Coulanges well applies to generalizations about the American labor movement. Here, swift and unpredictable changes make short shrift of generalizations that seemingly rest upon years of careful observation. But such is the social dynamism of American reality in this period of evolving, or rather erupting history; it is no respecter of hard and fast conclusions.

How does unionism bear upon the whole of American democracy?

In his inimitably simple yet clinching way, Abraham Lincoln, in a speech at Cincinnati, Ohio, in 1860, answered the question emphatically: "I agree . . . that the working men are the basis of all governments, for the plain reason that they are the more numerous." However, the highly technologized society of our time is not moved by numbers alone. Of course, the tenet of government by majority and due protection of minority rights is recognized, as ever, but in the words of the late Justice Oliver Wendell Holmes, "the life of the law is not logic but experience." And ever since the days of the Great Dissenter, the "law" has had to cope with unprecedented, incalculable, and truly devastating experience. It was the functional significance of labor that made possible labor's continuous rise from rung to rung on the ladder of public and social recognition, particularly in times of national crisis, as in 1917, 1933, 1941, 1950—this in spite of warnings about a dangerous drift to laborism and kindred horrors.

If Mr. John Q. American has been reading over this writer's shoulder, he probably came across the advice, some pages back, that he take stock of "what labor is to him or he to labor." These closing pages, perhaps not unreasonably, should look in on J.Q.A.'s thinking.

From what is generally known of Mr. J.Q.A.'s mental processes, and headwork, he is wide awake and intelligent but not always free of pet prejudices and not overburdened with detailed knowledge of relevant special facts and figures. A man of the world, J.Q.A. knows that human organizations are not congregations of saints—and that they couldn't long continue in business if they were. The nation's political history is not a closed book to him, and he has no starry-eyed illusions about the operation of the country's economy, past or present. And, although he does not justify crooked deals in politics, or buccaneering methods in industry, he considers himself "historically minded" with regard to such matters. Thus, he has observed that, had it not been for some of the robber barons in the past and even for some present-day hucksters, our extant great industrial plant and magnificent transportation and communication systems might have presented a vastly different aspect. Indeed, we would still be wearing our European ancestors' swaddling clothes. J.Q.A. likes to refer to Franklin D. Roosevelt's 1932 Commonwealth Club address and point out that although we would not try to rationalize roughneckism into a wise way of building a nation, we must remember that history rides no macadamized roads, and "boys will be boys." J.Q.A. follows F.D.R. in granting the malefactors of economic history the "Scotch verdict." He does not, however, apply similar hind-forgiveness to the builders of labor power.

To be sure, J.Q.A. does not consider labor an inferior who owes thanks to anyone for being alive, yet he feels labor should at all times avoid doing less than "the right thing." J.Q.A. is not above patting himself on the back for his "fairness to labor," and he feels that labor should neither forget nor abuse its neighbors' confidence and good will. He takes it that since he stood by labor, even though at a rather safe distance, when the latter was "in the doghouse," labor should keep its peace and avoid making itself too conspicuous now that it is almost "top-dog." It is true, though, that J.Q.A.'s labor reactions are not violent and do not generally last long; as the provocation causing his anger ceases, he desists.

Broadly speaking, J.Q.A. is against unions building up so much power that they might tend to become a directing rather than a contributory and cooperating factor in the nation's democratic setup.

Right or not, his bill of particulars runs about as follows:

1. The unions get in everybody's way too much. They concern themselves with everything under the sun. They should stick to organizing, to collective bargaining, and to their union agreements. Outside of that,

the workers are free citizens like everyone else; where do the unions come in? Of course, they should not commit their members to fixed political policies.

2. Labor has a right to strike—and sometimes strikes are unavoidable—but the public is being exposed to too many strikes, some entirely unjustified, such as jurisdictional strikes or those waged because of stubborn, ambitious union considerations and not on purely economic grounds. There ought to be a limit to this imposition.

3. The unions develop in their members an insatiable desire for more and more pay; they are just job and wage conscious, not broad-minded enough to consider other interests and other matters. They are Americans, too, aren't they, or are they only wage-earners?

4. Unions live by the grace of democratic law, but they do not practice democracy and protect civil rights in their dealings with members and other workers not willing to join. Theirs is a kind of double-standard morality. In many instances, they behave like exclusive clubs, charge prohibitive initiation fees and high dues, and bar people from employment because of color, creed, or opinion. Why not regulate their behavior by proper law?

5. True, the laws in the past were harsh on the unions, but now that they are the preferred wards of the law, why don't they live up to law, avoid violence, abuse, and obstructionist tactics during strikes, and quit waging jurisdictional wars?

6. Unions need money to meet legitimate operational costs, true enough. But their revenue should be subject to a public check and they should not have million-dollar treasuries; that much money tends only to develop recklessness and arrogance in their leaders and members. And it encourages "racketeering."

7. Union leaders have too much power. What with the closed shop and the dues checkoff—even though somewhat restricted by recent labor law—they are building up a labor monopoly. It was unavoidable that labor should grow big and powerful since unionism is an inseparable part of the gigantic national economy, but why do the unions oppose any regulative setup by federal law such as a Federal Labor Commission similar to those that exist in transportation, trade, or finance?

8. With union recognition under the law and collective bargaining now the customary way of doing business, the closed shop is really an unfair practice. Unions should not compel but should seek to convince workers to join and, failing that, hold their peace.

9. With full employment a national goal and a President's Council of Economic Advisers set up to make sure that plans are always ready to fight unemployment, there is no good reason for featherbedding practices. Productivity is what makes for higher earnings and consequently for more work and employment.

The essence of Mr. J.Q.A.'s "nine-point bill of gripes" is reducible to three sets of wrongdoing, according to his way of looking at labor matters. These are:

The unions do not keep their own house in good order;

The unions endanger national economic health by excessive demands;

The unions are throwing their weight around, are doing the Big Labor act, are the counterpart of the nation's major Me Firstists among business, farmers, and government, each husbanding its own power and special interest, and may the hindmost face his fate.

Mr. J.Q.A. would be less the fair-minded *homo Americanus*, in which he takes such pride, if he insisted that he is right all around. The desire to "tell 'em off" leads him into overstatement and overgeneralization. He knows that, and in a pinch he puts his brain on active duty.

So, in the course of argument he agrees that such matters as clear abuse, or loaded manipulation of officers' authority to the disadvantage of the union members are not, in their broader aspects, disabilities peculiar to unions, but represent one of many facets of a national problem: the growing obsolescence of some of our time-honored democratic devices; and that hence, the effective treatment of the evil goes beyond dreaming up restrictions upon union operation.

Mr. J.Q.A. is not likely, however, to be so amenable and so reasonable on the second score and on the third. These factors affect him directly and he is greatly concerned about the wider implications and the co-effect of the two: labor's growing and ever-more-persistent calls for a progressively increasing share of the "national cake," and the rising impact of labor's political strength.

This last point has been worrying him considerably. Yet, seeking to be fair to labor, he looked over one of the reports by the President's Council of Economic Advisers to discover that "in 1948 almost one-quarter of our 46 million family units had incomes below $2,000 a year; about two-fifths had incomes of less than $3,000; and almost three-fifths had incomes of less than $4,000." These are fairly high incomes by the standards of many other countries in the civilized world, but with the dollar cutting a not-very-impressive figure these days, we ought to be doing better. This is particularly true regarding our productivity: "output per man hour, measured in constant dollars, increased about 22 per cent from 1929 to 1939; by 1945 it was 19 per cent above 1939, and tentative estimate (in 1950) indicates that it is now running 13 per cent above the 1945 level—a gain of about 2.5 per cent compared with 2.1 per cent in the prewar decade." Labor has a case; it cannot be easily denied.

Down through the years leadership has been changing hands and character in the United States. And since such shifts have happened before—the United States has been run successively by the agrarian, the mercantile, the financial, the industrial bigwigs, and by just lawyer and politician combinations crowding in between—J.Q.A. has come to think that perhaps he should not be overimpatient with labor wanting a say in managing things American. Of course, they would have to show that they've "got what it takes" to play a part in the running of the old homestead. J.Q.A. once got so carried away by the idea, and by his probable part in the event, that he even tried to practice up a loud Demostheneslike challenge addressed to these would-be new leaders. He was thrilled by the sensation of acting as the people's tribune as he spoke up: [5]

Now that a dozen of the great unions have got the economic power to paralyze the nation at any time, you, their leaders, must stop simply calling for "more," even where you are entitled to it. You must begin to tell us, the people, what kind of society you are going to create eventually, after you will get all that you want. Yearly now you are getting nearer to a position of real authority over us and we want to know what you are going to do with your authority. We are listening, we are eager, we are ready to be led. We are not at all afraid of change, if it means change into something positive, some new ideal. . . .

We are patient, but our patience has a term. We are generous and will go far under the influence of a sob story. Yet our generosity will end if we find that your sob story, or your sheer power, is being used to take food out of our children's mouths and give it to yours, or, for that matter, to take cars away from the present rich in order to ride in bigger ones yourselves. . . .

We are growing progressively less concerned with the statistical dispute whether the auto workers are entitled to another raise, or whether GM has the capacity to give the raise without lifting prices. But we are quickly interested whenever Mr. Reuther shows flashes of a real and comprehensive plan behind his plan to have a look at the company's books. . . . Within the next few years, either you are going to show the whole country the way to a better world or the whole country is going to show you the gate. . . . Tell us what indeed you are for. Or, if there is anywhere today a high labor official who truly lacks the intelligence to have a broad plan for the future, if some of the top leaders are really as innocent of social intention as they claim to be, then in responsibility to their organizations and to the nation they ought to step down in favor of better men.

It is not very surprising that Mr. John Q. American does not hold fast to full-scale answers to the conflicting and confounding labor issues of the time. Who would in this mid-century era of flux and upheaval, which defies cataloguing and serial numbering of any basic assumptions and solutions, which is at loggerheads with fixity, unbroken continuance, and finality?

In 1950, the basic labor law, the Taft-Hartley Act, was still on the books with but a slim likelihood of being drastically altered in the near

[5] Chard Powers Smith, "Labor, We Are Waiting," *Labor and Nation*, Jan.–Feb. 1947.

future. Yet union leaders were called to take high place in the national councils of government at the first indication that Americans and the citizens of other free nations might be forced to do a repeat performance, to defend with their lives the right to practice freedom—for the time being on a small patch of land on the Asian continent. And the call was quite different from that of a decade before, under Roosevelt, in the face of the Nazi war. It was then deemed sufficient and wise enough for the White House to pick prominent union leaders and place them in advisory capacities in a few selected conspicuous positions, and thus achieve the recognition labor could expect. Not so in 1950, when authoritative labor officers and units were asked to have "representatives of their own choosing," and labor, in turn, replied by calling for participation beyond advice-giving: it sought a part on all levels of policy determination and performance.

Neither the coefficient of labor's political drawing power, nor economic labor arithmetic had been sufficiently altered since 1941 to account for the decisive change of attitude, but labor's internal cohesiveness and consciousness of aim had grown considerably. That the Taft-Hartley Act was still in force and its basic inspirations were probably as potent as ever did not seem to matter very much. Even as on earlier occasions, labor power burst out of the seams of paper law restraint. In consequence, the steady rise of labor in social stature was causing apprehension. Voices were heard from authoritative sources advising that a laboristic society was succeeding the extant capitalistic order, that "the labor movement which has developed in the United States in the last fifteen years is . . . the largest, the most powerful, and the most aggressive that the world has ever seen; and . . . the strongest unions are the most powerful private economic organizations in the country" and that "a community in which employees rather than business men are the strongest influence . . . will have its own way of looking at things, its own scale of values, its own ideas on public policies, and, to some extent, its own jurisprudence." [6] But—is that implicit in labor's growing power?

It is fair enough to speculate on what American society may come to be "in the course of human events," but there seemed little justification for a "laboristic" prognosis as of the mid-century years. Beyond the fact, neither new nor surprising, that the number of wage earners exceeded the number of payroll-dispensers in American society, as indeed it does in all industrial societies, there was no discernible proof by 1950 of a rising intellectual "laborism" and a corresponding laborist "set of values," as these words are understood, in extant or evolving American society. What appears to have happened is that labor had gone along with the

[6] "Are We Becoming a 'Laboristic' State?" by Sumner H. Slichter. *New York Times Magazine*, May 16, 1948.

Roosevelt Revolution, affected by it and measurably affecting it. The essential and inescapable effect of the "revolution" was the overhauling of the "standard" relations of forces in U. S. economy and polity, causing appreciable changes in traditional ways of life. It was not a labor but a national revolution. The whole nation, having found itself in the maelstrom of double-quick evolution (a revolution by consent), was casting up new concepts of social relations, developing different social appetites, casting out obsolescent notions of right and wrong, and was not hesitant to recognize new power when it rose in new places. Labor was one such power. The people's attitude toward labor altered. However, labor was neither the only nor the major engineer of the historic upheaval; the major force was, of course, the whole people and their government. Labor felt it was a part of the people; its actions were to give expression to that feeling.

Franklin D. Roosevelt's "we've had a revolution without making one" epitomized national history in the 'thirties, and labor's part in it. If new scales of values, or rather the old considerably revised, entered the consciousness of the American people, they were essentially classless, not made by "ideologues." They just "growed" in the process of living. No laboristic society was coming into being: the old social order was emerging with new trappings to replace the old ones that no longer served a useful purpose.

The consequence was that a labor movement came into being in the United States, "bone of the bone" and "flesh of the flesh" of the old, yet new and different, even as the country and the people emerged different from the upheaval. The simple, realistic truth is that while American labor had for some time since the Great Change been advancing in seven league boots, the reference to Big Labor, whether intended as an insult or as flattery of a kind, is not social-economic nor political truth. And although the membership and the leadership of labor have their "quota" of malcontents, actual or potential racketeers, would-be tycoons, and just plain Babbitts, even as these influences are found in any mass undertaking involving power and contests, unionism has grown progressively mindful of community responsibility and responsive to public and national duty in a practical, cooperative way.

The emergence of American labor as a contender for a dignified place in the local and national community is not primarily due to the fact that we in the United States have become a community in which "employees" prevail—we have been that community for decades; it is rather due to circumstances of scope and origin that transcend the American scene; to the fact, really, that the whole of human society, the United States along with all other nations and peoples, has been undergoing a great transformation involving political ideas as well as economic facts, concepts of rights as well as the realities of security, the ever-growing need for expanding production as well as the pressures from many sides for a reassessment of standard human values.

Any analysis of the course of labor unionism in the evolving pattern of mid-twentieth century American society cannot help taking into account, if it is to remain valid, that a worldwide revolutionary upheaval is in progress and that the U.S.A. is an active part of the world. The dashing to and fro of people aboard a rapidly moving train is not an independent determinant of the train's direction. The play of forces in American society under such circumstances "seeks its level" rather than follows fixed "rules of the game." The union movement is in the national and international marketplace for what it can get in exchange for what it has to give. The "goods in exchange" involve work and pay, cooperation and status, a share in power and assumption of responsibility for the exercise of power—all this as war and peace battle for a hold on history, and as all power groups in the world, and within American society, test their strength and seek out avenues of advance.

J. B. S. HARDMAN

PART TWO

Unions and Political Activity

Introduction

Unions and political activity

IF MAN IS A POLITICAL ANIMAL, THEN the vote-conscious American with his perennial enthusiasm and flair for solving all questions at the polls is the political animal *par excellence*. Therefore it would seem to be apparent, deductively, that the American trade unionist should have developed into the most highly specialized political species on the continent.

Indeed it was so. Early unionists showed a marked propensity for enjoying politics to the neglect of labor organization. For nearly 75 years in the nineteenth century, leaders as well as rank-and-file followers pursued this natural political bent with such fervor that trade union objectives were lost in the underbrush of visionary social schemes. They displayed a constant weakness for the blandishments of the third parties of reform. The simple goal of building permanent unions with economic power seemed never to have equaled in allure the attraction exerted by universal panaceas. When overemphasis on the ballot did not quite kill the unions, recurrent depressions, recalcitrant employers, unfriendly courts, and a conservative middle class united to administer the *coup de grâce*.

As the Knights of Labor lay gasping in the latter 1880's Samuel Gompers arose to preach his gospel of bread-and-butter unionism. Concurrently, he laid a restraining hand upon unbridled political zeal within the labor movement. Through the years, he converted a hitherto undirected social force into meaningful political heat on election day. To this hour, the American labor movement, in its political philosophy and action, is still his debtor.

Henry David's chapter "One Hundred Years of Labor in Politics," traces the painful evolution of labor's reaching out for political maturity and wisdom on the American scene. This chapter reveals that at no time did Gompers and his lieutenants minimize the importance of subjecting state legislatures and Congress to the most searching scrutiny of their sporting with labor's welfare and destiny. In this respect, they carried forward a policy already instituted by the Knights of Labor. The AFL merely perfected and extended its operation. But it had added a new dimension to scrutiny: economic power.

The accounts of two labor lobbyists, 60 years apart in time, supply a measure of the tasks and techniques common to both periods as well as an indication of the differences in labor's position before Congress to-

Ralph Beaumont, one of the its of Labor's Washington representatives, reports for 1890; W. C. Hushing, Chairman of the AFL's National Legislative Committee, reports for 1950.

As early as 1906, however, American labor learned that the labor lobbyist's efficiency in pleading and button-holing was not enough. Nor was labor's economic power, essential though it might be for gaining respect and an industrial hearing. Beyond the lobbyist and the collective contract, the American legislator seemed to respect the ballot box most of all. Today, neither the AFL nor the CIO leaves labor's voting habits to chance. They have organized their political activities (still respecting Gompers' dictum against independent political action: Reward your friends and punish your enemies) on a nation-wide scale, dipping down into every county and congressional district.

Since labor's first political awakening in the late 1820's began with high hopes at the local level, the circle of enthusiasm is now complete. Labor's political aspirations again center in ward and election district. But the journey around the circle has revealed the fundamental difference between starting and meeting place: the slowly growing respect of labor and its leaders for the process of careful planning and specialized knowledge even in the field of political and legislative action. Like all Americans, they once regarded this province as the playground for hunch, instinct, and oratory. In the contemporary labor movement, it is gradually becoming the arena of directed and rigorous hard thinking and work.

The day-to-day painstaking operations of Labor's League for Political Education are discussed by Joseph Keenan of the AFL, and Jack Kroll covers comparable activities for the CIO-PAC. How these top policies and plans are translated into local action is traced out, step by step, by George Wartenberg in "Political Action in a Congressional District."

Both top policies and their effectuation are already falling under uncomfortable scrutiny as a result of the 1950 election returns. Throughout the Roosevelt era and into the Fair Deal, labor leaders have acted as though this principle were a law of nature: the larger the registration rolls and the larger the ensuing vote on election day, the more liberal the voting of the nation will be. 1950 proved this assumption false. Labor leaders are now confronted with the truth they have avoided facing for a long time. The rank-and-file members of unions, unless educated during the intervals between elections, and particularly during the campaigns, in the social and economic realities of their nation and world, will reject exhortation and act independently at the polls, often without knowledge. In this respect they are no different from their non-union fellow Americans. Moreover, they will not support a nondescript candidate merely because he happens to be the candidate of labor and of the large city political machines to which labor has been wedded, albeit unwillingly. Another fiction has also perished. Because of the Roosevelt experience, labor leaders were inclined to think that the nation's press, essentially conservative, had lost its influence. The unhappy results of the 1950 elections (from labor's point of view) indicate forcibly that the role of the labor press, radio, television, and workers' education classes must be reconsidered. Profound as the changes in labor's political activities have been within the past decade, future developments will have to undergo an even deeper sea-change.

Perhaps a development of even more striking proportions than that experienced on the domestic political scene is found in the widening circle of labor's increasing concern with international affairs. For the first time in the course of our national life, labor leaders and officials have been recognized as proper and effective representatives of the United States in South America, Europe, and Asia. There they have shown the keenest understanding of the problems of peoples striving for economic and political equality; experience has equipped them with an attitude and language common to organized workers everywhere. No less a person than W. Averell Harriman—formerly ECA's Special Representative in Europe—has stated publicly that they are the best ambassadors America now has abroad.

Val R. Lorwin has traced the evolution of American labor's natural interest in world events and institutions against a background of the internal difficulties which hampered progress within labor's own ranks and the external handicaps which American isolationism in general set in the way. Eleanor Finger has provided a detailed account of labor's contribution to the success of the ECA program. She has described the specific tasks that labor leaders have undertaken in their world mission of extending the hand of workers in America to the peoples of all continents.

MAURICE F. NEUFELD

Chapter 5

One hundred years
of labor in politics

A MINOR CONCERN WITH POLITICS HAS LONG BEEN TAKEN TO BE A DISTIN-
guishing feature of the American labor movement. From the failure of
organized labor to establish a national party comparable to the British
Labour party, it has been commonplace to infer both political immaturity
on the part of its members and its own apolitical character. Both inside
and outside the labor movement, there seems to be general agreement
that organized workers first began to display a significant measure of
political consciousness and activity during the New Deal years.

These and similar assertions constitute a curious mixture of valid
judgments and conventional misconceptions. The first labor parties in
the world appeared in the United States, and for almost a century and
a quarter, organized workers have been engaged in various kinds of
political activities. It is significant that only one of the major labor
organizations created by workers since the early part of the nineteenth
century directly repudiated all forms of political action by labor. This
was the Industrial Workers of the World, but before the IWW assumed

this position, it had, during the first two years of its existence, called for independent political action by the working-class.

Three patterns of political behavior have been developed by organized labor. One turns on the attempt to establish and maintain independent parties, local, state, and national in scope, either alone or in conjunction with farmers or others. The ventures into the field of independent electoral politics may constitute a record of overwhelming failure, but the aspiration toward a distinctive labor party has managed to remain very much alive in the American labor movement.

A second pattern of political action grows out of the support given both by individual union members and labor organizations to revolutionary political parties. These have been Marxist-oriented, and although it is true that the various socialist parties that have existed since the last quarter of the nineteenth century have drawn some of their strength from middle-class elements, the essential core of their membership has come from the ranks of organized workers. Not only have these parties been "working-class" by self-declaration, but small segments of the organized labor movement have maintained that they have been the only genuine instruments serving the political interests of wage-earners.

The third pattern consists in what is traditionally called "nonpartisan political action." Nonpartisan political action turns largely on the use of pressure techniques and the lobby, and it rests on the possibility of exchanging labor votes for governmental behavior favorable to labor. The test of favorable behavior lies in the actual policies and actions pursued by legislators, executives, administrators, and the courts.

In a limited sense, nonpartisan politics may be viewed as an extension of the collective bargain to the area of government, with the agreements reached neither expressed in formal contracts nor, of course, enforceable. To the extent that it aims to win support on issues significant to labor from all political parties—in practice from the two major parties—and not at causing the parties to divide over these issues, it may be accurately described as bipartisan. Up to the present, this has been the dominant pattern in organized labor's political behavior. It has, of course, been traditionally associated with the American Federation of Labor, which has consistently repudiated independent electoral politics and has given primary emphasis to economic organization and action.

The Nonpartisan Pattern

Party politics of any kind are barred from the conventions of the AFL by its Constitution. In 1887, a year after the Federation was founded, its convention criticized the launching of political programs as "extravagant expenditures" of organized labor's limited resources. Behind this point of view and the nonpartisan policy adopted by the AFL there stood the experiences of the British trade union movement; the inability of the National Labor Union and of the Greenback Labor party in the U. S. to found substantial electoral organizations; the disappointing history of American labor legislation from the 1860's on; the effects of the political differences within the Knights of Labor; and finally, the difficulties caused the Federation by socialists within and outside its ranks.

But the AFL did not turn its back upon every mode of political action. In 1897, its convention reaffirmed the Federation's opposition to party politics, but it declared for "the independent use of the ballot by the trade unionists and workmen, united regardless of party, that we may elect men from our own ranks to make new laws and administer them along the lines laid down in the legislative demands of the American Federation of Labor, and . . . secure an impartial judiciary that will not govern us by arbitrary injunctions of the courts, nor act as the pliant tools of corporate wealth."

This declaration, however, did not point to the establishment of a separate labor·party, and the political policy pursued by the AFL is summed up in its familiar injunction: "Stand faithfully by our friends. Oppose and defeat our enemies, whether they be Candidates for President, for Congress, or other offices, whether executive, legislative, or judicial."

Nonpartisan political action is neither the invention nor an exclusive possession of the AFL. Today, the Congress of Industrial Organizations operates politically on nonpartisan lines, and independent unions, notably the railway brotherhoods, have done so for many years. It is, of course, also the characteristic mode of behavior of employer, business, farmer, and other more specialized interest groups.

Nonpartisan tactics were used by labor as early as the 1830's, when a New England convention of workers, artisans, and farmers proposed to secure legislative objectives by selecting friendly candidates. During the two following decades, workers' organizations pressed political candidates regardless of party for pledges to support their demands. The pledge and the lobby were employed by the Eight-Hour Day organizations of the 1860's to win passage of shorter-hour laws. During most of its existence, the Knights of Labor opposed the establishment of an independent labor party, and utilized the techniques of nonpartisan action. The AFL's predecessor, the Federation of Organized Trade and Labor Unions of the United States and Canada set up a "legislative committee" which attempted to influence the major parties on labor issues and lobbied for a federal eight-hour-day law. Individual unions, of course, lobbied for specific legislation long before the close of the nineteenth century.

The AFL began to lobby formally in national politics in 1895, when it appointed legislative representatives to serve in Washington, D. C. Two years later, the Federation moved its headquarters to the national capital, thus acknowledging its concern with national legislation, and during the next year, its Executive Council began to lobby directly for labor measures. In 1921, the AFL sought to enhance its political effectiveness by setting up a large legislative conference committee to meet monthly during Congressional sessions. This Conference Committee of Trade Union Legislative Representatives consisted of legislative agents of national unions and the Federation's officers and legislative representatives.

Up to 1906, whatever political pressure the AFL had been able to generate was directed toward individual legislators and the party organizations. For practical purposes, it played no role designed to affect the outcome of elections, and the returns from its political efforts were very thin indeed. Organized labor was not exempted from the provisions of the Sherman Act; the labor injunction was employed with increasing frequency and more injurious effects; the very existence of the trade union movement was being imperilled by damage suits brought against unions and the penalties for contempt of court imposed on union leaders. At the same time, the Washington lobby of the National Association of Manufacturers was enjoying real success in killing proposed labor legislation.

In consequence, the AFL was spurred to undertake a broader and more energetic campaign of political action. A meeting of the Executive Council and of representatives from 118 international unions in March, 1906, formulated Labor's Bill of Grievances, which demanded governmental action to effect a long list of reforms. When Congress blithely ignored the Bill of Grievances, the Executive Council decided to participate actively in the 1906 campaign. It urged all organized labor bodies to work for the defeat of the enemies of labor, to support friendly candidates, and to put up a straight labor candidate when the major parties failed to respond to labor's demands. A labor Representation Committee was designated to run the campaign, and provision was made to raise funds for it.

Subsequently, this committee became the Nonpartisan Political Campaign Committee, and was assigned responsibility for directing and coordinating the political work of the Federation, including the task of making national endorsements. Democratic platforms have been more frequently endorsed by the Federation than those of the Republican party, but this development should not be read as evidence of partisan bias. When the Nonpartisan Political Campaign Committee endorsed the LaFollette-Wheeler ticket in the 1924 election, it specifically pointed out that this action did not signify "a pledge of identification with an independent party movement or a third party, nor . . . support for such a party, group or movement except as such action accords with our nonpartisan political policy."

The characteristic mode of election operations followed by the Nonpartisan Political Campaign Committee appears in the circular letter issued by the Federation's President, William Green, on the eve of the 1926 Congressional elections, which urges "the organized wage-earners and their sympathizers" to prevent the defeat of progressive Congressmen and to prepare "to take an aggressive part in the primaries . . . and the elections. . . . A careful record of the votes made in the present session of Congress and previous Congresses will be compiled and sent to all organized labor. . . . It will be helpful to the American Federation of Labor Non-Partisan Political Campaign Committee if the various state federations of labor and central bodies will send in a list of candidates for United States Senators and members of the House of Representatives. . . . Every state federation of labor, every city central body, and every local union should appoint non-partisan political campaign committees. . . . Mass meetings should be held. . . . The campaign should not be confined to the organized wage-earners. . . . Much depends on the outcome of the primaries and the elections. . . . It is our wish that every campaign committee will write to the American Federation of Labor for information that will be of value as to candidates."

Throughout the existence of the Nonpartisan Political Campaign Committee, its appeals of this kind to the affiliates of the AFL and their memberships have produced widely varying responses. Until very recent years, the actual involvement of the Federation's rank and file membership in its election campaign activities has generally been extremely slight.

The nonpartisan political policy demands expenditure of energy and application of pressure when the major parties are engaged in formulating legislative programs and nominating candidates; when elections are in progress; when legislation is up for consideration; and at the point of the administrative process. Whatever shape activities take at these four points, they always rest upon the proffer of labor votes in exchange for office-holders, programs, and policies favorably disposed to labor. Nonpartisan action, thus, involves the assumption that the major parties are not wholly the instruments of employer interests and will serve labor when the latter offers payment in the common coin of politics— votes.

Application of nonpartisan policy has entailed a wide range of operations on the local, state, and national levels by the Federation and its constituent bodies. These activities, quite understandably, have been conducted with varying intensities at different times and at different points over the vast and complex political and geographical map of the United States. The conventions of the AFL, which take action on questions of public policy significant to labor, serve another political function in providing an audience for addresses by elected and appointed office-holders, including the President and the Secretary of Labor, in which at least some general expression sympathetic to the labor movement, if not specific commitments to pro-labor measures and policies, is expected.

Between election and lobbying activities, no firm distinction can be maintained. Both rest on bargaining techniques. Because labor is so vitally affected by state legislation, the state federations of the AFL engage in extensive lobbying in order to block harmful bills, promote favorable measures, and secure friendly administrators. The unions themselves, of course, also exert pressure for these purposes, and the central labor bodies reproduce the political functions of state federations in the area of municipal politics. The Federation's state and city units draw up legislative programs, may enter primaries, and finally, attempt to deliver a "labor vote" in elections. In some cases, these political activities have linked AFL bodies to state and local political machines and bosses. In Philadelphia, Kansas City, Chicago, San Francisco, and elsewhere they have at different times even operated as key cogs in dominant local machines.

State federations and central labor unions, like the affiliated unions of the AFL, differ widely in political activity and effectiveness. Some, notably the Wisconsin State Federation, can validly claim records of substantial achievements, but most of them cannot. In part, the very techniques upon which they depend set a limit to their effectiveness, as they do to the accomplishments of the Nonpartisan Political Campaign Committee.

Roll-call votes and attitude questionnaires offer no fool-proof means for the determination of "friendly" legislators. If candidates for office with undisguised antilabor records are defeated by mustering at least a portion of labor's voting strength against them, there is no surety that those supported and elected as the "friends" of labor will fulfill their promises. A moderately astute, or indifferent, office-holder can vote as desired on enough issues to establish a claim to labor support without being genuinely sympathetic to labor's interests. Moreover, each political campaign sees leaders of the Federation in the camps of the contending major political parties, generally occupying posts on labor bureaus or committees, where they serve unmistakable partisan interests.

There are impressive arguments to justify nonpartisan policy and consequently shun independent, electoral politics. The two-party tradition—no less weighty for being semimythical—and the strength of party loyalties operate against the creation of a permanent labor party. So does the absence of a corporate sense of class consciousness in the American labor force. In so far as the primary system offers organized labor a means, at least in theory, of seizing control of the major parties, it encourages nonpartisan behavior. Moreover, the major parties are animated by opportunistic rather than ideological considerations, and whenever it is necessary to insure victory, will be responsive to labor's demands. The federal system itself demands that an independent labor party do battle not only on the national front, but also on the forty-eight state fronts.

What may be called the official philosophy of the AFL also strengthened, prior to the New Deal years, the case for nonpartisan political action. The Federation maintained that what labor primarily wanted from government was freedom to pursue its program through economic means. When the latter proved impotent, or when reforms in the working conditions of workers unable to bargain collectively were imperative, then the AFL was willing to utilize governmental power.

Until 1932-1933, therefore, the Federation held that a full-blown program of social reform legislation would weaken the need for trade-unions and that the bureaucracy of a state providing welfare services would curtail freedom. In addition, it feared that should public utilities or basic industries be taken over by government, workers would lose the right to strike. To the extent that the AFL took the position that labor could expect only minimum benefits from the state—particularly where federal and state constitutions and the courts placed severe limitations on the exercise of economic functions by government—it was consistent in putting its major efforts into trade-unionism and in opposing the formation of a labor party.

Still other defenses of nonpartisan action were developed by Samuel Gompers and other AFL leaders. They asserted that even if the organized workers were united in a single party, there were not enough of them to play a deciding part in elections. They also argued that an independent labor party with a clearcut program would crystallize antilabor sentiment in the major parties and divide workers, rather than unite them, by compelling them to commit themselves on controversial issues. Employers, it was pointed out, would be more antagonized by a course of independent political action which threatened the existing political order than by collective bargaining, and this would result in sharper antipathy to labor.

Finally, it should be noted that the Federation's officials have rarely exercised caution in estimating the gains scored by nonpartisan tactics. Thus, the Executive Council's annual report for 1923 claimed that the AFL was responsible for the defeat of 11 reactionary Senators and the election of 23 members of the upper House "loyal to labor," of whom 18 were Democrats and the remainder Republicans. Among the candidates for the House of Representatives, "170 were elected," according to the Executive Council, "either because directly supported by the A. F. of L. National Non-Partisan Political campaign committees or by reason of the opposition of their opponents." (!) By the close of the

1920's, the AFL asserted that some 200 laws had been placed on the statute books as a result of its nonpartisan activities.

The most important innovation in the Federation's political conduct came in 1948, with the effort to apply its nonpartisan policy more effectively. Under the Taft-Hartley Act passed by the 80th Congress, union expenditures for political purposes were prohibited. In order to participate in the elections of 1948 and to defeat those members of Congress who had voted for the measure and were candidates, the 1947 convention of the AFL established an independent organization financed by voluntary contributions. This was called Labor's League for Political Education. At the AFL convention the following year, as at earlier gatherings, resolutions calling for the creation of an independent labor party were offered and turned down.

A. Philip Randolph, President of the Brotherhood of Sleeping Car Porters, proposed that the AFL establish a special political commission charged with the formulation of a twelve-year plan aiming at the establishment of an American counterpart to the British Labour party. The convention, however, voted to continue Labor's League for Political Education on a nonpartisan, expanded, and permanent basis with Joseph D. Keenan as director. The LLPE is, therefore, the Federation's equivalent to the CIO's Political Action Committee, to the independent International Association of Machinists' Nonpartisan Political League, and to the Railway Labor's Political League set up by the railroad unions.

At present, these organizations show a genuine disposition to cooperate on nonpartisan terms, and in the 1949 special election for United States Senator in New York, the AFL and CIO bodies did collaborate effectively in supporting Herbert Lehman's successful candidacy. In the following year, the AFL and CIO joined forces in a futile effort to prevent the reelection of Senator Robert Taft in Ohio. As the Federation's major political arm, LLPE is supposed to participate in campaigns with funds raised from voluntary contributions; to join with other organizations for common political purposes; to conduct research; and to issue public reports. Its educational and informational functions are supported by voluntary contributions from AFL affiliates. LLPE's goal was "a trade-union political steward directing an effective team of volunteer workers in every one of the 110,000 urban and rural precincts" of the country by the time of the 1950 elections. This was not fulfilled, but if it ever is, the Federation will have established its first grass-roots political instrument for implementing its nonpartisan policy.

In a statement on the 1948 election returns, LLPE not only claimed substantial gains due to its labors, but also, by implication, affirmed the wisdom of nonpartisan action. The box-score compiled by the LLPE showed that seventeen "enemies" of labor seeking Senate seats and 106 contesting seats in the House were defeated; that all the "friends" were retained in both Houses; and that 172 LLPE-endorsed candidates for the Houses were elected. No comparable claim of successes, however, could be made after the 1950 Congressional elections.

Criticisms of Nonpartisan Politics

Criticisms of nonpartisan political action had been registered before it was peculiarly identified with the AFL, and since then have been directed both from within and from outside the Federation. Almost since the foundation of the AFL, elements within it have charged that the nonpartisan policy is profitless, if not an actual disservice to labor. They have asserted that nonpartisan behavior splits labor's strength at the polls; that when union men are elected as major party candidates their loyalties go to the Democratic and Republican parties and not to the trade union movement; and finally, that liberals outside the ranks of labor are chiefly responsible for the gains ascribed to nonpartisan action. These critics have demanded partisan political action through either an independent labor party, affiliation with a third party built upon a broad reform base, or the channeling of labor's political energies into radical parties of Marxist character.

The radical parties have, of course, maintained that the major parties are dominated by the same capitalist interests, and constitute, so far as workers are concerned, a choice between Tweedledum and Tweedledee. With the Democratic and Republican organizations serving the few, and not the many, it follows that the salvation of the workers can only be found in a party of their own. Significantly enough, the nonpartisan policy is also anchored in the view that the major parties are not divided by questions of basic principle, are supported, broadly speaking, by the same kinds of people, and are concerned with winning elections and not with realizing distinctive programs.

The demands within the AFL, and later inside the CIO, for the creation of an independent labor party have been fed both by the conviction that only a socialist-oriented party could serve the cause of labor and by disillusion and even disgust with the performance of the major parties. At the height of the progressive upsurge during the second decade of this century, the Wisconsin State Federation of labor, for example, repudiated the major parties as instruments of "our industrial masters," and called upon the workers to elect members of their own class to all offices. A year later, in 1914, the United Mine Workers declared that the moment was at hand "for the laboring people to come together in a political party." There were lively demands in many quarters for American wage-earners to follow the path of European workers in moving toward social and economic reform through independent labor parties.

After World War I, sentiment for abandoning the nonpartisan line grew rapidly. It was argued that the huge corporations represented concentrations of political as well as economic power; they had, in short, become majority stockholders in the major parties. A maturer economy meant worker insecurity on so vast a scale that trade-union organizations could not cope with it. Only through a fresh utilization of the power of the state—which had served the propertied interests so well—could security be attained. From this it followed that unless labor entered politics on its own, or in combination with agrarian groups, it would be impossible to fashion government into an instrument for achieving working-class well-being.

Independent Electoral Politics

The nineteenth century experiences with independent labor or farmer-labor parties had not been very encouraging, although some local organizations had shown temporary promise of real strength. The first labor party in the world, the Working Men's party, was founded in Philadelphia in 1828 by the Mechanics' Union of Trade Associations of that city. Similar parties appeared shortly after in Boston, New York, and elsewhere. The early disappearance of property and tax qualifications for voting, as well as the specific demands put forth by these local parties, encouraged these ventures in independent electoral politics. They were long regarded as a significant source for Andrew Jackson's voting strength, but recent studies indicate that working-class districts in Boston and Philadelphia gave very slight support to the city labor parties.

Before its dissolution in 1872, the National Labor Union launched the short-lived National Reform party. The depressed years of the 1870's prompted organized workers to turn to independent political action in several cities. The Greenback party, which flourished during this period, made its appeal to both farmers and workers, and polled over 300,000 out of a total popular vote of over 9,000,000 in the election of 1880, its peak vote in the three presidential elections beginning with 1876 in which it ran candidates. Its chief strength, however, lay in predominantly nonindustrial areas.

The deep resentment felt by the workers in consequence of the unfortunate Haymarket Affair in 1886 stimulated the attempt to found the United Labor party in Chicago. At the same time, labor made possible the exciting Henry George mayoralty campaign in New York City in 1886, and the successes of the Union Labor party in Milwaukee. Both the Union Labor and the United Labor parties tried to become national organizations, but barely survived the presidential election of 1888, in which the first secured almost 150,000 popular votes out of a total of more than 11,000,000; and the latter, less than 6,500. During these years, labor parties in New England, the middle and northwest states, and Colorado polled comparatively heavy votes. Several segments of the organized labor movement, notably in Cook County, Illinois, and in Colorado, where the miners had a real stake in the free coinage of silver, joined forces with the Populists in the 1890's.

Not until after the close of the First World War was there felt once more a lively impulse among trade-unionists to fashion an independent labor party. Soaring prices, the ferment of postwar reconstruction programs, and the stimulus of revolutionary currents in Russia and elsewhere in Europe were important causes of the most vigorous expression of political militancy by labor during the twentieth century. It is significant that the lead in creating the numerous labor parties of that period was taken by officials and rank-and-file members of AFL unions, state federations, and central labor bodies.

When the first convention of the American Labor party met in Chicago in July 1920, 15 state labor parties were already in existence. The national organization changed its name to the Farmer-Labor party of the United States, and offered an extremely interesting and advanced program to the electorate in the 1920 elections. Its candidate, Parley P. Christensen, polled only a little better than 260,000 votes, but the state parties showed far more voting strength, scoring a number of Congressional successes.

Shortly afterward, a rival, communist-controlled organization appeared in the Federated Farmer-Labor party; and in 1922, the railway unions, together with other segments of the labor movement which wanted vigorous political action, but not an independent labor party, created the Conference for Progressive Political Action. This organization made possible Senator Robert LaFollette's presidential candidacy in 1924. Endorsed by the Farmer-Labor and Socialist parties, LaFollette and his running-mate, Burton K. Wheeler, ran under varying party names in different states. They rolled up over 4,800,000 popular votes, over 16 per cent of the total cast, with about two million coming from normal Democratic votes and about half that number from Republicans.

This show of seeming success actually marked the decline of labor's postwar political militancy. Prosperity; abandonment by the railway unions of the Conference for Progressive Political Action; the failure to maintain the temporary unity among western progressives, socialists, industrial workers, and agrarians, achieved through the personality of LaFollette; disintegration of the farmer-labor party organizations; and still other factors contributed to the passing of labor's political militancy. Of all the state labor parties that flowered after 1919, only the Minnesota Farmer-Labor party, which polled 40 per cent of the state vote in 1924, remained a significant political force. In a handful of other states, notably in Wisconsin, progressive coalitions in which workers strengthened an essentially agrarian base, also played roles of more than trivial importance in the later 'twenties.

The Impact of the Depression and the New Deal

Broadly speaking, the more intensive movements for independent political action have been related to periods of depression and serious dislocations in the relationship between wages and prices. Until recent years, labor's economic weapons were seriously weakened in depression years, and it turned to the ballot as another source of power. With the deepening of the depression after 1929, organized labor's interest in political action rose. The formation of local labor parties followed unsuccessful strikes during 1930-1931 in Philadelphia, in Kenosha, Wisconsin, in New Bedford, Massachusetts, in Elizabethton, Tennessee, and elsewhere. The intensity of a depression that appeared to threaten the very life of the economy compelled the AFL and other segments of the labor front to abandon their traditional views on the economic and social responsibilities and functions of the state. With 15 millions unemployed and hunger a frightening reality, it was impossible to maintain suspicion of a government that provided social or welfare services. It was no longer sufficient to hold that government fulfilled its primary obligation to labor when it left the unions free to realize their aims through economic means.

Up to the early 'thirties, as it has been observed, the AFL—which was roughly equivalent to organized labor—viewed the acquisition of political power as secondary to the attainment of economic power, and it maintained that the chief purpose of political action was to secure a climate favorable to economic organization.

The primary goal, therefore, had been to wipe out governmental restraints on the freedom to organize, to strike, to boycott, to picket, to bargain collectively. Governmental policies that were not regarded as bearing directly on wages, hours, and working conditions were given very slight, if any, attention. Tariff and immigration policies were, of course, objects of lively concern.

The resolutions acted on by AFL conventions prior to the 1930's, as well as its pressure and lobby activities, confirm the validity of this observation, but it is also clear that the Federation did not adhere consistently to its general anti-interventionist position on the functions of government. It has already been indicated that where economic power was ineffective, where gains through collective bargaining were very unlikely, as in the case of women, child workers, and seamen, the AFL was ready to utilize the power of government to secure specific benefits.

Primary among the minimum benefits sought from the state was legal recognition of the right to organize and bargain collectively. This had been secured for one small portion of the nation's labor force by the Railway Labor Act of 1926—a striking instance of success through nonpartisan tactics—which recognized the right of railway workers to form their own organizations and to designate representatives for purposes of collective bargaining. Not until the passage of the Wagner Act, however, was this sort of legal protection extended to a substantial number of organized workers.

With the remedial and reform measures of the New Deal, organized labor acquired a new stake in politics. Wages, hours, jobs, relief, unemployment insurance, a broad social security program, the conditions of organization and collective bargaining—all these were now affected with varying degrees of decisiveness by government policy. Everyday experience encouraged a greater political maturity and a range of political activities that transcended the traditional expressions of nonpartisan policy.

In the early 'thirties, therefore, organized labor was compelled once more to examine the old issue of the desirable form of political action. At this juncture, moreover, neither the Socialist nor the Communist parties could seriously claim that they were genuine political instruments serving the mass of the American workers. In spite of its local voting strength in such centers as Milwaukee, Bridgeport, Connecticut, and Reading, Pennsylvania, the Socialists were virtually impotent as a political organization and movement.

This fact was apparent in the vote they secured in the protest election of 1932 which carried Franklin D. Roosevelt into the presidency. Out of a total popular vote of almost forty million, the socialist presidential candidate, Norman Thomas, secured less than 900,000, a little better than 2 per cent. The communist total in 1932, on the other hand, with conditions more favorable to the party's appeal than ever before, barely topped 100,000. The Communist party, in short, had failed to establish a significant political bridgehead in the camp of labor. It had, moreover, won the enmity of most trade unions as a result of its name, its programs, and its attempts to capture control of the labor movement through the tactics of boring from within and dual unionism.

Radical Political Parties

The failure of Marxism to become a vital political movement in the United States has intrigued several students, but it still remains to be fully explored. For the purposes of this examination of organized labor's political activities, that question may be ignored. It will be sufficient merely to call attention to the socialist-oriented parties that have appeared since the 1870's, and which have claimed to represent the true interests of the American working class.

The first of these parties, the Labor party of Illinois, founded at the close of 1873, was Lassallean in its theoretical position, as was the Social-Democratic party of North America, which was born the following year. Both were less important than the Working Men's party of the

United States founded by a gathering of socialists in Philadelphia in 1876. Late the following year, this became the Socialist-Labor party, which still survives and which attained the height of its influence in the 1890's under the leadership of Daniel DeLeon.

Schisms in the socialist camp led to the creation of two new parties before the Socialist party of America was founded in July, 1901. The nucleus of its initial strength lay in former members of the Socialist-Labor party and recruits from the vanishing Populist cause. Until it was severely split by the issues created by the First World War and the Bolshevist Revolution, the Socialist party was roughly equivalent with the socialist movement in the United States. Its membership grew steadily to reach 125,000 in 1912, when its presidential candidate, Eugene V. Debs, polled almost 6 per cent of the total popular vote. In that year, over a thousand dues-paying members of the party were holding some kind of public office, among them 56 mayors and one Congressman, Victor L. Berger, elected two years earlier.

But the party's political strength was far less a product of conversion to socialism than of a widespread desire for "honest" and "good" government and of dissatisfaction with the major parties. It is significant that the positive response to socialist candidates was relatively greater in states that were not preeminently industrial. Thus in 1912, Debs scored 10 per cent or more of the total vote in Oklahoma, Nevada, Montana, Arizona, California, Washington, and Idaho. In only three industrial states (Ohio, Pennsylvania, and Illinois), did he register 7 per cent or more of the total vote.

A number of considerations, among them the loss of much of its nonreformist wing and the new political militancy of organized labor, led the Socialist party to explore the possibilities of collaborating with other left-of-center groupings for the purpose of establishing a labor party on the British model. The outcome of the 1924 election shattered this hope, and the party's political weight diminished over the remainder of the decade.

Meanwhile, socialist elements with a revolutionary, Bolshevist orientation were seeking to win political support from wage earners through the Workers' party, fused out of several competing organizations in 1921-1922. This group subsequently became the Communist party of the United States, and was the American section of the Communist International until the latter was formally dissolved in 1943. The Communist party then took the form of a political association. After the Second World War, it resumed its existence as a party, but not as a direct participant in national elections. Throughout its existence, the communist organization, which made its best showing in a presidential election in 1932, has drawn political support from a handful of unions in a few urban centers.

Their failure to win political power is no measure of the political influence that radical parties have exercised upon the organized labor movement since the close of the nineteenth century. They have helped to sharpen political awareness and to spur organized labor to political action; they have conditioned the drafting of labor's political programs; and finally, they have contributed to the splits and schisms that have marked the history of the labor movement.

Labor Politics since the 1930's

The mounting concern with political action that developed during the early years of the New Deal was reflected in the plea made by a delegate from the International Ladies' Garment Workers' Union at the 1935 AFL convention that labor build its own party and elect its own candidates. The objective was to realize a labor program "to balance production and distribution." This met with no success, and only one of the several labor parties then in existence could be counted on as a factor in building a national labor party. The solidly established Minnesota Farmer-Labor party wielded enough power to make a deal with the Democrats by which the latter withdrew their state ticket in 1936 in exchange for farmer-labor support of President Roosevelt. During the preceding year, farmer, labor, cooperative, and socialist forces drew together in Wisconsin to produce the Farmer-Labor Federation, which appeared to promise the emergence of a third party on the Minnesota pattern.

Labor's political stake and the formation of the Committee for Industrial Organization led to the founding of Labor's Nonpartisan League in the summer of 1936. To the encouragement of those who desired independent political action, the offspring of this body in New York was the American Labor party, which promptly concentrated its energies on the re-election of President Roosevelt and Governor Lehman. The ALP vote in this and following elections made it an important factor in state and city politics. Although the Democrats had enough margin to elect Governor Lehman in 1936, the ALP vote made possible his re-election two years later and gave the state to President Roosevelt in 1940.

This balance of power success of the ALP, however, left severe doubts concerning the wisdom of independent political action. Only when it embraced a major political figure—Roosevelt, Lehman, Fiorello La Guardia—did the ALP poll an impressive vote. Its affiliated trade union membership was not an accurate measure of its political weight, and more important, did not balance the lack of solid ward and precinct organization and of loyal, individual party membership. The tendency for some labor leaders to regard the party as if it were their personal property, and the policy and personality struggles between right wing and communist elements, were disruptive forces within the ALP, reducing its political effectiveness.

By 1944, the battle for control of the party resulted in withdrawal of the right-wing forces and the founding of a second political organization with a labor base in New York in the Liberal party. Between them, the ALP and Liberal party enabled President Roosevelt to carry New York in 1944, for the Democratic vote was only 39.4 per cent of the total, and the combined Roosevelt vote was 53.5 per cent of the total popular vote. When the ALP and Liberal party departed from a balance of power role by running their own candidates, and when they did not endorse a very strong candidate, the limits of their appeal were clearly set forth.[1]

When Labor's Nonpartisan League came to life in Washington on August 10, 1936, it claimed to represent the political interest of 85 per cent of the organized workers in the country. Primarily dedicated to the re-election of Franklin D. Roosevelt, its purpose was to continue as a permanent organization in order to augment the political effectiveness of the nation's liberal forces. Initially supported by the AFL, CIO, and independent unions, the League soon became another battle arena for the first two. In 1938, William Green urged AFL members to withdraw from the League, charging that it was a CIO agency manipulated by CIO leaders seeking to create an independent political party. Even before this date, the League and the Nonpartisan Political Campaign Committee of the AFL were operating as rivals, quarreling over the terms of the federal wages and hours law, over nominations, and over endorsements of candidates.

In spite of the political ferment it engendered in labor circles, the election of 1936 actually served to check the movement for independent political action on a national scale. For it was clear that labor stood to gain by throwing whatever weight it could muster to President Roosevelt. A labor party with an independent ticket would only divide the voting strength of the labor and progressive forces in the nation to the advantage of the Republican party.

Overwhelmingly, the leadership of organized labor was persuaded that the interests of their movement were inextricably linked to Franklin D. Roosevelt. In the President they possessed a "friend" whose program

---

[1] In 1942 the independent ALP candidate for Governor contributed somewhat to the election of Thomas E. Dewey. The Liberal party slate in the New York City mayoralty election of 1945 polled only 122,316 votes. Some 425,000 ALP and 180,000 Liberal party votes cast for the Democratic candidate for Governor, Senator Mead, did not prevent Dewey's re-election in 1946. By 1948, the ALP's balance of power position in New York City's politics was, for practical purposes, gone. The 1950 election demonstrated that the ALP had at maximum a nuisance value in the mayoralty and gubernatorial areas. The Liberal party, which contributed heavily to Senator Lehman's reelection in 1950, had been able to determine the Democratic mayoralty choice, but suffered with him and the Democratic gubernatorial candidate whom it endorsed. In spite of this limited success, the Liberal party clearly took third place among the parties in New York.

reflected their concerns and demands. He gave the Democratic party a progressive orientation. In organized labor the party and the President possessed an important source of strength.

This relationship seemed to fulfill the terms of the brief for nonpartisan tactics. Here, rewarding labor's friends and punishing its enemies promised maximum returns. By contrast, the launching of an independent party upon a labor base, or even the entrance of labor into a third-party movement more broadly conceived, invited risking the gains secured from the New Deal.

As long as Roosevelt was the Democratic standard-bearer, there was valid reason for maintaining an alliance by which labor bound itself to specific Democratic candidates and policies, but not to the party itself. The vast majority of organized labor's rank and file learned its non-partisan policy lessons very well indeed. Neither John L. Lewis's rancorous attacks upon F.D.R. and his support of Wendell Willkie, nor the opposition of the communists to the President's foreign policy substantially affected the voting behavior of workers, both organized and unorganized, in the 1940 presidential election.

In this context, it is worth noting that the labor vote in presidential elections since 1936 has constituted a relatively stable factor. In rough terms, around three-fifths of the AFL and about 70 per cent of the CIO voters have been casting Democratic ballots. At the same time, the fact that, in spite of the close ties with organized labor established by President Roosevelt, between 30 and 40 per cent of the votes of organized workers have gone to Republican presidential candidates underlines the enormous difficulties involved in detaching wage-earners from the two major parties and inducing them to vote for an independent labor party. Party loyalty, it is clear, operates for workers as well as for others.

The notion that the Political Action Committee of the CIO constituted a new departure in labor politics has had wide currency, even within the labor movement, although it patently represents still another expression of the nonpartisan policy. Behind the formation of PAC, in the summer of 1943, stood the losses in New Deal strength in the Congressional elections of the previous year, due in good measure to the voting indifference of organized labor. There were, however, also other causes at work. The rapid growth of membership in CIO unions meant an obvious increment in economic power and encouraged the hope for the acquisition of greater political weight. Political differences within that body were reduced by the Nazi attack upon the Soviet Union, because communist opposition to President Roosevelt's foreign policy ceased, and by John L. Lewis's resignation from the presidency of the CIO and the subsequent departure of the United Mine Workers from that organization.

To the extent that the positive purpose in founding PAC was to insure the election of the friends of labor and to realize a progressive program through nonpartisan action, it also operated against the flowering of an independent third-party movement. "We are not interested," declared PAC Chairman Sidney Hillman, in 1944, "in establishing a third party, for a third party would only serve to divide rather than to unite the forces of progress. We are not an appendage of either major political party. ... Like every other organization concerned with the affairs of government, we seek to influence the thinking, the program, and the choice of candidates of both parties." Twenty-four years earlier, Samuel Gompers, castigating the Chicago Federation of Labor for having abandoned the nonpartisan policy, warned that the new Farmer-Labor party would "hamper the success of labor in its efforts to defeat its enemies and elect its friends" in the elections of 1920.

Within the CIO, there has always existed a body of lively sentiment favoring independent political action. Some of its leaders, notably Walter P. Reuther, have made it quite clear that they look forward to the ultimate creation of a labor-based third party. But PAC's behavior up to the present time adds up to a militant application of the AFL's traditional nonpartisan policy.

For obvious reasons, until PAC set out to punish the members of Congress who had voted for the Taft-Hartley Act, most of its energy—apart from that devoted to the task of getting workers to register and vote—was spent to support Roosevelt and New Deal candidates. Both the PAC and the AFL labored energetically, openly and behind the scenes, at the Chicago Democratic National Convention in 1944. They were equally committed to Roosevelt for a fourth term. They fought the vice-presidential candidacy of James F. Byrnes. They employed the same techniques when they opposed each other on the vice-presidency, the CIO championing Henry Wallace, and the AFL Harry S. Truman.

It is worth noting that, in spite of the extensive publicity given to PAC, most of it bitterly unfavorable, about one-third of the adult population of the country said that they had not heard of it on the eve of the election of 1944, and only about one-half of the adult population knew that it was supporting President Roosevelt. In that election neither the CIO's PAC nor the AFL determined the outcome. But the votes cast by workers made a major difference in Roosevelt's popular vote. Only in New York did the President significantly exceed his 1940 vote, and here he would have run well behind Thomas Dewey had he not received approximately 825,000 ALP and Liberal party votes. In five states with heavy labor concentrations in the Midwest and New England (Illinois, Michigan, Minnesota, Connecticut, and Massachusetts), F.D.R.'s vote remained fairly stable compared with that of 1940. In other industrialized states, including California, Ohio, Indiana, and Delaware, his vote dropped below the 1940 levels.

Developments since 1948

The issue of an independent third-party movement was temporarily shelved by the policies and personality of President Roosevelt and by America's entrance into World War II. But later developments forced a re-examination of the courses of political action open to labor. The death of Roosevelt, the termination of hostilities, and the problems of making the peace at home and abroad affected the situation. The atomic bomb, the initial rightward drift of President Truman's administration, the victory scored by the British Labour party in 1945, and the real defeat suffered by the labor and liberal forces in the Congressional elections of the following year were also influential. So were the impressive weight of conservative and reactionary elements in the two major parties, the character of Soviet foreign policy and its reflection in the behavior of the communist-dominated segments of the labor movement, and the growing intensity of the cold war.

These considerations also shaped the dominant answer given prior to the 1948 election—that is, to continue with the policy of nonpartisan action. This decision was made easier by the narrowing of organized labor's political target around the defeat of the pro-Taft-Hartley Senators and Representatives, and by the effort of the communists to create a new third-party movement around the personality of Henry A. Wallace. There is no doubt that the Progressive party born in Philadelphia in the summer of 1948 was both conceived and delivered by the communists, but it is also clear that Henry Wallace's demand for the abandonment of traditional party affiliations made sense to many who were neither communists nor fellow-travelers. When, in announcing that he would run for President in 1948, he called for the formation of a "New Party" and assailed the two old parties as subservient to the same minority interests and undistinguishable except in their rivalry for office, Wallace was reiterating one of the oldest themes in American protest politics.

The Progressive party entered the presidential campaign with a catch-all program, the slogan of "Peace, Progress, and Prosperity"—used, interestingly enough, by the Democratic party in 1916—and the support of a handful of communist-dominated unions in the CIO. Officially the CIO continued its nonpartisan policy and together with the AFL threw its weight as an organization to President Truman.

The election upset that continued him in office not only embarrassed the professional poll-takers; it also foretold the proximate demise of the Progressive party. Henry Wallace's popular vote, 1,157,172, was about 2.5 per cent of the total cast. Moreover, almost half his vote, 509,599 was registered in New York, where his candidacy gave the state to Governor Dewey. The apparent failure of subsequent efforts to make it appear that the party is not communist directed and controlled and the decision made at the close of 1949 to expel the communist-dominated unions from the CIO have left the Progressive party virtually impotent. Early in 1950, with Wallace's future role very much in doubt and several internal differences over leadership not clearly resolved, the party decided to contest only a limited number of Congressional elections later in the year. The outbreak of the Korean conflict and the subsequent resignation of Wallace and other leaders from the Progressive party as a result of its support of the Soviet Union's position on Korea settled at least two questions. It reduced the party to a hard core of Communist and fellow-traveller members, and it took the party out of the 1950 elections.

Both the AFL and CIO quite understandably claimed credit for President Truman's surprise triumph, even though it was a shift in the farm vote outside of the South that made his triumph possible. He did not carry the key industrial states of New York, Pennsylvania, Michigan, New Jersey, and Connecticut, which fell to Roosevelt four years earlier, and the Truman margin was very slight in such critical states as Illinois, Ohio, and California. Yet, it does not appear that the decline in the Democratic urban vote in 1948 from that of 1944 was due to a change in labor's voting behavior, except in New York and California, where the Wallace vote mattered.

The Democratic labor vote appears to have remained fairly stable, and to this extent the two labor organizations were justified in claiming responsibility for President Truman's election and for reaffirming the wisdom of nonpartisan action. In 1948, as it has been seen, the AFL undertook a broader and more militant program. At its convention that year, the CIO found in the election full confirmation of "the correctness of our decision to abstain from and discourage any move in the direction of a third party at this time." Concerned with the consequences of a divided labor vote, the convention rejected "any and all proposals for a third party," and resolved to continue PAC in its existing form with Jack Kroll, who had replaced Sidney Hillman on the latter's death in 1946, as director.

Delegates from the communist-controlled unions that had championed Wallace and the Progressive party fought for the right of each affiliate to determine its own policy in respect to political party endorsements, and urged that the CIO spearhead a national coalition of progressive forces. The first proposal implied the abandonment of the CIO's nonpartisan policy and the destruction of much of PAC's effectiveness. Together with all the other recommendations of the communist forces in the convention, it was roundly defeated. The expulsion of the communist-dominated unions from the CIO during 1950 promises greater internal coherence on political matters within the organization. There still remains within the CIO, however, a body of sentiment which looks forward to an independent labor party at some future date.

At present, and in spite of the disappointing results which this strategy brought in the 1950 Congressional elections, the organized labor movement stands overwhelmingly committed to the continuation of nonpartisan action. And the very nature of the American party system seems to warrant this commitment. The major parties as vote-getting mechanisms have no firm ideological roots. It has been emphasized that they divide the electorate less by demanding adherence to fundamental principles and clean-cut programs than by contending for expressions of voting loyalties in contests for office.

As a vote-getting machine, each party organization is capable of absorbing within it virtually all the political elements in the nation. "Its one purpose," observes John Fisher, "is to unite the largest number of divergent interest groups in the pursuit of power. Its unity is one of compromise, not of dogma." [2] This policy gives American politics a disordered, illogical, and at times, even an irrational cast. But it means that nongovernmental power structures such as the unions, which appear as pressure groups when they act politically, are encouraged to remain, in so far as possible, within the orbit of both the Democratic and Republican parties and to attempt through them to shape the character and behavior of government.

HENRY DAVID

Popular Votes for Labor and Labor-Affiliated Parties in Presidential Elections

(The votes of state parties that endorsed major party candidates are not listed. Nor are the votes given to the People's party, which received labor support before and after fusion with the Democratic party in 1896. The vote of the coalition of parties that supported LaFollette in 1924 is included.)

Year	Party	Presidential Candidates	No. of Votes
1876	Greenback	Peter Cooper	81,739
1880	Greenback	James B. Weaver	308,578
1884	Greenback	Benjamin F. Butler	175,370
1888	Union Labor	Anson J. Streeter	146,935
	United Labor	Robert H. Cowdrey	2,818
1920	Farmer-Labor	Parley P. Christensen	265,411
1924	Farmer-Labor, Liberty Bell, Socialist, Progressive, etc.	Robert LaFollette	4,822,856
1928	Farmer-Labor	Frank E. Webb	6,390
1932	Farmer-Labor	Jacob S. Coxey, Sr.	7,309

[2] "Unwritten Rules of American Politics," *Harper's Magazine*, November 1948, pp. 32-33.

POPULAR VOTES OF RADICAL PARTIES IN PRESIDENTIAL ELECTIONS

Year	Party	Presidential Candidates	No. of Votes
1892	Socialist-Labor	Simon Wing	21,164
1896	Socialist-Labor	Charles H. Matchett	36,274
1900	Socialist-Labor	Joseph F. Malloney	39,739
	Social Democratic party of America	Eugene V. Debs	87,814
	Social Democratic party of the United States	Job Harriman	6,359
1904	Socialist-Labor	Charles H. Corrigan	31,249
	Socialist	Eugene V. Debs	402,283
1908	Socialist-Labor	August Gilhaus	13,825
	Socialist	Eugene V. Debs	420,793
1912	Socialist-Labor	Arthur E. Reimer	28,750
	Socialist	Eugene V. Debs	900,672
1916	Socialist-Labor	Arthur E. Reimer	13,403
	Socialist	Eugene V. Debs	585,113
1920	Socialist-Labor	W. W. Cox	31,715
	Socialist	Eugene V. Debs	919,799
1924	Socialist-Labor	Frank T. Johns	36,428
	Socialist	(endorsed LaFollette)	. . . . .
	Workers	William Z. Foster	36,386
1928	Socialist-Labor	Verne L. Reynolds	33,276
	Socialist	Norman Thomas	267,835
	Workers	William Z. Foster	21,181
1932	Socialist-Labor	Verne L. Reynolds	33,276
	Socialist	Norman Thomas	881,951
	Communist	William Z. Foster	102,785
1936	Socialist-Labor; Industrial Labor	John W. Aiken	12,777
	Socialist	Norman Thomas	187,720
	Communist	Earl Browder	80,159
1940	Socialist-Labor	John W. Aiken	18,677
	Socialist	Norman Thomas	99,557
	Communist	Earl Browder	46,251
1944	Socialist-Labor; Industrial Government	Edward A. Teichert	45,336
	Socialist	Norman Thomas	80,518
1948	Socialist-Labor	Edward A. Teichert	29,061
	Socialist	Norman Thomas	139,521
	Socialist-Workers	Farrell Dobbs	13,613

SELECTED BIBLIOGRAPHY

Anderson, Dewey and Davidson, Percy E., *Ballots and the Democratic Class Struggle* (Stanford, California: Stanford University Press), 1943.

Carroll, Mollie Ray, *Labor and Politics* (Boston: Houghton Mifflin Co.), 1923.

Childs, Harwood L., *Labor and Capital in National Politics* (Columbus, Ohio: Ohio State University Press, 1930.

Commons, John R. and Associates, *History of Labour in the United States,* 2 vols. (New York: The Macmillan Company), 1918.

David, Henry, "Labor's Bipartisan Political Thinking," *Labor and Nation,* vol. 5, no. 5, September-October, 1949.

———, "Labor and Political Action after World War I: 1919-1924," *Labor and Nation,* vol. 1, no. 4, February-March, 1946.

Davis, Jerome, and Stein, Emanuel, editors, "Labor Problems in America," Chap. 20. (New York: Farrar and Rinehart), 1940.

Fine, Nathan, *Labor and Farmer Parties in the United States, 1828-1928* (New York: Rand School of Social Science), 1928.

Gompers, Samuel, *Seventy Years of Life and Labor,* 2 vols. (New York: E. P. Dutton & Co.), 1925.

Hardman, J. B. S., "Labor Parties, United States," *Encyclopaedia of the Social Sciences,* vol. 8. (New York: The Macmillan Company), 1932.

Hesseltine, William B., *The Rise and Fall of Third Parties: From Anti-Masonry to Wallace* (Washington: Public Affairs Press), 1948.

Hillquit, Morris, *History of Socialism in the United States* (New York: Funk and Wagnalls Co.), 1906.

Laidler, Harry W., *Toward a Farmer-Labor Party* (New York: The League for Industrial Democracy), 1938.

Lorwin, Lewis L., *The American Federation of Labor* (Washington: The Brookings Institution), 1933.

Perlman, Selig, *History of Trade Unionism in the United States* (New York: The Macmillan Company), 1922.

———, *A Theory of the Labor Movement* (New York: The Macmillan Company), 1928.

——— and Taft, Philip, *History of Labor in the United States, 1896-1932* (New York: The Macmillan Company), 1935.

Stedman, Murray S., Jr. and Stedman, Susan W., *Discontent at the Polls: A Study of Farmer and Labor Parties, 1827-1928* (New York: Columbia University Press), 1950.

Ware, Norman J., *The Industrial Worker, 1840-1860* (Boston: Houghton Mifflin Co.), 1924.

———, *The Labor Movement in the United States, 1860-1895* (New York: D. Appleton & Company), 1929.

Chapter 6

The AFL-LLPE
and how it works

LABOR'S LEAGUE FOR POLITICAL EDUCATION IS STILL IN THE INITIAL STAGES of growth. The organization is being developed at national, state, and local levels.

The national LLPE office is located in Washington. Policy on the national level is determined by the Administrative Committee composed of national AFL and LLPE leaders. The chairman and secretary-treasurer are William Green and George Meany, respectively. The author of this chapter is the national director.

There are local LLPE's in every state and principal city, but still not in every congressional district. Geographically, the organizational setup follows, for the most part, the same pattern as that of the political parties. At the same time it takes advantage of AFL national, state, and local administrative arrangements.

But it should be understood that the administrative arrangements of local Leagues are very flexible. The local Leagues adjust their methods of operation to meet the conditions of their particular communities. They use all of the resources available in their areas—such as local AFL and CIO unions, PAC, and other interested groups—and coordinate the activities of the organizations working with them. They will also co-operate with the established political parties under given circumstances.

The policy committee on the state level is usually the State AFL Executive Council. The legislative body of the State LLPE is made up of delegates from the local unions and the local LLPE's. Voting quotas in some cases are determined on the basis of per capita tax payments to the State LLPE.

Local LLPE's are organized by area (comprising two or more congressional districts within the state), congressional districts, and city levels. There are also League representatives in local unions, union shops and plants, and election precincts. The officers of the local LLPE's are

113

usually men and women holding office at a corresponding level of the local AFL union structure.

The local LLPE may either establish separate headquarters or share them with the central trades union. Headquarters are staffed to perform many of the same functions undertaken by local political party headquarters. From these offices the local League publishes facts about the candidates it supports, arranges their radio programs, issues posters and flyers, sends out letters and telegrams, and arranges speeches throughout the area it covers. Direct daily contact with the voters is maintained through representatives in union shops and leaders in election precincts. For example, each shop under the jurisdiction of the ILGWU has a political steward who works independently of the shop steward. His duties are: to keep members informed of actions taken by Congress and state legislatures; to encourage members to write to their Congressmen and legislators; to make sure that members and their families register and vote; and finally, to explain the issues of the political campaign.

National Activities

The national LLPE therefore has a huge task of coordinating policy and activities. To finance its program, the national LLPE collects voluntary contributions from individual union members. Local union shop collectors receive from the national LLPE office receipt books (printed in triplicate) and League buttons. A button and the original copy of the receipt go to the contributor and the second copy is forwarded to national headquarters. The third copy is kept by the collector. The money is mailed to Washington weekly. The state LLPE is reimbursed for half of its collection. The remainder is allocated by national headquarters where it is most needed.

The national League provides the following services for the local Leagues and all other politically activated local AFL units:

1. *The League Reporter*, a four-page newspaper, is published weekly. It is sent to every AFL and LLPE affiliate and is available to anyone else who desires to subscribe. *The League Reporter* analyzes bills before Congress. It keeps its members informed of the voting record in the House and Senate. It reports national trends of interest to labor as culled from other sources.

In order to insure widespread dissemination of its news, this publication urges local Leagues, labor press, and union journals to reprint its articles. Mats and cuts are also available after publication in *The League Reporter*.

2. The national LLPE office prepares and broadcasts radio programs and gives assistance to the local LLPE's and the local AFL union radio stations in the preparation of their own programs. The national LLPE makes platters and distributes them to the local LLPE's for use on their stations. The local LLPE then prepares its own introductory remarks. These recordings are also made on phonograph records for use at local union meetings. And the national LLPE prepares programs for use on nationwide hookups. It is up to the local

LLPE's to persuade local network stations to carry the programs if they are not already doing so. At present, Frank Edwards is broadcasting over the Mutual network five nights weekly, reporting the AFL view of the news.

The radio department of the national LLPE advertises through *The League Reporter* the radio schedules of Congressmen and Senators friendly to labor and the local stations over which they will speak. In addition, the national LLPE supplies publicity material to the local Leagues for use in their localities, and suggests methods of using programs most fully, such as posting notices of radio programs on union bulletin boards and discussing programs at union meetings.

Effect of Taft-Hartley Act

At this writing, the LLPE is in its first stage of shaping organization to needs and policies. The LLPE is, for the AFL, a novel venture. Organized political action by the AFL had never been attempted before, and any new project requires the solution of many policy and administrative questions. Some policy and administrative practices are not yet fully formalized. Plans must necessarily be tested by trial and error, and I would say that we are still in the trial period.

Furthermore, working under the Taft-Hartley Act has created difficulties of administration and financing. Section 313 under Title III of the Act prohibits corporations and unions from making contributions or expenditures in connection with any election to national office. In other words, the trade union structure, as such, cannot be used for political action, and union treasuries as well as special assessments may not be used for political activities.

The discriminatory nature of this Act can easily be seen when it is pointed out that other voluntary associations of individuals supported by dues and assessments are not so restricted. The National Association of Manufacturers and the American Medical Association, for example, have complete freedom to use their regular treasuries or assess their members to help political candidates.

Obviously this section of the Taft-Hartley Act has not prevented trade unions from engaging in political action, but it does serve as a very serious hindrance. It has forced our State Federations and our Central Labor Bodies, which are the logical units for political action, to set up parallel organizations with separate facilities, separate titles, and separate financing. It prevents the ordinary union channel from collecting political funds, since the membership of a local union cannot vote by majority rule to have an assessment collected along with the next monthly dues. Each contribution must be collected on an individual basis. Complete sets of separate books with separate receipts and accounting systems had to be set up. In addition, complete records had to be kept of every single dollar contribution for purposes of reporting to Congress.

The League is scrupulously careful to operate within the terms of the Act as interpreted by our lawyers. Nevertheless, for certain important political activities, union funds and facilities can be used. For instance, between elections the activities of the League are devoted entirely to educational purposes. These activities involve informing our members on the legislative issues, action of Congress, and the voting records of Congressmen on specific pieces of legislation. For this purpose we use radio broadcasts and our weekly newspaper as well as special releases of various sorts. To finance these activities each International was asked to contribute 10 cents per member for the full period between December 1, 1949 and February 1, 1950. Since none of this money was to be used in behalf of any particular candidate, the contribution could be made from union funds. Another voluntary contribution drive was organized to finance our activities in the 1950 election when we were again bound by the Taft-Hartley restriction.

In addition, union funds and assessments can be used in behalf of state candidates and for the purpose of carrying on registration drives. Thus, in many areas the preliminary work of registering our members and establishing precinct committees has been financed from funds raised by assessment.

Regularly published union papers and journals are not forbidden from carrying partisan political stories. Through these union publications, financed largely from union funds, we are able to get our message into every trade union home.

In spite of the difficulties created by Section 313, the 1948 election and the special elections during 1949 demonstrated that the authors of the Taft-Hartley Act were not successful in preventing unions and union members from organizing for political purposes. AFL unions are obviously determined to assume their proper responsibility to the public and to their members as far as political action is concerned.

JOSEPH D. KEENAN

Chapter 7

The CIO-PAC
and how it works

*P*OLITICAL ACTION AND TRADE UNIONISM ARE, OF COURSE, NO STRANGERS. Virtually since the first day of our republic, working men and women have sought, with varying success, to use their democratic prerogatives toward improving their conditions of life.

This history of labor political action has had two distinct trends, and labor organizations have alternated periodically between these trends, seeking a path that would lead them to their goal. They either plunged with fervor into the building of a separate labor or "third" party or they religiously refrained from participation in the political processes and sought to exert their influence only in specific instances and on specific issues.

In many instances the obstacles to formation of a labor party were in the form of election laws, designed to keep upstart organizations from invading fields preempted by older political organizations. The more serious obstacles were the intangible ones resulting from the isolation of labor that occurred with the formation of a "labor" party. Other groups in the community regarded the labor party as an exclusive organization, and the older political parties took for themselves those planks of the third-party platform which carried the greatest appeal and left the outsiders with only minor objectives for which to campaign. Third-party politics also had the drawback of plunging the organizations into internal turmoil. Party politics became a matter of discussion, and frequently dissension, within the union organization and many resented the inference, whether warranted or not, that their free choice as citizens was being corrupted.

Abstaining from political action also had serious drawbacks. The most obvious was that the political influence of a large group in the population was neutralized while other groups, less numerous but better-financed and more active and vocal, were able to influence elections and legislation

117

to their own advantage. Without an effective method of enforcing their wishes, representatives of labor organizations could do little more than plead the justice of their cause in the state and national legislative halls. And justice was not always the compelling factor in the legislation that was passed. Economic and social justice more often appeared to the legislator garbed in a cloak of votes.

History of PAC

Against this background, the CIO Executive Board on July 7, 1943, established the CIO Political Action Committee. It was composed of the late Sidney Hillman, chairman; Van A. Bittner, vice chairman; R. J. Thomas, secretary; and Sherman Dalrymple and Albert J. Fitzgerald. Sidney Hillman was president of the Amalgamated Clothing Workers; Van A. Bittner, vice president of the United Steelworkers; R. J. Thomas was president of the United Auto Workers; Sherman Dalrymple headed the United Rubber Workers; and Albert J. Fitzgerald was president of the United Electrical, Radio and Machine Workers. David J. McDonald, secretary-treasurer of the United Steelworkers, was named as alternate to Mr. Bittner.

The purpose of the committee, CIO President Philip Murray reported to the CIO convention on November 5, 1943, was "to conduct a broad and intensive program of education for the purpose of mobilizing the five million members of CIO and enlisting the active support of all other trade unions, AFL, railroad brotherhoods and unaffiliated, for effective labor action on the political front."

"It is definitely not," the report of President Murray said, "the policy of the CIO to organize a third party, but rather to abstain from and discourage any move in that direction. For, even apart from the insurmountable technical problems of placing such a party on the ballot in 1944, a third party would only serve to divide labor and progressive forces, resulting in the election of political enemies. The primary political task today is to weld the unity of all workers, farmers and other progressives behind candidates, regardless of party affiliations, who support the war program of our Commander-in-Chief and enlightened domestic and foreign policies."

Following the establishment of the PAC in July, 1943, a series of regional conferences was held and plans were developed for launching registration campaigns. In September, a plan of organization was submitted to the CIO vice presidents calling for the establishment of a national headquarters in New York, an office in Washington, and 14 regional offices. Provisions were made for the financing of the CIO Political Action Committee in accordance with the requirements of existing law.

It was that organization that functioned during the 1944 presidential campaign. The full-time staff of 135 people consisted of 75 employed in the national office and 60 in the regional offices.

On April 12, 1945, the CIO Executive Board moved to expand the CIO-PAC and directed the establishment of Political Action Committees by the industrial union councils, state and local, to work under the supervision of CIO-PAC. In most instances each council used its state executive board as a nucleus for the committee with membership extended to include representatives from every union, council or other CIO entity in the area. The CIO Executive Board also directed the formation of Political Action Committees by the international unions with their own Political Action directors and with liaison representatives to coordinate their work with that of the CIO-PAC.

Sidney Hillman, chairman of CIO-PAC, died on July 10, 1946, and changes in the structure of PAC became necessary. The committee, by action of the CIO Executive Board, was enlarged to include the vice presidents of the CIO; and an executive board, consisting of the presidents and secretary-treasurers of the five largest unions and a director, was named.

Today the CIO-PAC Board consists of the presidents and secretary-treasurers of the CIO's six largest unions (United Steelworkers, United Auto Workers, Communications Workers, Textile Workers Union, Amalgamated Clothing Workers, and United Rubber Workers) and a director. It is responsible to the CIO convention and, in the interim, to the CIO Executive Board.

Organizational Structure

The basis of CIO-PAC, of course, is the men and women of the CIO. Operating through their unions, they are the people who do the political action work of CIO and the people who, in the final analysis, determine the political direction of CIO-PAC.

In this factor lies a great deal of the strength of CIO-PAC, for its organizational base is the union, in which men and women are bound together by economic self-interest, rather than the looser party organization in which the cement is patronage or self-aggrandizement.

The men and women of CIO who engage in political action do so as a matter of principle rather than as a matter of self-advancement. They are seeking the passage of a particular piece of legislation or the election of a particular candidate because they believe in the legislation or the candidate. They are not concerned with the governmental jobs that will be created by the legislation, or the patronage that might come their way as the result of their candidate's election.

The old notion of political machines built on an elaborate structure of patronage and a few dollars on election day has been destroyed. The wonder of the professional politician is that labor's political organization not only enlists the support of hundreds of thousands of energetic political workers, but that these workers also contribute financially to the organization.

The introduction of principles as a political factor on this level has led to introduction of principle as a political factor on higher levels. And there have been instances in which successful candidates, somewhat to their surprise, learned that they were expected to talk and act the same way after election day as before.

The formal structure of the local Political Action Committees varies greatly from local to local and from community to community. In most instances, the local union has a Political Action Committee with the president of the local acting as chairman, and a specially designated person does the actual day-to-day work. If the local is large enough to sustain paid officers, the political action worker may be a paid employee of the local. More often he is compensated for time lost from his job because of his political action activities. Other members of the committee include members of the local executive board, shop stewards, grievance committeemen, and other members of the local willing to work.

Above the local level there are the city and county Political Action Committees and the congressional district PAC. The city or county PAC parallels, in most instances, the city or county industrial union council, in that it is a delegate body composed of representatives of locals within the geographical area covered by the industrial union council. The congressional district PAC has no parallel in the industrial union structure, but it, too, is a delegate body concerned primarily with election of the congressional candidate from that district. It exists principally in the large cities of the nation represented by a number of Congressmen (such as Chicago and Philadelphia).

The city or county PAC directs the political action work within its geographical area and selects candidates to be chosen by the voters within that area. Thus mayors, city councilmen, sheriffs, municipal and county judges, and other public officials on that level are supported or opposed according to the decisions of the city or county PAC.

The congressional district PAC performs a similar endorsement function with reference to congressional candidates.

On the next higher level are the state Political Action Committees. These committees are often more formal in their nature than the city or county PACs or the congressional district PACs in that they have constitutions, by-laws, and procedures in accordance with a fixed pattern. Virtually all states now have Political Action Committees, formally established and operating under constitutions and by-laws.

One of the oldest is the Ohio State PAC. It consists of a state central committee composed of delegates from all CIO locals in the state and a steering committee of 17, including the CIO regional directors, the international union regional directors within the state, and four representatives from the smaller internationals. The president and the secretary-treasurer of the Ohio Industrial Union Council are designated in the constitution as the officials of the Ohio PAC.

The steering committee considers matters of policy and submits recommendations to the state central committee. The state central committee, in turn, submits its recommendations to the convention of the Ohio State Industrial Union Council or is empowered to act on its own if such action is required prior to the next state convention.

In the past, the Ohio PAC has made recommendations concerning state offices, national offices elected on a state-wide basis, and congressional district candidates.

The Ohio PAC employs three persons on a full-time basis whose function is to assist all CIO locals in the state with problems of political organization and political techniques. Moving about the state, they assist in launching registration campaigns, set up election day procedures, and in general, provide the know-how that may be lacking in the community.

The Ohio PAC is financed by a voluntary per capita tax of one cent per member per month from each of the locals affiliated with the Ohio CIO council. This money is used only for educational purposes or for elections for state office, the Taft-Hartley act prohibiting its use in connection with a federal election.

The office of the CIO-PAC, now located in Washington, D. C. in the offices occupied in 1948 by the Dewey-Warren Clubs, is the headquarters of the director and his staff. In contrast to the 135 people employed in 1944, the CIO-PAC national staff consists of eight people including the director, plus clerical staff, whose regular assignment is in the Washington office. Four additional people are on the CIO-PAC payroll as full-time field representatives and they cover the entire nation.

The Washington staff, all of whose members perform field work, is comprised of the director, the assistant director, a comptroller, two public relations people, and three research people. The four regional representatives cover the New England and Middle Atlantic states, the South, the Middle West, and the Far West and Mountain States.

From time to time the staff is augmented by the addition of part-time representatives for specific tasks; and the national office shares the salary and expenses of a political action worker with a state PAC.

Financing PAC

There are numerous legal requirements covering the financing of political organizations and with all of these the CIO-PAC and other PACs rigidly comply.

All of the work of CIO-PAC in connection with a federal election is financed by voluntary contributions from the members of CIO and others who feel inclined to contribute. These contributions are receipted from numbered books that CIO-PAC prints and furnishes to the international unions, which, in turn, distribute them to their locals.

The locals distribute the books to their collectors, who receive the contributions and fill in the receipts in duplicate. The duplicates are given to the contributors, and the originals, together with the money, are forwarded through international union channels to the CIO-PAC. Half of the money remains within the state in which the contributions were made, for application to political action work in that state.

Quarterly reports are filed with the Clerk of the House of Representatives and such state reports as are required by state law are filed by the appropriate officials with the appropriate state office.

PAC Operation

Perhaps the simplest means of describing the operation of PAC is to picture an imaginary congressional district. This hypothetical district is in an industrial area and there are many labor voters who are concerned with the kind of representation they have in the national Congress. They have a well-organized PAC and they are actively engaged in politics. The incumbent representative is a person whose voting record indicates that he is more concerned with the owners of industry in our hypothetical community than with the welfare of the individual workers and their families.

John Smith is a young attorney in town. He has held a few political offices and has established something of a record for himself. He believes he could represent the people of that congressional district more fairly than the incumbent and he has definite views on the particular issues of the day. He has, therefore, filed as a candidate for Congress. But he knows he lives in an industrial district and that his chances depend to a large extent upon the degree of backing he can get from organized labor.

John Smith, therefore, calls up one of his friends, a local union official. He tells him he is going to run for Congress and that he would like the active support of the PAC. His friend tells him to take the matter up with the local PAC, and he gives John Smith the name of the chairman. Smith and the PAC chairman make a date to talk things over. When John Smith and the PAC chairman meet, Smith finds that in addition to the chairman there are four or five other people present. They are the screening committee and it is their function to make the preliminary decision as to whether Smith warrants their support.

Together, Smith and the screening committee talk over the whole matter. They discuss at great length Smith's views on current political questions to determine, primarily, how well informed Smith is and how closely their views coincide. There may be differences of opinion between Smith and the screening committee, but the main question in the committee's mind is whether Smith and the people they represent are both going in the same direction. They are more concerned with his general outlook than with his specific views on the way in which to solve specific problems. They may also discuss the question of finances, the other support that Smith has, the record he has made in the public offices he has held, and his prospects of winning.

Following the talk, the screening committee makes its decision, and at the next meeting of the Political Action Committee, presents its report. The members of the committee have talked to Smith, Brown, and Jones and they believe that John Smith is the man who should be endorsed. He is an able man, they say, and his record entitles him to a chance at higher office. The PAC concurs in the recommendation of the screening committee and votes an endorsement of John Smith. This endorsement is reported to the constituent unions of the area PAC, to the state PAC, and to CIO-PAC in Washington. It is also announced to the newspapers.

Having endorsed John Smith, the area PAC proceeds to back up its action. It checks the membership files of all unions within the area to see if all members and their wives, adult children, and in-laws are registered to vote. If they are not registered, machinery is set in motion to get them registered. Caravans from workshops to the registrar's office are organized. Registrars are persuaded to keep late office hours. In some places, union members may be deputized as registrars.

Following the final registration day, the area PAC takes stock and lays plans for the coming election day. One of the most important jobs is that of educating the union membership and others in the community on the issues involved. Housing may be an important problem in the community. John Smith supports federal housing legislation, but the incumbent believes such legislation is an unwarranted intrusion of the federal government into the domain of private enterprise.

The PAC will get all the information it can about housing and about the proposed legislation. It may make a survey to determine the existing housing conditions in the district, the amount of private housing being constructed, and the amount of rental housing available, the scale of rents being charged, and the possibilities for erecting low-cost projects.

Then it will print and distribute literature on the question. It may provide speakers who can discuss the subject of housing and its various aspects. It may purchase radio time for a discussion of this issue. It will start people talking about housing, the pros and cons of public low-cost housing as opposed to privately financed housing. The voters will thus acquire some information on which to make up their minds about John Smith and his opponent.

Along with the educational campaign on the issues and the records of the opposing candidates, the PAC outlines detailed plans for election day.

All of these activities, of course, cost money. The area PAC may have some that it has raised in a local affair. It may also receive some money from the state PAC and from CIO-PAC. Because John Smith is running for federal office, all of this money is from voluntary contributions.

The big push comes on election day. Car pools are set up to transport people to the polls, and dispatchers are at hand to tell the drivers where to go. Baby-sitting service is supplied to mothers who cannot leave their homes unattended while they go to the polls. At the polls themselves, workers and challengers are on duty, and after the polls close someone is assigned to make sure that votes in the ballot box are the only ones that are counted. These poll watchers must be fed, and the drivers will need sandwiches so they can keep going throughout the day.

The objective of all of this, of course, is to ensure that every eligible voter, everyone who registered during the registration drive, follows through and votes.

And sometime in the early morning the weary PAC people will learn that John Smith has been elected to Congress.

PAC is an organization of flesh and blood that cannot be compressed into or explained by an organizational chart. It is an organization whose integral parts are interchangeable and well geared to form the political organization of the CIO. Within broad limits, the function of each of its parts is political action in its entirety, and no part of the organization is able to refuse a particular task on the grounds that "it's not my job." What is lost by lack of specialization is more than gained in versatility. That is not to say that PAC does not have its specialists. Rather, PAC specialists are required to have abilities over and above their specialties.

Only by maintaining this unity of purpose is the CIO-PAC able to fulfill its function with its necessarily small staff. Only this desire to achieve a common objective produces the enthusiasm and energy that make tasks more than routine, and in the end, provide success when defeat seems the probable outcome.

Nor is it mere imagination to say that this enthusiasm and energy do exist. In Durham, North Carolina, over 500 trade unionists from all over the state paid $5 each to attend a dinner at which the director of CIO-PAC and his counterpart from the AFL-LLPE spoke. The 500 unionists jammed into a small hall, many of them forced to stand, and the only immediate tangible return for their $5 was an average southern meal.

A similar meeting in Utah produced 400 people, with hundreds more turned away, each of whom paid $10 for speeches, dinner, and a contribution to the joint political action work of the CIO, AFL, and railroad brotherhoods.

In a small canyon city in the forests of Idaho, striking smeltermen sat in the bitter cold and cheered political action talk; and in the blistering heat of an Ohio summer hundreds of trade unionists sat beneath a tin roof to formulate political action plans. In dank Tupelo, Mississippi, a trade unionist proudly reported that his local of 100 members had contributed $98 "and I'm a-goin' back to get them other two."

A regeneration of the democratic faith is taking place in the nation. It is a result, perhaps, of the war and of its consequent challenges to that faith. But it takes its expression, if not its inspiration, from the CIO-PAC, from the feeling of union men and women that it is not politics that is a dirty business but sometimes the practitioners of politics. Through their union organizations, they have learned they can tackle and solve industrial and economic problems of more than individual magnitude, and now, through their political organizations, they are learning that application of the same spirit will solve social and political problems and that all of these problems have common denominators.

Thus, to CIO political actionists, the person who fouls the democratic nest by abandoning principle as a guiding rule in politics is polluting the whole of the community, and the community should be warned against him. In Philadelphia, for example, interparty corruption was met by the simple expedient of replacing Democrats who were on the Republican machine payroll with CIO-PAC people who carried through the assignments that were made on election day.

In the formulation and application of this political code of morals, the CIO-PAC feels it is contributing not only to its own welfare but to the welfare of the nation as a whole. It is replacing the cynicism and disrespect for democratic institutions and procedures that have, in the past, preceded the downfall of democracy, with a healthy determination to maintain in good repair that flexible system of democratic government which makes the best possible compromise between liberty and authority.

JACK KROLL

Chapter 8

Political action
in a congressional district

TO ARRIVE AT AN UNDERSTANDING OF THE "NEW" FORCE OF LABOR IN POLITICS, it might be best to view a small unit of our political life, the congressional district.

In 1946, as in many other parts of the country, the Republicans had taken over the congressional district with which we are concerned, as well as the state itself. Yet there were no clear-cut lines of party affiliation, and even in union ranks there were many who considered themselves Republicans. The Democratic party machine had virtually collapsed in this part of the state and showed no signs of gathering popular strength behind it.

Beginnings of CIO-PAC Local Activity

The unions in our district had not yet decided what candidates to back, and they were waiting for the endorsement of a Presidential candidate by the national CIO-PAC. But they were not idle. They knew that their first job was to get people to register. In 1947 and early 1948 the international unions and the national CIO-PAC endeavored to build local organizations on a precinct and ward level.

Here is how it worked. George, a union member, was working in Plant X and belonged to the United Steelworkers of America. His local union shop PAC representative had checked George's home address and reminded him that the registration place on Y Street was open from six to nine o'clock. George promised to go that very night. The local PAC man, a coworker of George's, also asked him to drop over to his house afterwards to discuss plans to cover the neighborhood and remind other people to register.

After George had finished his supper he asked his wife to come along and register at the same time. His wife said she had to wash the dishes. George felt too tired to argue, and went by himself.

The registration did not take very long. When George arrived at the home of the PAC representative, ten other men who also lived in the neighborhood were already there. Two worked in George's shop; three who belonged to another union worked in a pottery plant nearby; two more had just come along. They worked at the railroad yards across the street.

They were reading a little leaflet called *Political Action Techniques, Blockworkers*. Not everybody agreed on the techniques suggested in the leaflet. Joe, a friend of George's, thought that it would take too much time to run around to all the members in their union to see if they had registered. He thought it would be much better if each man were assigned a couple of blocks where he could visit every house, regardless of union membership. He could just ask the people if they had already registered and remind them that registration was open for only a few weeks.

They all discussed what to tell the people when asked questions. The PAC man thought the best thing to do was to talk about high prices, the Taft-Hartley Law, and the bad performance of the 80th Congress. If they couldn't answer some question or if they got into an argument, they should say they did not know the answer, but would try to find out. He impressed on them how important it was to get the people's names, to be friendly, and to avoid arguments if possible.

George, who was thinking of his wife at this point, said, "And how about the women?"

"My wife never votes," the railroad man said, "and neither does that brother of hers who has been living with us for the last three years."

The others had similar experiences. They decided to make it a special point to talk to their own wives and to the women in the houses they were going to visit. One of the men suggested that maybe their wives should make some of the visits to the neighbors, the grocer, and the other people with whom they did business.

The PAC man had a parcel of leaflets on high prices and the Taft-Hartley Law, which he distributed. "Don't let your wife light the furnace with those," he reminded George. "Leave one of each at all the houses you visit." He then marked out on a map the streets each was to take as his territory, and reminded all the men to come to a meeting in Union Hall where all the blockworkers were to decide which candidate to back in their congressional district.

The next day, at noon, while eating his sandwich, George talked with his friend Joe who lived on the outskirts of town. Joe had gone to a similar meeting of another local PAC where they had decided that all the wives should take an active part in visiting neighbors. Some of the girls from the sheet-testing department who had been there suggested that the blockworkers go in pairs. It would be more fun. During the last campaign one girl had found out that a man can do much better in some places and at some times, whereas at others, a woman can be more effective, depending upon who is at home at the time.

She also said that two together would not be so easily discouraged by an unfriendly response as would one working alone.

That night George lit his pipe, took some of the literature under his arm, and set out. He had been assigned to a couple of blocks some distance from his house, and didn't know the people there. George wasn't one of those big talkers, so he felt just a little bit apprehensive when he rang the first doorbell.

A woman opened. "I don't want to buy anything," she said. George explained that he hadn't anything to sell; that he had come around to find out if she had registered this year. She asked George what party he represented. He explained that he didn't come from any party. His local union was carrying on this registration drive. "Oh, them," she said. "They give nothing but trouble: higher wages, higher prices; we folks can't keep up with it." Her husband wanted to know who was at the door, so she asked George to come in.

George had seen her husband before; he worked at the local A & P on Main Street. George was asked to sit down, but couldn't help feeling a bit uneasy.

Her husband, Jim, wanted to know what it was all about. When George told him, he agreed. "Yes, if folks would take a bit more interest in the government, maybe they wouldn't have so many crooks down in Washington." George asked him if he had voted in 1946. "No, plumb forgot about it, but this time I will." George was satisfied with this, gave them a booklet about high prices to look over, and promised to drop by again before election.

"Come to see us anytime," they said, and he left with a friendly handshake.

The other visits were similar. Most people were friendly. Some asked him to stay for a cup of coffee. One woman knew George's wife; another man had worked at the shop some time before, but was now driving a truck; he also belonged to a union. George asked him to come to the congressional district PAC meeting.

After talking to about 10 families, George had enough for one evening and went home. There he made out 10 cards with names and addresses and a short remark about what happened. Eight of those visited thought they'd vote this time so that something would be done about housing and prices. Two said politics was none of their business.

Deciding the Issues

The next morning, George gave his cards to the local PAC man in the shop, who already had quite a stack of them from the other boys.

He smiled. "Well, George, we get 'em talking, and before you know it, they go down and register. Then we go to bat for our candidates and it'll make a lot of difference on Election Day."

George wasn't so sure. "You know, most of those Taft-Hartley boys are Republicans. It stands to reason we won't back them, but all the papers say Dewey is practically elected. Why do we waste our time?"

"Don't be so sure, George. If we get out all those votes, it won't be Republican. That's what it says in this *Memo from PAC*. It explains that if we bring in a big vote, it will favor the Democrats."

There were a lot of people at the meeting a couple of nights later. At the table facing the crowd was the president of George's local and a man from the regional office; also a couple of men from other locals, a man from the AFL, and some other men George didn't know.

The man from the regional office opened the meeting. He read a letter from the international office of the United Steelworkers of America saying that the CIO had come out endorsing Truman and Barkley. They liked what Truman had said in Philadelphia; also the Democratic platform was much better on Taft-Hartley, on the Labor Department, and on many other things. He passed out a platform comparison listing the stand of both parties and what the CIO thought about it. One man got up and wanted to know about Wallace.

A few men booed. The chairman explained that the CIO had come out against Wallace and it would only help Dewey if people threw their votes away by voting for Wallace. There was more discussion. "How about them Dixiecrats?" a colored worker wanted to know. "They're Democrats."

This was explained. Truman had taken a firm stand on civil rights. The Dixiecrats had walked out of the Convention.

The meeting was asked to come to order, and the chairman introduced a young man who was sitting up front.

"He wants to run for Congress from our district on the Democratic ticket and he is going to tell us tonight where he stands. We also asked the Republican candidate to come over, but he said he couldn't make it. Had to go to the Junior Chamber of Commerce or something," said the chairman.

The young man had been in the state legislature and had been mayor in one of the small towns. He had been in the war, and come out a major.

He talked about Taft-Hartley and about prices. He sounded all right and he looked like a good guy, tall and tough; not afraid to say what he thought. They liked him.

A show of hands was asked on whether this CIO-PAC congressional district meeting should endorse the man in his campaign. Most hands went up. The motion was seconded and carried.

"Now let's get down to business," the president of George's local began. "This campaign costs money. Those dollars for PAC in our local haven't come in so good. Anybody here who wants to pay up?"

He collected about $30 and gave each donor a receipt. "Now what about literature for our candidate?" A couple of guys had ideas on that. So a committee was appointed to draw up some drafts and present them to the next meeting for O.K.

How about the blockworkers? Do they need more help? George's local PAC man and a couple of others went up front and reported. They had found out that two people going together was a good idea, but they couldn't get enough women to go. A girl from a small plant got up and said, "Heck, they haven't even asked us." All the girls in her place would go.

"Well, let's all get together!" everybody shouted. How about the AFL? The man from the AFL said he was going along; his men hadn't done those things in previous elections, but they'd do what they could. Wouldn't we want to get together on an ad for our candidate in the local paper? His local union would pay half the costs. All agreed.

A committee was appointed to study the need for cars on election day and for poll watchers. It was agreed that they would report in detail later.

Getting Out the Vote

It wasn't the same everywhere. There was great variation in the procedure of political action. This variation was strongest in the "follow-through" operation in the weeks before election.

In many instances the impetus to arouse the membership was so strong that it got out the vote by conventional methods such as free transportation, last minute meetings, final distribution of literature. These methods were used almost everywhere where there were unions.

But in places where the results were startling, a planned step-by-step procedure had taken place. These steps differed from district to district. A comparison, if carefully studied, might lead to many future improvements.

In our case the following paper work had been accomplished:

George's card, which he had filled out when becoming an active participant, was printed in the form of a pledge. It read as follows:

I pledge my support and will do everything I possibly can to urge registration and voting in all elections by calling my friends and neighbors.

It also included checkmarks for George to fill in. "I will work as a blockworker on political action in my neighborhood" and "I will also work at the polls on Election Day." It listed George's name and address, ward, precinct, congressional district, and the number of his local union. It also carried the information that anyone living in the state might sign such a card.

Such cards, kept for future reference, will tell at a glance how many people can be counted on for serious political-action work.

Another card index went even further. It originated with the locals and was based on their membership lists. Usually it was kept up to date by the regional PAC office of each international union and coordinated on a congressional district level. Here a blue card was made out for every member giving all pertinent information as to name, address, district, local etc. There was space on the back of the card for changes and remarks. These cards were checked against local registration records, available to the public in most cases, and all names not to be found there were contacted.

Some members thought they had registered some years back in other elections and had fulfilled the necessary requirements. Where that was not the case, the proper procedure was explained to them and they were given slips to be taken to the registration board and returned to the union. The slip said, "You are eligible to register if you have lived in this state for one year, ... days in the county, ... days in the precinct, and if you are twenty-one years or over." This method produced an almost complete registration in George's local.

Such a system may sound complicated and certainly involves extra work and attention, but results indicate that it is worthwhile. When it is realized everywhere that political action is as important as other union business, such files will come into existence in many places.

The next congressional district meeting had a very large attendance and things really began to hum. The Transportation Committee reported. It was headed by a man who had been a dispatch sergeant in an Army motor pool during the war. He had worked out pickup points and time schedules, and reported on the number of vehicles he would require for full coverage on Election Day. This information had already been coordinated with the list of cars to be made available by the Democratic party in the district, and with arrangements for hiring several buses. A fund was set aside to take care of mileage expenses.

Girls from the telephone union reported that they had formed a group to handle phone coordination with headquarters, the polling places, and the motor pool, and to channel all incoming calls with requests for transportation, baby sitting, etc., to the proper persons.

Other girls had set up a baby-sitting group, available to all families with small children.

Additional assignments as poll watchers were given out at the meeting to a third group of volunteers. They would also see to it that open telephone lines were available near each polling place. Over these lines the names of the union members who had already voted would be called in every 30 minutes. This system would make possible a concentration of effort by the entire organization, during the last three vital hours on Election Day, to bring out the people who had not yet shown up at the polls.

There were a few talks of the usual pre-election nature, which were well received. But they were secondary. Somehow the people, like George, who had volunteered their services and who, up to this point, had already put in a lot of time, were more excited about their own political work with neighbors and friends than about anything an orator could possibly say. For many, it was the first time that they had been active in politics and it was a real experience. They called George "the spark plug of the Sixth Ward" in his shop, and he liked that title.

The last week was hectic. Union officials made arrangements with employers for time off on Election Day. Half-page ads were run in the local paper every other day. These ads, prepared by the local PAC man, lacked the advertising agency slickness of those run by Republicans in the same paper. Instead, they compared candidates and their stands on vital issues. All unions in the area, AFL, CIO, and Independent, were signed sponsors. A full-page ad on Election Day listed the complete slate endorsed.

One local radio station carried a 15-minute program on housing, prepared by national PAC on platters. The prospective congressman made effective use of some six jingles of thirty seconds each produced from the same source. He played them on his sound truck when covering some of the rural parts of the district. He also bought radio time for the jingles right after the sports news in the evening. One of the jingles was about a boy and a girl in a parked car. They remarked very leisurely what a wonderful evening it was. Then suddenly the boy said, "Oh, but this is the time!" "Time for what, honey?" the girl wanted to know. "Time to register and vote, of course," was the answer.

Union officials talked with farmer groups and a frank discussion between the groups as to their mutual problems and aims had achieved very satisfactory results. The farm leaders were going to back the same candidates as labor.

Election eve was spent in checking up on all details for arrangements. These men and women had been influenced very little by the national radio and newspaper campaign claiming that the election was in the bag. They couldn't speak for the nation, but they knew that in their own congressional district, free men were going to the polls the next day, doing what they thought right.

When somebody mentioned that nobody he knew had ever been approached by a pollster, George mentioned that he had. An efficient-looking girl with glasses who said she represented a research organization, had asked George a great many questions. "I answered most of her fool questions, but when she asked me whom I was voting for, I told her that the candidate for the Drys was my man. That startled her, but she took it down, and I went off to have a beer."

On Election Day the men on the night shift of the big steel mill were the first to get to the polls. Cars and buses had picked them up. George was a poll watcher and his eagle eye kept track of everything. Every union man in the city was at his assigned post. There were a few "snafus" here and there, but the plan, so carefully laid out, worked well. There was a heavy vote all over the city. When George saw the faces of the people, he knew his time had not been wasted. They were his people. The count later in the evening didn't surprise George. But when he got home that night and heard the results coming in from all over the nation, he knew that there must have been a lot of Georges in many other places. He lit his pipe and he felt good. "All is well in the U. S. tonight," he told his wife.

GEORGE WARTENBERG

Chapter 9

Labor lobbyist —1890

Introductory Note

ALTHOUGH HE MAY STILL RESENT THE SUPERIOR STATUS AND THE GREATER influences wielded by the spokesman for business, the labor lobbyist of today enjoys a measure of power and prestige that his predecessor of more than half a century ago would have envied. The two differ in their immediate legislative concerns and in influence, but in their function and basic techniques, they stand upon essentially the same ground. They both represent labor's interests at the point of the legislative process, and their effectiveness is largely a product of the strength of their organizations and of their individual skills.

In 1886, when the Knights of Labor was approaching its maximum membership, its General Assembly established a "permanent" labor lobby in Washington. Ralph Beaumont, John J. McCartney, and James Campbell were designated its members by the General Executive Board of the Knights, and set off for Washington in the fall of the year. The K. of L. lobby produced no notable successes, and perhaps its most important accomplishment was the introduction of a bill providing for government ownership of the nation's telegraph systems. With the decline in the power of the Knights after 1887, the labors of its lobby became even more difficult. Moreover, by 1890, the membership and leadership of the Knights were agitated by the issue of independent political action and affiliation with farmers' organizations.

Ralph Beaumont, for years important among the second-rank leaders of the K. of L., was active in labor politics as early as 1877. In that year, he ran on the Greenback Labor ticket in New York, and was the dominant figure in the party in the Elmira, Oswego, and Hornellsville region of the state. He was one of the founders of the national Greenback Labor party the following year, and at the close of the 'eighties pressed for independent political action by the Knights. Beaumont represented that wing in the Order which urged affiliation with the movements of agrarian protest that were then taking political form and subsequently produced the People's party. Beaumont urged Terence Vincent Powderly, the General Master Workman of the Knights, to call a convention for a third party in 1890, and in that year served as secretary of the National Citizens' Alliance founded at Ocala, Florida.

In the hitherto unpublished letter that follows, Beaumont reports to Powderly on his lobbying activities in the spring of 1890. His letter indicates the nature of those activities, and frankly sets forth the difficulties and frustrations that were an integral part of his job. The Powderly Papers, where this letter was found, were graciously released for study and publication by Mrs. Powderly before her death in 1940.

To avoid obscurity in a few places, punctuation marks have been inserted in brackets. The spelling remains unchanged. The footnotes to the letter deal with aspects of it that are not self-explanatory.

HENRY DAVID

OFFICE OF LEGISLATIVE COMMITTEE

Order of Knights of Labor of America
938 E Street Northwest
Washington, D. C.

May 24th 1890

Friend Powderly;

I enclose you a copy of the Telegraph Bill that has been agreed upon by the House Committee on Post Office and Post Roads.[1] This Bill I obtained from the Postmaster General.[2] He wrote us a letter and desired an interview. When we called upon him he asked what we had come to the conclusion upon. We informed him that we were willing to compromise between our measures and his, if he was willing. He asked us in what way. I informed him that if he would insert a clause in his bill asking for an approprition of $8,000,000 to enable the government to build and operate his line without any out side Capital. He informed us that he was sorry to hear us say that. Upon his saying that he informed us that no bill could go through that involved an appropriation. That the strength of his bill lies in the fact that he was not asking for any money to carry out the proposition. I informed him that while that was so I doubted very much the wisdom of such a move, arising out of the fact that it would take money to carry it on in his department and when the year was up his limited postal system would have to be met by a deficiency, and the result would be that that fact might put the real measure back for years. The oponents of the System would say that it was a failure in a limited way and it would be more so if the government went into it any farther. But he would not see it in that light. I told him that when he got it on to the floor he would find that there would be people who would say that the government was aiming

---

[1] This measure, HR 3319, "To provide for a limited Postal Telegraph Service," was introduced December 20, 1889. No further action was taken on it during the First Session of the 51st Congress, which Beaumont's letter covers.

[2] John Wanamaker.

at nothing only being a tender to some new scheme of Capitalists who were not able to cope with the Western Union, but would undertake it in case the government would undertake to give them a certain quantity of business. Then again, he would find the Western Union fighting them very bitter[ly] because this bill did not prevent that company that the government made the contract with, from doing a commercial business with the public, and of course, the Western Union would fight that to the bitter end, and that the Western Union if the case became desperate would then form a combination with us, and accept our bill in case we would amend it so that the government should purchase existing telegraph lines under the right of eminent domain and then it would result in our measure. He then said that would result in not getting anything. We informed him that we thought on the whole it were better to wait for the next Congress than it was to gain a half way measure, that would tie the government up for ten years to a contract. He then said that the Act of 1866 under which the Telegraph companies of the United States were formed gave the government the right to take hold and condemn the telegraph lines at any time, and that any company that organized to do the business with the government would have to organize under that law, that the Western Union accepted that provission of law in 1866. I told him that while that might be so, the vested rights of property and sacredness of contract seemed to be more powerful with the Judiciary to day than statute law. This he virtually admitted in substance in conversation later on when he was making a plea for the acceptance of his proposition in the following language. "This measure is an entering wedge; it opens the way to the final absorption by the government of all Telegraph lines. You had better accept this while you have a Postmaster General that is favorable to your ideas, as the next one might be a bitter oponent of the system. For instance if any thing should happen that I should leave this place and Mr. Clarkson [3] should come into my place you would not fare so well. Then again this telegraph measure is purly my own. I dare not even let this measure come before the Cabinet. It has never been the subject of conversation for a moment between even the president and myself. If I were to bring it up before the Cabinet I feel certain that it would be sat down upon, as they are all lawyers and the sacredness of vested rights and of property is strong with that class."

So here we are in that position. The comittee has been waiting to hear farther from Dr. Green [3a] and have not as yet reported the bill. At our first meeting with Mr. Wannamaker I informed him that I knew we had no chance with the Committee with our measure as against his, arrising out of the fact that the Chairman of the Committee Mr. Bingham [4] had at the early part of the session introduced a bill embodying the very ideas of his proposition. And I wish to say right here that this convinced me that the Chairman of the Committee and the Postmaster General had had an understanding before congress

[3] James C. Clarkson, first Assistant Postmaster General, was also a member of the Republican National Committee.

[3a] Dr. Norvin Green (1818-1893), was president of Western Union from 1878 until his death.

[4] Henry H. Bingham, Republican Representative from Philadelphia, had introduced the bill identified in Note 1.

met. This belief of mine was strengthened when I came to learn that Mr. Bingham, the Chairman, had for several years been the Postmaster of Phil [adelphia] and was virtualy promoted from that office to Congress. The only way that I had to get my bill considered was to put it in and then wait until the Postmaster General's measure came up for action in the House and then have the introducer of our measure, Mr. Wade,[5] the Chairman of the Commitee on Labor, get up and move it as a substitute, and thus precipitate the debate at once between the friends of the two ideas, viz. government ownership and a partial ownership. With this object in view I saw Mr. Wade and was to furnish him data to antagonize it with, and this course was agreed upon. In the mean time to strengthen our position I requested through the *Journal* [of the Knights of Labor] that petitions be sent to me in favor of our bill.

I had hoped that I would receive enough petitions so that when the time came I could dump them right on to Congress and by this means show that our idea had the people behind it. But I am sorry to say that it has failed to materialize as up to date the total number received is a few hundred over 16,000 and I have them here, and am in doubt as to what course to pursue with them.[6] If I put them in it will, I fear, only display our weakness. The opponents of the idea all together will say that the small number of petitions that have been sent in indicate that the people have no interest in the matter. Or whether it is best to keep them until the short session. My mind of late has turned upon the last proposition, arrising out of the fact that at the present the outlook is very slim for any action being taken on the question at all, as the majority party machine is running things with a high hand they are not going to let any thing go through that involves an appropriation except it is for pensions.

There were other matters that interfered with our telegraph measure. First came the postal Clerks with a demand for a reduction of hours of labor, and when the Committee sent to the Postmaster General for an estimate of the increased appropriation that would be needed in order to grant that request, he reported about $2,300,000. Then came a request for an increase of saleries of the letter carriers, an increase again of $250,000. Then came the request of an increase of saleries of Postal Clerks in the Railway mail service amouting to over $200,000. Then came the fourth Class Postmaster with their convention demanding an increase in pay, and on the top of all of it was the estimates of the Postmaster General for several millions of increase[d] appropriation for the department arrising out of the increased business of the Post Office Department. And when all this was bunched it has fairly paralyzed the Post Office Commitee, because the party Machine is at all times holding up the ghost of reduced expenses to go before the people upon. Now I have given you the situation in regard to the Postal Telegraph Measure.

The Pacific Railway steal, known as the extention of the time of payment of the debts to the government, I think is killed. The Committee are divided upon the question, and there are five that have signed a minority report. When

---

[5] William H. Wade, Republican Representative from Springfield, Missouri. The measure referred to was HR 7167, introduced February 18, 1890.

[6] Beaumont did not submit any K. of L. petitions during this session.

there are so many on the minority side it is sure to be defeated, or to be plain about all the chairman will do is to report to go on the Calender and will never dare to call it up under those conditions.[7]

The trade label Bill [8] was reported adversely by the Judiciary committee right in the face of the fact that in private conversation with members upon the question they agreed that it [the old law] was of no account without a penalty clause. But Bynum the introducer of the bill fought it out on the floor when the report was made and succeded in getting the House to let it go upon the Calender. But since then Bynum has got into a fight with the speaker and the republican party which has resulted in his being censured by the House.[9] So now I suppose that Reed will spite him by not recognizing him when he wants to call it up for action.

The Labor Committee of the House has several Bills before it. The eight hour back pay bill. The Bill to amend the Alien Contract Labor Law. A Bill to amend the eight hour law by adding a penalty for its violation. A Bill to make Legal Holyday of the 1st of Sept. in the District of Columbia,[10] and several other minor bills. And while every Committee in the House, and there are 57 of them, are supposed to have a day in their regular order except two (Ways and Means and Apropriations) there is not one fourth of them have up to this date been called and some of the members are talking of getting home by July 1st.

I saw Wade the Chairman of the Committee on Labor yesterday and he was nearly crazy. He had been to Reed in desperation, and said to him, "Do you want to kill me all together. Here I am chairman of the Labor Committee and the whole Labor element of the Country looking to me for results and I unable to even get a day for the consideration of my measures. When Congress is over they will say. Well we had Wade as chairman of the Labor Committee and he never done a dam thing." I never saw Wade so desperate; he was cussing the Machine and every thing else in General. The Machine he says is trying to

---

[7] This measure was HR 111, introduced December 18, 1889, "To amend an act entitled 'An Act to aid in the construction of a railroad from the Missouri River to the Pacific Ocean'" etc. On June 5, 1890, a substitute measure, HR 10756, was introduced in its stead.

[8] HR 260, introduced December 18, 1889, was designed to deal with counterfeiting of union and other labels and trademarks. Although adversely reported, it was placed on the Calendar, but no further action was taken at this session.

[9] William D. Bynum, Democrat from Indianapolis, Indiana, raised such a rumpus in the House on May 17, 1890, in connection with an earlier debate on schedules in the McKinley Tariff bill, that the Speaker was unable to repress him and the House censured him by vote. The Speaker was Thomas B. Reed of Portland, Maine.

[10] Eight eight-hour back-pay bills were introduced during this session up to the writing of Beaumont's letter. There were three bills to amend the Alien Contract Labor Law; Beaumont was probably referring to HR 9632, introduced April 23, 1890, reported out by the Committee in August, and subsequently passed by the House. The bill to amend the Eight-Hour Law was introduced by Wade, March 20, 1890, was reported back with amendments, and was placed on the Calendar. HR 3346, introduced December 20, 1889, by W. H. Crain, Texas Democrat, provided that the holiday be called "Artisan's Day"; it was referred not to the Committee on Labor, as Beaumont says, but to the Committee on the District of Columbia. No action was taken on it during this session.

force the Windom [11] Silver measure down my throat when it is political suicide with me in my District to support such a measure. Then he says there is Old Joe Cannon the Chairman of the Committee on Apropriations coming up and voting agnst the duty on lead ore, and my district the heaviest producer of lead ores in the country. Well if he was not wild it was a caution. Then the District Committee of 66 had the temerity to go before Reed in Wades behalf for to get his Committee a day. And I saw Hobbs last evening and he told me that he heard that Reed got on his ear about as bad as he does in the House when a Democrat undertakes to tell him that he is absent from the House when he does not vote.[12]

None of the Committees of the House are doing any business. They hardly ever get a quoram. You talk to a member that is on a committee about a measure before it as to when in his opinion the Committee will consider it and he will smile at you as much as to say "can't you read"[?] Things were never more demoralized worse than at any time during the last two congresses. The House has spent several weeks discussing a Tarrif measure,[13] and now it is over before the Senate Finance Committee and the first thing that they do is to lay it to one side and procede to form a bill of their own. The next thing that is to be brought up is a Federal Election Bill and that will be a strict party measure and will cause a more bitter fight than the tarrif. Lodge [14] framed one in his Committee of the House with the Australian feature in it. And he had to alter it. Notice was served on him by the Republican leaders of the senate that such a feature would not be considered for one moment by that body. There will be weeks spent by both bodies over that matter. And nothing from now on will have any show but that and the apropriation bills.

Our Farmer Friends, have had their Sub-Treasury Bill [15] introduced and they have been heard before the Senate Agricultural Committee and the House Ways and means Committee. It was realy amusing as well as agrivating to see them before the latter Committee. There was Macune, Livingstone, Wardall and Rodgers [16] of the Colored Alliance. It took them several weeks to get the consent of McKinley [17] and when it was given there was hardly a day that

---

[11] William Windom, Secretary of the Treasury. Innumerable silver measures were introduced in both Houses during this session. Windom urged the issue of treasury notes against silver bullion at the price of silver when it was deposited. This proposal was not accepted, and the compromise measure finally passed July 14, 1890, was the Sherman Silver Purchase Act.

[12] This refers to Reed's tactics as Speaker to secure a quorum in the House.

[13] The McKinley Tariff bill, HR 9416.

[14] Henry Cabot Lodge, chairman of the Select Committee on Election of President, Vice President, and Representatives in Congress. In the House alone, eighteen Federal election bills were introduced during this session.

[15] The subtreasury scheme was developed by C. W. Macune of Texas, a leader in the National Farmers' Alliance, as a means of providing cheap short-term credit for farmers. The bill referred to, HR 7162, was introduced February 18, 1890, by John A. Pickler, Republican Representative from Faulkton, South Dakota.

[16] These were leaders in the organizations of farm protest. For Macune, see Note 15. Alonzo Wardall was a member of the National Executive Board and of the national legislative committee of the National Farmers' Alliance. Leonidas F. Livingston was President of the State Farmers' Alliance of Georgia. J. W. Rodgers was Secretary of the State Wheel of Georgia.

[17] As chairman of the committee.

there was a quorum of the committee together, and it seemed as though it was under protest that they was heard. Mills [18] of Texas never was in the Room a moment save to pass through it. Bayne [19] of Pittsburg would come in and go out while they were talking and when he was in he would go right to writing or looking over some papers as much as to say by his actions what rot. And other members were most conspicious by their absence. And it was only three quarters of an hour each day; it took four days to get a chance to say what they had to say. There was one man who was there all the time. It was Roswell P. Flower from Wall St. in New York. He was there and interupted McCune so that he took up nearly one half of his time. He would beg to ask him a question and would then go on with a speech in favor of state banks as a method of relief for the farmer, and the[n] ask him if he had heard of the French Asignats and deliver a five minutes speech upon them. He was looking after Wall St. But when the old Man Livingstone got up he commenced the same game. But the old man give him to understand that it was he that was entitled to the floor, and said to him that if he, Flower, wanted to discuss this question that he Livingstone would pay for half the expenses of hiring a hall for that purpose and would be with him at any time that he desired. That ended his interuptions. Now Friend Powderly I opine that there will be some farmers in the next house, and if there is they will oppose any eight hour legislation or any increase of wages on the part of working men in New York. When these men come to congress to ask for that kind of legislation they will be told by these farmers that as long as they cast their votes for Wall St Bankers like Flower who come here to enact financial legislation which opresses the farmers and robs them that they must look to those bank representatives for their incrased pay measure.

As I see the matter with these people now it is this. I think that the Senate Agricultural Committee will make a report, and it looks to my mind that the Republicans on the Committee will let Senator George [20] of Miss. a Democrat write the report and he will write a report to the effect that the tarrif is responsible for the agricultural depression and so report and then the republicans will deny that and that just side tracks the money issue and brings to the front the Tarrif issue. In the House the other day they got a resolution offerred to the effect that the House should order the House Committee on Ways and Means ... [to] report to the House for discussion the subtreasury bill. This resolution goes to the Committee on rules composed of Reed, Chairman, McKinley and Cannon, Republicans, Mills and Blount, Democrats.[21] It has just about as much chance of being reported as I have of being a presidential candidate in 1892. And these fellows are now beginning to see what could not be told them that an individual member of congress is of but little account. It is the machine that they must move. They have been to see Reed and the president but all the satisfaction was the loss of their time.

Thus the condition that legislation is tied up here at the Capital and the

---

[18] Roger Q. Mills, Democrat from Corsicana, Texas.

[19] Thomas M. Bayne, Republican Representative from Bellevue, Pennsylvania.

[20] James Z. George, Carrollton, Mississippi.

[21] The Committee at this time consisted of the first four and John G. Carlisle, Democrat from Covington, Kentucky, who resigned from the House on May 26. Mills was not officially appointed to the Committee until June 11.

members of Congress in a devil of a stew about getting home I look at it as though between the desire of the members to get home, the Federal election Bill, Tarrif Bill in Committee on Conferences and the Apropriation Bills there is but little show for anything else. And by the 15th of next month I shall leave here as I can make my wages at lecturing [22] and the expense to [the] Order of my being here will be so much in the line of Economy. I do not see what I can do with this condition of affairs existing. The Farmers Representatives are more disgusted that I am at the situation....

I do not think of any thing more at present. Hoping this will find you and your family well.

I Remain Yours Fraternally,
RALPH BEAUMONT

---

[22] For the Knights of Labor.

Chapter 10

Labor lobbyist—1950

THE AFL LEGISLATIVE ARM IN WASHINGTON IS ITS NATIONAL LEGISLATIVE Council. Established by the 1948 convention, its membership consists of representatives from the 106 affiliated unions; the four over-all departments: Building and Construction Trades, Metal Trades, Railway Employees, and Maritime Trades; the 48 state federations of labor; and from some of the 650 central labor unions and 44,000 local unions. Sixteen of the standard railway labor organizations affiliated with the AFL also participate in the work of the Council, as does the International Association of Machinists, which is not now affiliated with the AFL.

This stage of development in AFL legislative organization has been reached after more than a half century of activity in the field. From the beginning, the AFL had a National Legislative Committee, which was presided over by Samuel Gompers for the first 14 years of its existence. In 1895, Andrew Furuseth, head of the Seamen's Union, became chairman of the Committee. When William Green succeeded Mr. Gompers as president of the AFL, he set up an additional body—the National Joint Legislative Conference of the AFL and Railroad Brotherhoods. The new Council established in 1948, with Mr. Green as chairman, and secretary-treasurer George Meany as secretary, has broader representation than the old Conference and also has made available on short order a larger number of persons for legislative work.

Stationed in Washington, and immediately available when needed, are seventy-five members of the Council. Forty others are available on 24-hour notice.

The work of this large body is executed by an Administrative Committee of nine members elected by the Council. Its chairman, the writer of this chapter, is also chairman of the National Legislative Committee, which carries on the day-to-day work.

The National Legislative Committee includes a chairman, several Legislative Representatives, and a number of staff members with legal training. The Committee takes its directives from the AFL's highest governing body, the Convention that meets annually and passes resolutions bearing on legislative action. The resolutions, often general statements of policy, are passed on to the Committee for translation into specific bills for presentation to Congress. Customarily, members of the Congressional Committee that is to consider the type of legislation covered by the bills are requested to sponsor these bills. Although at one time or another, the AFL has testified before almost every Congressional Committee, it is mainly concerned with the bills pending before the House Committee on Education and Labor, the Senate Committee on Labor and Public Welfare, the two Appropriations Committees, the two Post Office and Civil Service Committees, the Armed Services Committees, the Judiciary Committee, Ways and Means and Finance Committees, Interstate and Foreign Commerce Committees, and Public Works Committees.

The roster of AFL witnesses at Committee hearings has included William Green, President of the AFL, members of the Legislative Council, and occasionally representatives of the state federations of labor or city central bodies. Infrequently, the Committee has issued an appeal to the general membership of the AFL requesting that they contact their Congressional representatives in behalf of or in opposition to specific legislation. But this action is resorted to only in an acute situation.

In its offices in Washington, the Legislative Committee maintains a complete file of bills, Committee reports, hearings, Committee calendars, and all related material, to enable it to keep in close touch with the progress of a given bill or resolution. It maintains an up-to-date personal file on each individual member of Congress, and all public statements of interest are included in the file together with the lawmaker's voting record on all matters affecting labor, general welfare, and related topics.

After a bill or proposal is assigned to a member of the Legislative Committee staff, he is responsible for following it through to its conclusion and reporting on it to the annual AFL convention.

There are times when the legislation is of such moment that all National Legislative Council members may be required to turn their energies toward the success of the immediate enterprise. In such cases, the Legislative Committeemen personally contact "doubtful" members of the Committee or of the House or Senate, pressing our views and checking on reports that one or another legislator may be wavering from his position in our favor. Committee staff members also contact lawmakers known to be antagonistic to organized labor's position. This contact is for the twofold purpose of attempting to convert such legislators and of learning more accurately the details of opposition sentiment.

On some legislation, the National Administration lends support. In such cases, AFL efforts are coordinated with those of representatives of the White House and the Department or Agency delegated to do the Administration's liaison work on Capitol Hill. Toward this end, we find it practicable to compare notes and exchange information on informal polls of the members of the House or Senate upon a given piece of legislation.

The procedure followed during the long campaign for the repeal of the Taft-Hartley Act and on the new minimum wage illustrates this type of cooperation. At one point in the Taft-Hartley fight in the House of Representatives, the Wood Bill, which was regarded by many as fully as injurious as the Act itself, was substituted for the Lesinski Bill. The vote having been taken, a temporary victory was won when a motion was made to recommit the Wood Bill to Committee for further study, and the following day was set for the unfinished business of voting on this motion.

The entire National Legislative Committee and the members of the Council worked closely with the known friends of labor in Congress, and contacted every available member who had failed to vote the preceding day, as well as all members who could be classed as doubtful. The result was that the Wood Bill was recommitted by a margin of three votes.

Legislation sometimes calls for a rapid increase in manpower to contact the lawmakers. On these occasions, the AFL informs the state and central affiliated bodies and requests that delegates be sent to attend a meeting of the Legislative Council. Such meetings are sometimes held on short notice. Delegates are briefed on the situation upon arrival, and ways and means are discussed on what part the visiting delegates can best take in the campaign. It has been found helpful to call these delegates to Washington on occasion for the obvious reason that they come as constituents of the lawmakers from their own states.

It is not always possible, 12 months or more in advance, to formulate a legislative program admitting of no variation. For this reason, the Executive Council of the AFL is authorized to consider and approve any measure to meet the needs of the situation between Conventions.

In its contacts with lawmakers it has always been the policy of AFL legislative representatives to refrain from general political discussion. The AFL has maintained a record of nonpartisanship and supports or opposes candidates for Congress on their records alone. Many uninformed persons are of the opinion that labor organizations are formed for the purpose of combating employers and for causing them difficulties in every possible way. Insofar as the American Federation of Labor is concerned, this accusation is absolutely untrue. From its earliest days it has been interested in and has endeavored to promote the welfare of all the people of the United States. And in later years it has broadened its activities in behalf of the peoples of the world.

W. C. HUSHING

Section Two

AMERICAN LABOR ABROAD

Chapter II

Labor's international relations

THE VIGOROUS ROLE OF THE MAJOR AMERICAN LABOR ORGANIZATIONS IN the founding, late in 1949, of the International Confederation of Free Trade Unions is a vantage point from which to view the activities of American labor in world affairs. Another chapter discusses the part played by the labor movement in the European Recovery Program. This chapter will discuss the other activities of American labor in the field of foreign affairs and in its relations with the labor movements abroad.

Except in times of world crisis, in wars or other threats to the survival of the national community, foreign affairs are never a matter of great concern to the average man or to the community as a whole. This has been most true in the United States, separated by an ocean from an Old World from which most of America's immigrants were anxious to get away. There is, therefore, nothing surprising in the relative indifference to world affairs shown by the American labor movement during most of its existence. That was simply part of the prevailing attitude in the United States in a period when we were concerned with our own industrial development and our domestic social and political problems, and when, with the exception of the first world war, we felt safe—and aloof—from "Old World Quarrels."

On one international issue the labor movement took a strong stand—immigration. Out of the understandable desire to protect its standards against the competition of the millions of immigrants and potential immigrants from Europe and Asia, it worked for a ban on the import of contract labor, the exclusion of Orientals, and later for the restriction of European immigration. These campaigns succeeded in getting Congress to ban the importation of labor under contract (in 1885), to exclude Chinese (in 1882), and finally to close our great doors to all but a trickle of immigrants after World War I, in 1921 and 1924.

From this special concern, and the statement of Samuel Gompers after his return from Europe in 1910 that "the Old World is not our World," it is a long way to the activity of the labor organizations in the writing of the European Recovery Program, their current concern with the major issues of international affairs, and the leadership of the AFL and the CIO in the setting up of the new International Confederation of Free Trade Unions. In part, this growth of interest corresponds to the considerable growth in the awareness of the United States as a whole of foreign policy issues, and to our half-reluctant assumption of the world responsibilities which have fallen to us. In part, it reflects the changed position of labor within the American community, its emergence from a role of inferiority and a posture of defense to its present strength and responsibility in the American scene, which encourage it to play a role and secure recognition on the world scene.

During the first great war, to be sure, organized labor suddenly, and for a time, became far more important in the scheme of things. It attained great recognition in the war effort. Unionism grew in numbers and importance, and AFL leaders, particularly Gompers, "reached out for leadership in the international labor movement." Gompers headed the Versailles Commission which drew up the Labor Convention of the peace treaties, creating the International Labor Organization (ILO). But the American people returned to isolationism. The postwar depression hit the AFL hard. For both these reasons the Federation largely closed its international books in the 1920's. Since the end of the Second World War the postwar roles of the United States and of American labor have been altogether different.

Unlike most other groups in the nation, labor can not only attempt to influence general foreign policy, but it can also act internationally through its own international organizations. We shall first take a brief factual look at these organizations.

Almost as soon as labor unions began to struggle onto their feet in Europe, their leaders tried to develop international associations. While these efforts long remained essentially European, and while they were inextricably bound up with Socialist and other radical movements which gained little hold here, these efforts did touch the United States. Even the First International, with which Karl Marx's name is linked, moved its headquarters to the United States in 1872, after eight years of turbulent history, but only to expire. Unlike the First International, the Second International, founded in 1889, very soon began to function as an organization of the Socialist political parties, rather than of both unions and parties. Meanwhile, the trade unions began, in the last decade of the nineteenth century, to federate internationally along the two lines which have since marked their international efforts. One line was that of federations of national unions in single industries or trades, called "international trade secretariats" (which we may abbreviate as ITS). The first was created in 1889 by a meeting of printers' delegates from thirteen countries, including the United States. Miners' national unions created the International Miners' Federation; the dockers, seamen, and railway workers' unions of many countries joined in an International Transport Workers' Federation; the metal workers organized the International Metal Workers' Federation, and so on for organizations, which have continued to the present day, in a score of industries, trades or professions. Many American unions joined international trade secretariats of their crafts or industries.

The ITS have shown varying degrees of activity. Some have had only a mail box existence, doing no more than occasionally exchanging information among national affiliates. The most vigorous has been the International Transport Workers' Federation, operating in an industry which is international in character, with the clearest economic basis for federation. With the most effective leadership of the ITS, it has organized and lobbied, researched and published; it has fought fascists openly and underground, and fought communists. It has achieved an impressive measure of international improvement of the standards of its members, and built up an organization with a loyalty all its own.

International Federation of Trade Unions

The other line of federation, beginning a few years later than the first ITS, has been that of federation of the national trade union centers of many countries. What later became the International Federation of Trade Unions (IFTU) was launched before World War I, and in 1910 the American Federation of Labor followed Gomper's recommendation to affiliate, despite his own misgivings about the socialist character of the IFTU's European leaders.

The IFTU was revived after the first war and functioned, with high resolutions and modest activity, between the two wars. But the AFL dropped its membership soon after World War I out of alarm about the IFTU's socialist orientation, fear that it would encroach upon the

AFL's autonomy, and dissatisfaction with the per capita tax it was asked to pay. In the next two decades the IFTU came to look less dangerous to American labor leaders. They saw how far from revolutionary was its spirit, as it stood off the attacks of the Red International of Labor Unions, the trade union arm of Russia's Comintern. They saw how, after originally criticizing as inadequate the International Labor Organization which Gompers had done so much to set up, the IFTU became active in the ILO as coordinator of the Workers' group of delegates. In 1937, three years after the United States joined the ILO, the AFL reaffiliated with the IFTU. Since the statutes of the IFTU allowed only one national center from a country to belong, there was no real possibility of the newly-born CIO's affiliating.

The IFTU did not survive the second world war. Over the strenuous protests of the AFL, which argued that it could be recreated and re-invigorated, the IFTU was dissolved (in late 1945) in favor of an experiment in cooperation between Communist and democratic union movements, the World Federation of Trade Unions (WFTU).

World Federation of Trade Unions

While the war was still on, in February 1945, the preliminary conference which led to the founding of the WFTU was held in London. In September of that year the WFTU was officially established by a Congress in Paris.

The WFTU, it will be recalled, was the creation of a labor "Big Three," the British Trades Union Congress (TUC), the Soviet trade unions, and the CIO, then represented by Sidney Hillman. The attempt by the CIO and TUC to achieve common action with the Russian unions and with Communist-controlled labor movements in other countries was no doubt a natural development in the wartime and immediate postwar atmosphere. It was abundantly clear to many, however, even at the time, that the organization as such could not survive a deep cleavage among the nations whose labor organizations were represented at Paris.

The AFL refused to join the new organization and denounced any collaboration with the government-run "trade unions" of the Soviet Union. The Christian—chiefly Catholic—trade union centers also rejected affiliation.

Despite their absence, the WFTU claimed at its formation to include sixty-seven million workers—whatever might be said about the padded membership figures or bona-fides of some of its affiliates. Its structure was loose and recognized the autonomy of constituent federations, since the Soviet attempt to write the Communist concept of centralization into the statutes had been vetoed by the CIO and the TUC. In aims, the WFTU reiterated the traditional trade union objectives of bettering the standards of labor throughout the world, with some dashes of socialist phraseology about nationalization and workers' share in the control of industry. It demanded a part in the writing of the peace and in the determination of labor policies for the ex-enemy lands, and it proposed a vaguely articulated role of participation or consultation in the United Nations.

Through a combination of the increasingly clear Communist orientation of its secretary-general, Louis Saillant (of the French General Confederation of Labor), and the relative inactivity of the TUC and the CIO, especially after Hillman's death, the WFTU emerged more and more openly as a Communist propaganda instrument. By the time the CIO sought once more to become active in its management, it was too late.

Meanwhile, the ITS, most notably the Transport Workers, refused to be bullied or cajoled into amalgamation with the WFTU.

The espousal by the British and the American union movements of the European Recovery Program and the Russians' and Communist-controlled unions' opposition to it brought the uneasy conbination to the breaking point. In the early months of 1948, the refusal by the Communist majority in the WFTU Executive Bureau even to discuss the European Recovery Program led to the formation, by the CIO, the AFL, the U.S. railway labor organizations and the democratic labor groups of the ERP countries, of the ERP Trade Union Advisory Committee. This Committee was important less for what it did in the ERP than for what it showed about the changes in the international labor alignment.

In January 1949, the non-Communist members of the WFTU Executive Bureau (CIO, British TUC, and the Netherlands Federation of Labor) split from the organization, and were followed over the next half year or so by the other non-Communist affiliates. The WFTU was not destroyed, as some of its opponents over-enthusiastically proclaimed. But it was left as the indubitable trade union arm of the international Communist movement.

With the split in the WFTU, an effective democratic alternative became both essential and, probably for the first time, possible. Agreement between the AFL and the CIO was the first prerequisite. As soon as this agreement was attained, the TUC issued the invitations for a preparatory conference at Geneva in June 1949. This Conference called a Congress at London, in November 1949, which set up the International Confederation of Free Trade Unions (ICFTU).

International Confederation of Free Trade Unions

In scope, the ICFTU already includes almost all the non-Communist trade union centers of the world, with a claimed membership of some fifty million (if one counts those affiliates of ITS who are not members of national centers affiliated with the ICFTU). This includes the revived labor movement of Germany and most of that essentially new postwar creation, the Japanese labor movement. It includes both major non-Communist centers of India. Both national centers of Canada are, of course, members. The Australian TUC has pulled out of the WFTU, but has not yet joined the ICFTU. The solid British, Scandinavian and Low Countries' unions are here, as in the International Federation of Trade Unions.

In *organization*, the ICFTU preserves the principle of the autonomy of its constituent national centers. But it proposes to combine this with an effective headquarters, on the one hand, and, on the other, with vigorous regional activity. The headquarters, in Brussels, is under the energetic and canny secretary-general J. H. Oldenbrock (of the Netherlands), until recently Secretary-General of the International Transport Workers' Federation.

The ICFTU has recognized the importance of regional activity, with a large measure of regional autonomy, in the Far East, the Middle East, Africa, and Latin America. In the "underdeveloped" areas of low living standards and uncertain political democracy, trade unions (and other mass organizations), if they exist, are comparatively weak and inexperienced; unions are threatened by government and employer domination on the one hand, and on the other by the Communist drive through the WFTU. The ICFTU Congress stated the need for regional activity and organization, but left for executive action the development of organizational forms and programs. Regional conferences have already been called for Africa, Asia, Latin America, and Europe to develop the details of operation and regional structure in each of these areas.

Another major organizational problem is in the process of being worked out; the relations between the new Confederation and the International Trade Secretariats. These relations were a subject of irritation between the pre-war International Federation of Trade Unions and the Secretariats. A working relationship has now been reached between the two groups on a basis of mutual cooperation for a common end, working together as one international trade union movement, at the same time recognizing the autonomy of the several parties. Provision has been made for reciprocal representation on the governing bodies of the organizations concerned.

American Unions in the Lead

Previous leaders of the non-Communist labor movement have been the British, the Germans and the French, with the small democracies of Europe contributing much of the international labor personnel. Today the top personnel of the British TUC is more than fully occupied with the responsibilities of the British economy, battered by two world

LABOR'S INTERNATIONAL RELATIONS

wars, with the newly nationalized industries, and with the British state under a Labor Government.

Western Germany's own position is still too dubious for other labor movements to consider the leadership of its trade unionists. French non-Communist labor leaders, despite a long international tradition, are now a minority movement in their own country, and unable to offer leadership.

Their own vigor, their numbers and their superior financial resources, and the default of others, therefore, call the Americans to a leading role.

These factors are reflected in the objectives of the ICFTU. While leaving the constituent organizations full autonomy to develop their own national aims, the Confederation departs from the long socialist traditions of labor internationalism to state the demands of social reform within the framework of the existing order, along the lines of CIO and AFL philosophy in the U.S. European Socialists are generally too tired and unsure of themselves to contest this statement of aims. And the trade union movements of the underdeveloped areas are more concerned with nationalistic and anticolonial demands than with pushing their own socialistic or statist orientation.

There has been a healthy increase in mutual toleration since prewar days. American labor leaders no longer fear that European labor will (or can) seek to impose doctrinaire Socialist ideas upon the American scene. European labor leaders find that Americans have moved considerably from the simplest free enterprise ideas. European Socialists themselves, after a generation of governmental responsibilities, are less suspicious than they once were of American labor's basic acceptance of its society and government.

Cooperation between the AFL and the CIO is making possible this new world position of American labor. Their cooperation on the international scene will certainly make for greater cooperation of the AFL and the CIO on domestic affairs.

The International Trade Secretariats

American labor is playing an increasingly important role in the trade secretariats. American railway labor's affiliation with the International Transport Workers' Federation made it possible for this key group to resist assimilation by the WFTU. The affiliation of the Machinists with the International Metal Workers' Federation shortly after the war was followed last year by affiliation of the United Automobile Workers (CIO), the Steelworkers, and the AFL Metal Trades Department. The United Mine Workers are active in the Miners International, to note one other example.

The ITS will continue to deal with the economic problems of workers in specific industries, while the ICFTU represents the more general and the more "political" interests of workers as a whole.

Regional Labor Organizations

The ICFTU takes the center of the international stage, organizationally speaking, but it proposes to develop regional activities. American labor organizations have in the past made attempts to stimulate such activity, particularly in Latin America. Samuel Gompers, feeling frustrated in his hopes of cooperation with Europe, turned with great energy to organizing the Pan-American Federation of Labor, and it was on his way home from Mexico City that the valiant old fighter died in 1924. The Pan-American Federation, set up in 1918, was largely a Mexican-American affair, with a little strength in other Caribbean lands, and less in South America. Suspicion of American policy and of "dollar diplomacy" was then too strong for the AFL to overcome, despite its own fights against American intervention in Mexico. The radicalism of the Latin American labor movements alarmed the AFL, and the issue of Mexican immigration finally separated the Mexicans and the AFL. Practically, the Pan-American Federation ceased to exist after 1926.

When the AFL again turned to Latin America, the United States had shown by a decade and a half of the Good Neighbor Policy how far it had come from the dollar diplomacy days. Naturally all suspicion had not been erased south of the Rio Grande. But it was possible for the AFL in 1947, playing a major part as discreetly as possible, to bring together unions of North and South America in the Inter-American Confederation of Workers (CIT). In the CIT have been grouped, in loose confederation, most of the non-Communist labor organizations of Latin America (notable exceptions being the Argentines), and the AFL and the Canadian Trades and Labor Congress. In the polarization of labor alignments, the CIT stands opposed to the Communist-dominated Latin-American Confederation of Labor, which is the regional branch of the WFTU. The AFL maintains a full-time representative (Serafino Romualdi) for Latin-American affairs.

Both the CIT and the nascent Asian Federation will probably adjust themselves to existence as regional bodies of the ICFTU. The AFL now appears quite anxious that the CIO and the Canadian Congress of Labor become associated with the CIT.

Other AFL and CIO Regional Activities

The AFL and the CIO have since the war maintained several representatives abroad, on a full-time basis, in a development new in American labor history. The stationing of representatives abroad on a full-time basis of course adds an entirely different form of representation to that provided by the occasional trips of American union leaders abroad.

The AFL has had two men in Europe since the war's end, Henry Rutz in Germany, and Irving Brown with Brussels as his headquarters, and all of Europe as his field. Brown has thrown his weight against Communism wherever he has found it entrenched in the labor movement, encouraging and assisting non-Communists of all sorts to unite and fight the Communists and the WFTU. This fight he has carried on within almost every country in Western Europe. He has also aided the anti-Communist exiles of the Soviet orbit. The first of "labor's foreign service," he has been a tireless organizer and a fearless fighter. He was one of the first to recognize how the non-Socialist American labor movement might work with Socialist labor abroad. He has carried forward the concept that everything of importance in foreign affairs was American labor's business.

The AFL has since last year also had a representative (Richard Deverall) stationed in India, aiding the inexperienced, but potentially very important, trade union movement there.

The CIO representative in Europe is Elmer Cope, who was for a time assistant secretary-general of the WFTU, in charge of its colonial department—a role in which his chief function was to prevent the use of the WFTU for Communist "agitprop" in the colonial areas.

Nationality Groups' Relief Activities

One exception to the general loss of interest in world affairs after the first world war was the interest of various American nationality groups in the fate of their former compatriots or co-religionists in Europe. This was particularly true of Italian and Jewish labor groups, and helps to explain the continued interest of both big needle trade unions in European happenings.

Italian-American committees of the AFL and the CIO have carried on a variety of activities, ranging from aid to antifascists, and wartime and postwar relief work, to aid to the new unions and attempts to influence the direction of Italian trade union organization. In addition, the AFL Free Trade Union Committee, headed by Matthew Woll and David Dubinsky, has maintained a great interest in the post-fascist labor movement of Italy, and in the struggles against Communist control of Italy's organized labor.

Aid to the Jewish people has been generous and widespread among the labor movement, going far beyond the Jewish labor groups. It has included large relief and rehabilitation activities, aid to the victims of persecution and to refugees, and both political and economic support, first for the idea of a Jewish homeland, and then for the State of Israel. The Jewish-American Labor Committee brings together both CIO and

AFL representatives. Its work has also included aid to non-Jewish anti-totalitarians in Europe's labor movement.

These activities, of course, were only part of the tremendous relief activities and contributions of all wings of the labor movement, which attained hundreds of millions of dollars in the wartime and immediate postwar period.

As in most of the other fields of American labor activity there are special Communist organizations appealing to the various nationality groups, just as there were Communist affiliates of the Red International of Labor Unions in the dual unionism period between the wars. This chapter will not attempt to discuss them for lack of space.

Participation in the ILO

A major international activity of labor has been its participation in the International Labor Organization (the ILO). The ILO is an inter-governmental organization, and it is now a "specialized agency" of the United Nations.

Each of the two great modern wars has been accompanied by a great surge of labor aspirations and labor discontents. The revolutionary developments in Russia and the violence of the labor ferment in Europe impressed and frightened Allied statesmen into offering some satisfaction in the peace treaty to the aspirations of labor. The Versailles Peace Commission set up a Commission on International Labor Legislation which (with Gompers as chairman) drafted the Charter of the International Labor Organization. The Organization's purposes were to improve standards of living and working conditions, to lessen international competition based on the exploitation of labor, and to help assure world peace by curbing social injustice.

It was created as "an institution half way between a parliament and an advisory body," as a "compromise to reconcile the ideas and purposes of governments, employers and labor unions in various stages of development." It was not to be an international parliament with genuine law-giving powers, nor a "parliament of labor" alone.

Its structure is that of an annual Conference and a small executive Governing Body, on both of which governments, workers and employers are represented (in a 2-1-1 ratio), plus a large permanent administrative and research office at Geneva.

Like the other organisms born of each world war, the ILO fell short, in its immediate conception and in its later operations, of the more hopeful demands of the times. But, in thirty years of work—in the formulation and recommendation of labor standards, in the performance of basic research and the furnishing of legislative and administrative counsel, and in providing a forum for unlimited discussion—the ILO has made a modest but respectable contribution to the improvement of labor standards throughout the world. It has laid a solid, if unspectacular, basis for continuing international action on labor and social issues. It has developed patterns of international cooperation in its unique tripartite organization in which labor, employer, and government spokesmen discuss, compromise and vote, much as they share responsibilities within national communities. And the ILO has brought together labor union leaders from all over the world who might otherwise have never met.

The ILO was autonomous and essentially separate from the League of Nations, but the United States did not join the ILO until 1934. The American worker delegate to ILO conferences was then, and has since been, chosen from the AFL. At various times there have been CIO advisers to the AFL-named delegate, and for a time the CIO took an active part in some of the Industrial Committees of the ILO, committees each concerned with labor questions of a single industry, such as steel, oil, textiles. As the consequence of unsuccessful attempts in 1944 and 1946 to have the workers' representation shared on a basis of equality between the two federations, the CIO has for the last three years refused to take any part whatsoever in ILO work. This impasse, however, need not be permanent.

The AFL, vigorously represented by full-time international representatives Robert Watt, Frank Fenton, and now George F. Delaney, has taken a steadily increasing interest in the ILO. It has recognized the considerable American responsibility for any international effort to improve the conditions of working people. The reasons for its interest in the ILO are political and sentimental, in the best meanings of those words, rather than self-interested. Only indirectly and in the long run, does it see in the ILO any chance of improving the position of American labor by raising standards elsewhere and diminishing the competitive effects of low wages and poor working conditions abroad.

Within this country, the ILO conventions and recommendations have had no great effect. First, because most (although far from all) of the standards set by our legislation or by collective bargaining have been higher than those of the ILO. Second, the federal-state division of responsibility for labor legislation in the United States has made it difficult to secure action on ILO standards.

American representatives, labor and governmental, have taken a lead in moving the ILO toward its current emphasis on technical assistance to underdeveloped areas, and toward its present experiment in the protection of trade union rights and the freedom of association.

United Nations Economic and Social Council

In the Economic and Social Council of the United Nations (ECOSOC), the American Federation of Labor received consultative status as a "regional organization." The WFTU originally (in 1945) put in a bid for a seat with a vote on the 18-nation council. Soon persuaded of the absurdity of asking for a seat and a vote in a governmental council, it demanded consultative status. This was granted. At the time, as an offset to the WFTU, the AFL demanded and received the same consultative rights. That status lapsed when consultative status was recently granted to the ICFTU.

In ECOSOC the AFL has made as its chief issue the charges of a vast system of forced labor in the Soviet Union. In 1949, under the spur of reiterated AFL insistence, the United States delegation to ECOSOC sponsored a demand for a first-hand UN-ILO investigation of forced labor wherever it might exist. It looks as if such an investigation may never be launched, chiefly because of the unwillingness of most other countries to be investigated unless—as no one expects—the Soviet Union permits investigation of its territories. At the least, however, the AFL has focussed some moments of the world's harried attention on a great moral issue.

The WFTU has repeatedly aired charges before ECOSOC of violations of trade union rights in Greece, Spain, Portugal, Latin America, Africa and the Middle and Far East. The AFL has counterattacked, and demanded action on violations of trade union rights in countries behind the Iron Curtain (and elsewhere too). ECOSOC therefore asked the ILO, in its own behalf and that of the UN as a whole, to undertake a program of protection of trade union rights. This program includes Conventions already adopted on freedom of association and on the right to organize and bargain collectively, and an attempt at ILO investigation and conciliation where violations of trade union rights are charged.

The ICFTU also exercises its consultative rights in the various specialized agencies of the United Nations—the ILO, the World Health Organization (WHO), the United Nations Educational, Scientific and Cultural Organization (UNESCO). American labor has already taken a part in their work, chiefly through the Government's naming of labor people as members of general United States delegations to their meetings.

The labor organizations do not feel that they have adequate recognition in all the UN work. But they recognize that the problem of their participation has been complicated by the division of the American labor movement, and the difficulty of prying loose qualified labor men from their work at home. Meanwhile, notable service has been rendered on WHO and UNESCO delegations by Nelson Cruikshank and Mark Starr of the AFL and Kermit Eby and Stanley Ruttenberg of the CIO.

U. S. Foreign Policy

Beyond its own international organizations, or its participation in intergovernmental agencies, labor has taken a part in the shaping of the foreign policy of the American government, in all the ways in which a large conscious group in the community seeks to influence public policy.

Both the AFL and CIO have standing committees on International Affairs. Both maintain full time international representatives in Washington, George Delaney for the AFL and Michael Ross for the CIO.

CIO and AFL conventions lay down broad lines of recommended policy on international matters; this is not new, but the range of policies and the attention given to foreign affairs at the conventions have greatly increased in recent years. Officials of the AFL, the CIO, and the railway brotherhoods testify before Congressional committees, argue their case in the press and over the radio, and talk with the officials of government whom they want to influence—from the President or the Secretary of State or Labor down to the bureaucrats making or unmaking policies at the shirt-sleeve level. Because of the general recognition of the need for labor's support at home and abroad, these consultations are usually welcomed and sought by government officials nowadays. In addition to formal and informal consultation between State Department and trade union officials, there is a continuing mechanism of formal consultation in the Department of Labor, in the Secretary's Advisory Committee on International Labor Affairs, on which top leaders of the AFL, CIO and the Railway Labor Executives Association sit. One of that Committee's major concerns has been the labor policy of the United States in the occupation of Germany and Japan. (ECA activities are treated in the following chapter.)

The broad policies of the government in the postwar world—the containment of Soviet imperialism, aid to European reconstruction, "Point Four" technical assistance and economic development aid to underdeveloped areas, support for the United Nations—have had the support and participation of American labor. Even the policy of expanded world trade and reduction of our own trade barriers has received an impressive amount of support. But support has not been uncritical. Both the AFL and the CIO have attacked the Government on such grounds as allowing a return to power of reactionary industrial and bureaucratic elements in Germany and Japan, lack of programs to meet the resurgence of dictatorships in Latin America, softness towards the Franco régime, and the ECA's tendency in some countries to stress budgetary balances and production increases at the expense of equitable distribution and social reform. The AFL argued that a more vigorous policy might have saved China from Communist control. There also lingers in labor circles a good bit of the traditional American feeling that foreign policy is made by "striped pants boys." But this suspicion is gradually lessening as labor men themselves accept diplomatic assignments and, even more, as they get into the habit of mingling with foreign policy-makers here or in American missions abroad.

Much of the energy and assurance of American labor on the world scene comes from its wholehearted identification with the basic values of American democratic society and with the immediate goals of the American Government. If labor were to feel these values threatened at home, it would have little stomach or energy for the fight abroad, and its leadership abroad would be seriously undermined. But it is most likely that as long as the international responsibilities of the United States remain so vast, and as long as what we euphemistically call the "cold war" has the labor movement abroad as one of its warmest battle-grounds, the labor groups of this country will continue, expand and deepen their role in international affairs both at home and abroad.

VAL R. LORWIN

Chapter 12

Labor and European recovery [1]

THE ROLE OF U.S. LABOR IN THE MARSHALL PLAN IS SIGNIFICANT ON TWO counts. First, it indicates the ever widening interest within official trade union circles in government policies not directly related to domestic "bread and butter" issues. Second is the recognition by the U.S. Government that American labor has a unique contribution to make in the development of American foreign policy.

Labor's interest in the European Recovery Program is not in itself a new phenomenon, but rather part of a developing concern in international issues with its most recent roots in the last war.

Both the AFL and the CIO during the war established agencies to maintain contact with fighting trade unionists in the European antifascist underground. With the end of the war, American labor undertook a financial campaign to relieve the suffering of European trade unionists and their families. By the end of 1948, it was estimated they had contributed over two hundred million dollars to their fellow workers abroad.

However, the extent of war destruction and the suffering of the peoples throughout Europe called for aid on an international scale far beyond what any one single group could accomplish. In recognition of this fact, U.S. unions early supported government-directed international relief. The United Nations Relief and Rehabilitation Administration (UNRRA) offered the unions their first opportunity; the Marshall Plan for European recovery was their next and greatest chance to assist labor and the democracies overseas.

Labor lent its support effectively to the promotion of the Marshall Plan from the time it was first proposed by Secretary of State George Marshall at Harvard University until it became law, ten months later. Through the secretary-treasurers of both the AFL and the CIO, U.S. labor participated in the President's Committee on Foreign Aid (the Harriman Committee). This 20-member committee laid the groundwork

[1] The views expressed in this chapter are those of the writer and do not necessarily reflect the position of the Economic Cooperation Administration.

159

for American aid in the European Recovery Program. Labor representatives served as members on five of its eight subcommittees and as observers on the remaining three. Their major contribution to the Committee came in their insistence that the United States must not interfere in the internal policies of European governments by reason of Marshall Plan assistance.

In the weeks of Congressional hearings that preceded the passage of the Foreign Assistance Act, representatives of the AFL, the CIO, and the railroad brotherhoods testified on its behalf and against a threatened cut in the original appropriations.

Significance of Labor Participation in ECA

In no other government agency lying outside the traditional area of labor affairs has U.S. labor been given a role comparable to that in ECA. Labor participation, it was recognized, could be of advantage both to the government and to labor itself.

The government needed mass support for the program. The estimated cost of the Marshall Plan was heavy, averaging more than $100 for every man, woman, and child in the United States over its four year span. Although government officials felt the impact of large exports of goods to Europe could be borne by the American economy, they recognized that strains would be introduced into the economy in certain industries such as steel, fertilizer, and farm equipment, and that public support was essential both to stand the taxes and to put up with whatever shortages or price rises might occur in the course of American aid to Europe. Labor's support, representing the single biggest cohesive group in the United States, was considered vital.

Abroad, too, American labor had an exclusive contribution to make. Of the 16 ERP nations, half have either labor governments or coalition governments in which the Socialists or Social Democrats, traditionally the major spokesmen for democratic labor, play an important part. It was vital to gain their confidence.

Socialists have traditionally held American capitalism in distrust. Playing upon this historic hostility, the Communists sought to undermine the confidence of European workers in the Marshall Plan by labeling it "the creation of Wall Street," "an instrument of American capitalism," "American imperialism," etc. No better counteroffensive could have been provided than the support, and even more important the participation, of U.S. labor in the programming and administration of the European Recovery Program.

American labor has been among the most active supporters of the ERP for reasons of its own. That support stems from a realization that world peace and world prosperity are unattainable if Europe should remain bankrupt and thus open to political domination from the extreme right or the extreme left. U.S. labor wants no part of either. This cold logic has been supplemented by American labor's traditional humanitarianism, which many times in the past has responded to appeals for the relief of human suffering. In the case of Europe, this humanitarianism has become personalized through the long-standing friendship between the labor movements of the two continents. Such a concern in Europe's welfare inevitably led American trade union leaders to take an early and active interest in the Government's proposal for a European Recovery Program.

Structure of Labor Participation in the Marshall Plan

The Marshall Plan became law on April 3, 1948. Shortly thereafter, President Truman appointed Paul Hoffman to head the Economic Co-operation Administration, the agency set up by Congress to administer U.S. activities under the Marshall Plan. Two months later, Administrator Hoffman officially announced the appointment of two well-known trade unionists, one from the AFL and one from the CIO, to direct a Labor Division and serve as his labor advisers. A Labor Division was created in the Paris office of the ECA with an AFL trade union official in charge. The post of Labor Information Director in Paris was filled by the head of the American Newspaper Guild (CIO).

Directors of labor divisions, drawn from the American labor movement, are now serving on the staffs of 11 out of 16 of the ECA Missions [2] set up in each of the participating countries in Western Europe. All of the labor directors are assisted by labor information specialists. In addition, 3 out of 12 members of the Public Advisory Board, created by Congress to counsel the ECA Administrator on matters of public policy, are labor men drawn from the AFL, the CIO, and railroad brotherhoods.

Especially significant in the administrative development of ECA has been the promotion of two trade unionists from Labor Directors in the French and Norwegian ECA Missions to top posts as Chiefs of the Swedish and Norwegian ECA Missions. And another trade unionist has been appointed to head the ECA Mission to Greece. With these appointments has come the recognition that competent trade unionists have a contribution to make, not just in the field of labor, but in over-all policy on behalf of the American people. These appointments have set an important precedent for wider labor participation in government beyond that of merely representing one sector of the American public.

----

[2] The 11 ECA Missions where labor divisions are now in existence are: Austria, Belgium-Luxembourg, Denmark, France, Greece, Italy, the Netherlands, Norway, Sweden, the United Kingdom, and Western Germany. Those excluded at present are: Ireland, Iceland, Portugal, Trieste, and Turkey.

Labor's Task in ECA

ECA's major task is to promote European recovery. Inherent in this task are tremendous economic problems—the answers to which vitally impinge upon the workers' welfare.

Under the Marshall Plan, each country must decide what amount of its national income is to go for investment and what is to be left for consumption. Upon that decision rests the level of living that workers can enjoy now and in the future. In planning the way in which recovery funds are to be used, the initial decision rests with the European governments. For this reason, trade unionists throughout Western Europe have sought participation in the governmental administration of the recovery program. The extent of European labor representation ranges all the way from close participation in the governmental operation of the recovery program to virtual exclusion in those countries where the value and usefulness of labor's contribution are not recognized.

While the country's program is in the process of formulation, the ECA Mission staff within the country maintain a close working relationship with their counterparts in the government. It is at this point that the labor director can advise the ECA Mission chief as to how the program affects the workers' interests.

When each country's program has been formulated, it is transmitted to the Organization for European Economic Cooperation (OEEC). This is a European organization made up of top-level representatives from all the participating countries. Here European and American labor serve in an advisory role through an organization, independent of government, called the ERP Trade Union Advisory Committee.

At the Paris headquarters of ECA, the Labor Division has a part in assessing the OEEC-revised program, which is sent on to the Washington headquarters for final appraisal. At this point, the ECA Labor Division in Washington can advise the Administrator on matters of labor policy arising in the review of each country's program.

Certain problems lie exclusively within the labor divisions' sphere of activity. One of these is the question of labor supply. Within Western Europe both shortages and surpluses of labor may be found. The extent of labor surpluses, however, in such countries as Italy and Germany, necessitates finding outlets outside of Europe. This problem is the special concern of the Manpower Branch and the Displaced Persons Specialist serving on the staff of the Labor Director in the Paris office of ECA, and of the directors of Labor Divisions in those countries where the problem is especially acute. On this problem the Labor Division in Paris works closely with the Manpower Committee of OEEC, the International Labor Organization, and the International Refugee Organization in promoting more effective utilization of European labor.

The problem of vocational training is closely related to the problem of labor supply. Here again the initiative rests with the Paris office of the Labor Division to work with OEEC and ILO in setting up training courses and an intra-European employment service to widen the labor market for the unemployed.

Increasing Production in Marshall Plan Countries

A related problem and certainly one of the most important is that of increasing productivity. The greatest advances to be made in European production today must come through more efficient methods and modernized machinery. The initiative for this program rests first with European management; but it is the responsibility of the labor division directors within the ECA missions to work with trade union leaders within the country to win their positive support for a program of increased efficiency hedged with adequate protection to insure the workers a fair share of the benefits from increased production.

One important phase of this problem is the extensive technical assistance exchange program now being undertaken between Europe and the United States. On the theory that know-how can best be communicated by on-the-spot observation, teams of European workers, technicians, and foremen are touring the industrial centers of the United States. The Labor Divisions in ECA Missions have assisted European trade unionists in coming to the United States under this program. In Washington, the ECA Labor Division is responsible for planning the itinerary for labor teams in the United States to provide them with an understanding of American industrial methods and the American labor movement.

In the case of Great Britain, a special committee called the Anglo-American Council on Productivity has been created to assist Great Britain in her program to increase productivity. On the committee, labor and management are equally represented, with Great Britain providing twelve and the United States eight of its members. One major function of the committee has been to supervise the selection of workers, technicians, and managers to come to the United States under the technical assistance program to study American industrial methods.

Certainly one of the most useful services rendered by the labor division chiefs within ECA has been to act as a link between the ECA Mission and the respective European non-Communist labor movements. The labor division chief, coming as he does from the ranks of the American trade union movement, is in a strategic position to bring understanding of the recovery program to the Europeans. He is also in a position to interpret what is going on in the United States to European trade unionists who, even if some have had sporadic contacts with American labor leaders in the past, have been out of touch with much that has been happening in liberal circles within the United States. At the same time, the ECA labor directors can help to increase the understanding of American labor about the organization and activities of Western European trade unions.

To further this understanding on both sides, most ECA missions in Europe now have a labor information specialist on their staff who is responsible for providing a two-way flow of information between the United States and the country in which he is operating. He is concerned too with keeping labor informed about the operation and progress of the ERP. These information specialists have been drawn wherever possible either from editorships of American labor papers or from posts where they have come to know the American labor movement.

At home the ECA Labor Division conceives its informational function to be in part one of appraising accurately the labor situation in Western Europe and transmitting accurate descriptions to American unionists through customary channels; and one also of interpreting the U.S. labor movement accurately to Europe.

Cooperation Outside Government Channels

American labor's participation in the recovery program has not been confined to its representatives in the governmental machinery operating through ECA.

In March 1948 before Congress passed the Foreign Assistance Act, labor representatives from 12 of the participating countries met in London to discuss trade union participation in the recovery program. This meeting took place at the invitation of the British Trades Union Congress and the Benelux trade union centers. It followed the refusal of the Executive Bureau of the World Federation of Trade Unions (WFTU) to consider a CIO proposal to set up machinery to handle the labor aspects of the Marshall Plan. AFL representatives, although boycotting the WFTU, participated in the London meeting. A continuing organization, the ERP Trade Union Advisory Committee, was created to represent labor's interests both in Europe and the United States in the operation of the recovery program. To date the committee has been primarily concerned with: (1) increasing participation by European trade union representatives in the operation of the ERP within their own countries; (2) securing recognition from the Organization for European Economic Cooperation as the official labor advisory body (granted in December 1948); and (3) creating a permanent office in Paris to serve as a clearinghouse and a coordinating center among national trade union centers in participating nations and to maintain a liaison with OEEC.

Through this organization labor, both in the United States and in Western Europe, maintains an independent role outside the governmental operation of the recovery program. The ERP Trade Union Advisory Committee serves also to coordinate and solidify labor's position on common problems arising out of the recovery program. Through labor representatives in the European governments, through the elaborate machinery set up within ECA to secure U.S. labor a voice in the program, and through the ERP Trade Union Advisory Committee, European and U.S. labor have created important channels through which their point of view may be represented in important policy decisions affecting ECA policy.

Getting the Men for the Task

The top personnel of the Washington and Paris labor offices have been drawn exclusively from the labor movement. Prerequisite also to the job of labor director in the ECA country mission is a trade union background. Of the two deputies and ten labor division chiefs in ECA missions in Europe, seven come from the AFL, three from CIO, one from the Machinists, and one from the railroad brotherhoods. More than 20 additional trade unionists are now serving in the Washington and overseas labor divisions on the technical and informational staffs. Technical assistants to the top staff both in Washington and Paris have in some cases been drawn from other sources, reliance being placed more upon their specialized skills in the labor field, than upon a trade union background.

ECA labor directors have had little difficulty in coming to know European trade unionists because of their common bond in the labor movement. It is this characteristic that especially differentiates the work of ECA's labor directors from the labor attaches appointed to serve in American embassies throughout the world, including many of the participating countries. This post, which was officially created by the State Department in 1944, has been filled, with a few exceptions, by men and women drawn from academic and government fields where they have specialized in labor economics and have had contacts with the American labor movement. These people are technically trained to do a reporting job on the economic and political aspects of labor activities within their respective countries. As a result, the functions of ECA labor directors and American Embassy labor attachés serve to complement rather than compete with one another.

The very fact that a trade union background has been made a requirement for the most important labor posts within the ECA has caused a serious recruitment problem. In those countries where labor governments are now in power, the post of labor director in the ECA mission can carry considerable prestige and weight, depending upon the caliber of the man selected to fill the post. Where a labor government is not in power, the responsibility of the labor director is greater in protecting the interest of workers in the important economic decisions that must be made.

Recruitment has been hindered by two factors. First is the general lack of experience among trade unionists—as among most Americans— in international affairs. This lack of experience includes not only unfamiliarity with the European trade union movement and the special problems relating thereto, but also a lack of understanding of the more technical economic problems that touch upon the welfare of workers. Such economic problems involve an understanding of fiscal policy, public finance, price structure, industrial structure, etc. These problems call for a highly technical knowledge upon the part of labor directors whose responsibilities include making recommendations to the ECA mission chief on policies affecting the welfare of workers. At present in some country missions, the labor director is concentrating almost exclusively on trade union policy, overlooking the broader aspects of the job because of a lack of understanding and perspective into the true nature of economic problems. In other cases the labor chief either has some grasp of the broader economic problems or has at hand ECA or embassy personnel who can provide him with the information necessary for reaching a decision on such problems.

Secondly, those officials who through their ability and leadership qualities have been elected to responsible posts within a union are often not in a position to accept ECA posts that would take them away from their union for a period involving at least a year's leave of absence. This condition severely limits the area of potential candidates. It is a problem that applies more acutely to labor than to industry.

An additional problem exists within certain missions where the ECA mission chief has not yet accepted the labor director as an important member of his staff to be consulted on questions of policy that have some bearing, especially where it is indirect, on labor. This is proving less of a problem, however, than might have been expected. In a number of missions the labor director has come to be one of the key officials, thoroughly integrated into the work of the mission.

Keeping American Interest Alive

Another problem affecting labor's role in the Marshall Plan has to do with the degree of support upon which that role is based. Even if the general importance of European recovery may be understood by the trade union leadership, to a large proportion of the rank and file it is seen as a problem so far removed from their day-to-day living that they exhibit little interest in how the program is being operated. They are sympathetic with its goals but that is as far as their interest extends.

This leads to the second major problem, a source of weakness. Because of the vagueness of their understanding, large sections of organized labor, and industry too, are not yet fully aware of the implications of a European Recovery Program and the price they might be called upon to pay to maintain that recovery with the end of ERP. Unless the rank and file of labor, together with industry, see those implications the success of the recovery program is in grave peril in the years ahead. European recovery can be maintained upon a sound footing only if international trade is allowed to expand beyond its prewar levels and to find a pattern that in many respects will differ from the prewar channels of trade. The shifts of trade resulting under the new pattern, if allowed to assert themselves with a minimum of interference, will inevitably cause dislocations in industries both in the United States and Europe. The temporary unemployment and business failures occurring in certain industries will create a serious pressure to build up once again tariff barriers and bilateral trade—two trends inimical to world prosperity and peace. Workers need to realize that their real interests are better served through increased international trade and that a number of jobs are dependent upon Europe's ability to buy from the United States. In the same way, European workers must be made to realize that the temporary dislocations resulting from a more economically integrated Europe will be more than outbalanced by increased markets to absorb the greater production, lower prices, and therefore, higher levels of living. Upon this kind of understanding can be built a sound program for world prosperity—a prerequisite to world peace.

ELEANOR FINGER

PART THREE

Union Communication: Publicity, Public Relations

Introduction

Union communication: publicity, public relations

UNIONS ARE MASS ORGANIZATIONS. They are a *democratic setup*. They are *public institutions in the public limelight*, and a part of the nation's public institutionalism, in fact and in law.

Unions comprise large numbers of members. Even the local unions often have more members than can be convened in one hall, and frequently they do not live in the same locality. Hence, communication between the organization and the members is an important union problem. Even more compelling is the problem in the instance of national or regional unions, whose members live in various states and cities. Effective communication via traveling organizers and representatives is well nigh impossible, and communication through the mail hardly offers a satisfactory way out.

Press publicity is, of course, the answer to the needs of a mass movement. However, it has not been the full answer, since the big commercial press only recently discovered labor as an item of considerable "reader interest," and this recognition is not yet sufficiently widespread, nor is action upon that recognition always fair and satisfying to labor. As Marion H. Hedges and Gordon H. Cole point out in this section, the big press is almost always one-side-minded: "dishonestly neutral," as the saying was a generation ago, with regard to a certain American wartime attitude.

Hence, there came into being a union-owned press at a very early stage in union development, when the general press was virtually inaccessible to the union side in a controversy. However, the union press has continued and grown at an even more accelerated pace in more recent years when labor coverage has, in effect, become a journalistic must in newspaperdom.

Unions are *democratic* organizations at least in their own view of themselves, whether or not their operation of the democratic process always and in all instances follows the accepted political pattern. By logical sequence, their union press is the open road for two-way traffic in union communications. The union's own press presumably presents a more effective medium than the forum of the local union meeting for giving the members an opportunity to voice their opinions and to react to the opinions of others. There is no general ac-

171

ceptance of this view, however. Many union spokesmen take the position that internal union differences are best aired and composed in the local meeting, but they value the union papers as adequate means of vocalizing union news.

Furthermore, as union organizations tend to develop an institutional complexion, there arises an ever greater need for what are in effect house organs. Unions have a social life that needs to be recorded and reported but which produces the kind of reading matter that has little public news value, if any, in the practical estimation of the general press organs. There are also the problems of building union morale for battle, or when it is necessary, preparing the members for an unfavorable decision in a controversy. Tasks such as these cannot, as unions see it, be performed by an outside medium.

Finally, unions are *public* institutions. The union's own press has a well-founded and fairly well-defined function—as presented in the explicit statements by Marion H. Hedges and Henry C. Fleisher in this section—but there is also need for a wider means of communication, a meeting of minds with their neighbors. "Organization life" is but a part of the union's "day's work." Unions are obliged to live with all the people in the community, and they are concerned that there should be wide public understanding of union aims. Labor action affects the community. Action deriving from various segments of the community affects the course, and indeed, the destinies of labor. Labor unions are closely watched, and sympathy for or antagonism against unions are at times not necessarily due to common or contrary interest. In a particular instance, appreciation of a union's action may be withheld due to lack of adequate information, and the union wants to put that information forward. But it also happens that disapproval of a union action is due to the union's not taking the right course. The union may be impelled to recognize an error, to offer corrective action, and to make its position widely known. In such instances, publicity in the public press becomes necessary.

The labor press, publicity, and public relations are three interrelated aspects of union activity along the communication front.

Pursuit of the hard-worked task, *to make friends and to influence people*, ranks high on any listing of assorted activities of a present-day union. Labor has become community-minded.

Currently augmented union preoccupation with political activity has tended to accentuate union concern with community attitude toward labor, its mind, and its behavior. To be sure, not all unions are active in like measure, but few are unaware of the need.

Press publicity and public relations are the recognized means of attaining community understanding and sympathy for union labor. In a sense, both methods of reaching the community are facets of one problem, yet the two are not quite the same.

Going after press publicity appears to be a relatively simple undertaking —that is, simple in approach. It calls, on the surface, for providing the means and the proper person to head the department, and then to issue press releases. Of course, several points must be taken into consideration: What kind of publicity will be acceptable to the press? How well will the press play it up? What angle will it give the story? Nonetheless, the start is clear, and the union is reasonably sure to receive due notice in the press of what it wants publicized. Rather different and more difficult to perform is the task of developing effective public relations.

What is public relations? And more specifically, what is it in relation to unionism?

With disarming simplicity, the UAW-CIO monthly, *Ammunition*, answers: ". . . one man's mouth aimed at another guy's ear. Convey your message. What message? The specific message depends on what's cooking at the moment: contract negotiations; city, state or national election; strike vote; speed-up in the plant; campaign to improve unemployment compensation; Taft-Hartley repeal."

But that isn't quite it; surely not quite all. "One man's mouth to another guy's ear," whether it be whispered across a lunch counter or blared over the radio, still remains only publicity. It is talk. Public relations is more: it may be action. Of course, words and deeds are not strangers to each other, but they are not simply interchangeable. "Every organization, whether it is a labor union, a corporation, an industry or a political party, has two obligations today," wrote Elmo Roper. "It has the obligation, first, to see that its acts *are* good acts, that they are in the public interest; and, second, that the public *knows* what its acts are and, in so far as possible, what motivates them." [1]

Of course, the union should tell the world about itself, but it can gain little by either publicizing acts or procedures that happen to be bad, or by merely keeping silent about bad things of which the public is well aware. This introduction emphasizes the basic difference between the respective tasks of *publicity* and of *public relations*. The job of publicity is *to inform*. The job of developing good public relations may sometimes involve union action *to reform* what is not good in the union's practice.

The publicizer chooses what he wants to inform the public about. Of anything else he makes no mention. He picks the best foot to put forward. The task is not so simple in the case of developing or building a satisfactory labor-public relationship. It is more than dissemination of picked information or of composing the right text or of providing effective and "selling" photographs. The task of building friendships that would "pay off" in emergencies is sometimes a job directed inward, necessitating change, adjustment, or abandonment of acts, procedures, or policies in force, if the public is to be "sold" on the organization or the movement.

"Public relations" has developed into a major industry. The industry has developed its techniques, professionals, and business tricks. Unions are eagerly sought as a clientele. They are a good market for the industry: they have the money to pay for the service, and they seem to need the service often enough. Yet the public relations problem of the labor movement is vastly different from that of organizations less complicated and less endowed with social dynamism. The difference lies in both the *content* of the union function and the *direction* of its effort in public relations.

As to the content, unionism is a compound of "enlightened self-interest" and self-denying social idealism; and its day-to-day performance embraces bargaining, tricky diplomacy, statecraft at its best, and rough-

[1] *Labor and Nation*, October 1945.

and-tumble battling. Furthermore, since real interests are at stake at nearly every crossing of the social traffic lines, honest misunderstandings and conscious misinterpretations can be and are plentiful. The union's pursuit of good public relations, involving a complex educative performance, is a full-time engagement. It amounts to much more than creating a good market for a commercial commodity.

As to the direction of labor's effort at developing public relations, an outside as well as an inside orientation is involved. Labor's public is not all outside. Labor itself is, to a very great extent, the public. Unionism must prove itself to its own new millions by acts of value and of lasting good. For faith in unionism will not stay put; it will rise or fall in the measure that unions prove themselves deserving of the loyalty of their constituents. Labor-public relations, in addition to whatever else it may be, is also a problem of relations between union government and union members. Wise leadership will not take the whole membership for granted. But, as unions develop "good public relations" with their own members, they must bear in mind—and this is frequently their Achilles' heel—that concern for their members' special interest must be balanced with due consideration for basic community or national interest.

The key to good public relations is high purpose, service, integrity, intolerance of and battle against evil. These characteristics are also the key to building a union movement of impregnable moral force; one which will not fail to impress itself favorably upon its constituent units, as well as upon the community as a whole. The staying power of the labor movement, as of democracy itself, grows in direct ratio to its integrity and social morality.

How is union public relations work carried on?

An indication of some of the answers can be found in excerpts from a discussion several years ago by representative union leaders. Wrote Mr. Julius Hochman, a vice-president of the very public - relations - minded ILGWU-AFL:[2]

"If we are to reach the minds and hearts of the American people, a thorough clarification of the problem and, on that basis, a broadly conceived, comprehensive program needs to be carried on systematically over a period of years. I am not thinking primarily of meeting attacks from hostile quarters. Nor am I thinking of selling anything to anybody in the usual sense. What I am thinking of is a carefully planned, long-range effort to get across to the American people the fundamental truth that trade unionism is an integral part of the American way of life, that the achievements of labor are a major contribution to democracy, and that the aims and aspirations of the labor movement have their rightful place in the future of America."

And Walter P. Reuther, President of the UAW-CIO (vice-president at the time the statement was made), said: "I believe it is advisable for union leaders to make criticism of bad practices within their own and other unions. I do not believe we can protect the good name of the union movement by attempting to cover up the facts concerning such bad practices. I think it is much better to

---

[2] This statement and those that follow appeared in "Public Attitudes Toward Labor Unions," *Labor and Nation*, October 1945.

acknowledge such undesirable practices publicly and to act affirmatively to correct them. I do not believe that public regulation of certain phases of union activity will tend to allay antiunion sentiment to any significant degree, although I do believe that certain specific reforms such as compulsory public accounting for union revenues and expenditure might help."

Statements of policy are not necessarily or always an exact reflection of actual performance, but they are indicative of the trend in labor thinking.

It would seem certain, however, that since "public relations" has become a game played on all sides, and since some are able to buy and pay the highest prices for the most accomplished players, labor practitioners can win in a contest only by matching the artful performance of the party of the second part with convincing proof of its own socially valid service. "Some think," writes an expert public relationist, "that public relations is the main hope for preventing the decapitation of capitalism." If the statement is a gross exaggeration, however it is read, it can hardly be disputed that the survival of unionism as an effective progressive force in American democratic society depends upon a union policy of public relations stripped of professional cant and hokum, and instead rooted in action based upon equating labor interest with broad public concern.

There appears to be a growing union awareness of the rather complex and challenging realities attendant upon living with the public.

J. B. S. HARDMAN

Chapter 13

Why a labor press?

THE UNITED STATES IS GOING THROUGH A TRYING PERIOD INVOLVING major readjustments of democratic processes to meet the changing times. At the same time we are bending every effort to encourage the spread of democracy and its philosophy of freedom throughout the world. A free press is as basic to democracy as free speech, and our daily press should be one of the principal tools for selling democracy.

A Free Press and Its Role

We in this country have rigorously guarded our right to a free press. But we have done too little to assure that the press that is guaranteed freedom fulfills its responsibilities to the public. The literature on journalism in this country presents alarming evidence that our daily press falls far short of democratic functioning. In the eyes of too many Americans our vaunted "freedom of the press" has come to be an empty shibboleth—defended in the courts with a flourish of oratory, defended in the press with righteous indignation, but often breached in the every-day operations of our newspapers.

No one questions the right of an editor to support one side of an issue. But most citizens resent and condemn the editor who, because of bias or self-interest, fails to give the reader the full story—the cons as well as the pros. We condemn the editor who by any means takes unfair advantage of his great power to influence opinion. And yet our daily press continues to be rife with examples of this kind of action. This situation would be more serious than it is if it were not for the radio, which is doing a more efficient job than the daily papers as a discoverer and shaper of public opinion.

Public opinion polls offer one clear indication of the abject failure of the daily press to perform its constitutional and professional function. In an amazing number of instances, the polls of public opinion reveal that the people are thinking in a direction quite opposite to that indicated by the daily papers.

176

The small but influential labor press is an ameliorating force in this situation. The growth of the labor press has been stimulated by the urgent need to counter the controlled opinion of the daily press and its vested interests. It attempts to fill out the inadequate and biased reporting in our daily press on matters of interest to labor—and to combat the obvious antagonism of many daily papers toward the whole labor movement. It should be noted, however, that this special function does not give the labor press—any more than the daily press—the right to present only one side of an issue. Labor editors have the same responsibility to the public as any other editor to give a true account of all the pertinent facts on any given story.

No matter how effective the labor press might become, it could not hope to fill the need of a responsible, public-spirited daily press. In January 1950, there were 1,780 daily newspapers reported in the United States, with a combined circulation [1] of 52,845,551. This great propaganda force might be likened to so many little hammers beating upon the minds of the citizenry. In contrast, there are about 650 weekly and 250 monthly labor publications in the United States, and there is no strictly labor daily.

That my indictment of the daily press may not be branded as a labor executive's blast at "big business," I hasten to quote from Edgar M. Queeny's book,[2] *The Spirit of Enterprise*. Mr. Queeny is chairman of the board of Monsanto Chemical Company, a business man, and an officer in the National Association of Manufacturers, and cannot be accused of having leftist leanings.

"There are no businesses," says Mr. Queeny, "other than public utilities that approach as close to monopoly (as newspaper publishing), and as the market is public opinion, monopoly of the enveloping medium carries grave potential threats to free minds, at least to a well-informed public."

Mr. Queeny goes on to point out, "Editorial opinion is controlled by the publisher. Therefore, when the public is dependent on one newspaper, the public receives only one viewpoint—that of the publisher, who may be influenced by the effect that pandering to prejudice and ignorance has on circulation and his pocketbook, or the publisher may be influenced by prospective political reward."

Mr. Queeny feels this situation deeply. "It would seem," he says, "in the interest of an informed public opinion and free minds that Congress consider how to restore free competition to enrich and purify the newspaper business, and how editorial pages could be made into forums like radio, which is required to grant both sides equal opportunity to be

---

[1] See *Editor and Publisher*, 1950 International Year Book Number, p. 17 .

[2] Edgar M. Queeny, *The Spirit of Enterprise* (New York: Charles Scribner's Sons), 1943. Pp. 19 and 20.

heard. This could be accomplished without abridging the freedom of the publisher to say what he pleased, while guaranteeing to those subject to misinterpretation or attack or to those of opposing political faith, an opportunity to freely 'lay his views before his fellow citizens' also."

A more devastating indictment appeared in an objective analysis of the "present state and future prospects of freedom of the press" completed in 1946 by the Commission on Freedom of the Press. The Commission was composed of 13 leading Americans with unquestioned reputations in university and business circles—and none of this group was a labor leader. The Commission interviewed men and women connected with the press and members of the industries, government, and private agencies concerned with the press. Its unanimous report [3] "A Free and Responsible Press," warned that freedom of the press in America was in danger for three reasons:

First, the importance of the press to the people has greatly increased with the development of the press as an instrument of mass communication. At the same time the development of the press as an instrument of mass communication has greatly decreased the proportion of the people who can express their opinions and ideas through the press.

Second, the few who are able to use the machinery of the press as an instrument of mass communication have not provided a service adequate to meet the needs of the society.

Third, those who direct the machinery of the press have engaged from time to time in practices which the society condemns and which, if continued, it will inevitably undertake to regulate or control.

Proponents of the labor press will readily agree to these words of the Commission:

When an instrument of prime importance to all the people is available to a small minority of the people only, and when it is employed by that small minority in such a way as not to supply the people with the service they require, the freedom of the minority in the employment of that instrument is in danger.

This danger, in the case of the freedom of the press, is in part the consequence of the economic structure of the press, in part the consequence of the industrial organization of modern society, and in part the result of the failure of the directors of the press to recognize the press needs of a modern nation and to estimate and accept the responsibilties which those needs impose upon them.

The labor press is designed to help supply people with the service they require. There seems to be wide acceptance of the principle that if newspapers are to be guaranteed certain rights under the Constitution, they should assume certain responsibilities. One of these responsibilities

[3] Commission on Freedom of the Press, *A Free and Responsible Press* (Chicago: University of Chicago Press), 1947.

is to create a forum for free opinion. Failure on the part of the daily press to do this, of course, affects the labor press, forcing the labor press—in order to correct the one-sidedness of the daily press—to become an organ of special pleading.

Policies of the Daily Press

An examination of the curricula of the journalism schools in this country discloses a concern with the ethics of journalism as a profession. Principle No. 1 might be described as duty to the community; principle No. 2 has to do with allegiance to the truth and accuracy. Truth and accuracy refer not merely to avoiding libel suits but to placing facts in their right relationships. This is a task that many feel the press fails to perform—for individuals and organizations. And although the press is careful not to libel individuals, less care is taken to avoid libeling groups or whole blocks of the population.

Many examples of the way the daily press can build up prejudices in the public mind against groups of citizens may be found from a study of papers published during World War II. A widespread impression was created, for example, that labor was shirking in its war effort; that workers were profiteering through unduly high wages. A relatively small number of strikes was played up in news stories and editorials, but little attention was given to the magnificent accomplishments in maintaining good labor relations of the labor-management committees or to the tremendous overtime effort of labor unions.

Through press reporting on absenteeism during the war, the impression was widely created that labor was hampering the war effort for selfish and frivolous reasons. Yet there is evidence that absenteeism in no way reached a proportion beyond normal. The sound opinion of investigators and social-minded people was that absenteeism could be traced primarily to the wear and tear upon the human machine, and had nothing to do with unionism.

The public has heard little about labor's great achievements in the building of cantonments and barracks in a short space of time at a considerable sacrifice to union treasuries. Nor, when the dramatic story of the atom bomb and the way it was produced during the war broke, did the public read about the union's help in assembling skilled workers and persuading them to move to remote atomic production locations, nor of their agreement to refrain from union organization to assure that the project remained secret.

Some commentators take the position that the failure of the daily press can be traced to the disappearance of personal journalism. It has been said that Horace Greeley established his famous New York *Morning Post* with only $200 and his genius. His paper in those days really performed a social function, discovered public opinion and created a forum in which differences of opinion could be heard in an orderly way and could produce a resultant policy.

Personal journalism has not disappeared from the daily press, but is merely manifesting itself in a peculiarly antisocial way. One form of personal journalism that has survived is the one-family type of journalism where the views of a single family are set forth in one or more papers as principles and policies worthy of a great republic. Another type of personal journalism, of course, is that of the columnists, many of them syndicated in a great many papers throughout the country.

There are among the many columnists some who seem deliberately to create misunderstanding of labor's problems, its purposes, and its actions. At least one highly paid, widely syndicated columnist devotes most of his copy from year to year to vicious attacks on the labor movement as a whole. His technique—highly successful, but scorned by more ethical columnists—appears to be to magnify exceptional cases into generalities about the whole labor movement.

The report of the Commission on Freedom of the Press states that "Members of the Commission were disturbed by finding that many able reporters and editorial writers displayed frustration—the feeling that they were not allowed to do the kind of work which their professional ideals demanded, that they were unable to give the service which the community needs from the press. A continuation of this disturbing situation will prevent the press from discharging its responsibilities toward society."

Here again, many labor leaders will agree with the Commission. Many have had the same reaction from able, well-informed, and well-intentioned newspaper reporters and editors who have been assigned to cover stories involving labor.

The most cursory study of our daily press today shows that it tends to intensify group conflicts in an era when everything should be done by thoughtful men to break down barriers between economic groups and to work out economic policies for the whole nation by conference. Vilification of any group in the daily press erects barriers to reconciliation of differing points of view.

Labor Press Expanded and Improved

The first labor paper in the United States was started more than a century ago. Since then the labor press has grown by fits and starts. Now its influence is far greater than its size would indicate. The approximately 650 weekly and 250 monthly labor publications in the United States are estimated to have a readership of around 20,000,000. The size of this circulation is due in part to the intense loyalty of the readers, and in part to the fact that the papers are family circulated.

In addition to the weeklies and monthlies, there are several labor press services. They provide the same types of service for the labor press that are provided by the large number of special services available to the daily papers. There are a few labor newsletters run on a commercial basis that give a well-rounded story of labor to a comparatively small audience.

Technically, the labor press has improved considerably during the last ten years. In appearance, some of the monthly magazines of the international unions are comparable to commercial monthly magazines, and in the author's opinion are superior in their profound treatment of economic and social questions. Nearly all of the better monthly labor magazines are circulated outside of union ranks, placed in public libraries, read by employers, engineers, economists, and students. Editors of these magazines are usually trained in their profession, and they are fortunate in that they are not controlled either by advertisers or by subscribers, since union members automatically receive subscriptions.

Although the weekly labor press has not shown the widespread improvement of the monthly magazines, many labor weeklies are attractively edited and are doing a good job in their communities. A difficulty in a large number of weekly labor newspapers is that they are edited by men without special aptitude or training for their jobs. They have been chosen in some cases because the political exigencies of the situation in their particular community have given them the opportunity, and in some because of their outspoken support of the point of view in that community. Even though some of these editors are untrained in their profession, they still perform a valuable function because they keep alive the right of free speech in the community by providing an open forum.

The labor press lies close to the roots of American life, aiding materially in preserving the traditional right of free speech. But if the United States is a "newspaper democracy," as James Bryce said it was, the control of public opinion lies largely with the daily press and the great illustrated publications with their colorful appeal, and not with the less spectacular labor weeklies and monthlies. Occasionally the opinions of labor editors are quoted in the daily press. But it would be difficult for the average newspaper reader to name any labor editor or to trace his influence on the thinking of any individual or group.

The Future of the Labor Press

The outlook is not a cheering one, but it is not hopeless. If a democracy is going to function, it must somehow discover a way to have every public question properly aired; it must somehow present all the facts in their proper relationships. Whether democracy will be able to effect ways of fulfilling this need, no one can say, but there are certain possible courses of action that could be taken toward that goal.

First, and most important, is for the daily press to live up more nearly to professional standards. The Commission on Freedom of the Press noted that the "leading organs of the American press have achieved a standard of excellence unsurpassed anywhere in the world" although it finds that the press as a whole "is not meeting the needs of our society." It concluded that the press will have to improve itself. "The outside forces of law and public opinion can in various ways check bad aspects of press performance, but good press performance can come only from the human beings who operate the instrumentalities of communication." Labor recognizes that it cannot directly influence the daily press. However, one suggestion that all of labor would support is that publishers appoint to their staffs labor editors who have a social grasp of labor problems and then give them a free hand in presenting the news of the labor world in the great dailies. There are pitifully few labor editors in this country, and even fewer who are given a chance to do the kind of job they would like to do.

A second hope for our daily press lies with the American Newspaper Guild—the union composed of members of the working press. In the summer of 1950 at its 17th Annual Convention, the Guild strengthened this hope. A program was unanimously approved for promoting the publication of new dailies with high ethical standards throughout the country. The Guild members expressed deep concern over the monopoly of the press and over its "failure to live up to the ideals of our constitutionally guaranteed freedom, and failure of fair presentation and editorial examination of the news."

A special committee of the Guild was appointed to formulate a course of action and to invite other labor unions to cooperate in setting up a Labor Committee for Expansion of Newspaper Publications. In making suggestions to the proposed Labor Committee, the Guild stressed the need for the Committee to cooperate where possible with civic groups and individuals in setting up needed papers, but also said that where this was not possible, the Committee should undertake organization itself. The Committee was urged to establish a code of ethics to which each new paper should agree before aid is provided by the Committee. In addition, the Committee was urged to assure local organizations of newsprint, services, and technical advice necessary for the practical and successful operation of newspapers of general circulation.

Special emphasis was laid on the need for safeguarding the new publications against one-sided reporting. "Such newspapers should, whenever at all possible, be locally controlled and financed but with the provisions in their incorporation to promote the continuance of liberal policies. Among these safeguards should be provisions against ownership falling into the hands of one person or a small group of persons. Such papers should not be subject to the vagaries of union politics as would be the case should control be instituted and continue in the hands of the Guild or any other union or group of unions. Nor, in many communities, would such papers stand a chance for success, if set up as straight labor papers, or particularly if in the control of any labor organization outside of the community involved."

The Guild makes clear that the program cannot succeed just as a Guild project. "Only with . . . a determined and united effort by all the labor movement can this difficult task be successful in initial financing and subsequent financial operation and execution."

This is an inspiring and ambitious program that challenges the whole labor movement. Labor could well try again to establish daily papers in this country, even though precedents are not encouraging. The Seattle *Union Record*, the Milwaukee *Leader*, the Minneapolis *Star*, the New York *Call* are all skeletons on the sands of time. These were noble experiments, worth their cost as expensive failures.

There is nothing more costly to manufacture than a daily paper. It is a perishable product that must be ushered into the world quickly, perform its function, and pass on. It must concentrate in the short space of 24 hours a great deal of thinking and energy, which consumes time and money.

Even so, it is worth labor's time to try to find an answer to the question of how to produce a newspaper without subsidies from big advertisers, which will provide the sports news and entertainment that the average reader wants as well as the more serious reporting. If, for example, the labor unions became imbued with the idea of a national daily in Washington, one could easily be financed by one cent per capita tax a day, paid by the national and international unions. But labor will first have to recognize the vital importance of keeping the channels of public opinion open and clear. Labor has operated radio stations in one or two instances with considerable success. Labor can also operate a daily paper.

But there is an additional job that labor unions should begin—separately and cooperatively—to aid in meeting the problem of a free, democratic press.

Labor should strengthen and improve its existing press. Labor unions should seek out new editorial talent, raise up great editors, give recognition to the services that they perform for the movement and the community. The labor press may have as a basic objective the education of union members and the provision of a forum for them, but labor editors should recognize that there is an increasingly broad readership potential outside the unions. Such circulation should be encouraged as a means of extending the understanding of labor's problems and points of view.

Democracy today faces an unsolved problem. Democracy may find that the problem is so grave that some solution will have to be found through Congressional enactment. It is just as dangerous to national health to poison the public mind as it is to poison the public stomach. Pure food laws came after a colossal struggle to enact them. Pure news laws may come in the same way.

In the meantime, the labor press will continue to improve. It will come to grasp more fully its duty and its opportunity, and it will continue to influence the grass roots of the American population.

M. H. HEDGES

Chapter 14

The union press—an inventory

THE AMERICAN LABOR PRESS IS A HARDY INSTITUTION. IT HAS GROWN AND flourished during a period when commercial daily newspapers have been merging and going out of business. It has lived through the difficult period of war and postwar, when newsprint shortages and maldistribution enormously increased the normal burdens of publication. It has survived a period of rising prices and rising costs.

Despite this constant succession of economic problems, the labor press, by the middle of the twentieth century, has reached an apex of effectiveness and influence. Labor papers—national and local—have increased their circulation and maintained their readership gains. Their quality has generally, though by no means uniformly, demonstrated steady improvement. Perhaps more than at any other time in the past, the labor press is read by union members and by the general public; and the frequency with which it is quoted by reporters for daily newspapers, by editorial writers, and by columnists is an indication that the labor press has something to tell the American people.

Press Policy-Making

The effectiveness of the labor press, of course, is based squarely on the health and vitality of the American labor movement itself. The daily press is owned or controlled almost exclusively by corporations or individuals interested in marketing a commodity that will make profits. Accordingly, it is subject to a variety of pressures, influences, and even corruption stemming from the general economic relationships among its owners and the rest of the business community. The daily press—both the big chains and a high proportion of the individually owned newspapers—is in the hands of persons whose primary occupation is the publishing business. Corporations such as General Motors or the great Atlantic & Pacific Tea Co. or Macy's do not publish daily papers of their own. But the corporate viewpoint finds expression in the great majority of daily papers, on the editorial page and often in the headlines and

185

news columns, without the necessity of the direct link of industrial ownership.

The labor press, on the other hand, is an institutional type of publishing operation. There are few, if any, "independent" labor publications, and their circulation and influence are minimal. Labor papers, obviously, are either owned or thoroughly controlled by national labor organizations, by local unions or by community labor groups at the state, county, and city level. Their editorial policies adhere closely to the policies of the organizations for whom they speak.

This correlation of paper to organization is naturally flexible, and for one reason or another, there may be temporary exceptions or time lags. But one can safely predict, to choose an easy example, that praise of the Taft-Hartley Act in the official organ of the CIO, or a tribute to the principle of industrial, rather than craft, unionism in the columns of the AFL's publication, would lead quickly and certainly to an overhauling of the editorial policies of each publication, and almost certainly to the appearance of new names on their editorial mastheads!

If the general content and editorial position of the labor press can thus be determined by a knowledge of the policy positions of the organizations they serve, how then can one account for the increasing popularity and effectiveness of labor publications? The answer, I think, is simple: the labor movement and its press have a message of economic, political, and legislative liberalism that millions of Americans can find in few other popular media of news or opinion.

Occasionally, after unusually embarrassing debacles such as the election of Harry Truman in 1948, the daily press turns the searchlight on its own shortcomings and acknowledges that reforms are necessary to develop better recognition of the public's attitudes. But resolutions are soon forgotten under the impact of the economic forces that dominate the country's daily press. If there was a change from the generally conservative tone of the general run of newspapers between 1948 and 1949, it was so minuscule as to escape the notice of students of the press.

Thus American labor papers flourish because there is a strong, organized union movement, and because there is little more than a handful of liberal-minded daily papers throughout the country. The labor press is not perfect; there is great room for improvement. But labor papers as a group come closest to carrying on the great tradition of liberal expression handed down from earlier generations of journalists.

Function of the Labor Press

The labor paper does not exist solely, or even principally, to cry out against abstract injustice. It fills a variety of practical needs, and through its service to its organizational publisher, it justifies the expense of its existence. The labor paper is in some respects a house organ. It carries the organization's message to the general membership. It serves as a union-wide, or community-wide, bulletin board, carrying routine announcements, schedules, and programs for the rank and file. It reports a great mass of organizational news, some of it important *per se*, some of limited interest. On occasion, it becomes a means of personal aggrandizement for an officer or group of officers at the head of the organization. But one of its most vital functions is to serve as a vehicle of popular education for the aims and aspirations of its parent organization.

These functions of the American labor paper have existed almost from the time of the first pioneer labor organizations, in colonial times and throughout the nineteenth century. American workers have always placed strong reliance on the effectiveness of the written word. Foster Rhea Dulles, in his *Labor in America* (Thomas Y. Crowell, 1949), describes leaflets and circulars distributed in 1815 by the Journeymen Cordwainers. Protesting an effort to use the courts to declare their strike for higher wages an "illegal conspiracy," they circulated printed statements that declared "the name of freedom is but a shadow...if we are to be treated as felons and murderers only for asserting our rights to take or refuse what we deem an adequate reward for labor." It was an editorial theme repeated thousands of times in subsequent labor publications.

In 1836, the Workingmen's Party of New York was forced to issue its own magazine in order to answer the violent attacks of the conservative Manhattan press on the concept of labor political action. In 1837, Dulles recounts, a host of new labor journals sprang up on the heels of that year's financial panic, and by the time of the Civil War, the labor press was an established institution that began to put forward organized labor's views and to advocate economic and social reform.

Fincher's *Trades' Review*, the organ of the Machinists and Blacksmiths, was the most important of these papers and with representation on its editorial board from other unions, it became a national spokesman for the whole labor movement [Dulles points out]. Its editor, Jonathan Fincher, was an able and indefatigable reporter, and a forthright commentator on labor issues. Other labor journals were a new *Workingman's Advocate*, published in Chicago; the New York *Trades' Advocate* and the *Weekly Miner*.

The progress of the labor press from its humble beginning as a circular or throw-away has reflected constant rises and falls in the status of the American labor movement. The labor press was stimulated during periods of intellectual revolt against poverty and injustice; it declined in effectiveness during the apparent prosperity and very real political lethargy of the 1920's, as well as during the period of paralyzing poverty and demoralizing fears brought about by the 1929 collapse. With the coming of the New Deal, which stimulated the growth of unionism, and the creation of the CIO to tackle the organization of the mass production industries, the labor press bounded back as an effective medium.

In 1949, Herbert Little, director of the Office of Information, U.S. Labor Department, reported that that department had a mailing list of more than 800 labor periodicals. (*Editor & Publisher*, October 15, 1949. "800 Labor Journals on Government List.")

According to Mr. Little,

Their circulations have been estimated to total more than 20,000,000, possibly as high as 30,000,000. Eliminating obvious duplications, such as the machinist who gets his union's weekly newspaper, its monthly journal and the local labor papers, it is apparent that nearly all of the 16,000,000 labor unionists in this country get and probably read one or more labor papers. If their families are taken into consideration, the possible readership would be tripled.

These 800 papers have a wide variety of organizational sponsors. Papers or magazines are published by the national federations, such as the AFL, CIO, and the associated railroad brotherhoods; by national unions, like the Steelworkers, Auto Workers, United Mine Workers, Machinists, Carpenters and Teamsters; by districts of various unions; and by state, county, or city AFL federations and CIO industrial union councils.

Quite naturally, the three labor papers most widely read *outside* the ranks of organized unionism are those published by the national organizations of the AFL and the CIO, and by the railroad brotherhoods. The *CIO News* is a weekly tabloid newspaper of 12 pages; the *American Federationist* is a slick-paper monthly magazine devoted primarily to articles of interpretation and analysis by leading figures in the AFL; and *Labor*, published by the railroad unions, is a four-page, standard-size weekly newspaper that gives extensive coverage to the Washington scene and to general railway labor news.

The Central Publications

The circulation of none of these papers and magazines is as great as those published by the largest unions, which go into the homes of all members of the particular organizations. But because of the top-level nature of the labor federations or associations they represent, the *CIO News*, the *Federationist*, and *Labor* are closely read outside the ranks of organized labor. Each of them sells thousands of copies to libraries, teachers, professional students of the labor movement, people who "are interested in labor," trade associations, corporations, and undoubtedly, labor spy agencies. They are "must" reading for labor reporters from the wire services, for columnists, and for many public office-holders whose duties require a close knowledge of events, attitudes, and trends inside the labor movement. The views of these publications are frequently quoted, as an examination of the Congressional Record will show; and during 1949, a survey showed, almost every issue of the *CIO News* was quoted by one or the other of the major telegraph news agencies.

The *CIO News*, in addition to its national edition, prints about a dozen special editions for CIO national unions and local councils. These editions contain a mixture of pages, some from the national edition, some devoted exclusively to the news of the affiliated union that sponsors it. The national edition of the *CIO News* has about 90,000 subscribers gained on the basis of individual sales and block subscriptions purchased by organizations. The number is increased substantially by the circulation of the special editions, which in the case of national unions go to each member in good standing.

A staff headed by Allan L. Swim, editor of the *CIO News* and publicity director of the CIO, produces the weekly paper and handles the mechanics of publishing the editions. Material is prepared by the union or council for which it serves as official organ.

The *CIO News* has adapted many of the innovations brought to American journalism by the tabloids—although needless to say, it eschews stories of murder, sex, and spicy divorces. Its style is pert; its stories generally short and condensed; its editorial page breezy and vernacular; and it devotes considerable space to pictures and cartoons. The *CIO News* seeks to establish a balance of content among general news of interest and significance to labor; interpretation of developments in Congress; and publicity for the official views of the CIO on both organizational and external news.

The *American Federationist* underwent drastic changes during the 1930's. Once an almost unreadable labor version of the old *Atlantic Monthly*, down to and including a series of full-page advertisements from nonunion and hostile corporations, the *Federationist* was the subject of a complete overhaul about 1935. It emerged as a slick-paper, well-illustrated magazine, which under the editorship of Bernard Tassler offers the reader a well-balanced selection of articles by labor leaders, government leaders, and other friends of labor.

A newcomer, but an effective addition to the labor press, is the *League Reporter*, issued by the AFL Labor's League for Political Education. A weekly four-page tabloid, it concentrates on every phase of the AFL's political activity. The CIO Political Action Committee, although publishing no newspaper, issues an informative condensed weekly newsletter on congressional and political developments.

Labor, though more sedate in appearance and writing style, gives much the same type of news content to its readers—some 700,000 or more members of the "Fifteen Recognized Standard Railroad Labor Organizations" that own it and for which it serves as their "official Washington weekly newspaper." Edited by Edward Keating, a one-time member of Congress, *Labor* is written by a highly competent staff of experts on Washington affairs and on railroad labor problems. *Labor* carries little feature material, but some of its exposés of corruption in government and of questionable corporate practices have been widely quoted.

During election campaigns, *Labor* prints numerous special editions for distribution in states where candidates endorsed by the railroad brotherhoods are running for office. The circulation of these special editions has run into hundreds of thousands, and *Labor's* influence as a mobilizing force to get out the brotherhood's vote has long been recognized by public officials and office seekers.

The intense interest of labor papers in political affairs appeared directly threatened in 1947 with the passage of the Taft-Hartley Act. Section 301 of that unpopular legislation provided that expenditures, as well as contributions, by labor organizations "in connection with" primaries and elections of candidates for federal office would be considered illegal. The question at once arose whether a labor paper's endorsement of a candidate for such office would not be an illegal "expenditure," since the publication costs of the overwhelming majority of national labor papers and magazines are borne by the unions whose names they bear.

The issue came up for a test in the courts during the summer of 1947, when Philip Murray wrote a *CIO News* front-page endorsement of Edward A. Garmatz, a candidate for Congress in a special election in Baltimore. Copies of the *CIO News* were especially circulated in Garmatz's district. Some weeks later, the Department of Justice procured an indictment against both the CIO and Murray on charges of violating the Taft-Hartley Law. In the courts, the CIO argued that the particular section, at least, of Taft-Hartley was unconstitutional because of its obvious limitation upon freedom of speech and press, as the law was deemed to apply to labor papers. The U.S. Supreme Court, however, held during its 1947–48 term (*U.S. vs. CIO and Philip Murray*) that endorsement of a candidate for federal office in the columns of a labor paper, even when the publication is substantially subsidized by the publishing union, does not constitute a political expenditure within the meaning of the law. Thus, although assuring political freedom to the columns of the labor press, the Court did not act on the constitutionality of the particular section of the Taft-Hartley Act.

National and Local Union Press

The publications of the national AFL, the CIO and the brotherhoods are perhaps best known to the general public, but the paper best known to any single unionist is that of his own organization. These national union organs vary widely in format, quality, and general interest, but since they are in most cases distributed to each member as one of the union's services, they achieve tremendous circulation. Relating directly to events and problems of the worker's own industry and organization, they are carefully read.

Such publications as *The Machinist* (International Ass'n of Machinists); *Steel Labor; The United Automobile Worker; Trainman News* (Bro. of Railroad Trainmen); the *Rubber Worker;* the *Mine Workers Journal;* the *International Teamster; The Advance* (the Amalgamated Clothing Workers); *Justice* (International Ladies' Garment Workers' Union); the *Fur Worker;* and the *Despatcher* (International Longshoremen's and Warehousemen's Union)—to name but a few—offer widely disparate types of news and editorial judgments. All of them, however, compel the interest of readers, through skillful writing, good makeup, or stimulating expression of opinions. Some of these, like the *Mine Workers Journal* and the *International Teamster,* clearly reflect the by no means reticent attitudes of John Lewis and Dan Tobin. Some, like the CIO *Oil Worker* or the magazines of many of the brotherhoods, are almost exclusively devoted to news of the union and the industry. Others, like the *Despatcher* and *The United Automobile Worker,* give a larger proportion of space to national and world news, although obviously there is a deep abyss between the interpretations to be found in the papers of the unions headed by Harry Bridges and Walter Reuther.

The third general category is the local labor press: the regional papers —state, county, and local—and the usually more informal publications of individual locals. Ordinarily, the local labor paper is the official organ of the central AFL or CIO body in the community, county, or state. It advances the program of that body; carries news and notices of the central council and its affiliated local unions; and dabbles, in varying degrees, with legislative and political news of the community it serves.

Lacking the solid financing or the assured subscription-through-dues readership of the national union papers, most local labor papers must devote a substantial portion of their space to paid advertising. Even with the income thus derived, few local papers have sufficient funds to provide large enough staffs to fulfill the potential role that can be envisioned for a community liberal-labor publication, particularly in the growing number of "one-paper cities." With the editor often compelled to serve as reporter, advertising salesman, printing foreman, union organizer, and publicity man, the paper may understandably suffer from lack of careful attention to detail or the development of a good story into a real community issue.

Nevertheless, many local labor papers maintain high standards and produce editions that are influential and well-read. Among these are: the *Colorado Labor Advocate;* the *Michigan CIO News;* the *Wisconsin*

CIO News, the *Cleveland Union Leader;* the *Cleveland Citizen;* and *Kenosha* (Wisconsin) *Labor* (one of the few joint CIO-AFL publishing enterprises in the country).

The local labor paper is supplemented by hundreds of local union bulletins. Sometimes these bulletins are printed newspapers, or special editions of the national organization's paper. The *United Auto Worker,* for instance, publishes many such editions. More often, they are mimeographed bulletins of news, announcements, gossip, and jokes, all devoted to the arena of a single factory or shop. Usually edited by amateur talent, the local bulletins frequently take the shape of informal news letters. But if they are nonprofessional in appearance or writing style, they have a devoted reading public because the stories and quips are about the people they know. Their importance should not be minimized. Indeed, as a national magazine recently pointed out, smart corporation personnel managers read the columns of the local shop papers with careful attention for clues to developing grievances, intra-union politics, probable contract demands, and other matters of interest not only to the union but to the men who must work with it across the conference table.

Labor Press Services

A number of special services provide a national interchange of news, picture, cartoon, and editorial copy to the labor press. The *AFL Weekly News Service* contains one or two full-size pages of news and editorial clip-sheet material; its product is used principally by AFL and railroad brotherhood papers. The *CIO Union News Service* has for many years fulfilled a similar function for its affiliated press. Two cooperative agencies, Labor Press Association and the Federated Press, neither of them formally attached to either the CIO or AFL, sell five-times-a-week news and picture releases to the labor papers, and their product is widely used. Some government agencies, among them the Department of Labor, also send regular weekly releases to labor paper editors.

Through the medium of the labor news services and through reprints of important feature material from such papers as the *CIO News* and the brotherhoods' *Labor,* policy statements and attitudes of the national organizations filter through most of the labor union press.

The Editorial End

The labor paper editor thus becomes an important factor in the machinery of the American labor movement, for he administers one of the major channels of communication between the leadership and the membership. To fill its editorial positions, the labor organizations have in recent years turned increasingly to the ranks of professional journalism. This trend marks a considerable change from the past; twenty or thirty years ago, the editor of the union's official paper was likely to be a deserving brother, an ambitious local secretary, or a veteran organizer relieved of the more arduous physical tasks. The product of their editorial activity was more likely than not to be too heavily written, too long, and too ardently subjective.

The postdepression upsurge of the labor press brought an influx of experienced newspapermen into the labor publishing field. The change is easy to explain. The growth of unionism in the 1930's, accompanied by the CIO's challenge to the mass production industries, obviously called for modernized union public relations programs. A by-product of the New Deal's acceleration of union activity was the creation of a corps of news reporters throughout the country whose assignment was labor. In the decade after World War I, the labor assignment on all but a handful of daily papers had been haphazard and generally unrewarding. During the 1930's, newspapers found that union activity required the same sort of knowledgeful reporting as business, the courts or the state house; labor reporting acquired status. In addition, the formation of the American Newspaper Guild for the first time brought the meaning and philosophy of organized labor to thousands of newspaper employees. Thus, happily, skilled talent was available to the labor press at the time it was most needed, and the new generation of labor editors quickly discarded the somewhat encrusted traditions of the past in their effort to bring labor's new millions a clear comprehension of the issues in their union's fight for survival and advancement.

In most national unions, the editor is also the public relations director and he takes his place on the special advisory staff of the union's elected leadership, along with the lawyer, the research economist and the education director. The editor-publicity director must have a deep reservoir of knowledge about his union and his industry, for he is the person who will have most frequent contact with reporters, magazines writers, radio people, and other information seekers.

In some unions that have further enlarged their publicity departments, the managing editor of the official publication serves under the publicity director, who supervises not only the paper but the various other aspects of public relations work. Few organizations, however, have the resources for so elaborate a staff. Thus, on both the national and local levels, the editor must be a Jack-of-all-trades who prays for the time or energy to handle any one of his jobs as well as it should be done. Many unions have hired editors of high reputation, expecting them to produce miracles of journalism and public relations on a one-man basis, without the assistance or funds necessary to realize the organization's hope for a revolution in its public relations.

Every labor editor has been approached by eager youngsters fresh from college or from the basic training of the newspaper city room who wish to "get into" labor journalism. But with limited budgets and staff, it is not easy to find methods to place job applicants. Few "apprentice-ship" positions are available, and the landing of a labor press job is usually a matter of personal qualifications, contacts, and a generous dose of luck. Like other phases of professional work in and for the labor movement, the available positions are few in relation to the size and influence of the organizations. Much more than business, labor in America still relies heavily on happenstance for filling staff positions; it has not yet developed formalized methods for bringing up talented young people through its staff ranks.

The labor press compares favorably in readability, journalistic ap-proach, and attractive typography with many other classes of institu-tional publications. But the forward-looking labor editor may easily be dismayed when he compares his publication with the most carefully edited and highly groomed products of the commercial newspaper and magazine publishing industries. He is concerned with the growing abyss between the methods available to organized labor for reaching its members and the public with labor's program and philosophy, and the tremendous expense of fully utilizing new communications media now available to the corporations. Through its own publications, the labor union talks to its members for only a few minutes—at most, in the case of the bigger magazines, an hour or two each week, or each month. The daily newspapers, with their features, comics, sports—and often hostile news and editorial columns—command a much greater portion of his reading time. The union member tunes in his radio to a continuous round of commercial programs, which if they do not openly offer corporation progaganda, nevertheless pay tribute to the "success story" of the corporate sponsor. He hears a group of news analysts and com-mentators whose views, in sum total, are little less opposed to the thinking of organized labor than are those of the hostile newspaper columnists and editorial writers. Against this mass of programming, the occasional labor broadcast, either network or local, and the small handful of labor-owned FM stations provide a very feeble counterbalance. Now there is television, with its even greater impact on the individual. The number of television broadcasters may of electronic necessity be smaller than in either AM or FM radio. The investment necessary to place a transmitter on the air has, to the present at least, limited station licenses to wealthy corporations, and the cost of buying time on television far exceeds that of radio. Around the corner lie facsimile and other forms of transmission, which threaten to reorganize the methods through which Americans receive their news and opinions.

One cannot see how labor will be able to find financial resources sufficient to utilize these new media as they should and could be used to help the cause of unionism and of progressive, individualized thinking about our national problems. For several decades, workers and their union leaders have discussed the possibility of a national daily newspaper owned by labor and expressing its viewpoints. But the desire and the hope have always foundered on the difficult problem of financing and distribution.

The labor press has partially met the challenge. It has improved its contents, its appearance, and its circulation far above the levels of two decades ago. Copy by copy, it can stand comparison with the average daily or institutional publication in this country. It has something to say; it says it vigorously; it has the loyalty of its readers; it has been of vital assistance to labor's dramatic growth and development. So long as the general press continues to misjudge public opinion and public thinking, there will be a sizeable role for the labor press to fill.

To the men and women who staff that press, and to others who will join its ranks, the labor press offers a challenge to preserve the tradition of free, combative journalism; to use their energies and talents to build a better America; and to help search for new formulas to translate the freedoms of the press into the new methods of communication that are now wielding so great an influence on the American scene.

HENRY C. FLEISHER

Chapter 15

Reading matter for
15 million unionists

THE APPEARANCE IN THE 1820's OF THE *Mechanics Free Press,* OFFICIAL organ of the first Philadelphia central labor body, foreshadowed the development in this country of a journalistic phenomenon of considerable proportions, which by virtue of its extent and of its trade union rather than political inspiration, is uniquely American.

Almost every one of the 107 AFL, 33 CIO and 69 independent national and international unions in this country has its own publication, magazine, or tabloid, weekly or monthly. This does not take into account the numerous publications of local unions, joint boards, and other subsidiary bodies.

The extent of the American trade union press can be accounted for partly by the American talent for the lavish gesture that embellishes our trade union conventions with brass bands, banquets, and elaborate staging. More important, however, the trade union press, which by 1840 already comprised no less than 60 publications, has grown in response to the exigencies created for union leadership by the historical lack of class-consciousness and the hostile environment responsible for much of the characteristic pattern of American trade unions. Finally, in the last decade, there has been the need to utilize every means of contact and influence to assimilate the millions of newly organized nonunion-thinking men and women. This last circumstance accounts for the rise of many new publications and the strengthening of most of the older local labor papers.

With few exceptions, these publications are supported by an allocation from membership dues, and distributed free to each union member. Close to 15 million people are handed or mailed a labor paper, probably at least glance at it, possibly even read its contents carefully, and may indeed pass it along to friends and relatives. However, no one who has seen bundles of union papers gathering dust on the shelves of local meeting halls will want to measure the influence of the labor press by the circulation figures alone. But even at a conservative estimate, in terms of total number of publications, budget, feet of copy, and circulation, it reflects a substantial segment of public opinion and concern.

"The Same Stuff They Talk about at Union Meetings"

What's in the labor press? Back in the 1930's, when trade unions hung out their shingles on countless Main Streets for the first time, I went to a little town in Pennsylvania to write a story on a shirt-workers' organizing campaign. Girls and women drifted into the union hall after work, chatting in little groups as they waited for the meeting to start. At the front of the room, some of the active local leaders conversed earnestly with the speaker from the national office. Others fussed with the arrangements for the meeting, setting up the water and glass for the speakers' table, or busily untying the strings from large bundles of *The Advance* and distributing copies to the early arrivals. As the papers were handed around, the girls in a group near me interrupted their talk and looked up to see what was going on. "What's that?" asked a bobby-sox-aged worker as she was given her copy.

"The union paper. Take it home and read it," she was advised.

"What's in it?" asked the youngster.

"Oh, you know," another girl explained, "preachin'. The same stuff like they talk about at the meetings."

It would be hard to devise a more accurate description of what's in the labor press or a more succinct statement of the John R. Commons documentary approach to the study of the labor movement.

This young shirt worker's impression of what's in a union paper is borne out by a somewhat more scientific analysis of subject matter, arrived at with the aid of a ruler, a representative sample of union publications, and some arithmetic. The result of this analysis is presented in the table below, which attempts to give some idea of what is contained in a number of labor papers in certain categories of news and information. The sample, it should be noted, is arbitrarily, or at least casually selected, but without any intentional bias. It includes the publications of the national CIO and AFL, of national and international unions, and city and state bodies in both camps, as well as the publications of independent unions.

Four issues of each paper, one each for 1946 and 1947, and one each for 1949 and 1950, were measured and averaged in terms of actual printed matter, exclusive of display heads and the like. The figures for the four issues are combined in the table.

In Column I, *News of the Union and the Industry,* we have included all reporting of the daily life of the organization and of the conditions of the trade and industry: news of organizing campaigns, strikes, and negotiations and provisions of contracts; activities of national and local officials, union conventions and elections; news of union good and welfare, educational, and research activities; financial and membership reports; comment on economic trends in the industry; market developments; technological changes; the employment outlook; and special industrial problems facing the union.

Column II, *General Labor News*, covers news of other unions, and the national federations of labor; general labor problems and economics; and general industrial trends and developments—such items as cost of living, information about women workers, child labor, industrial homework, pro- and antilabor sentiment, etc. Separate percentages for domestic and for international and foreign news are shown here.

Column III, *Political News, Legislation, Public Affairs*, covers legislative action and proposals, congressional and state legislative debate and action, news of court decisions and administrative practices affecting legislation; news and editorial comment about the political parties and about the various organizations for political action, *e.g.*, the CIO Political Action Committee; news and editorial comment about elected officials; recommendations of specific political action, and editorial comment on political action in general; news and comment on government policy other than on labor relations, such as foreign policy, veterans, housing, etc.

Column IV, *Education and Information*, records those articles, features, and expanded discussions of economic issues, labor and social problems, and labor history, which may range over some of the subject matter of the other columns but whose approach is neither editorial nor strictly news story.

Column V, *Human Interest*, measures the amount of space devoted to personals about the union members, biographies of retiring workers, obituaries, social activities of locals, and nonlabor news of general human interest.

Column VI, *Entertainment*, includes fiction, comic strips, recipes, beauty culture hints, and children's pages, as well as jokes, maxims, squibs, and "filler."

Column VII measures advertising space.

No statistical table can go very far toward giving a live picture of the contents of a newspaper. Perhaps a glance at typical headlines and titles will add for the reader a little of the actual flavor. Consider, for example, the headlines of the July '46 issue of the *CIO News* and of *The Federationist*.

CIO News—July 1946. It was a Nice War for Congressman May . . . World Mourns Hillman. . . . May Denies Use of Influence. . . . It's Know Who, Not Know How. . . . World Mourns Hillman's Death. . . . PAC Head Was Global

Types of Reading Matter in Selected Trade Union Papers

(Figures represent average percentage of total space per issue)*

Publications	News of the Union and the Industry	General Labor News			Politics, Legislation, Public Affairs	Education and Information	Human Interest	Entertainment	Advertising
		Domestic	International	Total					
[1] Central Labor Union & City Council Pub'ns.	11	18	1	19	12	11	7	10	30
[2] National Labor Federation Publications	15	25	6	31	24	19	3	5	3
[3] Pub'ns. of AFL International Unions	42	11	5	16	14	10	13	3	2
[4] Pub'ns. of CIO International Unions	43	13	3	16	17	6	7	3	8
[5] Pub'ns. of Independent Int'l. Unions	40	11	1	12	12	11	9	7	9

[1] St. Louis Labor Tribune; Chicago Federation News (AFL); Toledo Union Journal; Kansas Labor Journal.

[2] American Federationist; CIO News; Labor (15 Railway Unions); AUA Report.

[3] International Teamster; Journal of the Electrical Workers; Justice (ILGWU); Typographical Journal.

[4] United Automobile Worker; NMU Pilot; Int'l Woodworker; The Advance (ACWA); Steel Labor.

[5] The Carpenter; the United Mine Workers Journal; Machinists Journal.

* Four issues of each paper, one each for 1946, 1947, 1949, and 1950, were measured in terms of inches of printed matter, exclusive of display heads, etc., and averaged.

Citizen.... Tribute from Truman.... America Has Suffered a Great Loss—
Murray.... Passing of a Great Leader—Editorial.... Looking Ahead—Column—
Len DeCaux.... To Remember in November—The Vote on the Wherry
Amendment to the OPA Extension Bill.... It's a Lie—Column—Mary Solow....
Farmed Out to a Flea Circus—Baseball Guild Progress.... Organizing—Column
—Allan Haywood.... To Put It Briefly—Column.... Woodworkers, Furniture
Workers Talk Merger.... Steel Union Wins Long Strike.... Case, A C Strikes
May Spread.... Hoeing Pays off for CIO.... OPA or More Pay—Says UAW.
... Glass Union Will Meet.... AFL at "Work" Says Toledano.... Law Guild
Hits Atty. Gen. Clark.... Report on WFTU—H. C. Fleisher.... Death to
Franco! .... Economic Justice—Southern CIO Drive.... Educators Meet CIO.
... ILO Sea Pay Gains Inadequate—by Seth Levine.... Tomorrow's Citizens—
Feature, Rose Alshuler.... Urges Anti Cancer Law.... Women Face Legal
Booby Trap—Harriet Bouslog.... Picket Line Verses to be Published.... Less
Women in US Industry.... Jim Barry—Comic Strip Page.... Senate Charged
with Gross Irresponsibility on OPA.... Wreckers Still at Work in Senate....
Brotherhood Takes a Beating—Report on FEPC.... Eager-Beaver Brass.... Let
Bosses Pay for Error says CIO.... CIO Protests Vet Firings.... CIO Backed
Men Win in Two Primaries.... Hush-Hush On Housing Probe? .... Gloves
off in Hawaii.... The DuPonts Don't Like It—PAC in Delaware.... The Poll-
Tax Must Die—Editorial.... Washington Guide.... No Time to Lose on Wage
Bill.... Housing in a Hurry! .... Keep Your Eye on Congress....

The Federationist July 1946. Skyrocketing Prices Bear Out AFL Warnings.
... Green Hails President's Veto of OPA Bill.... More Women Workers Than
Before the War.... Josephus Daniel's Paper Says Fight Against Labor Is Losing
Battle.... UNESCO Rejects Bid of WFTU As Exclusive Spokesman for
World Labor.... US Circuit Court Decision in Donelly Case.... Boilermakers
Union Radio Programs.... AF of T Charges NAM Seeks to Control Schools.
... Minn. Milk Drivers Help Veterans.... AFL Members Cooperate against
Europe Famine.... The Future—Editorial Quote—John Winant.... We Back
America—Our Country Is First with Us, Can CIO Say Same—George Meany.
... Communist Dominated WFTU Provides Russia with Global 5th Column;
US Branch is CIO.... Green Blames Congress for Much of Labor's Unrest....
Don't Blame Labor. Are Prices Too High? They Are But Building Unions Are
Not at Fault—Boris Shiskin.... The Communists Move in on French Labor—
Matthew Woll.... Convention Roundups.... W.D. Mahon Retires as Head of
Streetcar Men's Union.... Green Addresses Hatters Convention.... Musicians
Convention Important.... George Meany Addresses California State Fed. Con-
vention.... Building a Modern Union—Report on IBEW—Ed. J. Brown, Pres.
... Jewell of Railway Employees Dept. Retires.... Our Nation's Labor Policy
—Editorial—Wm. Green.... ILO and the United Nations—R.J. Watt.... The
Chemical Workers Union—H.A. Bradley Pres.... Cement Workers—A Young
Lively Union—by W. Shoenberg, Pres.... Freedom—Editorial Quote.... Labor
Men in the News—Column.... What They Say—Column.... Labor in Japan
Today—by J.J. Murphy, AFL Representative.... News of Pattern Makers....
Report on Maine Federation.... Report on Missouri Fed.... Report on Oregon
Fed.... Report on South Dakota Fed.... Report on South Carolina Fed....

Report on Virginia Fed.... Labor News Briefs—Column.... The Movement in Indiana—by C.H. Mullen, Pres. Ind. State Fed.... Junior Union Page.

There are some marked and interesting variations among the individual papers, but the general pattern is sufficiently similar to permit a valid generalization. If a man spends one hour and forty minutes reading his international union paper from cover to cover, and at a steady clip, he covers pretty much the same territory, be he carpenter or clothing cutter. He spends 42 minutes or almost half the time reading about the daily life of his union and conditions of the trade and industry, organizing campaigns, strikes and negotations, provisions of contracts, etc. Fifteen minutes is taken up with news of other unions and general labor problems; fourteen minutes of this hypothetical reading session is spent on legislation, political action and public affairs; nine minutes covers a characteristic feature of trade union publications, the "educational" or "factual" or background articles; ten minutes for human interest items; four minutes for entertaining reading matter, and six minutes of rather dull advertising complete the reader's agenda.

Thus, the emphasis appears to be first on the daily life of the union, second on the general labor movement, and third on legislation and politics.

A story is current about a union delegate to a meeting in Switzerland who sat glumly in his seat while fellow delegates admired the Swiss vistas through a train window. "Take away the scenery," he remarked with a shrug, "and what have you got?"

The scenery of the labor press—the slant and orientation of the news—varies widely. Without some discussion of this scenery, to go along with the tabular analysis of content, you haven't got much.

Aims and Orientations

The trade union paper is essentially a means of communication between the administration and the members. For the worker it is a means of keeping well informed about the trade in which he earns his living and the ways in which his elected union representatives deal with the problems involved in making that living as adequate and secure as possible. For the labor editor, the union paper represents an opportunity to cultivate and enrich the interest of the membership, not only in immediate issues and developments surrounding the job, but also in the wider arena of economic, legislative, and political developments that impinge upon a particular trade. It presents a challenge to widen the concern and solidarity of the membership to a horizon that includes the labor movement as a whole and the total national welfare. This mission is apparent in all of the papers, but the embroidery upon this basic purpose varies from paper to paper with the tradition, the ideology of the union, the characteristics of the membership, and the talent and budget of the editor.

The most apparent variations are of course those stemming from divergent political and economic programs, and the trade union press runs the expected gamut from extreme right to extreme left.

The splits in the labor movement also color the news, explicitly as well as by omission. For example, *Steel Labor* published a history of the union on the occasion of its tenth anniversary. This history recounts the dramatic offer of the Committee for Industrial Organization to aid the Amalgamated Association of Iron and Steel Workers, and describes the campaign at length. The fact is that John L. Lewis was then President of the CIO, and the drive was sparked by an organizing force and by funds supplied, to a great degree, by the United Mine Workers. Yet the name of John L. Lewis is as conspicuously absent from this history as is Trotsky's name from current histories in the Soviet Union.

That the labor movement is split and that trade unions vary widely with respect to political and economic program and tactics are points that need no laboring. A fact less well appreciated by the uninitiated is the extent to which the so-called "right-wing" unions are committed to legislative programs and extensive participation in both politics and public affairs. This is borne out by actual measurements that show that the amount of space devoted by all papers to legislation, political action and public affairs varies only negligibly. This fact seems worth pointing out if only because it is too frequently assumed that the CIO is for political action and concerned with legislation, whereas the AFL has its head buried in the economic sand and ignores the legislative field. The same general uniformity is observable with respect to space devoted to foreign labor news, which again reflects the fact that none of the customary lines can be drawn in describing the concern of American unions with the international labor movement. This is comment not to minimize ideological or tactical differences, but rather to suggest the need for their more accurate definition.

Personality

Back of union program and policies are also membership characteristics and human personalities. The style and the general atmosphere of a labor paper mirror these things too.

One cannot read the *United Automobile Worker* with its provocative headlines proclaiming the union's activity on every front, edited in the streamlined tabloid manner, without visualizing a meeting of this turbulent and dynamic organization, tense and faction-ridden on the one hand, vigorous and resourceful on the other, with every social, economic, and political issue having a legitimate place on the union agenda. Similarly, a glance through the *Federation News*, organ of the

Chicago Federation of Labor, just as inevitably evokes a picture that will be recognized by anyone who has ever attended a typical AFL central labor union meeting, and sat through the halting and undramatically presented reports of trade developments, the dull but detailed accounting for dues spent, the inevitable "good and welfare" hopper, customarily reserved for education, legislation, public affairs, and anything else not strictly "reports from the trades." The *Federation News* is no amateur job as labor papers go. It contains a wealth of news that cannot easily be found elsewhere. It reflects a deep concern for labor's stake in a variety of civic and public issues over and above legislation immediately affecting organized labor; it conveys by implication rather than assertion a deep conviction of the importance and dignity of the organized labor movement. Although its physical makeup and sometimes its writing—until a recent change toward modernization—have been on the dull side, it is a paper that anyone interested in the subject matter of labor might select to read. But it differs from a paper like the *United Automobile Worker* or *Steel Labor* exactly as a typical central labor union meeting differs from an auto workers' convention.

No generalization about AFL and CIO publications is safe. Some AFL papers sound like the CIO, and vice versa. However, on the whole, the CIO publications tend to resemble the late *PM* in style, whereas AFL union publications are more old-fashioned, and retain a flavor reminiscent of the *Workingman's Advocate* and *The Knights of St. Crispin*. The difference lies in a quality of journalism difficult to describe but probably of greater fundamental importance than issues of political or trade union tactics, a quality related to a respect for the intelligence of the individual worker and an old-fashioned faith in education. Some of the newer tabloids have retained something of this quality while utilizing the modern conveniences that characterize the new-model labor press. This development, and the fact that an "old line" AFL magazine like that of the IBEW has successfully adopted a sort of *Life-Time-Fortune* streamlining, promise that effective labor journalism need not be achieved at the expense of these values.

Limitations

Many observers are puzzled because the trade union movement has failed to produce a single publication of outstanding nationwide influence, despite the fact that it supports an enormous number of papers and magazines; and that these, while performing an important service, remain a network of information and policy outlets for individual trade unions. The answer is that in both the magazine and newspaper fields, the important liberal and progressive journals, although enjoying considerable labor support, have been outside the trade union movement in origin and control.

To understand this fact it is necessary to make a distinction between a labor paper and an official trade union organ and to regard the trade union publication as performing a unique and special function and operating within the limitations of this function. Most trade union publications, it must be admitted, are interesting only to those already interested. Very little space is accorded to news of general interest, and too much space is given to local and personal union items. The editor's temptation to crowd in as much serious and meaty stuff as possible does not attract the marginal reader who has only a limited interest in union and public issues.

The fact that an official union organ must constantly plead a cause and seek to influence the thinking of the membership immediately sets a monotonous tone. For the sophisticated reader, this monotony is not relieved by the flat, one-dimensional quality of news about controversial issues. The trade union movement is by its very nature full of inner debate and controversy, little of which boils over into print and then only in the most circumspect fashion. One does not expect to find in the *United Mine Workers Journal* a full-dress debate on the wisdom of Lewis's tactics in the 1946 strike; nor does one look in *The Advance* for a critical examination of the implications of the late Sidney Hillman's activities in the WFTU; nor seek in the *United Automobile Worker* a frank, two-way discussion of the Allis-Chalmers strike—yet these are all highly controversial issues, on which debate rages in every union corridor. This may or may not make for healthier and more unified organizations, but it is certainly not the stuff that makes one look forward eagerly to the next issue of one's union paper—it is not the stuff that builds circulation.

In the last 10 or 15 years, labor news has come to occupy a lot of space in the daily metropolitan press. Major union developments, interest in which extends beyond the membership, find their way into everybody's paper. And when a union leader fires an important policy gun, he releases the news via the metropolitan papers or the radio. By the time his own union paper is off the press with the story, its dramatic impact has already been discounted.

The union paper thus becomes supplementary reading, yet the official organ remains a necessity. There is a huge amount of detailed information that must be available to the membership of a democratic organization. Facts for shop stewards, grievance committee men, and for the membership at large are essential if collective bargaining is to function. It's "the same stuff they talk about at union meetings," but even when the meetings last until very late, there isn't time to say it all.

NORA PIORE

Chapter 16

The union's public relations

TWELVE YEARS AGO, KATHERYN LEWIS TOLD ME, "DADDY DOESN'T CARE what the newspapers say about him as long as they say something."

For years that was the policy of the greatest public relations genius the labor movement has ever known. Hostile newspaper headlines and disapproving radio comment advertised John L. Lewis and his activities. Constant, and frequently malicious, overstatement of Lewis' power helped to strengthen Lewis' position, and incidentally the position of all unions. The coal miners' struggles have been and still are convenient symbols around which all mass media—the newspapers, the radio, and the magazines—center their attack against organized labor.

The Nature of the Problem

During the period of organization and growth, union labor benefited from the overstatement of union strength. Eventually, the constant repetition had its effect even on some union members. A surprising number of Americans accepted the fiction that the employees of the nation's great business corporations had suddenly acquired greater power and greater resources than the owners of the corporations.

That fiction was the basic excuse for the Taft-Hartley Act. And that fiction is today the Number One public relations problem of every international union. The problem of the 200-odd international unions is to break through the symbolized thinking of the American public—the doctors and dentists, the storekeepers and salesmen, the farmers, the housewives, and everyone else outside the labor movement—with the true story of the aims and accomplishments of organized labor. If we fail, we will be confronted with more repressive legislation—subjecting union members to antimonopoly laws, taxation, and other restrictions.

It is still important to keep the name of the union where people outside the labor movement can see and hear it. But now that everyone knows that unions have arrived, it is even more important that we tell our neighbors the truth about unions, that we let them know that unions are organizations of plain people with American ambitions and American problems, varying each according to the trade or industry or community where its members work.

John L. Lewis realized this in 1947 when he established the United Mine Workers News Bureau to tell the story of the tremendous job of social work being done for coal miners through the Welfare Fund. The International Association of Machinists, the United Auto Workers-CIO, the International Ladies' Garment Workers, the Amalgamated Clothing Workers, and many other internationals were already at work improving their public relations.

Using Press and Radio

Every union develops its own approach to public relations. But the problems are common to all.

If we are going to get our story to our neighbors outside the labor movement, we must aim at the newspapers and the magazines they read, and the radio stations they listen to. If we had unlimited funds, we could advertise, but we can never expect to compete with management in this field. That means we must aim our story at the news and feature columns and the special events broadcasts.

A union's first step in developing good public relations boils down to the contacts its officers make with newspaper and radio reporters. Every responsible and properly functioning daily now has one or more reporters who specialize in labor news. The labor reporters are men and women who make their living by writing what they can find out about union activity in such a way that the editor will accept it for publication. They won't take "eyewash" for facts, but they appreciate help when they get it.

When a reporter comes to the union or calls on the phone, his employer expects him to bring back a story—something interesting that can be printed. If a reporter is on to something the union doesn't want printed, he won't be suppressed because the union officer refuses to talk about it. And, it may often be better to make sure the reporter has the facts straight than to brush him off with a curt "no comment." If no comment can be made, it is best to try to interest the reporter in another story that he can take back as a substitute. If they like the union representative, if they understand what he is trying to do, they will treat him with respect in their stories.

All this is very fine, it may be said, but everyone knows what happens when the editor gets hold of the story. Regardless of their personal predilections in a given instance, the editors also are managers. Their product, the news in their newspapers, is sold as impartial information. The editors have a responsibility to inform their readers, a responsibility that they take more seriously than the editors in any other country in the world. In most countries, remember, labor has its own daily press. Otherwise it gets no favorable mention at all.

A union's chance to get a story in a newspaper or an article in a national magazine reflecting credit on the union and its officers may depend on how active a conscience the editor has. There are ways to stimulate this conscience. If the paper or the magazine is struggling for added circulation—as most papers are—the editor will be especially sensitive to letters to the editor, polite protests, or legitimate requests for attention for union activity.

A union's chance for favorable publicity can be improved by personal contact between union officers and the editor. Most editors have never known a union officer. If a union representative can get acquainted and the editor likes him, the reporter who covers the union office will have a much easier time getting his stories into print.

The problems of dealing with broadcast stations are slightly easier because the broadcasters operate on a public franchise that requires the station to give every group in the community an opportunity to be heard on the air. The Federal Communications Commission has a Blue Book, regulations that are much more binding on the management of a broadcasting station than is the conscience of an editor.

A union's public relations program can be shaped to make it easier for both the editor and the broadcaster. I believe it is fair to assume that the newspapers are almost never going to applaud unions in their bargaining efforts with management. Not, at least, until unions publish their own dailies. As long as newspapers are supported by the advertising of business corporations, the newspapers are always going to favor the employer in any showdown. Furthermore, the management of almost every newspaper is in almost constant negotiations with one or another of the Printing Trades Unions or the Newspaper Guild, representing the newspaper's employees. No newspaper that I know of takes a position editorially that would raise the cost of its own operation. That's one reason why newspapers rarely favor higher wages.

This is the basic fact of life in the operation of any union public relations department. An impartial statement of union demands may be published in a newspaper. But when negotiations approach a climax, the newspaper will almost always be found on the side of the employer. If the union wants to argue its case before the public at that point, it should buy advertising space or radio time in which to tell its own story.

However, there are many union activities carried on between negotiations that a newspaper editor *can* applaud and support. And by publicizing these subsidiary activities, a union can get favorable attention in most newspapers. Labor's political activity, for example, has been carefully covered in scores of big dailies and by the network commentators. If anything, the newspapers have overplayed the political strength of unions just as they overplayed labor's economic strength 12 and 15 years ago. Certainly, if labor's political funds were only half as large as the newspaper reports, the Taft-Hartley Act would have been repealed long ago.

There are a score of other activities going on every day in most organizations that, if publicized, will help to show the union in its role as an American organization of American working people whose hopes and aspirations are no different from and no less admirable than those of any other group in the community.

Here are a few suggestions for legitimate news stories that will interest most editors, recently prepared by the International Association of Machinists for the guidance of its local publicity chairmen:

Reports of successful contract negotiations.

Reports of union activity to encourage the sale of products made under union contract.

Reports of union interest and activities supporting good government, registration drives, official endorsement of candidates.

Reports showing the skill and inventiveness of union members.

Reports of employment (or unemployment) conditions and job openings.

Reports showing participation of the union in community projects and drives.

Reports of women's activities in the union, especially women officers and shop stewards.

Reports on visits of officers from International Union headquarters.

Reports on the presentation of veterans badges or other honors to union members.

Any union that takes the trouble to let the newspapers and the radio stations know in advance of its activities will find it possible to get news of the union in the papers and on the air. Any union that takes this trouble to acquaint its neighbors with the many contributions it makes to community life, month after month, is going to have a lot more public support when negotiations become difficult and the headlines herald a strike vote.

If some groups in our country mistrust unions and union officers, it is because they know only a fraction of what the unions are doing, only the part that has been reported in the headlines just before and during the strikes. By and large, that shortcoming in union public relations is as much the fault of union officers as of anyone else.

As many union leaders have learned, it isn't only what you do that counts, but what people *think* you're doing. That's what every union's public relations director should be working on.

GORDON H. COLE

Chapter 17

The union press—an evaluation

AS OLD AS THE UNION MOVEMENT ITSELF, THE LABOR PRESS EXPANDED to a very great extent in the last two decades, following the movement's own phenomenal expansion. How well has the labor press utilized its enhanced opportunity for service? How much influence has it exercised within and outside of the labor movement? Has it been a contributing force in the intellectual expansion of the union movement, of its members and of the environment in which the union members live?

There are no statistically measurable answers to these questions, but convincing particulars have been presented in several preceding chapters of this part of *The House of Labor*. They are to the effect that, by and large, the labor press has done well.

The studies are of particular interest in the light of an inquiry along similar, if less ambitious lines, made in 1926. In that instance, the editors of 25 leading trade union publications were asked to answer a number of questions regarding the labor press: the best means of making it most effective; a desirable formula for content; an indication of the particular groups among the members at which the labor press is to aim (the most active members, the interested rank and file, families of members); and whether free discussion of policy, strategies, and basic aims is to be allowed, encouraged, or restrained.[1]

An Inquiry 25 Years Ago

The problems that concerned labor editors in 1926 have not, it appears, been altogether solved yet, as the following quotations from that inquiry seem to show. What did the editors in 1926 want the union press to be?

---

[1] The inquiry was conducted by Phil E. Ziegler, then Editor of the *Railway Clerk* (Brotherhood of Railway and Steamship Clerks), the results edited by Professor Willard E. Atkins of New York University, and published in *American Labor Dynamics* by J. B. S. Hardman and Associates (New York: Harcourt Brace, 1928; out of print).

As to contents, all but three favored the inclusion of "outside" matter in official publications, and these pleaded not enough space. Agreement was almost uniform that the order of importance was: (1) a discussion of the general labor-movement problems; (2) history and educational matters; (3) fiction; (4) popular science. Albert F. Coyle of the *Locomotive Engineers' Journal* voted against the inclusion of fiction with the comment, "The *Saturday Evening Post* is too cheap. I do print real stories of railroad experience, which are often more romantic and thrilling than fiction."

Cartoons, art pictures, and just amusing matter were favored in the order named with the answers running thus: cartoons, "yes"; art pictures, "especially for the frontispiece"; just amusing matter, "a very little, usable as filler material. Like spice, a little goes a long way."

On the matter of appearance, eight voted for an illustrated cover, one for illustrations on special occasions only, and six answered that their cover design was standardized. The question whether a standardized appearance was desirable led to a split of eight in the affirmative and seven in the negative, the reason given by two for the affirmative being that the publication should be readily recognized. All but one saw no obstacle to using good paper even if the paper looked rich. "Good paper by all means," and "but one thing restrains us from using the best paper—the price," were characteristic comments.

In those days the discussions on improving the union press by way of including illustrations centered on whether the cover or the front page should be so adorned. Labor cartoons were rare things and a luxury, even though such artists of a labor outlook as Art Young and John Baer managed to live on an apple a day. But apples had to be bought, and the engraver's cuts had to be paid for.

The replies to the question as to what might be done to make the labor press more effective and vigorous indicated considerable breadth and diversity of approach on the part of the editors:

Trouble is less with the papers than with the intelligence of the rank-and-file readers. The majority of editors are trying to reach boobs and dumbbells in the unions, and this necessitates catering to that kind of taste and mentality. Labor editors should deliberately aim to reach the intelligent minority. Even though the articles go over the heads of the majority, perhaps an occasional idea will swoop low enough to make an impression of some kind. But it is the intelligent minority who formulate policies. Appeal to them.—Cedric Long, *Home Cooperator*.

The making of a magazine is a highly technical job. It should be considered such and technical talent should be secured. We believe that education of our members in labor colleges is destined to raise the standard of journalism.—G.M. Bugniazet, *International Brotherhood of Electrical Workers*.

Carry more and better illustrations and photographs and print more readable and interesting articles on subjects not strictly pertaining to organization work. In other words, a more mixed diet.—F. Finnran, *Railway Maintenance of Way Employees' Journal*.

By developing a desire for greater responsibility for and control over the conduct of industry by the workers, (1) by the use of the labor press as an educational medium to that end; (2) by the encouragement of workers' education: educating the workers to be more political- and social-minded; (3) by the discussion of the effects of political, economic and social forces upon the lives and problems of the workers.—Phil E. Ziegler, *The Railway Clerk.*

I would say that what we need most of all is freedom from official dictation, more trained journalists on the job, and closer contacts with the rank and file on the part of labor editors. It might also be a good idea for union papers to give their printing to union institutions.—Oscar Ameringer, *The Illinois Miner.*

I would favor the coordinating and unifying effort along general educational lines—the propagation of trade union principles and ideals—the discussion of live economic and political subjects, etc. Such coordination could be made most effective through the medium of a central directing agency developed on the plan of the service at present maintained by our weekly newspaper *Labor* for the official publications of the different railroad labor organizations.—John F. McNamee, *Journal of Brotherhood of Locomotive Engineers and Fireman.*

More intensive study of national economics—less stress upon group interest or advantages.—Thomas F. Flaherty, *The Union Postal Clerk.*

The most badly needed material in the American labor press is brains, coupled with hard editorial work. The secretary of one of our largest international unions, who also edits its journal, told me that he spent four to seven hours monthly on the job, leaving the work largely to a stenographer. Secondly, our labor press is provincial; it needs a world outlook and a realization of the economic unity of the workers in every land.—Albert F. Coyle, *Brotherhood of Locomotive Engineers' Journal.*

Labor papers should be labor papers—not political or Communist propaganda sheets. Trade union publications should confine themselves to trade union matters and not waste space on outside "isms."—Ellis Searles, *United Mine Workers' Journal.*

A more liberal policy toward new ideas and forms of unionism is necessary to greater interest in labor organizations. Too much dry rot seems to prevail, due to set and inflexible policies.—Justus Ebert, *The Lithographers' Journal.*

I have studied the policy of labor publications in their effort to become of more value to our readers. A few of these stick so closely to purely organization subjects that their readers get but little idea of what is going on in the general trade union movement, and less concerning general public policies which affect the workers' standard of living. On the other hand there are one or two who reach the other extreme, and seemingly discuss questions of public policy or general problems affecting the workers as a whole, instead of devoting much attention to the immediate interests of their own membership. My own opinion is that there is a sensible medium between these two extremes. Members must be kept interested in the general questions affecting the welfare of their own organization. They must be kept informed as to what is happening within their own group. As no organization can live by itself satisfactorily, it is also necessary that the membership should be kept informed concerning general policies and movements affecting trade unionism as a whole.—John P. Frey, *International Moulders' Journal.*

I used to believe that labor journalism might be a great factor in building up the labor movement. I still believe that with all its limitations it is a factor of importance. Nevertheless, rather more definitely than ever I am of the opinion that we cannot expect labor journalism to arise under present conditions in sufficient force to be a principal factor in arousing and educating a more militant labor movement. Rather we must expect that a more intelligent and vigorous labor movement will establish a better labor press.—Norman Thomas, *New York Leader.*

Progress In Appearance and Content.

What is the state of labor's fourth estate now, 25 years later?

The content of the labor press surely is no longer what it used to be.

The review of a number of representative union journals, by Nora Piore in Chapter 15, answers the question: what is in the union press? *The union publication is an extended, written replica of the local union meeting.* Thus, even as the latter has tended in recent years to be "diversified," enriched with "human interest," so the union journal has accordingly developed similar diversifying features. There is the columnist as guest speaker; the comic strip as the light entertainment portion of the local gathering; the education page and the woman's page for the similar phases in the organization's life. Where, on the other hand, the union itself does not engage in any "frills," does not go in for education, culture, entertainment, and other union-streamlining devices, the union publication holds fast to the traditional content.

Hence, the UAW-CIO's modernity is reflected in its monthly *Ammunition,* a richly imaginative publication as to execution, yet soundly feet-on-the-ground in so far as policy orientation is concerned. Again, the tightly governed International Brotherhood of Teamsters publishes a monthly journal that is largely a sequence of monologues of the union president's opinions—lively and often vital and pugnacious, since that is the particular officer's personality.

The central journal of the AFL appears as the mouthpiece of those who have arrived: comfortable looking, well poised, and self-assured in tone, in content selection, and in general treatment of the world's evils—of which there are but few: the evil that is Russia, the surviving open-shop industrialists, and intransigent congressmen. In turn, the CIO's chief publication comes attired in work clothes, sleeves rolled up, no holds barred, all set to go and well aware that the going is likely to be rough.

There has been notable improvement in the labor press in point of typography, layout, and illustration. Regarding the last, the national labor union press, operating under sufficient and ready budgets, has been more fortunate than the local union press, which is obliged to live on limited and rather uncertain revenue. In both groups, the writing is far better than that found in most labor papers in the 'twenties, and the editorial manner is no longer studiously cultivated to make reading rather tough. The old practice of using labor journal editorial chairs as a dumping ground for superannuated or politically embarrassing v-p's appears to have been discarded, and the proverbial paste-jar-and-scissors, once the foundation of editorial equipment, have been reduced to the status of mere auxiliary tools.

The observation of Mr. Norman Thomas in the 1926 inquiry proved correct. The labor press, if any unit tried it, did not succeed in invigorating the union movement. It took the dog to wag the tail, not the other way 'round. If the union journals today, in most instances, are assertive, ambitious, and free of inferiority complex, that is due to the present-day vigorous state of the unions.

How strong is the influence of the labor press upon the members?

Henry C. Fleisher seems to think on the subject in positive terms. Nora Piore, with considerable field experience, is in a more speculative mood, but the consensus of opinion seems to be that the union press carries considerable weight with its readers. It stands to reason that it does in so far as the activist minority is concerned. Confirmation of fitness to be influential comes from an "outside" observer.

Martin Dodge, of Dodge & Mugridge, labor and public relations counsels, and publisher of *DM Digest—Gist of the Labor, Leftwing and Group Press*, compares the labor press favorably with the multitude of company house organs. There are about six thousand of the latter, with a circulation of 49,000,000 copies monthly. In an article, "Labor's Fourth Estate," which appeared in *Personnel*, January 1949, Mr. Dodge wrote

industry can ... benefit from a study of labor's journalistic techniques. . . . The labor press is the union man's advocate. . . . Blessed with a singleness of purpose, the labor press never leaves the reader in doubt as to where it stands. . . . The labor press talks the workingman's case in language that sends no one to the dictionary and puts no one to sleep. . . . The whole gamut of gripes, aspirations, and delusions that labor harbors. . . are all spelled out in the labor press.

A study of the content of 100 labor papers appearing in August 1948, made by Mr. Dodge and published in *DM Digest* on October 11th of the same year, showed the following topical space consumption: political issues, 25 per cent; economic issues, including collective bargaining negotiations and settlements, 23 per cent; internal union affairs and interunion matters, including educational and inspirational items, 22 per cent; "frivolous" matters or subjects in the lighter vein, covering cartoons, humor, household tips, and the like, 30 per cent. Mr. Dodge concludes:

...the labor press today deals most frequently with larger issues, with the relationship of trade unionism to society.... Ten per cent of our total population—15,000,000 union members—are exposed regularly to the labor press. No other comparable group has such a vital and persistent medium.

The Local or City vs. the National Journals

In point of appearance, and presumably, general comfort and security of living, the national union publications seem to have profited most by the general progress of the union movement, but the local or city union publications are making a more significant showing. With exceptions on both ends of the comparison, the city union journals are making a more effective bid for reader interest and attention. This progress is due not to editorial prowess but to the different circumstances attending the production of the respective group publications:

(1) The local publications are, in most instances, published weekly and in newspaper form, and produced overnight; the publications of the national unions, on the other hand, are mostly monthlies, and many appear in magazine form, which is slow in production. This difference enables the local publications to come to lively grips with current issues and to avoid the more general, ponderous editorial rather than newsy way of presentation, which is almost unavoidable in the less frequent and slowly produced national publications. Seemingly in recognition of this disadvantage, two important and politically-minded unions, the Brotherhood of Railroad Trainmen and the International Association of Machinists, recently began to issue also weekly journals, in tabloid newspaper form—both done in good, lively style and with a vigorous approach to immediate issues. Also, the new international unions, CIO mostly, are not magazine-minded; they publish what amounts to newspapers.

(2) The local publications serve readers in a limited area, and hence they apply themselves to issues of immediate concern to the readers who live and are active in the community. The writers thus are in a better position than the national monthlies to influence their readers' thinking and hence action on economic and political issues.

(3) Distant from and not directly under the control of the national unions, the city publications are in a position, assuming that their editors and managers are willing and able, to keep to a minimum presidential "statements" and "addresses" and other products of ghosted loquacity, and thus enliven and diversify contents.

In part because of these advantages, a number of local or area organizations have been producing labor papers of increasing merit.

Dissenting Opinions In the Union Press

A standard gripe in the union press ever since its inception has been that the "kept press," that is, the commercial newspapers and magazines, is closed to dissenting labor opinion. Perhaps the "kept" appellation was not an ideal choice of description, for the unions, too, "keep" their papers even though none too comfortably. That, at any rate, has been the charge.

How has the union press itself stood up on this issue? How much freedom to differ does a union journal allow the members of the organization with regard to officers' behavior and to contention for participation in policy making?

The rather touchy issue of free expression of dissenting opinion regarding policy, strategy, and basic aims was pressed in the 1926 inquiry referred to early in this chapter: was there to be free discussion? It brought affirmation from all but one. However, there were qualifications, such as:

Yes, within certain limits; but even this is not possible as all such are considered internal questions with us.—Justus Ebert, *The Lithographers' Journal*.

Some restriction is desirable. Many members are not well enough informed to discuss important matters.—F. Finnran, *Railway Maintenance of Way Employees' Journal*.

Depends on the views.—F.H. Pease, *The Railway Conductor*.

It limits its contents to news and matters directly connected with the coal industry and the miner's union. . . . It does not fool with politics, socialism, or any other outside subject.—Ellis Searles, *United Mine Workers' Journal*.

The attitudes of the union press have not undergone much change on this score, except perhaps that the *United Mine Workers' Journal* itself, and other labor journals have taken to considerable "fooling" with "politics, socialism, or any other outside subject." However, the issue of freedom to dissent does not appear to be of the same urgency as of old. Judging by appearances, the national union press has either not been faced with the problem at all, or it merely has not encouraged the practice of publishing discussion matter on issues concerning internal union matters of a possibly divisive character. To assume the former is rather a strain upon credulity.

The reasoning of prevailing union leadership—in enough instances to constitute a majority in the field—is not friendly toward airing in public any division of opinion in their unions or, for that matter, of any controversial material. Most union presidents have come up the hard way, having battled for union, then for recognition by employers, then for office in the union. They made sacrifices, perhaps suffered maltreatment. They learned to accept and later to demand "discipline." Even after they have got themselves entrenched in their positions, they remain fearful of "disruption" and "betrayal." And, although they continue to be manipulators and bargainers, and they are also, most of the time, preachers, and pontificators of unquestioned authority, they cannot see themselves engaged in the free intellectual give-and-take of discussion without calling upon the shibboleths and myths of authority, and the faith and sacred cows of the rights of leadership. Their frame of mind determines the ways of the union press.

Be that as it may, freedom to express dissenting opinion in matters of basic union policy is not an evident practice in the labor press. The journals of only very few national unions have in recent times allowed space and equal treatment to candidates opposed to incumbent national officers. Among these journals were the publications of the International Typographical Union, the American Newspaper Guild, and the National Maritime Union, where the writer saw expressions of "dissenting opinions" affecting basic power and policy before the dissenters actually took over. The exceptional freedom in the case of the ITU, with equal space and full rights allotted to opposition candidates, is time-honored, and it bespeaks the organization's generally democratic way of union life. It is less certain that the instance of the ANG can be so classified since the union is relatively young, but it would be strange indeed if a union, whose members' stock-in-trade is words, would ban for whatever reason the right to trade strong, winged words in an honest-to-goodness fight of ideas. As to the NMU, the liberality of the 1948–49 fight of contenders may have been unavoidable since both sides, however uneasily, were in power in the national setup, and there is no clear indication whether or not a "free press" will be the rule in the future.

A measure of inclination to be self-critical on occasion is observed in some of the publications run by or in behalf of groups of unions in various cities. Their lesser rigidity is due to their relative independence from the central union authorities and their greater dependence upon reader support. Their situation is unlike that of the national union journals; the latter are strictly mouthpieces of the national officers, and in matters of possible basic consequence to the "state of the union," traffic is strictly one-way. The local publications, as indicated earlier, depend upon support from circulation and upon revenue from commercial advertising, both of which are obtainable only if the readers are actively concerned about the publication. So these papers have to be interesting, must reflect reader orientation; must, indeed, show a measure of leadership and occasionally display spirit, "free discussion," "self-criticism."

To be sure, the local publications do not advocate rebellion or harbor sedition. They attack directly only when it is reasonably safe to do so. A high officer is likely to be "named" only if his union has no members or local unions in the city where the paper is published. Or—if his union's jurisdictional claim is openly defied. Thus, the miners' president might be castigated in a Minneapolis, Minnesota paper, or the teamsters' chief treated with less than the respectful deference due to royalty in a machinists' publication. Otherwise, just maldoings in general, not maldoers in particular, may be exposed to critical review. Nonetheless, the local publications are a refreshing and often a vitalizing influence.

Two samples of "telling off" will give an idea of what a local paper will do that a national paper will not.

Racine Labor, published by a mixed group of AFL and CIO affiliates, commenting in 1947 on the enactment of the Taft-Hartley law, observed:

The fact [labor's failure to prevent T-H] can be traced in large measure to labor's great blunder in not unionizing the workers it organized. And the blunder is the outgrowth of labor's single-minded devotion in the past to "pure-and-simple" or "business" unionism.... The result of this "business" unionism has been neglect of the economy as a whole and concentration on the narrow interests of particular groups....

The old way is dying.... Labor needs to sweep away the "business" unionism that has outlived its usefulness and embark on a new unionism, a politically-conscious, consumer-conscious, rank-and-file unionism.

The writer blames the unions' failure to make the transition from "business" to "militant" unionism on the deficient use, or the inadequate service of "the two great weapons by which labor wins battles—education and the press."

At about the same time, the AFL *Toledo Union Leader* castigated the "dictatorial guys" of the union movement for their haughty disregard of the little fellows in the unions:

It is the candid opinion of this editor that organized labor should do some housecleaning, and I don't mean the Communist bugaboo, either.... Some of labor's elected officials seem to regard it beneath their dignity to pay attention to any suggestion advanced by any of the lower mass, commonly referred to as "rank and file."

It is about time that a few of these dictatorial guys take stock of their own arrogant and domineering attitude and realize that in organized labor we have a reputation for democratic action to uphold.

The writer ends up on a clear threat:

Education of the rank and file can be carried on against reactionary leadership in our labor movement as well as that on the political field.

Why "Hell" Is or Isn't "Raised" in a Union

Obviously, broad discussion of basic union issues, and still less, specific consideration of current administrative policies, are not exactly invited by those who lead the union press. But would there be justification for believing that this kind of traffic in dissenting opinion is desired by many—but refused the green light? If, on the other hand, there is no call for it—at least none loud enough to be heard—why is there not? Where is that basic, good old American urge to "raise hell"—for "the hell of it," if not for cause? And at that, in the labor movement which is, by definition, an "agin" setup? Is everything so exceedingly fine on the labor Olympus, or is it a case of contentment on the part of unionists who have suddenly realized that "they were nothing yesterday" and "are all today"?

The answer, it is safe to assume, is neither that the millennium has come for the labor millions and left no room for criticism, nor that lily-livered men now tread softly where men of stout heart once marched.

The matter is more complicated than is seen on the surface, as may perhaps be illustrated by the following personal experience.

Way back in the early 'twenties, the writer undertook the responsibility of editing a weekly paper for a large (nonaffiliated) national union, with the stipulated understanding that he would work to develop the publication into a national labor weekly. The editor, generally accorded a free hand in running the publication, specifically asked and was given explicit assurance of an experimental six-months nonintervention, whether by the president or the city or area managers, in his plan to develop a free discussion page, no matter how "provoking" open-mindedness might turn out to be. The pledge was kept. In turn, the editor spared no effort in inviting and encouraging two-way discussion of matters that members had been heatedly talking about in private gatherings and at union meetings. It was slow going from the outset, and the response that was eventually kindled was no more than an exercise in repetition by a bare dozen political partisans who harped on the same points week in and week out. The project died of malnutrition after having been kept alive for a while by injection of synthetic discussion material.

Personal experimentation may not be a safe basis for generalization. There are, or may be, many deterring peculiarities in one situation or another to prevent a justifiable generalization. There were such in the situation cited. However, the following circumstances of union life bear upon the issue under consideration, giving the problem of free discussion and even of democracy in the union movement a peculiar twist. These generalizations are submitted on their respective merits:

(1) Workers join unions not as discussion clubs but as service organizations through which they propose to gain certain advantages: job protection, security, advancement, and the like. To some, not a large number of workers, the union may offer an opportunity for political advancement, that is, for securing standing and other gains as officers, spokesmen, and leaders of men in the organization, and via the latter,

in the community or even in the national political arena. Only gradually—and not by any means to all workers—the union may become a *movement* involving *values*.

(2) Possible occasions for dissatisfaction on the part of members, which may under certain stimulations—singly or in combination with other provocations—lead to opposition and stimulate "raising hell," are:

(a) The union's failure to protect work conditions provided for under union contract, or to improve contractual conditions when they are no longer in keeping with those offered elsewhere in the market, or with those provided by other unions for their members.

(b) Mistreatment or neglect of members by local officers in shop matters or in the local union setup.

(c) A sense of grievance built up by a contender for office or for other preferment who may either exploit a genuine offence by the officers in power, or play up some fancied injustice to build up support for his ambition. Part of the game in this sort of enterprise is to promise advantages to the party of the revolution when it becomes the party of the government. Officers are designated in advance—a shadow cabinet, as it were. Ambitious workers, envious of the progress and comfort of officers in power, are amenable to such urges.

(d) Political line-up by a party group seeking a base for influence. Such a group, however, does not play its hand openly: it usually operates by pursuing various divisive tactics, whether by "adjusting" facts, or playing on emotions, or playing up gripes; or by inflaming ideological stirrings, and sometimes also by subtly exploiting race or color prejudices or other sensitive reactions capable of producing division. Whatever may be the calculated motivations of the leaders of such factions, those who follow them may sincerely believe that they are battling at Armageddon in the cause of some particular "lord."

Significant facts and developments have tended, in recent years, to dull the edge of such appeals to mutiny or civil war, to undercut the sprouting of the seeds of rebellion—and to obviate its first manifestation, the call for open two-way discussion:

(1) Unions, in recent years, have been able to bring home the bacon, with fair regularity and in reasonable quantity, thus depriving most of the "outs" of their basis for effective appeal against the "ins."

(2) The mass-spread of unionism and the many positive contributions that union leaders have been able to make, on behalf of the growing membership, to many community and national causes have raised the prestige of functioning leadership, thus making drives "agin" rather difficult to initiate, and due to "delivery" by unions, even more difficult to sustain.

(3) Also, the high and ever-increasing cost of doing almost anything—

from renting a meeting hall to mimeographing circulars—has made the cost of setting up revolutions virtually prohibitive.

(4) The spread of unionism and the rise of membership from barely two million to seven or eight times that number between 1933 and 1950 have, in fact, opened new opportunities for advancement—officerships, and the like—for perhaps more persons than are in the field seeking such chances. There has been almost a dearth of rebel leaders, willing, fit, and ready to land on the payroll.

(5) The union movement, beginning with 1932 and to date, underwent a transformation from prevailing backsliding conservatism to progressive mobility. This change has come about under the combined effect of the hard sufferings caused by the depression; the sobering lessons of fascism abroad; the Roosevelt influence and that of other liberal forces in and outside government; the bracing labor upheaval at home that led to the rise of the CIO and to the resurgence of organizing energy in the AFL; and finally, the energizing and uplifting spurt given to unionism by the pro-labor legislation of the 'thirties: the Norris-LaGuardia Anti-Injunction and Anti-Yellow Dog Contract Act of 1932; the Wagner Act of 1935 (NLRA); the Fair Labor Standards Act of 1938. This internal revitalization of labor, considered together with the economic circumstances that have since the war's end kept labor fully employed most of the time, on the whole favorably and with but comparatively few, however explosive, breaks in labor-management relations, has brought about a greater than ever cohesion in the ranks of union members and has left little room for internal squabbles and no elbow space for petty rebellion promoters.

(6) The provision of the NLRA giving workers in the plants the right to be represented by "unions of their own choosing," and the availability of a supply from which to choose, no doubt tended, at least in the earlier years of the AFL-CIO schism, to emphasize the unions' service to their members, as a condition of winning and holding affiliation, and thus reduced internal combustion to a minimum.

(7) As to the "parties of the left" and their influence upon union divisions, the course of union events brought about a rather peculiar situation, in consequence of which the Socialists have abandoned all oppositionary orientation and the Communists have become a clearly reactionary influence. Briefly, the interesting about-face evolved in the following way:

(a) Continually declining in general strength ever since their heyday in 1912, the Socialists have exercised no appreciable influence upon the unions. On the whole, the Socialists have not been in sympathy with the idea of fostering opposition groupings around their theoretic views on unionism. In fact, they have become, almost everywhere, staunch supporters of the functioning leadership. This support has become most pronounced in recent years as unions have taken on a more advanced economic and political outlook than ever before, and as the Socialists have ceased to view their own party as a promising tool and as a political rallying center for exclusively Socialist objectives. The Socialists' support of union administrative authorities has grown firmer and indeed altogether uncritical as the latter have opened full-scale war against Communist penetration and maneuvering.

(b) Basically committed, with regard to other organizations, to the strategy of rule or ruin, the Communists had at first all but discarded that strategy—or at least so it seemed—in the years of 1936–1939 and 1941–1945. In the first of the two periods, they worked diligently and cooperatively in the organizing drives of the period, thus proving to be unionists without fear or blemish, and thereby succeeding in gaining impressive influence in many unions and virtual control of some. For a time, during the short interval of the Hitler-Stalin treaty and friendship, the union policy of American Communists turned toward the traditional double dealing and obstruction, and the more relevant tactic of sabotage in war industries, but that was abruptly ended as soon as Hitler broke his alliance with Stalin and marched into Russia. After that, during 1941–1945, the Communists in the unions were superpatriotic, opposed strikes and wage increases and anything that might have retarded the flow of men and matériel to where Russia might need them. And that came to a halt again when war was at an end and peace the Russian way set in. They have since played not the part of reform but of reckless struggle for power.

The exercise in strategic acrobatics did not enhance Communist prestige among unionists, whether among the rank and file or on the various administrative levels. Their attacks on prevailing union policies or criticism of officers have ceased to be viewed as matters of candid difference of opinion. In "their own" unions the Communists, of course, would brook no divided opinion: they were the government, without question. In fact, conservative leaders who did not care to tolerate anything less than complete obedience in their respective bailiwicks found comfort in referring to the Communist behavior as justification for oppressive methods ("Look what these radicals themselves are doing"). Or they merely branded all fair-minded dissenters as Communists and thus effectively silenced them, the Communists themselves having furnished the "reason" for illiberality.

How Relevant Is Democracy to Unionism?

The rather extended detour in this review of the issue of free discussion in the union press was developed here in order to show how it came to pass that the union press, a part of labor institutionalism, which was with so much difficulty erected upon nonconformism as a basic historic American right, has taken on so much of authoritarian character. The need for free traffic for dissent did not cease because an angelic quality has taken hold of all leader and officer mind and practice everywhere and left no occasion for any conflict of views and interests. It is only that the quality of dissent has been demoralized by the practitioners of a deceitful totalitarianism operating in the unions.

It may be asked, though: how important is it that there be a policy of free expression of ideas in the union press? Why not confine all discussion to union meetings? Indeed, a good many union leaders, otherwise of an advanced progressive orientation in matters social and political, see no need for it at all. Their reasoning is that the union is not a theoretic conclave, and that the union press is but an announcing device, an advertising medium, for the purpose of telling the members just what is being done and is to be done. Discussion is divisive, they say, and union action must rest upon unity; and to that end, an information bulletin, not pages of discussion, is all that is needed. Furthermore, open discussion—except inside, in the union hall or at the membership meeting—may involve disclosure of tactical moves and baring of plans, which in cases of developing industrial conflict, would only help the union-opposing employer or an inside union-disrupting clique, possibly one planted by the union's enemies. The argument, of course, is devastatingly similar to the rationalizations of all authoritarian outfits—although those advancing the argument in this instance are on record and in effect dead set against the communist or fascist varieties of enforced silence. At any rate something more workable than town meeting democracy is needed in such giant organizations as Local 600 of the UAW, or Local 3 of the IBEW or Local 48 of the ILGWU, of which the memberships run into many tens of thousands, or in such cases as the NMU, which has no local meetings at all. But something is wanted also in organizations even less populous than these.

A telling argument might be made against a limited, strictly information approach to the union press from the point of view of the union as a cohering, mobilizing, and fighting force. Indeed, no seasoned union organizer will deny that a union member who arrives at a conclusion in the light of open conflict of ideas is a greater asset to the organization; and that the man who is not talked down to, but is treated as a participant in the making of a decision, will be a more willing and devoted executor of the policy decision. Nor can it be denied that if antiunion employers and "internal disruptive elements" are preying upon the organization to discover its weak spots, the proceedings at a local union meeting never are nor can be a secret to them. Exclusion from the union press of basic and many-sided discussion of policy matters and of the state of the union itself—whether by active restraint or by failure to encourage—

does not help to make the union press an instrument for building the union organization into a union movement. One negative by-product of the one-way traffic in ideas is that it makes the union press, in so many instances, uninteresting, and indeed, lifeless. The young woman, in Nora Piore's analysis of the labor press, who characterized its function as "preachin' " was speaking the truth and unwittingly sounding a warning. "Preachin' " that fails to provoke mental participation produces no lasting loyalty. The way to carry conviction is to take the readers along on an excursion of reasoning why—not merely telling them that theirs is to do or die.

Conceivably, certain "human interest" features may attract some members to the publication. But such homey items as recipes for easy-to-prepare or easy-on-the-pocket meals, or charm tips, or poorly engraved line-cuts on poor paper of girls attired in contempt of ILGWU-AFL produced women's wear, cannot impress the readers very much or enduringly. They can get all they want of this kind of material, and in better quality, in the daily tabloid press.

Broader than the *pro domo* argument for discussion of basic issues of union life—as of life generally—is the point that fifteen million people are in unions, and probably no less than two or three million of them are actively engaged in its work. They should be given an opportunity for training in democratic procedure, training likely to be most fruitful since it would come integrated with the day-in, day-out doings of these people. And if it be asserted with a measure of truth that living in the union is living democratically, what argument can there be against the union press presenting to millions of member readers the experience in which only thousands of members had actively participated?

The Scope of the Labor Press

A writer in the lay Catholic magazine, *Commonweal,* some time ago analyzed "the scope of a Catholic paper," suggesting that the aims and objects of that press are "the *enlightenment* [of the readers] by telling ... things which [they] need to know ... or telling or reminding of things which are ... worth knowing; *enrichment,* by wise comment or information about any matters not necessarily formally religious, which play a part in our lives; *confirmation* in our faith and our determination to live by it, by careful ... exposition and explanation of principles or practice under attack. ..."

It is a good "scope": enlightenment, enrichment, confirmation. The union press might inscribe that on its masthead. But although unionism, not unlike religion, is an admixture of a faith, of an art, of a way of life, and of an institutionalism, there is nothing in it that is taken on faith. All things in unionism must prove themselves. Has the labor press proved to be the effective instrumentality of unionism within this "scope"?

The answer may be a matter of opinion. The question is of vitality at a time when unionism, like all facets of America's democratic way of life, are in compelling need of evaluation of values.

There are somewhere between 800 and 900 regularly published labor journals with a readership in excess of 15 million and, if the families of union members are considered potential readers the total is about one-third or better of the nation's adult population. It is a great sphere of operation and the labor press is, potentially, an influential force. Has it been so? A recent comment (1949) in the *St. Louis Post-Dispatch* referred to the labor press as "something for the commercial press to gaze upon in wonderment," and the daily observed that the enormous and expanding union press would not have been in existence or would not be growing "if the commercial press gave full expression to the needs and opinions of millions of trade unionists."

The opinion is not holeproof. For even assuming good will and wherewithal on the part of the entire commercial press to render that service, the "needs" of the union readers are in part beyond the logical scope of general publications, as was stated earlier in these discussions. That the particular needs of the workers as a functional group of the citizenry are real is well illustrated by the fact that while the commercial press is presumably able and willing to give expression to management's needs and opinions, there are in circulation, in the U.S. and Canada, according to a survey by the International Council of Industrial Editors, 4,050 industrial "internals," that is, publications intended to serve employees. These have a total circulation of 32,854,667 (*Personnel*, 1949). "Management spends on its 'fourth estate' $109,000,000 annually to make them [vital tools of communication]—and the investment is paying rich dividends," according to Mr. Steward J. Wolfe, of the Council.[2] Labor union publications probably do not cost more than 10 per cent of that sum.

The fact that there is a labor press and that it is expanding may be taken as proof that it is deemed a necessity, but the extent of its influence must be measured by other yardsticks than circulation. This is particularly important, since in most instances the paper goes to union members automatically, with their union enrollment; it isn't something they go out to get. The effectiveness of the labor journal is not determined by the horizontal spread—the number of members it reaches—but by its *vertical penetration*—how strongly it affects the judgment of those who read it.

The union press is charged with a two-way set of tasks. One is the

---

[2] Mr. Wolfe's circulation figure is lower than that given by Martin Dodge on an earlier page. The "house organs" referred to by Mr. Dodge apparently cover a wider reader area than the "internals."

carrying on of the usual assignments of house organs; the other is serving as battle arsenals in fighting for what the unions are out to achieve.

The aim of *enlightenment* is materialized less in preachment than in competent presentation of facts and argument. Writes a local AFL paper, the *East Bay Labor Journal*:

> The sooner labor papers develop the habit of arming their readers with facts, and not merely trying to kid them into thinking they are more powerful and perfect than they actually are, the sooner will the readers of labor papers go out and beat the blazes out of the readers of the *Wall Street Journal* in economic battles.

A healthy respect for facts, together with a sound interpretation of the meaning of static facts in situational dynamics *would* pay a rich dividend on the intellectual investment.

Enrichment is the second of the three objectives, produced by "wise comment or information about any matters ... which play a part in our lives." Wisdom is a relative thing. It is assumed by some in the field, Victor G. Reuther of the UAW-CIO, for example, that "union literature is read only by people who have a special interest in the subject of the publication, unless it is made as dramatic, as interesting, and as simple to understand as the newspapers and magazine features with which it must compete for attention." That fact but points up the difficulties of the performance, not its impossibilities. It really suggests that the labor journal is to seek to be not a five-and-ten but a department store, to serve variety and quality rather than to chase for the cheap and the easy to feed, the uncomprehending and him "who runs." The latter won't read, no matter what is given him. It is those who read without being lolly-popped who matter out of relation to the "percentage" they represent.

There also are those who would monosyllabilize all labor writing or bank primarily on labor comic strips to impart understanding, to which TWUA Education Director Larry Rogin suggests: "I am sure reading a comic strip doesn't change anybody's attitude."

The third objective, *confirmation*, "the exposition and explanation of principles or practices under attack," can be of cardinal significance if the labor press leaves the easy chair of a house organ to become the fighting instrumentality of an oncoming social force.

J. B. S. HARDMAN

PART FOUR

Union Research and Engineering

Introduction

Union research and engineering

ONLY DURING THE PAST GENERATION did research within American labor unions begin to assume the status of a recognized staff function best performed by professionally trained personnel. During this period, the research department was regarded primarily as a service agency dedicated to the affairs of the union itself. Since the end of World War II, however, labor research has become increasingly involved with the larger common good. It has made a first start toward stepping outside the boundaries of a single union's specific problems; it has attempted to equate its line of vision with the panoramic welfare of the national community. The opening chapter in Part 4 by Broadus Mitchell, "Development of the Activity," traces the historical development of union research.

Today, therefore, union research must be regarded as exhibiting a dual preoccupation. At the same time that it addresses itself to immediate and long-range problems that face a particular union (and the industry of which it forms a part), union research also reflects and acts upon the increasingly apparent obligations that the continued health of the national economy presses upon thoughtful labor organizations.

Solomon Barkin illustrates, in both of his articles, "Expanding Functions of Union Research" and "Preparing a Case for a Government Board," the kinds of research activities which are oriented primarily toward the problems of unions themselves. The article by Lewis Carliner, "Research Facts for Action," and the contribution by William Gomberg, "The Union and Industrial Engineering" give further details about this phase of labor research. On the other hand, the article by Alfred Braunthal, "Union Research and Democracy," and Katherine Ellickson's "Cooperation with Government Agencies" provide an insight into the broader-scaled responsibilities which labor research is now assuming.

Whether the wider activities of labor research departments or their more limited responsibilities are under discussion, it is obvious that these departments will vary greatly in the performance of their duties. The truth of this observation can be easily established when a survey is made of the number of national and international unions, of divergent types, recorded as maintaining research departments. Although in a number of cases the research director also doubles as the educational director, there are, all told, 81 formal research departments among the unions in the United States.

As large and important a union as the United Mine Workers of America reports no research director. But it hires outside services for specific jobs and, in addition, the editor of the *Mine Workers' Journal* sometimes engages in research work. Similarly, several of the large Railroad Brotherhoods do not maintain research departments. According to a research specialist in one of the railroad unions, railway labor research is on the decline rather than on the rise. This is in part due to the formidable experience of the railroad unions in the field of negotiation. It must also be remembered that excellent data have been collected over the years by the ICC and the Railway Mediation Board. These facts are available to the Railroad Brotherhoods. When necessary, however, wage briefs are farmed out by them to expert agencies.

For the 81 national and international unions that maintain some sort of research staff, the following table shows the breakdown by affiliation:

Affiliation	Number of Unions with Research Departments	Number that Combine Research with Education
AFL (107 affiliates)*	39	12
CIO (33 affiliates)*	22	7
Independent (69)*	20	8
	81	27

* Based on *Directory of Labor Unions in the United States*, Bureau of Labor Statistics, June, 1950.

The national offices of the AFL and CIO also maintain research departments. In addition, there are research directors in the AFL Departments of the Building and Construction Trades, the Metal Trades, and the Railway Employees. Four AFL State Federations of Labor and four CIO State Councils report research departments.

It is impossible to estimate from existing sources of information the total number of persons engaged in union research. The limited data here presented are based on material collected by *Fortune* magazine.

The International Association of Machinists (Ind.) employs a staff of 15 people in its research department; the International Brotherhood of Teamsters, Chauffeurs, Warehousemen, and Helpers of America (AFL), 10 research heads (one in each of 10 major cities; New York, the head office, has a staff of four); the Amalgamated Meat Cutters and Butcher Workmen of North America (AFL), three persons; the International Ladies' Garment Workers' Union (AFL), eight persons; the International Brotherhood of Electrical Workers (AFL), one person; the United Hatters, Cap, and Millinery Workers (AFL), two persons; the American Federation of State, County and Municipal Employees (AFL), two persons; the Brotherhood of Railway and Steamship Clerks, Freight Handlers, Express and Station Employes (AFL), one person; the United Automobile, Aircraft and Agricultural Implement Workers of America (CIO), 21 persons; the United Steelworkers of America (CIO), a minimum of five, maximum of nine persons; the Textile Workers Union of America (CIO), 15 persons; the United Rubber, Cork, Linoleum and Plastic Workers of America (CIO), three persons; the Amalgamated Clothing Workers of America (CIO), 13 persons; the United Packinghouse Workers of America (CIO), two persons.

MAURICE F. NEUFELD

Chapter 18

Union research

1. DEVELOPMENT OF THE ACTIVITY

RESEARCH WORK IN THE SERVICE OF LABOR UNIONS IS BY NO MEANS A new development. One hundred and twenty-five years ago, Francis Place, the "radical tailor of Charing Cross," began to collect in a most deliberate fashion all available information on strikes and on prosecution of labor unions in Britain. He formed an extensive labor library, which filled the back room of his shop. He kept two-score clipping books, which have been a mine of information for historical investigators since.

His immediate object in all this was to be able to present a convincing case on behalf of unionists in order to secure the repeal of the so-called "Combination Acts," which since 1799 had made labor organization exceedingly hazardous. The method of Francis Place was not that of declamation, but rather of painstaking preparation of the facts. When witnesses against the Combination Acts were to appear before a parliamentary committee, Place entertained them at his house, analyzed and systematized the information they were prepared to give. Moreover, Place supplied to Joseph Hume, chairman of the committee, a documented understanding of the problem, so that Hume could draw out more revealing answers from those giving testimony. This effort was successful in 1824, when labor unionism received its first great charter of liberties.

Since the time of Place, there have been other distinguished examples of economic and legal research in support of unions. An historic instance in this country was the work of Josephine Goldmark, presented in connection with the legal briefs of Louis Brandeis, in cases testing the constitutionality of labor legislation. Miss Goldmark and Mr. Brandeis fashioned a new kind of brief to be presented to the court. It did not cite legal precedent or consist of "pure" legal reasoning. Instead, it talked about muscular fatigue, about industrial accidents, about ill health resulting from long hours, about wise social policy. This type of material and argument has become much more familiar with the subsequent growth of administrative tribunals.

231

It is to be noted, however, that until 20 years ago, economic research did not appear as a regular function of unions themselves. There were some instances, doubtless, but one of the first to come to mind is the service rendered to the Amalgamated Clothing Workers by Dr. Leo Wolman. That workers entering wage negotiations should be as well informed about conditions in the industry as were the employers came as a new and surprising idea. In addition to statistical and documentary backing for the bargaining of the union, Dr. Wolman's research had a creative part in other plans of the union for service to its members, such as the Amalgamated Houses and the Amalgamated Bank. Several labor research bureaus were established.

It is not clear whether the establishment of research departments in unions was stimulated by the growth of industrial engineering, personnel management, time and motion studies, production efficiency schemes and the like; but if workers were to be a subject of scientific study by employers, why should not industry be the subject of competent scrutiny on behalf of labor? Certainly, the growth and size of the American industrial unit and the consolidation of ownership had a close connection with establishment of research departments in unions. Relations of the workers and of their representatives with the employer were no longer so close as they had been; the employer was in all likelihood a great corporation, the head offices of which were probably at a distance. Personal understanding could no longer settle basic issues between workers and management. Management, moreover, came to the bargaining table equipped with elaborate figures. It was prepared to demonstrate the impossibility of acceding to labor's demands without fatal injury to the industry and thus to labor itself. This kind of support of the employer's position could be met only by corresponding investigation and study from the worker's point of view.

This is not to say that the importance of the bargaining ability or skills of management or of union officers was reduced by the technical assistance that these bargainers received. The elements of economic pressure were not at all diminished. Threat and counterthreat were vividly present.

Appeal to public sympathy on behalf of capital or of labor in a particular controversy was anything but new. Picket lines, parades, boycotts, public meetings, newspaper advertisements, speeches in legislatures directed as much toward the galleries as toward lawmakers—these were familiar devices. But now the soliciting of public sympathy for one side or the other was augmented by analytical statement and statistical exhibit.

The depression following 1929 popularized and expanded research intended to assist management, labor, and the government agencies charged with administration of new and sweeping economic programs.

The National Industrial Recovery Act was the chief stimulant to this development. The pre-code and code hearings and the functioning of all the elaborate machinery set up under these industrial codes necessitated analysis at every step. Unions were now given, in law, the right to organize and to bargain collectively without interference, and this liberty conferred new meaning on the factual presentations that were made.

The important participation of government in the country's economic life placed emphasis on exhibit rather than mere exhortation. Government agencies dealing with industrial and labor matters had, of course, long been collecting and publishing statistical and other pertinent information; their resources were now brought fully into play, as were, of course, the huge research machines of industry. The health of industry, both of management and workers, was declaratively a matter of public concern. Moreover, many economic areas were being submitted to systematic study in order to meet pressing social problems. It had been only a few years since President Hoover was determined that relief of the unemployed should be accomplished through the familiar but totally inadequate methods of private charity. Now, however, the Federal Emergency Relief Administration and the program it brought forward required exact study and quantitative statement. Laissez-faire, with its traditional reliance upon hunches and partisan interests, was suddenly superseded by regulation and something like deliberate schemes.

NRA itself and attendant organizations in other fields, notably the Agricultural Adjustment Administration, were discontinued. But so long as the depression was not conquered and the responsibility of government for efforts to extricate the economy was clear, the method of full investigation lost nothing; instead it was extended, indeed, taken for granted.

The United States did not get out of the depression until its entry into the Second World War—first in the upsurge of the defense program, ultimately in full participation as one of the chief belligerents. Economic mobilization for World War II had an advantage not present in 1917-18; that is, the long depression had accustomed the country to widespread governmental intervention in economic life, and so inhibitions against public control were weakened or removed. If government agencies subsidizing and overseeing economic activities had been numerous during the depression, with our entrance into World War II they became ubiquitous, and the degree of their positive management was increased. This development further emphasized the need of economic research on the part of organized labor.

In the matter of wage adjustment, for instance, the situation was entirely changed from what it had been years before. The labor officer found far less room for his traditional skill in bargaining with the employer. As the search for jobs rapidly turned into a search for workers, as orders poured in, and government and consumer demand became avid, employers were prepared to grant to workers more than the War Labor Board would approve. The problem, therefore, became one not of table thumping but of presentation of statistical and economic exhibits and the accurate following of administrative procedures. This was not the function for which most union officers were particularly fitted. The unions, in increased numbers, called to their assistance research specialists who could serve the new demand. Soon some 35 unions had established research departments that were constantly presenting and prosecuting applications before government boards.

The first phase of the work of these research staffs dealt with claims to all the rights offered to labor originally and in immediate amendments. Under war conditions, this phase soon came to a close: all that could be extracted under the Little Steel Formula, for example, was taken from it. It became necessary to persuade public administrators and legislators of the need for alterations of policy. Thus, the labor research workers were compelled to go beyond day-to-day problems and to propose major changes and extensions. Most notably, the official index of the cost of living came under fresh, critical inspection, and union research staffs, inspired by the steel workers' demands, made their independent study of what the war had done to the cost of living in this country. This, however, was but one of many less publicized excursions into the wide field of economic regulation. Economic briefs were presented to administrative boards and congressional committees, and became increasingly informed and bold with the tightening of the wartime controls, particularly as manipulation of total manpower loomed.

Factors such as these sometimes give rise to the belief that research departments of unions do not engage in research, but function only as instruments of propaganda. They do more than this. They prepare arguments that are in the industrial and economic fields much what the briefs of lawyers are in the legal domain. Labor expects its arguments and exhibits to be met by equally competent and assiduous statements on behalf of employers, government, or both. It is not surprising that in presenting its side, labor will search for the truth rather than the whole truth. It would be gratuitous to do more, in view of the equipment and the motive of others to check labor's demands. This putting of labor's best foot foremost is done, of course, with a display of virtue.

It is important to notice, however, that as labor organizations have grown from a membership of 3½ million to 15 million in a dozen years, policies that are wise for labor and good for the public come much closer together. This merging of interests serves as a check upon the partisan pretensions on behalf of the unions and calls upon the union advocate to be very mindful of the total public interest. Thus, in spite of himself, the labor aide in research finds himself subject to a new demand upon his talents and conscience. Research people in labor unions are approaching the search for truth that has long been supposed to characterize academic students of labor. Indeed, there is a question whether a bias of one kind or another does not attach as much to the university scholar as to the union research staff.

And what is the relationship of the labor research worker to the officers of his own union? Some officers, with a generous appreciation of the knowledge and talents of their research assistants, say that they welcome research advice on union policy. They say that it is the business of the research department to "sell" a policy to the union officers if it is able to do so. Others do not go so far. They suggest that it is proper for research workers to lay before the responsible officers of the union both sides of the question without more than a suggestion of the position to be adopted. No specialized investigation of economic data, however full or skillful, and no aptitude in its presentation, can substitute for the knowledge and experience of responsible union leaders. We must keep in mind that there are no economic verities beyond the importance of advancing the well-being of the masses of the people, which is to say, the workers. We are likely to suppose that economic truth is absolute, and so may be discovered and quantitatively demonstrated. This belief has no basis. Economic wisdom is relative to time and place.

At a meeting of the Inter-Union Institute, Dr. William M. Leiserson called attention to an historic instance in which labor was right and the most vaunted economists were wrong for fifty years. This was the controversy involving the so-called "wages fund theory" in England. Academic economists, advisors to government in important cases, maintained that a general increase in wages was impossible without destroying British industry. They kept up this clamor for a half century during which wages did rise, the number of workers increased, and British industry dominated the world. Finally, the most self-assured savants admitted that they were wrong and that spokesmen of the labor movement had been right all along. The disputes over shorter hours and improved factory legislation are other cases in point.

Pressure groups, so much reviled, constitute the method of democracy. It is proper that the people know their arguments, be able to choose instead of being simply coerced. In this fashion useful policy may be hammered out. Organized labor has become such a powerful pressure group that it can no longer make merely selfish pleas. It is obliged to mix public benefit with peculiar advantage. We shall be having more and more situations in which labor will be held publicly responsible. In such instances, the client of the labor research staff is not simply the labor union or movement, but the general body of American citizens.

BROADUS MITCHELL

2. EXPANDING FUNCTIONS OF UNION RESEARCH

The functions of the research staffs vary among the unions, but generally they are conceived to be service bureaus. The services of research departments are not identical although their patterns are very similar. Their major function is the preparation of economic material and information for use by union officials at all levels in connection with normal union operations and collective bargaining relations. These services may be summarized as follows in relation to the particular phase of union activity a union research staff seeks to serve:

In connection with organizational work, research staffs prepare surveys of the communities and plants to be organized, details on their labor history, comparative wages and production costs, financial conditions of companies, and their relation to other companies. For negotiations with individual companies, the union staff is supplied with data designed to aid the negotiators in formulating their demands, presenting their case, and determining the practical limits of the concessions they may receive. The organizer or negotiator is likely to carry with him a careful outline of the industrial standards the union seeks to establish; and information on comparative wage standards, working conditions, finances, cost analysis, competitive position of the plants, and actual industrial standards and conditions secured in other contracts. He will be furnished with checklists of information necessary to be gathered for the plant so that he is thoroughly familiar with the peculiar problems of the individual plant.

For the administration of contracts, the research department will be called on for very similar data and assistance in the analysis of grievances, to define the problems and advise on the solution of difficulties, particularly if they are economic or engineering in character. When arbitrations arise, the department is very frequently called in to aid in the preparation of briefs and in the presentation of cases. Special studies may be made to strengthen the union's case.

To fulfill these functions, the research staff must consist of technically competent persons. They must have a reservoir of information to aid them. The union contract file and the systematic analysis of these contracts is the most fundamental of the research resources. Second in importance is a complete file on each plant in the industry, including all possible published data on every aspect of its operation—labor history, wages, working conditions, products, personnel, finance, technology, industrial relations practices, etc. Thirdly, extensive data are assembled and analyzed on economic problems and experiences of the industry including all available statistics and operational information. Independent surveys and investigations are commonly made to obtain the data. The informational resources of many trade union research departments are more extensive than those available to many trade associations. As a result, the union research staffs have become recognized authorities on many phases of the industry's economic problems and experience.[1]

In some unions, the service has been extended beyond these normal levels to problems of a more specialized character. The handling, control, and supervision of managerial techniques such as time studies, incentive wage plans, job evaluation, etc., are the function of several research departments. Some are also equipped to assist local unions in their cooperative programs with management or in the rehabilitation of specific plants. Aid is frequently given by research-staff members in the formulation of safety programs or in the negotiation of insurance plans. In these special fields, they provide union officials with the technical knowledge necessary to deal with the issues as they arise in the process of collective bargaining.

Beyond the realm of service is the field of research. The research operation includes, first, initiation of investigations and studies necessary to provide information not available from existing sources. The TWUA research department's 1944 pricing of the 1935-36 WPA emergency budget is an example of such studies. Second, research is conducted on problems likely to become important in the future. These projects are generally initiated by the research director. Such research is essential to outline impending issues and to develop alternative courses of action by the union. Preparation of reports on such issues long before they become critical affords the union officers the time to evaluate the data and to crystallize policies on the basis of careful analysis. For example, investigations as to methods of industry-wide wage stabilization were carried on in the Textile Workers Union research department, and reports appeared several years before the problem became a current union issue.

The value and usefulness of the research department to the union depend on the professional competence of the personnel. The research man brings to the union his knowledge of current lines of economic thought, his ability to analyze economic trends in specific industries, and his expertness and familiarity with current economic literature. His function is to integrate this knowledge, experience, and training with the fundamental philosophy and desires within the trade union movement and the daily requirements of the leaders and membership, and to bring it all to bear on the formulation of union policy, strategy, tactics, and the routine processes of collective bargaining.

SOLOMON BARKIN

---

[1] The writer of this article was selected as the Consultant for the ECA Mission to the United Kingdom to evaluate the ECA program for the British textile industry.

3. UNION RESEARCH AND DEMOCRACY

In a highly industrialized country such as the United States, labor unions are the mainstay of industrial democracy. To perform their fundamental function properly, they need machinery, of which their research departments constitute a vital part. The rapid growth in the number and functions of union research departments in the last few years is a striking symptom of the progress in industrial democracy.

The part that labor unions play in an industrial democracy has been illustrated by the role they have assumed in the determination of wages. If industrial democracy can be defined as a system in which all economic, social, and political factors share equally in the responsibility for the stability and growth of the economy and for an equitable distribution of the national income, the organized wage bargain becomes a matter of prime importance for the proper functioning of industrial democracy. The progress in industrial democracy is then reflected not only in the numerical growth of labor unions, but also in the "pattern" character that wage bargains have assumed.

The numerical growth of labor unions has expanded the area in which wages are determined by collective bargaining from a small sector of American industry to the entire range of key industries. But this quantitative change has also fundamentally altered the nature of the wage determination. So long as the workers in leading industries of the country were unorganized, wages generally followed the law of supply and demand for labor, with its deplorable effects on consumers' purchasing power and economic stability. Labor unions were able to raise the wages of their members above the general level, but their wage rates set no pattern for the country as a whole. Today, with workers in all leading industries organized, every wage bargain in any major industry is likely to set a pattern that is quickly followed by most other industries, although varying business conditions in different industries make for slight modification in individual cases.

This trend was amply demonstrated by the four great waves of wage increases after World War II. What this system of wage determination involves for the union leader in terms of responsibility for the economy as a whole is easy to grasp. Wages are a vital link in the chain of factors that determine the degree of stability and the rate of growth of the economy. If the leading labor unions, which set the pattern, should insist on wage rates that are out of line with the other costs of production, profits, and prices, the cumulative effect of the wage increases incited by this pattern would be inflationary and an economic setback would sooner or later be unavoidable. If the wage rates set should be too low relative to prevailing profits and prices, consumers' purchasing power would decline and a business depression become unavoidable.

Whether or not and to what degree an individual union leader is aware of this responsibility and whether, if aware of it, he acts accordingly, depend on many factors. These factors include his own personality, pressure on the part of the membership, his power within the organization, the status of the union treasury, pressure of public opinion and of the instrumentalities of government, and so on. Some of these influences may be rational, others irrational; but in any event, in a democratic nation where the effects of all actions by important economic and social agents become known to everyone and are subject to public criticism and the verdict of the people, the chances are that the wage policy of labor unions will to an ever-increasing extent be determined by the economic and social effects set by their patterns of wage bargains.

The chief functions and responsibilities of union research workers can be inferred from these general considerations. A mechanical view of the functions of union research departments would be inclined to see in the labor research worker nothing but an advocate of a party in a conflict of interests, whose business it is to supply his client with persuasive arguments for his case. This is part of his job, too, of course. But it is in supplying the union with the data on which to base its wage policy that the services of the union research worker are most valuable. It is a comparatively minor task to assist in preparing the arguments with which to support this policy.

It would be highly unrealistic to assume that a union's wage policy is ever determined by its research department. The functions of leadership are not assigned to research workers. But the union leader who wishes to discharge his responsibilities, both to his members and to the community, as conscientiously as possible, will use the services of his research department not so much to bolster his bargaining position by statistical arguments as to acquire himself maximum insight into those conditions which he plans to affect by his wage demands. What is needed is a thorough, intensive, and constant study of the trends of prices, costs, profits, and business conditions, both generally and in the industry over which the union has jurisdiction.

Thus union research, while starting at home and serving the peculiar interests of labor unions, reaches out into the national economy and works in this area, as an instrument of union policies, toward a dynamic equilibrium of all productive forces and in the interest of social progress.

ALFRED BRAUNTHAL

4. Labor Cooperation with Government Agencies

Through its activities in connection with government research programs, the labor movement has become the most important force supporting practical and sound economic research. The CIO's interest in broad programs of economic research is not accidental. We know that the achievement of full employment and sound government policies to raise levels of living depends on adequate information on basic problems. A modern economy, like a superfortress, must have sensitive indicators of changes in volume, level, and direction. Corporations, government and unions alike can plan more sensibly if they know that employment, expenditures, or investments have suddenly declined or risen 2 per cent.

An illustration of the value of labor's cooperation with government agencies is the experience several years ago of the Labor Advisory Committee set up by the Division of Statistical Standards of the Bureau of the Budget, similar to its Business Advisory Committee. Since the Division of Statistical Standards had broad powers to pass on all government questionnaires and research programs, as well as to propose essential new projects, the labor representatives welcomed this opportunity to outline problems on which they thought further government action was required. Indeed, the establishment of the Committee arose out of the suggestion of the CIO that since business was consulted, labor should be likewise.

Partly as a result of labor's urging, the Bureau of the Budget set up a series of interdepartmental committees that prepared a program of reconversion studies on employment and unemployment, incomes, family expenditures, and other vital problems. In consultation with the government experts who had been preparing the plans for these studies, the CIO urged a bold approach to fill vital gaps in information. It specifically suggested that industry-wide figures on wages be obtained for all important industries, that the family expenditure study include tests of adequacy of food, clothing, housing, community facilities, and medical care, and that in the field of employment data the monthly report on the labor force be expanded to permit estimates of unemployment by regions and states.

Although these recommendations were in many cases much wider in scope than the final plans adopted, the experience proved beyond question that many government people welcome labor's suggestions and that labor research directors can provide valuable assistance on the type of study to be made, as well as on the details.

Cooperation with the Bureau of Labor Statistics has on several occasions been very fruitful. For example, throughout the war period, and indeed since 1936, the B.L.S. had been including lockouts in its strike statistics but failed to reveal this fact in its monthly releases or in the *Monthly Labor Review*. When the CIO became aware of this inaccuracy, it was able to persuade the Bureau to state explicitly that lockouts are included. The CIO also made specific suggestions to the B.L.S. on its form and instructions for wage rate surveys. Here the practical experience of men who had worked for years for the unions resulted in concrete improvements in the Bureau's procedures.

Although union research directors can assist government agencies in these ways, their efforts should be supplemented by the direct employment by government research agencies of persons familiar with wage earners' problems and with trade union policies.

KATHERINE POLLACK ELLICKSON

Chapter 19

Preparing a case
for a government board

*I*N JANUARY 1944 IN WASHINGTON, D. C., THERE WAS A CONFERENCE OF all cotton-rayon locals of the Textile Workers Union (CIO). A decision was made there to ask the industry for a general 60-cent minimum wage; a 10-cent across-the-board increase; uniform industry-wide wage rates for specific jobs; a daily minimum; and vacation pay. Negotiations with the employers failed to bring an agreement, and the U.S. Conciliation Service certified the cases to the War Labor Board. The consolidated case involved 25 cotton-rayon mills in New England, 6 in New York and Pennsylvania, and 23 in the South. The group was considered by the War Labor Board to be representative of the entire industry, and subsequent proceedings proved this to be correct.

The TWUA research department prepared the material necessary for the presentation of the union's case. The critical goal was to get the War Labor Board to change its own definition of substandard wages. It had previously instructed Regional War Labor Boards that increases in wages to a 50-cent minimum could be defined as complying with the privilege under the Act to correct substandard wages. The special responsibility in this case, where a 60-cent minimum was asked under the Little Steel Formula, was to highlight the inadequacy of the current tests for fixing substandard wages. The research task was to amass sufficient testimony and argument to compel the War Labor Board to order a higher wage level.

The first step was to provide the War Labor Board with a test of standard wages and to illustrate the depressing effects of substandard wages and living conditions on workers and production by means of data on the conditions of workers in textile mill communities.

Field Surveys

To meet the first of these responsibilities, the research department priced the lowest budget devised by American budgetary authorities to prove that the textile workers' actual incomes did not meet even this extraordinarily low and inadequate test. The 1935 Emergency Subsistence Budget of the Works Progress Administration was chosen for this purpose as being, without question, the lowest budget ever compiled by American relief authorities.

The pricing of this budget was executed with the cooperation of the United States Bureau of Labor Statistics, which helped bring commodity specifications up to date. Three New England and two Southern communities were visited and investigated. To secure representative price quotations, field agents specially trained by the Bureau of Labor Statistics visited and recorded both prices and deviations from specifications for the articles on specially prepared forms. Each agent was required to make further notes on the type of goods available or inadequately represented in the store. These returns were checked by a national research representative for accuracy, reliability and usefulness. Where necessary, telephone calls and return visits were made to verify the data. Information on rent and services such as medical care, recreation, transportation, fuel, light, telephone, schooling, etc., was collected from appropriate local agencies. All data were checked with special workers' committees in the area to ascertain actual buying problems not disclosed by the budget-pricing approach. Local unions participated fully in the survey and made it a part of their activities.

The union representatives who made the field surveys prepared statistical summaries of their data, assisted in this work by the union research department. The prices were weighted in accordance with the yardsticks and methods used by the WPA Emergency Budget. The full results were summarized in a special publication issued by the department, entitled "Substandard Conditions of Living. A Study of the Cost of the Emergency Subsistence Budget in Five Textile Manufacturing Communities in January-February 1944."

The study established the minimum cost of commodities and services in the five cities covered to be $1,524.64 for a four-person family in January 1944, including adjustment for food buying habits, but exclusive of taxes. This budget aided the War Labor Board in determining a new minimum substandard wage level and helped congressional committees dealing with minimum wage levels. It also provided valuable data on local conditions, and subsequently served many other purposes.

A second field survey canvassed textile families to determine their size, constituents, the number of wage earners, total family and individual earnings, and number of dependents. Local union committees visited a representative sample of workers in a number of organized Southern textile communities and filled out prepared questionnaires. To assure accuracy of data concerning income, representative payroll checks were obtained. Usable returns obtained from 1,520 Southern families in 14 mill communities revealed the following facts: 72 per cent of the families had only one wage earner; in complete families, that is, families with both husband and wife, 66 per cent were with single wage earners. Out of 5,844 individuals studied, only 35 per cent were wage earners. Special analyses were made of the number of dependent children and net income available per adult and child.[1]

A third inquiry was addressed to cooperating employers to determine the proportion of gross income deducted by the employer from the employees' earnings for taxes, war-bond purchases, and other nonservice costs as were required under benefit programs. These deductions were found to amount to 11.7 per cent in the Southern mills and 18.2 per cent in the Northern mills.[2] The accuracy of these data was checked by a special survey made by the Treasury Department on actual bond deductions in all textile mills.

The fourth survey secured specific descriptive matter on the plight of the individual low-income textile worker. This study was intended to illustrate in human terms the conclusions drawn from the statistical surveys. Individual families were interviewed to get a full summary of their expenditures on food during a typical week, as well as their clothing expenditures and other purchases. These data enabled the staff to appraise the diet and its inadequacy. Special attention was drawn to the low milk consumption among textile workers. Detailed descriptive data on living conditions were obtained on the individual family in order to present a graphic picture to the Board. From the persons interviewed in this survey, witnesses were selected for the public hearings that followed.

The other data needed for the full presentation of the case were collated from written sources and special surveys made by governmental departments or from the union's intimate knowledge of the industry.

Besides relying on the argument that a 60-cent minimum wage was vital to meet the human needs of workers, the research department also believed it necessary to highlight the effect of low wages on production. The TWUA had warned the War Production Board, in March 1943, of the impending decline in production. In the statement to the War Labor Board panel that finally heard this case, the TWUA showed that the decline in production *had* taken place and outlined the nature of the textile shortages. Only by increasing the available labor in textile mills would the problem of increased production be solved. To support this conclusion, the TWUA research department offered evidence collected by the War Manpower Commission. Letters secured from the U.S.

---

[1] TWUA statement before National War Labor Board in "Matter of the Cotton-Rayon Industry and Textile Workers Union of America," Case No. 111-5110-D, March 27, 1944, pp. 38-39, Tables XX-XXIII.

[2] *Ibid.*, Table XIX.

Employment Offices in all textile areas invariably emphasized the difficulties that low wages placed in the way of recruiting workers for the textile mills. The North Carolina Unemployment Compensation Commission offered data on the extent of emigration of North Carolina workers to higher paying localities, which was draining the number of workers available for textile production.

To portray the substandard nature of textile wages, the workers' earnings were compared with those of workers in other industries, both throughout the United States and within the respective regional industries. They were found to be at the lowest rung of our wage ladder. The regional comparison helped to offset the arguments constantly made that wages of textile workers must be low because earnings were low in the region.

The final presentation of data summarized material collected by outside groups on the dietary deficiencies among textile workers. The 1940 housing census and the reports of local housing commissions which universally condemned the backwardness of housing within the South were all presented.

Further tests of the inadequacies of earnings were disclosed through the data collected from various communities on the amount of private, public, and union relief paid to textile workers' families. Textile workers were invariably dependent on outside relief as soon as they were confronted by any emergency. Mortality rates among the textile workers in several states were higher than those of other groups in the population. Evidence of high military rejection also emphasized the handicaps of low wages. The special sufferings of low wage groups during periods of rising costs of living were projected by a special analysis of the trend of prices for these special groups. Data on migration, community facilities, educational opportunities, community wealth, and general economic backwardness of low wage areas completed the general description of the handicaps of the low wage worker.

Relation to Broader Economic Issues

The textile wage fight was conceived as the spearhead in the battle to advance backward areas to the general levels of income within the United States. It became a plea for high wages to assure the industrialization of backward areas, and thereby provide a base for postwar prosperity.

Proof of the industry's ability to pay was effectively presented. OPA studies of profits were introduced. Publications of the War Department's Price Adjustment Board highlighted the enormous profits made by the industry. The trend of stock prices was also presented to supplement the profit data.

The other issues were presented by the union in terms of general industrial experience and War Labor Board policy. The proposal for uniform industry-wide occupational rates was supported as imperative in a highly competitive industry in order to attract labor to highly essential jobs. Attention was drawn to the narrow range of rates and the lack of opportunities for advancement for workers in an industry where rates failed to reflect comparative job content. The proposed guaranteed daily minimum for incentive workers was supported by reference to general industry practice and WLB decisions. Vacations with pay and shift differentials were, of course, necessary parts of the wage program, as they had become established WLB policy and general industry practice.

These voluminous materials were presented to three separate War Labor Board panels specializing respectively in New England, New York-Pennsylvania, and the South. The basic statement was that for the South. In the New England hearings it was supplemented by special material on labor shortages and recruiting problems and comparative rates of pay in other industries in that region. Because there was considerable experience in this area of the operation of uniform occupational minima, detailed summaries were presented on the practicality of this provision. The profit record of the Northern mills was highlighted. In the New York-Pennsylvania area, the same type of supplementary data was offered, plus a detailed analysis of the competition between the New York-Pennsylvania rayon mills and the New England and Southern mills, to prove that they were part of the same industry. Workers from each locality were produced as witnesses before the respective panels.

For the cross-examination of employers, and the rebuttal, the research director prepared special forms of inquiry to secure supplementary data. These helped to emphasize company practices, turnover rates, causes of production bottlenecks, personnel policies, and methods of wage payment. Through this systematic cross-examination, conditions in the mills were revealed to support the need for improvement in wages. The effect of unsatisfactory working conditions on production and recruitment possibilities was also highlighted.

Following the hearings, the panels considered the evidence and their findings. Special analyses of testimony were furnished to the labor members of these panels to point up conclusions. Every draft of a panel report was critically reviewed for these persons until the final one was produced.

The entire argument had to be recast for a summary presentation before the National War Labor Board. The union's position was greatly strengthened by the endorsement of its position contained in the panel reports. Attention was focused on the need for higher wages to increase production in the face of the widespread recognition of prevailing textile shortages. To support this presentation, government agencies were urged to supply the National War Labor Board with statements concerning their textile needs and the probable aid that higher wages would afford in solving this problem.

To forestall argument concerning the impact of these increases on prices, the research department supplied summaries to the Board of the profits enjoyed by the industry and the prevailing profit margins to prove the ability of the industry to meet the bill without price relief. The Board's attention was directed to the wage increases granted by Southern plants during the course of the hearings as further evidence of the propriety of a wage increase. Since the panel had disapproved of occupational rates, special emphasis was placed on this phase to show the chaotic character of the wage scales and their depressing effects on workers and recruitment.

Supplementary Research

The hearings over, the National War Labor Board took the case under advisement. The research department had then to perform new services. The first was that of following the course of the case, furnishing the labor members of the Board with summaries of the data and issues, and helping them evaluate various counterproposals. After the Board members had arrived at a conclusion favoring the 55-cent minimum, their interest turned to the problem of occupational rates. Research memoranda were presented on substitutes for the complete occupational rate structure. Beginning with a proposal for rate groupings of jobs, the occupational rate issue finally evolved into the principle of guidepost rates for collective bargaining. Memoranda were supplied suggesting the appropriate jobs to be used as guides.

The actual issuance of the decision was delayed until February 20, 1945, even though the major conclusions had been reached at the beginning of January. The employers had, in the meantime, applied all the pressure they could corral, both in the Administration and in Congress, to forestall the decision. To offset this work and to assure public understanding of the case, the TWUA presented frequent press summaries of union data.

The decision was finally promulgated in February, but its effective date was delayed pending approval by the Director of Economic Stabilization so that it became operative on April 17, 1945. Although the order affected only 54 companies, its terms were generally observed throughout the industry both by union and nonunion plants.

Responsibilities After the Decision

The order directed the parties to negotiate balanced wage schedules on the basis of the guidepost rates prescribed by the order: five in number for the Southern mills, four for the New England mills and three for the New York-Pennsylvania mills.

This placed a new responsibility upon the research department. To carry out the task, the research department, in cooperation with the union staff, developed a schedule of standard union rates for the major jobs in each area. The methods of staff cooperation, however, had to be adapted to each area separately. In the Southern area, after exhaustive field inquiries in a number of plants and discussions with union committees, the union developed its proposed balanced-wage schedule. A conference of all Southern union negotiators was then held. At this meeting, a full kit of materials was supplied to each of them with a full list of all official documents; technical materials describing each key job; memoranda on the reasons for the union wage proposals and methods of determining rates for all jobs peculiar to an individual plant. The union negotiators were furnished with forms for securing job descriptions and job patterns. Detailed instructions guided them in dealing with piece-work and incentive-pay jobs, and supplementary wage clauses. Work sheets for determining costs were especially prepared to assure the careful preparation of the union proposals. The negotiators had the local unions prepare the data under the guidance of one staff man who spent his time directing the committees. These data were supplied to the research department, which reviewed the first wage proposals made by each staff member for the purpose of criticism and improvement. In time, each mastered the technique so that relatively uniform proposals were submitted to all companies.

Following the negotiations, the differences that arose between the union and management in many plants were submitted to the Southern Textile Commission for resolution. The research director handled all of the early cases before the Commission. In presenting the case, he offered careful analysis of job characteristics and their conformance with established union wage patterns. The Southern Textile Commission finally accepted, and with only a few exceptions, ordered the union's proposed job wage rates to be observed by the companies appearing before it.

In the Northern area, a completely different course was followed. After the union pattern was determined, it was submitted to an employers' committee. Negotiations were carried on with a committee representing 40 mills, in contrast to the individual mill approach that prevailed in the South. Agreement was reached on rates for 19 jobs, but disagreement continued on the rates for an additional 26 jobs. Hearings were held by the Northern Textile Commission on these rates. For each job the research department prepared a special brief in support of the union's rate, appraising the skills, training, and exposure of the worker, as well as other phases of job content. Several rates were supported on the principle of sharing the benefits of technological advances. Some rates were derived from going wage levels. These repre-

sentations were supplemented by oral testimony of witnesses who described their jobs. These briefs were technical in character and closely
appraised the value of each job. After the decision was handed down by
the Northern Commission, further negotiations were necessary with
employer groups. Negotiations with individual companies then followed on the basis of the general pattern. They were carried on by the
local administrative staff. Here again, disputes concerning individual
jobs were brought back to the Commission for settlement. The briefs
and arguments were handled by the research department. These involved direct appraisal of the job values in each plant, in relation to the
customary job content.

In the New York-Pennsylvania area, another pattern was evolved.
Here the research representative participated in the negotiations of the
wage scale for each mill. The great variety of wages and lack of a pre-
existing wage pattern meant that detailed job descriptions and complete
work duty charts had to be obtained for each mill. These guides had
to be carefully appraised to take into account the difference between
plain and fancy goods. Close inquiries into styles of fabric and equipment
preceded each determination. Special inquiry forms were filled out by
the local unions for each plant. The research department representative
participated in these negotiations to assure substantial uniformity of rates
throughout the industry.

The research department helped to present forcefully the TWUA's
demand to eliminate substandard wages. Its main responsibility was to
bring to light data that would compellingly support the union's demand.
The briefs and arguments proved to be rallying points for the organized power of the union to press for the correction of substandard
wages. With respect to the development and establishment of balanced
wage scales, the task was different. The research staff applied its technical knowledge and insight to guide in the formulation of the union's
proposed wage schedule. Subsequently, it helped train the staff in its
use and application. Finally, it helped to get the schedule adopted by
the textile commissions. The major task of negotiating the local application of the basic schedule to the individual mill remained with the
union's administrative staff, except that the research staff was called
in for specific cases when its aid was required on some technical phases
of the negotiation.

                                                    SOLOMON BARKIN

Chapter 20

Research facts for action

THE TELEPHONE RINGS ON THE AVERAGE OF ONCE EVERY THIRTY SECONDS during working hours at the UAW-CIO Research and Engineering Department.

"Look," a fellow says over the phone, "we have just been in negotiations and the company turned their books over to us. They say they will have to close up if they pay us the wage increase. Can you send someone who can look over these books for us?"

The Research Department can and does. In one case, the company had a neat trick. There were two companies owned by the same man. The profits were drained off into one company and the books of the other company were used to mislead the people in the plant.

Or perhaps a regional director is on the wire. A plant in his region is about to shut down over a speedup grievance and the company has finally agreed to negotiate. "Can the Research Department send in an engineer to help on negotiations?" It can and will.

Or another group of locals is ready to go into negotiations, and they want an overhauling of the incentive payment program and some guarantees against speedup wage cuts. "Can the Research Department send an engineer to work with them?"

"Sure."

Long distance call. The maintenance men in a large plant want some dope on prevailing wages for their jobs; they have an idea they are getting less than the going rate. "Would the Research Department send out the wages for the area?"

Tool and die workers in Milwaukee want the same information and so do the tractor workers in Peoria.

"Can we get this information by Monday?"

Those are all fire alarm calls.

But the Research and Engineering Department of the UAW-CIO operates something more than a fire engine house.

The Research and Engineering Department of the UAW-CIO is a specialized technical service designed to help UAW members win a better life.

But it doesn't do the winning; it helps them win. It makes the organizing easier, the bargaining easier, it supplies the information they need when they are out trying to get people in Congress and government to represent them. It prepares the basic reports for effective cooperative or insurance programs.

But the organizing, the negotiations, the voting, the cooperating, the talking, the persuasion and the man-to-man and woman-to-woman work are done by the members and the officers of the union.

Routinely, the Research Department subscribes to most business publications, the publications of government agencies such as the Treasury Department, the Securities and Exchange Commission, the Labor Department, the Federal Trade Commission, in order to keep a running record on the operations and profits of the companies with which the union bargains. Business and trade publications are reviewed for information on UAW companies.

When the government lets contracts to UAW plants, the Research Department notifies the regional directors so that they will know what is happening and can work out plans with locals to meet changing situations.

In addition, the UAW-CIO has purchased a share of stock in many of the companies with which the union deals so that all reports made to stockholders are available to the UAW-CIO as well.

Special business services such as Standard Statistics and Poor's and the Moody Manuals are scrutinized for the specific information they have—not only on a company's financial position, but also for information on the relationships between companies and the inter-relationships that arise from interlocking directorates.

Here is a list of what the Research and Engineering Department does:

Analysis of company operations. It makes analyses of company financial statements. The information culled from these analyses is used in negotiations.

Wage rate studies. Under the union constitution, each local is required to send in the wage rates for its plants every six months. These rates are entered on wage rate cards so that in a matter of minutes it is possible to quote the rate for a particular job throughout the industry. When locals want the wage schedules in a plant somewhere else in the country, the Research Department uses a photographic device that reproduces the wage schedules and classifications for that plant in less than a minute. Copies of the schedules are then mailed out.

Contract analysis. This is a new program that is just now being put into operation. Under it the contracts that the recording secretaries of each local send in are analyzed and their provisions put on punch cards. This system makes it very easy to see at a glance what features of a contract—insurance, pensions, vacations, paid holidays, grievance procedure, and seniority—are below standard. The Department is able to determine readily how many workers are covered by various kinds of provisions and to make comparative analyses of contracts. It helps the local decide what to shoot for in contract negotiations.

As a quantitative measure of its activity, the Department's records show that it answered nearly 3,000 requests on the three topics listed above during the period December 1, 1947, through May 25, 1949. A breakdown shows that 1,413 of these requests were for financial information, 956 were on wage rates, and 499 concerned contract problems.

Negotiation aids. The department takes part in most union negotiations of any size, sometimes directly, by assigning a research worker to the development and presentation of facts and arguments. Sometimes it works in support of negotiations by supplying the negotiators with statistics, profit figures, wage figures and detailed analyses of company statements. (An example of this activity is the exchange between General Motors and the union during negotiations on incentive payment plans. GM offered a statement that called speedup plans Grass Roots Democracy, and the UAW replied with a Research Department brief called "Sweat Today, Starve Tomorrow.")

Corporation and occupational research. The department also operates a resource agency for each industry and corporation council. In this case the department continuously supplies facts and figures on the problems of specific groups of workers as they arise. In connection with both the agricultural implement and airplane industries, for example, it has surveyed wages and working conditions so that the negotiations and councils concerned with these problems could plan strategy not only for negotiations, but for organizing. In the same way the department works with the Competitive Shop Department to plan for dealing with runaway shops or low-wage competition.

Time study and engineering. Time study and engineering are major activities of the department. Engineers from the Research Department are available to local unions (through regional directors) to help on specific grievances involving time-study methods. Engineers are also available to assist in negotiations.

At the same time the UAW engineers cooperate with the Education Department in offering classes to train time-study stewards and in preparing basic manuals on time study for use by UAW members.

Behind these front-line operations the engineers work on time-study policies for the consideration of the International Executive Board. The engineers also prepare contract clauses on time study which are based upon UAW policy.

Special audits. Occasionally an employer pleads poverty during negotiations or will make some other claim that can be verified or disproved by looking at his books. Sometimes he offers to open up his books to union inspection. In these cases the Research Department supplies auditors, through the regional directors, to check the company books.

Model contract clauses. Besides preparing contract clauses on time study, the Research Department also prepares model contract clauses on the other features of a UAW-CIO contract. When the UAW-CIO membership, through council meetings, the convention, and the International Executive Board, adopts a program, the Research Department works out suitable contract language to put the program into effect.

For example, the guaranteed 40-hour work week was adopted as a union objective. When this objective was adopted the Research Department went to work and wrote an airtight contract clause that would provide the guaranteed 40-hour week without weakening the seniority clauses that had already been won. In the future the Research Department intends to publish a new edition of its compilation of contract clauses.

Classes. The training responsibility of the Research Department is not limited to classes in time study. At UAW summer schools and institutes, at meetings of councils and at regional conferences the Research Department, working with the Education Department, supplies instructors to teach economics; to instruct union members in the analysis of corporation reports; to teach the use of government reports and business and industrial reports; to explain the relationships among wages, prices, and profits; and to analyze the effects of monopoly on the lives of union members.

The training, of course, is intended to inform union members, but it also has a more specific purpose—to enable bargaining committees and the other union committees to win better livelihoods for union families and to supply UAW members with the technical economic information they need to solve union problems.

Program planning: basic studies on union programs and plans. To make it possible to plan not only from day to day, but from year to year and over periods of years, the Research Department carries on studies that deal with the long-range objectives of the union. Basic studies are made, for example, of probable employment in the auto industry four or five years from now; the effects of monopoly restriction of production on employment possibilities in years to come; the structure of the industries in which the union is organized so that future strategies can be worked out; and the effects of Defense Department plans on the location of plants in the industry.

Special projects. The department undertakes specific research projects. During the intense steel shortage, for example, the Research Department investigated methods by which aluminum could be substituted for steel in the auto industry and the probable effects of this substitution on steel requirements. And the department has assisted the Federal Social Security Department on studies of insurance programs, pensions, and the attitudes of union members.

Bulletins. Each month the department publishes a bulletin that is sent to the officers, regional directors, and union department heads. This bulletin reports on all government actions; UAW plants; government contracts awarded; the purchase of plants or equipment from the government; reports of the Wages and Hours Administrator; Federal Trade Commission findings; Securities and Exchange Commission orders; and similar government actions involving UAW plants.

Publications review. Additional information about UAW plants is compiled from a continuous review of trade publications. In this way, new products or new manufacturing processes can be seen and planned for before they actually affect the working conditions in a particular plant.

At the same time the Research Department reviews American, English, Canadian, and other foreign economic and technical articles that bear upon the working or living conditions of members or upon union plans and programs.

Library. Publications are indexed and filed in the UAW library. The library, besides serving as a reference tool for the Research Department, is also a basic resource for every local officer. Books bearing on the problems of UAW members are maintained along with references to arbitration decisions, labor laws, court decisions, and NLRB orders. The library also accumulates documents, books, and other materials that are the sources of a basic history of the auto, aircraft, agricultural implement, and associate industries and the UAW. Books and magazines of interest to particular departments are routed to them. The library, of course, is available for use by local unions.

Liaison with government and university agencies. The Research Department does not, of course, have the resources of a government bureau or a big industrial research agency. It depends for basic information on government agencies. And one of its important jobs is to work with government agencies in an effort to encourage them to compile information that will be helpful to the UAW. Sometimes, however, government information is biased, or even inaccurate. It is the Research Department's job to police statistics bearing on UAW industries for the purpose of keeping the statistics straight.

This job is more important today than ever before since wages in some plants are partially tied to the cost-of-living index. At present, for example, this index is not a true report of changes in these costs because of a failure to report rentals and housing increases properly.

RESEARCH FACTS FOR ACTION

The Research Department is currently attempting to correct this situation. Indirectly, most wages are hooked to government statistics, and keeping them accurate helps prevent all workers from being short-changed.

By working closely with other union research agencies and with the CIO Research Department, duplication of effort is avoided, common plans are worked out, and manpower is made more efficient.

At the same time, the Research Department works with university investigators, supplying them with information for their studies to balance the automatic bias they get from business reports. Universities are encouraged to work on subjects the union would like to see studied, but which it cannot afford to study because of lack of time or resources.

By taking part in meetings of economic and statistical societies, the Research Department makes sure that the problems of the man or woman in the plant are not lost to view when the professors prepare their articles and speeches or write their textbooks. The department's presence at these meetings enables it to answer the arguments of those who represent management's point of view.

Personnel

A majority of the Research Department staff is made up of people who came out of the shops, worked in the union, helped to organize the union, and took part in union activities as stewards, committeemen, and union officers. Some, of course, are technical people who believe deeply in the program of the union and who choose to work for the UAW rather than for a university or a corporation.

Each day the Research Department gets applications for jobs from statisticians and economists in government, in universities and in business. They recognize that the Research Department of the UAW-CIO puts scientific methods to work for the welfare of the people of the country.

Because this is so, increasing numbers of university students also write in to find out the qualifications for working in a union research department.

Essentially these qualifications are simple.

A research worker must be technically qualified. If he wants a job as an engineer or a statistician, he should know engineering or statistics. But in addition he must understand the problems of the people who have organized the UAW-CIO. And the best way to get the understanding is to be one of them, to work in a plant, to be a steward, to take part in bargaining, and to take part in the democratic life of the union. With this experience and technical training, he will have the necessary qualifications.

LEWIS CARLINER

Chapter 21

The union and
industrial engineering

LABOR'S INTEREST IN INDUSTRIAL ENGINEERING IS AS BROAD AS THE ENTIRE field of management. Sales policies, production control methods, and all of the other professional techniques sharply influence the smooth operation of the enterprise and labor's ability to make a living out of the industry.

There are five specific techniques of industrial engineering of special interest to labor because of their direct influence on the collective bargaining pattern. These techniques are (1) time study of production standards as a basis for a fair day's work; (2) design and administration of wage-incentive payment plans; (3) job evaluation; (4) merit rating; and (5) the installation of work simplification techniques through motion study.

Current Labor Attitudes

Trade union administrators faced with the problem of applying these techniques have often sought central guidance for a fixed labor movement policy toward the industrial engineering profession. Unfortunately, the labor movement has not had enough consistent experience to formulate such a policy. Also, many engineers have become involved in attempts to restrict the area of collective bargaining.

It is not the purpose of this chapter to offer a formal statement of organized labor's position toward the use of engineering techniques, since no such policy exists. But it is useful and proper to examine and discern trends of thinking current among labor union administrators charged with supervising these problems.

The application of time study to rate setting is fundamental in any collective bargaining relationship. Where workers are paid straight time work, time study is generally used to determine production quotas. If the method of compensation is a wage-incentive payment plan, then time study is used to fix the production standard at which the additional increment wage begins to be paid.

The problems that develop under time study vary widely according to the type of industry under review. They may be classified roughly as follows:

1. Rate-setting in industries where the processes are machine-paced and automatic.

2. Rate-setting where the processes are man-paced and the machine, if one is used, is only a power-driven hand tool.

3. Rate-setting in service industries, where it is difficult to find any meaningful standard of productivity.

A problem in the first category is found in the textile industry where machines are fully automatic, in cases where a worker is called upon to repair a thread breakage or machine breakage. It should be noted that the worker is generally active during the non-producing state of the machine's operation.

Examples of problems of the second type are found in the garment industry where the sewing-machine operator controls the speed of output. The sewing machine generally can be speeded so far beyond the operator's capacity that its full possibilities are seldom utilized.

Problems of the third type arise in the building service industry, where attempts must be made to standardize the work task in terms of areas serviced.

The problems offered by man-paced operations are generally much more difficult to solve than those that have a fixed machine pace. The wide adaptability and variability in human performance often elude an engineering solution. And it should be remembered that there is some overlapping of these problems. A good example of overlapping is found in machine-shop work. In analyzing any of the common machine-shop jobs, such as milling, the various classes of elements may be classified as setup time, cutting time, and put-away or cleanup time. The setup and cleanup or put-away times are man-paced. The machine cutting time is fixed by standard feeds and speeds. This factor can be determined with much more accuracy by the engineer than can the first two elements.

With regard to the problems raised in collective bargaining over work standards, labor experts are unanimous in the rejection of the position that the setting of such standards is a unilateral function of management or its engineers. Hill and Hook in *Management at the Bargaining Table*, (McGraw-Hill Book Co., 1945) support the doctrine that determination of the standard may be the proper subject for a grievance, but must remain nonarbitrable—*i.e.*, the disposition of the grievance terminates with a unilateral management investigation, which either revises or substantiates the original position. This doctrine is rejected by labor technicians.

The position taken by engineers, such as Carroll and Louden, for example, that "Standards must not be subjected to negotiation or arbitration, either in their establishment or in their change," [1] is likewise rejected. In rejecting this doctrine unanimously, labor experts accept time study as a collective bargaining tool but point out that the many undetermined variables composing a production rate cannot be left to the unilateral determination of management, but are proper subjects for collective bargaining.

Representatives of those unions whose bargaining position is not strong enough to compel management to acknowledge officially the workers' equity in setting production standards found that management actually negotiates production rates on the operating level. Top management and its legal staff hand down a policy and contract to the actual operating officials who have to get out the production and who know, as a practical matter, that if they attempt to set the rates unilaterally, they will be bedeviled by disturbance after disturbance that will cut down production. The result is that standards are negotiated unofficially. This approach is found in many areas of the automobile industry.

Following agreement on this fundamental doctrine of the labor union's equity in the matter of setting the production rate, opinion on subsequent points has differed. The following points of view are discernible:

1. Complete rejection of time-study techniques as a guide to setting a fair day's work.

2. Consideration of the rate proposed by the time-study engineers as an offer, the union reserving the right to determine whether or not it will accept the offer by any criteria, time study or otherwise, that it sees fit.

3. Acceptance of a time-study system mutually satisfactory to union and management as a means of setting rates.

4. Development of a system of standard data that will serve as a basis for rate setting.

Proponents of the first point of view deny any validity whatsoever to the time-study technique. They indicate that the wide number of variables influencing the final rate result, all subject to human judgment, make time study all but useless. Still others indicate disagreement with the very assumptions upon which a job description is standardized to make time study possible. They claim that there is no one best method for all workers in performing a given operation. The more complex the job becomes, the less possible it is to standardize an elemental job description that every person can be expected to follow. They point

---

[1] J. K. Louden, *Wage Incentives* (New York: John Wiley & Sons, 1944), p. 162.

out that this whole theory flies in the face of all that the psychologists have found out about individual differences.

The reasoning of most unions manifesting this attitude is that the employer has a right to expect a reasonable effort during the working day without any limitation on the amount of production expected. Unions in which this point of view prevails are the photoengravers and the railway clerks.

Others, conceding the soundness of these objections to the time-study method, nevertheless contend that unions must adapt the technique to their purposes until such time as they can offer an alternative method of measuring a "fair day's output."

One group takes much the same attitude toward time study as was adopted by Carl Barth—associate of Frederick W. Taylor, industrial engineer often called "the father of scientific management"—who described the accuracy of time studies in the following terms: ("Symposium on Stop Watch Time Study: An Indictment and a Defense," *Bulletin of the Taylor Society*, V. 6, 1921.)

It is hardly conceivable that two time-study men, however well equipped by training and experience and with physical means, would arrive at exactly the same time allowance for any job each might in turn be inadequately assigned to study. And still, the time allowance of either would be undoubtedly fully satisfactory for use in establishing a fair contract between the worker and the management, though the two would not be identical.

The one revision that would be demanded by the union officer is that the contract be bilateral instead of unilateral. In testing the acceptability of the management's offer, however, the union officer may wish to be guided either by his own experts' time-study methods or by historical production rates. In any case, he will not reject the management's offer because it is a time-study offer. At the same time, he will not be constrained by the technical practices of the management. He is willing to concede the initial rate-setting process as a management prerogative. This is the practice of the garment workers in those areas where standard data are unavailable.

Others have gone somewhat further in jointly determining the technical criteria for many of the time-study systems. For example, the steel workers have agreed with the U. S. Steel Corporation that a working rhythm equivalent to the pace maintained by a man walking three miles per hour shall be considered normal. Similarly, other variables, such as the fatigue and downtime allowance for different jobs, are likewise negotiable. The automobile workers indicate that they have used this approach in many cases. Other groups have also attempted to circumvent the harrowing day-to-day arguments about production rates by joint programs to set up standard data.

The standard data consist in assigning standard tasks that recur over and over again in different work patterns as a standard time allowance. The production standards for new products are developed by adding the times for these various standard parts. Thus, the New York Dress Joint Board of the ILGWU sets production standards on the basis of a table developed by engineers. That is, the tabular values are guideposts around which bargaining takes place, due regard being given to the inherent limitations of the data's accuracy.

Workers in the service industries, such as the Building Service Employees' Union, largely accept the job standards that they find in practice when the building is organized. Attempts to increase this workload are resisted. However, they point out that when it signs up a newly built structure, a union must propose a standard of work for its own protection.

Some sociologists take issue with the labor group, claiming that the informal working group sets its own standards, irrespective of the union and the management engineers. It is the opinion of labor experts generally that the sociologists' conclusions are based on extremely inconclusive evidence.

There is fairly universal agreement that one of the primary problems faced by all unions is how to secure able union technicians. Objection is raised to management offers to train union time-study technicians. The trouble lies in the fact that these training courses are seldom thorough examinations of various techniques, but mainly an indoctrination in the virtues of the clerical techniques employed by the specific engineering organization. These courses do not turn out able union time-study technicians, but only proponents within the union's ranks of the time-study prejudices of the teacher. All are agreed that if the union requires technicians, it is the union's job to train them independently or in cooperation with a sympathetic university.

Wage Incentive Payment Plans

Many unionists have indicated that the increasingly automatic character of many industrial operations (in which workers have become mere lever-shifters) raises the whole question of how important the problem of wage-incentive payment plans will be in the future. Much more fundamental than this question is the problem of relative employment security and the means of distributing the increment of increased productivity to these lever-shifters, who seldom control the speed of production. Wage-incentive payment plans were developed during a period when the overwhelming majority of industrial operations were dependent on the physical exertion of the worker. The evolving technology of American industry may very well change the relative importance of wage-incentive payment plans and the resultant emphasis placed upon them by trade unions. A tendency is seen in that direction in the developing emphasis on the annual wage.

Many trade unionists object to wage-incentive payment plans on principle. Such plans, they contend, are an endless source of grievances and make administration of a collective agreement immeasurably difficult. In addition, they feel that wage-incentive payment plans are merely a device for shifting many management risks, traceable to fluctuations in direct labor costs, to the shoulders of the workers. This is the position of the United Automobile Workers.

Other union representatives feel that wage-incentive payment plans have become so integral a part of the wage payment structure of the industries in which they operate that any attempt by the union to oust the plan would be frustrated. They are primarily interested in developing safeguards that would protect the workers' standards in the operation of these plans.

Still another group actively advocates these plans. They claim that the plans solve certain problems for the union. These problems generally arise when employers complain that variation in the productivity of workers puts them at a competitive disadvantage in comparative direct labor costs. The wage-incentive payment plan always pinpoints this direct labor cost. In addition, the variability of the operation of these plans has served as a means for securing increases that were otherwise impossible.

A fundamental change in the approach to wage-incentive payment plans is advocated by some of the members of these latter two groups. Exception is taken to the very term "wage-incentive payment plan." The implication of the term is that the worker is actually entitled, as a matter of right, to a fundamental wage payment only, the day rate or the base rate as it is called in the incentive-wage plan. The understanding is that as a reward—not as a right—a worker will be paid a bonus for additional effort. A much more acceptable approach to this problem would be to change the name of this method of wage payment to something like "productivity wages." Thus there would be a contract between the management and the workers, establishing management's obligation to furnish the workers with the opportunity to make a specified hourly wage at a normal working pace. The worker, in turn, obligates himself to meet the jointly set production standard.

The advantages of this method can be readily seen. If there is a management breakdown in production control, daily workers are not paid in terms of an artificially deflated base rate, but at the average hourly rate that they have demonstrated they are capable of earning. The argument that payment at such a rate abolishes the worker's incentive is untenable. It might as well be argued that this obligation on the part of management to pay the average hourly rate is an incentive to see that its factory management is operating properly. Most engineering consultants, under pressure from the unions, have in any case adopted this method of payment for idle time.

Abuses of Wage Incentives

The principal administrative problem that bedevils the operation of these plans, according to most labor experts, is the meaning of the statement, "The rate remains unchanged unless the method is changed." The practices of some firms have led to suspicion concerning the techniques of work simplification.

The techniques of motion study may sometimes be abused to simulate a new motion pattern for an old operation in order to justify setting a new production rate. This abuse would generally take place on an operation on which the management had committed itself that no cuts would be made so long as the method remained unchanged. The management would seek out operations to define as loose, and by redefining vague motion patterns, attempt to justify a much tighter rate.

This abuse is found particularly in the automobile industry. The UAW, in an attempt to control the situation, now insists upon a detailed elemental breakdown of the before-and-after operation, with the time saving specified for each element.

Still another abuse in installing wage-incentive payment plans comes in the attempt to apply them to operations that are fundamentally machine-paced. In this case again, production variation may be subject to a whole host of variables so numerous that they are uncontrollable. A good example is found in textiles, where the weather helps determine the number of thread breaks an operator is called upon to repair. Under such circumstances, more often than not, the wage-incentive payment plan is a device for shifting a management risk from the management group to the working force.

A third group which actively advocates wage-incentive plans finds that the plans are an invaluable device for stabilizing the highly competitive industries in which it has to operate. The union has a means of determining whether or not it is carrying free riders when an employer threatens to close down his plant because his labor costs are noncompetitive. It serves as an aid in establishing a nationwide collective bargaining policy.

Job Evaluation

Although formal methods of job evaluation developed somewhat later than did time-study techniques and wage-incentive payment plans, they must be examined first in any consideration of industrial engineering techniques. The engineer, in setting up an installation, thinks in the following terms: Job evaluation sets the relative base rate in the job hierarchy; time-study sets the normal productivity rate; and the wage-incentive payment plan sets the amount of so-called "premium pay." We have, however, examined each industrial engineering technique in its chronological order of development. Most trade unionists indicate that the ranking and classification methods of job evaluation are not new, and the techniques have been used on an informal basis for a long time by trade unions in negotiating a general wage scale. Each rate is related to a specific job description. The principal problem around which most of the discussion centers is the feasibility of using more complex techniques for the same purpose.

Three attitudes are discernible toward a proposal by management that job evaluation be used in setting up the wage scale. These three attitudes may be categorized as follows: (1) complete rejection; (2) "coyness"; (3) acceptance on the basis of full labor participation in the installation and administration of the technique.

Trade unionists agree that under no circumstances can the job evaluation plan be used as the sole determinant of the relative wage structure. In addition to the relative job content measured by job evaluation techniques, the following elements would have to be considered in determining the final scale:

1. Irregularity of employment.
2. Career prospects of the job—*i.e.*, how high the promotional sequence climbs.
3. Market supply of and demand for specific occupations.
4. Traditional wage relationships, as they have evolved in time.

There are three separate areas within which the job evaluation problem is considered:

1. The older, long-organized industries within which a long collective bargaining history has built up traditional wage relationships.
2. Old industries, newly organized, wherein a long history of lack of organization has led to complete disorganization of rate structures.
3. New industries with new technologies, within which wage structures have to be developed without any historical precedents.

One job evaluation problem that arises under the first category is created by the introduction of new technologies that change the relative skill content of different jobs—*e.g.*, introduction of section work techniques into a sector of the women's garment industry where previously the complete garment method of manufacture had prevailed. Traditionally, the method used to cope with this development was to set a single rate for all sewing machine operations; yet it is obvious that the sewing jobs carry different skill values.

An example of the way the job evaluation problem arises under the second category, old industries newly organized, is found in one branch of the communications industry. The job rates that the union finds in use are completely jumbled because of the industry's frankly avowed policy of purchasing labor in the local market at the lowest available price, irrespective of consistency or relative job content.

New industries, such as plastics, present a problem to both union and management in developing a joint wage structure without any historical precedents.

Several arguments are advanced in support of complete rejection of a job evaluation plan proposed by management: Acceptance of job evaluation encourages the process of job dilution. That is, the skilled jobs are broken down into subsidiary jobs for no other purpose than to purchase cheaper labor. This process of job dilution taking place in various industries—e.g., the nonunion sector of the printing industry— has not even the merit, on evidence, of demonstrating an increase in physical productivity.

Another line of argument is that the job evaluation plans proposed by management hampered the collective bargaining process: Management proposals for job evaluation generally relate to some method of copying the area rate, through local labor market studies. This is an attempt, the advocates of this point of view maintain, to graft the infamous industry-area wage theory, first developed by the War Labor Board, onto the postwar economy. All these techniques, it is maintained, are based upon unwarranted assumptions. For example, one of the assumptions is the existence of a permanent set of values by which relative job content can be measured. But the values, as expressed in the relative weightings assigned different factors, are the same for all types of jobs; thus the yardstick created makes no more sense than would measuring the height of a building in terms of gallons of water. All the assumptions and tendencies of these techniques seem to favor management instead of labor.

A good description of the coy or "show me" approach is found in the *U.E. Guide to Wage Payment Plans, Time Study and Job Evaluation* (pp. 77-80), issued by the United Electrical, Radio and Machine Workers of America:

Let the company use whatever method it pleases, but under close union surveillance. If the result is satisfactory, well and good. If it is not, the company will hear from us. The union should always reserve the right to challenge any job values which it finds unsatisfactory, and to utilize any and all factors bearing on the case.

This stand-off approach has been used with some success by both the United Automobile Workers Union, CIO, and the AFL Amalgamated Meatcutters and Butchers. Both groups found this technique useful primarily as a means of securing increases from the War Labor Board impossible to achieve in any other way. The AFL union permitted the

employers to propose rates on the basis of the management's job evaluation plan and then introduced other factors, independent of the job
evaluation study, to adjust rates they felt were out of line. The CIO
union took a similar attitude, feeling that joint participation is impracticable for almost all unions because they are handicapped by the lack of
competent technical personnel to cope with the experts engaged by
management.

On the other hand, the following arguments are advanced in favor of
joint participation:

1. Most of the over-all job evaluation plans, such as ranking and
classification, actually consist of a subconscious breaking down of the
over-all job into subsidiary factors. It is just as well to formalize and
recognize consciously what is being done unconsciously. Unionists agree
that most of the management plans are, essentially, defective because of
their pro-management bias. The remedy then, lies in union-developed
plans that will serve as counterproposals. Thus, for example, in the
conversion of the job hierarchy into a wage scale, the concept of the
going area wage rate is completely rejected. Unions insist that factors
be weighed differently according to the requirements of different departments.

2. The problem of setting relative wage scales within a plant is not
a problem confined to the management-employee relationship. In formulating the demands of the union upon an employer, the union finds itself
immersed in the conflicting claims of the various groups as they compete
with one another for their share of the expected total increase. Thus
the union itself may find the need of some common measuring stick,
however limited it may be, which will provide a means of resolving
disputes among its own members.

3. Some segments of labor favor joint participation rather than the
stand-offish approach because the union, lacking any other criterion
on which to base its arguments, has to confine most of its arguments
within the framework of the management's job evaluation structure.
Proponents of this theory believe that it is much better strategy to be
"in on" the project from the very beginning and thus lay the basis for
the union's position in terms of what it wants from the job evaluation
system.

The extent to which unions try to solve the engineering problems
in their respective fields varies according to the nature of the industries
involved, the attitudes of the workers and the union leadership, and the
receptivity of the employers. Likewise, the nature of the problems
presented varies according to these factors. In the automobile industry,
many employers make use of engineering techniques that vitally affect
the earnings of their workers, yet they stubbornly refuse to allow their

workers to have any voice in the application of these techniques. These employers are invariably shocked when the union suggests that it might be a good idea to talk things over and come to an understanding *before* such techniques are applied, rather than to wait for trouble to arise and then try to repair the damage already done.

Failure of employers in the auto industry to recognize labor's equity in setting standards, etc., has resulted in many of the situations featured on the front pages of every newspaper following the war. There was, for instance, the case of a manufacturer who clung to his prerogative of taking time studies and setting standards without any "advice" or "interference" by the union. There was a job in his plant that had been in existence over a period of many years. The standard on this job had been set by time study and had existed over a long period. When the war came, it was necessary to change the raw material upon which this job was performed. The change of material made no difference in the job except for one element or one part of the whole job. Instead of time-studying this particular element alone, the entire job was re-studied and a new rate set after the entire job had been "rated" or "leveled."

In following this procedure, the skill acquired by workers on this job over a period of years and the gains from it were automatically cast aside. The result of this incident may well be imagined. However, despite all the trouble growing out of this particular case, the employer still refuses to meet with the union and draw up a mutually acceptable code of time-study practice that would prevent such occurrences from clogging the regular union-management grievance machinery.

Examples of Union-Management Cooperation

Many unfortunate examples can be cited in which unions have put themselves into a difficult position by agreeing to joint participation in plans, the implications of which they neither foresaw nor understood when they entered the agreement. But some of the successful examples of joint participation are cited as follows:

The United Steelworkers Union of America, CIO, and the management of U.S. Steel have jointly negotiated an industry-wide job evaluation point plan, which is being used to resolve the problem of wage inequities. The engineer in charge of the project indicated that in 1942 there were 16,000 wage rate classifications at Carnegie-Illinois alone. When first approached by U.S. Steel to use a job evaluation system to resolve these inequities, the union representatives turned the proposal down because they feared it. They were afraid that the technique would be used to re-juggle wages, and that any man whose job was down-rated would turn on the union. In 1944, the union demanded similar pay for similar work. The War Labor Board virtually ordered the use of a job evaluation system.

The union sat down with the corporation and devised a manual of job descriptions for all the basic steel industry. Along with it, the union and the company's engineers devised a point plan that both parties felt would serve their mutual purpose. The manual was first applied to a plant in Gary, Indiana. After some revisions, the manual was adopted and is now generally effective in basic steel. Stewards and union representatives are trained in its use. The union does not care to revert to the old system, under which no sooner had one inequity grievance been solved than another appeared in its place. This method of "beating" rates up disorganized the union even more than the company. Since provisions were made for transferring those whose skill had been rendered obsolete to better jobs, or for retaining the former and higher wage rate, there have been virtually no complaints.

An experience of the UAW-CIO is also cited. Because the union agreed with the company on the installation of a factor comparison method of job evaluation, to be administered by a committee made up of both union and management representatives, the union was able to prevent inequities being used as a basis for wage reductions. The union representatives, by a judicious choice of the key jobs under the factor comparison method, were able to insist upon a wage conversion line that would have yielded the group a 12 per cent increase in wages. The company demurred on the very job evaluation system that it had itself suggested, because it objected to giving the increase.

In another case, where the workers' equity in setting production standards was frankly recognized, an altogether different and more constructive solution was reached. A dispute arose over a job requiring the use of boring machinery. The standard had been set at 1,000 pieces per hour, yet production was only 800 pieces. A representative of the UAW who was handling the complaint on the rate went into the plant one day and singled out the job for his careful attention. After watching a worker on the job for some time, he observed that at intervals the man was finding it necessary to bend over and twist his head sideways in order to observe some working of the machinery. It seemed to be a rather awkward and tortuous process. And, needless to say, it was time consuming. The UAW representative stepped up to the machine and asked the worker if he might examine it. Then he made a rough sketch of the part that was demanding this unusual attention. The upshot of the matter was that this particular part of the machine was removed and relocated in the machine in such a manner that the operator could watch it easily and from a normal work stance. In no time, the production standard of 1,000 pieces per hour was being met and surpassed.

The Management Engineering Department of the International Ladies' Garment Workers' Union has a most ambitious program designed to meet the problems in its industry. That program is built upon the basic assumption that if an employer makes money, his workers will be in better position to make money. It is as hard-headed as that. The department makes no wordy pronouncements about social contributions, industrial progress, etc. It simply believes that in a competitive economy, it is a good idea to have your industry in sound, competitive condition. To that end, the department performs a number of different kinds of functions:

1. It furnishes a consulting agency for manufacturers who have agreements with the ILGWU. Department staff members travel to factories where production problems have arisen and help straighten them out, using the accepted practices of the industrial engineering profession. In an industry where piecework is so prevalent, a smoothly running plant means money in pay envelopes.

2. It assists in cases where disputes over rates or production standards are in progress.

3. It endeavors to train shop committees in the fundamentals of the methods it uses, in order to promote a clearer understanding of its objectives. In some cases, shop committee members attend regular classes in time study and as a result are better equipped to discuss standards with the management.

In short, the department renders services to manufacturers who request them, keeps an eye on the engineering work being done by management engineers, helps settle disputes, and tries to bring about a clearer and more realistic approach to engineering problems by both the employers and the union.

In addition, its staff members are constantly studying the industry, gathering material on it, and serving as a central information agency for technical problems. It might also be pointed out that the ILGWU bears the whole expense of maintaining this service. No manufacturer pays for the services of the Management Engineering Department.

The following is a typical problem that the department finds in its visits to factories:

A group of operators enter a complaint on a piecework rate. The management of the plant maintains that the rate was set fairly, and refuses to change it; the operators claim they are losing money; and both sides are rapidly becoming more incensed. A representative of the Management Engineering Department steps in to study the case. He observes the operators at their work. Everything seems to be going smoothly until he notices an operator pick up a pair of shears and trim a part of the garment before she sews it. In a few minutes the operator next to her frowns, rips a garment from her machine, and stalks off to find the forelady. The department representative walks over to a bin and picks up a bundle of garments waiting to be stitched. The two operators have given him a clue. He examines the parts in the bundle. The parts are badly cut and do not match properly. This means that the operators who sew them will have to waste time in trimming them or will have difficulty in making the parts match up properly in their machines. Such difficulty naturally slows them in the performance of their work.

What started as a rate complaint turns out to be a matter of inferior cutting. The department representative traces the work back to the cutting room. He corrects the source of the trouble there so that the operators will receive work that is properly cut and requires no extra attention. With lost time eliminated, the rate becomes satisfactory to the operators.

There was another example. A rate complaint was entered. Investigation of the rate by a departmental staff member indicated that the rate was fair, provided a constant supply of work was available. But such was not the case in slack seasons. Examination of the firm's methods of routing and scheduling its work through the plant revealed that the ratio of work-in-process inventory to finished goods produced was 30 to 1. A revision of these methods resulted in a ratio of 2 to 1, thus assuring a constant and fast-moving supply of work throughout the factory and no time lost by the operators.

Meaning of Scientific Management

A review of the labor movement's attitude toward these industrial engineering tools reveals a purely pragmatic approach. Asking a trade unionist whether he is for or against scientific management makes no more sense than asking him whether or not he is in favor of having weather. Scientific management represents no organized body of doctrine. The results of its operations depend upon the people who are applying the technique. Introduction of industrial engineering into a plant no longer elicits the alarm or fear that it once did. On the other hand, the technician responsible for application of the procedures will find himself challenged continuously by the union in those areas where a collective bargaining interest exists.

Still, there has been far from uniform acceptance of industrial engineering by the labor movement as a collective bargaining tool. Whether the technique under discussion is job evaluation, administration of wage incentive payment methods, or use of time study for rate-setting purposes, the three principal points of view remain: (1) complete rejection; (2) observant, suspicious resistance followed by limited acceptance; (3) complete joint participation.

Where management has taken the position that the administration and installation of these tools remain a unilateral management prerogative, all groups agree that the union's policy is complete rejection when its collective bargaining strength can make such a policy stick.

But it cannot be said that there is a single general policy of the labor movement toward industrial engineering techniques.

WILLIAM GOMBERG

PART FIVE

Welfare, Health, and Community Services

Introduction

Welfare, health, and community services

A FRINGE ISSUE IN COLLECTIVE BAR-GAINING that began to manifest itself during the War Labor Board days—health and welfare benefits—is slowly being woven, as a pattern, into the entire fabric of labor-management negotiations. In a broad, historic sense, this development is but a current form of labor's perpetual interest in the general welfare of its members. The essential difference between the present-day welfare activities of unions and earlier attempts to achieve similar goals lies in the contemporary realization by labor that these plans can best be achieved within the economic and social framework of our culture rather than outside of it.

During the nineteenth century, escape from the industrial and commercial system had been the most persistent feature of labor's struggle for well-being and status. In the 1840's, this aspiration took the form of socialistic communities and co-operative workshops and distributive centers. When periodic depressions did not succeed in destroying all of labor's experiments, the rest perished in the vigorous fires of individualism

and opportunity that swept the entire nation in its rush onward toward the West.

Again in the 1860's, despite undeniable past failures, the National Labor Union offered a fresh program of producers' cooperatives to the small band of organized workers in the United States. It appealed to the continual yearning of labor for security and recognition, but, once more, did not succeed, so foreign was it to the prevailing economic reality of the times.

Later, in the 1870's, there emerged a league of consumers' cooperatives called the Sovereigns of Industry. Although the Sovereigns disbanded in 1880, the Knights of Labor revived their program, with emphasis upon producers' cooperatives, amid fervent anticipation of success. When it also collapsed, labor's hope of escape into a more equitable system of production and distribution gave way before the humdrum hours-wages-working-conditions philosophy of Samuel Gompers. He was convinced, and spent the rest of his life in convincing labor, that American workers could never cast off capi-

273

talism through heady dreams of a cooperative commonwealth.

Labor's banks and credit unions and its cooperative housing ventures, although considerably younger than the various benefit plans that unions set up for themselves more than 50 years ago, nevertheless partake more of the spirit of labor's earlier philosophy of escape than its later acclimatization to the American scene. Despite their anachronistic flavor, labor banks and credit unions, described in this Part by Maurice F. Neufeld, and cooperative housing, covered by A. E. Kazan, must be accounted for in the balance sheet of the welfare activities of unions. Although the first group of undertakings has suffered, for the most part, a drastic desolation of earlier hopes, cooperative housing activity has been gaining momentum. Yet both have to be recognized as non-representative of labor activities today.

The early benefit plans of unions, financed and administered wholly by them almost since the beginning of their existence as internationals, provided for the common welfare at the same time that they kept their actuarial feet planted firmly within the existing order. They may be regarded as the forerunners of the welfare plans, collectively negotiated, of the present day. "Union Welfare Plans" by Abraham Weiss presents an inclusive review of the size and distribution of the welfare funds wholly sponsored by labor unions, and provides, as well, a guide to the types of newly evolving plans sponsored jointly by unions and management. As Mr. Weiss points out, between 6,000,000 and 7,000,000 workers are presently covered by some type of health, welfare, and/or pension plan under collective bargaining. This is an astounding figure considering the short period during which this development has occurred.

John M. Brumm's "Unions and Health Insurance" surveys the historical development and present forms of health insurance plans, analyzing those aspects which follow already-established principles and practices and those characteristics which are unique. Dr. Warren F. Draper's "Health Programs of the United Mine Workers" presents one of the most controversial as well as comprehensive plans now in operation. Ruth Glazer's report on the International Ladies' Garment Workers' Union Health Center deals with the oldest institution of this kind and covers a type of activity which is spreading within the labor movement.

Turning now to labor's concern with community welfare services, it can be seen that this preoccupation is directly correlated with the growing strength of the American labor movement since 1935 and with the concomitant recognition of labor's prestige by the country as a whole. Unions have therefore moved from the restricted area of concern for their own welfare to the broader arena of community welfare services. One aspect of this interest in problems and issues that go beyond labor's traditional range of activities may be found in the growth of labor radio stations and programs. This pioneering field of union responsibility has been reported by M. S. Novik. Also in line with this development, both the CIO and the AFL, as federations, have turned their attention toward labor's increasing participation in community-wide affairs. Matthew Woll and Leo Perlis describe this work. Both the AFL and CIO also recognize the problems faced by minority

INTRODUCTION

groups. They are aware that these problems are not limited merely to the untoward effects of discrimination solely within industry but also extend to the entire social scene. Their efforts are depicted by Emanuel Muravchik.

Labor's direct participation in welfare, health, and community services is therefore an expression not only of an evolving concept of social justice within the American community, but also of labor's own growing sense of social responsibility.

MAURICE F. NEUFELD

Chapter 22

Union welfare plans[1]

PENSION AND WELFARE PLANS HAVE BECOME AN INTEGRAL PART OF THE collective bargaining program of most of the important unions in the country. This is in line with the broad goal of the labor movement for economic security for its members. Today, labor looks upon pension and social insurance plans won through negotiations as positive and constructive contributions to the general welfare of its members. Interest in these plans stems from various sources: The increasing desire by workers and their union leaders for economic and job security; the changed economic climate and public temper that made demands for "health and welfare" more strategic than demands for wage increases; the increasing proportion of aged employees which underscored the need for pension benefits to solve the problems of superannuated workers; gaps and inadequacies in governmental social security programs, and so forth.

Within less than a decade, negotiated "health and welfare" plans have become firmly imbedded in our industrial relations scene. Such plans, however, are not new; they have existed for decades. Records indicate that the first modern company-initiated pension plan was established in 1874. Though development was slow, by 1938 more than 1,000 private company pension plans were in existence.

Employers have for many years made available, both with and without employee contributions, medical aid to workers in the form of direct medical services, hospitalization, and cash payments during disability, as well as group life insurance and pension plans. Company-sponsored plans were never wholeheartedly endorsed by unions because of the belief that they were paternalistic and were adopted to win employees' loyalty, to chain workers to their jobs, and to discourage union organizations.

Unions, too, have maintained their own benefit programs for many years, financed out of members' dues, per capita tax, or special assessments.

---

[1] The views expressed by the author do not necessarily constitute the views of the Department of Labor, the Bureau of Labor Statistics, or the Division of the Bureau of Labor Statistics with which he is associated.

At least three national unions—the Molders, the Spinners, and the Typographers—had a benefit plan before 1860. For the most part, however, the union-financed plans offered modest benefits and were often shaky financially.[2] But there is little connection between these early efforts and the present-day programs of many unions, through collective bargaining, to protect the health and welfare of workers and their families.

Preoccupation of labor unions with "health and welfare" is, therefore, not a new departure in labor policy. The new factor is the inclusion of such plans under collective bargaining. This latter development coalesced and fused the then existing dual systems of company-sponsored and union-sponsored plans. This fusion occurred chiefly as a result of special wartime and postwar developments that diverted these programs into the mainstream of labor-management negotiations.

Therefore, health and welfare as bargaining aims of unions represent the culmination of a fairly long historical development in labor-management relations in the United States. Roots firmly fixed in American industrial history have been transplanted to a new institutional setting, that of collective bargaining. This represents a reversal of traditional union attitudes toward welfare plans in which the employer participates. The factors responsible, among which are to be included the experience of unions with their own benefit systems, are described in the following paragraphs.

Trade Union Benefit Activities

Many American trade unions have from the start established benefit programs on their own initiative, financed by membership dues or assessments. Many unions, in fact, started as fraternal or benevolent societies— the Typographers, Journeymen Cabinetmakers, Locomotive Firemen and Enginemen, Iron Molders. Their objectives were not only to raise wages and improve working conditions, but also to supply sickness, unemployment, old-age, and mortuary aid to the members or their widows. Welfare activities preceded the "bread and butter" activities of wages, hours, and working conditions.

In some cases, these plans were established because union members could not obtain insurance from the commercial insurance companies. Workmen's compensation laws were not, as yet, known in this country. In addition, these benefits were generally regarded as a source of union strength and as an organizing device. In lieu of cash benefits, some unions provided homes for aged and disabled members, sanatoriums, hospital treatment for tuberculous members, funds for relief, and the like. In one

---

[2] Murray W. Latimer, on the basis of a detailed study of trade union superannuation and total and permanent disability plans in effect in 1929, concluded that "unless drastic financial reorganization is made, they are almost certain to end in failure in the relatively near future." *Trade Union Pension Systems* (New York: Industrial Relations Counselors, Inc., 1932), p. 98.

way or another, welfare and mutual aid programs became a recognized feature of American trade unionism and helped greatly to give it a much needed stability in its early days.[3]

By the end of World War I, however, trade union welfare activities were definitely on the decline, owing largely to adverse experience. Since they were financed entirely by workers' contributions, it was difficult to build up adequate reserves and place the funds on a sound actuarial basis. Many unions found that the number of members eligible for benefits was outstripping funds available. In some instances benefits were reduced; in others, benefits were retained only by increasing dues and/or assessments. Some unions discontinued their plans. In view of the burdens that "benefits" placed on union finances, the American Federation of Labor warned its affiliated unions against the adoption of new plans: "Benefit systems, where they are still in operation, are a constant source of trouble. . . . Few union operations are today productive of as much woe and uncertainty as the benefit systems that remain in operation. Because they are unscientific they must continue to produce woe as long as they are allowed to exist. There is an endless chase in which assessments never catch up with benefits to be paid out. . . ." [4]

Even as late as 1929, however, about 60.7 per cent of trade union membership was covered by some provision for sickness and disability.[5]

These financial problems caused a number of unions, chiefly the railroad brotherhoods, to add regular insurance to their standard benefit programs. Other unions, such as the Boilermakers, Cigarmakers, and Sleeping Car Conductors, substituted such insurance for their traditional benefits, in effect transferring the maintenance of such other benefits to the local union level. Most of this insurance was placed with one of two union-owned companies doing a general insurance business: the Union Co-Operative Life Insurance Company, established by the International Brotherhood of Electrical Workers in 1924, and the Union Labor Life Insurance Company, started by the American Federation of Labor in 1925 and owned by its affiliated unions.

A number of unions, like the Brotherhood of Railroad Trainmen, operate insurance departments where members may take out insurance covering death, accident, or sickness, or all of these.

A study by the Bureau of Labor Statistics in 1927-28 of the benefit activities of 78 national and international unions disclosed that 63 paid benefits for death, 14 for disability, 12 for sickness, 13 made some pro-

---

[3] Nathaniel M. Minkoff, "Trade Union Welfare Programs," *Union Health and Welfare Plans*, BLS. Bull. No. 900 (1947), p. 12.

[4] "Why Trade Union Group Insurance rather than a Benefit Plan?" *The American Photo-Engraver*, April 1930, p. 451.

[5] Earl E. Muntz. *Growth and Trends in Social Security*. National Industrial Conference Board. Studies in Individual and Collective Security, No. 6 (1949), p. 117.

vision for aged members, and 20 had some form of insurance. Eight unions paid tuberculosis benefits or provided for treatment of the tubercular. Seven unions maintained homes for the aged and disabled, and two of these also maintained a tuberculosis sanatorium in connection with the home.[6]

The passage of the Social Security (and Railroad Retirement) Act in 1935 for the first time made old-age protection available on a broad basis. It modified the hostility of national labor leaders to private pension plans. Just as the Wagner Act provided the union with *organizational* security, so the Social Security Act provided a minimum measure of *old-age* security to the workers. It provided a base for future expansion—on the legislative front and on the bargaining front.

Union benefit programs were therefore revised, chiefly by discontinuing provisions for old-age pensions and unemployment. Group life insurance and sickness benefits grew more significant.

The new industrial unions organized after 1935 generally do not include benefits. Unemployment and old-age benefits were by then available as a result of government legislation. Even some of the old-line craft unions that have continued a benefit system have admitted members who pay lower dues and are, therefore, not eligible for benefits.

Trade union benefits have been consistently modest. The most common type—a death benefit—usually takes the form of a lump-sum payment and is, in effect, a contribution to funeral expenses and doctor bills, but is not, in most cases, large enough to be considered a provision for dependents. In 1928 the death benefits of individual international unions ranged in amount from $20 to $1500, and disability benefits from $50 to $800. The weekly benefits payable in case of sickness ranged in amount from $4 to $10, and in time from 7 to 16 weeks a year. Old-age pension payments paid ranged from $5 to $70 a month; in cases where the old-age pension was in actuality a lump-sum benefit, not a continuing annuity, the amount ranged from $50 to $800.[7] In 1931, the average pension was a little less than $300 a year.[8]

In 1949 a total of 73 national and international unions out of 112 reporting to the American Federation of Labor paid some type of benefit to their members. These 73 unions, with an estimated membership of close to 7½ million,[9] made payments amounting to more than 67 million dollars covering death, sickness, unemployment, old age, disability, and miscellaneous items. Death benefits amounted to nearly 28 percent of the total disbursement, as shown in the following table:

---

[6] "Beneficial Activities of American Trade Unions," BLS. Bull. No. 465, 1928, p. 12.

[7] BLS. Bull. No. 465, *op. cit.*, p. 3.

[8] Murray W. Latimer, *op. cit.*, p. 119.

[9] Membership figures as reported in BLS. Bull. No. 980, "Directory of Labor Unions in the United States, 1950."

DISBURSEMENT OF NATIONAL AND INTERNATIONAL TRADE UNIONS
FOR BENEFIT SERVICES, 1949 [10]

Type of Benefit	Number of Unions [11]	Amount (in millions)
Total	73	$67.17
Death	68	18.83
Sickness	22	7.29
Unemployment	12	.82
Old Age	23	14.94
Disability	17	1.38
Miscellaneous	38	23.91

In 1943, the latest year for which data are available, unions paid out close to 7 per cent of their receipts in death, sick, pension, and other benefits to their members or their dependents.[12]

In view of the financial problems that have beset trade union benefit systems, it is not surprising that benefit payments have been generally inadequate to meet union members' security needs. The depression underscored existing weaknesses in their voluntary benefit systems and the limited scope of their protection against the hazards of old age, sickness, disability, unemployment, and the like. Consequently, union leaders abandoned their traditional policy of "voluntarism" and turned to governmental social insurance to provide the necessary protection for their members.

An atmosphere was also created that, in short order, was to change the basic nature of union welfare plans from those financed by the workers themselves, through regular payments or assessments, to funds or programs financed, at least partially, by the employers under a contractual obligation arrived at through collective bargaining.

Benefit Plans Under Collective Bargaining

Although it is not generally known, provisions for health, welfare, and retirement benefits were included in collective bargaining agreements almost 30 years ago.[13] In 1921 in Cleveland and in 1924 in New York, the

[10] Report of the Executive Council of the American Federation of Labor to 69th Convention, Houston, Texas, Sept. 18, 1950, p. 84.

[11] Includes international and national unions providing benefits through the national organization or through their locals.

[12] U.S. Bureau of Internal Revenue, Supplement to Statistics of Income for 1943, Part II, p. 36 (Nov. 1945).

[13] In 1911 the United States Brewers' Association proposed to the Brewery Workers that by agreement between the two organizations each employer was to turn over 1.5 per cent of his payroll to a pension fund to which the individual employees were also to contribute 0.5 per cent of their pay. (Pensions were more or less incidental to a workmen's compensation plan which the bulk of the assessments was to support.)

International Ladies' Garment Workers' Union entered into agreements with employers whereby jointly-financed unemployment insurance programs were established. The Amalgamated Clothing Workers Union in Chicago entered into a similar agreement with employers in 1923.[14] In 1926, the Amalgamated Association of Street, Electric Railway, and Motor Coach Employees entered into an agreement with the Chicago Rapid Transit Company which called for an employer-financed program of $1,000 of life insurance and weekly sick benefits of $20 a week for a maximum of 26 weeks. In 1929 a pension and disability insurance plan was agreed to between Local 3 (IBEW) and the members of the Electrical Contracting Association of New York, with the entire cost borne by the employers.

But these examples were exceedingly rare. As recently as 1942, the Bureau of Labor Statistics, after a comprehensive survey of collective bargaining agreements, reported that health, welfare, and retirement benefit plans were rarely included.[15] By 1950, however, such provisions in union contracts covered about 7½ million workers in virtually every industry, including such casual employments as the building trades, trucking, and longshoring. Practically every union, excluding the railroad, postal, and other governmental employee unions whose members are covered by Federal, state, or local pension systems, has negotiated such plans and incorporated them in its agreements.

Many of the benefit plans placed under agreement were not created by the unions nor did they come into being as a result of collective bargaining. Many were existing plans, originally sponsored and established by the employers themselves, and financed wholly or in part by the employer. The significant change was that they were formalized, often liberalized, and brought within the scope of the agreement. In some cases, such as that of the AFL Electrical Workers, collective bargaining resulted in contributions by employers to long-established *union* pension plans, hitherto financed wholly out of union dues.

What are the factors that account for the remarkable growth of such plans during the last few years?

During World War II the limitations on wage increases caused unions to seek substitutes for such increases in the form of "fringe benefits," including insurance and pension plans. Workers considered such plans as a supplement to their actual earnings. The National War Labor Board ruled that employers could make contributions to welfare plans without violating wage ceilings providing the cost did not exceed five per cent of

---

Although approved by the conventions of both organizations, the union referendum rejected the proposal. Murray W. Latimer, *op. cit.*, p. 26.

[14] These unemployment insurance programs were abandoned after enactment of the unemployment insurance provisions of the Social Security Act of 1935. The ACWA plan was converted into a life and health insurance fund in 1939.

[15] BLS. Bull. No. 686, "Union Agreement Provisions (1942)," pp. 198-201.

payroll. Employers, therefore, turned to such plans as a desirable substitute for wage increases in attracting and holding workers in a tight labor market. Both the National Association of Manufacturers and the U. S. Chamber of Commerce recommended the acceptance of such plans, perhaps to ward off compulsory health insurance.

Much more significant for collective bargaining, however, were National War Labor Board decisions that such plans were within the sphere of collective bargaining: It directed employers to include an already existing unilaterally-established plan in the union contract; it held, in a number of cases, that the union was entitled to a written guarantee that for the duration of the war the employer would neither terminate nor amend the existing pension and benefit plan.[16]

Favorable tax regulations, combined with high wartime profits and high excess profits taxation, made the net cost of such plans very low and induced employers to install or liberalize them to attract scarce labor. In 1942, the income tax laws were revised to permit employers to deduct "reasonable" expenses for employee benefits from taxable income. The possibility of tax deductions interested employers in such plans; such interest, in turn, stimulated union activity in this field.

The period following the war's end saw an upsurge in labor's drive for "health and welfare." Older workers who had been allowed to continue working because of labor scarcity now were retired on inadequate pensions. Employee and union resistance to forced retirement mounted. The welfare fund obtained by the United Mine Workers, supported by a tonnage tax on coal,[17] inspired other unions to press for company-financed pensions.

Further impetus and support to this trend was given by a series of NLRB and court decisions that pensions were subject to bargaining;[18] and that the Taft-Hartley Act not only permits but requires the employer, upon union request, to bargain on employee benefit plans.[19]

A growing feeling that social security benefits no longer were adequate in the face of rising living costs, and the absence of any general program for health insurance furnished additional impetus to union demands for

[16] Western Union Telegraph Co.—2516-CS-D (1/13/43) 6 WLR 133.

[17] Employer payments into the Welfare and Retirement fund are now 30 cents per ton.

[18] Inland Steel Co. 77 NLRB 1; 170 Fed 2d 247 (1949); 336 U.S. 960; W. W. Cross Co. 77 NLRB 1162; 174 Fed 2d 875 (1949); General Motors Corp. 81 NLRB 126 (1949); Allied Mills 82 NLRB 99; Tide Water Assoc. Oil Co. (Case No. 2c-6907, September 8, 1949).

[19] The Taft-Hartley Act (Sec. 302) places the following restrictions on employer payments to a trust fund: The benefits must (1) be for the exclusive benefit of the employees, families or dependents; (2) be held in trust for benefit of payments stated; (3) contain specific details for payment of benefits; (4) provide for breaking deadlocks between employer and employee representatives administering the fund; (5) provide for annual auditing; and (6) if the benefits are pension or annuity benefits, be placed in a separate trust fund from the other benefits.

union-management welfare plans. After 15 years of experience under Social Security, during which time living costs had doubled, old-age benefits averaged about $26 a month for a single worker and about $40 for a retired worker and his wife. These amounts became increasingly less adequate for elderly people to maintain even a modest standard of living. For example, Social Security Administration–Bureau of Labor Statistics studies showed that the approximate annual cost of a budget for an elderly couple in 13 cities, at March 1949 prices, ranged from $1,440 in Houston, Texas, to $1,830 in Washington, D. C. Average annual payments under Federal Old Age and Survivors Insurance amounted to less than $500 to an elderly couple.

Although both AFL and CIO demanded increased social security payments as early as 1946, there was little likelihood of a rise in the general level of benefits. The Federal floor of social security protection had, it appeared, sunk to sub-basement levels.[20] Since Federal benefits were too small to give security, workers and their unions looked to the employer to support such plans. From 1946 on, annual conventions of the AFL and CIO adopted resolutions urging their affiliated unions to secure pension, health, and welfare benefits through collective bargaining.

The inadequacy of Federal old-age benefits loomed larger as the following facts about our aging population became known: (1) By 1950 an estimated 8 per cent of the population, or about 11 million people, would be 65 years or older—a proportion which is double what it was 50 years ago and in numbers almost 4 times as many; (2) the average life expectancy at age 65 had increased 2 years since 1900, to 13⅔ years; (3) in 1948, almost ⅓ of the 11 million people over 65 had no money income of their own and another ⅕ received less than $500 during that year; (4) older workers had difficulty in finding jobs, in securing re-employment, and in living on inadequate incomes. Soaring old-age assistance payments gave eloquent testimonial to these difficulties.

These facts gave support to the unions' contention that there was a compelling need for old-age protection that was not being met by present-day arrangements, and that workers could not save enough for old age out of wages in the face of high living costs. Union bargaining demands gained additional support when impartial employee opinion polls indicated that American workers are primarily concerned with security. As one labor spokesman stated:

Labor's position is that to the extent that adequate security for workers is not provided through governmental programs the problems of workers' security will be taken to the collective bargaining table. Economic security for the

[20] Monthly primary old-age benefits under the Social Security Act were increased in mid-1950 by about 70 per cent, or from an average of about $26 a month to an average of $44 a month.

worker when he is no longer able to work is as fundamental a concern of the union as wages and working conditions.[21]

From the standpoint of the "security" of the union itself, negotiated welfare funds were important as a stabilizing element by building up union morale and membership loyalty:

To the unions, industrial pensions are a prime source of the institutional security which is still their chief aim in life. Benefits delivered directly to the rank and file through collective bargaining always reflect more credit on the union than those resulting from an act of Congress. Joint administration of pension benefits gives the organization an additional function, a new role, in economic life. The retiring worker looks to the union, rather than a government official, to investigate his rights, certify him for his pension, and handle any disputes and problems concerning his status.[22]

At the state level, the failure of the Social Security Act to provide health benefits was recognized through enactment of state disability insurance laws, making mandatory provision of weekly accident and sickness benefits for workers. Rhode Island in 1942, California in 1946, New Jersey in 1948, and New York in 1949 enacted such laws. Except in Rhode Island, private plans meeting minimum standards are encouraged. At least in these states, practically every employer (and every union) has been drawn into the quickening welfare stream.

The economic climate in late 1948 and in 1949 also favored the spread of such plans as living costs levelled off, general business activity declined, and unemployment rose. With the "props" for a fourth-round wage increase demand weakening, unions shifted their bargaining emphasis from direct wage increases to indirect increases in the form of insurance and pensions. President Truman proposed to Congress the adoption of a broad program of social welfare. The unions could therefore expect greater popular support on the welfare front than on the wage front.

All these factors, then, led many unions to reverse their original views on employer financing of benefit plans and to request that employers provide such benefits. Collectively-bargained plans were pressed to provide supplementary benefits that would more nearly approximate the needs of workers in industrial and high cost of living areas. The traditional concern of unions with the welfare of their members, now channeled into the sphere of collective bargaining, is expressed in the following statement by Philip Murray, President of the CIO:

The basic reason for collective bargaining about social security ... is because labor organizations, if they are to meet the necessities of their members, and

---

[21] "Labors' Approach to the Retirement Problem" by Harry Beeker, Director, Social Security Department, UAW-CIO in proceedings of second annual meeting of the Industrial Relations Research Assn., New York City, Dec. 29-30, 1949, p. 118.

[22] Arthur M. Ross, "The New Industrial Pensions," *Review of Economics and Statistics*, May 1950, pp. 133-138.

they can have no other reason for existence, must participate actively in the formulation of plans for security which have become, and will as time goes on, be increasingly a matter of major concern to all those who work.

At the same time, unions continued to press for improvement and expansion of the Federal Social Security System to provide a floor of security for all people:

Needless to say, trade unions have entered the field of social welfare out of sheer necessity. The attitude of some employers with respect to the health and welfare of their workers and the past inadequacy of governmental plans left them no other course. However, it is hoped that the social security program of the Federal Government, which now offers only a limited form of protection, will eventually embrace all forms of sickness insurance and medical, mental, hospital, surgical, dental and prenatal care. When this happens, some unions will gladly turn over their responsibilities to the Government and continue to pioneer in other fields of social reform and economic justice.[23]

Similar views are expressed by the AFL Metal Trades Department:

If adequate old age pensions and death benefits are to be provided for all the workers of the land, it is imperative that the Federal Social Security law be amended without delay. When all of the workers and all of the employers contribute to a nation-wide fund, then all of the workers benefit directly and fully ... the answer may well be an all-inclusive social security law, covering all the workers, with adequate benefits in the case of old age, sickness, death, plus complete medical care.[24]

The "welfare" seed sown in the favorable economic climate of the war period and nurtured by the legal obligation to bargain, burst into full flower when a Presidential Fact-Finding Board enunciated the moral concept that employers must assume responsibility for providing pensions and welfare as a part of normal business costs. This principle was laid down by the Steel Industry Board appointed by President Truman to make recommendations in the wage and pension dispute between the United Steelworkers of America (CIO) and the major steel companies:

Social insurance and pensions should be considered a part of normal business costs to take care of temporary and permanent depreciation in the human "machine" in much the same way as provision is made for depreciation and insurance of plant machinery. This obligation should be among the first charges on revenues.[25]

This recommendation helped to establish permanent responsibility for security benefits as a charge upon business. It accelerated the movement

---

[23] N. M. Minkoff, *op. cit.*, p. 24.

[24] Bulletin of the Metal Trades Dept., American Federation of Labor, May 1948, p. 5.

[25] Report to the President of the U. S. on the Labor Dispute in the Basic Steel Industry by the Steel Industry Board, September 10, 1949, p. 8.

that had begun earlier. Pensions and welfare funds, the so-called "fringe benefits" became leading subjects of bargaining. The proportion of contract negotiations involving pensions and insurance rose sharply. Their significance during 1949 is indicated by the fact that these issues, either alone or in combination with wage demands, were involved in labor-management disputes accounting for 55 per cent of the total strike idleness during that year.[26]

The Ford Motor Company agreed to a noncontributory $100 a month pension plan (later increased to $125) shortly after the Steel Industry Board's recommendations. A work stoppage in the steel industry following the companies' opposition to the noncontributory feature of the Board's recommendations ended when the Bethlehem Steel Corporation signed a contract which became the general pattern for subsequent settlements throughout the industry. It contained noncontributory pensions ($100 minimum including primary social security benefits) and a social insurance plan financed jointly by employer and employee.

In effect, the Ford and steel settlements set a benchmark for subsequent negotiations on pensions and insurance. The great impetus given to such benefit plans continued into 1950 at an exceptionally rapid pace. Including the coal settlements, the number of organized workers affected by new pension plans or by increased employer contributions to established plans negotiated during the first 5 months of 1950 exceeded the total for the entire year of 1949, when more than a million organized workers were thus affected.

Extent and Characteristics of Benefit Plans

Health, welfare, and pension plans in collective bargaining agreements now cover about 7½ million workers. In some instances, such as coal, steel, auto, textiles, men's and women's clothing, furniture, tobacco, and street and electric railways, virtually the entire industry, or large segments of the industry, have established through collective bargaining various combinations of welfare and/or pension plans.

Health, welfare, and retirement plans assured through collective bargaining follow no particular pattern. They vary as to methods of financing and insuring. Likewise, there are differences in administration, benefits, eligibility criteria, and other details. The employer alone may finance the program or both employer and employees share in the cost. Administration may be vested in the employer, the union, or a union-management group. In addition, plans may be insured by an established private carrier, or an insurance company chartered for the express purpose of insuring a particular plan, or benefits may be paid directly from the fund. In many in-

---

[26] "Analysis of Work Stoppages During 1949," *Monthly Labor Review*, May, 1950, p. 497.

stances in which insurance is with an established private company, the company has a role in the administration of the plan.[27]

One of the most distinctive developments has been the creation of multi-employer welfare funds. A few plans, such as those of the miners, men's clothing workers, and electrical contractors, are on a national or industry basis; other plans, like those in the apparel industries and building trades, are negotiated on a regional or area basis. Union membership and a specified period of service in the industry is generally a requirement for benefits in these industry- or area-wide plans. Such plans are usually financed by uniform employer contributions—such as a fixed percentage of wages, or a fixed amount of money per month per employee, or a fixed number of cents per hour worked.

These pooled plans generally cover a large number of small employers who might otherwise be too small (or too insecure financially) to be able to provide pensions. This central fund concept has the double advantage to the workers of giving their pensions a broader financial base and of permitting transfers from one company to another without sacrifice of pension rights. Toledo employers have strongly rejected a proposal of the CIO United Auto Workers to establish an area-wide pension plan. On the other hand, Detroit tool and die shops, which have heretofore bargained with the same union on a multi-employer basis, have recently entered into an agreement embodying the pooled fund idea.

Some of the plans, such as the Ladies' Garment Workers' and the Hatters', are self-insured. At the other extreme are some employer-union funds which buy group insurance policies and turn over the acceptance and payment of claims to the carriers. The Amalgamated Clothing Workers has its own variant: Insurance is purchased from the Amalgamated Life Insurance Company, which was organized by the union with a board of directors having both union and employer representatives.

The negotiated pension plans differ from pre-existing employer-sponsored plans in that there is a contractual obligation to pay certain benefits, at least for the duration of the union agreement; employer plans usually contained a proviso that the company was free to discontinue or modify the plan at its discretion.

The issue of noncontributory pensions has been for all practical purposes settled in major negotiations in the steel and auto industries and elsewhere. Some unions, however, believe that pension plans are based on a sounder foundation if workers also contribute, and there is less likelihood of the plan being discontinued under such circumstances. Though many AFL and CIO officials consider that retirement benefits are a deferred compensation by the employer for service rendered by the employee, and, consequently, should be financed entirely by the employer,

---

[27] Labor-Management Relations Report of the Joint Committee on Labor-Management Relations. 80th Cong. 2d sess., p. 91.

others hold that no question of "principle" is involved concerning whether pension plans should be contributory or noncontributory. An AFL report states:

> As a matter of expediency, of course, it may be necessary or advisable at times to accept a contributory arrangement in order to get a stronger voice in the administration of the fund, or where the workers want a more satisfactory scale of benefits than can be financed by the amount negotiated from the employer, at the time.
>
> This is a purely practical matter, however, and not one of "principle."

The newly emerging negotiated pension plans show the following features:

As a rule, there is no compulsory retirement at age 65, although some major plans set 65 as the normal retirement age but permit the employee to work up to age 68 as long as he is able to perform his duties. The major steel contracts have no maximum or compulsory retirement age. A minimum of $100 a month (including ordinary Social Security benefits) after 25 or 30 years' service is standard, though the General Motors contract provides a pension of $117.50 monthly, the Ford contract $125, and long-service employees in the steel plans will be eligible to receive pensions in excess of these minimums. Employees reaching age 65 with shorter periods of service are generally eligible for pro rata minimum pension amounts.

There has been an increasing emphasis on disability protection in collective bargaining pension plans. The newer agreements negotiated for old age retirement plans in three of the mass production industries—namely, steel, auto, and rubber—and involving over 1,350,000 employees, include provisions designed specifically to allow retirement for permanent and total disability. This growing emphasis on disability protection is evidence of the concern of unions and employers for making more adequate provision available for the risk than now exists.[28]

Provisions for vested rights in the employer's contribution are virtually nonexistent in plans negotiated in 1949 and early 1950 with the larger unions. However, a number of pension plans negotiated by the International Union of Electrical, Radio and Machine Workers (CIO), including the Philco Corporation, provide severance pay for the worker ranging from 50 to 70 per cent of the employer's contribution.[29]

Most of the recent pension plans, such as in steel or rubber, are company-administered. The Ford and Chrysler plans are jointly administered but in both cases the company has complete control over the fund. In the

---

[28] "Permanent and Total Disability Benefit Provisions in Industrial Retirement Plans," Division of Research and Statistics, and BOASI, Social Security Administration, Federal Security Agency, June 1950, p. 10.

[29] IUE-CIO *News,* August 14, 1950, p. 11.

longer-established industry plans, such as in the garment trades, union administration, or joint administration is common.

Negotiated insurance plans generally offer a "package" of benefits: life insurance equivalent to about one year's pay; Blue Cross or similar hospitalization insurance policies; non-occupational sickness and accident benefits up to 50 and 60 per cent of average pay during disability for up to 26 weeks; surgical expenses reimbursement policies. Medical insurance —protection against doctors' bills aside from surgery—is still relatively uncommon.

ABRAHAM WEISS

Chapter 23

Unions and health insurance

A NEW FIELD OF TRADE UNION INTEREST AND RESPONSIBILITY, FREQUENTLY referred to as "voluntary health insurance,"[1] emerged during the war years. It covers a wide variety of medical and sickness programs, sought by unions as a part of their collective bargaining contracts with employers. These programs differ as to type and extent of benefits, method of financing, administration, and several other characteristics.

It is fair to say that unions usually have not immediately appreciated the full implications of their new ventures into this field and are only slowly becoming aware of the constructive role that the expert can take in this development. This chapter will survey these recent trends in trade union sponsorship of health insurance plans and indicate the outstanding problems, arising out of this sponsorship, that today are coming increasingly to require the services of professionally trained personnel.

During the war, the "wage stabilization" policies of the War Labor Board effectively restricted trade union bargaining for simple across-the-board wage increases even in situations where employers were favorably disposed toward granting them. As a general phenomenon characteristic of the war period, most union health insurance "plans" were the result of union effort to discover, in lieu of wages, collective bargaining demands that the War Labor Board would approve and that nevertheless would have an obvious monetary value for union members. Paid vacations and paid holidays, the most popular of these wage substitute demands, had by the end of the war become widely established throughout organized American industry. Health insurance, never as widely prevalent an item in union-employer negotiations, had not yet attained the status of a "fringe issue" that the War Labor Board might be expected to "order" in dispute cases, although the trend pointed toward the Board

---

[1] The term "voluntary" insurance is commonly used as a distinction from "compulsory" insurance established by legislation. However, many "voluntary" plans may in effect be compulsory for individuals in certain groups by virtue of membership in the group.

ultimately granting it that status. On the other hand, the Board never seriously considered disapproving these insurance arrangements when mutually agreed to by both parties, and in most areas the regional boards did not require that they be submitted for approval.

Health benefit clauses are now found fairly frequently in the collective bargaining contracts in the following industries: textiles, men's and women's clothing, coal mining, millinery, hosiery, textile dyeing and finishing, steel, bus and streetcar transportation, and upholstery. In the New York metropolitan area they are also well established in hotels, wholesale and retail trade, furniture, fur and leather, and laundries. Such clauses also constitute a noticeable trend in a great many other industries: *e.g.*, electrical manufacturing, paper manufacturing, automobile, shipbuilding, metal mining, and jewelry, to mention only a few.

Although a mild controversy exists over whether union-sponsored insurance in industry is a "new" development or whether it has not been rather a time-honored concern of the American trade union movement, the dispute can be resolved by definition and analysis. In two general aspects, health benefit plans are not new to American workers.

Early Health Benefits for Workers

In the first place, especially in the early days, trade unions were often constituted as "fraternal benefit societies" providing various kinds of "benefit" payments for their members in certain contingencies. Death benefits predominated. Only a relatively small number of unions have ever provided benefit payments in the case of permanent disability or of temporary disability (*i.e.*, sickness).

This aspect of union activities is of minor current importance because of the rapid decline in such activities after World War I. Whereas in 1908, 18 national unions financed sickness benefit programs from their own funds, by 1935, this number had decreased to seven. However moderately successful these programs may have been in their way, and whatever may have been the factors in their decline, the benefits were usually regarded as a member-getting and member-retaining device rather than as a component of a planned health security program.[2]

Secondly, companies themselves, both with and without employee participation in the costs, frequently have either provided medical service programs or sponsored group insurance plans. Many of the medical service type provide a high quality of care and have been run successfully for many years.

One authority has said that "the knowledge as to sound methods of meeting the need for protection against accident and sickness had to be

---

[2] Helen H. Avnet, "Voluntary Medical Insurance in the U.S.," Medical Administration Service, 1944), p. 6.

developed by experimentation over a period of years." [3] Fraternal benefit societies and employee mutual-benefit associations were two "experiments" in the slow evolution of the concept and practice of medical insurance.

The new trend toward union-sponsored health benefit clauses in collective bargaining agreements is likewise experimental. An important and often-neglected fact in this connection is that these trade union experiments constitute at most merely a small sector of the voluntary health insurance movement and can be evaluated only against this larger background.[4] Only one or two union plans have even attempted to be as comprehensive as the programs of several companies and of nonprofit medical care organizations in many parts of the country.

New Features of Today's Union Plans

For the moment, however, and viewed solely as a development in the labor movement, the new union plans are distinguished in several significant respects from earlier worker-benefit programs sponsored by unions or employers:

1. Established as a result of union-employer collective bargaining, current plans usually are specifically written into the union-management contract, often in considerable detail, and cover 100 per cent of the organized working force.[5] Fraternal benefits have occasionally been restricted to special categories of the union membership, and many of the employer-sponsored programs, particularly commercial insurance on a contributory basis, do not cover the entire working force.

2. Typically, these recent plans are sponsored by the union and financed by the employer, either completely, or on an employee contributory basis. Benefits are not paid out of membership-financed union funds as were the fraternal benefits; but active union sponsorship distinguishes them from the employee mutual-benefit societies.

3. In companies that previously sponsored an insurance plan on their own, collective bargaining has generally resulted in broader coverage, a reduction in the "restrictions and limitations" governing the payment of benefits, addition of new types of benefits, and an increase in the amount of benefits payable.

4. As distinguished from fraternal benefits, which frequently were

---

[3] Avnet, *op. cit.*, p. 1.

[4] A good survey of this larger movement is found in Avnet, *op. cit.*, and in E. L. Otey, "Cash Benefits Under Voluntary Disability Insurance in the U. S.," (Social Security Board, Bureau of Research and Statistics, Report No. 8, 1940).

[5] Although on the whole such developments date from 1940, a notable exception is the case of the Amalgamated Association of Street, Electric Railway and Motor Coach Employees, which as early as May 1926 had negotiated a contract with the Newburgh, N. Y., Public Service Corporation providing for the costs of a death and sickness benefit plan to be met totally by the company.

granted only when "need" could be established or as a result of a vote of the membership committee, current benefits usually are paid "automatically" as soon as the fact of a covered disability or expenditure is established.

5. In contrast to the earlier dominant emphasis on flat cash payments per unit-duration of illness, the recent plans have generally included hospitalization benefits, and frequently, surgical benefits. The trend is increasingly toward more comprehensive reimbursement for medical costs. In addition, provision is now more commonly made for some coverage, usually hospitalization, for dependents.

With a very few exceptions, the typical union "health insurance plan" today comprises the following elements:

1. Cash disability insurance to compensate for loss of income for nonoccupational sickness and accident, or provision for paid sick leave.

2. Hospitalization benefits covering all or part of the costs of room, board, and certain "extras" incidental to hospital confinement.

3. Reimbursement for surgical expenses in accordance with schedules that specify the maximum payments for specific operations..

4. Some provision for inclusion of maternity cases with limited benefits under each of the above coverages. Occasionally, dependents are also covered for hospitalization and surgery.

5. In addition to health insurance, the typical plan may contain a life policy and occasionally an accidental death or dismemberment policy which includes special lump-sum indemnity for loss of limb, finger or eye.

Factors Explaining the New Development

Health surveys have brought an increased awareness of the high costs of adequate medical care, the large proportion of the family budget that these costs consume, the inadequacy of medical care received by and available to industrial workers who cannot possibly budget for illness costs without a comprehensive prepayment scheme, and the sorry state of preventive medicine in a country that actually has a wealth of streamlined preventive techniques available for mass application.

In scattered localities and on a small scale throughout the country, medical care organizations have been slowly multiplying for many years.[6] Some have provided comprehensive preventive, diagnostic, and curative medical services. Occasionally, publication of a study of such

---

[6] Listings of existing medical care organizations with summaries of their administration, coverage, and services are provided in *Prepayment Medical Care Organizations*, Bureau Memorandum No. 55, Bureau of Research and Statistics, Social Security Board, and in *Voluntary Prepayment Medical Care Plans*, Council on Medical Service, American Medical Association.

a successful program helps break down traditional thinking about medical costs and methods of medical care.

Possibly stimulated by workmen's compensation legislation, the writing of group insurance by commercial companies has undergone an evolution over the past three decades. More recently, they have been forced by threatened competition of the prepayment movement to improve and standardize their group cash disability insurance policies and to add limited coverage for hospitalization and surgical expenses, and now occasionally for doctors' bills. Meanwhile, organized groups of hospitals in almost every state have demonstrated that the risk was basically safe and insurable by providing hospital care on a prepayment basis more comprehensive on the whole than that obtainable under the standard commercial policy. At present many of these hospital (Blue Cross) plans are being combined with medical and surgical service plans of varying degrees of comprehensiveness.

When brought into perspective with these and other contemporary developments in medical care programs, union plans are seen to be unique only in respect to their union sponsorship. This implies that union plans should be evaluated by the same standards as apply to all prepayment programs. Unfortunately, however, the relatively formal issue of who "controls" the benefit fund has usurped public attention in connection with certain recent union efforts to negotiate employer-financed health funds, to the exclusion of the much more fundamental issues of sound planning, financing, and administering the health program for which the fund is earmarked.

Two Approaches to Health Insurance

There are two different approaches to the problem of prepaying medical care on a group basis: (1) a cash benefit; and (2) a medical service approach.

The large majority of union-sponsored plans fall into the former category, typified by the standard commercial insurance policy under which the insured member is given certain cash benefits as reimbursement for certain expenditures and wage losses in connection with nonoccupational accident or illness. Under these plans the organization of available medical services remains unaffected, since the plans are devoted primarily to spreading the medical and financial risks of illness. They are not even superficially geared to the pressing problem of improving the health of the membership or reducing the incidence of illness and hence of medical costs.

The primary function of the second approach is to organize and distribute medical services to members in need of them. Emphasis is placed upon provision of medical facilities and services of high quality, on the prevention of disease, and on education in health care. An important incentive in taking this approach is the alleged excessive cost of group indemnity insurance, attributable partly to its inherent inability to provide adequate medical care.

As yet, very few union plans embody the service approach to any degree. Consequently, in the view of many public health experts for whom a service plan is the only one to be dignified by the name of a "health program," present union activities are not considered serious efforts toward dealing with health problems. Acquaintance with the unions' publicity about their plans, however, will dispel any doubt that they are seriously interested in health problems and often visualize their programs as first steps toward something more comprehensive. Since union plans are set up through the process of collective bargaining, it is quite understandable that certain problems related to this special process may have received attention out of proportion to their relative importance. The individual peculiarities of union-management negotiations have resulted in formal differences in the details of the clauses in the agreements creating the plans and in the various supplementary documents defining the roles of each of the parties. Yet a great many of these differences may have little or no relation to the substance of the plans themselves.

Characteristics of Union Plans

The absence of any well-defined patterns makes it difficult to summarize the existing variations among union plans. They have developed on local, regional, and national levels of union organization, and combine several types of benefits in a variety of ways. They may be based wholly or in part on the standard commercial policy for hospitalization, surgical and disability benefits, or may take the form of participation in some nonprofit organization, such as a Blue Cross plan (for hospitalization benefits) or the Health Insurance Plan of Greater New York (for a broad scope of medical services). In at least one case the union has even organized its own insurance company to provide disability, hospitalization, and surgical coverage. In a few plans the emphasis is on various types of medical services, such as can be provided by diagnostic clinics and panels of physicians made available either on a fee-for-service or salaried basis.

The benefits provided in the overwhelming majority of current union-sponsored plans, however, differ from one another only in minor details. By and large they follow the standard patterns developed by the leading commercial insurance companies, frequently modified by the inclusion of a local Blue Cross hospitalization policy. These commercial companies offer a scale of different benefits ranged according to premium costs and occasionally make modifications or "improvements" in what is offered at a given cost.

The methods of financing of these programs take a variety of forms. The employer may foot the entire cost through the contribution of a specified percentage of his payroll to a special fund or by outright purchase of insurance policies. The union may contribute to the cost, or a percentage of the cost may be defrayed by the employees through regular wage deductions. Where a separate trust fund has been set up it may be administered, or "controlled," by the union alone, by the union and employer jointly, or in combination with some representation from "outside." The money in the fund may be used to pay benefits directly to union members, to purchase commercial or Blue Cross insurance policies, or to finance a full-fledged medical service program.

Although neither a comprehensive survey nor an entirely satisfactory classification of these various plans has yet been made, there are several descriptive studies that may be referred to for details of individual plans and estimates of total coverage.[7] In its 1945 study, the Bureau of Labor Statistics estimated that 600,000 workers were covered by union-negotiated health benefit programs. An estimate in mid-1948 by the Bureau put the total at 3,000,000. Subsequent agreements in the steel and other industries may result in almost a doubling of this 1948 estimate by late 1950. The number of dependents, included in some of the plans, has not been estimated.

Some national and international unions have promoted a standard national plan, usually negotiated on an industry or branch of industry basis with groups of employers. Others have preferred to encourage their locals or groups of locals to negotiate programs independently of their national offices. In still other cases, locals themselves have taken the initiative. Although in most industries the plans probably have been innovations, in some industries they have been contractual outgrowths of pre-existing employer-sponsored plans.

Problems Confronting Unions

Interest in union health insurance programs did not wane following the end of the war. Unions heretofore without plans began looking for guidance in this field, and frequently turned to those with functioning plans for an appraisal of their experience. Many union leaders can undoubtedly be helpful, although it is an unfortunate fact that few unions have attempted any objective evaluation of their experience based upon

---

[7] *Group Health Insurance and Sickness Benefit Plans in Collective Bargaining* (Industrial Relations Section, Princeton University, 1945).

Royalties, Taxes and Assessments Industry-Paid and Union-Administered for Labor Welfare Benefits (Supplement to *Labor and Nation*, August 1945).

Health Benefit Plans Established Through Collective Bargaining 1945 (U.S. Bureau of Labor Statistics, Bulletin No. 841).

Medical Service Plans Under Collective Bargaining (*Monthly Labor Review*, January 1948).

statistics, which are the only means of providing a basis for the comparison of the various plans.

This deficiency appears to be due to several factors. Unions do not have the staff to devote to such statistical studies. Public information in this field, moreover, is relatively undeveloped, so that unions actually do not know how to attempt such evaluation. Lacking the guidance of experts, they often tend to overemphasize certain legitimate but minor kinds of problems to the neglect of more fundamental ones. Nevertheless, all unions have encountered problems; and out of their trials and errors in seeking to meet these problems, the outlines of a new department of union administration is definitely emerging. Already several unions have at least nominally created "social security" departments.

Several levels of problems confronting unions venturing into this field can be distinguished.

Collective Bargaining

Negotiation with the employer is on the first level. The employer may have to be "sold" on the need for and monetary value of a health benefit plan for his employees. Or the issue may be centered around the amount of money he is expected to contribute and the question of whether or not his employees are to participate in the cost. Occasionally the plan itself may be selected during negotiations and a decision taken to write it into the collective bargaining contract. This is especially likely where a commercial insurance plan is selected and the employer agrees to purchase policies providing specified benefits. The contract clauses may be simple and brief, or they may go into considerable detail; [8] for example, a union may consider it necessary to write in safeguards against employer failure to purchase and maintain the policies. A desirable flexibility, however, is attained when the contract provides simply for the establishment of a health fund. The possibilities can then be carefully studied and the plan worked out in a more favorable and less emotional atmosphere than frequently characterizes union-employer bargaining sessions. Of course the decision to set up a separate trust fund may be influenced by particular state laws.

Choice of Plan

A second level of problems is met after union and employer have reached general agreement in principle on some sort of program. If a commercial insurance plan is adopted, the union usually finds it advisable to participate in negotiations with the carrier company or companies,

---

[8] For description and samples of contract clauses that unions and managements have written to provide for health insurance, see: "Employee-Benefit Plans; Part I— Health, Welfare, and Insurance Plans," chapter for a revised edition of Bulletin 686, *Union Agreement Provisions* (Bureau of Labor Statistics, U.S. Department of Labor).

not only in order to secure the best general terms but also in order to modify certain details of the standard commercial policy to fit the needs of the particular situation. Even where the employer is the sole contracting party to the policy, unions have found it highly advantageous to participate in these negotiations. Obviously the union representatives in these sessions must be well acquainted with the field of health insurance and with the concessions that other unions have been able to obtain from insurance companies. Among the problems with which unions are usually concerned in their negotiations with insurance carriers are: (1) definition of eligibility under the plan; (2) provision for coverage of members when temporarily laid off; and (3) provision for settling disputes over the interpretation of the policy or over the facts of a particular case.

The detailed formulation of a medical service program requires much more deliberation than the commercial insurance situation. Success or failure of a service program depends primarily upon the care given to its planning at this early stage. Consultation with experts in the public health and medical economics fields is an absolute necessity. In most cases, a survey of characteristics of the union membership to be served and the community medical facilities available is a prerequisite to any further decision as to how the available funds can best be used.

In several states, unions desiring to establish their own medical service plans are hindered by laws that prohibit medical care plans set up under nonmedical auspices, or that place other restrictive conditions upon their organization. In an effort to meet these problems, some union representatives have attempted to work out agreement with representatives of organized medicine on legislation designed to remove some of these restrictions while preserving guarantees for recognized standards of medical practice.

Basic Administration

The next level comprises a wide range of problems best termed "administrative." In situations where a trust fund has been set up, the issue of control arises. It has been roughly estimated that programs establishing funds are about equally divided among the three alternatives: (1) sole union control, (2) joint union-employer control; and (3) control by a board on which there are representatives from the community in addition to the union and employer. Although this is a subject that has aroused widespread discussion, there is no definitive evidence that one type is in practice more satisfactory than another. Success or failure of a plan seems to depend much more on the nature of the plan itself than on the ultimate source of control.

Where there is no provision for a fund and the plan is financed by direct employer payments to an insurance company, the insurance company becomes the real administrator of the plan. This is equally true in cases where the trustees of a fund decide on a commercial insurance plan.

Day-to-Day Administration

Frequently confused with this problem of basic administrative control are certain procedural and day-to-day administrative problems in which the union may or may not become involved. These constitute the fourth level. Indemnity claims, for example, can be handled through union offices, employer offices, or some special office set up by the insurance company. Many unions consider it desirable to have claims pass through their offices both in order to give their members a greater feeling of participation in a union-sponsored plan, and in order to exercise a degree of vigilance over the enforcement of the terms of the policies. On the other hand, some unions take the view that they should be separated from the administration of the plan in the eyes of their members so that in the event of complaints they can more readily play the role of champion of their members' interests.

Under any program, difficulties may arise in connection with the procedure for filing claims or requests for service, routing benefit payments, instructing union members in the rules of the plan and their rights under it, handling complaints, settling differences of contract interpretation with the insurance company or agency providing services, determining criteria for occupational and nonoccupational disabilities, etc.

Actuarial Studies

At the fifth level the unions become aware of a need for an analytical breakdown of the amount of benefits received by members, the reasons for their illnesses, differentials between significant catagories of members, and similar data. By combining such information with figures on premiums paid or expenditures made for services, unions can obtain an accurate picture of the over-all costs of a program as well as the relative costs of its separable parts. With such statistics on the operation of a given plan, unions can observe how much of the money expended actually reaches members in the form of benefits (i.e., the "loss ratio") and how fairly these benefits are distributed among the members who have the medical needs and suffer the losses of income through temporary disability.

Research Problems

Once unions have advanced to this actuarial analysis of their plans, they slowly come to appreciate them as something more than mere schedules of potential benefits. Health plans become institutional arrangements resulting in certain distribution patterns of average benefits to members over a given period of time. These are the living plans. In comparing one plan with another, unions can learn how certain formal elements in plans may be correlated to actuarial experience. A normal industrial population having no prepayment plan is expected to make such and such average expenditures over a year's time for specific medical services. Since low-income groups, in particular, normally do not obtain all the services they want or need when ill, the existence of a prepayment plan relieving them of some of the incidence of high medical costs is expected to increase their utilization of available medical services.

Certain scientific problems are then posed: What kinds of arrangements of the various elements in plans encourage best utilization of medical services? What kinds of arrangements discourage this utilization? What are the medical and health needs of a given membership, and how can the available money be utilized most efficiently to meet and ultimately reduce these needs? (It will be noticed that this last is quite a different problem from the one of obtaining the greatest return in benefits from the premium dollar.) This type of problem occurs on what can properly be termed the "research" level. The variable elements in health insurance plans become the objects about which knowledge is sought in order to determine their effects upon the total operation of a plan.[9]

How Unions Meet These Problems

Having decided upon a *medical service* program, unions are confronted at an early stage with a majority of the types of problems outlined above. Medical service programs of necessity must be concerned with the organization of medical facilities and the quality of these facilities.

Commercial insurance or Blue Cross policies, on the other hand, come in neat packages that can be purchased and then neglected; union officials need to concern themselves only with the first two levels of problems, which are of relatively short duration, prior to establishment of the plan. Minor administrative problems, however, may soon come to the attention of union officials and take up enough attention to warrant the designation of one or more staff members to meet them. A staff man's first duties would probably involve interpreting policy rules to union members, and adjusting disputes between members and employers or members and the insurance company.

The specialization of interest resulting from preoccupation with purely administrative problems leads readily to concern for the actuarial and basic health aspects that require specialized research. These aspects are not so easily handled as the former, and to date, very few unions

---

[9] For an excellent statement of the kind of research needed and its importance, see Franz Goldmann, *Voluntary Medical Care Insurance in the United States* (New York: Columbia University Press, 1948), Chapter IX.

have attempted to do anything by themselves in this field, although some have hired special outside consultants to do limited research.

Through trial and error and interchange of experiences, unions are learning to develop special techniques in negotiation, writing of the agreement clauses, and solving some of the minor day-to-day administrative problems. But when unions finally become aware of the fact that their programs could be so organized as to improve the health status of their members, they will recognize the need of measuring the extent to which their plans actually accomplish this aim. Availability and quality of medical service, previously neglected, will be emphasized.

In this light, administrative arrangements assume importance not in and of themselves, but only because of the way in which they may help provide the essentials for better health. Here the qualitative experience and opinions of union officials and staff are of little value. It is impossible to find out how an insurance plan actually "works," that is, what kind of benefits an average member receives, without accurate statistical data. These data cannot be obtained, moreover, unless careful preparations have been made to provide for their continuous collection. A purely technical problem in those cases where all records of claims and payments pass through union control, it becomes a more difficult one when claims are received in employers' offices or only recorded by insurance companies. Some unions provide in their contracts with employers for regular monthly reports on all benefits paid out during the month. Another source of data would be reports from the insurance company, although insurance companies are known to be reluctant to furnish this information on any detailed basis.

Although statistical studies of individual plans may provide some helpful data, unions will not get the full value from their statistics until comparative studies of the various types of plans can be made. Comparative studies require standardized statistics, and consequently, collaboration among unions. Moreover, union experience will become significant only when related to the experience of the many other groups operating prepayment plans. Unions that are seriously interested in this phase will find it highly desirable to call upon outside experts specializing in the study of prepayment plans for advice in establishing a distinct administrative and research department devoted exclusively to the health insurance field.

JOHN M. BRUMM

Chapter 24

Health programs of the United Mine Workers[1]

IN THE LATTER PART OF 1948, A MEDICAL PROGRAM FOR THE UNITED MINE Workers became possible through the Welfare and Retirement Fund. Facts and figures on health conditions, gathered by the United Mine Workers over a period of many years, together with the *Medical Survey of the Bituminous Coal Industry* conducted by Rear Admiral Joel T. Boone and his associates in 1946-1947,[2] provided authentic information regarding the conditions with which a health and medical program would be faced. Some of these facts were as follows:

The United States death rate from all causes for 1946 was 10.0 per 1,000. For coal miners it was 15.1.

The average age at death of miners for whom death benefits had been paid was 55.8 years as compared with 64.2 years, the average age at death for the population as a whole.

The number of miners killed from all causes annually from 1906 to 1945 averaged 1,981, which means that for every working day at least five men were killed. The total for the period was 79,240.

The number of miners injured each year during the 14 year period 1930-1944 averaged 66,968.

From 1944 to 1948, an additional 234,923 men were killed or injured in the mines.

It is significant to note that even during the first six months of 1949, when working days were curtailed to some extent and the annual vacation period was in effect, deaths in the bituminous mines were as follows: January, 65; February, 44; March, 45; April, 50; May, 46; June, 41.

Complete and accurate data regarding the incidence of disease among

---

[1] This chapter is based on Dr. Warren F. Draper's article, "Voluntary Health Insurance on the National Scene—The United Mine Workers' Health Program," which appeared in the April, 1950 issue of the *American Journal of Public Health*.

[2] U.S. Department of the Interior. U.S. Gov. Ptg. Office, Washington, D. C., 1947.

coal miners and their dependents were not available. However, with the woeful lack of public health measures and medical service in many mining communities, it could scarcely be conceived that the prevalence would not be high. Studies of infant mortality rates showed a significantly higher rate in mining counties than in nonmining counties. In medical certifications for disability benefits, tuberculosis, pneumonia, "miners' asthma" or silicosis, together with arthritis and rheumatism, played an enormous role.

The best hospitalization and general medical care plans that had been observed did not provide all-inclusive medical service and contained so many limitations that provision for all major illnesses was not possible.

About 70 per cent of the miners and their families received their medical services through prepayment plans of one sort or another. The administration and operation through some of the larger companies were outstanding, but at a majority of the mines the services ranged from adequate to very poor. Practitioners were overburdened and at a number of places there was a tendency to give more consideration to profits than to the quality of medical care. Poorly qualified physicians and others not properly licensed were receiving large sums through deductions from the wages of the men. In one instance, a druggist with no medical training whatever was practicing medicine in an isolated community and receiving a share of the payroll check-off along with two qualified physicians.

All in all, it will not be surprising to hear that life insurance rates for miners are 277 per cent higher than for workers in nonhazardous industries and are of course prohibitive.

There was no program for the rehabilitation of disabled miners of the soft coal industry. Some 400 miners with broken backs, paralyzed from the waist down, were bedridden, helpless, and forgotten in their hillside cabins. Their workmen's compensation exhausted, they were ekeing out an existence of indescribable misery and torture with no prospect in the world of anything more than an agonizing death.

Such were some of the conditions that had to be faced and on which immediate action was necessary.

The Objective and the Plan

The objective was to secure for the mine workers a good quality of medical and hospital care at as reasonable a cost as could be attained, and the first step toward providing immediate services was to arrive at satisfactory terms with the physicians and the hospitals.

The hundreds of thousands of mine workers and their families were distributed in communities of varying character in 22 states, extending from Pennsylvania in the east to the State of Washington in the west, and to Alabama in the south. To conduct the work throughout this extensive area, 10 Area Medical Offices were established at locations selected with reference to the numbers in the mining population to be served, medical and hospital facilities available, and accessibility to the mining centers. The places chosen were Beckley, Charleston, and Morgantown, W. Va.; Johnstown and Pittsburgh, Pa; Knoxville, Tenn.; Louisville, Ky.; Birmingham, Ala.; St. Louis, Mo.; and Denver, Colo.

A physician trained and experienced in organization and administrative work was placed in charge of each office, with the title Area Medical Administrator, UMWA Welfare and Retirement Fund. Provisions were made for a staff adapted to his needs. The Area Medical Administrators are responsible to the Executive Medical Officer at the headquarters of the Fund at Washington, D. C. He in turn is responsible to the Director of the Fund, who carries out the policies determined by the Board of Trustees. The Board of Trustees is appointed in accordance with contractual agreements between the United Mine Workers and the operators.

The functions of the field offices are, as described by one of the Area Medical Administrators:

1. Specifically to arrange for a high quality of medical and hospital care for members of the United Mine Workers of America.

2. To arrange for free choice of physician and hospital and concomitantly free choice of patient.

3. To utilize for the benefit of the United Mine Workers all of the health services made available by other organizations in the state and country.

4. To develop rehabilitative services for disabled miners.

5. To perform this service with a minimum of administrative detail and cost.

6. To provide a leadership which will direct the impact of the program into channels that will stimulate the highest quality of medical service, both for miners and for other members of their community at the most reasonable costs.

The inauguration and extension of the program were planned in four stages.

First were hospitalization and medical care in the hospital for members receiving grants from the Fund in the form of pensions, or disability benefits because of injury or disease that prevented them from working in the mines. Their dependents were included. As such grants are sufficient only for the bare necessities of life, these people were without means to pay for hospitalization and related professional services. It was recognized also that the experience gained in working out arrangements with physicians, hospitals, union officials, and the miners themselves would be extremely useful as the services were extended later on.

Second was the provision of home and office care, including drugs on a physician's prescription, for the same group of people. It was anticipated that this stage could not be long delayed because of the numerous cases in which discharge from the hospital would not be advisable unless outside medical care were provided. It was obvious that, otherwise, hospitalization would be required for numbers of persons who could be adequately cared for by home and office visits.

Third was the extension of hospital care and medical care in the hospital to all working miners and their dependents. This of course meant coverage for hundreds of thousands of persons. The number who would apply for such care could not, of course, be foreseen.

Fourth was the development of a program of public health and preventive medicine in cooperation with existing agencies, to correct the serious deficiencies and improve the deplorable living conditions which the *Medical Survey of the Bituminous Coal Industry* had revealed in a majority of the coal mining communities.

The first three stages have been in operation. The fourth is just beginning.

How the Plan Operates

The Area Medical Administrators arrange with individual physicians, hospitals, and drug stores within their respective areas to provide services to beneficiaries of the Fund upon presentation of accepted forms of identification.

Physicians must be in good professional standing and acceptable to the union members. They must indicate their willingness to render services in accordance with operating procedures established by the Fund and at reasonable charge. In determining a reasonable charge, they are asked to consider the following: (1) payment satisfactory to the physician will be made for every patient cared for (many beneficiaries could have paid nothing for themselves, and others could have paid only part of the usual fee); (2) payment will be reasonably prompt; (3) paper work will be kept at an irreducible minimum; (4) free enterprise and competition will be insured by the right of the patient to go to the physician of his choice and the right of the Fund to discontinue services of physicians whose charges are excessive as compared with similar services by others of equal standing.

The names of physicians, including specialists in all fields of medicine, who indicate their desire to participate under these conditions are placed on a local list that serves to inform the beneficiaries to whom they may apply for treatment. Physicians may refer cases to any other physicians on the local list for specialist services.

When the specialist care essential to the best interest of the patient is not available from physicians on local lists, the Area Medical Administrators may arrange for the services of the specialists required, wherever they may be located.

Dental and optical services are limited for the time being to persons who, the physician believes, require these services in the treatment of a specific illness.

Hospitals must agree to provide the best services they are capable of rendering. Unfortunately, satisfactory standards do not prevail in some institutions and the decision must then be made as to whether to deal with them on a restricted basis and make intensive efforts to bring about improvements as rapidly as possible to make them more nearly acceptable. Progress in this direction is being made. As far as possible, the Reimbursable Cost Formula is the basis used in determining rates. Lists of the hospitals with which agreements are made are sent to participating physicians and to the local unions.

Members and their families who are recipients of grants from the Fund may receive prescribed drugs and medical requisites. Drugs are limited to those listed in the *U. S. Pharmacopeia, New and Non-Official Remedies* or *National Formulary*, and new drugs accepted for inclusion in *New and Non-Official Remedies*. Arrangements are made for conveniently located drug stores to fill prescriptions presented by members, upon proper identification, and to bill the Fund at reasonable rates. Lists of the drug stores with which agreements are made are sent to participating physicians and local unions. Comparable arrangements are made with vendors of orthopedic and other appliances.

Bills are reviewed in the Area Medical Offices and forwarded to the Washington office for audit and payment.

A member receiving a grant from the Fund and in need of medical care is given the following instructions: .

1. Select a doctor from the list available at your local union.
2. Go to the doctor you select and present your identification form.
3. Medicine prescribed by the doctor may be obtained from any drug store listed at your local union.
4. If you need hospital care the doctor will give you a note to your local union which will issue a Hospitalization Slip.
5. Take the note from your doctor and the slip from your local union to one of the hospitals listed at your local union.

Arrangements are made with the State Offices of Vocational Rehabilitation to provide services for patients who can benefit by them, either during or after their hospital treatment.

The Medical Advisory Board of the Welfare and Retirement Fund, with Dr. R. R. Sayers as Chairman, was appointed in September 1947. It consists of 10 members of recognized authority in the fields of medicine and public health. The members of the Board are consulted with regard to administrative procedures and technical problems. The program that has been adopted is in accordance with principles viewed as sound by the members of this Board.

Progress

About six months prior to the adoption of the Medical, Health, and Hospital Program as outlined, the Fund, through Dr. Sayers and his associates, undertook to locate and hospitalize a number of its beneficiaries who were in most desperate need of immediate attention. Among these were many paraplegics paralyzed from the waist down from spinal injuries and broken backs. Some had been in this condition for as long as 30 years; others for lesser periods of time down to a few months. They had received whatever care was afforded at the time they were injured but had long since been forgotten and given up to die. The condition of most was so frightful that physicians at leading medical centers to which they were transported for treatment stated that they had never before been confronted with such problems, and were compelled to organize teams of specialists and devise new techniques for salvaging the remaining tissues of these diseased and wasted bodies.

The institutions that could undertake the intensive care that such seriously diseased and injured persons required over a period of many months were practically nonexistent. Every facility that could be adapted to the job was utilized and others were developed. Approximately 200 of these patients were sent across the continent to two medical centers in California in chartered cars with physicians and nurses in attendance. Arrangements were made with hospitals at frequent intervals en route to which patients could be removed, should emergency need arise.

A total of 496 cases of this type have either been discharged from the centers or are still under treatment. Their transition from helpless, bedridden, literally rotting creatures to men in wheel chairs and on crutches and artificial limbs is one of the most dramatic stories in medical history, and a monument to the physicians and institutions who undertook this seemingly hopeless task.

The experience with these and other special cases was extremely useful in the program that followed. The union members became more confident of the ability of the Fund to enlist the interest and cooperation of physicians and institutions of national renown in their medical problems. On the other hand, physicians and medical centers gained an insight into the medical needs of the miners and their families, which did much to awaken a favorable response to the extension of the work.

As the general program has been developing, step by step, for less than a year at this writing, and is by no means yet complete, sufficient data for accurate appraisal of results have not accumulated. Impressions have been gained and trends have been observed and are summarized here for what they may be worth at this beginning stage.

Some 6,500 physicians and 600 hospitals are already listed as participating in the program; also 1,287 drug stores. From January 1 to September 1,

1949, 39,000 persons were hospitalized and 375,000 days of hospital care were provided. A total of 180,000 home and office visits were made.

The response of the medical profession and the hospitals is excellent. In many instances, liaison committees have been appointed by state and local medical societies to insure proper understanding and good working relationships with the Area Medical Offices. These committees have been of great assistance in matters pertaining to reasonable fees, maintenance of proper standards of medical care, eliminating bad practices, encouraging well qualified physicians to settle in mining areas where greatly needed, and the like.

Satisfactory relationships with the physicians throughout the extensive coal mining areas are due in no small part to the time devoted by the Area Medical Administrators to making direct personal contacts and giving talks to medical societies on the objectives of the program and methods of procedure. Emphasis has been laid upon the responsibility of the profession to see that a good quality of service is rendered, and for policing that service itself. The simplicity of the methods followed by the Fund in relation to paper work and the payment of bills has also aided in gaining support.

The matter of fees is in process of being resolved. The objective of the Fund—to secure medical care of good quality at as reasonable a cost as such quality could be provided under any system—has been accepted without question. The Fund may already rely upon outstanding members of the profession with whom it deals throughout the country for 100 per cent cooperation in this respect. They are cognizant of the medical problems of the miner and of the spirit in which a great union is approaching the medical profession and seeking its cooperation in a plan that holds promise of a high degree of satisfaction to both. They voluntarily determine the fees they consider proper under the circumstances. It would be too much to expect that there would not be marked deviations from what the majority of physicians feel is right and proper. Bills are submitted occasionally that are out of all proportion to what experience has shown might be expected. When this occurs, the physician is frequently willing to modify his charges when the facts are brought to his attention; otherwise it is assumed that he is not interested in receiving patients of the Fund and he is no longer bothered.

In general, it has been the experience of the Fund that excessive fees tend to occur with physicians who rarely receive the miners' cases, or do so for the first time, or have little interest in continuing to serve them. They fail to appreciate the aim of the program, and they do not share in the constructive interest of the others of the profession who are supporting principles they consider sound and hope will work. With sufficient time and the continued aid of the profession, it is probable that most of these difficulties can be overcome.

WARREN F. DRAPER, M.D.

Chapter 25

Unions and health care

*I*N NEW YORK CITY, 200,000 MEMBERS OF THE INTERNATIONAL LADIES' Garment Workers' Union belonging to 29 different locals are covered by a unique health plan providing prepaid medical care at the Union Health Center. Under this plan, some 40 different medical services are available to workers at the Center, which occupies six floors of a modern twenty-seven-story office and loft building in the heart of New York's garment district. The clinics are manned by 175 physicians who attend on an hourly basis and an additional staff of over 200 persons including nurses, technicians, and pharmacists. During 1949 as many as 2,700 services were being rendered daily, and over 454,000 were provided in that year. Each of the 48,000 patients using the Center in 1949 received an average of nine services.

This use of the Center represents the peak of the 34 years of its existence. The badly needed physical expansion of facilities, which had been delayed during the war, has now been completed and a carefully planned reception and routing system makes possible the daily treatment of this large number of persons.

The Health Center began under very different circumstances in 1916. It then occupied two rooms adjoining the office of the Joint Board of Sanitary Control, which had been set up to inspect sanitary conditions in the industry. Several locals of the ILGWU had banded together in that year to finance a Union Health Center in New York. The high incidence of tuberculosis among garment workers and the inability of workers to bear the costs of medical care when they became ill were some of the motivating factors. The Health Center's function, at first, was to examine members who claimed sick benefits under the systems instituted by individual locals. By 1919 the Center had begun to include treatment as well as diagnosis in its services and the demands upon it were so great that the sponsoring locals bought and equipped a building for its use on 17th Street.

From its inception to 1929, the Center provided its services solely for members of ILGWU locals. However, the period from 1926 to 1933 was a time of setback for the Center. Internal union difficulties and the severe depression of those years combined to rob the union of financial support and patients. Rather than close the doors of the Center the Directors made arrangements with other unions in New York to serve their members. Contributions from the Rosenwald Fund also helped to cover the costs.

Under the stimulus given union organization by the National Recovery Act in 1933 new members came into the ILGWU increasing its strength. Interest in the Health Center revived and the 1934 Convention of the ILGWU voted to take over the Health Center. This time it was to be run by the International rather than by the combined efforts of several local unions. Since that time the Center has moved to its present quarters and has greatly expanded its services.

Until 1944 the Center was supported by union members who paid an annual premium of $4.20 a year for sickness insurance. Because of the low premiums it was necessary to have strict medical administration of the insurance fund and each new member was examined upon application for insurance. Since 1945, when the employers began their contributions to the fund it became possible to offer sickness insurance to every union member, regardless of health, age or sex. This change is reflected in the frequency of claims which rose from 5.7 per cent in 1944 to 10.4 per cent in 1947.

Today the Center is supported by funds from three main sources. The payroll tax on employers, which many locals have incorporated into their contracts, makes up more than half of the income. As increasing numbers of locals are able to include this clause in their agreements, more and more of the costs of medical service will be defrayed directly by the employer. The national ILGWU also contributes to the expenses, and a small percentage is made up from fees paid by the patients.

Health on Credit

Most of the workers are covered by a system of health credit. They receive from their locals "Health Credit Books" for medical care which entitles them to a specified amount of medical service at the Center. The credits range from two free medical examinations a year to $25 worth of medical attention. Each service at the Center has its price, albeit a low one, and a member "pays as he goes," as deductions are made from his health credit book. If he uses up all his credits, he pays cash for succeeding visits and treatments. The charge for all services, however, is much below that found in standard private practice. The charge for a visit to see a doctor, general practitioner or specialist, at the Center is $1.25. The actual cost to the Center for this service is $3.00.

A distinction should be noted here between the medical aid financed by the local unions at the Center and the sick benefit programs. The purpose of the sick benefit programs is to provide a sick worker with a weekly income when he is too ill to go to work. The union-financed medical care which workers receive at the Health Center is given to *keep* them in good health or treat complaints which do not confine them to bed, e.g., arthritis, diabetes, neuralgia, sinus trouble, hay fever, etc. Doctors from the Center, however, go out to the homes of persons who are ill and in bed to certify them for the sick benefits which they are entitled to receive from their local union.

Members of the family of ILGWU members covered by the plan may use the Center, but they are required to pay for each service.

Organization and Equipment

A large variety of services is available to workers at the Center. Nineteen special departments are in operation, the most active of which are the eye, ear, nose, and throat, allergy and hay fever, social hygiene and physio-therapy consultation departments. Two types of therapy, six kinds of diagnostic services (e.g. audiometry, electrocardiography) and twelve special services including minor surgical operations are available.

To supplement its low cost treatment, the Center has established a pharmacy which dispenses medicines at 40 to 50 per cent less than the standard cost. The pharmacy has a standardized formulary which enables it to buy drugs in large quantities. Instead of stocking several brands of B Complex vitamin tablets, for example, the doctors at the Center agree to use only one type, thereby simplifying and economizing ordering procedure. In 1949, 123,567 prescriptions were filled.

The Center also maintains a medical records library where records are available to physicians for checking of cases and morbidity records and where other medical data are kept for study purposes. The Statistical Department codes and tabulates the records using the latest IBM equipment and provides a continuous analysis of the patients and cases treated at the Center. Study of these data is instrumental in pointing the direction of the development of services. The Center is headed by Dr. Leo Price.

Members who wish to come to the Center make an appointment in advance. The Center is open from 9 A.M. to 7 P.M. on weekdays and from 9 A.M. to 2 P.M. on Saturdays. Evening hours and Saturdays are the most popular times, although many workers make appointments during their lunch hours because of the convenient location of the building. They are interviewed when they arrive by registered nurses who fill out their medical case histories, thereby aiding the doctor who will examine the patient. If an individual returns to the Center, an effort is made to give him the same doctor. The procedure, briefly, is as follows: The patient comes in either for a general examination or because of a specific complaint. He is interviewed by a nurse and then is examined by a general practitioner. If he has a special complaint or if the general practitioner discovers a special condition he goes to see one of the specialists employed at the Center Laboratory tests for complete diagnosis of the patient's condition, medication, and much of the treatment are all available at the Center. When cases arise which seem to require surgery or other services which the Center is not equipped to supply, patients are referred to institutions which can meet their need.

It has been observed that the extent to which workers use the services provided by the Center varies with the amount of free medical care to which they are entitled, rather than with how much they need. Thus members of a local which provided a liberal allotment of free treatment per member came more frequently than members of a local who would have to pay cash for most of the services.

Forecasting

In addition to treating patients for the specific complaints which bring them to see a doctor, the Center attempts to detect the presence of disease among workers before they are aware of it, and also to provide special care for the chronically ill so that they can continue working. For some time now the Center has been giving chest X-rays to each new patient. This procedure has proved a valuable case finding device, since the X-rays permit the discovery of some abnormal conditions of the heart and great vessels and other pathology of the chest. Analysis of the first 40,000 X-rays revealed 31 active tuberculosis cases and 676 cases of pathology of chest organs. The use of this X-ray makes possible the early discovery of illness, thereby making quick recovery more certain, and also lessening the loss of working time to the sick person.

A large number of the workers in certain sections of the industry are older men and women, many of whom are afflicted with chronic illnesses, but must continue to support themselves. In one cloakmakers local, for example, a study of a selected sample showed that the median age of the members was 57.5 years. An analysis of disability claims in 1947 indicated that diseases of the heart and circulatory system are the most common among ILGWU workers, and it may be noted that 92.5 per cent of those disabled by heart disease were over 40 years of age. Dr. Price has commented that "Long experience has shown that workers suffering from heart disease can be gainfully employed in this industry which, as a rule, requires no special vigor or physical effort." To help these workers preserve their health, and consequently their earning power, the Center has initiated special services for their care and protection. There is, for example, the cardiac clinic. As soon as a case of coronary disease is discovered the patient is advised to attend the clinic where he is helped to reorganize his working and living habits to suit his condition. Workers with other disabilities can also receive regular treatment at the Center.

Although the ILGWU Health Center is now more than 30 years old, the notion of medical care on a year round basis to keep workers well, and to arrest incipient illness which may become more serious is still a new trend in union health programs. If the standard union procedure of insuring the *wages* of a worker by sick benefits is supplemented by a program of continuous health care, much will have been done to improve the health and increase the security of American workers.

RUTH GLAZER

Chapter 26

Banks and credit unions

LABOR BANKING LUXURIATED (IF A KINDLY EXPRESSION IS PREFERRED) IN the wholesale abundance of the 1920's. Superficially, it might seem to have been related only to the boom behavior of that flush decade. But the history of American labor, as it reaches down into profounder meanings, must also root this movement in the traditional, periodic, and ever-futile endeavors of trade unions to free themselves from the rigors of factory life and the capitalist system.

Although the credit union drive within the ranks of labor took its start during these same dollar-happy times, it was always more modest than its banking companion in uttering claims for salvation. Yet it too shared—along with labor banking, cooperative housing, and producers' and consumers' cooperatives—a common ideological weakness for a nineteenth century of Jeffersonian shape and tint. Therefore the credit union movement can be realistically described only as a less virulent variety of that lower-middle-class escapism to a utopian past that oozed, from time to time, into labor's welcoming heart.

For 1950, the historical truth of the matter is fixed: neither labor banking nor credit unions have attained today the importance of a recognized major effort within the labor movement. They represent as yet merely interesting, minor, and peripheral ventures. By their very feebleness, they lend dignity to those trade union institutions which are more enduring and robust.

Labor Banking

Despite Samuel Gompers' far from gentle efforts to convince American workers that they could never successfully sever their destinies from capitalism, as early as the 1904 Convention of the AFL a proposal to found labor banks in the United States was urged. With Gompers in command, it failed of passage. The notion nevertheless persisted through the 1910 and 1914 Conventions, only to meet defeat again. An even more grandiose plan calling for the establishment of a central labor bank had to be vetoed by the AFL as late as 1924. As a result, the labor banking movement was fated to pass its short frisk in the sun largely outside of the unions affiliated with the AFL.[1]

Beginning in 1920, a bevy of confident American labor unions disinterred the least successful script of their nineteenth century repertoire and proceeded to polish up the old routine. The lead was taken by the International Ass'n of Machinists, which purchased a majority stock interest in a bank in Washington, D.C. During May of 1920, the curtain was raised in the nation's capital on the first labor bank in the United States. Later that year, the Locomotive Engineers founded a bank in Cleveland, Ohio. Florence Peterson records that from 1920 to 1926 the Locomotive Engineers "owned and controlled 14 banks, a holding company, an investment company, 6 security corporations, a realty and mortgage company, an insurance company, and several 'thrift' companies, besides having an interest in a Wall Street bank and another in Florida. They also started a real estate development in Florida covering 50,000 acres, and including three hotels." [2]

During these fat years, the following unions also took banks unto themselves: the Amalgamated Clothing Workers, the Brotherhood of Railway Clerks, the Printing Pressmen, the Railroad Telegraphers, the Flint Glass Workers, and the International Ladies' Garment Workers. Altogether, various international and local unions, state federations, and city centrals owned 36 banks with total resources of over $126,000,000.[3]

The reasons for labor's banking enthusiasm were as contrasting as the colors, lights, and shadows that merge to form the American Dream. (1) To some unions, the chief purpose for venturing into the banking field was the lure of profitable investment for union funds that had burgeoned during World War I.[4] (2) A factor thought more compelling by Royal E. Montgomery in luring labor into the banking business was the "alleged participation of the regular banks in the open-shop drive of 1920-1921." In many of the large industrial centers of the country, the deciding influence in the open-shop battles was the availability of credit to anti-union firms.[5] (3) Closely bound to this reaction against the conservative banking fraternity was its corollary: labor banks would

[1] Harry A. Millis and Royal E. Montgomery, *Organized Labor* (New York and London: McGraw-Hill Book Company, Inc., 1945), pp. 344–345.

[2] Florence Peterson, *American Labor Unions* (New York and London: Harper & Brothers Publishers, 1945), pp. 177–178, footnote 2. See also Industrial Relations Section, Department of Economics and Social Institutions, Princeton University, *The Labor Banking Movement in the United States* (Princeton, New Jersey: Princeton University Press, 1929), chart facing p. 46.

[3] Florence Peterson, *op. cit.*, p. 178. See also *The Labor Banking Movement in the United States*, pp. 17–54.

[4] *The Labor Banking Movement in the United States*, pp. 56–60.

[5] Harry A. Millis and Royal E. Montgomery, *op. cit.*, p. 345. See also *The Labor Banking Movement in the United States*, pp. 60–63.

be in a position to aid unions in the event of strikes or lockouts. Actually, this purpose was never realized, for as soon as union banks had funds in hand, the natural reluctance to part with hard cash easily overpowered labor's sense of solidarity.[6] (4) Banking advocates delighted to paint in phosphorescent strokes an imaginary mural of labor Galahads striking an heroic pose of supporting union-minded employers—an attitude that some surviving union banks, even today, never tire of assuming, although actual instances of such aid are rare enough to be noteworthy.[7] (5) Then, too, it was thought quite possible that labor could eventually control the basic industries of the country by becoming large shareholders of banks and corporations. The strike would disappear forever. In its stead would spring up the banker-investor-labor leader who would call the millennial tune like some latter-day Carnegie or J. P. Morgan in reverse.[8] (6) The labor movement, during this early period of naïve enthusiasm about the almost boundless potentialities of union banking, was equally enthusiastic about cooperative enterprises. It seemed natural, therefore, to zealots in the cooperative movement and to some labor unions that loans to cooperative ventures should be included in the programs of the labor banks. It should be noted, however, that once the banks were in operation and had acquired financial experience, most of the labor bankers, with one striking exception, were distinctly opposed to such loans.[9]

A union like the Amalgamated Clothing Workers of America, however, was more modest in its demands upon American life. It saw its banks primarily as service institutions for workers in its own industry and for other union members in the community. It thought largely in terms of financial security for the average unionist who might find it difficult to obtain a loan at an ordinary commercial bank. Consequently, character loans were provided at lower rates of interest, without collateral when endorsed by other union members. Loans and assistance to home builders also became part of the services offered. Investment advice of a sound nature was proffered. Hours more convenient to the factory worker than those of the usual banking day were instituted. Furthermore, a labor bank could assure the cooperative sharing of profits among savings depositors through a limitation on dividends.[10]

The causes of the disastrous failure of all but a handful of labor banks by mid-depression must be sought not only in the romantic inflation of their goals and the general sickness of the times, but also in the nature

[6] Harry A. Millis and Royal E. Montgomery, op. cit., p. 346.
[7] Ibid., p. 346. See also The Labor Banking Movement in the United States, pp. 108–111.
[8] The Labor Banking Movement in the United States, pp. 63–65.
[9] Ibid., pp. 111–114.
[10] Ibid., pp. 191–202, 224–226.

TABLE 1

CONDITION OF LABOR BANKS AS OF JUNE 30, 1948,* AND DEC. 31, 1949

Bank	Capital, Surplus, and Undivided Earnings	Deposits	Total Assets
All banks:			
June 30, 1948	$5,119,499	$89,181,399	$95,156,593
December 31, 1949	4,916,424	88,571,474	95,396,635
Amalgamated Trust & Savings Bank, Chicago, Ill.:			
June 30, 1948	$1,760,000	$33,415,032	$35,561,530
December 31, 1949	1,765,000	34,444,050	36,770,765
Brotherhood State Bank, Kansas City, Kans.:			
June 30, 1948	542,728	10,375,827	10,953,876
December 31, 1949	558,148	9,883,592	10,494,989
Union National Bank, Newark, N. J.:			
June 30, 1948	716,771	11,010,302	11,761,175
December 31, 1949	391,841	7,971,597	8,772,186
Amalgamated Bank of New York, N. Y.:			
June 30, 1948	2,100,000	34,380,238	36,880,012
December 31, 1949	2,201,435	36,272,235	39,358,694

* Information supplied by Industrial Relations Section, Princeton University.

TABLE 2

DEVELOPMENT OF LABOR BANKS IN THE UNITED STATES IN SPECIFIED YEARS, 1920-1949

Date	Number of Banks	Capital, Surplus, and Undivided Earnings	Deposits	Total Assets
December 31—				
1920	2	$ 1,154,446	$ 2,258,561	$ 3,628,867
1925	36	12,536,901	98,392,592	115,015,273
June 30—				
1930	14	7,217,836	59,817,392	68,953,855
1935	4	2,051,943	17,262,281	19,692,385
1940	4	2,684,911	23,847,294	26,931,651
1945	4	3,428,078	72,776,529	76,509,121
1947	4	5,052,138	89,549,666	95,245,931
1948	4	5,119,499	89,181,399	95,156,593
December 31—				
1949	4	4,916,424	88,571,474	95,396,635

of unions as institutions and in the character of American union members. The desire of labor leaders for prestige often resulted in immeasurable harm to the labor banking movement. Jobs, loans, and easy earnings were made available to friends of the particular union group in power. Competent managers were a rarity, not only because men with experience, who were also sympathetic to union banking, were scarce, but also because of the inherent distrust of the self-made union leader of an expert and trained staff. Moreover, as the most definitive study in this field points out—*The Labor Banking Movement in the United States*, published by Princeton University in 1929—the average workingman or union member was never sufficiently impressed with the idea of a labor bank to help the movement build up a sufficiently large number of customers in relation to fixed costs. Hours geared to the workers' convenience, higher interest rates on deposits, the possibility of making deposits by mails, and advice to small investors were not sufficiently attractive offerings in a highly adaptable and competitive field to make the venture a success. Probably the fast pace with which labor banking in the United States was launched and the absence of proper education for a membership that possessed no inherent class-loyalty also help to explain the record of almost complete failure.[11]

At the present time four labor banks are still among the living: two are owned by the Amalgamated Clothing Workers, one in New York City and the second in Chicago; a third bank in Newark and a fourth in Kansas City are owned by several unions that cooperate in these ventures. For the 18-month period from June 30, 1948, to December 31, 1949, according to the reports of the U. S. Bureau of Labor Statistics, the combined capital, surplus and undivided earnings of the four labor banks showed a decrease of 0.4 per cent. Deposits also decreased 0.7 per cent. Total assets, however, increased 0.3 per cent.

The two summary tables reproduced on page 317 are taken from the July, 1950, issue of the *Monthly Labor Review*.

Credit Unions

Ideally, because of its nature, the credit union should find ample opportunity for functioning at its best in the trade union movement. Since it is a cooperative investment and loan association, it enjoys and encourages a more intimate relationship with its members than does the average bank with its customers. Members are known to each other, they have a personal interest in the institution they have created, and they are able to accomplish their business, as far as labor credit unions are concerned, under a union atmosphere of leisure and friendliness.

Despite the earlier sanguine conviction by enthusiasts that credit

---

[11] *Ibid.*, pp. 238–263.

unions and labor organizations were meant for each other, credit unions sponsored wholly by organized labor groups do not today constitute even an important minority segment of the entire credit union movement.

Data for 1948, the latest year for which statistics are now available, showed a total number of 9,329 credit unions with a membership of 3,767,839: 4,058 federal credit unions with 1,628,339 members and 5,271 state-chartered credit unions with 2,139,500 members.[12]

Unfortunately, the Bureau of Labor Statistics no longer reports separate data for credit unions sponsored by labor organizations. The only source of limited information is the Social Security Administration's Bureau of Federal Credit Unions. Consequently, available figures deal only with federal credit unions under labor sponsorship.

Of the 4,058 federal credit unions reported in 1948, 102 were classified as composed wholly of trade unionists. There were 29,532 members within this group, compared with 1,628,339 members for all federal credit unions.[13]

The total assets reported for all federal credit unions in 1948 were $258,411,736; for federal labor credit unions, $3,158,386. The total of loans to members for all federal credit unions amounted to $137,642,327; the total for federal labor credit unions [14] was $2,130,118.

From their date of organization to December 31, 1948, all federal credit unions had made loans amounting to $1,308,563,785; federal labor credit unions had made loans amounting to $15,690,151, or 1.2 per cent of the total.[15]

As has already been indicated, no figures are published for labor credit unions chartered under state laws. Estimates for the total number of labor credit unions (both federal and state) range from 500 to 1,000 and should more justly be characterized as guesses rather than estimates. Nevertheless, the figure 500 may be a safe one (at least to think about) since the United Automobile Workers reported in the March, 1950, issue of *Ammunition* that "In something less than three years, more than 250 UAW credit unions have been organized." [16]

Whether there are 500 or 1,000 labor credit unions in a country that boasts of 15,600,000 organized workers is a fact of less importance than the inescapable conclusion that within the credit union movement, labor credit unions have not as yet begun to play a role of any considerable importance.

MAURICE F. NEUFELD

[12] *Monthly Labor Review*, September, 1949, Vol. 69, No. 3, p. 276.
[13] Federal Security Agency, Social Security Administration, Bureau of Federal Credit Unions, *Federal Credit Unions—Report of Operations for the Year 1948*, Table 10, p. 10.
[14] *Ibid.*, Table 10, p. 10.
[15] *Ibid.*, Table 17, p. 17.
[16] *Ammunition*, March, 1950, p. 27.

Chapter 27

Union cooperative housing

THE AMALGAMATED CLOTHING WORKERS OF AMERICA (CIO) BEGAN TO develop an active interest in housing in the mid-twenties. This interest was precipitated by the acute shortage of housing and the constantly rising rentals that followed World War I. A number of active union members, mainly grouped around the Amalgamated Credit Union in New York, decided to try cooperative action to solve their personal housing problem.

Many thought it was a bit too daring for working people without money to dream of building "homes of their own" under the circumstances of the time. But there was no law against dreaming, and what's more, these members secured the promise of the Amalgamated Clothing Workers to take the lead in the venture. In 1927, the first units in this new field of cooperative enterprise, housing 250 families, were completed. Since then, the housing project has expanded greatly, in two sections of New York: the Bronx and the East Side in Manhattan. With the completion, by the end of 1950, of the construction at present underway, the cooperative housing development will have produced the following housing facilities:

Amalgamated Housing Corporation, Bronx, N. Y.—1,450 families. Cost: $10,000,000.

Amalgamated Dwellings, Inc., Grand St., Manhattan—236 families. Cost: $1,500,000.

Hillman Housing Corporation, Grand St., Manhattan—800 families. Cost: $8,500,000.

The three corporations, operating the union-sponsored activity, thus enable 2,500 wage earning families to live in their own cooperative communities costing $20 million dollars, of which roughly one-third represent their own equity interest.

Of the three operating corporations, the Amalgamated Housing Corporation and Amalgamated Dwellings, Inc., are Limited Dividend Companies under the New York State Housing Act, and Hillman Housing Corporation is a Redevelopment Company under the supervision of the City of New York. In each case, partial tax relief is granted by the City and the State of New York for a limited number of years. Both Amalgamated Dwellings and Hillman Housing Corporation are slum clearance projects, located in substandard areas of New York City.

Financing

A similar method of financing, with minor variations, is used in all three developments by the operating corporations. Basic is the cooperator-tenant's payment on the purchase of his apartment, which takes the form of subscribing to the stock issued by the respective corporation in amount equal to what is required to pay for his apartment. In the instance of the Amalgamated Housing Corporation in the Bronx and the Amalgamated Dwellings, Inc. on the lower East Side, each cooperator pays, as the purchase price, $500 per room in the apartment he will occupy. In the new additions to the Amalgamated Housing Corporation, the equity investment was advanced to $650 per room due to the prevailing high cost of construction. In the case of the Hillman Housing Corporation, downtown, the cooperator-tenant's investment is $600 per room.

The balance of the funds needed to cover the cost of the land, improvements and building, is secured by a first mortgage loan. Since no stock is issued to anyone who does not live in the development, the member-cooperators collectively own the project. Individually, each cooperator is a tenant as well as a stockholder. Members who find it difficult to supply the required equity investment are assisted through loans to the extent of 50 to 70 per cent of the total investment required, to be repaid in the course of 5 to 10 years. Upon the completion of the entire construction program the three housing companies will have equity funds invested by their members totalling approximately $6,000,000, and loans of about $7,000,000 each from the Bowery Savings Bank and Mutual Life Insurance Companies.

An estimated budget to cover the cost of operations is generally set up at the time the project is conceived. The average maintenance per room for the entire development is then determined and a fixed rental is set for each dwelling unit. The rental in the buildings erected by the Amalgamated Housing Corporation in the Bronx prior to World War II was $11.00 per month per room; in the buildings currently under construction by AHC the average charge will be $15.00. Amalgamated Dwellings in Manhattan operates on an average rental of $12.22 per room. The Hillman Housing Corporation has set $15.00 per room as the average maintenance charge. In total the three housing companies have an annual rent income of approximately $1,325,000.

322   HEALTH AND WELFARE SERVICES

Organization

The ACWA-sponsored housing companies are cooperative organizations. Each member has one vote regardless of the number of shares of stock he may hold or the number of rooms he occupies. Surpluses, or profits, if any, are shared in proportion to the annual rent (maintenance and operation charges) paid. Meetings to discuss the affairs of each corporation are held frequently. At an annual meeting, the stockholders elect members to the Board of Directors, the senior governing body. The Board, in turn, appoints the manager who is in charge of operations. At the end of the fiscal year a detailed statement, covering the financial and general operations, is submitted to the stockholders for discussion and approval. Decisions of the Board of Directors are subject to review by the membership. The stockholders also elect a House Committee, which assists management in dealing with local problems. Maintenance charges, or rent, originally fixed for each apartment (except for occasional minor adjustments) remain in effect unless changed by the member-stockholders. There is no direct legal or financial relationship between the three developments. Each operates as a separate entity and has its own Board of Directors and standing committees.

To safeguard the cooperative character of the enterprises and to create greater financial stability and confidence, a rule has been set by each housing project to the effect that no one may sell his stock equity before offering it first to the corporation for repurchase. The incentive to purchase housing stock for speculative or profiteering purposes by those who do not intend to live in the community has also been effectively eliminated by the corporation's practice of never declaring dividends on stocks. If a surplus exists at the end of a year it is distributed in the form of a rebate on rent. Special reserves are also established by each development to make it possible to purchase the equity from members who wish to leave the community. In no case is a member entitled to more than the par value of the stock that he holds.

Membership is limited, as much as possible, to wage earners and those of moderate incomes, but is not confined to members of the Amalgamated Clothing Workers. It was realized from the outset that a housing development involving the investment of large sums of money would be a poor financial risk if tenancy were limited to workers in any one industry. It was also recognized that a community made up of people engaged in a single kind of occupation would be less interesting socially than one comprising a variety of engagements. Thus, contrary to the impression held by some, and in keeping with the basic cooperative principle of "open membership," the Amalgamated-sponsored housing developments are occupied by a majority of people other than members of the union.

Two-Fold Benefits of Cooperative Community Living

The benefits that cooperative housing offers to its participants can be divided into two groups: material and social. The underlying motive for the promotion of a cooperative organization is the natural desire for material benefits. In the field of housing, however, the social benefits to be derived by the individual, as well as by the community as a whole, outweigh to a certain extent the purely material gains, important as the latter are.

Broadly considered, the social and psychological forces that influence the tenant-member of a cooperative housing society and his family may be summarized as follows:

Cooperative housing builds homes for its members, not apartments for profit and speculation.

Cooperative housing engages the interest of the member by imposing on him the responsibilities of part ownership of the development in which he intends to live for a long time. He is made to realize that the success or failure of the enterprise depends on him.

By virtue of the common interest in the undertaking, cooperative housing creates a common bond among the members even if the group is not a homogeneous one at the start.

The democratic form of organization inherent in a true cooperative enterprise offers the tenant-owner a liberal education in how to care for the needs of his immediate community. The acquisition of the habit of thought and action for the good of the community is a progressive social asset.

The indifference of the city inhabitant toward his neighbors, which prevails in the private commercial apartments, is almost impossible in a cooperative project. Here one member of the community meets another as a co-owner. Their common financial interests bring about a closer social relationship as well. Before very long, cooperators develop a pride in their community and in its accomplishments. Moreover, ownership of property and the sharing of responsibilities make the tenant-owner a more independent and self-respecting citizen, and thus a better and more useful member of the general community outside his immediate project.

The beneficial effects of the mutual influence of the individual and the community are considerable. The results of over two decades of operation prove that, given proper surroundings and decent environment, a good many of our personal and social problems can be reduced to a minimum, if not entirely eliminated. The fact that after twenty-two years more than 70 per cent of the original member-cooperators remain in the community, and nearly one hundred young couples, children of these "pioneers," have chosen to settle among them, is eloquent evidence of the continued attractiveness of the enterprise.

Related Co-op Activities

The establishment of the cooperative housing development has led, of course, to several related cooperative activities. Right from the start the Amalgamated Housing Corporation developed cooperative food stores and cooperative distribution of milk. Similarly, cooperative distribution of electricity was set up at the outset. When difficulties developed with the public utility company years later, the cooperative installed its own three-motored diesel plant and operated it for a number of years. Also, a nursery school and summer day camp for the children in the community, to mention but two of the many social activities, are conducted on a cooperative basis. These and other activities are carried on under separate corporations, the A. H. Consumers Society, Inc. and other similar setups, with each member-stockholder of the housing company holding one share of stock. According to established cooperative principles, the surplus or profits of the various business activities are distributed to the members in proportion to annual purchases.

The most recent example of this matter-of-fact cooperative expansion in the Bronx unit is the purchase of a full block of buildings housing 22 stores which is being converted into a modern cooperative shopping center with a supermarket designed to take care of about $15,000 worth of business a week. Still another is the building of a two-hundred-car garage (also in the Bronx development) to be financed and operated cooperatively.

Fertile Field for Union Action

Cooperative housing as successfully demonstrated by the Amalgamated "pilot" projects is no longer a dream and a risk. Others, in New York City and elsewhere are following the example, notably the State-sponsored, all-veteran Bell Park Gardens project and the privately sponsored "Queensview" development, both 800-family undertakings and cooperative all the way. Large financing institutions no longer hesitate to lend substantial sums to soundly organized cooperatives. Public confidence in cooperative housing, badly shattered by the several failures in the past—the result of poor financing, poor management and too much politics—is now restored, and tenants, by the thousands, are ready and anxious to make the necessary equity outlay. The successful operation of the various Amalgamated projects, it is but fair to emphasize, has made possible this revived confidence in cooperative housing.

Incidentally, it is not true, as many seem to think, that the Amalgamated Clothing Workers of America (ACWA) "owns" or "controls" the housing corporate bodies that bear its name in their designations.

The union lends its name, its prestige, and occasionally acts as a guarantor in financial matters, but it does not own a single share of stock in any of the housing corporations. Jacob S. Potofsky, President of the ACWA, is a Director in all three cooperatives, and the fraternal relationship between the union and the housing development is very close. But control and ownership rest entirely with the tenant cooperators.

What the Amalgamated has accomplished can be duplicated by other large and progressive labor unions with no financial involvements whatever, provided they are willing to apply themselves to the task and lend competent guidance to member groups. Private builders are not likely to enter the unprofitable field of housing for wage earners or white collar families of limited income. Either government housing or cooperative housing is the answer to the urgent need for homes of the urban middle-income groups. Our experience and that of government housing in the New York area, in addition to the experience of cooperative housing programs developed in Sweden and other European countries, lend strength to the conviction, held by most practical, nonpolitical observers, that the cooperative approach is most desirable, both socially and financially.

It would no doubt prove helpful if a chain of central cooperative housing agencies were established in the larger industrial cities, equipped to provide the planning, construction and management personnel as well as financial assistance to those unable to raise the full amount of their equity.[1] This is where trade unions, fraternal organizations, liberal endowment foundations and social-minded citizens generally can render great service to a social end without "risking" a dime.[2] Cooperative housing bonds can be both a sound financial investment and a dynamic contribution to better housing for the middle and lower middle income groups, in fact, even for the so-called "poorer" wage earner. Today, this last category of citizens must qualify for government "poor man's" housing with the social stigma it bears, but, given assistance in the form

---

[1] In 1948 the National Cooperative Housing Association was organized to help integrate cooperative housing information throughout the country, and may in time become the effective agency for such integration on a truly nationwide scale.

[2] In addition to the Amalgamated housing projects, another union-sponsored and successfully operated housing project is the Carl Mackley Houses in Philadelphia, sponsored by the American Federation of Hosiery Workers (CIO). This project is owned and managed by the Juniata Park Housing Corporation, a limited-dividend corporation. The resident here never becomes owner of either his apartment or of equivalent stock in the Association.

There are other examples of union-sponsored housing projects where the union has acted as the agent for joint buying of land and building of homes. Among these are the 50 Stonewall Heights Houses in Front Royal, Va., sponsored by the TWUA; and five houses built under the sponsorship of the Tulsa, Oklahoma, Building Trades Council. (Source: Nonprofit Housing Projects in the United States, Bulletin 896, U.S. Dept. of Labor, Bureau of Labor Statistics, March 1947.)

of long-term, low-interest loans as practiced in Stockholm and Antwerp, even the poorer family can enjoy the advantages of a cooperative home with the sense of independence and self respect that goes with it.

The trade union movement certainly did not wait for government to do all the union organizing for it; why not apply some of the same independent, democratic people's action to housing?

ABRAHAM E. KAZAN

Chapter 28

The unions, radio, and the community

*I*N THE EARLY DAYS OF RADIO BEFORE THE CONCEPTION OF FM AND WHILE the standard-band wave lengths were sparsely tenanted, labor was too busy trying to stay alive to worry about radio. Later, after the Wagner Act had given labor a lease on life, the trade unions were too busy coming of age to have any awareness of radio and its value as a public relations medium.

By the time labor had come of age and begun to appreciate the need for, and opportunity to do a community service job, the standard, or AM, band was overcrowded. Consequently, of the 2,000 AM stations in the United States, only one, WCFL in Chicago, is labor owned; that license was issued to the Chicago Federation of Labor in 1926.

There is one other AM station, WEVD in New York City, which comes close to this labor-owned category. In 1932, a group of outstanding citizens, such as John Dewey, Hendrik Willem Van Loon, and Morris Hillquit, inspired by the late B. Charney Vladeck, general manager of the *Jewish Daily Forward*, set up the Debs Memorial Fund which advanced $100,000 for the operation of WEVD on a non-profit basis.

Labor was not alone in missing this opportunity to move into AM radio back in the days when wave lengths were available. Many an educational and noncommercial organization now regrets not having thought of radio.

When the Federal Communications Commission, after the war, decided to open a new band for FM stations, labor's hopes zoomed. At last the dream of having a medium for presenting a fair treatment of labor's activities and goals was within reach. And four different labor unions (ILGWU, UAW, ACWA, NMU) filed applications with the FCC; of these only the International Ladies' Garment Workers' Union (AFL) and the United Auto Workers (CIO) received grants.

Today there are 5 FM stations owned and operated by labor. These are the three ILGWU (AFL) stations—WFDR, New York; WVUN, Chattanooga, and KFMV, Los Angeles—plus WCUO, Cleveland, and WDET, Detroit, of the United Auto Workers (CIO). In Washington, D.C., a group of individuals interested in co-ops have financed WCFM, and these six stations, plus KWIK, an AM station in Burbank, California, which the ILGWU purchased to plug its Hollywood FM station, operate as a non-wired network.

These stations exchange programs of public interest (examples: 30th Annual Conference of the American Civil Liberties Union in New York; ADA Convention in Washington; program on TVA from Chattanooga, etcetera). They also use, daily, some programs like "A Liberal Look at the News"—this being a daily commentary on the news done by such liberals as Robert Nathan, Mrs. Raymond Clapper, John Herling, and Wallace Campbell.

Most of the special programs heard on these stations originate in either Washington or New York simply because most of the newsworthy things happen in those two cities, but each station does its own local programming as well as originating special programs for the other stations.

With these stations as a nub, the radio coverage of important labor conclaves has been improved. Most recently the ILGWU's Golden Jubilee Convention in Atlantic City was heard over the aforementioned six key stations and over a station in Boston, Massachusetts. Some months earlier the CIO's national convention in Cleveland was heard over a special network of about 75 different stations.

These programs were actually 30-minute digests of tape recordings of the daily sessions of the convention and were fed to some stations by tape, to others by telephone line, and were carried by some as a public service and by others as a straight commercial, sponsored by some local of the union.

During the organizing of the International Confederation of Free Trade Unions in London, WFDR in New York arranged with the British Broadcasting Corporation to receive a daily commentary from London and sent these programs, via tape recording, to the 5 other outlets.

This type of program has resulted in two national commercials on the six stations and more are in the offing. The first of these was the Kaiser-Frazer "Washington Report" program, using Marquis Childs and Joseph C. Harsch on alternate nights in a quarter-hour of news comment. The second was the delayed re-broadcast of the American Federation of Labor's Frank Edwards newscast heard coast-to-coast over the Mutual Broadcasting System.

Programming

In the few years since labor has been operating FM stations, it has already learned that they must be run in the community interest and not for ulterior purposes like augmenting organizational operations. They have also discovered that functioning in the community interest means doing a full schedule of special events programs, covering the important developments and functions of the community, organizing debates and forums on civic problems, working with local groups and showing them how to get their story across in radio. In short, these labor stations have become aware that:

1. The interests of labor are the interests of the community.
2. The station must be used as an instrument to present the interests of the community as a whole, rather than one point of view only.
3. Programming is the lifeblood of a radio station. Labor-operated radio stations must have programming that meets all the rules of good radio—whether or not the other radio stations do. And especially is this true of news and special-events programs.

Unions not yet in the radio field must also consider seriously several alternatives before entering it.

Choosing Broadcast Outlets

Television, already an established rival of radio, is considerably more expensive to build and operate. And the number of locations available is severely limited. Moreover, it is probable that most cities where interested unions are located already have all the TV stations they will be permitted by the FCC, or that applications have already been made for all the available allocations. Hence, even if a union can afford a TV station, it is likely that it could not get a license. And even though TV is rapidly increasing in popularity, the number of TV sets in use is still far less than the number of radio sets.

FM, newest method of radio broadcasting, uses different equipment from AM, and requires a special radio receiver. Its attributes are a high-quality signal, no static, no fading, and no distortion. Handicapped by the phenomenal growth of TV and the lack of good sets, the story of FM, during these last two years, has been anything but encouraging. Nevertheless, many in the trade still think FM will eventually supplant AM. And in many areas, FM is the only radio system with room for newcomers.

Amplitude Modulation, radio signal with which we are all familiar, is probably the best medium for a union, because 98 per cent of the homes in the United States have at least one AM radio set. But because it has been operating for more than 25 years, AM radio is also the most crowded medium. In some areas, however, it is possible to apply for low-powered or part-time stations, and such opportunities should be investigated. Another possibility is the purchase of an AM station now in operation. This procedure will be expensive since most AM stations are at their financial peaks, but any AM stations for sale should be carefully evaluated and appraised by the radio-minded union.

Therefore, when the question arises, "Which medium shall my union select?" these facts should be considered:

1. Television requires too high an investment for too long a time for any trade union.

2. AM radio, if a spot can be found on the dial, or if a station can be bought, is the goal to strive for. But if and when a union finds someone willing to sell, it is necessary to examine the property carefully.

3. FM radio may offer the only opening. Then, by all means, the union should get into it.

At this point, the step-by-step procedure for applying for a license must be considered:

1. A decision must be made whether to operate a commercial or a non-commercial station. A commercial station is advisable for the following reasons:

 (*a*) A radio station is expensive to build and operate.

 (*b*) On an outright subsidy basis, it can become a serious financial drain after a number of years.

 (*c*) A successful commercial station can sell time to advertisers and so cut down the amount of the subsidy.

2. A radio committee should be set up in the union, staffed by some of the top policy-making people: the education director, the newspaper editor, and the business manager. This committee should be as small as possible, so as to expedite its functioning, yet it should be kept broad enough to represent the needs and knowledge of the union.

3. One person must be in charge of the station and that person must be held responsible to the radio committee.

4. The person named and the committee designated must have the time and the authority to deal with financial and legal problems that will arise.

5. The advice of other unions now in radio must be sought for suggestions and guidance. These unions have gone through the experience of setting up a new station and will undoubtedly be glad to help.

6. A radio attorney, someone qualified to practice before the FCC, is needed. The unions with radio experience can also offer guidance here. But two rules-of-thumb are in order: (*a*) when possible, an attorney who represents another station in the community should not be retained; and (*b*) an attorney familiar with and friendly to labor should be sought.

7. The advisability and possibility of interesting other unions in the community in participating in the station should be considered.

8. A radio engineer must compile and prepare data for the application sub-

mitted to the FCC. Here again, the unions with radio experience can be of help. One of their engineers might be able to do preliminary engineering work on a per diem basis, thus effecting considerable savings.

Budgeting a Station

Once the application for a station is approved, the cost of construction, equipment, and operation must be considered:

A site for a transmitter is easier and cheaper to buy, or rent, in a small town than in a larger town. The same is true of space for studios and offices and for the cost of building, power, water, and telephone lines.

Depending on the area to be covered and the size of the community in the heart of that area, building and equipping a station will cost at least $35,000 in a small town to $100,000 in a large city. If a Radio City type of building and studio, air conditioned offices, and a midtown location are wanted, the minimum will have to be increased.

Operating costs can be figured along the same lines. The more hours per day the station is on the air, the more staff is needed. The more staff, the higher the operating cost. For guidance, there follows a list of the minimum staff required to operate a station 10 hours daily in a nonmetropolitan community:

Engineering

Chief Engineer
4 Staffmen
1 Part-time Secretary

Programming

Program Manager
3 Announcers
1 Part-time Announcer
1 Secretary-Traffic Girl
1 News Editor and Special Eventsman

Sales

Sales Manager
Secretary
Salesmen on commission

Promotion

1 Publicity-Promotion Man
1 Secretary

Department heads, qualified in terms of experience, and convinced that the labor-liberal point of view is correct and worth fighting for, are available. They do not require excessively high salaries. The staff listed costs a total of $1,215 in salaries per week. This amount breaks down as follows: engineering, $425; programming, $500; sales, $145; promotion, $145.

Mail, telephone, overtime, and essential sundries will add at least another $250 to these salary figures. So it is best to figure on at least $1,500 a week, or $78,000 a year for an operating budget. And again, this is a minimum figure based on the ability and willingness of the staff to improvise and cooperate. The smaller the town in which the station operates, the more opportunity there is to double up on assignments. The chief engineer may be able to take regular duty at the controls; the program manager should double as announcer and special events man; one of the announcers should also serve as assistant to the news editor; announcers can write continuity; the sales manager and program manager can prepare commercial copy and programs.

Eventually, as the station develops, this doubling up will have to stop. The time comes when advertisers start to use the station. At that time, someone will have to concentrate on continuity, on traffic, on production as full-time duties.

Department heads should be allowed to select their own aides, but they must be held responsible for the people they hire.

Operating Policy

Community service is the key to the eventual success of a trade union in radio. Unions should not operate labor stations. They should operate community stations, since the interests of labor can never be separated from the interests of the community. No radio station, and especially no labor station, should present only one point of view.

The programming of a labor station must include a balanced and complete schedule of news, popular and serious music, plays, sports, and service programs. The station should develop local talent, local groups, public information and education, and it should hold forums on a wide range of public issues, including labor-management relations, consumer-farmer relations, and community-civic relations. News must be presented without bias or prejudice, so that all listeners will have faith and confidence in its reliability. This means the news must be true, factual, and comprehensive. A pro-labor bias is as bad as anti-labor bias.

Labor stations have an obvious additional job in their news coverage: to present labor news, news of labor legislation, and news about the accomplishments of labor throughout the nation.

A labor station, motivated by the concept of community service rather than by the drive for profits, should be able to resist the temptation of overcommercialization so prevalent among commercial stations.

In conclusion, a labor station must service the community on a sustaining *and* a commercial basis. By so doing, it can set so effective an example as to provide a yardstick by which the other stations in the community can be measured by the listener. And it will thus accomplish something of everlasting credit to the highest ideals of unionism.

M. S. NOVIK

Chapter 29

Unions and community services

1. THE CIO COMMUNITY SERVICES PROGRAM

*T*HE COMMUNITY SERVICES PROGRAM OF THE CIO IS, FIRST OF ALL, A BREAD-and-butter program. It helps to find and bring together available services in the community and CIO members and their families who need them. It is also a social action program. Wherever needed services are missing or inadequate, the program is geared to obtain these services and see to it that they are sufficient for their needs. It is, at the same time, a community organization program, a community relations program, and a public relations program.

Establishment and full utilization of adequate services demand the careful development of group cooperation, mutual understanding, and comprehensive planning on a community-wide basis. This requires what the experts call "community organization." Here public relations is both a means and a by-product, but never an end.

Principles of Operation

To help promote the program, several principles have been borrowed and developed:

1. There shall be representation with taxation.
2. Meeting the basic needs of the people is a governmental responsibility.
3. Relief services shall be made available to all on the basis of need, regardless of the cause of that need.
4. The union is responsible not only for the welfare of its employed members but also for the welfare of its unemployed members.
5. The job of the union extends beyond the plant gates.
6. The community is the world.

To help implement the program, an organizational structure has been devised. First there are the community services committees of local industrial union councils. Then there are the labor participation committees of councils of social agencies. But the very heart of the program is the counsellors of the local unions.

Six years ago there were only 90 CIO men and women serving on the boards and committees of our community social service agencies. Today there are more than 5,000 CIO members and an equal number from the AFL serving in this capacity. This, we are assured, is progress. Still, there are few workers, few farmers, few Negroes serving as trustees of our hospitals, as members of our boards of education, as directors of our Red Cross chapters, as commissioners of our parks, playgrounds, public assistance, and unemployment compensation bureaus. It has been the objective of the community services program to encourage year-round participation of CIO members in community affairs and active representation in community agencies and organizations on all policy-making and operating levels.

The CIO looks toward these agencies for services.

There was a woman in Kansas City who thought she had cancer.

There was a man in Camden who could not fill out his income tax return.

There was a boy in Denver who was stricken with polio.

There was a family in Chicago who could not get along.

There was a girl in Detroit who was alone and homeless.

There was a striker in Indianapolis who could not pay his rent.

There was a worker in Washington who was without food for the weekend.

There was the neighbor in Elm Trees who needed a lawyer.

There was the man in Philadelphia whose brother-in-law deserted from the British Navy, entered this country on a six-month pass, overstayed his time, and was being sought by the U.S. Immigration authorities.

These are only a few of the many problems that CIO members—like others—face beyond the plant gates. The collective bargaining agreement does not cover them. The political action program does not cover them. The legislative program does not cover them. The union treasury—even if it should—does not cover them. Still, these problems must be solved. Their solution cannot be postponed until a new collective bargaining agreement is reached or until appropriate legislation is enacted. The needs are now and they must be met now.

Role of Voluntary Agencies

CIO members will not be satisfied with the adoption of a resolution in support of a national health insurance program tomorrow, when they require hospitalization and medical care today. CIO members will not be satisfied with signing a petition for full employment tomorrow, when they need a job today. To help meet these immediate needs, the community services program looks to existing community agencies to provide, as swiftly, as adequately, and as efficiently as possible, the essential services and assistance.

These services may include marital counseling, summer camps, recreation, hospitalization, medical care, legal aid, child placement, old-age benefits, unemployment compensation, public assistance, emergency food allotments, housing, and many more. Aid and services of this kind may be obtained from both public and voluntary agencies. The CIO gets them from both while the need is immediate, and it does not waste time by joining in the academic debate on the shop-worn subject of public vs. private welfare.

The challenging fact is that, in this century of the so-called "common man," it is still necessary for American workers to take the means test to get on relief. The CIO directs a needy worker to public assistance, not because it likes to but because the needy worker needs it as a last defense against hunger.

To some, this means that the poor will always be with us and that charity begins at home. To the CIO, it means that Elm Trees alone cannot solve all its problems, but that the people of Elm Trees, joined together with the people of other communities, can take action to solve their common problems. Employment, health, social security, education, prices, wages, housing, and much more are problems as common to New York, Los Angeles, and Mississippi as they are to Elm Trees. Since they are basically common, they can be solved only by common action. It makes little difference, then, whether these problems are solved in Washington, Albany, New York, or Sacramento. In the long run, they are solved by the people of Elm Trees—acting as one through their own organizations and chosen representatives.

The community services program does not concern itself directly with such union activity as organizing the unorganized, collective bargaining, political action, and legislative lobbying. It does concern itself with social action that leaves its mark on all other phases of trade union activity. The CIO takes such action on its own initiative and in cooperation with other community groups. Such action takes various forms.

It may be the establishment of a Citizens Commission for the Public Schools in New York.

It may be the formation of a Citizens Housing Committee in Washington.

It may be the creation of a Neighborhood Committee to Eliminate Mosquitoes in Paterson.

It may be presentation of testimony before a legislative committee on hospital construction, or organization of a delegation to Washington, or signing petitions or sending letters, postcards, and telegrams.

This is the people in action. This is the community in action. This is democracy in action. It is this action that points to needs, that stimulates interest, that inspires planning, that encourages solutions and services.

The CIO recognizes that the basic needs of the people can be met only by the people themselves acting in concert through their government. Yet its community services program encourages active participation in the affairs of voluntary health and welfare organizations. Even if the government should assume its full responsibility in safeguarding our most important natural resource—the people's health—there still will be an important job for the voluntary agency to do.

First, the voluntary agencies are part of our democratic way of life, offering, as they do, a chance for citizen participation through board and committee membership and through volunteer service that government agencies have not been able to provide.

Second, the voluntary agencies are more flexible than the public agencies and can play a valuable supplementary role to government in pioneering experimentation and research.

Third, the voluntary agencies, properly coordinated within councils of social agencies, can do an invaluable job of planning and social action, which public agencies have found traditionally difficult.

Fourth, the voluntary agencies, because of the flexibility of their rules and the comparative absence of red tape, can provide emergency and supplementary services when needed.

Fifth, what some social workers like to call "character-building" organizations, such as the Girl Scouts and the YWCA, should always be on a voluntary basis and should never be replaced, in a free and democratic society, by government-controlled Hitler Jugends or Red Fronts.

Sixth, voluntarism retains, to some degree, the spirit of good neighborliness and mutual help, which is especially important in a highly complex society such as ours.

Seventh, voluntary agencies play an important educational role and often arouse public opinion in support of governmental measures designed to meet human needs.

Contributions to Voluntary Agencies

There are literally thousands of voluntary agencies across the nation. They include such organizations as the Boy Scouts, Camp Fire Girls, Family Service Society, Salvation Army, Red Cross, Child Welfare League, the "Y's," and the Community Chest. CIO members support these agencies with voluntary contributions. From 1942 through 1949, CIO members contributed more than $275,000,000 to such organizations as the National War Fund, Red Cross, Community Chests, National Foundation for Infantile Paralysis, American Cancer Society, American Heart Association, and others. Throughout this period, the community services program has been concerned with the multiplicity of fund-raising drives and the resultant duplication, inefficiency, waste, and confusion. Philanthropy is big business, and much money has been raised from the people on the basis of sound organization and heart-rending emotional appeals.

Let us take three health agencies, for example, heart, cancer, and polio. These three, like many others, raise their funds through organized independent national campaigns. Each spends a considerable sum of money every year to administer its campaign. Each has its own fund-raising and promotion departments. Each calls upon the people, at different times of the year, to contribute dimes, quarters, dollars—as much as they can. Each enlists countless volunteers to solicit contributions. Each tries to get into the union halls and plants with cans and pledge cards. Each implies that it alone saves the people from a fate worse than polio, worse than cancer, worse than heart disease, worse than death. One out of every five gets this, and one out of three gets that, and one out of one finally dies. It is a sad story. It is sad because there is so much waste, inefficiency, and confusion. It is sad because the funds are not contributed on the basis of relative need, but on the basis of better organization and greater emotional appeal.

There really isn't enough voluntary money around to do the total job. The mistake that private health agencies make is in appealing to the people on the basis of meeting the people's needs rather than on the basis of meeting the agencies' needs. No single voluntary agency can hope to cope with the total job of cancer research, detection, prevention, cure, and terminal care.

The major portion of this job belongs to the government. The private agency may have a supplementary program that should be financed on that limited basis by voluntary contributions. Under the system of free enterprise in fund-raising, the polio organization gets more money than the heart and cancer organizations when, at the same time, many more people are ill or die of heart and cancer disease than of polio. Under these circumstances, the CIO Community services program has been promoting federation in fund-raising and the budgeting and allocation of funds on the basis of relative need.

Voluntary contributions were not so voluntary at one time. In many industries, management made "voluntary" contributions to such agencies as the Red Cross and Community Chest a condition of employment. In too many cases, workers were forced or shamed into giving for charity out of all proportion to their meager earnings. At the same time, many a company, publicly and for what it considered sound public relations reasons, took full credit for the gifts of its employees. Since the agencies were controlled by the same people who controlled industry, the quotas for the plants were set by management, the standard of giving was set by management, solicitation was handled by management, and contributions were allocated by management. Workers, however, were given the privilege of contributing.

The community services program has helped to change this picture. It has encouraged the widely accepted principle that those who give should determine for themselves their own quotas, their own standard of giving, their own solicitations or payroll deductions. It has also sponsored the widely accepted principle that employees' gifts shall be credited to their unions rather than to their companies.

CIO members do not contribute to the voluntary agencies in the expectation that their gifts will be returned to them in services. But they do expect to receive assistance and services from these agencies in the event of need, regardless of the cause of that need.

For many years, voluntary agencies and some governmental bodies, such as public assistance bureaus, have refused to grant assistance to needy strikers. They donned the noble cloak of impartiality and suggested that it would be unfair to the community and to their own consciences to subsidize strikes. This approach has been largely changed by the CIO community services program, which took the position that, with respect to relief, the word "strikers" is secondary to the word "needy" and that it is the responsibility of the community to minister to the needs of all its citizens.

In most cases, however, needy workers preferred not to apply for relief. Taking the means test is an indignity to the human spirit that no proud person can stand. Workers don't want handouts and charity. They want jobs and insurance against rainy days. Still, in a system such as ours, where jobs are somewhat insecure and insurance is either nonexistent or limited, public assistance and other relief services become, at times, the only means to survival.

The community services program takes the position that the people are entitled to these services as a matter of right. They pay taxes to finance the public agencies and they make voluntary contributions to finance the private agencies. Therefore, the services provided by these agencies in time of need are, in a sense, a form of social insurance against starvation.

CIO Community Services Committees of industrial union councils and local unions implement this program in their own communities. They know the needs and resources of their own communities. They join forces with other groups, through labor participation committees of councils of social agencies and other community-wide committees. They press forward on all fronts to make the community a better place to live in. In their fight for better schools and parks, for better and more hospitals, nurseries, recreation centers, for better and less expensive medical care, and for other facilities of service to the people, the CIO works with management, other labor groups, and anyone else who believes in the same minimum program for a better and more democratic community. This work, then, has many by-products. In the first place, it provides an opportunity for the CIO to put its best foot forward in a more receptive atmosphere of good will and mutual understanding. Once an area of agreement has been discovered in the comparatively less controversial field of community services, it may be possible to discover other areas of agreement—in the fields of race relations, labor-management relations, and others that are interrelated and often react to the same influence.

The program also has educational implications. People who were isolated from the mainstream of community life and whose knowledge of their community often came from the vague and wishful theories of their grammar school text books on civics, now, for the first time, learn about their community, its politics, its economics, its sociology, its problems, and its potentialities, by doing and by actively participating in its affairs.

The union counselor training program has reached many thousands of rank-and-file workers in 54 industrial communities with the ancient philosophy that we are our brother's keeper and that we had better do something about it.

Union counseling has been taught, in intensive training sessions, to 6,000 steel workers, radio workers, textile weavers, shipbuilders, and others. They are trained to refer the needs of their fellow-workers and neighbors to the appropriate agency, to follow up for a speedy and effective solution, and to file the required reports with the local CIO Community Services Committee.

To discharge his duties, a union counselor must know about the facilities and resources of his community, their functions and responsibilities. In discharging his duties, a union counselor often learns of the community's specific shortcomings and limitations, not only in the fields of health and welfare services but also in the related fields of financing, budgeting, planning, administration, and politics. An interested union counselor is often excellent material for agency board and committee membership. Such a counselor soon discovers, too, that active participation in social and political action is essential if the basic health and welfare needs of the people are to be met.

Union counseling is an education in responsibility to our fellow men, in community consciousness, in citizen participation, in human relations, and in basic trade union and social work principles. It is also an education in the need for social, political, and legislative action for the eventual elimination of the basic evils of our society: poverty, disease, slums, and crime, all of which today provide a fertile field for patch-up social work.

It is reasonable to expect that the union counselor soon will take his place in the forefront of grass roots political organization for the single purpose of helping to build an economically just and politically free society for all. Knowing his community as he does, helping his neighbor as he does, thinking as he does in broader terms, he is now in a better position to replace the old-time ward heeler and district captain of the boss-ridden political machines in our industrial communities.

The community services program has been called, at times, a "fringe" offshoot of the Congress of Industrial Organizations. In theory, it is. In practice, it is part and parcel of the over-all CIO program, simply because it is part and parcel of our everyday life. You can no more separate the community from the union than you can separate the union member from his community. The fact is that there is nothing novel about the community services program. It is as old as the American trade union movement itself—except that, today, it is more sharply focused and more clearly defined.

LEO PERLIS

2. The AFL Program

One one occasion, speaking of the aims of the American Federation of Labor, President Gompers said, "We want more school houses and less jails, more books and less arsenals, more learning and less greed, more justice and less revenge—in fact, more of the opportunities to cultivate our better natures, to make manhood more noble, womanhood more beautiful, and childhood more happy and bright."

In the early days of the AFL, organized labor did not approve of many of the activities in which we now find ourselves. But the program and activities of the American labor movement have altered with the changing times. Early in this century, social welfare work and plans were of little concern to the American wage earner, and much less to the trade unions. Today we are actively involved in many forms of welfare activity. We are identified with the Community Chest; we are actively concerned with every community activity that works for the welfare of the citizen and the community, of the state, and of the nation.

The AFL has, of course, always cooperated with other progressive and civic-minded groups in the struggle for advanced social legislation. Union action and achievement have figured prominently in legislation restricting the use of child labor; in the elimination of sweatshops; in safety regulations in factories and mines; in workmen's compensation; in universal suffrage with the elimination of the property holding rule; and in the establishment of free public schools. The AFL was also in the forefront of the fight for federal aid to education, old age insurance, social security, establishment of the minimum wage, extension of civil liberties, slum clearance and public housing, fair employment practices, and the regulation of life insurance.

Our activity now extends to the planning and programming of community welfare, joining our activity with that of other freedom-loving groups in the community.

At its convention in St. Paul in October 1949, the AFL unanimously recognized the need for establishing and developing a sound, constructive program in community health and welfare. The following paragraphs from a convention resolution state the position of the Federation:

RESOLVED, That the American Federation of Labor urge Community Chests and Councils to inaugurate or expand the participation of American Federation of Labor members in the year-round activities of Community Chests and Councils, and be it further

RESOLVED, That the international unions, city central bodies, state federations of labor and federal labor unions of the American Federation of Labor cooperate with Community Chests and Councils in an effort to accomplish the maximum results through this program.

There are three essential phases in the relationship of the Community Chest and Council movement and its affiliated Red Feather agencies to the community. The agencies render services to the people of the community; the people of the community voluntarily contribute funds for the support of the agencies; and the Community Chests and Councils conduct an educational campaign to make the community aware of the services and of the need in the community for these services.

In developing a program with the voluntary health and welfare agencies, such as those affiliated with Community Chests and Councils, the AFL has adopted a basic, four-point program of supporting and sponsoring: (1) A year-round Labor-Management Committee of the local Community Chests and Councils; (2) Red Feather Tours; (3) AFL-Management-Social Work Institutes; (4) Speakers from agencies addressing union meetings. The four parts of this plan have been successfully developed, with the local membership of the AFL, into an effective year-round program.

This program is put into effect in each community by the local AFL Central Labor Union made up of the local AFL unions, in cooperation with the local Community Chest and Council. These Central Labor Unions have responded to communications from the national AFL officers who work in close cooperation with the national AFL staff representatives on the Community Chests and Councils. Usually a committee, such as health and welfare, within the Central Labor Union is responsible for carrying out the details of the program.

The Labor-Management-Social Work Institute is a very important part of the AFL four-point program. Here is an example of its usefulness. In 1949 the Connecticut Federation of Labor, AFL, sponsored such an Institute. The activity was started under a grave handicap, since there had been little AFL participation in the work of local Community Chests, outside of fund raising, and in some communities the drives had met with a very apathetic reception. However, as a result of the Institute and of a conscientious follow-up, a number of AFL members assumed positions of responsibility on boards and committees, not only of the Community Chest

but of other agencies—including some that had previously drawn the
sharpest attacks from the AFL. In 1950 the Connecticut Federation of
Labor conducted another Labor-Management-Social Work Institute, developing a program designed to reach not only the leading officers of the
unions—that was accomplished in the previous year—but also the membership in the more than 400 local unions in the state. Through the program
set up at this Institute, every member of every local union knows why he
contributes to Community Chests and what services in the community are
available to him.

Red Feather Tours are another highly valuable means of telling the
membership of the work of the voluntary agencies. On a Red Feather
Tour, representative union members are taken to visit the agencies. Management cooperates by giving the worker time off from his job to take
part in the Tour. The Tours are conducted under the direction of the
AFL staff representative with the Community Chest, who trains lay
volunteers to act as guides for the individual groups. In St. Louis, for
example, 265 Red Feather Tours involving 3,161 employees were made
during the first ten months of 1949. As a result, the AFL is represented on
the boards and committees of virtually all of the Red Feather agencies in
St. Louis. In 1948, 82 firms, in cooperation with the unions in their shops,
arranged for their employees to make 206 tours involving 1,814 workers.
In the campaign that year, the employees of these firms contributed
$66,000 more than they had the previous year, a gain of 19 per cent.

The AFL in St. Louis is very proud of its record of year-round participation as well as contribution, but it should be borne in mind that this
is an AFL-management program of cooperation with the Community
Chest. That management recognizes its value is indicated by a statement
of an official of one of the largest firms: "We feel that these tours have
given our employees a better view of the accomplishments of the Greater
St. Louis Community Chest and also shown them what their contributions
do to help this great organization in the work it is doing." The experiences
in other cities could be cited, but the St. Louis record will serve as an
illustration. What should be emphasized is that the Red Feather Tours
are planned on a year-round basis, not confined to campaign time.

A unique activity has been developed in Seattle, Washington, and
Kansas City, Missouri. In both cities, motion pictures of the agencies' work
were shown at union meetings. In Seattle, the building trades cooperated
in building some of the sets used in the picture, and the AFL Motion Picture Machine Operators contributed the services of a union technician to
show the picture not only to local unions but also to other citizen groups.
Within a few months the picture had had over 700 showings.

At times the American Federation of Labor selects a particular activity
for the purpose of a "control experiment," to ascertain the response of the
AFL membership. For example, a special brochure was prepared for our

members by the Boys Clubs of America and sent to all Central Labor Unions with an accompanying letter from President William Green. It was also distributed to every Boys Club in the country. As a result, committees from the Central Labor Unions have visited Boys Clubs to learn about their activities and their needs at first hand. Representatives of the Boys Clubs have addressed union meetings; AFL members have told their fellow-workers about the purposes and achievements of the Clubs. AFL central bodies have provided instructors for shops and classes, and given their aid to other specific projects. They have also sponsored Boy Scout troops.

The experience in Toledo, Ohio indicates the value of cooperation by all groups in the community, particularly labor and management, in a sound community health and welfare program. Toledo had been growing very rapidly as an industrial center, but little had been done to keep abreast of the recreational needs of the city. The Toledo Council of Social Agencies, with an AFL member on the board, studied the situation and took action. It organized all groups: management, labor, churches, civic groups, into one great sponsoring team and put an adequate recreational program into effect.

The labor press helps considerably in the work of the Community Chests through articles, stories, and pictures that go to the many millions of labor paper readers. In a letter of thanks to the International Labor Press, the Executive Director of the national office of Community Chests wrote: "We are thinking of the descriptive articles and pictures that appear weekly throughout the year in your papers. This type of publicity, not connected with any fund raising, is of real value in making known to the public the day-by-day services rendered by the voluntary services."

The monthly journals of the AFL national and international unions and the weekly AFL labor papers serving the entire community have done a really excellent job. But there is another division of the labor press that should be drawn into this sustained educational enterprise. The bulletins of the local unions and the house organs of firms having contracts with AFL unions could, under the direction of a labor-management committee, reach the members of the unions on an industry or plant level, acquainting them with the available services and encouraging them to take part not only on committees but in the very activities of the agencies, such as Boys Clubs and Boy Scouts.

Today, approximately 30,000 AFL members are serving on the boards and committees of Community Chests and Councils and the Red Feather agencies. In one city a member of the Teamsters Union is Secretary of the Community Chest. In a midwestern community a member of the Carpenters Union is President of the Chest. In another, a Typographical Union member is a Vice-President of the Chest. When a member of the Plumbers Union and President of the Central Labor Union was elected

President of the Community Chest in this area, the local newspaper congratulated him editorially and pledged full cooperation.

There are many instances of good AFL relationships in the community that have been built up by participation in the work of voluntary agencies. A West Coast Central Labor Union reports, as part of a Union-Management Relations Study made by the official AFL bulletin, *Labor's Monthly Survey*, that "The Central Labor Union and delegates take part in all civic affairs and have representatives on all social agencies. We have built up good will for the AFL throughout the city and our labor-management relations are of the highest."

There are some who would call all of this "good public relations." I prefer to call it "good human relations." That does not mean getting your picture in the paper. It does mean taking an active part in anything that affects the welfare of the community. It does mean maintaining and improving living standards. It is a challenge and an opportunity to do a real, constructive job in human relations, to promote good will and good work in each community, because it is in the community that this must first be done.

MATTHEW WOLL

Chapter 30

Unions and minority discrimination

THE MAJORITY OF THE TRADE UNIONS OF THE UNITED STATES ENFORCE NON-discrimination, oppose racial and religious prejudice, and support civil rights when the opportunity arises in the normal course of union activity. There are many instances of failure to counter discrimination but they are exceptions to a basically democratic pattern. In our nation, churches are characteristically segregated, colleges and universities normally have quotas for minorities, and community organizations practice exclusion of one or another American ethnic or racial group. In the face of this, unions organize workers employed in their respective jurisdictions on the basis of equality without regard to race, religion, or national origin. In general, unions whose membership includes diverse ethnic groups use economic pressure on employers to break down the discriminatory patterns. They try to enforce hiring and upgrading based on seniority or on some other objective standard that does not permit of racist application. Most unions, even those whose membership does not include members of minority groups, give support to civil rights legislation and pay at least verbal homage to the principle of equality for all persons regardless of creed, color, race, or national origin.

The diverse trade union policies and practices in the intergroup relations field are discernible in the following areas:

1. *Collective bargaining:* combatting discrimination and segregation in employment through provisions or practices under collective bargaining agreements.

2. *Education and propaganda:* seeking to advise union members on labor's reasons for being opposed to discrimination and prejudice, and otherwise seeking to reduce the incidence of prejudice among union members.

3. *Community action:* participating in drives for civil rights legislation, in community-wide civil rights councils and in other community efforts at improving intergroup relations.

4. *Internal practices:* liberalizing union policies on the admission and status

of minority members and on the interrelations of groups of members of varying ethnic origins.

The following basic factors must be kept in mind in order to understand
the practices of some sections of the labor movement in intergroup matters.

1. Union organizations are influenced by the national and local community
patterns. The fifteen million union members are "average Americans," and
tend to share the attitudes dominant in the communities in which they live.

2. There are strong equalitarian ideological undercurrents in the American
trade union movement. These stem from: (a) the general equalitarian philosophy which has characterized American society, exemplified by the role of the
trade union organizations during their formative stages, and (b) the powerful
influence of socialist ideology in a number of American unions, and the union
officials and activists oriented towards this ideology.

3. Among industrial workers there have always been large numbers of
foreign-born Americans who have themselves experienced ethnic discrimination, and many had been raised in a socialist or trade union environment.

4. In many industries, employers used nationality, religious or racial differences as a means of dividing workers and preventing unionization. This
often resulted in an appreciation of the need and the desirability for unity
across ethnic lines. At times, however, the effects of antiunion activities carry
over the implanted prejudices, and discrimination is practiced even by local
unions.

5. The ethnic employment patterns in most industries and trades were set
by employer decisions, not by the unions. The ethnic character of the union
membership in an industry invariably reflects these decisions. For example,
the exclusion of Jews from employment in nonselling capacities in insurance
companies, but their inclusion in employment in retail trades; or the exclusion
of Negroes from skilled railroad jobs, but their inclusion in sections of the
auto industry, are reflected in the composition of the unions in these industries.

6. The policy of maintaining "closed membership books," in some skilled
crafts, in order to keep down the number of workers competing for jobs,
serves to perpetuate the ethnic patterns previously established in the industry.
This means that if, in a given skilled craft, members of any particular group
were excluded from employment 25 years ago, they are likely still to be excluded today.

Combatting Discrimination Through Collective Bargaining

Unions play their most important role in advancing or retarding nondiscrimination in the United States through their direct dealings with
unionized employers. It would be a safe guess that more opportunities for
minorities have been opened by union economic pressure than by the state
FEPC laws. Large sections of American industry that practiced discrimination in advancement or hiring, prior to unionization, have been brought
into line by the pressure of the unions in their industry. From the needle
trades to the auto industry, from maritime to coal mining, millions of
workers are employed at jobs in which the unions have abolished pre-

viously practiced discrimination. Today, thousands of workers in these industries hold jobs that no member of their race, religion, or national group could have held prior to unionization.

The breaking down of discriminatory patterns in unionized industry is handled, most frequently, not as a separate issue, "discrimination," but as an incidental result of the enforcement of "seniority provisions" within a plant, or the enforcement of "union hiring" provisions. The refusal by management to up-grade an employee who is a member of a minority group will in most cases be handled by the union as a violation of the seniority provision rather than as a violation of some general clause in the union contract banning discrimination. One international union that has kept a record of progress reports that during the last ten years, through their system of plant-wide seniority, over 100,000 jobs from which minorities were previously excluded are now filled exclusively on the basis of seniority and competence.

Eight state FEPC laws in force give the aggrieved individuals the right to file complaints against employers who discriminate on the basis of race, creed, color, or national origin. Attempts have been made to have these laws revised to permit complaints by organizations. This would make it possible to use the laws more effectively as an additional pressure on a unionized employer to follow a nondiscriminatory policy. The law could likewise be used to force the nonunion employers to conform to fair employment requirements.

Discrimination could be eliminated in most unionized employment provided there already are members of minority groups employed within the jurisdiction of the local or by the plant concerned. Experience shows that where the local union leadership stands squarely for equal enforcement of union contract provisions, previously established discriminatory patterns break down. In one large local union in St. Louis, Missouri, a strong position taken by the leadership broke down in that industry the rigid segregation patterns practiced generally in the community. The union officials responsible were repeatedly re-elected over opposition candidates.

Certainly, many union officials avoid the issue, feeling that they would jeopardize their chances of re-election if they fought a battle in the interests of minority rights. The president of one of the large railway brotherhoods, which excluded Negroes, often expressed himself publicly in behalf of equal rights for people regardless of creed or color, but never raised this question within his own union. An administration entrenched with its membership can almost always enforce established nondiscriminatory patterns. Thus discrimination against Negroes gave way in the border and southern states in coal, maritime, steel, needle, textile, and in some building trades local unions.

In the majority of unionized industries in which discrimination is still practiced, one of the following conditions may prevail:

1. Plants do not employ members of any minority group, so that the problem of the seniority rights of a minority worker never arises. Or there are no members in the local who can complain of discrimination against members of their group. As hiring in most mass-production industries is exclusively an employer prerogative, both in contract and practice, the unions do not usually attempt to bargain for nondiscriminatory hiring.

2. Seniority in the plant operates only within a department, or within a skill, and hiring is planned so as to keep all the members of one ethnic group in one department and all the members of another group in another department. The members of a given group thus can rise on the basis of seniority only within one department. This means that the least favored minority is limited to the least skilled and most poorly paid department.

An effort has been made, particularly among CIO unions, to popularize a nondiscrimination clause in contracts and to establish a Fair Practice Department. One major industrial union claims to have written a nondiscrimination clause into 80 per cent of its collective bargaining agreements. Various model clauses have been drawn. Typical is one that reads: "Neither the employers nor the union shall discriminate in hiring, upgrading, transfer, layoffs, or rehiring against any employee on account of race, creed, sex, color, or national origin."

The Fair Practice Department is a department of an international union charged in part with the responsibility for spreading the union's fair employment policy to plants where it is not fully enforced. The first union to establish a Fair Practices Department was the UAW-CIO. In 1946, the union adopted a formalized set of procedures for handling fair-practice matters through this department. A number of other unions, both CIO and AFL, have followed suit. During 1949, there appeared to be a definite trend in this direction, and it is likely that by the end of 1950 close to 20 international unions will have functioning departments or national committees. Among these are the American Federation of Teachers-AFL, the United Steelworkers-CIO, the United Rubber Workers-CIO, the United Automobile Workers-AFL, the National Maritime Union-CIO, and the International Union of Electrical Workers-CIO.

In 1942, the National CIO established a Committee to Abolish Discrimination in Employment, and through its director, George L. P. Weaver, it has been an active force in encouraging antidiscrimination activities among the CIO affiliates.

During 1949 and 1950, various training programs were put into operation to aid union officials in meeting the problems of discrimination, segregation, and prejudice that arise in the shop and local. This training has taken the form of workers' education courses, trade union institutes, and the publication of training materials. It indicates the recognition of this area of action as a distinct field for union activity, even as community services has become an accepted trade union function.

On the negative side, there are a few instances in which unions have resisted employers' efforts at change in the direction of nondiscrimination or have tried to force discriminatory practices where they did not previously exist. The Federal Circuit Court has ruled, for example, against any attempt by the Brotherhood of Locomotive Firemen and Enginemen to eliminate Negro firemen who have in the past performed firemen's duties on the Gulf, Mobile and Ohio Railroad. Such incidents, however, are very rare.

Checking Prejudice Among the Union Members Through Education

The position that "race" prejudice is contrary to the policies and traditions of organized labor and that ethnic divisions are a serious menace to trade unionism and to the standards of living of the workers is found in both AFL and CIO constitutions, and in many published statements of William Green and Philip Murray, as well as in the printed and verbal propaganda and education that reach the union membership.

Many unions have published one or more pamphlets under their own imprint dealing exclusively with these problems. The AFL and CIO nationally have published a number of materials on discrimination and prejudice. Such publications are exhibited at most major trade union conventions, and efforts are made to encourage the education of local union membership on these problems. These activities are aided by the efforts of the Jewish Labor Committee and the National Labor Service which offer the unions various types of assistance in these matters.

Surveys of the coverage of intergroup relations items by the labor press indicate that normally one out of every five issues of these periodicals contains material aimed at improved intergroup relations. This material is made available through several syndicated press services including International Labor Press, Labor Press Associates, Federated Press, and two press services specializing in human relations, Labor Reports, and National Labor Service.

Discussion of intergroup relations has been a part of every labor- or university-sponsored workers' education training program. It has been found that effective discussion of these problems can arise normally in connection with courses on shop steward training, collective bargaining, labor history, labor economics, political action, and so on. Even courses in public speaking, discussion techniques, labor journalism, and other essentially technical subjects allow for the discussion of related intergroup problems. Moreover, many schools have established the practice of conducting one session on civil rights or fair practices for each group of students.

The value of handling intergroup relations through workers' education programs is limited by the small percentage of trade unionists—not more than one in a hundred—who are reached by these programs. However, those who do participate are generally drawn from the ranks of the union officials and active union members so that their influence cannot be measured in terms of numbers alone.

Participation in Community Antidiscrimination Efforts

The two federations, the AFL and the CIO, have given firm support to all major civil rights efforts. Both were represented on the President's Committee on Civil Rights, which wrote the Civil Rights Report—the AFL by Boris Shishkin, its Research Director, and the CIO by its Secretary-Treasurer, James Carey.

Through public pressure, financial contributions, lobbying, and insistence upon a strong civil rights plank in the Democratic Party platform, the national leadership of the AFL and CIO has played a major role in the struggle for a federal FEPC law—second only to that of the national organizations of the Negro and Jewish communities. A. Philip Randolph, Chairman of the National Council for a Permanent FEPC, and the only Negro president of an AFL international union, has been a leading figure in the fight for a fair employment practices law. Of the international unions, few have played as active a role as have the national CIO and AFL, but almost all have lent formal support to the civil rights program and FEPC. Most active have been the unions with long progressive records, and those which regardless of politics, count among their members large numbers of Negroes or Jews. Even those unions which would have to change their rules or practices to meet the terms of a federal FEPC law have rarely opposed it.

The national CIO and AFL and several of the international unions have also been particularly responsive to the needs of the Jewish minority not only in the United States, but in other parts of the world. They have participated in the various American activities to aid in the establishment of the state of Israel. In the drive for liberal DP legislation the AFL and the CIO have reversed traditional positions against immigration to favor such legislation.

The positions of the state and local bodies have not always paralleled those of the national federations. In several notable instances, state federations of labor and AFL central bodies have been distinctly cool to state and local FEPC and other civil rights legislation. In one or two cases there has been outright opposition, and in a number of others there has been either silence or unfulfilled promises of public support.[1] However, these

---

[1] The reasons usually given by the responsible AFL leaders have been either that, locally, the given measure is CIO sponsored; or that the proposed measure contains an "injunction" provision, which word is anathema to organized labor. In this connection the Research Department of the national AFL at one time issued a model state FEPC law that presumably avoids any objectionable provisions.

instances are exceptional, and under the leadership of the AFL national office, these state and local groups have in most cases changed their views. Almost all of the state and local councils of the CIO have stood solidly behind civil rights.

The actions of the individual locals, trade councils, and local joint boards have varied greatly. Again, active support for civil rights has usually come either from those with progressive and socialist traditions, or those with large numbers of minority workers among their members. Most local unions and joint boards have given at least formal support.

In a few areas there has been active opposition from local building trades councils to regulations outlawing segregation in public housing or in private limited-dividend, partially tax-exempt, housing. In these instances, the legislative representatives of the building trades councils appear to be guided by the building trades employers' associations in their communities.

Many city and state governments have official committees aiming at improved intergroup relations, such as the Mayor's Committee on Unity, and the Governor's Council on Human Rights. Most of these committees have broad advisory and educational functions, but receive little or no funds, and are consequently limited in their operations. There is no established pattern in regard to labor representation on these committees. In general, labor participation seems rather minor except in areas such as Chicago and Detroit, where the trade union movement has been aggressive in promoting improved intergroup relations. On the other hand, almost all of the boards charged with the enforcement of the eight state FEPC laws and the several local FEPC ordinances have active labor participation.

Generally more important than the so-called "Mayor's Committees" and "Governor's Committees" are the joint councils of local organizations set up in various communities, dedicated to the adoption of civil rights legislation and the improvement of intergroup relations. Labor is usually not an active participant, largely because the leadership of these groups is drawn from religious, educational, and social work circles that are not in contact with the trade union leadership. Where labor has been represented, the participation has usually been "formal" rather than active. Exceptions can be found in areas such as Los Angeles, Chicago, and Detroit where the unions have on their own initiative taken an active interest in civil rights matters, or where there are active Labor Committees to Combat Intolerance or similar bodies that participate in community groups representing organized labor.

Internal Union Discrimination Policies and Practices

It has already been indicated that where members of all groups are employed within an industry, the unions have commonly followed a policy of including them on a basis of equality in union locals. It is estimated that there are approximately 1,400,000 union members drawn from the minority groups in the United States. This figure includes approximately 800,000 Negroes and about 500,000 Jews. The largest concentration of Negroes is in the United Automobile Workers-CIO, the United Steelworkers-CIO, and the United Mine Workers. The largest concentration of Jews is probably in the International Ladies' Garment Workers' Union-AFL, the Amalgamated Clothing Workers-CIO, the Retail, Wholesale and Department Store Union-CIO, and the Retail Clerks International Association-AFL. The participation of Negroes in union leadership has been steadily increasing in the past two decades. In unions that have large numbers of Jewish members, the Jewish workers have always been substantially represented among the leadership elements.

A number of international unions, in industries that at one time employed few, if any, workers of a minority group, established and have continued exclusionist policies, keeping a policy of discrimination alive where changes might otherwise have taken place. In the majority of cases of racial discrimination by unions, the victims have been Negroes. But exclusion has also been practiced against Jews, Mexicans, and Orientals. One small international union in a highly paid trade pursued a policy of exclusion of Jews from employment. Under powerful pressure from strong segments of the labor movement, and threats of public exposure, this policy was dropped. There are, of course, a number of local unions, particularly of the "closed book" variety, that in practice exclude Jews from membership. They would no doubt insist that the absence of Jews from their membership is entirely accidental.

In the southwestern part of the United States there are occasional instances of unions excluding persons of Mexican extraction. During World War II there were also a number of unions that excluded Japanese from their membership.

In the past, a number of major unions, and almost all of the railroad brotherhoods, specifically excluded Negroes by provisions in their Constitutions, among these the Locomotive Firemen and Enginemen, the Trainmen, the Yardmasters, the Conductors, the Switchmen, the Locomotive Engineers. It probably would be safe to estimate that these policies are maintained by unions having between 10 and 20 per cent of the union membership of the United States.

The exclusionist policies of the unions mentioned have begun to break down under the combined pressures of public opinion, the wartime FEPC order, and the new state FEPC laws. The International Association of Machinists, which at one time had a "lily-white" pledge in its oath of membership, has in many areas organized large numbers of Negroes into its locals, on the basis of complete equality.

Following adoption of the New York State FEPC law, the State Commission Against Discrimination conferred with those international unions which had pursued openly exclusionist policies. As a result, all of the unions concerned made changes in their regulations. Some eliminated all discriminatory regulations. Others inserted clauses into their constitutions that made the discriminatory policies inoperative in those states in which they are illegal (*e.g.*, Railway Mail Association). The practical results of these changes vary sharply from union to union. In many of the locals in the New York area, there has been a real change of attitude toward the inclusion of Negroes. No doubt many of the union officials regard the constitutional amendments as mere paper revisions, but at least one large railway union that previously granted Negro locals "auxiliary" status has inaugurated a policy of both organization and education aimed at ultimately breaking down the pattern of discrimination in its craft. It seems safe to predict that within the next few years, we will see the end of international-union-enforced policies of discrimination, although discrimination will no doubt continue for some time to be the dominant pattern in the locals.

A number of unions that have admitted all races to membership have, however, maintained separate locals for Negro workers. In a minority of cases, the legal rights of these locals have been less than those of white locals. In some instances, the Negro local has been attached as an auxiliary to a white local and has had little or no part in negotiations, selection of officials, or representation at union conventions.

The segregation of workers into Negro and white locals has been a dominant practice in the South and has also characterized many unions in the northern and western parts of the United States. In general, chartering of segregated locals prevails where one of two conditions exists: either the workers are racially segregated in the industry or plant, or they work in crafts where hiring is done on the basis of crews employed to do a specific short-run job, as, for example, in the building trades and among longshoremen.

As to the first, the influence that a segregated industrial pattern has on segregation in the unions, particularly in the South, may be illustrated by the experience of the American Federation of Teachers. Teachers throughout the border and southern states are employed in a strictly segregated pattern. The result of this has been that the American Federation of Teachers has chartered separate white and Negro locals throughout the South. Despite serious and sincere efforts and declarations over a period of several years by the union's conventions, executive board, and by its Committee on Democratic Human Relations, no amalgamation of colored and white locals has been achieved.

It would be an error to think that the general social pattern of the South is such as to exclude the possibility of common organization of Negro and white workers. There are hundreds of union locals in the South to which both races belong and in which they both participate actively. Here again, we can see the significance of the employment pattern and the stand taken by the local union leadership.

In crafts where crews are hired for specific jobs, it has frequently been the practice for the workers of each race and in some cases for the workers of varying national origins to organize separate locals. The employer or the foreman will hire workers from *one* of these groups so that one job will be done entirely by Negroes and another by whites. Similar practices may be pursued in connection with Italians, Irish, Jews, and Poles. This practice violates state local FEPC laws, but no real change seems to be in sight.

Even in union locals in which persons of all races, religions, and nationalities are joined together, there remain intergroup problems such as participation of minorities in union activities, discrimination and segregation in union-sponsored recreational and social activities, and conflict between groups of workers in the shop.

No characteristic description can be given of the problems or practices of union locals with mixed membership. In some locals, ethnic lines have been largely obliterated and participation in union activities and election to office are entirely on the basis of other individual or political considerations. In others, each ethnic group is organized and all groups are unofficially given proportionate representation on the various offices and committees. There are union locals where a dominant ethnic group tends to exclude all others from participation in union activity and leadership. Sometimes an ethnic group not previously represented among the workers in a local fails to be properly integrated into the union because of the difficulties of communication, and significant differences in point of view and allegiance between the old and new members.

Among the most common problems faced by unions of both Negro and white workers is that of joint social functions. The inhibitions that exist in our culture against the social mixing of the two races, especially when both men and women are involved, have caused concern even in many very democratic locals. On the other hand, where this question has not been regarded as a menacing problem, these situations have usually been met without incident. As an outstanding example, an extensive interracial recreation program has been carried on without conflict for years by a joint board of a union having segregrated locals, in St. Louis, a border city.

Characteristically, unions provide equal treatment for all members. The shop and trade union situations, the sharing of work experiences and economic struggles make for equalitarianism across ethnic lines. Nonetheless, wherever various nationality, racial and religious groups belong to the same union local, intergroup relations problems are bound to arise. So long as union locals operate in the atmosphere of prejudice common to our nation, so long as the membership is recruited from a cross section of the American people, prejudices must occasionally show themselves in the union membership. The encouraging sign is not only the decrease in discrimination and prejudice and the heightened concern for civil rights found in the labor movement, but also the fact that the labor movement is developing methods and machinery for coping with these problems on a continuing basis.

EMANUEL MURAVCHIK

PART SIX

Union Administration

Introduction

Union administration

THE MOST NEGLECTED ASPECT OF the labor movement's institutional life, overlooked by scholars and union research experts as well as by the general public, are the day-to-day operations that constitute the administrative process through which organized labor's varied programs are brought to fruition. Indeed, sufficient attention has not been paid even to the basic union structure within which these operations take place.

The chapters in Part 6 cannot hope to cover adequately the large, unmapped areas of a pioneering discipline in the social sciences, but they can lead the way in exploring the few small paths now open with the hope that they might soon become highways of entrance, survey, and applied knowledge.

With these ends in view, J. B. S. Hardman has taken as his task an exploration of the financial resources of labor unions. His chapter provides an estimate of the "dollar-worth" of the institutions whose administrative processes are being described.

Eric Peterson's chapter describes fully the structure and operations of the International Association of Machinists, a large, influential union whose long history and development is of the highest significance. Maurice F. Neufeld has surveyed in detail the governmental structure and processes of Local 3 of the International Brotherhood of Electrical Workers. This Local was chosen not only because it enjoys a distinctive relationship with its employers and administers its operations efficiently, but also because its size (30,000 members) makes it a unique institution for study.

Sidney Shulman's article, "Labor Union Accounting" provides a clear statement of the important features of this specialized activity. He also makes evident the relationship between union accounting and a system of modern budgetary and administrative controls.

W. P. Kennedy contributes an appraisal of the tasks that face the general counsel of an international union, while Joseph Kovner performs the same service for the union lawyer who is brought in, from time to time, to deal with legal problems. Because these activities cut through every segment of a union's responsibilities, the vistas opened by the two discussions are broad, and sweep beyond legal preoccupations.

Morris Sackman's article illustrates, step by step, the administrative consequences of adopting a health and vacation fund plan for the internal operations of a union.

MAURICE F. NEUFELD

Chapter 31

Administration of a national union

THE INTERNATIONAL ASSOCIATION OF MACHINISTS, WITH A MEMBERSHIP OF over a half million, is one of the six largest unions in the United States. Size determines the complexity and variety of administrative problems of a union at the national level, but the structure of the labor organization is a basic determinant. The huge, sprawling frame of the IAM rests on 1,750 local lodges in a thousand cities and towns in the United States, its possessions, and Canada. A small local lodge may have as few as 15 members, the constitutional minimum, and there are giant lodges numbering as many as 10,000 members. Lodges differ not only in size; they also cover many varied industries. Though the majority of IAM members are employed in manufacturing, a sizeable part, about 200,000, work in the nonmanufacturing industries. The latter group includes mining, construction, retail and wholesale trade, transportation, communications, public utilities, services, and government.

But a union is more than merely the sum of local lodges. It is a living organism. Without the national headquarters, the vital functions of circulation and communication would be impossible. Union administration performs these functions by means of a complex chain of human links—personnel, and a mountainous load of paper work. To keep in constant touch with its seven regions, 1,750 locals, and more than 500,000 members, national headquarters operates through 600 representatives.

Government of the Union

The primary source of authority in the IAM is the quadrennial convention of delegates elected by the local lodges. The Executive Council of 11 members—the International President, the General Secretary-Treasurer, and nine general Vice-Presidents—is the governing body of the IAM between conventions. Election of Grand Lodge officers takes place every four years. These officers, who comprise the Executive Council, together with the delegates in attendance at a convention, constitute what is called the Grand Lodge. All major decisions of the convention are subject to approval by a vote of the membership through referendum. But the convention is not the sole body that can initiate referenda. Proposals to be decided by referendum vote may be placed before the membership between conventions by a number of locals through a procedure provided for in the Constitution.

For administrative purposes, the Grand Lodge of the IAM is divided into seven territories, including Canada. The International President assigns a General Vice-President to supervise the activities of all the lodges within his territory. Where the needs exist, local lodges may band together into district lodges. Where districts exist, they are serviced by one or more representatives. Thus the pyramid of authority is built upon the broad base of the local lodges, above which are the district lodges.

On the next level are the Vice-Presidential territories. Its top, the pinnacle of administrative authority, is vested in three elected officials at National headquarters: the International President, the General Secretary-Treasurer, and the resident General Vice-President. It is at this point that the responsibility for unraveling the tangled mass of communications, delivered daily at the Machinists' Building, is delegated to the respective heads of departments.

Within this setup of authority and administration are found the appointed officers called Grand Lodge Representatives. They are assigned either to work under one of the General Vice-Presidents or to some special task under the direct supervision of the International President. These Grand Lodge Representatives serve as links between the local or district lodges and General Vice-President of a given territory. National headquarters keeps in constant touch with all its subordinate bodies as well as with the Grand Lodge Representatives. Although each individual Vice-President is subordinate to the International Officers at headquarters, the Executive Council as a whole is the union's supreme governing body between conventions.

Administration

The bulk of the administrative work falls on the General Secretary-Treasurer's Department. It requires the services of 145 out of the 200 clerks employed at headquarters. Of the remaining 55, half are employed in the International President's Office and the other half in the Journal Department.

The General Secretary-Treasurer's Department has the responsibility of maintaining the Machinists' Building in which the IAM is housed. It must make most of the purchases and operate the stockroom. It receives all monies for dues, initiation and reinstatement fees, profits on investments, and miscellaneous income. On the disbursement side, it takes care of donations to business agencies, strike donations, and payment to elected and appointed officials of the union, professional and clerical staffs.

This Department handles the investments of the organization, both in the United States and Canada, subject to the approval of the Executive Council. It must take care of the payment of all fees for affiliation to various national and international bodies. It provides for auditing finances of the local lodges, and a staff of traveling auditors is maintained for that purpose. Each local lodge is required to file with National headquarters an audited quarterly financial statement.

Other duties performed by this Department include:

1. Organizing new lodges.
2. Disbanding defunct lodges.
3. Issuing emblems and pins for veteran members with continuous good standing.
4. Issuing certificates of exemption.
5. Operating Beneficiary Department.
6. Paying Death Benefits.
7. Arranging conventions.
8. Making election arrangements and counting ballots.

The General Secretary-Treasurer is assisted by a staff set up on a functional basis. First, he has the help of an Assistant General Secretary-Treasurer, who is an appointed official and serves as Deputy to the General Secretary-Treasurer in administrative matters. The Department is broken down into three main divisions: (1) membership records; (2) mail receiving; and (3) bookkeeping and accounting.

The Accounting Division is in charge of accounting, auditing, and supplies. The Correspondence Division receives and distributes all mail. Reports from the local financial secretaries are distributed among the clerks who check the reports and fill the orders for dues stamps.

When these reports have been checked and the orders filled, they are taken up by the Barometer Unit, (staffed by two clerks and a statistician who is a member of the research staff). The pertinent information is entered upon a specially designed membership record card. From this card the basic information concerning membership, dues payment, gains and losses, and types of membership are secured for a permanent record and statistical analysis. These forms can be used for manual sorting, enabling the General Secretary-Treasurer's Department to obtain information that otherwise would lie hidden.

There is one card for each local lodge. These cards are maintained separately from the mechanically operated punch cards used for individual members. When all the records of individual members have been transferred to punch cards, it will be possible to secure hitherto unavailable information concerning the composition of IAM membership.

From the Correspondence Division the financial secretaries' reports go to the Membership Records Division. The chief function of this department is to keep an accurate record of dues and other fees paid by each member. The Outgoing Mail Section is also part of this division. This section is in charge of outgoing bulk mail and maintains a mailing list of all local and district lodge Business Representatives, Special Organizers, and all Recording and Financial Secretaries. The main duplicating equipment is operated from this section.

The Accounting and Auditing Division has the following responsibilities:

1. Purchases.
2. Payroll.
3. Payment of all other bills.
4. Supervision of investments.
5. Administration of referenda.
6. Supervision of field auditors.

The administrative setup of the IAM is the product of 60 years of evolution. Primitive equipment stands side by side with the latest electrical devices. But in one division after another, the old is giving way to the new, and the whole administrative process will soon be modernized.

Finances and Membership Records

Unions grow and prosper in modern industrial society because they perform an indispensable service for their members. This service is the development and administration of collective bargaining. The union contract is the goal of collective bargaining. For this service the union member pays dues to his local lodge, which, in turn, pays per capita tax to national headquarters; *i.e.*, Grand Lodge, IAM.

Grand Lodge renders a multitude of services. The nature of these services and the way the Grand Lodge is linked to the subordinate units and individual members determine the quality and extent of its administrative responsibilities. Since, among other provisions, the IAM Constitution calls for a number of financial benefits for its members, Grand Lodge headquarters must keep a complete up-to-date record of all its members.

As previously stated, the General Secretary-Treasurer's Department is responsible for keeping the membership records in order. One-half of the clerical staff (100 clerks and four supervisors) at Grand Lodge is engaged in the task of recording the dues payment of each individual member. The Membership Record Division occupies the whole fifth floor of the seven-story Machinists' Building. Stored there are huge Membership Ledgers with the names of millions of machinists who were initiated in the IAM during the 62 years of its growth. Hundreds of filing cabinets contain the dues records of members in good standing, as well as the lists of the lapsed members of all local lodges. Modern punch-card systems are used to post more than a half million cards a month. The recently installed tabulating machines make it possible for Grand Lodge and the local lodge financial secretary to have identical records of good-standing membership.

Of the IAM's 1949 income of $5.6 million, 99.44 per cent came from the per capita tax and fees. Some of the money provides for pensions, death benefits, strike donations, and other contingencies. The major part is disbursed for current expenses. Remaining funds are invested in government bonds.

As in most unions, the members pay their dues to the local lodge financial secretary. Each month he sends to the G.S.-T.'s Department a report giving the name, classification, membership card number, last month and number of months for which dues have been paid for each member. Also included are the total amounts due as per the report and a membership summary. In addition, the financial secretary lists all new members initiated, furnishing name, classification, card number, date of initiation, age and date of birth of the new member.

Another section of the report gives a record of members accepted from other lodges. Dropped members who are reinstated must be listed separately. All members three months in arrears are listed as lapsed and entered in the proper place on the report. Expelled members are listed separately. Withdrawals of members who obtained employment outside the trade or who have been appointed to supervisory capacities are also listed on the report.

The report of the financial secretary is a basic, original record. It initiates a series of diverse actions in behalf of individual members in all areas. Since so much depends on this record, great pains are taken to check and compile its contents accurately and quickly. The process is rather involved.

After the financial secretary's report is properly digested, the Membership Record Division at the International Office furnishes him with a machine listing of all the members in good standing as recorded by Grand Lodge. This listing, with space to indicate the dues payment for 18 months, serves as the starting point for the financial secretary's next report. It is a great time-saver for him, since he does not have to enter by hand the names of each member in good standing. By making a cross in the appropriate boxes he indicates the months for which dues are paid.

The financial report serves as a source of varied statistical information. The data are of great importance, both for policy making and administration. The problem of turnover illustrates this fact. In 1949, close to 100,000 members were initiated or reinstated into locals of the IAM. The overwhelming majority of the gains were new members. Accordingly, the Educational and Research Department had special jobs to do along the lines of informing new members in the rudiments of trade unionism. And the publications had to be aware of this element in their audience.

Organization Division

Membership gains are, unfortunately, also associated with membership losses. Since the peak of World War II membership, annual losses have, at times, exceeded gains. The turnover can be accounted for by a variety of factors. There is, first, the ordinary turnover in every plant and industry. The union exercises no control over such gains and losses. But national headquarters is gravely concerned with the gains and losses over which it *can* exercise control. Every union strives to increase its membership and keep losses down to a minimum. It is the task of the Organization Division to accomplish these purposes.

By constitutional provision, the International President is the chief organizer of the Grand Lodge. The constitution also provides that he "shall have full control of all Grand Lodge Representatives and of all organizing. He shall provide suitable literature for organizing purposes and have the authority, when conditions warrant, to appoint Grand Lodge Representatives and assign them to such localities and for such particular terms and duties as shall be for the best interests of the Organization."

The staff of 130 Grand Lodge Representatives is but a small part of the IAM's organizing staff. Grand Lodge makes regular contributions to the local and district lodges, in order to enable them to support full-time Business Representatives. A local or district Business Representative is elected by either his local or district lodge. But, part of his salary is paid by Grand Lodge.

Despite this monetary contribution, Grand Lodge does not control the local or district Business Representatives. Representatives are responsible to the membership of the local or district lodges. Local and district Business Representatives are required to send weekly activity reports to the International President and copies to the Vice-President in their territory. Semiannual reports are also required from these Business Representatives as well as from Grand Lodge Representatives.

Like any going concern, the IAM must maintain its present organization and make gains to counter losses, which naturally occur because of industrial conditions and internal situations. It is, therefore, constantly looking for new fields to organize. This function is performed by the International President together with the General Vice-Presidents, who make requests for assistance from Grand Lodge. Not only must financial assistance be granted, but the facilities of the Publicity, Research, and Educational Divisions must be made available to the field staff in organizing campaigns. The national office maintains a stock of organizing literature, which is constantly revised and is furnished upon request. Special organizing newspapers are issued with the aid of the Publicity Division. New organizing material is designed by the Education Division with the assistance of the Art Division. The Educational Department is in charge of training organizers, and has prepared an organizing manual and work book.

Collective Bargaining

Being primarily a collective bargaining agency, the union must constantly negotiate agreements. Though most of the negotiating is done on a local basis, some of it must be performed through Grand Lodge. This is especially true in the case of the railroad industry, where the International Association of Machinists negotiates jointly with other railroad unions. In air transport, the IAM negotiates alone but on a national company-wide basis. This is also the case where companies have plants scattered throughout the country, a situation which makes company-wide bargaining necessary.

Whether negotiations take place locally or nationally, a copy of each agreement is sent to Grand Lodge headquarters, where the Research Division analyzes, records, and files these agreements on specially designed statistical cards. They become a treasury of information for future negotiations, and are used in granting strike sanction. The Agreement Section of the Research Division is constantly publishing surveys of agreements, which are requested by the field staff in the negotiations. Its findings also served as a basis for a model agreement developed by the IAM for internal use. The Research Division is, of course, called upon to supply all relevant information in connection with collective bargaining.

Processing of Union Action

The handling of strikes may, perhaps, serve as the best means of illustrating the processing of union action. Article XXI of the IAM's Constitution covers strikes. Its nine sections include the following items: approval of strike; method of declaring strike; discontinuance of grievance; calling off a strike; handling unfair work; strike and victimization donations; method of payment; deduction of arrearages; and strike stamps.

From the very beginning, unions realized that effective collective bargaining required sanctions against recalcitrant employers. The right and power to strike constitute the ultimate sanctions. In adhering to the policy that to be prepared for strikes is one of the most effectual means of preserving peace, the IAM has succeeded in keeping its strikes down to a minimum. Ninety-nine per cent of the agreements are negotiated without strikes. To achieve such results, the IAM has worked out an elaborate procedure. It is well worth dwelling on the subject at some length.

The Constitution provides (Article XXI, Section 2): "No strike shall be declared by an local lodge or the members thereof without first obtaining the consent of the International President or the Executive Council." The only condition under which the International President may authorize locals to strike is specified in Section 1 of Article XXI: "In an extreme emergency, such as a reduction in wages or an increase in the hours of labor, where delay would seriously jeopardize the welfare of those involved, the International President may authorize a strike pending the submission to, and securing the approval of, the Executive Council."

The recording secretary of the local is required to prepare a statement and history of the matters in dispute and forward it to the International President. For this purpose, Grand Lodge has developed a form, called the "Investigation of Grievance" blank. The Grievance Blank is processed by a Grand Lodge Representative, assigned to work in the International President's Office. There a digest of all information pertaining to the controversy is prepared. In addition to the information submitted in this form, the Strike Section examines the union contract and the relevant files.

A Proposition is then drawn up for submission to the Executive Council members. Reproduced here is an actual case with only the names omitted.

OFFICE OF INTERNATIONAL PRESIDENT
Washington, D. C.

PROPOSITION NO. _____ –1950 _____

EXECUTIVE COUNCIL MEMBERS June 6, 1950

Dear Sirs and Brothers:

We have received an Investigation of Grievance Blank from Lodge # _____ in which strike sanction is requested against the _____ _____ Association _____, _____, which Association is made up of the following shops: _____, etc.

We have had previous contractual relations with these employers; our labor relationship has been very poor. The contract recently in effect expired on May 1, 1950.

Our members and the employers are in dispute over a 10¢ an hour wage increase and eight paid holidays.

The prevailing wage rates are: journeymen $1.70, specialists $1.53, and helpers $1.40.

There are 46 journeymen, 1 helper, and 1 apprentice, members of our Organization involved; of this number, 40 members would be entitled to strike donations.

The provisions of the Taft-Hartley Act have been complied with. Business Representative _____ served a 60-day notice on each employer on February 27, 1950; he served a 30-day notice on the Federal Mediation and Conciliation Service and the State Mediation Service on April 7, 1950.

Grand Lodge Representative _____, Business Representatives _____ and _____ and the committee met with the Association's committee on March 23, 30, April 20, 28, May 3, 12, and 29, but were unable to arrive at a satisfactory settlement.

A strike vote was taken at a meeting of the Lodge held April 5, 1950. There were 37 members present; 29 voted in favor of strike and 8 opposed.

The question for the Council to decide is:

Shall strike sanction be granted to Lodge # _____, under the conditions stated above, against the _____ _____ Association, _____, _____.

With best wishes, we remain

Fraternally yours
/s/ Elmer E. Walker
Elmer E. Walker,
GENERAL VICE-PRESIDENT

        /s/ Eric Peterson
GENERAL SECRETARY-TREASURER
/at

The Proposition is issued from the "Office of the International President" but is also signed by the General Secretary-Treasurer. Before any Proposition is drawn, the local lodge must meet all the Constitution's provisions as to strike procedure. Furthermore, in order to write up the Proposition, it is necessary for Grand Lodge to maintain an efficient system of agreement analysis. The Proposition is mailed to every member of the Executive Council, along with a "Voting Blank." The office copy of the Proposition indicates when the vote was received and how each council member voted. Upon return of the voting blanks, a letter announcing the results is sent to the Recording Secretary of the lodge concerned, to the Business or Grand Lodge Representative connected with the lodge, and to the members of the Executive Council.

If the local lodge fails to receive the sanction of the Executive Council, it is required by the Constitution to hold a meeting and "declare the grievance at an end." It continues: "continuing such grievance, after failure to receive the sanction of the Executive Council, shall be considered sufficient cause for the suspension of any local lodge, and the members thereof from all rights and privileges, at the option of the Executive Council."

However, even when strike sanction is granted, a strike may still not take place. In such a case, a progress report on the negotiations or a signed agreement is forwarded to headquarters. Should a strike or lockout occur, then the recording secretary must send a "Report of Strikes and Lockouts," along with a "Strike List," giving the names and card numbers of all members of the IAM who are on strike. Here the work of the G.S.-T.'s Department begins.

It is this Department's responsibility to determine which members are eligible for "Strike and Victimization Donations." To be eligible, (1) members must have been in continuous good standing for at least six months; and (2) strike must have continued for a period of more than two weeks. The amount of strike donations that a member receives is determined by his classification. Since there are three levels of dues payments, there are likewise three rates of strike benefits.

Though the strike donations are modest from the point of view of the recipients, they can be staggering for the Grand Lodge Treasury. For example, a strike may involve 10,000 members and continue for six months. A million dollars is disbursed quickly under such circumstances.

Service Functions

Ever since the establishment of the National Labor Relations Board, Grand Lodge has found it necessary to maintain a section on NLRB matters. A former NLRB Regional Director is on the staff as counsel. Most of the agreements provide for arbitration, and a Grand Lodge Representative has been assigned to assist the local lodge in selecting arbitrators, and must furnish them with pertinent information regarding arbitration decisions.

Because of the special problems that exist on railroads, the chief task of one Grand Lodge Representative is to handle matters pertaining to this field. Certain matters, however, are handled by the top elected officials. This is true of the relationship with the railroad unions, chiefly the Railway Labor Executives' Association. Here the International President or his designated deputy attends meetings and makes decisions on policies in the railroad field. One of the General Vice-Presidents is designated by constitutional provision to handle IAM needs in the railroad field.

Another function performed by the International President's Office is that of liaison with government agencies. Much of this work is done through the legislative representative whose job is not only to advise Congressmen on the position taken by the International Association of Machinists on certain issues, but also to call to the attention of government agencies the needs of various segments of the union. This type of work is very often done in cooperation with employers who have agreements with the IAM. The legislative representative alone could never perform his duties properly. Many of the contacts with government agencies are made directly by the elected officials in Grand Lodge and by a number of the Divisions. Likewise, all phases of governmental research relating to the work of the union are handled through the Research Department. One member of the staff serves in an advisory capacity to the Bureau of Labor Statistics, and to the Division of Statistical Standards in the Budget Bureau. Another member of the Research Staff covers hearings on minimum wages that are to prevail under the Walsh-Healy Act.

The Journal Department is responsible not only for publishing the *Machinists' Monthly Journal* but also for maintaining an accurate and up-to-date mailing list for itself and for the weekly newspaper of the IAM, *The Machinist*. To maintain one of the largest mailing lists in the world, the *Journal* uses automatic punch card equipment. Correcting addresses is, in itself, a tremendous task, since in a single month there may be as many as 50,000 changes in the mailing records. Each member of the IAM automatically receives a copy of the monthly *Journal* and the weekly newspaper. The *Journal* is edited by an official elected directly by the membership, who conducts his affairs under the general supervision of the Executive Council. The editor of *The Machinist*, on the other hand, is selected by the International President with the approval of the Executive Council. The two publications operate as independent units except for the mailing list.

In response to the needs of the organization, many services are being performed by Grand Lodge. From the very beginning, the union published its *Journal*. In time it was found necessary to publish a weekly paper, *The Machinist*, to help in organizing campaigns and public relations. With the rapid growth of unionism, the IAM could not function properly without staffs in Research and Education. The Wagner Act created the need for a specialized section to handle NLRB matters. The phenomenal growth of collective bargaining in the past 15 years has multiplied the usefulness of agreement analysis. It is not surprising, therefore, to find the Agreement Analysis Section to be the largest division of the IAM's Research Department. It takes up one-half of a floor, employs 10 workers, and uses the most modern procedures for gathering, analyzing, and disseminating information contained in 12,000 agreements.

Thus the march of events and the voice of the members have shaped the administrative setup of the IAM.

ERIC PETERSON

Chapter 32

Administration of a local union

LOCAL 3, IBEW: DAY IN, DAY OUT

LOCAL 3 OF THE INTERNATIONAL BROTHERHOOD OF ELECTRICAL WORKERS is a New York City industrial federation of 30,000 members. This largest of building trades locals in the United States garners its flying-wedge vigor and effectiveness from the great heartland of its wide jurisdiction: the electrical construction contracting fields, which are scrupulously tended by 8,000 of its prime workers. These top craftsmen possess high vocational skill and earning power, intelligence, independence, perseverance, sympathy, and sense of solidarity for less fortunate workers (as well as for themselves), and probably of most importance, toughness of scruples and techniques. These formidable qualities, when joined together, signify full control of electrical construction jobs. Because of them, Local 3's skilled members and officers have survived to lift their union from a faction-torn agglomeration of 7,000 dues-payers in 1932 to its present tightly (although shrewdly and therefore humanely) administered eminence among locals in America.

This chapter is not concerned with the historical, social, psychological, industrial, and economic factors that might help to isolate and explain the noteworthy characteristics of Local 3. It is intended, instead, to present a brief description of the day-to-day administration of this unique industrial-craft local.

1. The Membership

The 30,000 members of Local 3 are as heterogeneous in race, national origin, and religion as the rest of their fellow citizens in the variegated metropolis where they live and work. Administratively, their basic classification, set by Section 9, Article II, of the International's constitution, is twofold: "A" and "B" charter members. In conventions and referenda of the parent body, the "B" charter members are under-represented and their voting strength is proportioned downward. Furthermore, "B" charter members do not enjoy union-sponsored pension and benefit rights since they make no contributions in dues for these purposes, nor may they vote at conventions on these matters.

In meetings of Local 3 itself, however, "B" charter members possess the same voting privileges as "A" charter members. Moreover, the history of Local 3 has shown that the lower-paid workers first come in as "B" charter members, and as their wage scale rises, they become "A" charter members. The wire and cable workers, for example, started in 1936 in the "B" category; by 1940, they moved into the "A" category. The same course of evolution was followed by the switchboard and fixture workers.

The next most inclusive grouping into which the membership of Local 3 is classified are the Divisions: (1) Construction, (2) Maintenance, Manufacturing, and Supply, and (3) Marine. Into these three Divisions are distributed the 23 classes of trades and crafts under the jurisdiction of the Local. Of these 23 classes, 19 are formed by "A" charter members who comprise 70 per cent of the total membership of Local 3. The remaining 30 per cent fall into four classes made up of "B" charter members.

2. The Elected Officials and Their Staffs

Most of the elected officials and boards of Local 3 are common to all building trades organizations: the president, the vice-president, the executive board, the financial secretary, the treasurer, the recording secretary, and the examining and election boards. The business manager is also an elected official, but under his supervision and appointment operate four assistant business managers as well as a score of business representatives who function under the assistant business managers. The editor of Local 3's bi-weekly newspaper, *Electrical Union World*, the director of the union's School, and the office manager, who is in charge of the clerical, fiscal, and stenographic employees, report administratively to the president. The Finance Office is also administered by the office manager who is responsible, in this added capacity, to the financial secretary of the Local.

All of the officers, with the exception of the business manager, are elected for two-year terms. The business manager is elected for a period of four years.

The election procedures recently used in choosing the officers have been widely publicized. The 1948 elections were conducted and supervised by Father William Kelley, formerly Chairman of the New York State Labor Relations Board. He had a staff of 40 people to aid him. Father Kelley also conducted the elections for choosing delegates to the conventions of the IBEW. The officials of Local 3 are very proud of the fact that voting machines were used and that these machines were of the same type employed by the City. Manhattan Center was rented for the occasion and the polls were open from 8 A.M. to 4 P.M. on Saturday when the men were not at work.

The scrupulous passion for mechanized honesty that these careful and commendable election arrangements represent is but one of the many administrative reflections of Local 3's self-consciousness when it contemplates its own past history and faces the future of its position within the IBEW.

The business manager, and not the president, is the most important official in Local 3. The three occupational Divisions of the Local are under his direct supervision. His responsibilities in this vital area of the union's activities are described in Sections 4 and 5. The business manager is also recognized as the union's most potent spokesman by the Joint Industry Board of the Electrical Industry in New York City (briefly described later). The parent body, the International Brotherhood of Electrical Workers, has itself, through its public utterances, testified to the unrivaled power of the business manager of Local 3. It has also avoided a genuine showdown with him, and for good reason.

The president of Local 3, although a full-time officer, occupies a position of secondary importance in the union's hierarchy and might possibly possess even less actual power than the assistant business managers who are appointed by the business manager himself. Nevertheless, the president performs functions that require considerable knowledge, experience, and skill.

Three of the activities for which the president of Local 3 assumes constitutional responsibility are particularly noteworthy. They concern the role of the office manager, the work of the Compensation Office, and the apprenticeship training program.

The Office Manager. Apart from professional personnel, like the editor of the union's newspaper, and executive personnel, like the assistant business managers and business agents, Local 3 employs about 30 people who might be classified as clerical, stenographic, and fiscal. These employees fall under the supervision of the office manager to whom the president has delegated this authority. They include four private secretaries; eight stenographers; two typists; six clerks engaged in general clerical work, filing, and posting; one telephone operator; one head bookkeeper and two bookkeepers; three cashiers; one mail clerk; and two men who work in the addressograph room where plates are on file for each member of the union.

All of these employees belong to Local 153 of the Office Employees' International Union (AFL). Local 153 has a membership of 5,000. Local 3, of course, maintains contractual relations with Local 153.

In addition to supervising this staff, the office manager is also in charge of hiring personnel, keeping personnel records, preparing the payrolls, and supervising the purchase of supplies. The most remarkable fact about the office manager, as far as union administration is concerned, is that he should exist at all.

The work of the *Compensation Office* forms a part of the president's duties because of the historic circumstance that the president has always had the task of following local and state legislation. Due to his knowledge of the various laws with which the Local was concerned, he came to have the chief responsibility for processing the workmen's compensation claims of members.

At the present time, there are two full-time representatives and one full-time secretary in the Compensation Office. The two representatives came up from the ranks of the Local, prepared themselves for the state examination that must be passed in order to qualify as workmen's compensation representatives, and were licensed by the State Workmen's Compensation Board. Since July 1, 1950, they also have been handling cases falling under the new New York State sickness and disability law. Through them, Local 3 assumes all responsibility, both administrative and financial, in handling the workmen's compensation cases of its members, including the assembly of pertinent data, interviews, and the entire process of judicial appeal.

From 1927, when Local 3 assumed the administrative responsibility for following through on workmen's compensation cases, until March 31, 1950, the total amount awarded to injured members of Local 3 was $1,943,496.07.

Statistics, such as those cited, are readily available in monthly, annual, or cumulative form for any period since 1927.

The Apprenticeship Training Program. The formula used by Local 3 for establishing the proportion of apprentices to journeymen is not unique nor are the methods it employs for selecting and training apprentices wholly distinctive. The School, operated by Local 3 in cooperation with the New York City Board of Education, is recognized as excellent. But there are other union apprenticeship programs that are equally good. The striking feature of the program, however, grows out of the official encouragement the apprentices receive to foster their own initiative (naturally within bounds). For example, the apprentices bargain with the contractors through their own negotiation and policy committee. It may be assumed that the committee receives help and support from Local 3's skilled negotiators. This committee consists of ten apprentices who are selected by the business manager on the basis of the best letters submitted for this purpose. The choices of the business manager are then presented for approval to a meeting of the apprentices. As a result of their most recent negotiations with the Joint Industry Board, Class A apprentices were granted the following wage rates, effective April 17, 1950:

		Per day	*Per hr.*
1st year—First six months		$ 6.00	$1.00
	Second six months	6.60	1.10
2nd year—First six months		7.80	1.30
	Second six months	8.40	1.40
3rd year—First six months		9.30	1.55
	Second six months	10.50	1.75
4th year—		11.40	1.90

3. Dues Payments and the Finance Office

All of the bookkeeping and accounting arrangements within Local 3 are highly mechanized, receipt-proofed, and double-checked. In part, this precaution owes its potency to the Local's unsavory past, which the Local has been anxious to live down. In part, it derives from the union's armed-truce relationship with the International which, in any case, lays down stringent constitutional provisions regarding financial matters. In part, it stems as well from the large size of Local 3's membership, which logically and technically requires mechanical posting. In part, too, this preoccupation with punctilious methods certainly springs from the business manager's psychological enjoyment of administrative procedures that have a businesslike sheen. At any rate, the monies of the membership are virtually never touched by human hands.

Dues in Local 3 are collected *in advance*. Of the 23 classes, 14 pay dues on a quarterly basis, 4 semi-annually, and 5 annually. There is a direct correlation between high or low wages and the amount of dues and the time period of prepayment. The highest total dues, $96.80, are prepaid on an annual basis by the top craftsmen in the union. The lowest total dues, $12 a year, are prepaid quarterly by a group of unskilled or semiskilled workers. To complicate Local 3's bookkeeping arrangements still further, the employers of certain classes of the membership have agreed, under the terms of the collective bargaining contract, to refund to the individual member that amount of dues which the member pays to cover the death benefit and pension plans of the International and Local 3. For five classes, this employers' refund amounts to $50.40 per year, returned semi-annually.

Somehow, these involved details of dues collection (as well as of other related activities) must be flawlessly recorded and receipted. This is the rigorous task of the *Finance Office*, which functions from day to day under the direction of the office manager.

The employees in the Finance Office have had considerable experience, outside of Local 3, in the type of work they are performing. Each of them, including the office manager, has worked for mercantile, industrial, banking, insurance, or railroad establishments. All of the employees are bonded by outside bonding companies. These bonds range from $1,000 to $25,000.

All dues, in the form of checks or money orders, must be mailed to the Finance Office by each member. The only exceptions to this rule are made for those shops or groups where arrangements have been approved for a checkoff by the employer or for collection of dues through the shop steward.

DUES PAYMENTS BY MEMBERS OF LOCAL 3

Class	Period	Total Periodic Rate	Inter- national Office	E.W.B.S.* N.Y.C.	Local 3 Dues
A	Annual	$96.80	$21.60	$28.80	$46.40
D	Quarterly	10.50	7.50	none	3.00
DBM	Quarterly	10.50	7.50	none	3.00
DH	Quarterly	10.50	7.50	none	3.00
DMS	Annual	85.80	21.60	28.80	35.40
E Switch- board	Semi-annual	30.00	15.00	3.00	12.00
E	Semi-annual	27.00	15.00	3.00	9.00
EM	Quarterly	10.50	7.50	1.50	1.50
EW	Quarterly	10.50	7.50	1.50	1.50
F	Semi-annual	24.00	15.00	3.00	6.00
FC	Quarterly	10.50	7.50	none	3.00
G	Annual	96.80	21.60	28.80	46.40
H	Quarterly	12.00	7.50	1.50	3.00
J	Annual	96.80	21.60	28.80	46.40
L	Quarterly	9.00	7.50	none	1.50
M	Annual	96.80	21.60	28.80	46.40
MS	Quarterly	9.00	7.50	none	1.50
N	Quarterly	9.00	7.50	none	1.50
S	Semi-annual	24.00	15.00	3.00	6.00
BC	Quarterly	4.50	1.50	none	3.00
BL	Quarterly	6.00	1.50	1.50	3.00
BU	Quarterly	3.00	1.50	none	1.50
BW	Quarterly	4.50	1.50	1.50	1.50

* Electrical Workers Benefit Society, New York City.

Three basic records are kept for all 30,000 members. These records are now maintained through four custom-built machines designed by the National Cash Register Company. They have been in operation since 1942. (1) The *ledger card* provides columns for eight different categories of financial data on one side and contains detailed information about the member's history on the reverse side. (2) The member's individual *dues book* is an exact duplicate of the financial side of the ledger card. As soon as the machine has recorded the payments on the ledger card

and on the member's book, the book is folded in half, placed in a con-
venient-sized envelope (since the members complained about the length
of the unfolded book) and returned by mail to the member. (3) An
individual *receipt* is also printed at the same time. It duplicates pertinent
information for the benefit of the parent body, the IBEW. This receipt
protects the member and the Local, and at the same time, affords the
International Office with a view of the individual dues payments as
well as a check upon total payments.

In addition to the ledger card, the Finance Office also has on file the
obligation card and the application card for each member, past and
present, in alphabetical order.

The Finance Office provides each official of Local 3 with a weekly
financial resumé, detailing the status of membership, the number of
members who are in arrears, by classes, and the cash balance.

Bank deposits must be made daily.

All disbursements by the Finance Office are made by voucher warrants and checks and require the signatures of three bonded officers.

The books of the Local have been covered by independent audit
since 1934. Each member, every three months, receives a printed financial
statement, as reported by the Theodore R. Wiese Company, certified
public accountants, covering the balance sheet and the income and
expenses of the general fund.

4. *The Construction Division*

The administration of the Construction Division is wired so intricately
to the structure and activities of the Joint Industry Board of the
Electrical Industry in New York City that it is difficult at times to
discern when the functions of Local 3 leave off and when those of the
J.I.B. are brought into play.

Although the J.I.B. is surely an administrative invention of considerable importance in New York City, its structure and operations cannot
be described because of limitations of space. Its *Rules and Regulations*,
however, are printed and available to the public.

So far as the Construction Division is concerned, one of the most
important functions of the J.I.B. is represented by the operation of the
Employment Plan, inaugurated on January 3, 1939. The plan attempts
to establish an eligibility list for the rotation of employment in an industry plagued by seasonal crests and dips. Administratively, it comes
to life in three forms used by the Employment Department of the J.I.B.

(1) Each worker is given a bound pad of weekly time cards, self-
addressed to the J.I.B. Pertinent employment status and wages and
hours items must be checked. (2) An Employment Termination Report
on a printed 4 x 6 inch slip must be forwarded to the J.I.B. by every jour-
neyman or apprentice. He is asked to check lines that indicate the types of

work installed and the reasons for termination of employment. (3) A third form required by the J.I.B. is the Contractors Weekly Payroll Report. It is due each Tuesday before 3 P.M.

These forms are really marriage certificates that join together, perhaps not always in sickness but certainly in health, the Joint Industry Board and the Construction Division of Local 3. Even a casual observer cannot fail to realize that the distance between the offices of the J.I.B. and those of Local 3 is only deceptively 20 city blocks in length. The administrative distance between these two centers of electrical activity fades away especially as the operations of the Construction Division are contemplated.

Although the business manager assumes ultimate responsibility for the operation of all three Divisions, an assistant business manager is appointed by him to take charge of the day-to-day operations. The assistant business manager of the Construction Division is aided by seven business representatives who are assigned to specific boroughs within the City. These administrators look after the affairs of 8,000 electrical construction workers employed by 509 contractors (who bargain through the J.I.B.) and 200 independent contractors (who sign individual agreements and abide by the provisions of the J.I.B. contract). These craftsmen are engaged in electrical alterations, repairs, jobbing, and heavy construction. The Division maintains a complete list of all past and present members in each of the eight administrative classes under its jurisdiction.

All but one of these classes hold separate membership meetings once a month. Fines of 50 cents per meeting are imposed for nonattendance. Because it has a membership of 6,200, Class A (skilled construction journeymen and apprentices) holds its meetings at Manhattan Center. Better than 50 per cent of the membership is usually present. About the same proportion of the other classes attend their own membership meetings.

Class A is the controlling group not only in the Division, but in Local 3 itself. At the time when the business manager assumed office, the Local consisted almost wholly of Class A construction workers. Although the Local has expanded its jurisdiction and influence widely since then, the officers still identify themselves, at times unconsciously, with the affairs and welfare of Class A. This identification takes many forms, often unintended. For example, the provisions of the By-Laws regarding explicit meeting dates and stipulated membership dues refer to those which apply only to Class A journeymen and apprentices. As a consequence, too, of this close alignment, Class A has no officers of its own; in reality, its officers are those of the Local. Nor does it have a need for an elaborate committee system. Many of its problems, since they are regarded as *the* problems of the entire Local, are cared for either by Local 3 or the J.I.B. But to paraphrase a familiar song, it is well to forget what Class A is not and concentrate on the things it's got: job control.

Two types of membership committees are especially noteworthy because of their intimate relation to job control. On Saturdays and on week-days after 3:30 P.M. when work is over, members of Class A's Record Committee report to headquarters to systematize information about the various jobs where men are employed, the type of work members are engaged in, the hourly rates of pay, and the picketing records of members.

District Survey and Organizing Committees exist in each borough, usually set up along election district lines. A captain is appointed for each district to guide members of the committee in their surveys of nonunion jobs and working conditions. These committees are of inestimable value to the business representatives in checking facts about employment and calling unfavorable conditions to their attention.

So far as the administration of the Division itself is concerned, the fundamental task of the assistant business manager and business representatives is also centered in the control of jobs. Although the employment procedure, as has been mentioned, is handled through the Joint Industry Board, the Division is given access to the three types of basic records on file there. In addition, the Division receives, on its own, a foreman's report that provides a further check on all jobs in New York City.

To fortify this control procedure even more strongly, the Division subscribes to the Dodge Reports published by the F. W. Dodge Corporation. These reports cover in detail all new construction and alteration jobs, and provide key information about the contractor to whom the job has been awarded, indicating, as well, whether the contract concerns electrical, bricklaying, carpentry, plumbing, steel, or heating work, or any other classification in the building trades. These reports are received in duplicate. One set is kept at headquarters. The other set is divided according to boroughs and districts and given to the business representatives. The business representative uses the Survey and Organizing Committees of his districts to check the name of the contractor (who may change from the time the report was made), the beginning date of the job, and how many stores, for example, might be erected and who the tenants will be (such information is of future value to members of Local 3 who are engaged in commercial sign work).

Problems of job control do not end with record-keeping and survey reports. In many ways, the work of the Construction Division actually begins at this point. If a nonunion electrical job has been discovered by a Survey Committee, the business representative will appear at the job. If the facts warrant such action, he calls a grievance on the job through the Building Trades Council. Through the intervention of the

Council, the electrical work is turned over to Local 3. This step might seem to conclude the matter. But not necessarily so. The next morning the Local 3 member who has been sent to the job calls the Construction Division. The work has already been started and he does not know where to pick up. The contractor, he explains, wants him to go ahead in a certain way. The Construction Division then assures the member that a business representative will stop in at the job to investigate.

There are also many difficult problems involving jurisdictional disputes. If the problem does not fall within the province of the Building Trades Council, the Construction Division will try to work out the difficulty with the owner and tenant.

The work of the Construction Division points a moral. It is not enough for a modern union to organize effectively; to provide high wages, moderate hours, and satisfactory working conditions; and to be solicitous of the health and welfare of its members. It is also necessary for an astute modern union to think in administrative terms that guarantee effective job control rather than to coast along casually on past triumphs.

5. *Maintenance, Manufacturing, and Supply Division, and the Marine Division*

The Maintenance, Manufacturing, and Supply Division encompasses 18,000 members. If the Construction Division is the heartland of Local 3, this Division represents the Far West, which the skilled electrical workers have settled since 1932. These craftsmen assessed themselves generously to organize the neglected territories. This casting of assessments upon the frontier may yet prove a boon to the Local during a period of severe unemployment when the building trades proper are the first to suffer. The maintenance, manufacturing, and supply workers are then likely to be a slightly more stable element in the union so far as the intensity of unemployment is concerned. Perhaps this thought lay behind the Local's total strategy when it laid out the master plans for its expanding domain.

The Maintenance, Manufacturing, and Supply Division has contractual relations with 800 to 900 employers. The variety of the trades and crafts they engage in is so great that the Division faces the most complex administrative task in the Union. The assistant business manager is aided by 12 business representatives. Responsibility for directly servicing the 10 classes in the Division is apportioned among them. The largest number of representatives assigned to any one class is three; in several instances a representative is shared by two or three classes.

Class F, which manufactures and assembles fixtures, provides an excellent example of the Committee structure in this Division. A full membership meeting is held once a month. At a meeting especially called for the purpose, a chairman, vice-chairman, and a recording secretary are elected. The elected Advisory Board, chosen from the ranks of the shop stewards, serves as the policy committee of Class F. There is also a Shop Stewards Committee. Like Class A, Class F has Organizing and Survey Committees, which work closely with the business representatives.

The Pension Committee represents the union side of the Joint Pension Committee. The Label Committee has the authority to issue labels to members who are given the responsibility for distributing union labels to the proper firms. The Entertainment Committee runs the large dances for the group. After these affairs, the resulting profits are turned over to the Welfare Committee, which arranges to visit the sick, attend funerals, and care for those in financial straits.

The School Committee advises on the program of classes which are taught by the foremen of Local 3. There are at present four classes in operation devoted to blueprint reading, fabrication, and theory—two at Brooklyn Tech and two at the Metal Trades School. An advanced class in layout is limited to journeymen and is conducted in Local 3's own School.

The Trustees Committee of Class F supervises the expenditure of welfare monies. Two members must sign each check. The Newspaper Committee keeps the editor informed about Fixture events. The Labor-Management Committee concerns itself with suggestions for new methods and changes. The Records Committee performs the same functions as its Class A namesake. The Athletic Committee arranges for bowling contests and soft-ball games between shops and among the Divisions.

The administrative problems encountered daily by the assistant business manager and the business representatives must be discussed for each of the main groupings within the Division. In Maintenance, the Survey Committee functions as a perpetual organizing group. For example, it ascertains how many buildings a company manages; it visits the buildings to discover whether the electrical maintenance men are union or non-union; if the finding is negative, the campaign to organize is laid out and inaugurated.

Again, the Survey Committee might find that electricians have been organized by Local 32B of the Building Service Employees' Union. The business representative must then convince the other union to surrender jurisdiction. The same situation might also exist in relation to unions of firemen and oilers and must be corrected.

In short, the large number of scattered units in which maintenance workers are employed makes the administration of their affairs trying and perpetually troublesome.

In Manufacturing, the owners of those shops which are under agreement give Local 3 preference in hiring. Unemployed members register at headquarters, and their names, card numbers, class, and type of ex-

perience are recorded. Under the rotation system in effect, when a job
appears, telegrams and telephones are used to tell them to report to headquarters. A business representative, who has a list of available jobs, meets
with them and tries to select the right man for the right job. To keep
all of the business representatives aware of the employment situation,
the Division rotates them each week. In this way, each representative
acquires fresh experience in handling unemployed members.

In addition to this task, the representative assigned to a certain number
of shops assumes the responsibility for ascertaining that all conditions
stipulated in the contract are observed. He is concerned about the improvement of conditions as well. The assistant business manager has
also attempted to introduce rotation into this area of responsibility. One
of the representatives who normally handles Fixture members recently
went to work in a wire and cable shop in order to vary his knowledge
and experience.

The Supply group is perhaps the most difficult to administer. The
gamut of jobs ranges from an employee who might be an experienced
buyer to a boy who works as a stock clerk. Somewhere in the middle
of this distribution are the typists and clerical workers.

By organizing the manufacturing and supply workers, Local 3 has
become a full-scale industrial as well as craft union.

The Marine Division. Prior to 1943, there were no marine workers
in Local 3. (Occasionally, Construction Division contractors performed
marine jobs.) In August 1944, the Division was formed and consisted
of 300 marine electricians. Not until 1945 did Local 277 of the IBEW,
which dealt with 30 odd marine contractors, merge with Local 3. Later,
those workers who were employed not by marine contractors, but by
shipyards, became part of the Division. They merged with Local 3 on
November 30, 1946.

The employment situation in marine construction has been grave during 1949 and 1950. The administrative task of the Division is further
complicated by the fact that contractors who normally engage in regular
construction work are capable of operating in the marine field. Too,
unoccupied marine contractors are equipped to perform construction
work. In that event, they have to hire Class A members and not Class
M members. However, when there was a shortage of construction
workers, the Marine Division obtained permission for its members to
work in the construction field. Since 1947, because of increasing unemployment, the jurisdiction of the Division was broadened to cover
jobbing, repair, and maintenance work in an effort to afford greater
work opportunities to its members.

The assistant business manager also supervises the affairs of Class N,
the Holmes Electric Protective Company employees. Class N has its
own chairman, vice-chairman, recording secretary, and an executive com-

mittee composed of one delegate from each of the main groups in the company: electricians, guards, patrolmen, repairmen, and switchboard operators.

A fourth assistant business manager does not administer a Division, but is left free to handle problems concerning special groups which need attention.

6. The Welfare Union

Because of the color of its jacket, the printed description of the *Pension, Hospitalization and Benefit Plan of the Electrical Industry* (administered by the Pension Committee of the J.I.B.) has come to be called the "Golden Book" by members and officers of Local 3. It is hard to believe that the selection of this color was fortuitous.

Eight types of benefits are provided. The classes qualified to receive these benefits, and other technical details are fully catalogued in the printed plan already cited. The benefits afforded by the J.I.B. provided an example to the Maintenance, Manufacturing, and Supply Division. Six classes of its members are also covered by benefit plans jointly administered by Local 3 and the employers through labor-management committees. The first plan was inaugurated in 1944 and the latest in 1947. Each provides for four kinds of benefits: a standard pension of $50 per month; a disability pension of $50 per month; hospitalization payments of $28 a week, not to exceed 15 weeks in any fiscal year; and insurance premium payments of $1.70 per month (which the worker himself would otherwise have to contribute to the IBEW ($1,000) and Local 3 ($500) death benefit plans).

The welfare activities of Local 3 go beyond these formal contractual benefits (to which should be added vacation of two weeks with pay provided by collective bargaining agreement, free dental care to Class A members, and an annual contribution by employers of $50 to Class A members to cover depreciation of tools and work clothes).

In May, 1950, ground was broken for the first of four housing projects in Queens County. The First Housing Corporation (there are four in all), with a capital of $1,050,000, has undertaken to develop 2,000 apartments of the garden type. Three thousand members of Local 3 subscribed $100 notes; the employers of the J.I.B. invested $300,000 with each employer limited to $5,000; the J.I.B. as such subscribed $200,000; and $250,000 came from the Joint Pension Fund. Occupants will not be limited to members of Local 3.

Employers have also agreed to set up a fund of $250,000 for Class A members from which their workers may borrow money, without interest, to purchase homes or cars.

But all this is not all. Local 3 headquarters buzzes with charitable activities during the late afternoon. The union encourages voluntary committees to solicit funds for the drives of Jewish, Protestant, and Catholic agencies, the Heart Association, the New York University-Bellevue Hospital, and the parade of other worthy causes that the metropolis features. Nor has the National Urban League nor the American Association for the Advancement of Colored People escaped the eye or aid of Local 3.

Of even more importance is the spirit of unaffected comradeship among the members. If one of them without family ties is dissatisfied with his hospital facilities, the chairman of a voluntary committee immediately takes up the task of transferring him to a more pleasurable spot. If debt overtakes a member, the first appeal is naturally made to the offices at 25th Street. By transforming itself for at least part of the day into a social agency, Local 3 has bound its members even more closely to its job-controlled bosom.

A member of the staff aptly described the character of the union's inner life, a quality that transcends its outward structure and administrative processes. Local 3 is virtually a small town with a strongly masculine flavor, into which wives, mothers, and sweethearts occasionally enter. But more frequently the boys enjoy being among themselves and there is a perpetual round of Communion breakfasts, Christmas parties, bowling games, baseball contests, turkey raffles, and when necessary, dances, wakes, and weddings.

Yet, the importance of the outward structure and administrative processes cannot be minimized. Whatever their relationship to the spirit of Local 3 might be, one fact is certain. Above structure, administration, and spirit rises that rainbow of union happiness: job control.

MAURICE F. NEUFELD

Chapter 33

Labor union accounting

UNIONS WERE STARTED BY HANDFULS OF WORKERS WHO DUG INTO THEIR jeans and came up with the dollar or two necessary to mimeograph the first leaflet or to pay for the first meeting hall. It is only recently that larger and better-financed groups of workers have been supporting the organization of new unions.

From the moment the first dollar was collected, and subsequently expended, it was necessary for someone to record the donors and to keep a record of the money spent. Even the rudimentary records had to be reviewed so that each member would know that his money was not wasted. Thus accounting practices were started in the unions.

In the early days of the labor movement, men were elected to office whose sole function it was to "go over the books." They were called "trustees." The function of the trustees was to look over the books and to manage collectively such property as the union possessed.

A sample excerpt from the by-laws of a local union, will show that this practice still exists.

The Trustees shall audit the books of the Secretaries and the Treasurer monthly and report their findings on the same to the Union, and they shall attend to the bonding of the Financial Secretary and Treasurer in a surety company. [Taken from the Constitution and By-Laws of the Radio and Television Workers' Union, Local Number 101.]

As the union movement grew, these primitive accounting practices could not and did not suffice. Accountants were hired who tried to adapt the accounting practices and procedures of industry to the needs of a union. These attempts failed, basically because of a lack of understanding of the operations and purposes of the union. The accountants were accustomed, by training, to look upon auditing as a device to be utilized, consistent with the needs of an industry, to cut costs and to increase profits. They did not realize that a trade union was a collective institution, primarily concerned with service for its members.

385

Labor unions were then forced to seek from within their own ranks persons who could be trained to keep records that would reflect the utilization for service of the union's dollar. Procedures were developed on a trial and error basis. Meanwhile, accountants whose relationship with the labor movement was somewhat more than professional were drawn into the orbit of labor unions. A marriage took place between standard accounting procedures and the understanding of the labor movement. The union leaders provided philosophy for the bone and flesh structure of accounting practices, and the procedures developed were designed to serve the primary purposes of the unions.

For instance, it might be poor business practice to spend a hundred thousand dollars to organize a small group of workers whose sole return to the union in dues and per capita might be a thousand dollars a year, for this would mean only a 1 per cent return on the capital invested. From a trade union point of view, however, the small group of workers might be essential to the maintenance and protection of the conditions of the larger group of workers. The small group, independent and unaffiliated, might have to work for lower wages, thus endangering the rate structure won by the larger group of workers. An accountant had to understand this. His job in the union was not merely to add and subtract figures, and to discover whether or not books were properly kept. The labor union accountant became an advisor to the union officers and, in many instances, the author of the financial reports and recommendations submitted by the union's leaders to its members.

It was the function of the accountant to see that financial operations were efficiently conducted; that there was maximum utilization of each union dollar to provide the best possible service and protection for the members. On the basis of audit reports and analysis, the labor union accountant was frequently able to show how the union's objectives might, by better planning, be more readily realized.

He was also able to point out to the union the need for acquiring and increasing reserves in order to bolster its financial position and its bargaining strength. By a professional, objective analysis of the operations of the union in all of its phases, from clerical to organizational, he could define inherent weaknesses in its administrative procedures or make recommendations for their strengthening. The accountant was able to assist the union in building up a sound investment program, by advising not only on the investment of funds, but on the husbanding of resources.

Union leaders discussed investments with the same earnestness they gave to the discussion of their other problems. Union reserves grew locally and nationally through sound investments, in interest-bearing federal, state, or municipal securities.

Periodic Audits

As union membership expanded and returns to the various national organizations in initiation fees and regular monthly per capita taxes grew in volume, the necessity for careful utilization of each union dollar was sometimes overlooked in the great growth and the attendant pressures. But the unions realized that if they were to benefit from this growth they would have to develop realistic auditing programs to guide the handling of the unions' funds.

Some did this by hiring "outside" accountants. Others by developing an internal accounting program. Invariably, the objective of both of these programs was to conduct a periodic audit of the union's books and of the books of its affiliated locals. These reports and the auditor's recommendations were submitted to the international and local unions concerned, where they were studied, analyzed, and considered.

For a better understanding of the foregoing, an outline of what is contained in the accountant's reports to the union is printed below:

1. Comparative statement of assets and liabilities.
2. Statement of cash receipts and disbursements.
3. Analytical comparison of operating receipts and the relationship of the disbursements thereto, by amount and percentage.
4. Comparative statements of expenses and receipts allocated to divisions, sections, regions, or shops of a union.
5. Percentage statement of relationship of direct cost of collections to income (where applicable).
6. Comparative statement of receipts from divisions, sections, regions, shops of the union.
7. Statement of per capita tax status and payments.
8. Analysis of a membership standing by sections, regions, divisions, or shops.
9. Statement of per capita stamp inventories, where applicable.
10. Statement of investments and their allocations to various funds.

It is evident that each of the above ten points has a definite relationship with the day-to-day functioning of both the local and the national union.

For instance, if the auditor's report shows, under points 6 and 7, that there is a drop in collections, this indicates either a "lay-off," or where the check-off and/or the union shop does not prevail, a loss of interest in the union by the workers.

This information is checked with the research, education, organization, and publicity departments of the union and the necessary steps taken either to offset a lay-off or to stimulate interest and loyalty to the union.

An auditor's report becomes the basis for all planning of future activities, for it analyzes, and evaluates the past in terms of hard, cold figures.

The Monthly Local Financial Report

Since the regular audit reports were made annually or semi-annually, union accountants developed the monthly financial report designed to foster closer and more sustained communication between the locals and the national organization. These monthly reports were simple forms that could be prepared by any worker of average schooling and intelligence. The monthly report and the audit report together indicated the progress of the union.

A sample of the kind of monthly financial report utilized by the Industrial Union of Marine and Shipbuilding Workers appears on pp. 390-391.

An example from the writer's experience illustrates a phase of the accountant's problem. In a recent audit report, my firm recommended that the local union cut down on "lost time" payments by better planning. A "lost time" payment is the money paid to a union official who is not a full-time paid employee of the union for time actually lost from work while on union business. In this particular instance, our analysis of the local union's finances indicated that there was an excessive expenditure for lost time in relation to the actual need of the local, especially since there had been a marked drop in membership because of "cut-backs." This recommendation was carefully studied by the national secretary-treasurer of the union. He pointed out to the local that it was spending its funds excessively, and imposed upon them a restriction on lost-time expenditures. This he could do because past experience had taught this union's members that the national union had to have some "veto" control over local expenditures.

In another audit, to cite one more example, we pointed out that the local union office was overstaffed. The overstaffing was a result of the sudden, sharp growth of the local, induced by war production. There was duplication of effort and an unsystematic method of recording the financial business of the local. As part of our accounting function, we developed an efficient administrative and office procedure and submitted it to the national and local union. The national secretary-treasurer, exercising his constitutional prerogatives, asked that the local conform to these procedures. This was done. The accounting staff trained the office help and assisted the local leaders in establishing the procedures and seeing that they were properly followed and supervised. As a result, there was a marked cut in the cost of the local union operations. The cases cited show that an old technique can be successfully applied to a new situation.

The Union Budget

Since labor unions cannot exist on a day-to-day basis, but must plan and save in the fat years for the lean, budgets had to be developed to serve as a guide to expenditure, as a means of anticipating and providing for the needs of the union. Budgets were developed in terms of percentage relationship to estimated income, and allowances were made, in advance, for any possible eventuality.

Expenses for local delegates to national union conventions were apportioned in advance over an entire year, instead of draining the local treasury during the month of convening. An emergency fund equaling 10 per cent of the monthly income was set aside for use in the event of a strike or a costly legal process. Funds were set aside monthly to cover the costs of negotiating a new contract, even though this took place only once a year. A margin for error was included and every reasonable allowance was made for declining membership due to lay-offs. No budget was made hard and fast, as subsequent paragraphs will show.

It is the function of the union, in principle, to budget. It is the function of the auditor to relate those principles in terms of dollars and cents. In developing the budget, the first costs to be determined were the fixed costs such as per capita taxes, salaries, rents, legal fees, convention expenses, election expenses. Variable costs of administration, such as telephone, office supplies, printing, postage, heat, light, publications, committee expenses, and general members' welfare, were estimated on the basis of past experience. A tentative budget was drawn up based upon a realistic understanding of the operations of the past several years, and on an estimate of future needs. Past operations were analyzed: expenditures for negotiations, processing grievances, organization, educational, administrative, and publication activities. Figures were arrived at which showed the relationship between these and the members' welfare. This tentative budget was submitted to the union's financial officers. It was discussed and revised, and then presented to the membership for adoption.

As the union grew older and stronger loyalties developed among its members, certain portions of the functioning expenditures of the union could be curtailed.

For instance, a local in existence for five years could be expected, at little or no cost, to organize the remainder of the workers in its immediate locality. Although the unit cost of organizing might increase, the over-all cost could be cut down. A realistic budget would reflect this change. A well-established union, more secure in its relationships with both management and its own members, might want to develop education and recreation activities in order to sustain interest in the union. These projects, too, would have to be reflected in any realistic budget.

Other Functions of the Labor Accountant

In the investing of funds, the role of the union is similar to the role of a trust. The union officer is much like a trustee who is charged by law with the function of protecting and increasing trust funds through nonspeculative and nonrisk investment.

For example, an analysis of various union statements will show that the

INDUSTRIAL UNION OF MARINE AND SHIPBUILDING WORKERS OF AMERICA

MONTHLY FINANCIAL REPORT

Local No._____ at _____ Month of_____, 19 ___

CASH RECEIPTS

OPERATING INCOME		
Working Dues (No.)	$	
Out of Work Dues (No.)		
Initiations and Reinstatements (No.)		
Assessments		
Fines		
Sale of Supplies to Members		
Investment Income — Interest		
Investment Income — Rent		
TOTAL OPERATING INCOME		$
OTHER RECEIPTS		
Refunds to Treasury (List)		
Exchanges (List)		
TOTAL RECEIPTS		$

SUMMARY OF CASH ACCOUNT

BALANCE — Beginning	$	
Add — Total Receipts (above)		
Less — Disbursements (page 2)		
BALANCE — Close of Month	$	

PER CAPITA TAX PAYMENT

Red Stamps	@ .65	$
Green Stamps	@ .05	
Blue Stamps	@ $1.00	
Supplies		
Bond Premium		
Other Items (List)		
CHECK No. Herewith	$	

STAMP ACCOUNTS

	Red	Green	Blue
ON HAND — Beginning			
Received from G. E. B.			
Total to be Accounted For			
Issued For Cash — Gross			
Issued Free			
Total Issued — Gross			
Reclaimed by Refunds			
Total Issued — Net			
Indicated Balance			
Actual Count			
Over or Under			

Signed:

_____
Financial Secretary

_____
Address

Form No. 112

Courtesy Industrial Union of Marine and Shipbuilding Workers of America.

MONTHLY FINANCIAL REPORT.

CASH DISBURSEMENTS

PER CAPITA TAXES		
General Executive Board		
Affiliations		
SALARIES		
Officers		
Employees		
Pay Roll Taxes Apportioned		
ADMINISTRATIVE EXPENSE		
Rents		
Taxes, Insurance and Building Maintenance		
Telephone and Telegrams		
Supplies, Printing and Office Equipment		
Supplies G. E. B.		
Postage		
Petty Cash		
Shop Steward Dues		
Heat, Water and Electricity		
Legal and Audit Fees		
Miscellaneous		
NEWSPAPER EXPENSE		
Salaries		
Printing and Publishing Costs		
Distribution		
Pay Roll Taxes Apportioned		
LOST TIME AND COMMITTEE EXPENSE		
Grievances and Arbitrations		
Negotiations		
Organizing		
Officers Duties		
Shop Steward and Department Meetings		
Pay Roll Taxes Apportioned		
CONVENTION EXPENSES		
I. U. M. S. W. A.		
Affiliations		
ELECTION EXPENSE		
Local and Department Elections		
Convention Delegate Election		
GENERAL EXPENSE		
Members Welfare		
Contributions		
Dues and Initiation Refunds		
INVESTMENTS (STATE NATURE)		
EXCHANGES (LIST)		
TRANSFER TO EMERGENCY FUND		
TOTAL DISBURSEMENTS		$

MONTHLY FINANCIAL REPORT (*cont'd.*).

majority of union funds are invested in (1) government bonds; (2) federal credit unions; (3) savings banks to the extent of $5,000; and (4) in rare instances, in high-type industrial bonds and even less frequently, in high-type industrial stocks.

A new function for labor accounting has recently developed. At the present time, union negotiations with employers are in many instances primarily concerned with the institution of pensions and welfare plans. Many of these plans are developed by union research and insurance departments, but the labor accountant has a specific part in pension planning.

Where the union administers the fund, the union accountant is charged not only with the responsibility for auditing the books, but also with helping to guide the investments of the fund so as to maintain the actuarially computed soundness of the plan and to assure the maximum return, in a safe manner, for each dollar invested.

The labor accountant helps in analyzing the income of the fund from employer and/or employee contributions, and from investments, and in analyzing the expenditures in relation to that income. Although there is much talk at this time about the depletion of one union's pension and insurance program, it is the exception, not the rule. Most union-administered programs have proved to be sound and have continued to function both effectively and efficiently.

The accountant fills essentially the same role in funds jointly administered by management and labor.

A labor union may, by state law, be prohibited from owning property. A corporation must be set up, which is primarily a legal procedure, but the labor accountant plays an important part in helping to set up the books and plans in connection with taxes.

The labor accountant's report can be read as a barometer. It can register clear weather ahead or it can show storm signals. He must help, on the basis of the union officers' analysis, to develop administrative procedures that will function effectively. He must understand that if a strike takes place income virtually stops and expenditures continue and perhaps increase. He must help to plan, with the union's financial officers, procedures that will enable the union to have money when no dues are forthcoming, either because of layoffs or work stoppages. He must anticipate with the union's leadership, perhaps months in advance, what may occur at the next collective bargaining session. For he must assure the liquidity of the union's funds so that they may be available when they are needed.

All this planning is not done with a crystal ball. It is done on the basis of constant and continuing analysis of past practices and past situations. A corporation accountant makes sure that his company's reserves are being maintained. A union accountant has much the same function, except that the corporate device of cutting costs to meet a decline in income may not always be followed in a union.

The total monthly income from the 15 million union members in the United States runs to about 30 million dollars. This vast sum of money involves an enormous amount of bookkeeping, analyzing, investing, and financial planning. It calls for the development of necessary and appropriate techniques, and has created a wide field for professional labor accounting.

SIDNEY S. SHULMAN

Chapter 34

The union and problems of law

1. THE LAW DEPARTMENT OF THE BROTHERHOOD OF RAILROAD TRAINMEN

THE MODERN UNION IS A MASSIVE ENTERPRISE WITH MANY COMPONENT parts and comprising many thousands of individuals, all functioning under a body of internal union law and within the framework of the laws of the state and nation. Its legal department or legal staff is a natural development stemming from the need for expert guidance in complicated legal procedure. It also derives from the realization that only through adequate knowledge of existing laws and of proposed legislation can the labor union protect the interests of its members, and in fact, continue to survive as a free democratic organization.

The labor union of an earlier day carried on its struggle for existence largely without benefit of legal counsel. It could—when it had the funds—employ a lawyer to handle a particular situation, but legal assistance was an emergency measure and the situation had to be crucial. Attorneys looked to business for lucrative employment, and a corporation counselship was the goal of most ambitious young lawyers.

Today, the Brotherhood of Railroad Trainmen, like most large labor unions, has a legal department, presided over by a general counsel. Lawyers are also engaged for special purposes and special occasions throughout the United States and Canada, but the general counsel's and legal department's duties are most closely associated with the everyday activities of the union.

By and large, the duties of the general counsel of the BRT are to advise the President and the Associate Grand Lodge Officers on matters pertaining to federal, state, and local laws, as well as to the laws governing the union under its Constitution.

One of the functions of the legal department is to prepare briefs and petitions for presentation to the Interstate Commerce Commission and to state public utility institutions whose operations are of direct and immediate interest to the members of the organization.

The union is frequently asked to give testimony before such public bodies as Senate and House committees and corresponding groups on the state level. Legal experts on the BRT President's staff prepare the material for presentation, and in many instances, represent the union at the hearings —especially before national congressional committees. Testimony before state legislatures and other state bodies is generally presented by the state legislative representative of the union in the state involved.

It is, of course, important for every union to know the law if it is to operate as a law-abiding part of the community, but it is especially important that it be thoroughly versed in the effect and ramifications of labor legislation. The operation of the Brotherhood of Railroad Trainmen is closely affected by such laws as the Railway Labor Act, the Federal Employers' Liability Act, and the Taft-Hartley Act. Intercity bus operators and employees of industrial plants, who are members of the Brotherhood, come under the last.

Bad laws make good lawyers particularly essential. Enactment of the Taft-Hartley law made it more difficult than ever for a labor union to conduct its business in a lawful manner. Naturally, so harassing a law involves much more work for the legal department.

The Jennings Bill is an example of the kind of legislation the union lawyers must watch for and guard against. The Federal Employers' Liability Act, which made it possible for workers or their families to receive more reasonable compensation for injuries sustained in the service of our industry, was broadened in 1910 to permit injured workers to bring suit anywhere the railroad was doing business. The Jennings Bill, passed by the House of Representatives at the same time that it was acting favorably upon the Taft-Hartley Act, would have repealed this provision and required that suit be brought only in the jurisdiction where the accident occurred or where the worker lived. This would have made it extremely difficult for the injured workmen or the dependents of those fatally injured to bring suit under the Federal Employers' Liability Act. In fact, the provisions of the Jennings Bill would have had the effect of making it easier for a farmer to sue for the loss of his hogs in shipment than for the brakeman on the freight train to sue for the loss of his legs in the same accident. Although the Jennings Bill did not become a law, the Federal Judicial Code was amended in various ways to accomplish substantially the same purpose.

The legal staff cooperates with the union's insurance department in conducting the BRT's $150 million life insurance program. When the Brotherhood was organized in 1883, it was almost impossible for the railroad workers to obtain life insurance in commercial insurance companies because their work was so hazardous. Today, through the union's insurance department, our members are able to obtain actuarially sound insurance at rates that are comparable to the standard rates of commercial insurance companies.

One of the most important phases of the union's work is carried on by the Grievance Department, which is composed of the general grievance committees. The legal staff advises this department on matters of union and general law.

It is one of the major responsibilities of the legal department to see that the laws of the organization itself, as embodied in its Constitution, are properly drawn and equitably administered. Under this nation's democratic system, the people are free not only to form and to join democratic organizations, such as labor unions, but also to formulate the organic and procedural laws of their organizations. Such laws have full force and validity as long as they are not contrary to the laws of the nation or the states.

The courts, of course, are jealous of their prerogatives and watchful of the conduct of private organizations to see that there is no overreaching or inequity in the treatment of their members. Yet the courts have frequently sustained the right of such bodies to enforce their own laws on their members. There are many cases on record in which the plaintiff in a court action has been required to return to his labor union and to exhaust its remedial procedures before having his day in court. The union's legal department must see that the laws of the organization are drawn to provide adequate machinery for the proper adjustment of disputes so that the member can obtain full justice within his union without recourse to litigation in the courts. It must also see that the union's elaborate appeal procedure is scrupulously applied so that every member obtains a fair hearing; and, of course, it must insure faithful compliance with the laws of the union.

The legal staff acts as adviser to the union's Legislative Department which is composed of the legislative boards in the various states of the U.S. and in the provinces of Canada.

W. P. KENNEDY

2. THE LABOR LAWYER

Of all the professionals serving unions—economists, teachers, publicists, artists, and now doctors, psychologists and social workers—the lawyer is the most intimate member of the union household. The lawyer was the first professional to be regularly employed by unions and in recent times his influence and functions have increased. Morris Hillquit, a labor lawyer of Socialist beliefs, was the rival of Samuel Gompers in intellectual and moral influence upon the labor movement in the early 1900's. In 1946, the CIO Packinghouse Workers Union elected its chief lawyer as its president.

It was said of the Taft-Hartley Act that it created a paradise for lawyers, a purgatory for employers, and hell for unions, but that statute only enhanced the always important role of law and legislation in American labor relations. Unions have had a constant need for lawyers. When oppressed by a law, they need lawyers to defend them against criminal prosecutions and civil suits; when favored by a law, they need lawyers to extract the full benefits of the legislation.

Position and Influence

Lawyers defended the early unions from the charges of criminal conspiracy; they became the champions of their clients, close to the economic struggle against employers, when they fought the labor injunction. The need for defense continues even with the passage of favorable laws. The Wagner Act protected the right of organization, but it did not save the Steel Workers Organizing Committee, for example, from the necessity of defending five hundred of its members from criminal indictments brought by the local authorities in the wake of the Little Steel Strike of 1937.

Favorable laws have strengthened the position of the lawyer in the labor movement. With the passage of the Wagner Act in 1935, a few lawyers were as indispensable as many organizers to the building of new unions. The leaders of the CIO unions always included a lawyer in their inner councils, and the strategy of an organizing campaign often turned upon legal points.

There was a time when, having overcome the legal obstacles to its establishment with the help of lawyers, a union conducted its everyday affairs with no further need for legal advice. But today legal regulations of employment, labor relations, and internal union affairs have expanded into a vast assortment of federal and state laws. They cover workmen's compensation, health and safety standards, minimum wages, overtime requirements, social security systems, labor board proceedings, and tax returns. Lawyers are necessary not only for momentous issues but for everyday matters.

As a result of the impact of these laws, the lawyer takes an ever-increasing part in the vital business of unions, negotiation of collective bargaining agreements, and their interpretation and administration. The trend of union-management pension plans and other insurance benefit schemes will lay new responsibilities upon the union lawyer.

As unions grow stronger and labor laws more numerous, internal union affairs become more complex. The first constitution of the Bricklayers Union was written by their own pioneer leaders; the courts overruled certain of its provisions in the course of litigation flowing out of internal disputes, and the constitution has been revised with the benefit of legal advice. The constitutions of the new CIO unions were drafted entirely by lawyers.

The United States Supreme Court, in 1946, decided that a union cannot settle individual grievances unless it has been authorized to do so by the individuals concerned, and that such authorization can be granted by the union constitution or by-laws. Lawyers pored over the decision and drafted amendments that were adopted by union conventions to meet this judicial ruling. Contrary to the general practice, the CIO Auto Workers Union permits lawyers to represent the parties in disciplinary trials within the union.

To the outside world, the lawyer is often the public representative of a union, as in hearings before legislative committees, lectures, debates, and radio forums. This is an important phase of union action. Samuel Gompers built the office of president of the AFL on just these functions.

The lawyer's influence within the labor movement is intensified in times of changing law. Changes have rolled in great waves over industrial relations and union organization. There was the development of the labor injunction in the 1890's; application of the antitrust laws in the 1900's; the exempting provision of the Clayton Act in 1914; the anti-injunction act of 1932; and the accelerating innovations since 1935. In 1914, upon the eve of the Clayton Act's passage, the AFL relied upon its counsel to approve the proposed language exempting unions from the antitrust laws. In 1949, William Green withheld comment on the government's bill to repeal the Taft-Hartley Act until he had consulted counsel. And the CIO general counsel manages its strategy on the repealing legislation.

Qualities and Conditions of the Labor Lawyer

The lawyer's place in the labor movement is securely fixed not only by the functions he performs, but by the way they are performed. The typical labor lawyer, one who devotes all or a great part of his practice to union clients, is characterized by his personal identity with the sentiments and character of the union he represents. The leadership of a union with definite political views chooses a lawyer of the same beliefs. A new union hires a young lawyer and they grow old together. To many labor lawyers, the union is much more than a client to be competently served, if he wishes it to prosper. Often, the lawyer sees in the labor movement the hope for improving society by bettering the economic welfare of the masses. Consequently, he gives devoted and aggressive legal services.

This mutual sympathy of ideals is augmented by a practical force: the successful labor movement can offer substantial support to individual political ambitions. This attraction is an inducement to lawyers in smaller cities and towns who cannot expect to make a livelihood out of union practice, and it is an inducement to influential lawyers to take at least an occasional case for a union. Many congressmen, senators, and governors were at one time counsels to unions.

The economics of a labor lawyer's practice ties him closely to his clients. The labor lawyer is confined to the union side of labor relations law. With few exceptions, unions will not retain lawyers who represent employers; and employers are suspicious of union lawyers. The reluctance of unions to entrust their affairs to outsiders tends to concentrate their legal business in the hands of a small number of practitioners. In Chicago and Boston, each with hundreds of locals, the bulk of union legal business is concentrated in two firms, one representing most of the AFL locals, the other, most of the CIO locals.

In addition, there is little turnover. If he loses a union client, the labor lawyer is not likely to find another. There are fewer possible union clients than employer clients. A single local has dealings with a number of employers; it has one lawyer. The legal business of the employers is divided among several attorneys.

Many lawyers representing unions must have other clients to complete their livelihood, and often they secure the business of union members, on cases such as workmen's compensation, divorces, personal injury claims, and small property matters. The late Joseph H. Padway, for many years the AFL General Counsel, told of the early days in Wisconsin when members were notified at union meetings that the union lawyer would give them a discount on legal services.

A comparatively small number of lawyers enjoy a full-time union practice: 150 are listed by the general counsel to the AFL and the CIO. (There are an estimated 170,000 lawyers in the United States.) A number of national unions have legal departments and retain their lawyers as part of their employed staffs. This arrangement provides intimate day-to-day service and is efficient for handling recurring legal matters, but it sometimes results in a loss of professional independence and objectivity. While many business organizations also employ "house" counsel, they regularly secure the advice of outside attorneys on important matters. Unions would also find it advantageous to follow this practice.

Outstanding Legal Contributions

Others besides the full-time or regular counsel have rendered important legal services to the labor movement or aided in its development. Unions owe much to the liberal lawyers who helped them when they could not afford to pay the customary fees for first-class legal talent. Justice Brandeis welcomed labor cases when he was in private practice. The law is significantly influenced by intellectual criticism, and in writing *The Labor Injunction,* Justice Frankfurter, then a professor, did as much as any single individual has done to end the abuse of legal process against unions in labor disputes. His work is only one example of the power of scholarship and intellect in law.

These qualities have served unions in another form. In critical lawsuits, unions have engaged lawyers on the strength of their professional competence and repute. Thus, in 1920, the United Mine Workers faced a ruinous suit for treble damages under the antitrust laws, as a result of a violent strike. The national union retained Charles Evans Hughes, who with great legal skill successfully argued the principle that a parent body is not responsible for the acts of its locals and districts unless it has clearly authorized, participated in, or ratified the action.

An important form of legal contribution to the labor movement has been rendered by the lawyers in government agencies administering protective and beneficial legislation. These lawyers are not labor lawyers—they are public servants; the benefits to labor from their work was incidental to the discharge of their duties. It is a large group: the United States Department of Labor and the National Labor Relations Board together employ a total of 420 lawyers in Washington and field offices. The original National Labor Relations Act of 1935 stated in general terms that employees had the right to self-organization free from employer interference and the right to bargain collectively through their freely chosen representatives. These general rights were elaborated into a detailed code of rules protecting unions and collective bargaining. There were few precedents. To win judicial approval of the new regulations, the lawyers had to make skillful use of legal principles and methods of analysis. The process was an exceptional triumph of legal ability. It was the work of a group of lawyers headed by the then NLRB chairman, J. Warren Madden, and General Counsel Charles Fahy, who were inspired both by a sympathy for the values of free labor and by the moving spirit of professional competence.

Service in government has conventionally been a training ground for private practice in the same field; employers and unions have recruited lawyers from the NLRB legal staff.

It has not always been easy for unions to secure legal services. In 1937, the United Shoe Workers Union, striking at Lewiston and Auburn, Maine, could not obtain local counsel even in nearby Portland. In that same year, the Steel Workers Organizing Committee had to pay premium prices for lawyers to defend its members against criminal charges in Pennsylvania and Ohio towns. These conditions are rare now that unions are successful institutions.

Unions have been provided with a variety of legal services, by a devoted group of lawyers specializing in labor law, by liberal lawyers and law professors, by eminent counsel in special cases, and by government lawyers. Personal connections, personal beliefs, political ambitions, and professional competence have determined the choice of lawyers. The nature of unions has molded an unusually narrow and intimate attorney-client relationship. The distrust of union leaders for outsiders and "intellectuals," though considerably relaxed in the case of lawyers, still operates to diminish the receptivity of unions to independent professional advice. The relationship will improve because unions are winning a secure place in law, and because many law students and lawyers are ready to serve unions.

JOSEPH KOVNER

Chapter 35

Administration of a union welfare fund

IN ADMINISTRATING A HEALTH AND WELFARE FUND, THE MAIN AREAS OF administration lie in collecting employers' contributions, establishing financial policy (deposit and investment of funds), and disbursing benefits. Generally these matters are determined in the collective bargaining agreement establishing the fund or in the trust agreement outlining the administration of the fund. In this way the administrative relationships that are to exist between the parties are established.

Collecting the Employers' Contributions

In the Greater New York dress industry with 2,444 shops employing 82,177 workers producing an estimated 78,000,000 garments, (January 1, 1949 figures), collecting contributions to the Health and Welfare Fund is a serious problem. The decision that the jobbers and manufacturers would contribute not only for the workers in their own shops, but also for those in the shops of their contractors, made the problem even more difficult. This problem was finally resolved by utilizing the experience and services of the two departments previously concerned with checking employers' employment and payroll records for contract enforcement.

The Health and Vacation Fund Department collects the payroll reports that each firm must submit to the Dress Joint Board, making certain that all the employers make their proper contributions. From these reports, it determines the level and volume of production and employment, sales, earnings, and other similar statistics. The Accounting Department checks the employers' books to make certain that the proper rates are being maintained, and to investigate violations of or noncompliance with their contribution requirements. Investigators in this department check the records of the firms with the reports filed with the Health and Vacation Fund Department.

All firms are required to file copies of their payrolls every month with the Health and Vacation Fund Department. Jobbers and manufacturers are required to contribute 4.5 per cent of the earnings of all of their workers for the period, or the equivalent rate for jobbers based on payments to their contractors. Where a contractor is working for a nonassociation jobber, the contractor is expected to make the contribution. The Department will not process a jobber's or manufacturer's reports without accompanying checks, nor process checks without accompanying reports. Here, the problem is to get the employers to submit their reports accurately, regularly, and promptly.

The Health and Vacation Fund Department then separates the jobbers' and manufacturers' reports from the contractors' payroll reports, to scrutinize them, and to note and attend to any discrepancies. Next, the payrolls are tabulated to obtain the average weekly earnings by crafts. The Kardex file on which the receipt of reports is posted is brought up to date, and then a daily record of the reports received is made out. Next, the jobbers' and manufacturers' reports are turned over to a bookkeeper who makes out individual ledger sheets and an annual earnings card, called the Shop Payroll Summary, for each shop in the industry.

The contractors' accounts are listed in a separate ledger, and a complete record of collections from contractors for work done by nonassociation jobbers is kept. A contractor's Record Card is maintained to check the contractors' reports.

The employers' contribution checks are tallied and deposited, and the receipt issued by the Bookkeeping Department of the Joint Board is the final check on the accuracy of the Health and Vacation Fund Department's figures. Careful records are kept of all shops under collective bargaining agreement with the Dress Joint Board to make certain that no firm escapes its liability.

Financial Policy

The employers' contributions and the interest on the investments of the Health and Welfare Fund constitute the only income of the fund. It has been the policy of the Dress Joint Board and each of the out-of-town departments, and a requirement of the International Ladies' Garment Workers' Union, that the locals keep their health fund incomes, reserves, and investments separate from their regular union incomes, reserves, and investments.

That part of the income not disbursed in benefits or spent for administration is retained in reserves. The amount of the reserves to be retained is determined at the beginning of each year by the Health Fund Committee, made up of representatives of each of the four Locals affiliated with the Dress Joint Board, subject to the approval of the Dress Joint Board. Responsibility for investing these reserves is vested in the Health Fund Committee.

Distribution of Benefits

For all the rules and regulations that exist and for all the procedures that are established for checking eligibility and paying the benefits, the disbursement of benefits, in the end, nevertheless remains a matter of human relations; human beings make the claim for benefits and other human beings handle the claims, determine the eligibility (within the framework of the rules and regulations), and disburse the benefits. In dealing with the members who come to claim benefits, there are many cases not specifically covered by the rules and procedures that must be settled "on the line" by clerks in the local union sick benefit departments. Rules and procedures do little more than establish boundaries, limits, and frameworks within which a multitude of cases are to be settled. This process is dynamic and does not lend itself easily to static descriptions.

Vacation Benefits

The Dress Joint Board is responsible for paying vacation benefits. This takes place about June 1st of every year. Distributing these checks among 55,000 to 60,000 workers in over 2,000 shops in New York City itself, and determining the eligibility of the workers for vacation benefits require considerable attention. The shop chairmen, business agents, the Joint Board administrative machinery, special clerks and typists, and the equivalent of the full time of about five persons are devoted annually to distributing vacation-benefit checks and to checking the eligibility of the members.

Every March the Dress Joint Board sends Vacation Payment Registration forms and instructions to the shop chairmen. The chairmen fill out the forms, giving the information requested for each worker, and return the forms to the Dress Joint Board. The Registration lists are checked, and if they are in order, the vacation checks are made up and prepared for distribution. On June 1st, they are picked up by the business agents who distribute them to the workers on presentation of their membership dues books showing that their dues have been paid up to May 1st of that year. Undelivered checks are returned with a special form to the Dress Joint Board, where they are then picked up.

There are some special cases that must be handled differently. Members who were not registered when the eligibility lists were made out or who changed jobs during the registration period must make out a special form. There are also the members of other locals of the ILGWU who have worked in Dress Joint Board shops, who may be entitled to all or some of the vacation benefits. Finally, there are the members who have left the trade because of illness or pregnancy. They are entitled to vacation benefits earned before the date of their withdrawal.

The Health Fund Committee has appointed a special subcommittee to act as an appeals board for members who feel that an error was made and who wish to make a complaint. After all the special cases and mistakes have been disposed of, the original Vacation Payment Registration forms are amended. Finally, the Dress Joint Board makes out for each firm a form that is a financial registration control sheet and becomes a part of the Board's permanent records.

Health Benefits

The disbursement of health benefits is the responsibility of the sick benefit departments of each of the affiliated locals and not of the Joint Board. The locals receive and verify claims for health benefits. Preventive medical care benefits, maternity benefits, and eyeglasses require little verification, but the general disability benefits require extensive verification to prevent the possibility of abuse. Each affiliated local is given a revolving fund with which to pay health benefits, and this fund is replenished every month by the exact amount that is spent each month.

General disability benefits. The methods for determining the eligibility of the members for the general disability benefits—sick, hospitalization, and surgical benefits—are essentially the same, except that such benefits are now paid as required by the New York State Disability Benefits Law. The member files his claim by calling in person, writing, sending in a special form, telephoning, or sending somebody in to the sick benefit department of his local union, notifying the department of an illness. Upon the receipt of the member's union book, his ledger card and all previous sick benefit cases are pulled from the files and checked. If he is eligible to establish a claim, a case is made out for him. The Union Health Center is notified of the illness either by mailing it an IBM Union Health Center Claim Card (if the member is unable to travel) or by sending the member to the sick benefit department of the Union Health Center with the claim card (if the member is able to travel). At the time the case is made up, the sick benefit department of the local also arranges for a leave of absence with the member's employer and obtains information on his past employment.

If the physical examination by the Health Center reveals that the claimant is not sufficiently disabled to receive benefits, the member's union book is returned and his case is closed. If the claimant is sufficiently disabled and is eligible to receive benefits, the local sick benefit department receives from the Union Health Center an award indicating the nature of the disability and an estimate of the number of weeks of sick benefit the member is to receive. If the member is sick beyond this estimated period of disability, the local union arranges for a re-examination either at the Union Health Center, at home, or in a hospital. If the member returns to work before the end of the estimated period of disability, the member or shop chairman informs the local union sick benefit department of the date of return to work, and the member is paid only for the actual number of weeks of disability. The union book is then returned to the member and the case is closed.

The Union Health Center also makes the awards for surgical benefits upon the submission of a surgical certificate, stating the nature of the surgery performed. Hospital benefits are usually awarded directly by the local union sick benefit departments, if the nature of the disability is clearly one that is not excluded from benefits and if there is no surgical information on the hospital certificate. Otherwise, the certificate is sent to the Union Health Center for an award. This hospital certificate must state the member's date of admission and the date of discharge from the hospital.

The member may appeal any unfavorable decision of the local sick benefit department or of the Union Health Center. This appeal is filed through the local sick benefit department with the Joint Board Committee on Appeals, which is a subcommittee of the Health Fund Committee. It is composed of two members each of the four affiliated locals of the Joint Board, together with the Secretary-Treasurer of the Health and Welfare Fund, who is chairman. These members (except for the Secretary-Treasurer) are all shop workers whose only compensation is supper money. This committee meets once every other week, or more often if necessary. It is the appellate body of the Fund. This committee calls the claimant to appear for a hearing and informs him of the evidence that he must bring. The local union sick benefit department does not take sides; it merely files the appeal for the claimant and gives the history of the claim. If a claim is denied on this appeal, the claimant may further appeal to the General Executive Board Health and Welfare Fund Committee, which is the court of final appeals. Few, if any, appeals have been carried to this committee.

Maternity benefits. In filing a claim for maternity benefits, the claimant must submit a birth certificate or some medical certification of a still birth. She will then get a check for $50.

Eye and medical care. Each member who has belonged to the Union for at least six months and who has not been dropped from membership for being in arrears in dues for over nine months is entitled to a pair of glasses and a medical credit book each year. These must be claimed in person and the membership book must be submitted at the time the benefit is claimed.

Retirement and death benefits. Claims for monthly retirement benefits, or $50, are made to the Retirement Department of the Joint Board. Each member sends his application to the Retirement Department of the Dress Joint Board. He is interviewed and a determination of eligibility is made. There are provisions for appeal in case of a denial of retirement benefits. The administration is completely in the hands of the Dress Joint Board.

The local unions pay a death benefit of $500. This amount will be increased to $1,000.

Administrative Responsibility of the Parties

The administration of the Health and Welfare Fund during negotiations or during a strike, if one should occur, will remain unchanged as far as the Dress Joint Board is concerned. Sufficient reserves have been set aside to pay benefits for three years without income, and the Fund's disbursement of benefits would not be impaired at such time because the administrative machinery of the Joint Board constitutes the administrative machinery of the Fund. The employers do not participate in the day-to-day administration of the Fund. There is employer representation on a Health Council, which is composed of six employer representatives and six union representatives, presided over by the Impartial Chairman of the dress industry; but this Health Council has only limited functions, none of which is concerned directly with the collection of the Fund's income, administration, or disbursement of benefits.

The Dress Joint Board is required to file with the Health Council any rules and amendments it may adopt. It must also report to the Health Council periodically on the accomplishments of the Fund concerning the health and vacation benefits. However, there are no requirements either in the rules of the Health Fund or in the collective bargaining supplemental agreements that indicate whether the Health Council can refuse to accept the report or what action it may take if it disapproves. There is also complete silence about if, when, and how often, the Health Council is to meet, and except for its functions of reviewing, criticizing, and changing, there is no mention of the nature of its agenda.

Actual administrative responsibility is vested in the Health Fund Committee of the Dress Joint Board. It consists of eight members: the General Manager of the Dress Joint Board, the Secretary-Treasurer of the Board, the Secretary-Managers of the four affiliated locals, the Manager of the Eastern Out-of-Town Department of the ILGWU, and the Manager of the Northeast Department of the ILGWU. The General Manager of the Dress Joint Board serves as the chairman of the Health Fund Committee, and the Secretary-Treasurer of the Dress Joint Board serves as the Fund's Secretary-Treasurer.

The top administration of the Health and Welfare Fund is, therefore, the responsibility of a small number of persons who are the political leaders of their respective units, and who are also the administrators of the Health and Welfare Fund. Below them are the Dress Joint Board delegates, the local union officers (of whom the Fund administrators are the top ones), the local union executive boards, the departments with their supervisors and clerks, and finally, the local union members who express themselves in the local union meetings. Above the Health Fund Committee are the ILGWU Welfare and Health Benefit Department, the GEB committee concerned with the activities of the Health and Welfare Fund (and other such funds), the General Executive Board itself, and finally, the international conventions held triennially.

With the enactment of the New York State Temporary Disability Insurance Law, there were some changes in the regulations of this Fund (all included above), but not in its administration. The Fund is now a carrier under the Law.

MORRIS SACKMAN

Chapter 36

"Dollar worth" of the unions

1. REVENUE

UNION OPERATION COSTS A GREAT DEAL OF MONEY. MONEY IS NEEDED TO carry on organizing activities, to finance strikes when such are in the day's work, to maintain offices and officers, to meet legal costs, research, publicity and education expenses, and costs of all forms of communication within and without. There are fewer strikes in this era of enlightened labor-management relations, but the strikes that occur are usually bigger and costlier.

Mr. Eric Peterson, General Secretary-Treasurer of the International Association of Machinists (Ind.), reviewing the problems of union administration elsewhere in this volume, suggests that even with very little support given a strike, "a shutdown of work in a plant, or an industry involving 10,000 men for a period of six months would be staggering to the union's treasury: a million dollars would be quickly disbursed." The million would be no more than pocket money, not real help. It would provide $16.67 to support a striker for a month. And support of the strikers is generally only one item in the heavy costs that a strike of such magnitude would involve.

Industrial warfare is expensive. But industrial peace is costly, too. Eric Peterson refers to the union's field staff of 600 full-time representatives, servicing the organizing and enforcement needs of his union's 600,000 members. The figure is in line with the average requirement of union administration: it generally takes about one union officer to service 1,000 members. The need in industries with small or widely scattered shops is for even greater staffs. The General Office of the IAM requires the aid of about 200 clerks, and that is not more than is generally the case. Unions that extend their activities beyond strictly "trade matters"— and it is a rare union that is willing to or can remain so "pure-and-simply" chaste in the present state of national and world affairs—make an enormous outlay of funds.

The 1950 Financial and Statistical Report of the International Ladies'

Garment Workers' Union (AFL) throws interesting light on the union money matter. The Report shows the steady increase of the union's operating staff (for both the General Office and affiliates):

1943	1,098	1946	1,338
1944	1,150	1947	1,394
1945	1,217	1948	1,446
	1949	1,522	

The following schedule shows the number of employees engaged in the administrative, organizing, enforcement, and clerical work of the union, the total payroll for such classification and the average weekly wage per employee within such classification:

	Number of Employees	Weekly Payroll	Average per Employee	
			1950	1947
Organizing and Enforcement Staff				
Locals and joint boards	440	$ 40,383.00	$91.75	$82.00
International general office	251	19,433.00	77.50	66.00
Total organizing and enforcement staff	691	59,816.00	86.50	76.50
Office and Clerical Staff				
Locals and joint boards	700	35,295.00	50.50	44.00
International general office	131	7,994.00	61.00	62.00
Total office and clerical staff	831	43,289.00	52.00	47.00
Totals	1,522	103,105.00	67.75	60.50
Summary				
Total—locals and joint boards	1,140	75,678.00	66.50	59.25
Total—International general office	382	27,427.00	72.00	64.50
Totals	1,522	103,105.00	67.75	60.50

The ILGWU reported 423,010 members as of January 1, 1950, and a national "organizing and enforcement" staff of 251, proportionately smaller with respect to membership than that of the IAM. That may be due in part to the fact that better than one-half of the ILGWU membership is centered in and close to New York City, in which the union has its General Office, a condition that facilitates enforcement tasks; also, in this area, the union's position is rarely and little challenged. However, it will be noted that the ILGWU local organizations engage a considerably larger organizing and enforcement staff—440 to the General Office's 251.

The union's total disbursements over the three-year period covered by the report (April 1, 1947, to March 31, 1950) amounted to $13,903,665.47. Administration and organizing consumed about 55 per cent of this sum.

Administrative expense includes salaries, operation of all departments, such as auditing—$425,214.69; education—$222,239.09; research and engineering—$231,899.14; publications and publicity—$854,695.82; convention, standing committees, affiliation dues—$648,416.57; and general maintenance—$992,992.17. The three-year total was $3,883,894.98.

Organizing expense includes salaries, travel, and organizing expenses, strike benefits and expenses, legal fees and publicity, and totaled $3,691,352.78.

Another item in the report quotes contributions to the labor movement and institutions at home and overseas, by the General Organization and by the affiliated Local Unions and Joint Boards, in the total amount of $4,596,921.23 over the three years, and a grand total of $13,614,354.77 in ten years (April 1, 1940, to March 31, 1950). There are not many unions "Marshall Planning" on so grand a scale, but a considerable number are now following this path, laid out by the pioneers, such as the Amalgamated Clothing Workers, the ILGWU, and several lesser units of the labor movement.

The ILGWU revenue to meet the almost $14 million cost of three years' operation was $15 million. Over 80 per cent of the revenue came from the share the General Office receives from membership dues or tax and initiation fees, which members pay to the local union. One-third of the funds for Contributions to Institutions and Causes were derived from a special assessment for that purpose, and two-thirds from direct cash contributions, or from money paid by employers to members for overtime work done to finance this need.

The total general funds of the ILGWU General Office and affiliates exceed $21 million. The various reserves, covering such funds and commitments as sick and death benefits, tuberculosis benefits, health, welfare, and retirement funds, administered either by the union or jointly by the union and the employers, stood at above $90 million as of December 31, 1949.

The ILGWU average annual revenue from dues and initiation fees, as it appeared on the quoted report, was about $4 million, from 400,000 members. The annual income of the International Association of Machinists, as reported by Mr. Peterson, is about $5.6 million, all but one-half of one per cent from the per capita dues, paid by the 600,000 members of 1,750 lodges (local unions) to the national organization.

Union activity is financed by proceeds from "union dues," a tax on union membership. The amount assessed is determined and legislated by each national organization, and varies from union to union. Other items of revenue are special levies or assessments on members to meet particular emergencies, and the initiation fees that unions charge new members. The money so received is generally divided into two parts. One part, per capita tax, goes to the national organization. The other part goes to the local unions and such other area organizations as there may be—district councils, joint boards, and the like.

The amounts of the tax, the methods of allocating the proceeds, and the basis of the tax imposition, whether it be a percentage of the earnings, an otherwise graduated tax, or a flat sum, differ in the various unions and trades. The tax is usually heavier in the better paid crafts than in the mass-production industries where unskilled and semi-skilled work prevail. The amount varies from $1.50 to $5.00 a month, in the largest number of unions, with $2.00 and $4.00 respectively in the CIO and the AFL, the prevailing figures for most of the large unions. In some of the highly skilled crafts, union dues are much higher.

Calculation based on a table, prepared and published in 1948 by *Life* magazine and covering 18 CIO, 20 AFL, and 6 independent unions, which together account for about two-thirds of the total United States union membership, would show the total income to all unions, from regular dues, to be about $400 million a year. The estimate agrees with this writer's own calculations, based on as yet unpublished, personally gathered information. In all, these data come close to the available official figures of union gross income of $389.7 million reported in 1943, and of $477.7 million in 1946 reported by the Bureau of Internal Revenue. Examination of the dues figures of the two unions previously mentioned essentially corroborates the $400 million estimate.

The ILGWU per capita tax of 18 cents a week is probably representative of the great majority of unions with large memberships. If all internationals collected on this basis, the dues intake from 15 million members in one year would be ($0.18 × 52 × 15,000,000) $140,400,000. The share of the local unions and joint boards in the ILGWU is about twice that of the national per capita, and if that division of dues is applied to the whole of the 15 million union members, the over-all total of dues should come to about $400 million.

The IAM, as stated by Mr. Peterson, takes in annually $5.6 million, of which 99.44 per cent is per capita tax. The reported IAM membership roll is 600,000. Allowing for a 10 per cent lag between membership census and membership according to actual dues payment, we get approximately $5.57 million from 550,000 members, or about $10 annually for each member. Assuming that local and district lodges take in about $20 annually for each $10 received by the General Office, and calculating total union income on the basis of $30, the over-all amount would be ($30 × 15,000,000) $450 million. There is the reasonable likelihood that the machinists' dues are a bit higher than those of the garment workers.

It is reported that unions have lately been raising dues payments. That is quite likely, but there will probably not be a great change in the top figures of income.

Unions derive income from two sources other than dues: initiation fees and emergency assessments. There is little reliable material available on which to estimate the totals of those items.

Initiation fees charged to new members, like the regular membership dues, vary greatly along similar lines, except that in a good many instances, more particularly in the mass-production industries, initiation fees are nominal—one dollar or so—and frequently this charge is applied to the first month's dues payment; in some instances, there is no initiation fee at all. Where such fees are collected, as in the skilled trades, the sum may range from $5 to $50. And it may at times be as high as $300, or even as high as $1,000 in some particularly highly paid or sheltered occupations. Sometimes high initiation fees are imposed, but are not really expected to be met, since they are used merely as a means for staving off the entry of new workers into a well-organized trade that is not likely to expand. These fees are anti-immigration legislation. The total revenue from initiation fees is not large.

Assessments to meet emergencies usually reflect the climate that prevails in industry on the union-management relations front. As recognition of unions becomes an industrial way of life, there is less occasion for unions to resort to emergency taxation. Generally, members do not like to be so taxed, and union administrations are reluctant to call for such revenue. However, the practice is an important part of union fiscal policy. In 1948-49, the Chicago Typographical Local 16 struck for the union shop, against all the newspapers in that city. The strike lasted over one year, and was maintained by the entire union membership outside of Chicago paying a regular percentage-of-earnings tax, which went as weekly wage to the strikers. The tax yielded many millions of dollars for the strikers. Likewise, the 100-day strike of the automobile workers against Chrysler Motors Corporation (1949-50) called for a similar supporting tax, which was estimated by the union to yield several million dollars.

Unions sometimes derive revenue from sources other than those reviewed above, although the sums thus received are not very significant. One such source is returns on investments, since many unions have large operating funds and accumulated resources at their disposal. The ILGWU, for example, reported $515,381.74 in interest on bonds, loans, and savings accounts over a period of three years, or $170,000 a year. Assuming speculatively that the ILGWU instance of resources and investment policies is representative, which it may or may not be, this type of revenue for the whole trade union organization would not exceed $5 million annually.

In all, it is fair to assume that the earlier estimated total of $400 million represents pretty closely the annual intake from all sources by the entire union movement.

This dependable and calculable revenue adds greatly to union stability and makes possible union expansion work within and without. Money, to be sure, isn't all that's needed. The human element in the labor-management equation, the members' and leaders' willingness, readiness, and ability to fight for set objectives is paramount. But assurance that the union won't be stopped in its tracks and that no major activity will be halted because of exhaustion of motive power is virtually a condition of survival in the supersensitive atmosphere of present-day union functioning. Furthermore, financial resourcefulness helps unions, with the growing interdependence of functional groups in the community, to better their position with their neighbors.

All of this discussion is on the positive side. But concentration of big funds in union treasuries is not an unmixed blessing. The growth of union finances calls for managerial astuteness on the part of union officers, which complicates the task of selecting proper personnel. Some otherwise good leaders may not be good financial managers. And others thus fit may not possess leadership quality. The head officers have the additional power that comes with authoritative proximity to large funds of money. As a rule, they do not have authority to divert funds at discretion. And they are more particularly restricted with regard to the "big money" that comes within the union's operational sphere through the health and welfare, and pension and retirement funds. These funds are earmarked and nearly always are either under joint union-industry control, or under strict regulation by insurance authorities, or both. Nonetheless, union officers are in a position to place orders for work and business, to plant numerous persons in all sorts of jobs, and to decide upon investment of large funds. They have *power*. That kind of power is bound to try the best intentioned union officer, and it subjects him to strong pressure from those who would seek to profit by its exercise.

It does not follow that unions should shy away from strong treasuries. But it is clear that the problem of union government is no more free of democratic headaches than is any other form of government. It will take the labor movement more than casual concern to solve this problem.

2. Resources

The unions' "wealth" has been given considerable attention in recent years in the business pages of the press. This consideration was prompted partly by investment interests, partly by the thought that unions could, by utilizing their rich resources, buy ingress into industrial management. The issue was raised by a privately conducted "survey of the probable resources of labor unions, their investment policies," which received much publicity in the labor press as well. The survey was conducted by Dr. Alexander S. Lipsett, an economist, on behalf of a public relations firm with various investment firms among its clients. The report was published as a pamphlet: *Labor's Partnership in Industrial Enterprise* (Floyd L. Carlisle, Inc., New York, 1950). The author's major conclusions were:

A net wealth of three to four billion dollars.

Large and almost exclusive investments in government securities and bonds.

Virtually no investments in corporate industrial enterprise.

An influx of billions of dollars annually from pension levies, the main burden of which is borne by industry and in the final analysis by the public.

These funds must be put to work—an investment of no mean size.

This plethora of money threatens grave dangers to the national economy, as well as to labor itself. Upon the wise employment of union assets depends whether organized labor is to become a cornerstone of industrial financing or to remain wedded to outworn investment concepts and the uncertainties of tomorrow.

As the author of the pamphlet saw it, the country was slipping into the embrace of a "laboristic economy" although capitalism could still be saved if the unions would but do their duty. "The era when so-called big capitalism supplied the means for the growth and expansion of American industry is past. Its place has been taken in a sense by the workers and their organizations, with an ever increasing share in the nation's wealth."

There is no law, of course, against imagining things. But, as to the accuracy of the estimated "$3 billion net union wealth," and "possibly double the sum," the unions would underwrite Mark Twain's famous remark apropos of his reported death. But what is it actually, if viewed unfancifully?

The 1948 effort by *Life* magazine to ascertain the unions' worth in dollars had 32 unions accounting for $224 million, and since the reporting unions represented about 55 per cent of the 15,000,000 union members, the total union wealth could be estimated as approximately $400 million, about equal to the estimated yearly union intake from regular revenue. However, two of the 32 unions covered in *Life* magazine, the United Mine Workers of America ($62 million) and the Brotherhood of Railroad Trainmen ($49.9 million) included in their reports the sums in their health, welfare, and life insurance funds—probably $90 million out of the $112 million. And it is quite possible that the other reported union resources likewise included similar money that is in no way "union resources," whether or not some of it can be viewed as investment capital. Thus, the estimated $400 million is more likely to fall below $300 million. It is, however, true that the union reports in *Life* covered only the national treasuries of the reporting unions.

No reports are available as to how much accumulated money there is likely to be in the local and district organization. But perhaps, here too, the ILGWU 1950 report offers a clue. There the total audited resources of the entire organization, national and local, is given as $21 million. This amount is exclusive of the major health, welfare, and insurance funds. Assuming that the 15 million unionists or organizations are of financial standing equal to the ILGWU, which is hardly warranted since the latter is admittedly wealthier than most others, the total "worth" of all unions would be about $787.5 million. A businessman buying this at the face figure would be a gambler, not an investor.

This concern with the unions' "wealth," coming in the years following World War II, recalls an interest in investments that developed in the union movement in the wake of World War I. But in an interesting way, the two situations differ. Unions were at that time, temporarily at least, in a pretty strong position, and some had accumulated substantial funds due to wartime prosperity and to wartime government aid to union organization and collective bargaining. Several unions launched labor banks (see Part V, Chapter 26). The Brotherhood of Locomotive Engineers was the outstanding organization to go in for a variety of business ventures, including grandiose real estate developments on a city-wide scale. With the exception of the ACWA banking venture, the "business" flurry ended in disastrous financial consequences for the unions, and in many instances for their members. The labor business collapse came while the mid-twenties' Golden Glow still seemed real. The promoters of the labor excursion into "primitive accumulation" spoke of cooperation as their social pattern. But they ran their undertakings, most of the time, pretty much according to the rugged-individualistic recipe. The miners union could not get the locomotive engineers' brotherhood to take on collective bargaining in the mines they operated. Labor in business did none too well.

If many union leaders are receptive to the idea of buying their way into a junior partnership with business, they have not made their wishes known. However, there is one important circumstance to be considered with regard to the unions' worth as investment capital: the total sum of union money, whatever it may be, is not owned by one organization but by many thousands of local and central units, and only here and there are substantial sums owned by a single organization.

Money in the view of all unions is a weapon, not an industrial power leverage. It is helpful to have funds, but reserves are not appreciated as a revenue-producing device. The source of revenue that matters most is the union itself. Some investment of funds is in the day's work, but is considered seriously only when all else is taken care of; and at that, it is for safekeeping rather than for "attractive return." And, of course, easy convertibility of savings into ready cash is a dominant consideration. Money thus viewed is not in the market for partnerships in industry.

It is well to seek a sense of proportion while viewing the unions' "wealth." Millions tend to look and feel like thousands, when confronted with billions. The estimated annual revenue of less than half a billion dollars by all unions would have been quite impressive in the years when total national income was below $40 billion, but it is not so awe inspiring in the face of the present $200 billion and rising national income. Professor Edwin E. Witte, of the University of Wisconsin, recently observed that the General Motors Corporation and the American Telephone and Telegraph Company each possess several times the total wealth of all unions together, and likewise that the annual net income of each is greater than the annual revenue of all the unions combined.

J. B. S. HARDMAN

PART SEVEN

Union Education Activity

Introduction

Union education activity

THE SELECTION OF MATERIAL FOR THIS part of *The House of Labor* included a call for three kinds of reporting and analysis by the contributing writers:

1. *The general function of the union educational activity and of the problems with which its practitioners come to grips in the course of their operation.* The discussion of function and problems as they face both the union and the educational staff person is presented by Mark Starr, Victor G. Reuther, and J. B. S. Hardman. Mr. Starr also examines the scope of the activity throughout the field.

2. *Description and analysis of what the educational leaders in a number of unions or auxiliary organizations have found to be either their most successful or their most interesting form of activity, or which raised particularly important issues.* Under this heading, Messrs. John D. Connors, Larry Rogin, Joseph Glazer, Herbert B. Jackman, and Mark Starr report on what they consider the best and most workable part of their respective labor education undertakings.

3. *Information and analysis of phases or departures in the labor educational field, of which relatively little is known, or which sought to effectuate a formulated policy, principle of, or approach to labor education, and which produced interesting results.* "Education Package" is the account of an Amalgamated Clothing Workers (CIO) experience, as carried on several years ago by the cultural activities staff of that organization: J. B. S. Hardman, Esther Peterson, Arthur Stark, Lawrence Levin and Agnes Martocci Douty. The writers present in detail ideas of plan and performance different from prevailing practice.

How Much Education?

Labor education is a recognized tenant of the *House of Labor*, but there is no law that assures each tenant adequate and satisfying quarters.

On the record, as presented by the U. S. Labor Department's Bureau of Labor Statistics, in its 1950 Directory of Labor Unions, 48 national and international unions—under one fourth of the total—maintain education departments: 21 of these are AFL affiliates, 14 are in the CIO, and 13 are unaffiliated unions. In addition, both the AFL and the CIO maintain national education departments. The BLS neither invents nor investigates information of this kind. It merely passes on what it receives, and does

419

not mark off the actual record of fulfillment as against a statement of intention. If it had done the latter, the resultant figures would have shown that a number of unions consider it no disgrace to have the title, education director, appended to a person on the staff or to an officer who is quite content to let the title remain purely ornamental. Indeed, most often the person so pedigreed is loaded down with more responsibility than he can carry, and education is not likely to receive a high priority.

However, if not a great many national unions have done so, the two labor federations have made labor education a function that is carried on by special setups and by appropriation of considerable funds. And there are several national unions whose education intentions are being carried into effect, in some instances on a large scale.

What Kind of Education?

The AFL Workers Education Bureau, made a formal part of the Federation in 1950—some 27 years after the founding of the Bureau—reports service to 500 national and international unions, state federations of labor, central bodies, local unions, and workers' educational enterprises. At the 1948 convention of the AFL, the Bureau reported that during the year it had sponsored 21 institutes on economic and industrial problems in 14 states, in cooperation with its local constituent organizations, universities, and community associations. It also conducted educational meetings at a number of conventions of AFL affiliates and participated in conferences sponsored by other organizations. The Bureau services its affiliates and cooperating groups by circulating literature and information of various types. It also publishes a monthly education news letter.

In the same year, the CIO Department of Research and Education conducted five regional conferences in Oregon, Massachusetts, Indiana, and Wisconsin, and sponsored leadership training courses in Maryland, Missouri, Colorado, and Tennessee. The Department acts as a clearinghouse for CIO education directors, and as part of this function, has arranged quarterly meetings for these staff members to consider current problems. The Department maintains a rental library of 60 films, which were seen during 1948 by more than 50,000 CIO members. Over 400 albums made up of three 12-inch records of the CIO's "America's Favorite Union Songs" were sold during the year.

The following variety of educational effort appears among the things the various union groups across the land are doing, either regularly or with some frequency.

Institutes. During the summer months, union members are brought together for periods of time, from a week end to a fortnight, to discuss union problems, to learn techniques of public speaking, collective bargaining, etc., and to hear experts on important subjects. These institutes generally combine a vacation atmosphere with the classes and are set away from a city. In the winter months, institutes are held over week ends. This type of activity is intended for shop stewards or others who are potential union officials, and sometimes the officials, too, are included in this type of activity.

Lectures. Local unions frequently sponsor individual lectures or a lecture series. These are generally offered to the members at local union meetings or at special gatherings, and usually cover current events, consumer problems, labor legislative issues, labor-management relations, and community relations.

Courses. Courses are conducted for smaller groups than the lecture series; the topics, however, are usually the same. In some instances such courses tend to be more detailed and require more participation from the attending members. This may be true, for example, of labor law, job analysis and evaluation, leadership training courses for shop stewards, techniques for union legislative committees, and other "tool" subjects designed to equip union officers and committee members with specialized competence. Courses on political problems, social security, and health and welfare plans have been offered more frequently of late. Courses on the history of the labor movement, and more particularly on the history of the respective union, and explanations of economics fall into the category of background material.

"Outside" Union Education

The American Labor Education Service (ALES) is the leading lay labor education auxiliary operating in the field. Not formally affiliated but generally recognized as a bona fide union setup, it sponsors institutes, arranges conferences and seminars, provides various counseling services for interested unions, and publishes a *Labor Education Guide.* It also conducts an annual Summer School for Office Workers (80 students in 1948). The ALES Annual Conference of Leaders and Teachers in Workers' Education, held each February in New York City, has become a well-attended national center for workers in the labor education field, directors of workers' schools, education directors, and members of interested government and public agencies, where they have the opportunity for discussion of significant related problems and study of new techniques in the use of movies and film strips, radio, and other educational devices and aids.

The Rand School of Social Science in New York and its branch in Northern New Jersey offer a variety of courses ranging from "tool" courses such as public speaking and parlia-

mentary procedure, to economics, social psychology, and political philosophy. The Highlander Folk School in Tennessee and the Hudson Shore Labor School in upstate New York are the two best-known residence schools. The latest venture in the field is the International Ladies' Garment Workers' Union Officers Training Institute, widely recognized on the very day of its opening as a West Point for union staff members, organizers, and the like. It is a one-year resident school situated at the ILGWU national home office.

Universities in various parts of the country have also shown an interest in workers' education. Several universities permit unions to use their facilities for summer institutes or for evening classes. Others have incorporated labor education courses into a special part of their regular program or have set up extension services for workers. Since 1925, the University of Wisconsin has been operating a resident summer school for workers who have been selected and whose expenses are paid by their unions. It also conducts extension courses during the winter. At Cornell,

New York State sponsors and finances the State School of Industrial and Labor Relations; and at Harvard a nine-month curriculum has been organized for specially selected trade union Fellows whose tuition and other expenses are paid for by their unions. Now in its seventh year, the course of study is being condensed into a 13-week program. The Institute of Management and Labor Relations organized in 1947 at Rutgers University in New Jersey reported in May 1948 that over 10,000 persons had been reached by its program. Other universities and colleges cooperating with unions are: the Industrial and Labor Relations Institute of the University of Illinois, the Labor and Management Center at Yale, Workers Education Service of the University of Michigan, Scranton University in Pennsylvania, Labor Education Division of Roosevelt College in Chicago, the Institute of Industrial Relations of the University of California, the Institute of Labor Economics of the University of Washington, the Industrial Relations Center at the University of Chicago, the Labor Extension Service at Pennsylvania State College, and the University of Minnesota, which offers extension courses and occasional workers' institutes. There are a number of others—perhaps 50 in all —that carry on workers' education in greater or lesser degree. (See Caroline Ware's *Labor Education in Universities*, published by the American Labor Education Service, 1946, and supplement, *Trends in University Programs for Labor Education*, reprinted by ALES from *Industrial and Labor Relations Review*, October 1949.)

J. B. S. HARDMAN

Chapter 37

The task and problems
of workers' education

COLLEGES AND UNIVERSITIES NORMALLY, IN THE PAST, PROVIDED MEN AND women with the training necessary to help employers and corporations keep labor in its lowly place. The law schools trained the lawyers who fought the workers in compensation cases for the benefit of the insurance companies. The injunction-granting judges, the industrial engineers, the speed-up experts, the personnel and welfare experts were given, in the universities, the skills necessary to uphold the *status quo*.

The failings of standard, formal education in grade school, high school, and college are, in part, the cause of workers' education. Only reluctantly have many schools talked about labor unions in their civics classes. Not until 1944 was a high school textbook available that covered the American labor movement. In school ceremonies it is rare to find representatives of labor participating. Only a small fraction, less than 5 per cent, of the school boards have a labor representative appointed or elected to them. Furthermore, only a small proportion of the school teachers are organized, preferring to remain in professional organizations or not to be in any organization whatever.

The New Deal decade brought a changing attitude toward workers' education from the grade school to the college. Although there is a growing recognition of trade unionism in American schools, and textbook references become more accurate with each edition, and although the educational associations are now anxious to gain the support of labor, as a matter of fairness and good sense this interest should have developed before. No institution in the United States has such a record of consistent support for public education as has the organized labor movement.[1] This new attitude will develop more rapidly than in the

---

[1] In *Labor Looks at Education* (Inglis Lecture at Harvard School of Education, 1946, republished by the League for Industrial Democracy in 1948) I made detailed criticisms of the public school system and suggestions for reforms in method and aims.

older European countries. In the United States, the possibility for the individual to move from one social stratum to another has meant that our universities have not suffered from the rigid caste system of Europe. For example, the British struggle between "independent working class" education financed and controlled solely by the unions, and "workers' education" supported by the state and the universities' extension divisions, did not reappear on this side of the Atlantic. The ideas represented respectively by the *Plebs*—National Council of Labor Colleges—the worker-sponsored schools, and the Workers' Educational Association, an extension of university work supported by government funds, became articulate here but they never became the basis of a long continuing organized conflict.

It is difficult to produce an adequate and agreed definition of workers' education. With general education it shares the purpose of preparing people for life in addition to preparing them to earn a livelihood. It shares too the current dilemma of either concentrating upon imparting skills for immediate use or training the powers of judgment by giving courses in the general philosophy and history of the labor movement. It must guard against "compartmentalism," which would try to separate short- and long-term aims. In the hands of good teachers, however, workers' education serves as a *discipline* in scientific methods of thought; as a *directive* for immediate action in the light of an ultimate goal; and also as a *dynamic* impelling the students into action.

The general workers' education movement in the United States has never clearly professed a revolutionary objective as it has in other countries. Here we study the social sciences and related subjects for the purpose of increasing the knowledge and effectiveness of the workers in their economic and political organizations rather than to help descry means of achieving socialism.

As farmers are given a knowledge of the problems of agriculture, so the trade unionist is given an insight into the problems of society, of wages and hours, of the structure of business, and government agencies that now materially affect the policy of the unions. For immediate effectiveness, tool courses, such as parliamentary law, English, speech and writing, and research methods, are necessary to a union's education program. Participation in forming the program and providing satisfactory controls by the representatives of the workers' organizations is essential to a successful, democratically functioning workers' education program.

Workers' education grows up to meet the specific needs of the workers' group, endeavoring to relate its activity to other groups within the community. That problem of integration is not easy because it depends upon circumstances that cannot be foreseen. For example, should there be a relapse into the old-time opposition against trade unions, then obviously the role of workers' education would have more to do with a psychology of conflict than with cooperation. However, if farsighted management and intelligent labor continue to cooperate in industry, there is no reason why, in the realm of ideas and intellectual studies, there should not be a greater interchange. Unions, for example, will use the experts from the university and trade union history and problems will find a place in the teachers' colleges and in the economics courses.

The position of workers' education inside the unions also presents a difficult and complicated problem. Many unions still suspect intellectuals and use the term "professor" as one of mild contempt. For many years the residential schools, such as Brookwood and Commonwealth, founded by private groups to train individuals for work in the labor movement, were looked upon with suspicion as the work of intellectuals who were outside the labor movement and trying to capture or control it. These residential colleges were, to some extent, intellectual hot-houses in which criticisms of the existing trade unions were developed by faculty and students who, in the main, were in the left wing of labor. This criticism, of course, did not endear them to the trade union officials, although Brookwood particularly endeavored to serve all sections of labor, and many of its graduates are now to be found in administrative union positions. Most of the colleges were, therefore, largely dependent for support on individuals who thus satisfied their social consciences. By the time the American labor movement developed its present power and strength, those individuals had been deflated by the depression, and the residential colleges disappeared for lack of financial support just at the moment when the great expansion of the labor movement and the need for more organizers provided them with their great opportunity. The Highlander Folk School, in Tennessee, continued mostly as a base for CIO training institutes in the South.

With but a few outstanding exceptions, the unions gave only lip service to workers' education. Both the CIO unions and the AFL unions, until recent years, praised education but were not prepared to pay for it in any adequate way. Now, however, according to the U. S. Dept. of Labor's *Directory of Trade Unions* (1950), 48 of the 209 unions employ education directors (in 27 instances, however, the same individual is both education and research director).

The Role of the Educator in the Unions

Lack of a clearly defined function influences the status of workers' education activists in the labor organizations. For example, in some unions the educational director as a "catch all" has to take over all the miscellaneous functions that have not yet been allocated to a specific trade union officer. These duties may include publicity for the union and its leadership, writing speeches, preparing resolutions, and publishing a newspaper. The educational director may have the job of dispensing information about workmen's compensation and security benefits; he may be the administrator of both the union's credit union and its sick-benefit provisions.

In some cases education is looked upon by the union officer as a show-case proposition—something that can be used for the purposes of advertisement but that serves no real fundamental purpose in educating the members or officers or determining policy to attain the immediate or ultimate ends of the organization. In some unions the educational directors and staff members serve as ward heelers for the administration. Their job is to see that their boss is re-elected. This attitude, of course, makes the educational staff and the classes nothing more than a yes-man chorus for the administration, destroying independence of thought and scientific inquiry.

In other cases, educational activity has been monopolized by an opposition group and thus workers' education has again become suspect. Usually the younger men and women of an organization attend classes to learn the challenging facts and the power to express them; in a hidebound organization such activity, however innocently conceived, is regarded as opposition—or less politely, as Stalinism. The ideal would be a middle position between the two extremes of amen-chorus and opposition. In classes studying the labor movement, there should naturally be a frank examination of the mistakes as well as the merits of each union and of unions as a whole. But if the union class becomes merely a sounding board for grievances, then its usefulness is seriously impaired.

Despite these difficulties, a great deal of useful educational work is being carried on. New members are introduced to the union, given information on the rights and benefits of their new status. The philosophy and history of the labor movement are studied with great profit. Refresher courses are given to officers, and in a few unions, would-be officers are put through qualifying courses.

The uncertainty and difficulties of trade union educators arise also from the fact that there is no code or agreement about the pay, the responsibilities, the hours and the tenure of such educational activitists. Pay ranges from nothing to $150 a week and is generally less than that paid to industrial organizers. The hours depend upon the amount of activity and sometimes go far beyond those usually listed in any trade union agreement. Some of the educators are members of the union that employs them. Others are not allowed to join the union (or may join only in an honorary capacity) for fear that they would become political rivals to some members of the administration. Tenure in too many cases depends upon the attitude of the manager, and there is serious need for a standard agreement safeguarding the right of the union educator to decent conditions and appropriate notice to terminate employment.

This would be the ideal situation for the educator working in a union:

He should feel free at any time to make constructive criticism and to have complex and difficult problems freely discussed in his classes by all shades of opinion within the union. He should be able to use workers' education to enrich and improve the democratic procedures inside the union by stimulating an alert rank and file. It should be possible for him to secure discussion of possible changes in the structure of the union without jeopardizing the educational program by criticism from vested interests that feel menaced by an alteration in the *status quo*. He should be allowed to coordinate the research, recreational, and health activities of the union with the educational work. He should be able to feel that procedures discussed in the classroom would add to the administrative efficiency of the individual union leader and the union as a whole; and to educate actively against any factional, racial, or religious discrimination that might be practiced in any section of the union.

In addition to such internal work, the union educator should be able to discuss freely the relation of the particular union to the labor movement as a whole, and ways and means whereby unity in the labor movement could be obtained. Additionally, the Educational Department should be able to be active in presenting labor's position to professional, religious, civic, farmer, and consumer groups.

Educators working for trade unions should be granted appropriate freedoms and security of tenure at rates at least equivalent to what their work would obtain in other educational fields.

Current Trends in Workers' Education

World War II brought considerable changes in the over-all picture of workers' education [the reader is referred to the John Dewey Yearbook, *Workers Education in the United States* (New York: Harper & Bros., 1941), for the prewar picture]. Some unions lost a number of their members and of their staff to the armed forces, which meant a decline in their activity. Other unions grew rapidly, accentuating the need for classes for new members and for training inexperienced officers. There has been generally a strengthening of this activity by short courses, institutes, special pamphlets, and handbooks. The Division of Labor Standards was helpful to a number of local groups, particularly in the Machinists' Union, in preparing such handbooks for the use of shop chairmen in the more efficient execution of their duties.

Later there was the training of "union counsellors" to deal with out-plant problems. There were institutes on racial understanding, full employment, housing, price control, minimum wage, and other postwar problems, but not to the extent that the postwar problems demanded.

Cooperation with Government Agencies and Universities

As suggested in the first part of this chapter, there has been in the United States no sharp controversy in workers' education on the matter of independence. The Workers Education Bureau, largely composed of AFL affiliates, for example, in its inception was largely influenced by the ideas of Albert Mansbridge, founder of the English Workers' Educational Association, but the WEB gave greater emphasis to the necessity of workers' control and direction for any educational programs adopted by the universities. For practical purposes and because of its limited funds, the Workers Education Bureau, in addition to publishing pamphlets and its journal, has been able to do no more than run yearly institutes on the premises of some 30 to 40 universities.

A few institutions of higher learning, notably Wisconsin University, Bryn Mawr College, and Barnard College, have developed summer schools for workers. In California, the universities have provided similar facilities for the Pacific Coast School for Workers. The Southern Summer School for Workers in earlier years utilized, in turn, various smaller colleges for its six- to eight-weeks school. The Wisconsin School for Workers, the Hudson Shore Labor School, the White-Collar Workers' Summer School, and Highlander School carried on during the war.

In many instances the unions have looked upon their educational work with a certain amount of institutional pride. Unions have been prepared to pay money much more willingly to support activities carried on under their own aegis than to contribute adequate funds for the provision of nationwide organizations, such as the Workers Education Bureau and the American Labor Education Service (a service organization combining AFL and CIO affiliates, publishing lesson outlines and bibliographies and running conferences and institutes). Theoretically this local effort seems a wasteful overlapping, but there has been a good deal of cooperation among the unions most active in the fields of workers' education. They have cooperated in the use of material and have pooled their knowledge at regional conferences organized by the ALES. The Annual Washington's Birthday Conference on Workers' Education, originated by Local 189 of the American Federation of Teachers at Brookwood College, has been taken over jointly by the ALES and Local 189. The record of these conferences mirrors the changing problems, methods, and ideals of workers' education activists.

Within recent times, the CIO has developed considerable activity in publications and in assisting its constituent unions to develop educational plans. But here as in the AFL, the unions prefer to meet their own specific needs in an independent fashion. Closer general cooperation among unions, and especially the coordination of their educational activities, would greatly help to advance workers' education and thus make possible the production of many necessary aids, such as labor films, textbooks on labor history, economics, etc.

Institutions of higher learning in the last few years have recognized a potential field for their expansion in the provision of training for union officers. The greatly increased strength of the unions, with over 15 million members, the permanency created by the improved legal status of the unions, combined with the lack of regular students in wartime were some of the factors behind this recognition.

From Harvard University in Cambridge, Massachusetts, to the University of California, in the Far West, programs have been developed for schools in industrial relations. This and other attempts have already been discussed.[2] There is a great deal of experimentation to be made in this field before any specific conclusions can be drawn.

If the barometric social pressure indicates fair weather in industrial relations generally, then we can expect that the colleges and universities, either on their own campuses or in their extension divisions, will endeavor to discover and meet the needs of organized labor for skilled and trained administrators. However, should the barometer show stormy weather, then alongside the breakdown of labor-management cooperation would come probably a breakdown in the overtures now being made to place the facilities of the institutions of higher learning at the disposal of the trade unions. Undoubtedly, in many industries, labor-management cooperation will be continued and the attempts at cooperation in education are likely to be strengthened. In 1948, an ominous fall in the barometer was the suspension of the Workers' Education Service by the regents of the University of Michigan, at the request of General Motors.

One hitherto undeveloped field for cooperation between the institutions of higher learning and workers' education activity is the training of teachers for the educational and recreational activities of the unions. Good progressive education in general uses the methods that are indispensable in efficient operation of workers' education. The schools of education in the various universities are becoming aware of the need and importance of adult education, and logically, should be prepared to study the methods necessary in classes run by the trade unions.

Generally speaking, work for trade unions is more closely associated with the extension divisions of the universities than with the courses carried on in the college classrooms where students attend for credits for degrees and take written assignments that are normally impossible in part-time study and evening classes.

Workers' education in the United States achieved its greatest strength

---

[2] "Education Discovers Organized Labor" (*Current History*, October 1944); "Higher Education for Labor Leadership?" (*American Federationist*, January 1945); "Cap and Gown Meets Overalls" (*Guidance, Practical Arts and Vocational Education*, January 1945); "Education for Workers" (*Forum*, July 1946).

and spread with the help of the WPA. Many of the people who participated in that boom were anxious to set up, either through the U.S.
Department of Labor or through the U.S. Office of Education, a similar
nationwide plan with the help of federal grants. Mrs. Clara Beyer, of
the Division of Labor Standards, interviewed the permanent Education
Committee of the AFL and representatives of the CIO on this matter,
and increased allocations in 1946 made it possible to enlarge the staff
of the Division for this purpose. But all this work was lost with the
slash made by the 80th Congress in the appropriations for the U.S. Labor
Department. Late in 1945, the U.S.D.L., under Secretary Schwellenbach,
called a conference of university leaders and trade union educators to
discuss plans for an education extension division in the Department of
Labor. These efforts culminated in July 1946, when Representative
Andrew J. Biemiller introduced H.R. 7108 to authorize a labor extension
division to be operated by the U.S. Department of Labor. The attempt
was revived in the next Congress, but the Bill, after lengthy hearings in
1948, never came to a vote.

There is, of course, no logical reason why the specific needs of organized labor cannot be recognized in the same way as the Extension
Division of the U.S. Department of Agriculture provides extensive educational facilities and 3,000 county agents for the farmers of the United
States. But it seems likely at the moment that such attempts will meet
with obstacles for some time yet. Meanwhile, the unions will develop
their own independent educational work, and let us hope, federate them
into a nationwide organization. Among the promising developments
are the summer institutes of the United Steelworkers, the Georgia
Workers' Education Service, and the program of the Kentucky State
Federation of Labor.

Despite difficulties created by apathy among the unions, lack of clarity,
and inadequate finances, which in turn produces personnel problems,
workers' education has achieved permanent recognition and will play
an increasingly important role in the American community.

MARK STARR

Chapter 38

The labor institute

EIGHTEEN YEARS AGO, THE WORKERS EDUCATION BUREAU OF AMERICA pioneered in establishing the Labor Institute as a means of bridging the artificial gap between the world of labor and the world of learning. It was a cooperative project, an "experiment in understanding," planned by workers and by educators together, for a realistic and objective discussion of the problems currently facing labor. It is not the function of the Labor Institute to adopt motions or resolutions or to formulate policies: it is fundamentally educational in character and is designed to teach labor not *what* to think but *how* to think. The Institute explores all sides of questions of vital concern to labor, under the guidance of experienced leaders of labor and education in the quiet atmosphere of the college campus.

In June 1931, the Bureau set up on the campus of Rutgers University in New Jersey the first Labor Institute in the country, which was sponsored by the New Jersey State Federation of Labor and the University. This Rutgers Institute of Labor has been held every year since that date and has won the approbation of leaders of labor, industry, education and the government throughout the land. From this humble beginning on the Rutgers campus in New Brunswick the Labor Institute Program has spread throughout the country until today the list of such institutes conducted with the assistance of the Bureau is over 150, with a distribution in some 40 states of the Union, among these—in addition to New Jersey—Colorado, Kansas, Montana, Minnesota, Indiana, Connecticut, and Massachusetts. This expansion has proved the soundness of this educational technique, and the validity of the pattern thus established for serving the economic and intellectual needs of trade unionism.

In general, the Labor Institute is set up on a state-wide level under the sponsorship of a state federation of labor and a state university with the cooperation of the Bureau. There have of course been modifications: occasionally a city central body and a municipal educational institution cooperate in an institute on a local level; or as has happened in some instances

431

of late, labor and industry together set up an institute with the help of the university.

The Bureau's major emphasis in planning and conducting the Labor Institute is always upon the mutual character of the undertaking. It is not something handed down from above, from leaders either of labor or of education. It is a cooperative endeavor in which scholars and workers set up the program together in a joint committee, working as equal partners in the project.

The democratic pattern thus established carries over into the actual conduct of the institute. The result is complete freedom and objectivity of discussion, too often lacking in other meetings in both the labor and the educational fields. Many of the institutes include very few formal ad- dresses in their programs; rather, they depend on panels to present the topics under discussion. However, in either case—panel discussion or prepared address—opportunity is given for audience participation and general discussion.

The success of the institute depends to a great extent upon the personnel of the joint committee. The university is usually represented by the di- rector of the extension division, some administrative officer, and members of the economics, political, and social science faculties. An equal number of labor representatives are usually appointed by the state federation, rang- ing from state officials to members of local unions.

The university provides the use of its facilities, and the sponsoring labor group in turn accepts the responsibility for promotional work and prelim- inary publicity. Institutes vary in duration from one to five days, usually being held over the weekend. Attendance varies from 100 to 500. Although the vast majority of the participants come from the ranks of organized labor, all sessions are open to the public and representatives of management, the farmers, and government, as well as the general public, are welcome. Thus the institute serves not only as an instrument of educa- tion but as a very effective public relations medium.

A study of the programs of the 150 and more institutes that the Bureau has helped to plan and conduct during the past 18 years reveals that they have taken their color from the contemporary scene and have given con- sideration to the questions that are currently of supreme importance to labor, and indeed, to all groups in the community. With the passage of the National Industrial Recovery Act in 1933, we carried on a series of 27 Labor Institutes to discuss specifically the provisions and implications of that Act. Eleven institutes centered their discussion around the Social Security Act and in 1935 and 1936 the National Labor Relations Act was the focus of attention in 10 institutes. With the outbreak of war in 1939, the defense program and labor's contribution to the war effort were re- flected in the institute discussions. Since the war, most of our institutes have been concerned with the problems of reconverting to a peace economy and the responsibility that labor has to help build permanent peace throughout the world in this Atomic Age.

It cannot be claimed that these institutes, held at 12-month intervals, are in themselves an effective continuing educational program. But the enthusiasm engendered at these annual "experiments in understanding" has been carried back to the local union and has resulted in expanded workers' education programs in the local community. The delegates have taken back to their fellow-members a better understanding of labor's own problems and of the service that the university can render to labor in our democracy.

And the seeds sown at these institutes that the Bureau started back in 1931 are now showing evidence of bearing still another kind of fruit. The wall of misunderstanding and prejudice that has existed between labor and learning is being breached. The university has gained a deeper appreciation of the important place labor holds in our American community and of the responsibility the institution of higher learning should assume in expanding its educational services to include the organized labor movement. For several years there have been sporadic instances of labor education projects under university auspices, but more recently, programs of workers' education or industrial relations have developed extensively in our American universities, until today there are more than 80 publicly supported, privately endowed, and sectarian institutions of higher education throughout the country offering their educational services to organized labor, either through resident courses or through activities under their extension divisions.

The Workers Education Bureau, as it looks at its Labor Institute Program developed over the years, feels that all its efforts have been justified by the results achieved and that it has made a significant contribution both to labor's understanding of its problems and to the bridging of the gap between labor and learning. We look forward to further expansion of the program, to developing still more cordial relationships with the university world, and to affording the labor movement still greater opportunity in the days ahead for free and open discussion of all aspects of its problems and of its increasingly important role both at home and abroad.

JOHN D. CONNORS

Chapter 39

The resident training institute

THE ONE-WEEK GENERAL RESIDENT TRAINING INSTITUTE IS REGARDED BY THE Education Department of the Textile Workers Union of America as its most effective work. This report describes exactly how such training institutes are run by one great union. Other organizations, we are confident, will find this information helpful. TWUA also conducts specialized or advanced institutes that are not described here.

Obviously, a one-week training period will not make an expert negotiator or an ace organizer out of a shop steward. So we don't attempt to do that kind of job. Our objective is more modest.

This is what we *do* attempt to do:

1. We try to improve the tools the shop steward or union officer uses in his everyday union job. He gets this kind of help in courses where he learns how to run a union meeting, how to settle grievances, how to get the local union to function effectively.

2. We try to make the student understand how the international union works. To that end, we seek to give him facts about the industry in which he works. A course in textile unionism covers these topics.

3. We try to take the blinders off his eyes so he sees more than his own union as the beginning and end of all things union. We try to get over the idea that he and his union are part of a potentially all-powerful force called the "labor movement," and also a little bit about political and economic problems and how the labor movement can use its power to build a better world. The program includes such subjects as labor history, labor economics, political action, and international affairs.

4. One of our most important objectives is to build union enthusiasm and loyalty. We try to give old-timers a sense of the importance of the job they are doing so they will be inspired to keep right on going. We hope the newcomers to the union will go back to their local unions anxious to become more active than ever before. This union spirit and loyalty the student gets partly from participating in the classes but mostly from talk-

ing, eating, playing, singing, and living with fellow-unionists with varied experiences from many states and many branches of the industry.

Recruitment of Institute Students

Several months before an institute takes place, letters and circulars are sent to all local unions in that area announcing the institute and urging them to select students. At the same time, letters and circulars are sent to all staff people in the area urging them to follow up the letter sent to the locals.

Each student fills out a questionnaire in advance of the institute. This gives us information about the mill, the job he does in the mill and the union, and what phase of union education he is interested in. This kind of information helps us know what points to emphasize in our program.

Who goes to these schools? Primarily shop stewards and local union officers and executive board members. All students are full-time workers in the shops.

How are they selected? This depends on the local or joint board that is sending them. In many cases, the students are elected at a regular union meeting. In some cases the membership gives the executive board the power to choose the students. One large joint board set up a special committee of top union officers who screened applicants for the school, and chose those they thought best qualified, and who would get the most out of the school.

The problem of getting students who will really get something out of the week's instruction—and of eliminating those students who come along just for the ride—has not been completely solved, and probably never will be. In the TWUA setup the local union or joint board pays the major share of the school expense and thus the decision of who goes to school must be made on the local level. In any event, we feel it would be unhealthy for the choice to be made on the national level. Fortunately, we have been successful in getting a high percentage of serious students anxious to learn and with the capacity to do so.

Repeaters, or students who come back year after year are not allowed at these general institutes. Such students are encouraged to attend advanced institutes that specialize in one particular subject, such as political action, collective bargaining, or union administration.

We try to keep the institute to about 40 to 50 students—then we can split them up into two sections of 20 to 25 each. We feel this is about the best number with which to do a really effective teaching job.

Where to Hold the Institute

The location of an institute plays a large role in its chances of success. The place should have an educational atmosphere that is friendly to labor, clean and comfortable lodging, physical surroundings that make informal recreation easy, and plenty of good food. TWUA has found these in labor schools, church conference grounds, colleges and state universities, and at a resort owned by one of our joint boards.

Food is perhaps the most important of the above considerations. No matter how good the classrooms and teachers, we have never found a hungry institute that was a successful one.

For educational purposes, the best institute is run at an isolated spot where the students are closely associated with one another. This isolation builds a strong feeling of solidarity, and gives those who attend a better opportunity to learn from one another. When the institute is held in or near a large city, there is a tendency to scatter to the bars and movies during the free hours, rather than to participate in the valuable informal discussion that takes place.

Recently TWUA has held an increasing number of institutes at colleges and universities that are developing labor education programs. Attendance at a university has a strong appeal to the average worker, which helps to open his mind to new ideas. The physical facilities also lend themselves to an institute program, and the university faculty forms a reservoir of speakers on a variety of topics. Cooperation with the university provides good public relations for the union and for the university as well.

Program of the Institute

The program is developed by the Education Department in consultation with the union officers, and other staff members of the union.

The complete program for each institute is planned well in advance. We have not found it profitable to come to an institute and ask the students what they want to study. We are flexible enough, however, to meet any special demands that may be raised.

The following courses are usually offered:

Collective Bargaining. How to settle grievances; duties of a shop steward; putting the contract to work; work-load and time-study problems; arbitration; economics of collective bargaining.

TWUA and the Labor Movement. Where our unions came from and where they are going. The history of the labor movement and the story of textile unions.

Issues of the Day. We analyze the political and economic issues of the day such as: Taft-Hartley, social security, civil rights, full employment economics, international affairs.

All the courses listed above are taken by all students. Students also have a choice of the following workshops:

Public Speaking. How to talk effectively at local meetings, union conferences, and conventions. A major part of the course is devoted to practice speaking.

Parliamentary Law. How to use parliamentary law to make union meetings more efficient and more democratic.

Making Your Union Work. How to make the local function effectively; getting union committees to function properly; making the union a force in the community.

Political Action. How to conduct a political campaign: block and precinct work, registration, getting out the vote, explaining the issues.

The program usually includes three morning classes (about 70 minutes each) and afternoon workshop (90 minutes) plus an informal evening program.

A typical daily schedule is:

7:15	Breakfast
8:00	Collective Bargaining
9:20	TWUA and the Labor Movement
10:40	Issues of the Day
12:15	Lunch
1:30	Choice of a workshop (Public Speaking, Parliamentary Law, Political Action, Making Your Union Work)
3:00 to 6:00	Free time, recreation, swimming
6:00	Supper
7:15 to 9:00	Evening Program—singing, speakers, movies followed by dancing, recreation, games

Afternoon & Evening. The recreation programs for the afternoon and evening are organized under the direction of a staff member. The 7:15 to 9:00 P.M. program is obligatory. This usually consists of singing labor songs, a guest speaker followed by discussion, and a short movie. Sometimes a longer documentary movie takes the place of the speaker. A definite attempt is made to integrate the speeches into the general program. The school runs from Sunday evening through Friday evening. There are five full days of instruction.

Institute Teaching Methods

Many different teaching techniques are used during the institute—but the basic method is classroom instruction. However, the teaching is completely informal and the discussion technique is used throughout.

There is plenty of "how to do it" practice in the regular classes and workshops. For example: In collective bargaining, mock grievance and arbitration hearings are conducted. Mock union meetings and congressional hearings are used to get practice in parliamentary law and public speaking. Mock union committee meetings are held in "Making Your Union Work."

At most institutes we have a newspaper workshop where a group of students turn out a mimeographed newspaper, which they write and put together themselves (advised by a staff member).

The town-hall type of forum is used to discuss controversial topics like "Should Labor Start a Third Party." Movies are used regularly at all institutes, usually as part of the evening program. Students are not encouraged to take notes in class because it is difficult for an inexperienced note-taker to do so and concentrate on the discussion at the same time. In lieu of notes, many pamphlets are distributed, which contain much of the material discussed in class.

On Friday night (graduation night) the students usually put on a variety show of skits, songs, and imitations, which they have rehearsed during the week under the supervision of a staff member.

Because the program is such a full one, there is no formal "homework" or outside class assignment except for the workshops (rehearsing with mock committees, newspaper work, preparing speeches, rehearsing for the show).

For the most part, teaching is done by the TWUA national Education Department staff, assisted by local TWUA Education Directors. We believe the most effective job can be done by an instructor who knows the union, its problems, and the kind of workers he is teaching.

Staff members of other TWUA departments are called on to teach special phases of some of the courses. For example: the Research Director or one of his staff teaches work-load and time-study problems in the collective bargaining courses.

We try to get at least one "outside" instructor for each institute, to lend some variety and broadness to the program. We have successfully used instructors from the U.S. Department of Labor, other unions, or from labor schools, such as the University of Wisconsin School for Workers. We have occasionally used regular college instructors, but there are not many who are effective teachers of workers.

For an institute of 40 students, the staff consists of four or five full-time instructors (including the director).

How the Institutes are Financed

The average cost per student is about $120 for the week. This figure includes food, board, tuition, fare, and one week's lost wages. Most of this cost is paid by the local union, the remainder by the international.

Occasionally, workers come to school during their vacation week. This saves the local union the expense of lost wages. However, the Education Department emphasizes that the institute is not a vacation school where you can learn something while on vacation, but a training school where you are expected to participate in a solid program of seven hours a day of classes, guest speakers, discussion and workshops. The institute is usually a lot of fun, but it is not a vacation.

LARRY ROGIN
JOSEPH GLAZER

Chapter 40

Training for union service

THE PHENOMENAL GROWTH OF THE INTERNATIONAL LADIES' GARMENT Workers' Union presented it with the problem of introducing young Americans to progressive trade unionism. This orientation began in mass membership meetings with educational talks and with songs and skits created and used on the picket line and in strike meetings.[1] Later the techniques of successful collective bargaining and of cooperation with intelligent manufacturers were studied. Union members were developed as chairladies, as business agents, and union officers, both paid and unpaid.

This practical emphasis upon immediate problems was not allowed, however, to exclude a study of the larger aims of the labor movement. The ILGWU has always maintained a cordial relationship with community agencies and was able to extend this cooperation. Further, it endeavored to instill into the minds of the new members the ideals of labor solidarity and opposition to all forms of racial discrimination and bigotry.

The strength and intelligence of the union has for 20 years made resort to large-scale strikes unnecessary. Thus a great deal of constructive energy has been released to deal with shop problems, increased productivity, and new work methods, and also to develop the welfare activities of the union itself. This shift in emphasis, of course, changes the climate of union educational activity but increases the need for intelligent understanding and participation of the union member in the life of his organization.

Education for New Members

As soon as a worker joins the union, the *welcome* leaflet is sent to him by central headquarters or by his local union. This leaflet describes, partly

---

[1] The work of the Educational Department of the ILGWU, as formally set up in 1916, is fairly and adequately reported in the official convention reports and in the histories of the union: *The Women's Garment Workers*, by Louis Levine, the *Needle Trades*, by Joel Seidman, and the most recent *Tailor's Progress*, by Benjamin Stolberg.

Since 1935, statistical records of classes and students have been maintained and are available in biennial reports and in such pictorials as *Growing Up* and ... *And the Pursuit of Happiness*. The *Monthly Labor Review* (August 1945), in the reprint Serial #R-1768, described the wartime development.

in pictures, what the union has done in its 50-year crusade against the sweatshop. The Kansas City, Mo., Joint Board sends a supplementary form letter to every new member explaining exactly the benefits and the costs of belonging to the Union, describing the union meetings and introducing the union officers. The next stage in the initiation of the member is a small illustrated 12-page pamphlet *Meet the ILGWU* followed by the pictorial *Story of the ILGWU*, and the filmstrip, "You and Your Union," based upon the *Pictorial Union Dictionary*, published by the Inter-Union Institute.

During wartime, when formal classes were difficult to run, the union tried to get a monthly message on every machine by means of attractive colored leaflets, such as *Watch Out for the Wolf* (a popularized advocacy of social security supporting the Wagner-Murray-Dingell bill), and *Brother Can You Spare a Finger?* (safety methods in the shop). These leaflets were also used to introduce the new member to the list of 140 publications in which the economics of the industry and the institutions of the Union are explained in greater detail.

Use of the printed word is supplemented by classes for new members, Officers' Qualification Courses, and scholarships ranging from weekend and two-week institutes to the Trade Union Fellowships at Harvard for one year.

The new members' classes have been best developed in St. Louis, Minneapolis, Dallas, and Chicago. The outline prepared by the St. Louis educational director in 1941 has been widely used and adapted by other locals. This outline is a seven-page syllabus ending with a check quiz. The first talk deals with "Why Do We Need a Union?," and includes duties of a union member, and privileges and protection for union members. The second talk is entitled "The Union as a Way of Life," and covers the credit union, the cooperative buying club, sick and death benefits, the union press, the summer institutes at the University of Wisconsin, and educational and recreational activities. Talk No. 3 describes how the Union works on a local and national basis. It explains the jurisdiction of the Union and gives a summary of its history. It finally exhorts new members to carry on and extend what they have been fortunate enough to inherit. Talk No. 4 is devoted to a recapitulation of the earlier talks and to questions about local activities.

The director, Doris Preisler, gives additional operational details:

The lectures were repeated regularly every month. We always skipped the fifth Friday so that the same lecture could be expected every first Friday of any month and the same thing was done for the second, third and fourth lecture. They were not dependent on each other so that a person could enter the class at any point in the series or could make up the next month for any one of the series he missed. This systematized attendance. I found that with the outline as a guide, one of the experienced officers could do a very good job of teaching the class.

Originally I introduced the class as a voluntary idea and gave the Executive Boards cards to give new members with the announcements of the classes. Needless to say, attendance was not large. However, the Joint Boards liked the idea and voted to make the classes compulsory in 1940 and it has been accepted routine ever since. New members come in asking where they go to school. Chairladies say that it makes their task much easier for them.

When new members appear before the Executive Board to apply for admission, they are told about the classes and told they must attend before they can get their union membership books. When they attend the class they are given a card marked 1st Friday, 2nd Friday, etc., which they keep until they have attended the four different lectures. The teacher rubber-stamps the date after the appropriate day each time they attend and retains the card on the fourth time. She signs the card and turns it over to the office manager who does not give out the book until she gets that card. If the office manager has to hold the book for more than six or seven weeks, she reports the fact to the proper Executive Board, which investigates. They are as strict about it as they are about the payment of initiation fees.

The Southeastern Regional director, John Martin, has had a series of lessons mimeographed for use in new members' classes. He recommends that the text be read aloud by the class leader and discussed with the new members and the officers. This is an attempt to overcome the common difficulty of finding experienced teachers available at convenient hours to teach the new members' classes and the difficulty of getting union officers to come to the class and describe their experiences. Even when teachers are available, their lack of practical acquaintance with the detailed operation of a modern union creates difficulty. The three lessons, as circulated in the Southeastern region, cover 32 mimeographed pages and have been distributed to all the ILGWU educational directors, again with the emphasis, as in the Preisler outline, that they must adapt them to their own locals. Finding out by experience that members with family responsibilities, and especially those living at widely scattered points from the factory and union hall, did not come to meetings, Mr. Martin printed the leaflets and distributed them by mail.

In Chicago, the late Morris A. Goldstein, secretary-treasurer of the Chicago Joint Board, prepared an instructors' outline for the "Union Applicants' Course." This outline describes in detail the duties of the union officers and the relationships among the members, the local, the Joint Board, the General Executive Board, the Convention, etc. This leaflet, too, has been made available to other joint boards and locals.

In Dallas, Texas, the same ground is covered. The locals there have voted to make the classes compulsory, and members must attend three class periods and receive a certificate upon completion of the course. A local officer comments: "I find that the members who attend these classes are more appreciative of what the union has done." And one of the largest manufacturers in Dallas says, "The good union members in Dallas are the best producers as well as the peacemakers in the shop."

All the new members' classes used *Pictorial Union Dictionary* (ILGWU edition) whose 42 drawings to illustrate the stages "Working Without a Union," "Winning a Union," and "Working Under Union Contract" were later available in the filmstrip "You and Your Union."

Classes for Officers

In addition to the new members' classes, the ILGWU Educational Department organizes classes for newly elected Executive Board members. This course exploits their new sense of importance and their desire to shoulder their responsibilities in an effective way. In Indiana, to help new chairmen, a mimeographed outline and agenda were supplied so that the officers made sure that the union meeting effectively covered all details. In New York, refresher courses have been held for business agents; and in 1945 the Officers' Institute invited outstanding industrialists and government representatives to deal with the general problems of labor in its relation to the community. Speakers included Eric Johnston, Henry Kaiser, Senator Joseph H. Ball, William H. Davis, and Professor Selig Perlman. As a follow-up to this program, but outside the work of the Educational Department, a series of lectures was given in 1946, at the Central Needle Trades High School, in cooperation with the industrial engineers of New York University. It dealt with efficiency methods as applied to the garment industry. Union officers and executives in the women's garment industry attended as students.

Returning to direct union training, the Officers' Qualification Courses were an experiment that carried through since 1935. These courses were made compulsory by Convention decision in 1937, for elective full-time officers who have not previously held office. These courses were described in the pamphlet *Training for Union Service* and also in the *Educational Report ILGWU, 1948–50*. As of May 1950, 472 members in New York City had completed this work. The Officers' Qualification Courses now include the History of the Union (9 periods), the Economics of the Garment Industry (9 periods), Structure and Functioning of the Union (6 periods), Trade Union Techniques (15 to 18 periods), and Parliamentary Law (3 periods). This 45 hours of work is a minimum course and can be extended. The periods are usually 1½ hours in length. The students are given tests. They are expected to attend 75 per cent of the sessions, and to secure a 75 per cent rating in their examinations.

All the institutes (20 in 1947–48 with 951 students, 19 with 1,485 students in 1948–49 and 19 with 1,999 students in 1949–50), which ran from one day to two weeks, stress preparation for union activity.

The Harvard Union Fellowships have been described elsewhere, notably in the recent study of workers' education at universities by Caroline Ware. The ILGWU has sent 17 students, and all but two of the Harvard students returned to active service in the Union. At the request of the ILGWU, whose membership is 75 per cent female, the Fellowships were opened to women in 1945. In 1948, the duration of the Fellowships was reduced from 9 months to 13 weeks.

The ILGWU Educational Department has been in close contact with other institutions of higher learning that are endeavoring to provide opportunities for trade union training. While certain phases of the training work for new members, such as relate to the union and the industry, must obviously remain a direct responsibility of the Union's Educational Department, in other matters of a general or a general labor character the ILGWU can well cooperate with other institutions. Furthermore, it should be remembered that this current emphasis upon the immediate needs of union training leads naturally to the larger vistas of the general labor movement and its aims for bettering the lot of the worker, in cooperation with all intelligent and social-minded elements of the community.

The Officers' Training Institute

To meet the immediate need for trained union officers, the ILGWU Officers' Training Institute began to operate on May 1, 1950. In 1947, at the Cleveland convention of the ILGWU, the labor college idea which had been repeatedly advanced at earlier conventions was made a reality. President David Dubinsky declared:

In the earlier years of the ILGWU, our leadership element was nourished chiefly in the traditions and the idealistic atmosphere of the old-time radical and Socialist movement. That reservoir has gradually become exhausted. It is characteristic, too, that this gradual drying up of the old-type sources of leadership has run parallel with the profound changes in the old production patterns in our industry, which are also rapidly disappearing. The fact is that our employers are realizing the necessity of devising new methods and developing new craftsmen.

The development of new leadership material, in quantity as well as quality, however, is not a problem for our union alone. It is a serious matter, and it faces the entire labor movement. The trade union movement, furthermore, plays an important part in the life of the nation. Who will lead and guide the trade union organizations in the future, therefore, is a matter of prime concern to the general American community.

Several schools of higher learning have been experimenting in recent years with training for trade union leadership. Regrettably, the trade union movement, as an organized body, has not given this matter of leadership training the attention it fully merits, nor has it supported these experiments as systematically as they deserve.

Basically, nevertheless, it is a union problem. It is my opinion that our union must devise new methods and employ new techniques in the development of its future leadership; that it must sponsor an educational project and attract to it other sections of the labor movement in a labor college or other such project for the purpose of training leadership for our union and for the trade union movement in general.

The union's General Executive Board reports, in part, on the launching of the institute:

The ILGWU Training Institute is a day school and offers a full one-year course, seven months of which are to be devoted to indoor class work, broken up into three periods, two of three months each and one lasting one month. Five months of the scholastic year will be given over to field work, broken up into two periods, the first of three months and the second of two months.

Field work will be carried on by the staff in cooperation with the affiliates of the ILGWU and will entail visiting shops, observing at close range the work of organizers, business agents and managers, the impartial chairman machinery wherever it exists, the procedures in organization, and following up labor relations cases. In addition to such field work, students will be given regular assignments and be required to submit reports periodically.

In addition to a regular staff, the Institute has engaged outside lecturers and key people familiar with the various angles of industrial education. Also, the heads of the various departments of the ILGWU are expected to give the students as part of their regular class work the benefit of their experience and accumulated information.

Applicants who are accepted for admission to the Training Institute will not be required to pay tuition fees but will be expected to provide for their own subsistence. A subsistence allowance may be made by the ILGWU to students who are assigned to union offices outside the New York City area for work experience during the training course.

Each student is carefully screened to assure his interest in and devotion to the objectives of the Institute. Candidates are expected to have had a reasonable prior education—at least high school.

Students are offered an assurance that on the satisfactory completion of their course at the Institute, they will be given suitable employment by the ILGWU or one of its affiliates.

The Training Institute opened its first academic year on May 1, 1950 with 37 students, 32 men and five women. Ten are members of the ILGWU; 19 are related to our union's members; three have other union connections; and five have no union connections but were regarded by the Committee of the GEB as qualified and desirable Institute students.

The ages of the students range from 21 to 30, and most of them have had a higher educational background than the required minimum of high school: 18 had full college education, 11 part college education. Arthur A. Elder, formerly head of the Workers' Education Service of the Extension Division of the University of Michigan, is the director of the Institute. The

General Executive Board voted an initial annual budget of $100,000 for the training school.

The experiment will surely give important leads for future training for union service.

MARK STARR

Chapter 41

Education on the local level

THE CONSTITUTION OF THE UNITED AUTOMOBILE WORKERS-CIO REQUIRES only that a local union have an education committee. It does not say how large the committee should be or how it should be selected. The by-laws of most local unions provide for an elected committee of from five to seven persons.

In practice, the chairman is elected and the rest of the committee is made up of people who are just attracted to the work. This practice is satisfactory, but it is a good idea to make service on the education committee official by confirming it with an official letter or card.

Every unit in an amalgamated local should have an education chairmanand committee who work with the chairman and committee for the entire local.

What Does the Education Committee Do?

The three major activities of an education committee are union building, pioneering, and teaching. Union building means projects to get members to attend meetings: bulletin board posters, leaflets announcing meetings, attendance prizes, and interesting programs. It means aid to organizing drives. It means helping members to understand what their dues accomplish for them, and the importance of voting in union elections, in the election of officers, in strike votes, in union shop elections, in national, state, and city elections.

The committee sponsors activities to make the union hall more attractive and pleasant as a center for the members' use. It sees to it that the local has a dignified initiation program that explains to new members what the union stands for; that new members are properly introduced at the union meeting; and that they receive new-member kits. It supplies new committee members and officers and stewards with pamphlets and materials that will help them on their jobs.

Pioneering means that the education committee does the spadework for new union activities until they are well enough organized to carry on by themselves. For example, until a credit union is organized, the education committee distributes pamphlets and organizes preliminary meetings until the credit union committee is ready to take over on its own. In the same way, the education committee would prepare the ground for cooperatives (not just for groceries, but for housing and health, insurance, fuel and gasoline, and anything else), for blood banks, a teen-age canteen, a Saturday morning child-care program, a summer camp program for children, a camera club, a buying club (in cooperation with the recreation committee), a theater group or chorus, a local union newspaper if it isn't already in existence, health and safety committees, and union counseling.

Teaching, for an education committee, means:

Training programs for stewards, where grievance procedure and the contract are discussed;

Classes (or weekend institutes) for newly elected officers;

Union hall classes in grievance procedure, time study, parliamentary law, public speaking, political organization, labor history, union counseling, workmen's and unemployment compensation, shop safety, radio, and journalism;

Union hall classes for women members and wives in nutrition, first aid, family problems, consumer problems, millinery, dressmaking, interior decorating, cooking, crafts, and similar subjects;

Classes for children in music, dancing, story telling, arts and crafts; children's activities like Boy Scouts, Sea Scouts, Campfire Girls;

Classes for union members in recreational and cultural subjects, such as fly-tying, dancing, photography, shop mathematics (if public schools don't offer night classes in this subject), contemporary literature, silk screening, and drawing;

Articles in the local union paper on important union and community issues, and labor history;

Regularly issued leaflets, distributed at the plant gate, which explain union, community, and national issues;

Use of bulletin boards to carry information on important issues;

Visits to new members to welcome them and to explain what the union is about;

A monthly new member class for all those who have been initiated into the union during the past month;

A union hall library and display of books and pamphlets, or a reading corner with comfortable chairs and magazines;

The display and distribution of pamphlets and books at each union meeting;

A radio program;

Forums and panel discussions;

Sponsorship (in cooperation with the international or regional education offices) of summer school training;

Sponsorship of a speakers' bureau to supply union speakers to churches and community organizations and schools;

Distribution of union publications and posters to schools, teachers, professional persons, and ministers;

Working out cooperative programs with libraries and schools that provide for special reading or discussion programs for union members and their families or that provide for union sponsored exhibits in public libraries;

Sponsorship of exhibits at county fairs;

Organization of joint forums and discussions with farm groups;

Placing union posters and exhibits in store windows;

Showing movies at union meetings and arranging for the showing of union movies to community groups;

Supplying newspaper editors and teachers with pamphlets dealing with specific issues while they are news;

Calling community conferences on specific subjects, such as school problems, recreation, transportation, or housing;

Preparing regular reports in cooperation with the PAC committee, on the activities of the local representatives in Congress and in the state legislature.

Money for Education

The Constitution provides that a local must allocate two and one-half cents per month per dues-paying member to education and recreation, but there is nothing to prevent a local from allocating more. Actually, the two and one-half cent allocation is not enough for most locals. To overcome the short budget, many local unions require the education committee to pay for running expenses out of its dues allocation. Major expenditures are paid for out of the general funds of the local. If a local has a good project that is beyond its budget, the education committee can ask the executive board and the membership for an appropriation.

Local unions also raise money for education through raffles, dances, theater, movies, circus, rodeo, or skating parties; the proceeds of bingo games, receipts from refreshment bars, and in one case, the profits from the automatic canteens in the plant help pay for education programs.

A local union education committee does not start from scratch. It can draw upon the educational resources of the UAW-CIO Education Department. For example, here is what it can use:

Ammunition, a monthly magazine that is intended specifically for the use of union committeemen;

More than 100 basic pamphlets on all the subjects and issues on which a committee will want to educate;

A leaflet handbook that tells how to prepare leaflets, and provides more than 100 sample leaflets and hundreds more workable ideas;

Big wall posters on union and historical themes featuring quotations from Lincoln, Roosevelt, Jefferson, and Wilson;

A continuous supply of bulletin-board-size posters on educational and historical themes;

Illustrated posters, bulletin-board size, designed to advertise union elections, union meetings, and union classes;

Radio scripts;

Study outlines and discussion guides on basic subjects;

Postage-stamp-size leaflets for plant distribution;
An initiation ceremony for use in any local union;
Recordings of union songs;
Turnover Talks (a series of poster-size illustrations for a talk on a basic subject: the Union, Dues, Cooperatives, and Fair Practices);
Films and filmstrips on union subjects, social security, sports, and a wide range of other subjects, including special children's movies.

The UAW Education Department has a Regional Education Representative assigned to work in a UAW-CIO Region. He will help organize a local union education program. The International Representative who works with the local will also help. And assistance in a specific education program can be obtained from one of the several other International Union Departments:

For economic information and information and assistance on time study—UAW Research and Engineering Department;
Fair practices, women's problems, civil rights—Fair Practices and Anti Discrimination Department;
Cooperatives and credit unions—Cooperative Division, UAW Education Department;
Recreation activities—Recreation Department;
Social security, insurance, health and safety—Social Security Department;
Books—Union Bookstore in Detroit;
Union counseling—Social Security Department;
Veterans' problems—UAW Veterans' Department;
Women's auxiliaries—UAW Women's Auxiliary Department;
Housing—Housing Department;
Political action and legislation—Political Action Department.

In addition, there are a number of government agencies that can help; the State University can provide instructors for classes; the public library may put a circulating library in a union hall and work with the local on reading lists; the Social Security Board in an area will be able to supply speakers and literature on the Social Security program, as will the State Unemployment Compensation and Workmen's Compensation agencies. Films are frequently available through the State Extension service and sometimes through the public library and commercial distributors. In Canada, besides working with government agencies, locals find it worthwhile to work with the Canadian Association for Adult Education in Toronto and with the National Film Board and local film depository.

How Does a Local Get Started?

If a local has an effective education committee, it can spread out and undertake new projects. If an education program is just getting started, its bare beginnings should include:

An initiation and training program for new members, and distribution of new member's kits;

At least a 15-minute education program at each union meeting;

Dressing up the union hall and making it attractive (if this has not already been done);

Setting up an attractive bulletin board;

Putting posters announcing union meetings on the board;

Displaying suitable posters; displaying and distributing literature at each meeting;

Working out an education program for the stewards—that is, planned discussions of grievance procedure or the contract at each meeting of the stewards' council;

Publishing an article on education in each issue of the local union paper, or distributing, not less than once a month, a leaflet on a subject in which the education committee is interested;

Getting people to work on the education committee;

Sending people to Summer School so that they can get the training they need to carry on key union activities.

The education committee should begin by holding a meeting to work out the education program to be undertaken. Locals should attempt only what they can actually get done, thus avoiding failure and the discouragement that comes with it.

The program should be presented first to the executive committee of the local, for ideas and approval; then to the membership for final approval. Going through channels in this way is extremely important. A program for stewards should be worked out with the bargaining committee. A political leaflet should be worked out with the Political Action Committee. In this way the committee gets new ideas and additional help. It also avoids offending people and builds good will.

Many education committees complain that they have too few people who will give active support. They say people are not interested in education. But the real difficulty is that no way has been found to interest them. The way to get someone to work is to go to him or her with a specific project.

A beginning can be made by asking someone in each department of a plant to distribute a particular leaflet. Then, if the assignments are given regularly, the chances are these people will eventually become interested in other activities as well.

Education Councils

As young people become active in a committee, an effort should be made to find out what they do best and what they like to do, and to give them that kind of assignment. It is important to give each volunteer a job that he can recognize as useful and helpful. In past years some locals failed on PAC because they actually got more volunteers than were used effectively. The people who were not used, naturally, became cynical and skeptical about the entire program. It is also important to assign work that fits the volunteer's capabilities and experience.

Very often a local cannot afford the kind of education program it should have. At the same time, it may be that other locals in the community are struggling with the same problem. In Racine, Wisconsin, the UAW dealt with the problem very effectively by organizing an education council financed by the dues allocation to education from each local union. Although no one local had enough to finance a program of its own, all of the UAW locals in Racine combined were able to employ a full-time education director and to sponsor an education program. Besides organizing the usual classes, institutes, and forums, this local program also set up cooperatives that built homes and are distributing goods at low cost. Similar education councils are operating in Jackson, in Grand Rapids, and in many Ohio cities.

Checking up on the Committee

Each education committee should submit a progress report every three months to the executive committee of the local and to the membership. The necessity for making the report will compel the committee to measure for itself how well it has worked. The report should relate what has been done in the past three months and what is planned for the next three months. The measure of a committee's success is not in the number of leaflets distributed or the number of forums and institutes run (although they indicate something). Better measures are:

Has it helped increase the membership of the union?

Has it helped in turning dues-paying members of the union into working members of the union?

Do more people understand the contract in the plant?

Are the officers and stewards better trained to carry on their duties?

Has the committee instituted activities that add to the well-being of the members—*e.g.*, credit union, co-op, children's activities, etc.?

When important issues came up in the plant and in the community, did the committee help people understand what was at stake?

Can the committee point to people in the local or in the community who have been helped to leadership by the committee?

Has attendance at membership meetings increased?

Is the proportion of people who vote in union and community elections increasing?

VICTOR G. REUTHER

Chapter 42

Education package

A Successful Educational Experience

FOR SEVERAL YEARS, FROM 1938 TO 1943, ONE PART OF THE GENERAL CULtural-educational activity, carried on for over 20 years on a national scale in the ACWA-CIO, stood out as the most genuinely successful project of the several the union had tried to develop. From the outset, that part of the activity drew a greater degree of response from union members than had been elicited by any earlier effort made in the same organization and under the same direction. It quickly proved capable of expansion on an impressive scale. The undertaking did not contain the customary assortment of "attractions," entertainment, promises of "lots of fun," and other "loss leaders" usually thrown into the education package to make it palatable to indifferent consumers. This unit of the union's general cultural activity embodied a coordinated program of labor education plainly offered as education. It included: weekend regional educational conferences; "active workers" schools (25 day periods); a series of eight correspondence courses, and a Monthly Readers' Packet—all four parts of an interrelated whole, as reported in subsequent pages. The activities were considerably reduced in 1942 and 1943 because of wartime restrictions upon rail and automobile travel, but good response continued even within these limitations.

The several phases of the activity were developed in a number of centers, from New York and Philadelphia to Minneapolis and St. Paul and points South—in fact, in as many places as could be undertaken by the available education-organizing staff and without upsetting other projects in a fairly large program of cultural activities.

There was nothing exceptional in the nature of this particular union's situation to warrant a conclusion that the experience was exclusive and that similar efforts could not be made in another union or would not meet with like success. Of course, the union administration was generally friendly and it was progressively cooperative when it appeared that the members "took" to the program.

The director of the activity was fortunate in securing a staff of gifted persons able and willing to bring a strong conviction of the living value of the general undertaking to bear upon their work, a circumstance of major moment in labor education.

The basic assumption was that labor education was a function of the union movement. The member-participant was invited to engage in the activity not solely because of the good that education might do him, but also because it was his duty and to his interest to assert himself as a citizen in a democracy, to find his place in the social and political setup, and to play his part in it as a member of his union. The functional relevancy between union member and citizen in the national democracy is a condition that involves rights and imposes duties. It is his duty, for example, to make himself aware of the contest of ideas, and alert in defense of what he deems to be right. Labor education was presented as having a broad national aim derived from the socio-economic location of labor in the nation.

The union administration was willing to have its director of education try various ways of making it a success. Any union starting out on an educational program is willing to give the person in charge a chance, or it would not have gone in for it. So eventual success was no less due to other reasons. Of moment in the particular venture was the experimental, open-minded approach to the selection of methods, program, and immediate tasks. There was no tight commitment to standardized patterns of procedure, and shifts and changes were considered and made as soon as a change in the situation necessitated a reorientation.

Such, for instance, was the shift in the composition of the union's membership in the course of a decade and a half. In the late twenties, that membership was predominantly immigrant, a considerable part approaching middle age, and largely located in a limited number of big cities from Boston to Chicago and not farther south than Baltimore and Cincinnati.

In the late thirties, with the immigrant influx a matter of the past, and the wide unionization of labor under the impact of the New Deal, the membership of the union presented a considerably different picture. It was younger, mostly native, whether of American-born, immigrant, or mixed stock, scattered over the greater part of the USA, and located, in addition to the old centers, in numerous small towns.

The meaning of the change insofar as shaping an educational program was concerned involved a number of points: (1) The older contingent was, to a considerable extent, union-minded, primarily socialistic-minded, having come from European lands with a developed, mostly radical, labor movement. Its call for education, whether by many or by relatively few, was for study in history, economics, American labor history, and citizenship, always with a radical slant. There also was the problem of a multitude of languages, and of giving consideration to a variety of national cultural backgrounds. (2) The new members required, of course, "union indoctrination," but that was to be differently presented. The educational program was, furthermore, to take into account the rise of fascism and nazism abroad and the corresponding "ideational" repercussions at home; later on, also, the developing unionist vs. communist conflict was important. (3) The general political reorientation and activization of most unions since 1936 has tended to give greater political and legislative content to labor activity. Consequently, the educational program was called upon to strengthen "agitation" as well as information and understanding, affecting a reasonable balance between the two. The reality of such need was well expressed years later in a labor publication, *Toledo Union Journal* (1947):

> Isn't it strange that at a time when the unions have attained the most remarkable growth in their history and when they are enjoying their strongest financial position, Congress and many state legislatures are arrayed against them?
>
> Instead of excusing ourselves and presenting alibis for our own failure, we would do better to sit down and seek to discover the reasons why we can add wages to the worker's pay envelope, but have failed to add union thinking to his mind.... To be sure, the labor unions have preached political action, but even that isn't enough. If economic action requires "education" and technique, so does political action.

The experience reported by the conductors of the program, of course, had to reckon with a variety of difficulties that involved "salesmanship" of the activity to the members as well as overcoming other "resistance." But out of the total development a number of do's and don't's appear that merit consideration, since their observance had some bearing on the success of the undertaking.

1. "Sell" education as education, not as "fun," entertainment, or as anything that it isn't. Most union officers are people who wouldn't be misled by labels.

2. Make sure the members know what they are to receive when they pick out an activity by its headline. They are likely to misread the meaning of nomenclatures, and then comes the disheartening "falling off of attendance."

3. Interrelate, do not mix, education and utility, or enlightenment and entertainment. Each on its own has merit and may lead toward the other more readily than when camouflaged.

4. Keep "ivory-towerites" and propagandists away from the work: both are boring to union members who want both emotional and mental stimulation.

5. Engage the union's best thinking timber to work out planned action and to head up such phases of the activity where practical wisdom is sufficient. However, in working out the program, do not dress education in "publicity" or "public relations" garb unless such is the aim in view and "education" is but a pretext.

6. If at all possible, endeavor to locate activity in the union building, even if it offers less attractive facilities. There the administration people see and are seen by the membership you seek to involve in the activity. But remember—good light, clean air, a touch of color, warmth of all kinds, are as essential as are good teachers. If a modicum of entertainment is on the program, see that it is to be wholesome, clean, engaging, not intoxicating.

7. Do not seek to save money for the union when it is necessary to spend some. If what is undertaken is successful, nobody will mind the cost. If it is unsuccessful, the economy argument will be a lame, ineffectual excuse.

8. Fall back as little as possible on such flat truisms as: "people are tired of speeches" or "discussion is the thing." Good speeches are listened to eagerly; flat discussions are exasperating. Make sure that what you offer is good and likely to be helpful.

9. Any project presented should be calculated on a limited duration run: an anxious "*encore*" is preferable to a tired "*enough*." However, each engagement should be conceived in a sequence to all or most others: they are to be battles in a war.

10. There is no such thing as "workers" or "union members" *in general*. They are all humans of individual distinction and each person is a distinct entity at a given time, in a given place and under given circumstances. Hence no education planning can be done usefully *in the abstract*. Not every program is good for all people. It should be calculated to meet a specific audience.

A story that went the rounds of upper level officers several decades ago may illustrate this point. A leading labor chief went as a member of a U.S. government mission to visit several allied nations, Russia included, during World War I, in 1917. Russia was at the time in the mid-honeymoon period of the revolution that had overthrown czarism and was painfully searching its road ahead. Bolshevism was battling to overcome the forces of social democracy. The mission was received in grand style by the Moscow Soviet, which was then the battleground of contending theories of state and of contrasting ways of life. The U.S. labor man held forth at the State gathering with a prepared speech. The address, however, evoked snickers while it was being delivered in English, and downright laughter when done into Russian. Puzzled and annoyed, the labor man asked his fellow-members on the mission what was so funny about his address.

"Well," they told him, "the union label in Russia, now . . ."

"O heck," the labor leader exclaimed, "that was the union label speech I had planned to deliver in Japan!"

There at that time it might have been well received. And perhaps not. It was a sure winner at a Rhode Island labor picnic, though.

J. B. S. HARDMAN

1. The Regional Cultural Conference

Educational activity can be initiated by union officers and—with good luck—it may "take." Or such activity may develop in response to a clear call from the rank-and-file membership, something that happens very rarely. But, however the germ enters the union body, the most essential element to educational success and continuance is the strong feeling for union participation that the activity succeeds in arousing in the members of the union. Feeling for the union, rather than a "thirst for knowledge" is the driving force in union education, at least as it is carried on in the present setting of unionism.

If it is to "take," the educational project must be able to engage the interest of the more alert and hence more responsive workers, those not yet fully absorbed in the day-to-day activity of the organization, but with a developing interest in unionism. The "mandate" of the union educationalist is to make the enrolled worker "a better union member," his work beginning only after the worker "joins up." The union educationalist's job is to cultivate in the unionized worker a sense of intellectual and emotional cohesion, a clear consciousness of union purpose coupled with broad appreciation of the duties as well as the rights of a citizen in a functional democracy. To put it differently: to link the feeling for the *organization* with a conscious commitment to the *movement*.

Locating Educational Timber

Unions have a kind of unrecorded social register, the people who invariably serve as delegates and fulfill other functions of distinction. Those are the members who have arrived. And then there are those who are interested in getting there but who are either not ambitious enough or not confident that they are adequately equipped. They are the educational prospects. The problem of the educational organizer is to meet them halfway, while they are eager, before they have hardened. The reference here is to education with a union content, not to entertainment, however legitimate the latter may be in its own right.

One means of locating and "processing" educational timber that proved to be very effective was the Regional Cultural Conference, devised and developed by the ACWA from 1938 to 1944.

Announcing the first six Regional Cultural Conferences, the union's national education department formulated its purpose in the following manner:

Amalgamated members know well that anything they can do separately they can do better together.

Many of our local organizations have maintained very successful recreation and educational activities—but their neighbors next door know little about it.

Locals wanting to start out with classes, or baseball, or dramatics, had to start from scratch, feeling their way along the same problems that other locals had already met and solved successfully.

Those days are over. All those efforts will be pooled together, experiences exchanged. And the result will be a coherent, streamlined cultural program for all of our members everywhere.

Information and know-how could presumably be passed on via organizers, but the real task was to find the local force among the slightly above the rank-and-file level of union members. They were sought out and identified in the process of launching and running the cultural get-togethers in the various regions. The conferences brought out hundreds of men and women eager and ready to try to educate themselves for union activity, and of these a great many proved of considerable value. In subsequent years, to meet wartime urgencies, the device was used to rally and to mobilize rank-and-file strength in the effort to locate and defeat fascist trends at home, making the whole membership conversant with the issue of broad democracy and bringing the problems of defense, maximum production, and national unity in war right into the factories and the homes. With wartime restrictions on travel, the character of the conferences had changed from inter-city to intra-city meetings, with delegates chosen from the shops within each city. The term *delegates* is not literally correct since participants were largely chosen—not elected—by the local organizations. Yet they were expected to, and nearly always did, report back to the local unions and sometimes to shop meetings on what they had done at the conferences and what was planned for the future. Soon after the conference, each delegate received from the national office a report of the proceedings of the conference, thus enabling him to fulfill more effectively his function as carrier of the educational message.

The number of conferees at each meeting was calculated to reach but not exceed 150. The area from which a conference was convened was kept at a radius of some 150 to 200 miles, making it possible for delegates to reach the gathering and to get back home within a weekend. Conferences generally started at 1 o'clock on Saturday and adjourned by 2 P.M. on Sunday.

The standard program for the Regional Cultural Conferences, as worked out by the national education department, and modified in many instances to suit the requirements of the locals, was conducted along the following lines:

First Session: Saturday, 1:30 P.M.

1. Opening of the Conference—Call to Order
                              Appointments
2. Dedication of the Conference
3. Mass Singing—"America"; "Solidarity Forever"
4. Welcome by Local Union Manager

5. The National Education Department Program—Presentation by General Office Representative

6. Reports from Local Units

7. Discussion of Education Program

8. Financing of Cultural Activities—Raising Funds
                                        Appropriations

9. Appointment of Committees on: Sports; Social Activities; Chorus; Dramatics; Dancing; Correspondence Courses
    Adjournment at 5 P.M.

Second Session: Saturday, 8 P.M.

10. Program by Delegations—Choral Numbers; Dramatic Skits

11. Delegates' Get-Together—Games; Dancing; Refreshments
    Adjournment at midnight

Third Session: Sunday, 9:30 A.M.

12. Committee Reports

13. Inter-City Meets

14. Publicity—Notices for the Press; Posters; Use of the Union Press; Popularizing Activities

15. Broadening the Program—Using WPA Facilities; Cooperation with Other Unions; Acting in Civic Matters

16. Luncheon, 1 P.M.

17. Summary of Conference Work by the Director of the National Education Department

Local group representatives presenting reports and delegates participating in the work of the various committees and engaging in the general discussions were keenly observed for a show of educational material. A report to the union's convention by its General Executive Board states that 862 delegates from 197 local unions in 80 cities in 19 states took part in these conferences in the fall and winter of 1939–40.

"The national leadership of the ACWA," states the report, "made a point of linking the cultural program with the major concern of the union movement: with freedom, security and democracy." A report to the 1944 convention, four years later, is outspokenly enthusiastic: "It is no exaggeration to say that these conferences were a brilliant success. They achieved, virtually in every instance, a degree of intellectual and emotional cohesion unsurpassed in other forms of similar activity. Other unions have followed the example."

The reading of the *Dedication* was an impressive part of the program of the Regional Cultural Conferences. It was first used to open a cultural conference in the Fall of 1938; it was later used on a number of different occasions as well as at succeeding conferences:

Dedication

We are citizens of a democratic nation, the sons and daughters of a democratic people. We are born of democracy, we live by democracy. We stand sworn to defend it, expand it and preserve it as the heritage of those who shall come after us. Though all the powers of earth strive to take it from us, they shall be shattered against the unbreakable rock of our resolution.

We shall defend our democracy as citizens, as workers, as a labor movement. We shall practice democracy within our own ranks. We shall be bound together by unbreakable ties, one living, harmonious whole, unbroken by differences of nationality, race, creed, sex or color.

We shall prepare for our battles through building our organized strength, through the constructive use of our leisure hours. United in the Amalgamated Clothing Workers of America, we take this pledge:

That our minds shall be quickened by study of the world around us;

That we shall be refreshed and our bodies strengthened by sports and healthy play;

That our lives shall be made rich by the cultural achievement of the ages;

That drama, music, art in every form, shall stir our hearts and broaden our vision;

That as we work together, so shall we relax together;

That our union shall grow strong through the ties of fellowship;

And that our hearts, our brains, our strength, our courage shall grow in the cause of the common good.

Thus shall we serve our free nation and the free peoples of the earth. To this cause we are dedicated.

It is no overstatement to say that to many of these delegates to the regional cultural assemblies, the experience remained a cherished memory. The immediate reward to the union was greater participation in its work, a keener sense of adhesion to the national community.

In the years that followed the war, the activity was continued.

ESTHER PETERSON

2. Active Workers School

The Active Workers School was intended primarily to put across education without facing the usual handicaps of classroom education: —dull sessions and declining attendance. To that end, the program was concentrated into a three to four week period, each of the several classes meeting twice a week. High officials of the union and prominent local educators were pressed into service for this relatively short period, thus achieving a blend of theoretical knowledge and practical union experience. The faculty worked on the basis of carefully prepared outlines of studies.

Teaching Staff

Engaging the union officers in discussing the program was one way of making the venture a part of "the union's business." Another means to that end was keeping the Active Workers School at the union building even if it was not always the most comfortable arrangement.

Good teachers for adult education are not always readily available. Competence is, of course, of cardinal significance; but of especial importance in this case of speedy education was a working familiarity with union people and their industrial and economic background. Accordingly, efforts were made to engage persons thus equipped for the undertaking in each city. In this respect, government employees and men and women in the newspaper field were of help. In Chicago, for instance, the faculty included a department head in the Illinois State Department of Labor; the Chief Supervisor and another member of the Wage and Hour Division; a professor of the University of Chicago who was a City Alderman and subsequently became a U.S. Senator; the foreign editor of a large daily newspaper; and the head of Hull House settlement.

The faculty met to consider specific requirements of teaching in the three-weeks course, and exchanged views as to the peculiar requirements of the students.

School Program

The program of courses was laid out by the national education center and included the usual variety with such modifications as were deemed advisable by the faculty in each city. The prevailing curriculum of the Active Workers School, prepared by the union in the year 1940, included:

Lecture Courses:
  1. This World of Ours—a History of Civilization
  2. Democracy, Aims and Practices
  3. The Old and the New Deal

Officers' Institute:
  1. Labor in the Defense Emergency
  2. Evolution of ACWA Policy

"Learning How" or "Tool" Courses:
  1. Public Speaking and Writing
  2. Collective Bargaining
  3. Parliamentary Procedure

Central in the program of the Active Workers School was the *Officers' Institute*, in which all local union Executive Board members, Joint Board delegates, and officers were asked to take part. In six sessions, over a period of three weeks, the assembled union workers studied the evolution of union policy over three decades of the union's history with regard to strikes, wages, collective bargaining, arbitration, politics and legislation, organizing tactics and methods. Brief but pointed statements leading up to the discussions were made by the guest speaker of the evening, usually a member of the General Executive Board, a general officer, or a leading out-of-town union manager. After that the floor was opened for discussion and only in rare cases was there enough time to satisfy the demand for more discussion. The sessions of the *Officers' Institute* were among the liveliest in the school's experience.

Enrollment and Operation

The rapid-fire method of the undertaking aimed, of course, at escaping decline in attendance or a slackening of interest. But it was for a considerably longer period than three weeks that the educative process was kept afloat. What follows is a typical extension of the schooling in 1949:

October 11, Tuesday: the education representative of the union's national office appears before the Board of Directors of the Joint Board to suggest the launching of the undertaking. Following all-around discussion, favorable action is taken—recommend the proposition to the Joint Board.

October 13, Thursday: the Directors recommend to the meeting of the Joint Board that the matter be acted upon favorably. The national representative outlines the program as the kind of campaign to assure good enrollment, to be completed before the school gets going. Delegates of the various local affiliates ask questions, receive answers, express opinions, make suggestions as to plans of the drive and character of the program. The recording secretary spreads the essence of discussion and the decision "upon the minutes" and the latter are mailed to the affiliated local unions, to be supplemented by oral reports to be made by the delegates. Each local is urged by the Joint Board to appoint an educational recruiting committee if it does not already have one; the locals also are supplied with necessary "literature," posters, folders, subscription blanks and the like. School is to be run from November 12 to December 9, the time between October 18 and November 11 to be utilized to popularize the school. In the meantime, the educational staff and faculty are properly cornered, teachers are secured, and programs and instruction methods gone over— all paraphernalia are prepaid. The classrooms are put in order with a clear concern about making it all attractive and comfortable: good chairs, effective lighting, a touch of color here and there, writing paper, blackboards, folders, etc.

November 12, Saturday: all the enrollees assemble; also present are the prospective teachers. Each head in charge of a course describes what his subject will deal with, and members who might have registered for a course they thought was something different are free to shift enrollment.

The occasion, plus a quick service of coffee and sandwiches, is used for getting acquainted—"students" with "faculty."

In several cities where local unions hold meetings more often than once a month, the union administrations agreed to call off all but one for the School's duration so as to enable local executive board members and active workers to attend classes without neglecting their organization.

November 14, Monday, through December 2, Friday: classes are in progress five days each week, each class meeting twice a week, and students asked to take on not more than three courses at most.

December 3, Saturday: in the morning of the day and for as long as wanted, the students and teachers meet to re-examine the entire venture in the light of the experience just gone through. In most cases these "alumni" gatherings evoke great interest, plans are set for other educational ventures.

December 9, Friday: commencement, as it were, at a dinner affair with appropriately contrived entertainment by educational and cultural talent of the organization; "diplomas" are presented by the teachers; the union heads and invited guests take part, say the things that fit the occasion.

The Net Result

The experience with the short-term Active Workers Schools and Officers' Institutes gave confirming emphasis to several points of moment to the problem of adult workers' education. These are:

1. Regular and full attendance is not attainable even in the short-term school, but more persons attend a proportionately larger number of sessions in the short-term schools than in classes drawn out over a number of months.

2. The short duration of the educational enterprise keeps the participant's interest alive over a *proportionately* longer period of time, and hence more is accomplished in the six sessions in three weeks than in six sessions in three months.

3. The concentrated method that induces the participant to take up two and more subjects at the same time results in greater mental activity and gives him a broader view of the general field with which the educational project deals. If greater penetration into the depths of a particular subject isn't achieved, more interest over a wider area is aroused. And—depth is not reached anywhere and anyhow.

4. To a considerable degree the venture was successful because the local union administrations did more than give consent: the leading officers actively participated and gave close personal attention to various phases of the program. Real success would hardly have been possible on any other basis. There was no failure in securing interest on the part of the members where the officers were willing to make the program a part of the union's program of action.

5. Because a large number of people are generally engaged in the school period, hundreds meeting each other, working together over several weeks, participating in the opening and closing exercises, something in the nature of a collegiate or encampment fellowship is developed.

6. A vital sideline of the venture was that the union's headquarters became, for the duration of the "college term," a "campus" with attendance in some instances running up to 500 men and women going eagerly from class to class, listening, speaking up, taking notes. In fact, to make studies useful and interesting and to make active participation by all possible, parallel classes in the more popular courses were run. There was no overcrowding. That fact, together with the general discussion sessions at the start and at the end, and the closing jamboree graduation exercises, again with several hundred assembled over tables and no front-benchers' segregation, tended to bring officers and members into the kind of contact for which business as usual offers no occasion.

ARTHUR STARK

3. Education by Mail

Many persons active in the field of adult and workers' education recognize the fact that, despite a very real enthusiasm that may attend the first session of a purely voluntary class, attendance among adults drops off fairly rapidly. It is not at all unusual for a group of 30 to drop to 10 after the second or third session. This decline in attendance in many instances bears little relationship to the quality of the instruction.

Advantages and Disadvantages of the Method

People who live far from the meeting place of the class are discouraged by the inconvenience of getting to and from. Others drop out if they miss a session or two. And many other factors play a part in the failure of adults to maintain attendance at classes. Initiating the correspondence method of education, the Department of Cultural Activities of the Amalgamated Clothing Workers of America hoped to remove the deterrents of physical inconvenience and of missed sessions. Its purpose was to bring education to the interested union member, directly into his home, via the postman. It would leave to him the decision as to time and place in which he could devote himself to studying the printed word. This method of education, of course, has both advantages and disadvantages, which are stated here as economically as possible.

The advantages of the correspondence method of study are obvious. Members are able to do their studying at home in their leisure time. If they had to attend a class they might find that 8 o'clock of a Tuesday evening would be unsuitable; but through the correspondence method, the material can be studied and answered at any time of the day, any day of the week.

Should a student fall behind in his work, he has his back chapters on hand and can catch up in a few hours of diligent work. Moreover, the member who lives in an isolated community can have access to union education without waiting for a class to be formed.

In addition to the advantages of time and place, he also has the convenience of individual learning pace. The correspondence course student proceeds at his own pace without embarrassment to himself because of undue slowness and without the irritation so often experienced by the rapid learner who is held back in a classroom by the not so quick and bright.

There is also no need to strain to catch the concept in the teacher's spoken word before it fades upon the hearing. The student can refer to the printed page as frequently as may be necessary for clarification or verification.

Then there is the individual attention that can be provided, since each set of responses is individually graded and points that are not clear to the individual student can be straightened out through the correspondence between grader and student.

It is also possible, as has actually happened in a number of instances, that other members of the family become interested in one of the union correspondence courses and study it along with the union mother, or father, wife or husband. In one year there were three instances of high school and in one case of college age children studying the courses along with the parent.

As to the disadvantages of the correspondence method, these are largely in the unavoidable absence of personal contact between member and instructor and the lack of the stimulation brought about by such contact. There is also the absence of sharing ideas and comparing similar and dissimilar experiences with other union members, which tend to enrich direct educational activity and make it more interesting. Statements, concepts, or conclusions that might, in a study class, be the subject of extended analysis and discussion, are eliminated in the correspondence method or, at best, are condensed into a categorical sentence or paragraph in the correspondence course or the grading letter.

The advanced student may often be at a disadvantage because he cannot pursue the subject by class discussion of finer points. Inasmuch as the courses are prepared so that every average-educated and intelligent member of the organization can participate if interested, the material has to be elementary in language and fairly limited in scope.

The correspondence student can, of course, raise the various points in his course with the Department of Cultural Activities, but articulateness with pen and paper is not easy even for the advanced union member. The hardship of writing may have played a large part in the gradual decline in questions answered at the end of each chapter.

Also, although the freedom to choose the time and place to study is an advantage for many, it may be a disadvantage for many others, since the presence of other household members is likely to be a distracting deterrent. It requires a good deal of self-discipline to study at home unless one has a room of his own, a luxury not enjoyed by many workers.

Processing the Study Material

Two groups of correspondence courses were developed and offered through the several years of the experience reported here: *tool* courses, intended to provide a background for trade union work, and *cultural* courses, intended to help the member express himself more effectively in his union meetings or to be a source of purely personal gratification. The tool courses included collective bargaining, trade union problems, clothing unionism and economics, labor in American history, and the history and program of the CIO. The cultural courses were public speaking, aid to writing, and reading to advantage.

Most courses were divided into 10 installments or chapters, mailed to subscriber-students spaced about two to three weeks apart to enable the recipient to study and to carry out the exercises or answer the questions which went with each unit. Students were not to subscribe to more than two courses at a time.

In most cases the material was prepared by the staff of the Department of Cultural Activities. In a few instances, the course was written by a specialist in some phase of economics or history, not himself of the union staff. Preparatory to work on material, the director outlined the course, discussed the program, made assignments of chapters to members of the staff best qualified to do the particular chapters, and then the writing was done. As many as five different staff members, including the Director, might author a particular course. To cite the Public Speaking Course as an example, it had eleven chapters, Chapters 1 and 8 were written by one staff member; 2, 4, and 10 prepared by another; 6 and 11 by yet a third, Chapter 3 by another staff person and Chapters 5, 7, and 9 by the Assistant Director. Chapters were frequently read by all the participating staff members and suggestions made for conformity of style and language, and level of instruction. All the contributors to the public speaking course were given the following instructions by the Director as a guide in preparing the text:

Instructions to staff members cooperating in the preparation of the course in public speaking:

1. *This is not a general course in public speaking.* We want to render *first aid* in speaking at meetings to our active members; we also hope that our advice may prove of value to those who are recognized as good speakers but haven't had professional training.

2. The advice given and the examples drawn to illustrate or emphasize

points should come, if at all possible, from ACWA union practice and experience.

3. As examples for analysis and study we will take excerpts from a few of the best speeches of FDR, John L. Lewis and Abraham Lincoln.

4. An installment should contain from 2,000 to 3,000 words; 12 is the maximum of installments.

5. Each installment is to call for one or more *exercises*. Since subscribers will be urged to set up local study groups for this course, the exercises ought to be devised to be workable in such gatherings.

Production of the study courses on the premises had its disadvantages. Delivery was not always prompt. It was frequently a nip and tuck race between fingers at the end of the typewriter and the calendar date on which installments were scheduled to go out. On the other hand, because it was "homemade" by persons with a knowledge of the background, environment, and needs of the prospective students, the material was free from certain defects that ordinarily go with academic manufacture. It was handled more realistically, more adequately adjusted to the mental equipment of the users. Furthermore, the fact that staff members were contributing authors of the studies as well as "graders" of the students' replies was particularly helpful at the end of the year when the contents of each course were reorganized, reedited, often rewritten in the light of the past year's experience.

On the whole, courses were revised each year. On the basis of the subscribers' answers, an attempt was made to weed out or clarify sections of a chapter or to restate or to remove questions that proved to be some trouble or were misunderstood. These were rewritten for clarification, and of course, all facts and figures were brought up to date. Frequently fresh examples were introduced for better illustration. In some cases a new interpretation of material was given because of changes in economic and political circumstances or currents.

Correspondence course students were expected to answer comprehension-test questions or carry out exercises assigned at the end of each course installment or unit. The answers were read and marked or graded immediately and sent back to the subscriber with a letter explaining where the student went wrong. In grading the papers, the grader tried to avoid discouraging the student. This task took the time of several staff members of the Department of Cultural Activities. If there had been no change in personnel, the graders were the persons who had written the courses. The traditional A—Excellent, B—Good, C—Fair, D—Poor were used to grade the papers.

Of course, a record was kept of the entire proceeding. As soon as a subscriber's name came in, a master record card was made on which all subsequent data of the correspondence courses were entered. Other cards were made out for each subject and addressing stencils cut for each subject. When the grader finished marking the answers, he turned the report over to the girl in charge of the record cards. Each card showed the number of answers that had been received, and the grades given for those answers.

Student-subscribers, on completing a course, were given a *Certificate of Merit* written and designed in the manner of school diplomas. Whenever possible, the certificates were presented in impressive ceremony at a union meeting accompanied by the leading officer pointing out the value of study.

Recruiting Correspondence Students, and Response

Student-subscribers were secured in a number of ways:

1. Writing letters to members of the union, particularly in outlying districts and small towns;
2. Addressing the members of the local union executive boards and committees urging them to subscribe, such urging often done by the local union managers;
3. Distributing attractive descriptive leaflets and displaying posters at local gatherings;
4. Soliciting subscription by staff members of the Department of Cultural Activities in the several cities where such were on hand;
5. Graduates of previous years calling on their friends suggesting that they join: little pins were given to members who secured the subscribers;
6. Calling for subscription in the union's central publication *The Advance;* a few months before the courses were scheduled to begin, application blanks were printed in the journal and members were urged to subscribe.

The last two methods were the most effective. There was no charge to the subscribers of the courses in the beginning. Later on a charge of 50 cents was made to each subscriber, whether he took one course or two. The purpose of the charge was to eliminate subscription out of mere curiosity. However, this did not turn out to be a real test. The fee made no difference in the percentage of the subscribers who failed to answer questions when they had received the study course. When the charge of 50 cents was imposed, the office added a loose-leaf binder notebook and a record card to the material mailed to each subscriber.

In 1938–39, five courses were offered and 900 members responded, taking 1,600 units in all.

In 1939–40, six courses were offered and the response was: 1,500 members, 2,200 units.

The figures for 1940–41 show seven courses, 1,700 subscriptions, and close to 2,500 units. In that year, for the first time, the charge of 50 cents was made.

In the winter of 1941–42, promotion of the correspondence courses was suspended since the workers were pressed to work long days and also urged to engage in civilian defense activities in their spare hours. However, subscriptions continued to come in. The work was carried on that year on a considerably reduced scale.

In the first of the three years for which enrollment figures are here indicated, 250 people received *Certificates of Merit*, compared with a total enrollment of 900 in 1938–39; and about 500 in 1939–40 against 1,500 enrollees.

The percentage of "graduates" is really higher than it appears at first glance, in view of the fact that about one-third of the enrolled consistently failed to respond right from the start. The rather heavy number of those failing to carry on correspondence—or more accurately, to do the required exercises—did not testify to that much lack of interest. Investigation brought evidence that many students felt that they were gaining much through receiving and reading the chapters, even though they lacked the energy or the time to complete the assignments. Considerable numbers specifically requested that they be continued on the mailing lists stating that failure to respond did not indicate disinterest, only that they could not do the required homework.

Seasonality of the industry in which the activity was carried on almost invariably divided the courses in half. Ten installments of a course took about 20 to 25 weeks and that period was often interrupted, somewhere in the middle, by the pressure of long work days in high season. In fact, it was usually around the fifth installment that responses started slackening.

The activity incurred considerable expenses. It involved receiving from 250 to 350 letters a week all the year 'round. Most of the time, direct answers were required in addition to exercises to be checked, graded, and recorded. The material was mimeographed in the earlier years, but later was printed on loose-leaf ledger sheets with illustrations added to the texts. The spread of 1,498 subscribers over the states in one year was as follows: New York—384; Pennsylvania—230; Massachusetts—108; New Jersey—52; Indiana—88; Illinois—61; Michigan—44; Maryland—80; Connecticut—37; California—26; North Carolina—26; Ohio—52; Virginia—39; Iowa—38; Kentucky—44; Missouri—28; Minnesota—23; Texas—23; all others—115.

Possibilities and Limitations of the Method

Study by correspondence will always have the inherent handicap of having to give accurate and full information or concepts within a limited number of words in a chapter and of having to hit all levels of intelligence and schooling at the same time. Planning from the outset for elementary and advanced courses in a subject might overcome that difficulty to some extent. It is also possible that any one course might be broken up into two integrated units of five chapters each with an adequate interval between the units so that the student who falls behind in answering his chapters in the first unit might feel less overwhelmed if he tried to catch up with the first unit before embarking upon the next group of five chapters.

The stimulation of group study might be achieved if within a local a group of subscribers to the same course could be encouraged to meet together on receipt of their chapters and use a group secretary, discussing the content, answering the questions, and receiving a group grading. In two instances, that did happen one year and the groups held up comparatively well. A list of the subscribers in any one locality might be made available to each individual subscriber, so that they might discuss their studies.

The correspondence course has no adequate substitute as a means for reaching the remotest hamlet and the union member isolated after working hours from his fellow-members. Letters from subscribers in small locals and in isolated towns indicate gratitude and pleasure at the opportunity to learn about the union, and show that the correspondence course satisfied a real need in these instances. Many unionists confessed in their letters that the courses cleared up their misconceptions about the purposes of unions in general and theirs in particular, and gave them insight into the labor movement hitherto unrealized.

The correspondence course has a real place in the education program of a union. It is by no means the complete answer, and should not be, but is one of the as yet comparatively unexplored channels for reaching a farflung, scattered membership with a uniform, coherent expression of the international union's educational philosophy, method, and content.

Monthly Readers' Packet

Closely related to the *Education by Mail* part of the program was the Monthly Readers' Packet, which consisted of a monthly mailing to subscribing members (at $1.50 a yr.) of an assortment of selected pamphlets, an occasional small book that seemed to be timely and to merit attention, and specially prepared items of reading matter that appeared to be interesting and relevant. Each month the Packet also contained a 32-page supplement presenting in pro and con argument-discussion the essential points of the major public issue of the month.

The Readers' Packet cemented by its continuity the work of the other three units of the Education Package: the Active Workers School, the Regional Conference, and the Correspondence Courses.

The Packet supplemented the Education Package in that, besides presenting reading matter, its function was to induce and encourage members to get together for talks and intelligent sociability. The material formulated points of discussion, suggested exercises, offered a quiz.

Readers were urged to send in clippings from the press, references to broadcasts—anything that offered a basis for discussion and for clarifying issues of union policy, union economics, defense matters, democracy, and the like.

In the years since the war, as reported by the ACWA Director of Education, "the book club [an adaptation of the earlier Packet] has become surprisingly popular with the membership."

AGNES M. DOUTY
LAWRENCE LEVIN

Chapter 43

The union educational film

ACCEPTANCE OF THE MOTION PICTURE IS WIDESPREAD IN LABOR UNIONS; BUT the role that the film can play in our everyday operations is not so widely understood.

We are all familiar with the "movie" in the neighborhood theater. Most of us would like to see the program, the ideals, and the problems of labor presented to our own membership, as well as to the nonunion public, through the medium of the film. Without question, the film can command the undivided attention of an audience while our story is being presented in an interesting and entertaining way. The possibilities of arousing an emotional reaction, or putting across essential information are unlimited with the use of the film. The film can be the "show-how" of labor union activity.

Labor faces two big problems in the use of film. The first is tying the use of the film to our union program—as an essential rather than as an incidental feature. The second problem is stockpiling films that treat the problems and interests of labor.

The United Automobile, Aircraft and Agricultural Implement Workers of America (UAW-CIO), through its Film Division of the Education Department, is tackling both of these problems with considerable success. But the satisfactory solution to the problem of getting more labor films will hinge on combining the efforts of more than one union, even though that union has over a million members. And this solution, in turn, will depend upon a more widespread knowledge of effective use of the film in the union program.

About 30 16mm sound films have been produced by various unions in the United States. Add the films produced by labor groups in other countries; the films produced by labor-minded groups in this country; and all those films that have been produced on subjects of interest to labor, and we have a list of about 400 films. Figuring in the entertainment films pushes the number of useful films well over the 2,000 mark.

Most of these films can be rented or purchased through one of the 250 film libraries in the United States. Most of these film libraries are operated commercially; many are operated by universities; and more recently, the public libraries have made the distribution of films a part of their program. Distribution of labor films is more limited. A number of democratic organizations and a few labor unions have three or four prints of film on hand for their own members and interested groups. About six of the commercial film libraries carry labor films on a rental basis. But there are only four labor film libraries of any size in our country: the UAW-CIO Film Library, the CIO Film Division, the ILGWU Film Library, and the jointly operated Amalgamated Clothing-Textile Workers Film Library.

The UAW-CIO Film Library has been operating since 1938. The longtime interest of the UAW-CIO in the use of film has developed the best-stocked union film library in the world. During the war, the UAW-CIO worked closely with the 16mm National Advisory Committee. Over 15 million persons saw films presented under the UAW-CIO auspices from 1942 through 1945. Since the war many of our films have been retired, and we now have 650 prints of over 400 different films. The present valuation of our films alone is $12,500.

About 375 local unions use these films regularly for meetings, classes, or other occasions. A total of 195 sound projectors owned by local unions are available for showing films. Other locals rent or borrow projectors for their film programs. The UAW-CIO has established an equipment-buying service to enable local unions to purchase satisfactory projection equipment at the lowest costs. Twenty-three sound projectors have been purchased in the last six months.

In addition to servicing the needs of local unions, the UAW-CIO Film Library is distributing films to schools, churches, public libraries, and communities all over the country. The importance of showing films with a labor message outside our unions can hardly be overestimated. Many local unions are called upon to bring their projectors and films to the rescue of a community program.

Brotherhood of Man, an animated cartoon on fair practices, produced by the UAW-CIO, has had an interesting history of community acceptance. This film has achieved the honor of being the most widely distributed informational film of its type. Four hundred and fifty prints of this film have been sold to film libraries, schools, churches, and community organizations for rental or loan to thousands of film users. The income from the sale of these prints has already defrayed about half of the original cost of production.

Of course, this film has been discriminated against in many places, particularly in the South. Southern gentlemen in our War Department have blocked the overseas distribution of foreign-language versions of *Brotherhood of Man.* On the other hand, we have the unprecedented case of securing 35mm theatrical distribution after three years of 16mm showings.

The UAW-CIO has had other success in producing 16mm films and filmstrips. *Building Industrial Democracy*, *United Action*, *Saga of 666*, *Svenson's Seniority*, and others have built up a better understanding of unionism with UAW-CIO members. Our film *Brother John* explains what the rank-and-file union member finds behind the union meeting. *Brother John* is also headed for a wide distribution. Several prints are going overseas under ECA sponsorship.

Our present film in production, *Workers' Security Through Collective Bargaining*, which explains the UAW-CIO 1949 demands, introduces new techniques of the automatic sound filmstrip medium. This new medium compares favorably with the effectiveness of movies and promises a partial answer to the production of more films that are specific to union needs. Low-cost production of films means that more films on more subjects will be available. And it also means that unions cannot afford to pass up the use of films in their regular program.

Most union users of film start out by using the movie as an added attraction to membership meetings. They soon find that the film offers far more than entertainment. The film becomes a vital tool in the hands of the local education committee. Films in membership meetings, in committee meetings, in discussion groups or film forums, in union hall or summer school classes, in political campaigns, and in community organizations offer a new horizon for action. And organized action is the life blood of union growth and achievement.

HERBERT B. JACKMAN

Chapter 44

Labor education a
complicated thing

*I*N THE 30 YEARS [1] SINCE ITS RECOGNITION AS A DISTINCTIVE UNION ACTIVITY, labor education has gained considerably in scope and volume. Yet it still remains a "thing of the future."

Progress was conspicuous in the mid-30's when new unions arose in many industries. These unions saw utilitarian merit in the "intellectual" engagement that had hitherto been considered immaterial and irrelevant. Because of this wider recognition and somewhat more generously allotted material resources, the activity was able to reach out into new and more attractive fields.

Educational workers received a new lease on life, to be sure. But it cannot be said that they were convinced that union education was really making significant headway. Indeed, the story of the American labor educational effort is one of intermittent attempts to overcome union officers' "sales resistance'" by offering well-diluted "useful" education while at the same time struggling to retain a modicum of intellectual quality in what was handed down to the union members as education.

Resistance and Counterresistance

Except for certain instances of sheer ignorance, union officers' resistance to "educational fancies" has had a not altogether implausible *raison d'etre*. Belief in the essentially satisfactory service rendered by our system of public schooling has been one reason for less than ready acceptance of labor education. Free, democratic, and obligatory, our public schools really prepare and equip our youngsters much better than is done anywhere else to face the tasks of mature life. And an ever-growing number of workers' children in this generation, as our living standards rise, are

---

[1] Earlier efforts had been made in the labor movement, but had been limited largely to the several unions in the so-called "needle trades."

474

enabled to enter and complete high school or vocational training school. Having played an historic part in bringing our system of tax-paid and universal public education into being, labor has confidence in the institution. If justified criticism is made of certain phases of the public educational performance, the job to be done, say the labor leaders, is to seek to reform the system rather than to try to supplant or to duplicate it by developing an educational institution of labor's own. And the union officers further point to the growing number of universities that are extending their facilities and staff cooperation to labor groups for conferences and institutes and even offering to union-selected trainees access to regular study courses in politics, economics, and industrial relations without the usual academic admission requirements and, of course, without degrees.

Labor educationalists, accepting this fact of United States reality for what it is, have nonetheless continued to see a need for doing a supplementary job within the union movement, a job distinct and different from the assignment of the public educational system and from what is being offered by the universities. The public education system, the labor educationalists maintain, fails to prepare their pupils for realistic and progressive coping with the social and political situations they are bound to meet as they enter mature life and join in the struggle for economic sufficiency and gain. That failing of the public education system cannot be easily remedied since issues of social and political orientation are at stake, and action upon such issues is unavoidably slow and must be prodded from the outside by pressure and competitive example.

The current concern of the institutions of higher learning with the problem of training aspirants to jobs in union administrative service and leadership is no doubt helpful, but it does not meet the total bill nor does it seek to do so. There is room, the labor educationalists have maintained, for a kind of coordinated, cooperative action by the union administrators, the labor educational enterprise, and those in the related university setups who appreciate what is happening in the political and economic recesses of American society, what Professor Sumner H. Slichter calls the emergence of the Laboristic Society. Together they could test, pragmatically and experimentally, the changes in educational practice made necessary by the need for ever more millions to "live with the union." Cooperation is wanted, not the substitution of university handouts for union-made labor education. This kind of cooperation has not often been practiced.

The argument failed to convince the mighty. The men of union "action" do not care for "theory"; they distrust the "long-hairs." Some fear education will "run away with the union." Others say, not without a measure of truth, that the study class "graduate" is likely to view the "certificate of merit" he receives as a license for a paid union job.

It is not likely that Yale President A. Whitney Griswold's "education is a part of the process of government" would be underwritten by the run-of-the-mill union officer. If he did go along with it, the "process of government" would not be turned over to "outsiders." However, the rapprochement between action and theory is a basic postulate of all education. To quote Mr. Alexander Meiklejohn: "Theory which does not guide action is idle and worthless. Action which is not guided by theory is stupid and self-defeating . . . As men seek to live intelligently, theory and action are bound together in holy wedlock."

This holds water in relation to modern unionism even if the older variety could have read itself out of any connection with "ultimates," "long-range issues" and other such "sophistications." And, true as it may be that organization is itself education, "the school of hard knocks" is not the total source of union wisdom. At some point in the unionist's empirical educative process, the acquiring of actual knowledge, the kind that comes through learning, is needed to supplement orientation through experience. With every day of our time, the business of being a responsible unionist grows in complexity, calls for exercise of judgment, for possession of a sense of values. Yet labor education has not recognized the importance of formal learning. The union as a whole is getting even more deeply involved in the mainstream of the intellectual contests and encounters that actuate national life, and to a constantly increasing degree, international life as well. And the individual unionist worthy of his membership card cannot in safety stay out of intellectual contact with the realities of twentieth century labor life. It is the function of labor education to achieve that "holy wedlock" of theory and action—or it just isn't education.

Utility and Value

Utilizing the favorable climate in the mid-30's and in the years immediately following and up to the war, the educational effort was broadened to include in the curriculum training courses for minor officers and shop stewards, weekend institutes, and area conferences, activities generally approved by union officers. And the addition of recreational and cultural activities, from bowling to dramatic performances, brought the serious aspects closer to the people, and what held out even greater promise for the future, legitimatized education in the eyes of at least some union administrators. In fact, the shrewder men in that category sensed in the education enterprise, thus brought "down to earth," an unexpected chance for discovering prospective rank-and-file leadership. That wasn't altogether new inspiration. Early proponents of education as a union activity had frequently pointed to the possible development of new sources of leader material as a redeeming by-product of the investment. They reasoned that knowledge of labor's fighting background, familiarity with the jargon of economic argument, general understanding of the mainsprings and urges of the political and social order, all buttressed by a workable comprehension of parliamentary rules and labor law, would equip workers who had a natural endowment for leadership with helpful practical and theoretic wherewithal.

However, these arguments on "intellectual-theoretical" prowess as a base upon which to build new leadership failed to click. Officers objected that those closeted exercises would attract only the bookish, the narrow-minded, and the stubborn—not at all leadership timber. But the new education-entertainment approach proved more appealing to union administrators. It attracts, they have held, the young, the mobile, and the not too sophisticated; the good mixers and the manageable. Observation of people in these activities should easily enable local leaders to discover those with apparent—or perhaps latent—qualities of mass appeal, those capable of carrying conviction and commanding a following. Singled out and given the needed polish and briefing, these would be the men and women the union needs as organizers and builders on the local level, not grumblers, fault-finders, and disturbers.

Considerations of utility made labor education acceptable over wider areas than before, but it cramped its content. No doubt publicity gained with the aid of educational work is a valuable asset to the union movement, but it is not education. Turning labor education into a sort of vocational training program is nothing derogatory to education, and such training is helpful to the organization, but labor education is more than vocational training. There are values of intrinsic merit in labor education that need to be produced if the undertaking is to find its true expression. The term, labor education, is a misnomer if it does not address the attention of the worker, as a member of the union, toward the broad realities with which the union must cope, both alone and in common with other unions.

Teaching the rules of parliamentary procedure, or how to file a complaint against management for violation of certain provisions of the trade agreement, or familiarizing the workers with their rights and duties under the union's constitution are important items on the labor educational program, but labor is not just a personnel problem. There is more to unionism than the business of hiring, firing, and collective bargaining. Labor as a whole, and the individual worker through his union, are a constituent part of our complex American society. The clear function of labor education is to bring the unionist into the vortex of ideas and socially significant interests that motivate the nation and impinge upon labor. There lies the central value of labor education. It is not very effective if it fails to meet the old perplexed complaint: "I wish yer'd tell me what a eddication is fer ef it don' help us ter live right an' guide us in time o' trouble"—only that "time o' trouble" now is all the time.

The Ordeal of the Labor Educationalist

Briefly, the ordeal of labor education and of its men of burden, in the lean years and in the years not so lean, comes down to the following:

1. Most unions do not see that education is what their members either need or want, or that setting up labor education is among the duties that fall upon union officers.

2. Even where union leadership, whether on the local, or the national, or on both levels, is in a mood to take on the educational commitment—and it is rarely more than a mood—the motivation is nearly always of a strictly utilitarian character. It varies from a rare, somewhat wistful "Oh, if one-tenth of them understood the movement, we'd have a powerful union" to the more frequent and realistic "A little education would be good for the new members; they'd learn union rules"; "It is good publicity"; "It brings the union in contact with useful people in the community [invited as lecturers or guest speakers or as honored visitors] and tends to improve public relations." The emphasis is on window dressing or utility rather than on basic educational value.

3. Members may in some instances have a vague notion that they'd like to learn this or that, but it is not easy for most of them to attend a study class or to do a bit of assigned reading after a full day's work. And sometimes the subjects discussed in the classroom are "too deep" and find little response in minds unaccustomed to serious thought on matters of no immediate or practical point. At this stage they lose interest and thus supply a seemingly unanswerable argument against labor education.

4. Quite often the union members in a study class, capable of participating in the "abstractions" of analysis and careful generalization, indicate that they would rather try their skill on the tangible and living problems of internal union matters. They are more interested in the realities of the industrial relations of which they are a part; but they are told that union matters must be taken up at the local meeting. Education in the classroom is not to get involved in intra-union matters or union politics. But, if union education is not education in union matters, why is the union in education?

5. The educational person on the union staff is, in many instances, met with the suspicion generally accorded the intellectual, unless he is of the widely publicized variety, and is looked upon with open cynicism by the administrative or organizing force (why doesn't he do a real job of work instead of fooling around with this kindergarten stuff?). He is not readily given sufficient means to carry on the work on a proper scale, and he is expected to show "results" not in units and values of educational progress but in publicity or in a kind of response not directly derived from the activity. Since approval is essential to the continuity of the work, the efforts of the person in charge of education are unavoidably diverted toward showy and newsy rather than educational ends.

The essence of the labor educationalist's task, within the prevailing difficult circumstances, is to produce as satisfactory a program as possible and to find ways of seeing it through with a measure of educational success while at the same time gaining sufficient appreciation by the union administration to ensure a promise of re-enactment and expansion of the program. That the resolution of this task will necessitate a compromise of certain educational concepts with union realities is quite unavoidable, but unless a limit is set on compromise, the end-product is futility with a union label on it.

Lack of wide penetration and of intellectual growth, the fact of labor educational history thus far, has not driven the workers in the field to abandon hope. In this stubborn clinging to what, at best, is a most difficult and thankless job, they have proceeded from the traditional teachers' attitude to pupils' failings: not to turn from the pupils in disgust or despair, but to seek out and try new methods of putting their ideas across. The significant difference is that it is not the pupils but the school principals who make the task so difficult.

"Emotion, Interest, Volition"

"Education is a complicated thing," wrote Mr. Frederick Lewis Allen some time ago. "I have long been amazed and amused to see how many people there are who, when they talk and write, and presumably think, about education, think of only one thing at a time; people who argue furiously for one educational principle, or educational reform, and seem to believe that if you only hold fast to this one principle, or achieve this one reform, everything else will somehow take care of itself."

Labor education faces the same phenomenon of one-track-mindedness. Its strongest adherents are likely to emphasize a single phase and see salvation in that alone. The union officer, of course, has his preference for what is "useful to the organization," for what is really vocational training. Those other things on the educational program, he thinks, can be taken care of elsewhere, by others. The intellectual, in turn, who is primarily interested in the generality of the social problem and the union's part in correlating ideas and social forces, tends to minimize the "tool" parts of labor education. He is likely to overlook or fail to appreciate fully the advantages of linking the solely "useful" with the otherwise valuable.

On the other hand, the union rank-and-file member, when he becomes education-minded, wants to learn some bigger truth than how to be a good shop steward if he should ever become one. "History of Trade Unionism," a subject for which many educationally awakened union members call, appears to most of them as a sort of eye-opener, a teacher of ways of living in a world none too friendly to them. But more often than not they are disappointed. Taken without living and driving contact with day-to-day reality, history offers no lessons applicable to an ever-changing present. To make digging into the past profitable for the future, it must be accompanied by an unhindered dissection of the present. But the latter may be and often is a touchy subject. And what is good for "the movement," as seen in the classroom, rarely coincides with what is good for "the organization" as viewed by many union officers. So the educationalist seeks to skirt the surcharged areas, but with no good results. The educationalist loses student confidence, and the student loses interest in the history of the movement, and in union education. Vital statistics of labor study classes do make disheartening reading.

What is to be done?

"Sell it to the union manager?" wonders the embattled, weary, and now cynical labor educationalist.

Well, yes, even though sales resistance is strong, and the market is the buyer's. There are but very few national unions that make a continuous practice of labor education. However, the hard-worked reference to "grass roots" applies. Local unions and interunion setups are labor education's mobile frontier.

Perhaps there has been too much readiness on the part of educational workers to fall for utility vs. value with the almost inescapable result that, having failed to carry the imagination and the enthusiasm of rank-and-file workers, they have unwittingly convinced the leaders that the members "just don't care for the thing." Union leaders shrewdly watch members' reaction; they won't sell enthusiastic response short. Educationalists could do better than clip the wings of their engagement in the search for down-to-earth "security." Part of their assignment is to create for their activity a mental climate in which the facts of social contest and conflict are subjected to open-minded and cold-blooded analysis; something akin to the Biblical "flame of fire out of the midst of a bush ... the bush burning with fire, and the bush ... not consumed."

Difficult? Certainly. Yet a reasonable way in this "line of business." In the commanding words of John Dewey, neither propagandist nor ivory-tower philosopher:

There is no education when ideas and knowledge are not translated into emotion, interest and volition. There must be constant accompanying organization and direction of organized action into practical work. "Ideas" must be linked to the practical situation, however hurly-burly that is.

Education, whether lay or labor, will thrive neither on canned goods nor on canonized truths. To succeed in the U.S. union movement, labor education must descend from the misty heights of abstract reasoning and substitute the study of the terse realities of social-economic and industrial life for the lofty rhetoric of socialist or liberal sermons on the mount. But that implies no espousal of pure "organizational" obeisance.

In a thoughtful essay on "Educating the Half-Educated" (the title referring to former Columbia President Nicholas Murray Butler's dictum: "America is the best half-educated country in the world"), Mr. Alvin Johnson observed:

The adult student has faith in the plain English language and does not like a professional vocabulary.... The adult student thinks he can live without [that].... He has an incorrigible predilection for freedom of instruction. Publish the fact that an adult educational institution selects its instructors for political and economic orthodoxy, or liberalism, or radicalism, and you soon lose all but convinced adherents, who are prompt to weary of a propaganda they are capable of promoting themselves.

The reference is to different "clients" but it fits the measure of labor education altogether adequately.

Content and Control

Two central questions bear gravely and deeply upon the problem under consideration. One is the *content* of labor education; the other is *location of control*. The two are interrelated.

As to control, the activity, to be effective educationally, must find a way of operating within the union movement yet free from the upsetting effects of prejudice by which at least sections of the movement are governed. It is quite possible that joint enterprise, by various unions, in educational work would create the necessary climate and opportunity for freedom from spirit-arresting orthodoxy, but unions have thus far not gone in for joint education, except by way of utilizing the very few summer schools for workers now in existence. It is in these that education comes closest to being itself.

It has been observed, however, that union officers, unwilling to stand for less than orthodoxy in educational endeavors when carried on at their home premises, take a more tolerant view when the adventure is cooperative and outside the union walls.

As to content, although long out of its 'teens, labor education has not yet in any final way found itself. And it really could not, since unionism itself is still in search of its detailed relevancy to the many dimensional totality of American and international living. But there is no doubt of the driving logic of the search of both unionism and education—"help us ter live right and guide us in time o' trouble." "Help" and "guide" are interrelated functions best discharged in integration.

Mr. Alvin Johnson wrote recently that Daniel Webster, one of this nation's most distinguished fathers,

...never heard of the phrase "collective bargaining."...He could not have defined the "standard of living," nor could he have conceived of the dynamic force of the phrase in the industrial relations of the nation.

Today any dictionary offers ready definitions of these terms and concepts, but how far do definitions carry one who wants to know? How well and for how long do definitions stand up in the flux of American dynamism?

Labor education is a "complicated thing" for the most abiding reason that it operates in an environment that is one of the most complicated things in the social order. Presumably a realistic "bread-and-butter" economic adventure, unionism is elusive of hard and fast definition. It is many things to many kinds of people. Living, fighting, advancing or retreating, extending in ever-varying directions, affecting multiple and conflicting interests, it is effecting sets of conditions deemed unthinkable only yesterday, reshaping economics, politics, the cultural life of the nation.

J. B. S. HARDMAN

PART EIGHT

The Union Staff—Function and Aim

Introduction

The union staff—
function and aim

*A*s UNION ACTIVITIES EXPAND IN RANGE and in scope there arises an ever greater call for expert services by trained personnel: researchers, editors, writers, teachers, lawyers, engineers, medical personnel, insurance specialists, sports and recreation directors, and possessors of various other skills and competence. On the face of it, unions do not appear to be coping with the problem in any markedly different way from that of other organizations, such as business, governmental departments, social institutions, and the like, when they are in need of men and women with a special know-how.

However, unions claim to be, or are—a matter of opinion—a movement with broad social aims, and hence their requirements are different. Except for the achievement of purely routine, if specialized, tasks, the union officers' call is for the particular competence or skill, *plus*. What is more, many among those who seek professional positions in labor unions look upon the prospect of "working in a union" as a professional job, *plus*. What is that *plus*? What does it really mean on each side of this employer-employee relationship?

A round-table discussion was arranged, presided over by the writer, to secure an insight into the union staff problem. Concise summations of the participants' statements, with "privilege to extend their remarks," were then secured, and these are presented in the following pages together with two additional statements made on another occasion but bearing on the same problem. As formulated, the problem to be clarified was: *the function and the aim of the specialized intellectual, or professional, or technician, in the performance of service in the union movement.*

The word "staff," in this instance, applies to all persons engaged by unions to perform services requiring preliminary training and either involving contact with union members, or relating directly or indirectly to union action or policy. There are no certain figures on the number of persons actually engaged in union staff work within this definition, but the number runs into the thousands on the many levels of union organization.

The nine participants in the symposium were, by occupational background: one national union leader,

485

one national union director of research, one national union education
director, one professor of economics
who was for some time Chairman of
the National Mediation Board and
member of the National Labor Relations Board, one professor of economics and for some time research
director of a national union, one editor
and for many years director of education of a national union, one professor
of industrial relations with a background of union organizing activity,
two professors of sociology with long-
standing interest in labor and related
matters.

They speak from many years of
experience and observation.

J. B. S. HARDMAN

Chapter 45

The union staff—
function and aim

1. WANTED: RESPONSIBILITY AND INITIATIVE

*L*ABOR LEADERSHIP AT THE TURN OF THE TWENTIETH CENTURY HAD A MAIN concept of force in its procedures. This was not a fault of the organized labor movement. It was the natural development of the long exercise of force, economic and political, that had been exerted by business management against unions of every sort and description. There is no need here to retrace the path of violence and denial of human rights that marked the long campaign of labor for basic recognition of the fact that workers had the right to speak collectively in matters affecting their wages, hours, and working conditions. Therefore, it must not be construed as criticism when we recognize frankly that the labor leader of 1900 needed only a few qualifications that were, however, extremely important. First and foremost was physical courage and stamina; second, intelligence that could direct the physical courage; third, the psychological ability to win and hold leadership for groups of workers who had been rendered almost inarticulate by the injustices of the economic system. The ability to seek out the suppressed thoughts of the rank and file and translate them into spoken words was important.

The labor leader's troubles were many. Leeches within the union movement called for stern repression by honest leadership, which as events have long since demonstrated, was in the majority. The ex-convicts and racketeers who sought to prey on unionism took their guidance, of course, from the current practices of industrial management. Management feared unions because they were a growing economic force with resources of their own, and racketeers sought to capitalize upon those fears and get control for their own selfish ends of those same union resources. Until management force without and criminal force within could be suppressed, the concept of force had to be given first place in union organization.

In the course of the last 50 years, this picture has gradually changed for the better—not in the sense that physical courage, intelligence and understanding of men have become any less important. They are as important as ever, but there have been added to them an ever-increasing number of new qualifications that today set the leader of labor in a social category that is as distinctly professional as the position of the lawyer or the architect. This evolution has been matched step by step by industrial management with the development of techniques designed to meet the menace of informed labor leadership. The result is that there have grown up in both labor and industry new agencies that can be designated on the labor side as "the union staff."

It should be stated at the outset in unequivocal words that the union staff is not in any sense a substitute for incompetence or mental immaturity on the part of the leader. An incompetent and immature leader cannot possibly assemble anything in the way of group organization other than an incompetent and immature staff. This conclusion means that the leader must be possessed of rare executive ability with a sufficient all-around knowledge of technical fields, and above all sufficient confidence in himself to select competent technical men and women who will comprise his staff.

Such has been the progress within the labor movement toward realization of labor's aims that today we find this field expanding to a degree that would have baffled the labor leader of 1900. Some of the old-timers, still around this present day, concede that labor staff organization has scored tremendous gains for workers, but they still express confidentially a fear that the labor movement may become a bit panty-waisted. This apprehension is only natural. It is a simple human tendency to look back on the old days as good. No doubt it was fun to drive a horse and buggy over the countryside, but one can easily forget both the time it took to get somewhere and the time spent in chamber-maiding the horse. We entertain strong doubts that any of the old-timers would suggest a return to the good old days when force and force alone made the decisions between labor and management.

In addition to being an executive, the modern labor leader must in effect be an economist, a psychologist, a public relations expert, an editor, a sociologist, a legislative lobbyist, a politician, a commentator on international affairs, and an analyst of domestic affairs in the fields of education, religion, agriculture, race relations, and a dozen other categories. Obviously, because he cannot specialize in each of them, it becomes his grave responsibility to construct a staff of experts in these various lines of endeavor. His task is far from being as easy as it sounds. It is no great problem for an industrialist, for example, to hire an economist. Industry, long in control of educational resources, has an ample supply from which to fill its needs in that regard. It can take almost any graduate of economics and get from him precisely the advice it needs from its point of view,

because virtually all standard economic texts and courses today are built
on the concept that business is the cause and profits the end-aim of human
life. Selecting a labor staff economist thus becomes one of the most difficult
tasks of the labor leader who is primarily concerned with human values
as against property values, not in a sense that denies the value of property,
but from the point of view that he rejects its superiority over human
values.

The economist who becomes a union staff member, therefore, must be
one who has proceeded far beyond the textbook reasoning of Adam Smith,
John Stuart Mill, David Ricardo, and their multitudinous successors. In
addition to knowing all of the arguments that modern industrial management advances to support its case, the labor staff economist must be
equipped to set forth the sound moral principle that holds to the contrary.

Likewise, the staff public relations man must be more than a mine-run
press agent as industry visualizes him. He must be a person knowing all of
the tricks of the industrial press agent, and in addition he must be fully
aware that he represents no tremendous advertising appropriation that so
often smoothes the path of the ordinary press agent to the editor or the
radio station director. It is what the labor public relations man brings to
the public attention that counts, not how much space or time he obtains.

Another staff functionary whose background must be carefully considered is the editor of union publications. There are thousands of trained
newspapermen in the United States today, and many of them are members
of unions. But more is required of a staff editor than technical knowledge
of the newspaper business. He must also understand the labor movement,
and his understanding must come from a knowledge of its history, its
victories, and its defeats over the decades. As simple a matter as a single-
page mimeographed handbill for distribution among the workers in any
given plant calls for the services of a trained staff editor. The written word
published on a handbill under the name of a union organization can be just
as destructive as similar words used in other lines of endeavor. Every
leader of labor can recall instances where improperly prepared mimeographed handbills have created a most difficult situation.

To the casual observer, a legislative expert and a politician may seem to
be the same thing. However, from the union standpoint there is considerable difference. The union staff legislative expert must have a fundamental
grasp of legislative affairs. Briefly, he may be said to be an expert in the
formula by which the political machine is operated, whereas the political
expert is concerned with actual operation of the machine.

The expert in legislation must be more than a mere lobbyist. It is true
that he must have a keen eye and ear to discern and appraise what is happening in legislative quarters, be it the Congress, a state legislature, or a
city council. He must be trained in civics and in constitutional structure,
and have more than a mere nodding acquaintance with the history of

legislation generally. In addition, he must be familiar with the philosophy of legislation. His qualifications must be such that even legislators themselves will turn to him for information and advice. He must have a power of analysis to grasp quickly the significance of any piece of legislation and its relation to the worker. Finally, he must have the facility to boil down into readily understandable abstracts legislative information that may be required on a moment's notice by the union leader.

Few persons are more important in the entire labor movement than a competent staff man on legislation. Every bill that is thrown into the legislative hopper bears in varying degree upon all of the people, especially those who belong to labor unions. Every authorized governmental appropriation, for instance, passes sooner or later into the hands of working men. It must not be assumed that labor's interest in an appropriation is by that very fact limited to what is paid in wages. Equally important is the service rendered by the government appropriation. Public money expended in the building of a dam to control irrigation might be considered beneficial to labor, but the benefit might easily be submerged because the dam in question, when completed, would serve to irrigate only the vast acreage of a single stock-raising corporation.

Turning now to the union staff expert on politics, we find that where the staff legislative expert has been concerned with representatives of the people known as legislators, the political expert must be an individual in close direct contact with the people themselves. He must be an expert on group thinking, or what is more important, on the refusal of people to think. In brief, his concern is with the state of the public mind, and his function is to translate the thinking of the people into concrete programs of government that will satisfy the people. He must be able to analyze the ethical motive of politicians. His principle concern, however, extends far beyond a knowledge of politics as politics; he must have a knowledge of politics in relation to the needs of the people.

At this point the fields of the staff men who serve as legislative experts and as political experts can be said to merge. In the final analysis the success of any legislative or political program depends upon mass action by the persons for whom the program is devised. In everyday language, the objective of both is mass pressure by groups. Adverse newspaper editorials to the contrary notwithstanding, the United States has always been governed by pressure methods. The right of the people to assemble peaceably and petition for redress of grievances is a cornerstone of the American system of democracy.

Another highly important staff activity is a research department under the direction of a competent director. This department must serve all other staff divisions, but most of all it must render tremendous service to the union leader in the basic activities of the union: collective bargaining with employers for improved wages, hours, and working conditions. The time has long since passed when collective bargaining was narrowly confined to wrangling over a few cents an hour. Collective bargaining these modern days proceeds on a basis of logic and both sides are required not only to offer proofs of their own contentions but to furnish the other party with certain information that is obtainable from no other source. This latter point has been determined by the National Labor Relations Board and it has been given an affirmative support of the federal courts. Management, of course, has long had its statistical data and when it became apparent to industry that its exercise of force was being matched by the growth of unions, it turned to its superior statistics for new support. The union research department is therefore the corresponding agency that the union leader must bring to his support at the negotiation table.

Still another important activity of the union staff is maintenance of an education department. Collective bargaining for the union is no longer conducted by a single leader; it is participated in by committees that extend all the way through the union structure from the international executive board down to the shop committee in a plant that may be three thousand miles from the international union headquarters. This huge increase in the number of negotiators has made it imperative that the union maintain constant training programs at every level. Here again, labor has had to meet the challenge of industry. The management of even the most remote plant has at its beck and call local representatives of employer associations and attorneys for use as negotiators. Obviously, no union has sufficient funds to proceed along the same lines; the union must rely upon workers called in many instances from their benches, and those workers must be trained carefully in the techniques of negotiation. But the matter of education within the union does not stop with a course in collective bargaining, because working for a living, not merely for wages, is the chief material activity of men. All other questions of everyday life are related to it. The function of the union organization in itself presents a vast educational field in all subjects.

In addition to these various activities, the modern labor leader must have the assistance of a legal staff to guide him through the intricacies of social legislation and the rules and regulations of many federal and state bureaus that are established by law. There is, of course, a limited field in which representation by lawyers is imperative, but for the greater part, workers are represented in legal proceedings by their leaders, not by lawyers. If an analysis were made of proceedings before the National Labor Relations Board and its national offices established under the Wagner Act, it undoubtedly would be found that labor leaders, not attorneys, had conducted proceedings in the majority of all cases. It is the union staff attorney's function to keep the union leader apprised on every point that will aid him in his work as a quasi-attorney for his union.

Another function of the union leader that has of necessity been delegated to a staff member is that of financial accounting. The matter of keeping books may seem to be a dull and drab everyday affair, but no union leader can ever permit the accounting methods of his organization to get far from his thinking. Carping critics are ever on the alert to prove either that the union is tremendously wealthy or that it is a vehicle operated by the union leader merely to exact dues and assessments from the members. Not only must the union leader be certain that the accounting methods of his organization are sound, but also he must be familiar enough with them to discuss them publicly. He dare not indulge in the chicanery of corporation accounting. His methods in this field must be simple enough for his membership to grasp readily.

Thus far we have considered the union staff as related to the domestic field of operation. Present world conditions make it imperative that the union leader be informed on international affairs, political and economic. Here again the pace has been set by industry. Business interests over many years have maintained close international relationships between and among themselves. Recent years have made "cartel" a word familiar to the average newspaper reader. The extensive international agreements for price fixing, limitation of output, shelving new technological processes and withholding new products from the market have been brought to light through a long series of indictments in our American federal courts.

All of these pernicious activities have had their impact, not only on American workers, but on the workers of every other land as well. It therefore becomes imperative that the modern union leader concern himself with international affairs. It follows naturally that his first concern must be to seek cooperation with the labor unions of all other countries. This cooperation is by no means a simple problem. It is fully as complex as the efforts of national governments to deal with one another. Labor, like government, finds itself confronted on the international plane with a variety of political systems, different traditions and customs, and differences in language. Virtually every problem that confronts the United Nations Organization confronts the International Confederation of Free Trade Unions, the delegates to which are union leaders from the free democratic nations. To meet those problems, the union leader must have competent staff assistants.

It must not be assumed that the various activities discussed represent all of the fields with which the labor leader must concern himself. Neither must it be assumed that any of these activities are separate ventures. One field overlaps the other and hence the union staff must be completely integrated. Staff members must serve not only the union leaders who direct them, but also one another.

Union staff members must be strong advocates of their point of view; they are not hired to say "yes" to every idea the labor leader advances. No labor leader wants to have around him a Hollywood setup. He wants the views of his staff members expressed to him in a challenging way. A union is not operated by a soulless corporation for the production of money profits; it is conducted by human beings chosen by other human beings to function for the betterment of their human interests. Staff members must be persons capable of keeping this thought ever in mind. They must bring to their jobs along with technical knowledge and a knowledge of the union movement the same willingness to sacrifice time and energy for a great cause that is demanded by union members of the union leader himself.

It is obvious that the Victorian educational structure that largely persists in the United States has neither the desire nor the capability to train persons for union staff positions. There has been more advance in this field over the last 20 years than occurred in the previous century, yet educational facilities to develop union staff members still are grossly inadequate. Tremendous work is being done by some of our higher institutions, by some excellent specialized schools, by voluntary independent labor school systems, and by the educational departments of various unions, but it is far from filling today's needs. A major objective of organized labor still is to provide educational facilities that will meet its requirements.

There is nothing radical in labor's demand for labor education. Public funds have long been expended through state-endowed institutions for teaching business administration. Whole institutions are devoted solely to teaching agricultural administration. Specialized schools and courses are established and maintained to educate people in the fields of their other special interests. Labor alone is not given full recognition as the most powerful group numerically in American economic life. This condition must be changed. Education must meet the needs of the people, and most certainly there is no greater need than able direction of the business of securing a living.

JAMES B. CAREY

2. "To Raise Questions; Not to Run the Union"

The unions and the labor movement are vast governments of their members. The place of the expert in the labor movement parallels closely the place of the civil servant in government. But in the labor movement his functions are hardly defined.

What is the place of the intellectual or the expert in the union movement? Is he to lead or to serve? If either, in what way can he fit himself best into the scheme of things? What is the union's attitude to be toward him?

Take the economists. I think the worst thing that could happen to the labor movement would be for it to take economists' advice on its union policies. Any economic expert that the labor movement employed would come with the point of view of his science. The point of view of the labor movement must come from common people, ill-informed people, perhaps. However, on the questions of their vital interests they are wiser than the experts.

In England of some years back, any well-educated person knew, for example, that unions just interfered with production and with the whole economic system. Therefore, workers couldn't really be helped. What one group of workers gained they took away from other workers. So it is very fortunate that the working people of England didn't go to training classes and didn't learn that kind of economics. They kept pressing for trade unions and built a labor movement.

The unions, of course, have some very complicated matters to deal with. Some seemingly simple things are not at all simple when they are carefully examined from the point of view of the consequences that are likely to follow action. If, for instance, a union wants to maintain its wage scale, that may cause some increase in unemployment. That involves a question of policy: Do we want to reduce wages low enough to give everybody a job, or should we keep high scales of wages and then, if that causes unemployment, get the government to deal with the unemployment problem? Working people and economists are likely to differ on policy matters of this kind.

Unions should not decide such questions without understanding all that is involved. A statement in the London *Economist* said that the trouble with the British unions is that they haven't acted like the American unions. The American unions, said the article, have pressed for high wages regardless of the consequences. They have forced employers and manufacturers to find ways of reducing costs other than by cutting wages. But the English unions have been reasonable, and they have kept their wage demands down. The unions should demand high wages all the time, the *Economist* implied.

I don't know whether that's the best policy or not. But do the members of unions discuss questions of this kind themselves, or do they let experts or friends commit them to a policy and then go to meetings to get mass approval? And will they sometime later find that they have adopted a policy they really didn't want?

In this respect what is the place of the expert—the lawyer, for example? Shall he, in the way he argues cases, commit the labor movement to a philosophy that might get into court decisions? Or should the labor movement itself develop its philosophy consciously, and predetermine its policies before it gives its support to something intellectuals have worked out?

Many problems, economic and political, need the attention of labor. But it is dangerous to commit the labor movement to answers until the labor movement has deliberated them carefully. Perhaps unions would be wiser on policies about which their members are divided if they would say, "We'd better wait before we commit ourselves."

The professionally trained intellectual clearly has a place and a job to do in the labor movement. But there ought to be a clear understanding of the nature of the job he is to do and of the place he can occupy without jeopardizing his usefulness and perhaps even doing harm to the movement.

To take the instance of the labor press, we talk about 15 million wage earners in unions, covered by collective bargaining agreements. With their families, they represent households of some 25 million people. Where is the press that expresses the philosophy, aspirations, the program, or the point of view of this mass movement, which we are told, has reached its maturity?

I am very much interested in a journal like *Labor and Nation* that is something more than a house organ of a union or a partisan-propaganda paper. How is such an over-all journal to be run, what direction is it to be given?

When a movement reaches maturity, it has to assume responsibility. A journal of the kind needed ought to reflect that maturity and responsibility. It cannot feed on a menu of inspiration, wishful thinking. The inspiring programs that such a journal might think up and present aren't enough. Inspiring programs are fine. They are to me like architects' drawings or planners' blueprints. But if the labor movement is to go into such things as an international program, a program of production in cooperation with management, an educational program, etc., the journal has to find out and enlighten the movement on how it can participate in and work toward these purposes without disrupting the union organizations. We have to inquire about the philosophy of this movement—what kind of an organization *is* the trade union movement, how does it function, how does it move ahead, how does it determine its policies? It needs more than professionally competent writing or editing to make a good labor journal. Also, more than sympathy for labor is required.

Or—we talk about training people for labor leadership: education. This reminds me of discussions we used to have on training for public service. I used to say the most important thing is to learn how to get elected to office. Otherwise, we will be training a lot of people who won't find an important place in government, and untrained people will be running the government. The same thing is true in the labor movement. It is a government as well as a union—an association of people with many purposes. To speak of it as if it had but one purpose is a mistake. To speak as if labor could go into politics, educational programs, international programs, etc., as other movements do is also a mistake. If a cooperative movement goes into such bigger movements, it must remember to sell groceries. Similarly, if the labor movement is going into these things, it will have to make its contributions in its own way. It must always remember to attend to the business of handling grievances and doing all the other little things in the shops that hold the workers together in an organization.

Let's take some concrete illustrations. I attended the CIO and AFL conventions in 1944. At the CIO convention I heard President Murray saying "The War Labor Board has destroyed collective bargaining in this country."

Perhaps Mr. Murray didn't mean that extreme statement: he probably meant that the WLB had very much weakened collective bargaining. I heard R. J. Thomas of the autoworkers say that "it may seem funny to hear me, a member of the WLB, denounce it the way I have been denouncing it." But he gave this as his reason: "We labor members took our jobs on that board under a misapprehension."

The CIO convention of that year was a victory convention. Four days were mostly taken up with demonstrations celebrating victory in re-electing the Roosevelt administration, and the last day was devoted to denouncing the Roosevelt administration's handling of labor. Had that been done before the election, the Roosevelt administration might perhaps not have been re-elected.

As a matter of fact, as an outside observer, I was of the opinion that the labor movement was as much responsible, perhaps more responsible than any other group, for the bad policies it was now denouncing.

The labor movement has always depended on the right to strike. It gave that weapon up during the war. It should have given up that right for the duration, there is no question about that. But *how* did it give it up? Did it ask what was labor going to get in its place? No, it just left it to the government to appoint a board, as if a board is a substitute for the fundamental thing upon which labor organization rests. What a board would do might be a reasonable substitute for the strike, but no inquiry was made as to what the board might do.

The board was not in advance committed to certain policies acceptable to unions. Now, when the labor movement didn't like the stabilization policy or the policy based on the Little Steel formula, what did it offer in its place? Labor did not like the way the War Labor Board was handling cases: it charged regimentation. But if the labor movement offered a method that accomplished the purpose without regimentation, how would it get this done?

What an educational program might bring to the labor movement is a strong conviction that the labor movement must have clear policies, and administrative organs for determining policies. Do the unions inquire what existing organs there are and whether they are designed to make their policies work successfully? If unions are committed to giving up the right to strike, can the official family commit the labor movement to that, or should the question be thoroughly discussed at every level in the organization until it gets to the top?

To use another illustration: the break between the farmers and the labor movement. In the early days of the New Deal, the farm organizations and the farm lobbies worked pretty well with the labor organizations and the labor lobbies. They had their differences, but they would iron them out and support each other's legislation so far as they could. But in 1940, a farmers' bill was up before Congress. It was intended to modify the parity price formula by including farmers' wages in the calculation of cost. It would have lifted farm prices but not so much as they have risen since. The President decided to veto it. He asked the AFL and CIO for support. They did support the veto. Whether the membership and the governing organs of the labor movement were consulted about that support, I do not know. But the fact was that within a few days the legislative agents of organized labor were up on Capitol Hill helping get that veto sustained. The farm organizations have been sore ever since, with one exception: the National Farmers' Union.

Here's another point: unions went to the government and got the Wagner Act passed. The enactment of the law and its operation changed the character of the union movement and added to the public standing of organized labor. It made a union a statutory representative of all the people in the bargaining unit. The law established authority for the majority to choose representatives who represent the others who aren't members, or don't want any representation, or don't like the particular representation. The employer must bargain with all people in the unit through the statutory representative. Unions hadn't been operating with statutory rights. Did any one inquire "what is that going to mean?" We all got on the band wagon, saying we wanted the law. The British Trades Union Congress after a thorough discussion rejected a proposal for such a law.

Under a Supreme Court ruling a statutory representative can't discriminate among the men he represents. They argued that a union is an agent of the state. On the other hand, in the UAW-Thomas case in Texas, the union contended that unions are a special kind of organization and argued on this basis that the government cannot regulate unions at all. But, are the unions business organizations, or are they something else? Their development shows that they are taking on the character of business organizations—but it seems to me that the trade union movement needs to watch what's happening to itself and decide what it wants to be and what it really wants to do.

There is one function the intellectual can usefully perform, and that is to ask questions. Here is an illustration from not so long ago. The leader of the Political Action Committee announced that the PAC-CIO would support men who supported Roosevelt's international program. Isolationists, even with good labor records, would be opposed. Was that the right policy? The labor movement has members who are isolationists: is not their point of view deserving of consideration? There are in the union movement members who believe in free trade, who have a direct material interest in free trade policies, even as there are others whose point of view and interest are in the direction of a protective tariff policy. For which is the union as a whole to stand up?

I suggest that raising questions and emphasizing discussion of the many serious matters and problems with which the union movement must cope is more important than hammering away at seemingly wise solutions. By so applying his training and expert knowledge, the professional intellectual on the union's staff will help the union clear its mind on what is the best policy in its considered interest.

WILLIAM M. LEISERSON

3. "More than a Paycheck"

The first intellectuals who made places for themselves in the labor movement really came in through the back door. When unions first began organizing, they had no resources of their own to count on in emergencies, and had to call on the general public for help. They appealed for financial help, but they needed more than that. They needed people to help man the picket lines, to run the mimeograph machine, to make posters, to distribute coffee and sandwiches, and do all the odd jobs that go into running a big strike.

The people who responded to the unions' call then did it because they were imbued with a certain amount of social idealism and saw the labor movement as a struggling, pioneering, crusading movement. When, after the strike, some of the volunteers who had demonstrated their worth were asked to stay on, they were glad if they got a modest maintenance wage.

Today, the intellectual can't serve his apprenticeship on the picket line. The unions have achieved great size and power, and their needs have become specialized and professionalized. A young idealist cannot, without skill and training, put out a newspaper or prepare a brief. The effect of this situation is that "outsiders" find their way into the union movement because they have skills that the union leader needs.

The movement needs the help of technicians, but it hasn't fully thought out the relationship between itself and the technicians. This fault is due, in part, to a hangover suspicion of intellectuals by the union practitioners. The result of this mistrust is that the intellectuals (editors, researchers, engineers, legal workers, education workers) are often hired on a hit-or-miss basis although in most cases monetary rewards offered are below those offered by business careers. Thus the labor technician still must have a "feel" for the labor movement and its ideals.

This situation can and should be remedied. It is clear that the specialists whom the unions need will be drawn from the colleges and universities. It would be the better part of wisdom for the unions to keep in touch with sympathetic professors at schools who could send people when there are jobs to be filled. Promising students could be selected as interns. Experienced union leaders should be prepared to give time to such beginners.

The union, in turn, must define its policy toward the intellectuals it is using in increasing numbers. It must decide what it wants from its professional men, how much "academic freedom" they can have, and conversely, how much they are to be bound by the union. It must then go on to face the relationship between the professional and the movement. To what extent, for example, should the professional men represent the union in the eyes of the outside world? Can professionals become leaders of the union: should they influence union policy?

Although a complete theoretical policy has not yet been hewed out by union leaders, attitudes have grown up in the course of day-to-day contact. At the moment it seems that the position of the intellectual in the labor movement is frequently the same as that of the intellectual in industry. The union leader wants service when he asks for it, and on the whole, isn't interested in advice. What, then, is the difference to the intellectual between being "in the service of labor" and in the service of industry? The answer probably is—idealistic motivation.

The people who go to industry are interested primarily in a job. The people who seek out union jobs are, on the whole, interested in more than drawing a weekly paycheck. But on what will their rather vague idealism feed? Can our universities be depended upon to place, under a special rubric, training courses in social awareness and idealism? Or should the unions just absorb the people that the universities turn out in the routine way and not care whether they have social idealism or not? The labor leader must face the question every time he adds to his staff. As matters now stand, the unions' requirements on the skills wanted have become very specific. The union officer expects the specialist who comes into the labor movement to be competent, reliable, with a good scholastic record and a measure of administrative ability with which to perform his job.

We are thus facing a vital gap in the intellectual-union situation, and it is up to both the union movement, as represented by the union officers, and to us who are on the movement's staffs to work out this problem in a rational way.

We won't be able to solve this problem without making a thorough examination of the function of the intellectual in the union movement, his opportunity and his responsibility, in the light of the need that the union movement has for his skills, energy, and social idealism.

A first step in that direction is to define the difference between being in the service of labor and being in the service of government or in the service of business. Is there a difference? We ought to get trade union people to describe what their functions are; what, for instance, a trade union research department does, or an engineering or a press and publicity department does or ought to be doing. Is an idealistic motivation wanted, or have we gone beyond that stage? What skills are essential? What sympathies and social understandings are necessary?

Next point is that we ought to think out a reply to the question: Is the trade union movement bureaucratic? If so, to what extent? We should get a picture of the facts. Some unions are so determined to be democratic as to be inefficient. The picture is difficult to draw. If there are bureaucratic tendencies, to what extent are they eradicable? To what extent can we build up antidotes? How can an enlightened "rank and file" combat bureaucracy? There are indeed people who are in the service of the movement who know that power degenerates, that permanency means bureaucracy, and who recognize nevertheless that we must have a certain amount of permanency for efficiency.

We may not have the answers to all this. But posing the questions and seeking answers will make us conscious of the problem and alive to the dangers ahead.

MARK STARR

4. "Continually to Offer Advice"

The number of people who are interested in becoming associated with the labor movement in this country is large but only the smallest fraction of it ever appears at the threshold of the union to converse with people in it about jobs. Moreover, the opportunities are so limited that only a few of these who appear or meet trade unionists ever get jobs. The field is most limited since ours is the country in which the labor movement is confined to trade unions, in contrast with other countries where the labor movement consists of a political party, cooperative organization, and intellectual organization, in addition to the trade unions. These other outlets provide a wider range of opportunities to the professionals interested in working in the labor movement.

As unions developed from small local organizations that could be run by one full-time office employee, the need for dealing effectively with public bodies became important. Unions need representatives to present their views, argue cases, secure positive administrative action and affirmative administrative rulings, interpret certain administrative procedures, laws, and guides, varying all the way from a National Labor Relations Board or a wage case to a safety ruling in a single industry locally, or any of the other matters that might infringe on the well-being of the union. Most of the early leaders of major stature, such as Gompers and Mitchell, were thoroughly capable of dealing with public bodies.

However, as organization grew and the union problems became more complex, labor leaders were no longer able to rely on their own information even in the immediate field of negotiating contracts. Moreover, most unions in the 1920's and until 1933 were local in character; that is, their market areas were mostly local: the competition and the scope of their problems were local; and most union leaders were thoroughly conversant with their own problems. It was not necessary to gauge the problems beyond the restricted market area they knew quite intimately. They knew the price problems. They knew the ability of industry, and they also knew the methods of economic pressure by which they could enforce their demands on the employers.

An altogether new state of affairs developed after 1933. With widely expanded organization in national industries, the negotiating problems became national in scope. Union officers realized the need for a full-time research staff to study market conditions, to gather exact data on every firm with whom they dealt, to help prepare careful and effective presentation of data. Their own daily experience was insufficient to provide them with the data they needed, which they could get in local industries. The research department was the result.

The work of a union research department is detailed elsewhere in this book. In a general way, the research staff, like every other special staff enlisted by the union, is there to give service to the union officer on any of the questions it is equipped to handle. Strictly speaking, it is a service agency without any policy-making functions. And yet by executing these functions it sometimes cannot help being very close to actually directing policy. When organizers for a particular area are scouting out the area, for example, they will choose, first, the town or mill where the workers seem most incensed against their employer, or where the pro-union feeling is running high. Although they may be able to sign up the workers, they may run into a situation where the employer "cannot be found," where ownership or the final financial controlling authority is confusing and concealed. The guidance of the research department will help where the organizing department is handicapped. In some cases, the research department gets a listing of all the plants in the area and finds out who owns each plant and what the financial ties are in each instance, which is no simple matter. Then the department marks out the plants owned by companies with which the union has contracts in other states. With the workers in those plants organized, the union is in position to secure contracts in the plants hitherto not unionized.

The professional in the union is not hired to participate in making policy and has no official place in the policy-making setup. But he can influence policy. When the research department, for example, is working on a current problem, preparing a brief, or conducting a survey, that is a service. But if the research department, at the same time, spots a problem that may arise in the future and proceeds to gather material on that problem, its influence in shaping opinion on the problem as it arises is considerable. It has already developed a point of view as it has worked up the data that will be brought to bear upon the development of policy. Frequently the executive board or the president of the union may present a long-range problem to the research staff. The kind of solution that the department recommends cannot help but affect the final policy.

The professional faces the eternal staff problem of getting its influence accepted and ensuring that the administration's experience is calculated into and absorbed by the research staff.

Originally, as Mr. Starr has observed, a large number of staff people came into the union for idealistic motives. Unfortunately, a large part of people without that drive are coming into the labor movement, because the bureaucracy is increasing and the salaries are beginning to resemble a living wage. But no matter what the incentive for the staff person, his influence depends in part on his persuasiveness, but also on the particular persons heading the union. On the whole, the trade union more nearly reflects the spirit and the personal peculiarities of the person who leads the union than do other institutions in our society.

The professional influences the shaping of policy affecting the future of the union through the officers and trade union leaders. In specific cases, staff members "represent labor" on numerous public and trade union occasions. They are, by now, permanent fixtures, yet union leaders have never stopped thinking of them as experimental additions. Perhaps organization of the professionals in the labor movement might help in gaining recognition of the staff's existence and functions. Labor leaders should be induced to deal with staff members in a defined administrative manner, to maintain continuous, organized contact between officers and staff.

In the long view, the function of the union staff can be to provide the long-range planning that will interrelate the immediate work with future objectives. This is an important task that every large organization must undertake. In the United States, particularly, this lack of integration between the immediate and the long-range trade union aims is especially pronounced. In other countries, where the unions are tied up with the political parties, the unions are continually being prodded to consider the political and economic problems in the making. Thus, an awareness of the country's or the industry's outlook at a given time must play a part in negotiating for wage changes.

The union research man cannot determine how much of a wage increase the union should ask for. But he can make suggestions, and depending on the personal confidence of the president, executive board (or any other determining body), his suggestion will be considered and may prove to be effective. Despite the fact that the union officer may not check with the research man on each step he takes, the research man ought to be continually offering his advice, whether it is accepted or not.

SOLOMON BARKIN

5. THE JOB IS—COOPERATE

The staff member does not frame basic union policy. That function properly belongs to the union officers and the union's General Executive Board. Beyond that essential and altogether proper arrangement there still remains a great deal of leeway for the staff professional to bring his influence, via his competence, to bear upon the situation. This point can be seen from an instance taken out of our experience.

At some time early in the war, the General Executive Board of the ILGWU had the foresight to appoint a committee on postwar problems of the industry as related, of course, to the union. The chairman of that committee came to the Research Department with some topics in mind that he wanted to see explored, and he invited the Research Department to add other topics. With that suggestion we worked for some time on such things as the possibility of expanding exports of our industry, particularly to Latin America, and of using air transportation. It became necessary to know which of our manufacturers had been exporting and what their experience had been.

Accordingly, the New York Association of Commerce and Industry suggested that they call a conference on the question, and this conference prompted the United States Department of Commerce to ask the commercial agents in Latin America to make detailed reports on the character of demand for women's and children's apparel in those countries and the manufacturing facilities that they had, their tariff structures, the procedures of getting North American goods through the customs, and so on.

When that research had been completed, the president of the union determined that we couldn't move farther than that until the employers took a more active interest in it than we had been able to discover or to arouse. This decision, naturally, put an end to that particular exploration.

Now, the General Executive Board had no clear idea of what industrial and market conditions might be after the war. It was the function of the Research Department to explore potentialities and to give the General Executive Board some starting points from which practical thinking could start.

Illustration might have been drawn from developing trends in location of shops in our industry, which raised the whole question of decentralizing the industry and spreading it from New York, as the dominant center, to many other markets and to small communities, in sections of the country where the industry never before had a foothold. The Research Department worked on this problem in cooperation with the management engineering department, because it involved introducing better equipment in the shops where the products were more standardized and the workers had less skill. Our study of the issue brought us face to face with the problem of section work against the craft system, which led to a report to the General Executive Board on the outlook for location of the industry and technological developments in the next 10 or 15 years, so far as we could forecast it.

Many of us serving on a staff in the unions come from college and university training, and in some cases, from teaching experience. Our old colleagues on the campuses are likely to assign to us a much more creative role than we can actually fill; and the friendly criticisms that come sometimes, or the hopes expressed by our old academic colleagues, overlook the fact that nine-tenths of our work, exacting as it is, is of a day-to-day and fairly immediate routine character. They forget that most of their own is of that character; that they give dreary lectures and read dreary papers and hand in dreary marks. They are likely to think of us as acting constantly in the creative intellectual capacity in which they like to think of themselves as acting in their best moments.

When they consider the equipment of staff members, they forget that the officers of the union have their unique equipment in knowledge of what the membership is prepared for, of the extent to which their fellow-officers will cooperate with them. They have to inform the staff people of the feasibilities in a particular situation. We would read ourselves out of court if our suggestions as to policy were not constantly mindful of the superior equipment of the officer as leader of a mass movement.

The unions have sometimes been willing to take great decisions at the prompting of some public figure, who is not connected with the union, as for instance Justice Brandeis. Why is the advice of a Justice Brandeis followed, although he is an outsider, while the opinion of an inside staff member may remain unheeded? It is because of the greater public standing of the outsider in this instance.

By the very nature of his position in the union, the staff member is under the necessity of considering what may seem to be politically feasible under the particular set of circumstances. I offer this suggestion in defense of the staff people who are sometimes blamed for not instilling a more fervid idealism and inducing a swifter progress than the unions show. The temptation of the union officer, when his research director comes into his office, is to say, "Behold, this dreamer cometh." We are inclined to avoid having that said not because we mind back-handed compliments, but because a wide separation between us and those to whose policy and judgment we should contribute would make us ineffective.

BROADUS MITCHELL

6. The Light that Fails

Since the earliest days of the nineteenth century, when feeble local unions began to appear sporadically on the American urban scene, organized labor has been trying to teach industrialists in the United States a simple lesson: You can't hire a hand. Temple Burling, the industrial psychiatrist at Cornell's School of Industrial and Labor Relations, has explained this phrase by adding: "You cannot hire his labor without hiring him, the whole of him."

With the exception of James Carey, whose views about the role of the labor staff are heart-warming, although wholly unrepresentative of labor leadership, the several participants in this discussion actually serving as full-time experts in the pay of unions intimate that members of the labor staff are, for the most part, treated as hired hands by labor officials. More significant, however, is the interlinear revelation that these experts tend to consider themselves as properly categorized hired hands. Since, as intellectuals, they are very much at home with words and ideas, they never express themselves quite so baldly. Instead, they tuck the generally recognized unpleasantness of their professional thralldom behind the curtained pronouncement that the job of ultimate policy making (an infinitely complex, ramifying, and many-echeloned operation in reality) is the sole responsibility of union leadership and higher executive boards rather than the task of experts. After enunciating this unrealistic dichotomy in the name of realistic appraisal, they go on to imply that it is even undesirable, if not downright unethical, for experts to approach the arcanum of policy formation a step nearer than the possible influencing (at a respectable distance) of decisions. But a partnership in direct policy formation—never!

This is not the occasion for an exploration of the multifarious ways in which policy is determined from day to day within various American institutions, both private and public. Yet even from a glance at the newspapers, one fact is clear: although a designated person or group may have the ostensible responsibility for setting policy and making the final decisions in case of strong disagreement, the process by which such an individual or group arrives at ultimate determinations has evolved, during the past thirty years, into a partnership with informed and expert collaborators—an association of the most intimate nature. So close, in fact, has this collaboration become that except to the public eye (when President Truman delivers his State of the Union address to Congress or Henry Ford 2nd speaks to the press about the plans of his company) it is impossible to discern with any accuracy where the contributions of top experts leave off and where the deciding judgments of top policy officials begin.

It is therefore amazing to hear deludingly simple principles about policy formation (what happens to be the practice in labor unions today is, *ipso facto*, correct or healthy) pronounced by labor experts who occupy some of the leading professional positions in labor unions. They are not, after all, statistical clerks, junior economists, occasional teachers in a workers' education class, or reporters on a labor newspaper. As nationally known experts in their respective fields, they are undoubtedly aware that the highest type of policy in both industry and government today is constantly being formulated by their counterparts in various fields. I need only allude to the position that George F. Kennan and his Policy Planning Staff have occupied in the State Department and to the influence that Dr. Irving Langmuir, the distinguished scientist, has exerted in the General Electric Company. The administrative assistants to members of the United States Senate and the counsels of legislative committees (we can all recall the yeoman service Leon Keyserling rendered Robert Wagner), however anonymously the results of their labors might appear in speech or print, are employed specifically to aid in the formulation of policy. The strength of these illustrations springs from the contemporary circumstance that these instances are not rare. On the contrary, they are becoming the prevailing mode of operation in government and in industry.

The answer to the problem posed: what should be the position of the expert in labor unions?, must be found less in fancy, hedging phrases regarding ultimate responsibility for the declaration of policy than in the personal history and development of both American labor leaders and their presently hired hands, the experts. The generalizations I am presenting as possible answers must obviously be considered merely as untested hypotheses to be subjected to more detailed observation and analysis. For the moment, however, they can serve, usefully I hope, as bases for discussion.

First, let us examine what we know factually about American labor leaders. This is important because they hold the whip, and consequently, the chief solution to the problem at hand. In Part One, Chapter 2, by C. Wright Mills and Helen S. Dinerman, gives us statistics about the origin, education, experience, and superficial political beliefs of labor leaders. But we are provided with little insight into the social and psychological complexities that confound the inner life of labor leaders, and which, in turn, plague their relationship with staff experts. Most labor leaders today still chew morbidly at their past when most other people taste only the very illustrious present of these union officials. As a result of this preoccupation, labor leaders are retarded in their administrative thinking and actions by at least a full generation as contrasted to their counterparts in government and industry.

Like most *arrivistes*, in whatever milieu or era they find themselves, top labor leaders have not been quite able to attune themselves psychologically or vocationally to the stupendous fact of their own position and power. In both their public and private appearances (like actors, they often assume roles even while purportedly out of costume), most of them perform as though their eminence cannot quite be real. Their persistent and obvious sense of intellectual, psychological, and social inferiority (unjustified as it is) alternates constantly with their conviction of superiority as men of action, shrewd bargainers, and successful manipulators of instinctive knowledge. These opposing pulls of character tear at their behavior each day and manifest themselves as personality patterns of humility and almost sentimental idealism combined with arrogance and opportunistic pragmatism. At one moment, temporarily forsaking their vaunted mission to the working class, they often cherish companionship with the learned, the modish, and the great; at the next moment, recovering their self-imposed balance, they feel only contempt for those who have not been tempered in the heat of pioneering strikes, lockouts, beatings, and intra-union warfare.

The daily frustrations of top labor leaders, actually, are painful and ulcerating. They are men of ambitious will and plastic shrewdness who, by dint of vision, sometimes brawn, and often real intelligence, managed a fundamental revolution on the American industrial scene. By habit they are more exhilarated in strife, whether on the picket line or at the collective bargaining table, than in the slow, detailed, consolidating, administrative operations that large, established, and responsible organizations are inevitably forced to undertake in our contemporary society. Labor leaders would be more than human if they could readily admit that their proclivities and training did not prepare them for this emerging phase of painstaking, modern institutional management. Whether they admit it consciously or not, they sense only too well that manifold knowledge, rather than moral indignation and the chance hunch, will play an increasingly more vital role in labor's future rendezvous with management.

What, then, is the prospect that a large proportion of top labor leadership can adapt itself to present exigencies? In many important unions, the possibility of change, except through death itself, is slight. Since able successors are rarely trained either by labor leaders or political chieftains, given the nature of politics, even the contemplation of death grants but an attenuated hope. Moreover, it is highly questionable whether present leaders, with their understandable limitations, could possibly prepare younger men for the type of responsibilities we have in mind, even if the will to do so existed. On the other hand, William M. Leiserson is more sanguine and has stated parenthetically that the development of unions "shows that they are taking on the character of business organizations—but it seems to me that the trade union movement needs to watch what's happening to itself and decide what it wants to be and what it really wants to do."

If hard-driving labor leaders, goaded by past insecurity and affronts, could be forced to slow down and become more contemplative; if they might be cajoled into a real understanding that they can no longer afford the psychologically exclusive emphasis they place upon admittedly necessary organizing campaigns and strikes and bargaining tactics; if there were some way to force upon them a knowledge of the evolution of industrial management during the past 50 years, then perhaps Mr. Leiserson's injunction, devoutly to be prayed for, might have an even chance of being realized.

Top labor leaders could then be expected to see, in the quiet of their imaginary studies, a parallel between status-and-power-haunted activists like themselves and the tribe of industrial pioneers that roamed America, in pyrotechnic fashion, during the managerially innocent days before Frederick Taylor. Even after the turn of this century, a man like William C. Durant, one of the most imaginative organizers of an automobile empire, rapidly turned into an industrial anachronism. His manipulatory skill and energy created the General Motors Corporation. But the basic cast of his personality made it impossible for him to halt his promotion schemes. When, after a few years, consolidation of resources and informed, skillful planning became a necessity, financial and engineering experts had to be rushed in to save a deteriorating situation. Charles W. Nash, a production man, took his place. General Motors was subsequently transformed from a mere holding company into a giant manufacturing enterprise.

Business history of the past 50 years is filled with similar examples of industry's gradual transition from operation by loud-voiced promotion, instinct, and rule-of-thumb procedures, to management by research in engineering, science, sales, and administration. It was high time a generation ago, when industry began to streamline itself, for labor leaders to have become solicitous about the institutional future of their organizations. To meet the coming challenge of their adversaries effectively (a contest that industrial development placed obviously in the cards), they should have sought out the ablest experts in the country and offered them a partnership in the solution of the geometrically compounding problems, both administrative and industrial, that they were certain to face. Unfortunately, what they never did then they are still not doing.

In suggesting a partnership, I am perfectly aware that I shall be presented at once with the old-bearded chestnut of an argument that labor unions are political as well as economic institutions and that men who make policy must continue to be the elected officials. However, in our increasingly oligarchical American institutions—labor, management, and government— this principle carries little weight except as an excuse for the inability or unwillingness by leaders to share the pleasures of prestige and power. Even within labor unions we have seen this sacred principle violated, although not frequently enough. Those who followed the intricacies of the hearings in 1949 before the President's Steel Fact-Finding Board have no illusions about the constructive policy-forming role of Arthur Goldberg, both on and off the official scene. David Kaplan's modest and quiet performance for the Teamsters cannot detract from its salutary effectiveness. Despite Solomon Barkin's distinction between the experts' right to influence policy as contrasted with the formation of policy, I would certainly add him to the list of policy-makers, perhaps over his public protest.

Because these examples of using experts to their fullest capacities as partners in a common enterprise are still so uncommon in the labor movement, I despair that anything short of impending disaster will ever convince most top labor officials to change into modern administrative garb. They took on economists 20 years ago only when their own ineptitudes became so apparent that they could no longer be concealed. Perhaps they consoled themselves with the thought that, after all, they could not be expected to have the knowledge of economists. Their talents, they believed, lay elsewhere.

Unfortunately, as our technological years pass, the areas of skill, where labor leaders formerly possessed indispensable, exclusive knowledge, narrow relentlessly. Despite this phenomenon, common to all institutions, these officials still remain humanly blind to their own shortcomings, to the sociological and institutional changes that the passage of time and the decline of their youth have wrought. Organizing the unorganized, for example, still remains one of their fancied monopolies of supreme talent. Yet a recent, highly publicized drive by a nationally respected international—a project also heartily approved by the national federation of which it forms a part—symbolized the disaster that can overtake modern unions by hard-headed reliance upon old hunches, antiquated methods, indifferent public relations, inadequate recognition of social differences between occupational groups, and relationships with employers which were unrealistic for the industry involved. Even the surprising nonchalance of announcing the drive publicly, without any semblance of an existing administrative organization to back it up (an inexplicable failure in our highly administered age), can be politely described only as unfortunate. Yet I doubt whether the top leadership of this international will seek expert advice or change its ways from those learned only too well when the first bricks were thrown in 1910.

Labor leaders have also publicly displayed their limitations in another vital area of union activity—the burgeoning field of political action. Here, too, they still fancy themselves as natural experts. Especially in the tightly controlled unions, the leadership has deduced from their success in sending orders down the line that they are entitled to eminence as geniuses in the arena of local, state, and national politics. Even their defeat in 1946 has not really taught them the fundamental lesson of political victory. Their proclivity for shouting orders, calling large meetings, getting out press releases, and inspiring zeal among the already fervid confuses their thinking about politics. They do not seem to realize that these dashing activities do not convert a single union membership list into a roll of unionized voters classified according to election districts. This grubby task possesses no glamor. Although labor leaders pay lip service to its importance, they have failed as yet to spend any considerable sums of money on making its performance an all-year-around task assigned to people hired for that purpose. They still walk in the dream that this job can be accomplished by committees that they have decreed to exist.

Nor have labor leaders shown political distinction, or even shrewdness, at the higher levels of political affairs. The behavior of some rather prominent labor dignitaries in 1948, when they called upon General Eisenhower, whose social views were completely unknown to them, to serve as presidential standard bearer, hardly bestows eminence for political sagacity. And, continuing the tradition of political naïveté, labor leaders in New York City at the beginning of 1950 appeared to be outraged that the Mayor had not followed their advice in certain appointments. It would seem clear enough to an outsider that a candidate who needed labor's support as much as this one did to be elected might have been signed and sealed before the event.

To be sure, the realm of politics is discouragingly complex and no one has the sure answer. But this is the very point. What labor leaders have failed to recognize thus far is the simple truth that in this field they are as amateurish and badly advised as the professional politicians themselves and the nation's press. They could all listen to men with ideas and knowledge a little more frequently. Even Farley proved less shrewd than Roosevelt who cupped his ear, instead, in the direction of a social worker.

Disasters, like the election of 1946, may seem like a high price to pay for learning a lesson written in history, but it certainly seems to be the way that humanity learns most of its lessons, if ever. I doubt whether labor leaders can be an exception to this basic law of social evolution. As types for the future they are extinct even now. With them may go their unions.

Just as labor leaders have been called upon to act in one era while still bound to the loyalties, customs, and frustrations of a dying one, so, in reverse, labor experts have been trained in the ways of the new, but are summoned to function each day under the shadows of the old. And like labor leaders, they also suffer from psychological impairments that dull their effectiveness in dealing with barking men of action who must be brought around to consider them as partners.

Most important, they accept from the bottom of their souls the labor leaders' notions of superiority through long suffering in labor's cause. It is obvious that they would never have chosen the labor movement as a career unless they were idealists. They are therefore naturally prone, especially when they first enter the unions' sanctuaries, to accept the semi-religious doctrine of their secondary moral roles. Even after their eventual and inevitable disillusion about the labor leaders' infallibility and ascendant merit in all fields of human conduct, they cannot quite break away from the movement, especially those who are most idealistic or who have little iron in their systems. This condition creates, therefore, a tendency for the law of the survival of yes-men to operate. It is largely they who stay on in the expert jobs. Those with independent turns of character and mind leave and bear prosperously the scorn (reserved in all of history for apostates) that labor heaps upon them when they become vice-presidents in charge of labor relations. But at least these revolters secure for themselves the opportunity of utilizing their fullest capacities in the employ of industry or government.

Also of leading importance is the fact that labor experts are not usually trained, before they enter the service of labor, in the intricacies of a political way of life. Perhaps, too, by temperament they are stripped of this rare trait of personality so necessary for survival in the labor movement. By the time the experts learn the political tricks (if they can learn them), it is usually too late for at least two reasons. Either they have already antagonized their superiors and are on the way out, or they have already established such a pattern of subservient behavior that a fundamental change would be regarded by their employers as treason.

Labor experts today are undoubtedly the creatures of labor leaders in the deepest sense: their attitudes and actions are created by those who command them. Unless labor leaders metamorphize themselves into a new breed of men, labor experts can never exert the kind of frankly acknowledged partnership that the very future of the labor movement demands. Sometimes I think that it would be well if all labor experts banded together and refused to serve the house of labor except on a basis of dignity, honor, and partnership. But their bosses, we know, and not they, are the men who make revolutions. In this sense, labor leaders are superior beings, and perhaps labor experts are right in their psychological, if not always vocal, admiration. There are, even today, a few labor-expert Hopkinses to labor-leader Roosevelts, yet the health of the desk brigade is not psychically sound. The disease, I fear, originated in the front offices where labor leaders sit shouting orders into long-distance telephones.

MAURICE F. NEUFELD

7. Can Labor and Intellectuals Work Together?

Labor has ample reason for eying "intellectuals" and the universities askance. The record of the middle class, including that section of the middle class who teach and do research in our colleges and universities dominated by business money and ideas, has not been such as to inspire the confidence of labor. In general, social scientists have sold their talents to the highest bidders; those bidders have been, directly or indirectly, business corporations; the problems on which the latter wanted work done were problems in which business corporations were interested, and social scientists have, for the most part, worked at such partial problems in the name of "objective research."

This state of affairs has not in all cases resulted from deliberate choice on the part of the social scientists. The academic world is a competitive hierarchy in which men struggle to get ahead. Their training for the

Ph.D. has involved at least six years of education beyond high school, plus the back-breaking period of research and writing on the dissertation. In some eastern colleges and universities, the young instructor who is not canny enough to "marry money" starts at a disadvantage. He begins at a modest salary in a world that expects him to be both a scholar and a gentleman. How and where he lives, how his wife dresses, how she entertains— these and many other criteria applied by the "faculty wives" (a competitive hierarchy dominated by the older, better-off wives of department heads and full professors) largely determine his fate as a "gentleman." The other criterion, his scholarship, is determined by another footrule. This measure is, especially in the universities and graduate schools, the man's research output.

In the nineteenth century, "research" meant mainly sitting in one's study writing books. To an increasing degree since then and especially since World War I, research has involved field work and statistical computation. These cost money. Where does the money come from? In general, educational institutions have not kept pace with their demands upon social scientists for productive research by providing the needed funds. Where they or the endowed foundations do provide funds, the cautious conservatism of trustees and university elder statesmen tends to allocate funds to "safe" research. This situation not only operates against the approval of funds for "questionable," i.e., "radical," research, but it operates to select "safe" men for promotion and even discourages candidates for the Ph.D. from selecting "dangerous" topics (likely to prejudice their job-finding) for their dissertations.

All of this is simply the educational phase of the general problem of all institutions in democracy living within the belly of capitalism. And such education and its research output are not surprisingly something less than labor would wish. We live in a society in which "money makes the mare go" and it is not surprising that as research has become more and more empirical and therefore expensive, research men, requiring output for advancement, have done those jobs for which funds were available. Even men with strong democratic interests and considerable independence of spirit find themselves faced with the difficult choice between no funds for research and doing research the market will buy; and they rationalize the latter alternative by the hope that it will yield incidental bits and pieces relevant to labor and other unorthodox issues.

Confronted with this situation, labor tends to throw in the sponge and to give up trying to get research help from university people. More than that, there is a general mood of active suspicion of academic people who want to "work with labor." There are ample grounds for this attitude, but it does not make sense when applied indiscriminately.

The fact is that we have moved along into an era in which, from now on, both business and labor will fight increasingly with the help of research. Table-pounding in conferences and congressional hearings is giving way to briefs supported by accurate—and expensive—fact-finding. Big business is prepared to spend "what it takes" to finance research, and big labor is being forced to match business' blue chips for research with those of its own. Some of the more urgent studies organized labor will do itself in its growing research departments. Business will not confine itself to its own research bureaus, but will also take its problems and money to the research men wherever the latter may be found. Since labor is, for reasons already stated, on the short end of this matter of access to research men and their data, failure by it to utilize available manpower, to be found here and there throughout the academic world, hurts nobody so much as itself. Over the long pull, it means also that labor is losing the seed corn of able young graduate students that would develop around those academic men who might work on problems of direct interest to labor.

If, therefore, research is increasingly a thing that has to be paid for, labor will do well not to interpret this relationship too narrowly. Two points are important here: (1) The kind of academic man who resists the pull of conventional problems and business money is likely to do so in part because he has somewhat more than average interest in things like "democracy" and "the social relations of science." He is not, therefore, so likely to be capable of being bought and paid for. (2) The academic professional who does work at unorthodox problems unpopular with his middle-class environment is highly vulnerable to charges of partisanship and unscientific bias or superficiality in performing his research. Not surprisingly, he is more vulnerable on these grounds than is his colleague whose bias is enlisted in the cause of business. All of this means that, if labor is to use academic research men and their students, labor must be prepared to respect them as scientists and not merely to use them as hired men.

Is organized labor prepared to do this? Can union officialdom "take" the steady scrutiny of science? The research director in a powerful union known to the writer frankly states that he defines his role simply as limited to implementing the policies the top men in his union elect to follow—*i.e.*, he gets the facts they need to make *their* cases. Without insisting upon absolutes, one may still say that such a role is considerably less than satisfactory for the research man.

At this point, the veteran trade union man picks up his hat in disgust, remarking: "Just like I told you—you can't work with these professors. They don't know what the score is."

Here one faces the fact that politics, including trade union politics, and scientific research are two different things. Both functions have to be carried on, but labor will ruin its own case if it assumes that the labor research man is merely the handyman of the labor politician. Nor is it an answer to point to the fact that not a few social scientists who have worked for business have been content to implement uncritically the political ends of the business system.

Let's grant most of the charges that labor levels at the men who work in universities. Let's face the fact that many academic people do not know what the score is, and as middle-class people would be timid in facing it if they did know it. Let's also face the fact that there are, scattered through the American university world, *some* professors who are primarily concerned with trying to find out what the score is, who regard that as the thing society pays them to do. Some of these men recognize the importance of labor and of labor's own problems and want to work on these problems, and around these men are larger numbers of selected graduate students who also are beginning to realize that there is a job of work to do in the field of labor research. These people do not want to "high hat" labor, for it is out of their interest in and respect for labor that they turn toward problems in labor's field. Does it make sense for labor to "high hat" them?

Over the long pull, a larger issue is involved in the potential relations of American organized labor and academic intellectuals. This issue concerns not what academic people are after, but what organized labor itself is after. This is no ordinary time in which we are living, and some intellectuals who are prepared to work with labor are concerned as to whether union officialdom itself is aware of the magnitude of the issues democracy faces. It is probable that liberal capitalist democracy's straddle between private economic power and democratic political power cannot persist. State and economy in industrial society are being forced into permanent merger for mutual strength and protection. This sharpens the issue within each nation as to who shall control the government. And I mean *control*; for the focus is moving beyond competitive efforts to influence government action on isolated issues, because both industry and labor are making new demands for built-in stability, and only continuous control can yield that. The choices ahead seem to be narrowing to but two optional directions of movement: toward a big-business-controlled state with a business version of welfare and with democracy sharply diminished; *or* toward democratic socialism with private business power replaced by a democratic planning state.

If organized labor and academic intellectuals join hands, the question is sure to arise: where does labor stand as regards such larger questions? Is American labor thinking today beyond the restricted limits of traditional liberal capitalist democracy? Does it assume, in the light of current developments here and abroad, that capitalism is a durable system, and that big capitalism intends democracy? What is labor's version of democracy, and to whom does it apply besides labor itself? Is labor's strategy viewed as riding the tail of big-business' kite, accumulating, as did German labor before Hitler, increasing concessions from management? Does it assume that labor can become an equal partner within capitalism? Or is it content to become a "kept" junior partner? Does labor think it can defeat increasingly organized and alert big-business power at the polls and then go on to create a thoroughgoing democratic version of welfare? And when labor "thinks" in answer to questions like these, is it labor that is thinking or only the top labor bureaucracies?

Here again labor union presidents may pick up their hats in disgust. This time the professors are—of all things—"too radical"!

Again, however, the fact has to be faced that the situation we confront involves not merely politics, but also stubborn facts. If labor and academic intellectuals work together, clashes are sure to arise. The labor man will accuse the intellectual of "trying to think too far ahead," and the intellectual will charge the union leader with "playing ostrich." Maybe the intellectual can't "take it" in such a situation, but he is prepared to try. But what worries him is: "Can labor take it?"

ROBERT S. LYND

8. "No Mean-Sized Opportunity"

Labor leaders shy at the word "intellectual." It makes them feel uneasy. Yet there are men in and around the unions who can't very conveniently be called anything else. Intellectuals are people who are pretty well educated and who spend their time using that education in talking and writing, and sometimes thinking, about various problems. They are always trying to find problems, and the problems they deal with do not have to be "theirs."

Most men are geared into a job with rather fixed duties. But many intellectuals have jobs that allow them to be a little freer. You will find them doing all sorts of work in order to earn a living, but one job you are not very likely to find intellectuals doing is running labor unions in the United States. Nevertheless, many pro-labor intellectuals have ideas about how labor unions ought to be run. This is the center of the problem.

We must distinguish at least four types of intellectual, who in one way or another are concerned with trade unions and their leaders. These four differ in the kinds of skill they possess and in the relations they have to the policy-making decisions made by union leaders. Each type tends to have different aims so far as labor unions are concerned; in trying to achieve these aims, they tend to use different means; and each of them tries to influence the policy-making leaders of the trade unions.

1. The first type of intellectual—*the official or the active member of a radical or third party*—has been in and around unions since unions began in this country. Labor leaders are not only aware of this type, but many of them tend to generalize their experience with him, and to think of all intellectuals as being the same.

The radical-party intellectual naturally follows the "line(s)" of his party in working within unions. He is not usually skilled in research techniques. He turns toward the factory workers and the unions in which they are organized. He is out to gain power within the unions by organizing "party cells" or developing party followers within various locals and plants, quite often directed against the majority leadership of the union. And he does so in the name of an ideology.

Sometimes he operates at quite a distance from the organized source of power, thus trusting the magic of his own speech and the "spontaneous will of the class-conscious worker" to win out in the end. As a *party* intellectual, however, he actually directs struggles for power within unions: He acts as a publicist and a politician within the union.

2. Labor leaders have been using *professionally trained intellectuals* as staff members for some time now. They have had to. Big business and big government have employed such men, and the unions have had to follow suit in order to do battle in the way battle is now done.

The union staff intellectual of this type may be a research or educational director, an economist, or a lawyer. He is concerned with the week-to-week problems the labor leader faces, and which he is to help solve. And in his business relations with the leader, the staff intellectual tries to influence the leader by presenting phases of a problem that the leader himself does not see. The staff intellectual tries to spot problems in advance and, by setting them up in one way rather than in another, he often does exert some influence over the leader. To have influence on policy, he has to be an expert in spotting and in presenting concrete problems that are in line with those in which the leader is interested but which go somewhat beyond the range of the leader's own perception. He is often a man quite skilled in research; but such power to influence affairs as he may possess depends upon the leader's attitude toward him and his proved usefulness.

This personal dependency on the leader means that the staff intellectual is typically in a quite insecure position. The caution with which such men proceed when policy-relevant issues arise is an aspect of the strong tendency among them to become technicians rather than all-around men of ideas. For they are trusted, and their advice is considered only insofar as they do not go too far beyond the leaders' range of interests and values. Insofar as they do not go beyond these limits, staff intellectuals act as technicians implementing laid-down policy rather than as direct influencers of policy.

3. Such influence as *the intellectual who works in a government agency that deals with labor unions* may have on union policy comes from his governmental position and not from his character as an intellectual or his skill as a research man. He follows the "line(s)" of government policy in dealing with the unions. He deals out rights and privileges in whichever way he thinks the law holds or allows. He tends to be an economic technician

with legally defined restrictions upon his thinking and research. Most labor leaders are now well acquainted with such types, and know how they work.

4. Not many labor leaders know the fourth species of intellectual—the *free-lance researcher*—and certainly they are not aware of what he can do for them and for labor unions. The facts are that such intellectuals have not been around very long and insofar as their skills have been used by power groups, they have largely been used in the service of big business, and not in the service of labor.

The free-lance research intellectual is "free-lance" only so far as labor unions, government agencies, and political parties are concerned. He is not usually an employee of any of these three, although he may drift in and out of all of them. He is perhaps most often a college professor in some social science department; but he may also be a journalist, or perhaps more likely, a research technician for one of the mass media or for their adjuncts. By definition, however, he has no constant foothold in the institutions of labor or in institutions that continuously deal with the unions.

During the last decade or so, American social science has made research advances that are of tremendous practical relevance to the problems the unions now face. The fact that should be stressed about this fourth type of intellectual is that he is very highly skilled in these newer research techniques. However, the free-lance research intellectual who is pro-labor is not usually "merely a technician." Very often he is also an all-around idea-man, whose research imagination is enlivened by the problems of labor.

Such intellectuals have virtually no influence on the policy makers in labor unions, and the simple reason for this is that they have no power within the union and no means of influencing it from without. They are highly skilled and autonomous—and powerless; they are pro-labor, and they want to work in the service of labor, but somehow they seldom do.

Intellectuals and Policy Making

The free-lance is not only powerless, he is often quite naïve about the kind of power needed to influence a labor leader. Such intellectuals do not see that the policy maker in a union has hold of a kind of power, and that this power also has hold of the policy maker. And so the intellectual often fumbles around with uninformed admonitions and is frustrated when nobody pays any attention to what he says.

Neither knowledge alone, nor experience alone, leads to the power of policy making in a trade union. And certainly, such power is not often influenced by admonition or the force of logic. Power in a union is determined by voting strength, by manipulation of influence, by strategic and intimate association, or by control of political machines within and among the unions.

The "third party" intellectual and the union staff intellectual are usually much wiser about the facts of power than is the free-lance intellectual. The party intellectual usually knows that the only way he can influence the union official is to organize a power base on party members in specific locals or plants. And it may take the staff intellectual years before he begins to influence policy. The free-lance intellectual seems to want to influence policy without paying the price the third-party professional, the staff intellectual, or the labor leader himself is willing to pay. He often seems to think he can get it by the sheer magic and wisdom of his talk. But that just does not happen.

The pro-labor research man who does not have power and does not intend to get it the hard way ought to recognize his limitations. If he is also a political-minded person, he must recognize that this alone does not make him a politician. And he should get the difference clear: he has no power with which to act; the trade union leader does. If the intellectual doesn't like that situation, then he ought either to go all out for leadership and shoulder the responsibility this stand involves, or go about his own work as best he can. But he ought not to expect power to be given to him by labor leaders.

The labor leader often puts his question to the intellectual in this way: "Why should you who have *no practical experience* in my line of work try to sell your ideas and your research to me? And why should you try to tell me what I'm supposed to do?" These are fair questions. The labor leader has the power to ask them that way. I think they are really at the bottom of many labor leaders' objections to free-lance intellectuals, and I want to tackle them. First, what does the term "practical experience" mean today in the field of labor action?

Practical Experience and Social Research

A lot that labor leaders say about their own practical experience and its absence among intellectuals is pretty much beside the point. Trade union leaders are constantly grappling with day-to-day facts and realities, but most of the facts they know and the realities they handle are specific facts and realities. These facts wouldn't necessarily be true for other industries or other unions or for similar unions in other types of communities. You have to "locate" and organize specific experiences in order to make further *practical* use of them. And many labor leaders don't see these particular experiences as just *one* kind of experience faced by one kind of wage worker or one kind of labor leader in one kind of situation. Thus his very experience often blinds the labor leader to facts and realities that happen to lie outside his immediate domain.

In his emphasis on practical experience, the labor leader often assumes that to be of practical value, experience has to be direct; that it must be had by the man who is going to make use of it. That is the notion of experience the labor leader assumes every time he uses "practical experience" to beat the intellectual over the head. But this is not an adequate notion of practical experience. The figures in an industrial census or in an opinion poll or in a content analysis of a radio script are based on experience just as much as is the report of a business agent to a union vice-president. Today, the really effective labor leader has to know how to get and to use such systematic and over-all experiences. And these are the kinds of experience that the research intellectual has the skill to organize for practical use.

The practical experience available in any one union no longer provides the most practical guide line for running even that one union. The scene in which any union operates today is big and highly complicated. And this means that a wider and bolder and more skillful approach is necessary on the part of the leader than what he can derive from his personal and direct experience. That is true economically and socially and politically—as a lot of labor men have learned during the late war.

The union leader must act on the basis of experiences that are much broader than any one leader usually has had, for three reasons:

1. The opposition—organized big business—operates more and more on over-all plans and over-all labor policies. And those plans and policies are more and more based on *research*.

2. With its improved public relations methods and techniques, organized big business is telling the public a rounded-out story, not just the story of one plant or one industry. And these public relations are based on careful *research*.

3. The government's intervention in business-labor affairs has become very wide in scope and very decisive in character. And government, too, has its arsenal of *researched* facts.

The labor leader is up against these three big facts, and to meet them *practically*, he is going to have to adopt more over-all plans and long-range policies. He is in a situation where the *only* practical approach to his problem is to go beyond his immediate practical experience. The experience of one man in one type of spot must be enlarged by the kind of thinking that draws upon the experiences of many men, each trying to get out of particular spots. And that kind of experience and thinking is another name for good research.

The U.S. worker has to depend upon the labor leader to see that his interests are protected. That puts a large responsibility upon the labor leader, and he cannot shoulder up to that responsibility all by himself. He has got to learn to use the experience of the research man if he wants to do the job in the optimum manner.

The skills of the research intellectual of which I speak have not been and are are not now used in the service of labor. They have been used and are being used more and more in the service of big business. Now, you can make that statement in two ways: "in the *service* of business" or "in the service of *business*." If you agree that you can say it the first way, then you have to admit that the research intellectual is no mere impractical theorist. Make no mistake about it: the intellectual who is the kept man of big business usually earns his keep: he *is* of service to business. If you say it the second way, you have to ask yourself why the research intellectual serves business. There are a lot of reasons, of course, but there are plenty of intellectuals now serving business who don't want it that way, who would gladly place their skills in the service of labor.

Part of this situation is the fault of the labor leader who shies away from the intellectual. And yet, it's not really his fault either. He simply doesn't know what the intellectual can do; he doesn't know how to use the intellectual to the top advantage of his organization. If labor leaders have been much slower than big businessmen to see the value of the research intellectual, the latter has been deficient in making out a convincing case for his latent, unused ability to render valuable service. He ought not to neglect this exercise in self-revealment. It is the key to no mean-sized opportunity.

C. WRIGHT MILLS

9. SUMMATION OF STAFF DISCUSSION

We have discussed the place of the professional intellectual in the union movement. By that term we designate the men and women who are engaged on a staff of a union or who carry on professional-intellectual work related to union activity by some other arrangement as to authority and compensation.

Our discussion has been concerned with two facets of the problem: (1) what are the chances of the professional worker on the union staff to do a creditable job in the field of his particular competence; and (2) what is he to do, or is he to do anything, besides executing his assignment properly so that he may stay employed and advance in status and pay?

Our general assumption is that the intellectual entering union service has more at stake than employment, the rate of compensation and tenure; that being on the job in the union also means being "in the fight," that of course in a broad social sense; and consequently we have sought to define how the professional, in the union's service, is related to the "fight"; and finally, we have sought to determine what should be his orientation and ways and means of going about participating in the fight.

The professional intellectual, generally, is sought and engaged by the union to bring in his trained competence where the union leader's "inspired" competence appears to be insufficient to the needs of the situation: what, then, is he to make of his assignment? Is he to be a helper, a tool, or also a cooperating fellow-combatant? Is he to try to bring ideas of his own to bear upon the course of union policy even outside the sphere of his hired competence? He does not represent the members of the union as the union officer does. He was hired as a specialist, a civil servant. Is he to stay confined to a limited assignment, or is he to seek to broaden out the application of his hired talents to a point where "report" and "advice" take on the character of a bid for leadership?

Service Plus Purpose

Any competent management in a business enterprise will seek out ability in a minor executive and play on that ability to the advantage of the business and the benefit of the able person. Is this likely to be the case in the union? And if not, if brow-raising or even expressed displeasure meets the attempt of the hired intellectual to transgress the technical limits of his job, should he "cease and desist," or is he to keep on pushing his ideas forth if he believes he is right?

The discussion has brought forth the following points:

1. The labor union movement is increasingly in need of professional services of a steadily expanding scope. The call is for research workers, editors, attorneys-at-law, engineers, experts in legislative pressuring or lobbying, educators, publicity and public relations specialists, health and life insurance experts, finance accountants and "political actionists."

2. The basic requirement of the persons in these categories is for information and assistance to the functioning union leadership along the respective lines and areas in which the service setups are instituted. The staff person is not asked to participate in policy making. The latter is the task of the union leadership and the higher executive boards.

3. Competence is a primary qualification for a job on a union staff. Vague pro-labor sentiments or smooth talking talents are not acceptable substitutes or even likely to prove a "bargaining" advantage. Yet, keenly felt concern with labor's long-range progress to which Mark Starr referred as social idealism, and willingness to do something about it is an asset likely to contribute to eventual growth on the job. It may make the difference between mere performance of duty and an opportunity of exercising influence.

4. Although a growing number of unions realize the need of professional service setups, a very considerable number of union officers, indeed, look with mild distrust upon the intellectual called in to serve the union. Even if the intellectual is not suspected as likely to "run away with the organization," he is viewed as "immature," in a practical sense, as one who "doesn't know the score." He is not accepted into the inner circle until he proves great devotion to his job and ability to make his general competence applicable to concrete situations. By and large, "acceptance of

intellectuals" does not go along with intellectual assertiveness on the part of the staff member. Self-restraint is a virtue, however, that more often than not defeats all purpose beyond that of achieving job security.

5. Generally, the relation of the professional intellectual to the labor unions' leadership setup is still unsettled, and it remains to be seen what may be the outcome of the growing influx of trained specialists into the union movement. There is a good deal to be done on both sides to turn this aspect of technical proficiency into a social dynamic.

James B. Carey's introduction to this discussion is a cogent orientation that should be shared by all labor union leaders and administrators. But that is not the case. Mr. Carey is not in a majority among his peers when he declares: "Union staff members must be strong advocates of their point of view; they are not hired to say 'yes' to every idea the labor leader advances."

Another vital point of the problem under consideration is touched off in Mr. Carey's declaration: "They [staff members] must bring to their jobs along with technical knowledge and a knowledge of the union movement, the same willingness to sacrifice time and energy for a great cause that is demanded by union members of the union leader himself."

Generally, the staff member who takes employment in the union in preference to a job in a business setup wants a relation to "a great cause." He rarely starts out as the regulation "pie-card artist" or "pork-chopper." But how does he discern the cause back of the requisites of the professional job?

Where the Cause Is

The staff member does not, in the nature of his assignment, ride a storm or reach out for the clouds. His work is mostly intramural. He is not dealing with multitudes of people; he does not march at the head of legions. The problems on which he is to work are not posed as alternative courses in basic social conflict. He is called upon to do a research job where he is to deal with payrolls, cost figures, and marketing data—not battle cries, although his research may give substance to big words. He may be sent out lobbying, pressuring, or to argue the union case before a wage or labor relations board, or to try to break down the resistance of a publicity-hoarding newspaper manager, or to discuss a health protection or sickness indemnity program with a cold-blooded, fact-minded insurance expert.

In these and other instances in which he is likely to work at his assigned chores, he deals with staid, solid persons of this day and this social-economic setup, and no Kingdom Come nor Revolution Absolute is in sight or even remotely at stake. He will find it exceedingly difficult to see the "great cause" behind the facts-and-figures contentions at the conference table or in the wranglings of lawyers and statisticians before a government board or a congressional committee; or, for that matter, at the conference table, after the agreement is reached, with shop committees, management, and local union officers bickering over payrates, charges for lost time, "feather-bedding" rules, sick leave, adjustments of grievances. All that is important, of course, but likewise important is the struggle that the corner grocery store man is waging for survival, whether when he is threatened with the competition of other shopkeepers themselves fighting for their lives, or when the gigantic chain-store corporation is undercutting his price level and competing him out of existence to establish price monopoly. What makes the labor job socially significant?

And it happens, ever so often, that in the search for "the cause" the intellectual in unionland runs into the petty or heavy uninspiring politics that the "bigshots" and the "small fry" of the "union crowd" play, jockeying for position, cliqueing together, or knifing one another, the aim of the game being either immediate advantage or to curry favor with some higher up of the union's "top brass." The young man in search of "the cause" has the choice between devastating despair and cynicism—no great comfort.

It takes time, patience, and opportunity, unless he is trained in advance and prepared to understand, for the outsider looking in to discover that the immediate union office environment is rarely, if ever, the proper terrain in which noble impulses and self-sacrificing determination are likely to be provoked into being unless under extraordinary stimuli. The union office is not much different from other offices, and cannot be. The office is not the union. The office only registers, but neither causes nor liquidates the upsurges of the dynamics of human relations, the conflicts and the strivings of the living people whose names, numbers, and addresses are recorded in the union office files, and who are the union. At times, the verbal expression of the conflicts and solutions is made at the office even as the living, vibrant voice of the singer is heard from the recording; but the artist isn't on the phonograph table and the union isn't in the office. The office is but the union's public address; from here the union gives expression, purpose, and direction to the play of forces outside the walled container. The union is outside the office and so is the cause. Does the intellectual on the staff need an Aladdin's lamp to find it?

It was not intended that the discussion should result in a recipe for "proper" behavior for the professional entering the service of labor. The task has been to point up the problems relevant to the "staff profession," if you please; for that is what it has become, now that unions with 15 million members call for an ever greater number of professional aids.

Solomon Barkin and Mark Starr, drawing upon the experience of their respective great unions (TWUA-CIO and ILGWU-AFL) which have quite a number of professionals on their staffs, emphasize the urgency of coping with the problem. C. Wright Mills, a trail-blazer in labor research, indicates new areas of application of the professional skills of those who seek not only a job but also a purpose. And whereas Robert S. Lynd is concerned about the union officer's ability to "take it" when the staff man opens angles and vistas not readily compatible with the routinized ways of unionism, William M. Leiserson insists, however guardedly, that the staff professionals should "raise questions" all right, but had better not try to "run the union" for they are not there for the task and it is well that they aren't.

Maurice F. Neufeld is rightly convinced that many "experts" do not wish to assert themselves. And he is equally right when he says that most union officers, especially the "higher brass," do not welcome staff assertiveness. But even if that is true in more cases than not, it is not the law of the land from which there is no escape.

William M. Leiserson very aptly puts the essence of the matter when he says raise questions, but do not seek to run the union. Raising questions can be, if they aren't of the foolish variety, a very effective means of assertiveness. Solomon Barkin urges: offer advice, again and again. That is no self-effacement.

As to Partnership

Maurice F. Neufeld would have the staff member—expert, as he designates him, but the term is perhaps not always applicable—assert himself as partner with the labor leader in policy making or have the guts to quit for greener pastures. The discussion has registered no disagreement if the "partnership" idea is not stressed too powerfully. Barkin, Mitchell (for a spell of time), Starr, this chairman, all field men as it were, suffer from no mental inferiority. But they cannot help knowing that the union is the members' to make or break, not the staff's. Conceivably, the union leader may not be doing right by the union members in denying them full say-so, and possibly he is overstepping the authority implicit in his assignment, but he does have clear powers. Not so the staff member. Claiming the power of partnership with the union leadership, he is attempting an usurpation.

The psychological analysis introduced by Mr. Neufeld would make staff-leader conflict appear inevitable. The leader, suffering from inferiorities and frustrations, conditioned by the circumstances attending his rise to power, compensates himself by seeking to humiliate his intellectually superior aide. And the staff member suffers equally from frustrations conditioned by his idealism—"or he would not have gone on a labor staff" —and hence he "is naturally prone . . . to accept the semireligious doctrine of their secondary moral roles."

The labor leader and the labor expert thus psychologically dissected may claim with good ground that "the report was exaggerated." For the ingredients of this leader-expert situation are not easily compressed into the psychological analyst's catalogue of labels. The union is more than the president and his staff. There is the vast element in the equation that just won't be ignored: the union members. Whatever the formality of the democratic performance evidenced in a union, be it ever so depressed, there is an essential give-and-take in the basic operation of the thing or it wouldn't wash. There is more than statistical tables, legal authority, or editorial prowess in the leader-member relationship. There is the human element, a weighty element that is real, and the staff member is but tangential to it.

It is not perhaps an incontestable truth that being "idealistic" is synonymous with "gutlessness," or that it takes real guts to shift from labor service to a vice-presidency in a business corporation, or to a desk in a government office; or that corporation vice-presidencies carry automatic license to partnership. Indeed, vice-presidents are more often than not upper-class underdogs in corporate hierarchies, unless they have either invested heavily in the business or otherwise made themselves valuable. So, too, is the staff "expert." He does not bring along as he "joins the firm" any claim to partnership. What he carries, as competence, is initially met by the reality and the continuity of the payroll listing. His title to greater recognition gains only in the measure as he shows growing quality and interested service. It is true, the "desk brigade" could do worse than heed the Neufeld advice and make the resolution he suggests: "refuse to serve the house of labor except on a basis of dignity, honor, and partnership," and, as happens in all revolutions, settle for less than all. But if partnership in a full sense is not attainable, and not due, striving to play a part in policy determination is the objective essential to Maurice F. Neufeld's other survival conditions—dignity and honor.

There are no hard and fast demarcations among service, advice, and leadership: one grows into the other without a formal declaration. Participation in leadership is not a right for the staff member but a grant on merit, and it lives on a continuous delivery of greater service only. That places the "hired intellectual," as I see it, in a preferred status.

The Essential Sense of Orientation

The professional intellectual who is not pleased with doing only a competent job but also wishes "to be in the fight" for an objective beyond the evils of the day will not be disillusioned by the petty and the seemingly aimless and incidental disturbances that appear to occupy the center of the union stage. To that end, his equipment for the job needs to include a broad sense of orientation, ability to discern the over-all significance in the flow of events, to spot the general in the specific, to see the far-flung objective in the pursuit of arm's-length immediate aims. The greedy, the loud-mouthed, the mentally inert, and the seekers of preferment are the warp and woof of the movement's substance—as are the pioneers and the martyrs, the master strategists and the self-denying rank-and-file builders, those whose overwork and undernourishment were the cornerstones upon which the power edifice has been built, and who, in no small measure, continue crucial. The bad and the good are all in the total setup. He who enters the field, if he is not to get lost or to be unnerved, needs to possess or develop a sense of the whole, akin to what the social-historian brings to his task as he studies the course of a process through the labyrinthine chaos of contradictory and inaccurate accounts of happenings, or personalized and biased testimony of contemporaries, and statesmen's doubletalk. This prescription is not likely to make the labor staff member's life very easy, but it may make it interesting—which is no small prize to snatch from living.

J. B. S. HARDMAN

APPENDICES

Appendix I

.Whether strikes are considered good or bad, or, discarding value judgments, whether they are regarded as persistent concomitants of modern industrial life, it is obvious that they have become an integral part of the institutional pattern of labor relations in the United States.

Certainly about one aspect of the nature of strikes there can be no controversy among informed persons. The strike, for better or for worse, is as natively American as our Revolutionary forefathers, the covered wagon, and apple pie. The first recorded strike occurred in 1741. Since this strike was a protest by master bakers in New York against the municipal regulation of the price of bread, labor historians tend to date the first genuine strike of wage workers from 1786 when printers in Philadelphia struck for a minimum wage of $6.00 a week. Even if the ancestry of strikes is traced from this later date, the American strike must be recognized as older, by a few years, than the Constitutional Convention itself.

Despite the indigenous character of strikes, the right to strike, along with the right to organize and to bargain collectively, suffered manifold vicissitudes until the enactment of the Wagner Act in 1935. Today, however, the right to strike (although it does not enjoy absolute protection under the law in all cases since there are important qualifications to this right) is recognized.

The accompanying Table of *Work Stoppages in the United States, 1881-1950* presents available statistics concerning strike action in this country. A glance at these figures will reveal that at no time in recent years did the number of workers involved in strikes, as compared to the total number employed, ever reach the proportion recorded for 1919, 20.8 per cent. The comparable figure for 1946, when the headlines of the nation seemed to indicate that our industrial foundations were collapsing, stands at 14.5. Even in this same year the number of man-days idle (because of work stoppages), as compared to the total estimated working time, achieved a percentage of only 1.43.

Since the right to strike (with qualifications) is now accepted in all

WORK STOPPAGES IN THE UNITED STATES, 1881-1950 [1]

	Work Stoppages		Workers Involved		Man-Days Idle		
Year	Number	Average Duration (in calendar days)	Number (in thousands) [2]	Per cent of Total Employed [3]	Number (in thousands)	Per cent of Estimated Working Time [4]	Per Worker Involved
1881—	477	[5]	130	[5]	[5]	[5]	[5]
1882—	476	[5]	159	[5]	[5]	[5]	[5]
1883—	506	[5]	170	[5]	[5]	[5]	[5]
1884—	485	[5]	165	[5]	[5]	[5]	[5]
1885—	695	[5]	258	[5]	[5]	[5]	[5]
1886—	1,572	[5]	610	[5]	[5]	[5]	[5]
1887—	1,503	[5]	439	[5]	[5]	[5]	[5]
1888—	946	[5]	163	[5]	[5]	[5]	[5]
1889—	1,111	[5]	260	[5]	[5]	[5]	[5]
1890—	1,897	[5]	373	4.2	[5]	[5]	[5]
1891—	1,786	[5]	330	3.6	[5]	[5]	[5]
1892—	1,359	[5]	239	2.5	[5]	[5]	[5]
1893—	1,375	[5]	288	3.2	[5]	[5]	[5]
1894—	1,404	[5]	690	8.3	[5]	[5]	[5]
1895—	1,255	[5]	407	4.4	[5]	[5]	[5]
1896—	1,066	[5]	249	2.8	[5]	[5]	[5]
1897—	1,110	[5]	416	4.3	[5]	[5]	[5]
1898—	1,098	[5]	263	2.6	[5]	[5]	[5]
1899—	1,838	[5]	432	3.9	[5]	[5]	[5]
1900—	1,839	[5]	568	4.9	[5]	[5]	[5]

Year		Number of work stoppages		Workers involved (thousands)		Percent of total employed		
1901—	5	3,012	5	564	5	4.6	5	5
1902—	5	3,240	5	692	5	5.4	5	5
1903—	5	3,648	5	788	5	5.9	5	5
1904—	5	2,419	5	574	5	4.3	5	5
1905—	5	2,186	5	302	5	2.1	5	5
1906-1913	5	5	5	5	5	5	5	5
1914—	5	1,204	5	5	5	5	5	5
1915—	5	1,593	5	5	5	5	5	5
1916[2]—	5	3,789	5	1,600	5	8.4	5	5
1917—	5	4,450	5	1,230	5	6.3	5	5
1918—	5	3,353	5	1,240	5	6.2	5	5
1919—	5	3,630	5	4,160	5	20.8	5	5
1920—	5	3,411	5	1,460	5	7.2	5	5

[1] The data contained in this Table are based upon four sources published by the Bureau of Labor Statistics, United States Department of Labor: (a) for the years 1881-1915, *Handbook of Labor Statistics*, 1941 edition, Volume 1 (Bulletin No. 694), page 320; (b) for the years 1916-1948, *Work Stoppages Caused by Labor-Management Disputes in 1948* (Bulletin No. 963), page 1; (c) for the year 1949, *Work Stoppages in 1949—Final Data* (mimeographed, undated), page 2; (d) for the first six months of 1950, *Work Stoppages in the First Six Months of 1950* (mimeographed), November 9, 1950, page 3.

[2] The exact number of workers involved in some strikes which occurred during the period 1916 to 1926 is not known. The missing information is for the smaller disputes, however, and it is believed that the totals here given are approximate.

[3] "Total employed workers" as used here refers to all workers except those in occupations and professions in which there is little if any union organization or in which strikes rarely, if ever, occur. In most industries it includes all wage and salary workers except those in executive, managerial, or high supervisory positions or those performing professional work the nature of which makes union organization or group action impracticable. It excludes all self-employed, domestic workers, agricultural wage workers on farms employing less than six, all Federal and State Government employees, and officials (both elected and appointed) in local governments.

[4] Estimated working time was computed for purposes of this table by multiplying the average number of employed workers each year by the prevailing number of days worked per employee in that year.

[5] Not available.

WORK STOPPAGES IN THE UNITED STATES, 1881-1950 [1] (cont'd)

Year	Work Stoppages		Workers Involved		Man-Days Idle		
	Number	Average Duration (in calendar days)	Number (in thousands) [2]	Per cent of Total Employed [3]	Number (in thousands)	Per cent of Estimated Working Time [4]	Per Worker Involved
1921—	2,385	5	1,100	6.4	5	5	5
1922—	1,112	5	1,610	8.7	5	5	5
1923—	1,553	5	757	3.5	5	5	5
1924—	1,249	5	655	3.1	5	5	5
1925—	1,301	5	428	2.0	5	5	5
1926—	1,035	5	330	1.5	5	5	5
1927—	707	26.5	330	1.4	26,200	0.37	79.5
1928—	604	27.6	314	1.3	12,600.*	.17	40.2
1929—	921	22.6	289	1.2	5,350	.07	18.5
1930—	637	22.3	183	.8	3,320	.05	18.1
1931—	810	18.8	342	1.6	6,890	.11	20.2
1932—	841	19.6	324	1.8	10,500	.23	32.4
1933—	1,695	16.9	1,170	6.3	16,900	.36	14.4
1934—	1,856	19.5	1,470	7.2	19,600	.38	13.4
1935—	2,014	23.8	1,120	5.2	15,500	.29	13.8
1936—	2,172	23.3	789	3.1	13,900	.21	17.6
1937—	4,740	20.3	1,860	7.2	28,400	.43	15.3
1938—	2,772	23.6	688	2.8	9,150	.15	13.3
1939—	2,613	23.4	1,170	4.7	17,800	.28	15.2
1940—	2,508	20.9	577	2.3	6,700	.10	11.6

1941—	4,288	18.3	2,360	8.4	23,000	.32	9.8
1942—	2,968	11.7	840	2.8	4,180	.05	5.0
1943—	3,752	5.0	1,980	6.9	13,500	.15	6.8
1944—	4,956	5.6	2,120	7.0	8,720	.09	4.1
1945—	4,750	9.9	3,470	12.2	38,000	.47	11.0
1946—	4,985	24.2	4,600	14.5	116,000	1.43	25.2
1947—	3,693	25.6	2,170	6.5	34,600	.41	15.9
1948—	3,419	21.8	1,960	5.5	34,100	.37	17.4
1949—	3,606	22.5	3,030	9.0	50,500	.59	16.7
1950⁶—	2,023	⁵	1,060	⁵	24,200	⁵	⁵

[1] The data contained in this Table are based upon four sources published by the Bureau of Labor Statistics, United States Department of Labor: (a) for the years 1881-1915, *Handbook of Labor Statistics*, 1941 edition, Volume 1 (Bulletin No. 694), page 320; (b) for the years 1916-1948, *Work Stoppages Caused by Labor-Management Disputes in 1948* (Bulletin No. 963), page 1; (c) for the year 1949, *Work Stoppages in 1949—Final Data* (mimeographed, undated), page 2; (d) for the first six months of 1950, *Work Stoppages in the First Six Months of 1950* (mimeographed), November 9, 1950, page 3.

[2] The exact number of workers involved in some strikes which occurred during the period 1916 to 1926 is not known. The missing information is for the smaller disputes, however, and it is believed that the totals here given are approximate.

[3] "Total employed workers," as used here refers to all workers except those in occupations and professions in which there is little if any union organization or in which strikes rarely, if ever, occur. In most industries it includes all wage and salary workers except those in executive, managerial, or high supervisory positions or those performing professional work the nature of which makes union organization or group action impracticable. It excludes all self-employed, domestic workers, agricultural wage workers on farms employing less than six, all Federal and State Government employees, and officials (both elected and appointed) in local governments.

[4] Estimated working time was computed for purposes of this table by multiplying the average number of employed workers each year by the prevailing number of days worked per employee in that year.

[5] Not available.

[6] The figures for 1950 pertain to the first six months of 1950 and are preliminary and subject to revision. They are based upon figures issued by the Bureau of Labor Statistics, United States Department of Labor, November 9, 1950.

democratic countries as an inalienable one, and, conversely, since strikes
are never tolerated under totalitarian regimes, the figures in this Table
might be regarded as a record of the price which a dynamic, democratic
society pays (sometimes unwillingly) for industrial freedom.[1]

---

[1] For a comparative study of strike statistics and an analysis of the factors involved
in differing national strike patterns, see Arthur M. Ross and Donald Irwin, "Strike
Experience in Five Countries, 1927-1947: An Interpretation," *Industrial and Labor
Relations Review*, April, 1950.

M.F.N.

Appendix II

The Extent of Collective Bargaining in the United States

The latest material now available on the extent of collective bargaining in the United States dates from 1946. There has not been a large increase in union membership since that date. Therefore, it is felt that the data presented below, while not current, will provide an approximate indication of the pattern of collective bargaining today.[1] (Ftntes. 1 & 2 on p. 537.)

Approximately 14.8 million workers were employed under conditions determined by written collective-bargaining agreements in 1946, an increase of a million workers compared with 1945. The workers covered by agreement represent 48 per cent of the 31 million [2] engaged in occupations in which the unions have been organizing and endeavoring to obtain written agreements. The percentage covered was the same in the previous year, but fewer workers—approximately 29 million—were eligible for agreement coverage in 1945. Nonmanufacturing industries accounted for much of the increase in employees eligible for agreement coverage.

About 7.9 million production workers in manufacturing were covered by union agreements in 1946 (69 per cent of those employed) compared to 8 million (67 per cent) a year earlier. In the nonmanufacturing industries 6.9 million workers, or 35 per cent of the potentials were employed under union agreements. Part of the decrease in total coverage in the manufacturing industries can be accounted for by changes in employment in such industries as aircraft and shipbuilding, in which a large proportion of the workers are covered by union agreement. In the nonmanufacturing industries the increase in the number of workers can be accounted for by higher employment in such industries as construction, in which the proportion of workers covered by collective bargaining is very high.

The extent of union agreement coverage in the various manufacturing and nonmanufacturing industries is shown in Table 1. Because each group covers a range of 20 per cent, it is possible for the proportion of covered workers within an industry to increase several per cent and still remain within the same group. During 1946 the percentage of workers covered by agreements in the dairy products industry increased enough to bring

Proportion of Wage Earners Under Union Agreements in 1946

Manufacturing Industries

80-100 per cent	60-79 per cent	40-59 per cent	20-39 per cent	1-19 per cent
Agricultural equipment.	Book and job printing and publishing.	Baking.	Beverages, nonalcoholic.	(None.)
Aircraft and parts.	Coal products.	Chemicals, excluding rayon yarn.	Confectionery products.	
Aluminum.	Canning and preserving foods.	Flour and other grain products.	Cotton textiles.	
Automobiles and parts.	Dyeing and finishing textiles.	Furniture.	Dairy products.	
Breweries.	Gloves, leather.	Hosiery.	Silk and rayon textiles.	
Carpets and rugs, wool.	Machinery, except agricultural equipment and electrical machinery.	Jewelry and silverware.		
Cement.	Millinery and hats.	Knit goods.		
Clocks and watches.	Paper and pulp.	Leather, luggage, handbags, novelties.		
Clothing, men's.	Petroleum refining.	Lumber.		
Clothing, women's.	Railroad equipment.	Paper products.		
Electrical machinery.	Steel products.	Pottery, including chinaware.		
Furs and fur garments.	Tobacco.	Shoes, cut-stock and findings.		
Glass and glassware.	Woolen and worsted textiles.	Stone and clay products, except pottery.		
Leather tanning.				
Meat packing.				
Newspaper printing and publishing.				
Nonferrous metals and products, except those listed.				
Rayon yarn.				
Rubber.				
Shipbuilding.				
Steel, basic.				
Sugar.				

Nonmanufacturing Industries

80-100 per cent	60-79 per cent	40-59 per cent	20-39 per cent	1-19 per cent
Actors and musicians. Airline pilots and mechanics. Bus and streetcar, local. Coal mining. Construction. Longshoring. Maritime. Metal mining. Motion-picture production. Railroads. Telegraph. Trucking, local and intercity.	Radio technicians. Theater–stage hands, motion-picture operators.	Bus lines, intercity. Light and power. Newspaper offices. Telephone.	Barber shops. Building servicing and maintenance. Cleaning and dyeing. Crude petroleum and natural gas. Fishing. Hotels and restaurants. Laundries. Nonmetallic mining and quarrying. Taxicabs.	Agriculture.[3] Beauty shops. Clerical and professional, excluding transportation, communication, theaters, and newspapers. Retail and wholesale trade.

[1] The succeeding paragraphs are taken from Bulletin No. 909, United States Department of Labor, Bureau of Labor Statistics, *Extent of Collective Bargaining and Union Recognition, 1946*, June 24, 1947, pp. 1–2. (Philomena Marquardt was in immediate charge of assembling the information.)

[2] This estimate of 31 million includes all wage and salary workers except those in executive, managerial, and some professional positions, but excludes all self-employed, domestic workers, agricultural wage workers on farms employing less than six persons, Federal and State Government employees, teachers, and elected or appointed officials in local governments.

It should be noted that the number of workers covered by union agreements is not the same as union membership. Except under closed or union-shop conditions, agreements cover nonmembers as well as members employed within the given bargaining unit. On the other hand, some union members may be working in unorganized plants and many civil-service employees and teachers are members of unions but are not employed under the terms of bilateral written agreements.

[3] Less than 1 per cent.

it from the 1-19 per cent into the 20-39 per cent category. Chemicals, excluding rayon yarn and the paper products industries, moved from the 20-39 per cent into the 40-59 per cent group. Canning and preserving foods, dyeing and finishing textiles, and leather gloves increased in the proportion covered so that they shifted from the 40-59 per cent to the 60-79 per cent column. Moving from the 60-79 per cent into the 80-100 per cent group were the electrical machinery and the rayon yarn industries.

M.F.N.

Appendix III

1892   *Eight Hour Law.* Act of August 1, 1892, as amended 1913, and Act of June 19, 1912, as amended 1917, 1940, U.S. Code 1946, Title 40, Sections 321-326; 1950 Reorganization Plan No. 14, effective May 24, 1950, 15 F.R. 3176. This law limits to 8 a day the hours of employment of laborers and mechanics employed by the Government or by contractors or subcontractors upon public works of the United States or the District of Columbia or by contractors or subcontractors in connection with the performance of any contract to which the United States, any Territory, or the District of Columbia is a party, except contracts for transportation, communications, supplies, materials or articles as may be bought in the open market, or the construction or repair of levees or revetments necessary for protection against floods, provided, however, that any contractor or subcontractor may employ such persons more than 8 hours a day if time and one-half is paid for overtime.

1908   *Federal Employers' Liability Act.* April 22, 1908, as amended on August 11, 1939. It covers every employee of common carriers by railroad, employed in interstate or foreign commerce, since such employees are not subject to state workmen's compensation acts. The Jones Act of 1920 made the provisions of the Liability Act applicable in suits for injury and death of seamen.

1926   *Railway Labor Act.* Act of May 20, 1926, as amended 1934, 1936, and 1940, U.S. Code 1940, Title 45, Sections 151-164 and 181-188. The Railway Labor Act governs the labor relations of railroads and airlines and their employees. The act makes it the mutual duty of

---

[1] Material in this list has been quoted or paraphrased from information contained in *Federal Labor Laws and Agencies,* Bulletin No. 123, August 1950, United States Department of Labor, Bureau of Labor Statistics. The *Prentice-Hall Labor Course 1951* has also served as a useful guide.

carriers and employees to make and maintain agreements, guarantees and provides for the exercise of labor's collective bargaining
rights, and prescribes methods for the settlement of various types
of disputes.

1927   *Longshoremen's and Harbor Workers' Compensation Act.* Act of
March 4, 1927, as amended through 1949, 33 U.S. Code 1946, Title
33, Secs. 901-950; Reorganization Plan No. 19, effective May 24,
1950, 15 F.R. 3178. The law covers all maritime employment on the
navigable waters of the United States (including dry docks), except
the master or member of the crew of a vessel. The principal employments covered are longshoremen and ship repairmen while on
board a vessel. The law has been extended to other employments,
including all private employment in the District of Columbia and
employment outside the United States in the service of contractors
with the United States at military, air, or naval bases or on public
works.

1931   *Prevailing Wage Law (Davis-Bacon Act).* Act of March 3, 1931,
as amended 1935 and 1940, U.S. Code 1946, Title 40, Section 276a,
as affected by Act of May 14, 1947, U.S. Code 1946, Supp. III, Title
29, Section 251, and 1950 Reorganization Plan No. 14, effective
May 24, 1950, 15 F.R. 3176. The Davis-Bacon Act requires payment
by contractors and subcontractors of wage rates determined by the
Secretary of Labor to be prevailing in the locality on construction,
alteration, or repair of public buildings or public works performed
under contract with the Federal Government or the District of
Columbia.

A similar requirement is made in connection with construction of
hospitals and airports by State agencies using Federal funds under
the Hospital Survey and Construction Act of 1946 (60 Stat. 1041,
42 U.S.C. sec. 291h) and the Federal Airport Act of 1946 (60 Stat.
170, 49 U.S.C. sec. 1114), respectively, in connection with the construction of rental housing projects insured by Federal funds under
certain sections of the National Housing Act, as amended (48 Stat.
1246, 53 Stat. 807, 12 U.S.C. sec. 1715c), and in connection with the
development of projects assisted under Title I (slum clearance and
community development) and Title III (low rent public housing)
of the Housing Act of 1949 (63 Stat. 419, 430, 42 U.S.C. sections
1459 and 1416 (2)).

1932   *Anti-Injunction Act (Norris-LaGuardia Act).* Act of March 23,
1932, U.S. Code 1946, Title 29, Sections 101-115, as modified by
Act of June 23, 1947, U.S. Code 1946, Supp. III, Title 29, Section
141 (Labor Management Relations Act, 1947). The Anti-Injunction
Act declares it to be a public policy that the worker shall have *full*

freedom of association, self-organization, and designation of repre-
sentatives of his own choosing to negotiate the terms and conditions
of his employment, free from employer interference in these or
other concerted activities for mutual aid or protection.

The act defines and limits the powers of the Federal courts to
issue injunctions in labor disputes, in conformity with this policy.

1933   *United States Employment Service Act (Wagner-Peyser Act).* Act
of June 6, 1933, U.S. Code 1946, Title 29, Sections 49-491, Act of
1947, Public Laws Nos. 40 and 646, Eightieth Congress, 1949 Reorganization Plan No. 2, effective August 20, 1949, 3 CFR, 1949
Supp., p. 136. Reorganization of the United States Employment
Service on a cooperative basis with the states, thereby establishing
a permanent and national system of public employment offices. This
system was further expanded in the Social Security Act of 1935
when Employment Offices were connected closely to the administration of unemployment compensation.

1933   *National Industrial Recovery Act,* Section 7a, 48 Stat. L. 195, was
the predecessor of the main provisions of the National Labor Relations Act of 1935, supplemented by the National Labor Board,
August 5, 1933 to July 9, 1934 (strengthened by executive orders
of December 16, 1933 and February 1 and February 23, 1934).

1934   *Anti-Kickback Law (Copeland Act).* Act of June 13, 1934, as
amended 1949, U.S. Code 1946, Supp. III, Title 18, Section 874,
Title 40, Section 276-c; 1950 Reorganization Plan No. 14, effective
May 24, 1950, 15 F.R. 3176. The Copeland Act imposes a penalty
on any person who by force, intimidation, threat of dismissal, or by
any other means, induces any person employed on public construction work, or on work financed in whole or in part by Federal
funds, to give up any part of his compensation.

1934   *Anti-Racketeering Law (Hobbs Act).* Act of June 18, 1934, as
amended 1946, U.S. Code 1946, Supp. III, Title 18, Section 1951.
The anti-racketeering law makes it a felony to *obstruct, delay, or*
affect commerce, or the movement of any article or commodity in
commerce, by robbery or extortion.

1934   Executive order of June 29 creating "First" National Labor Relations Board, pursuant to Public Resolution No. 44, approved by
President on June 19, 1934. Board functioned from July 9, 1934
until May 30, 1935.

1935   *National Labor Relations Act (Wagner Act).* July 5, 1935, c. 372,
49 Stat. 449, U.S. Code, Title 29, Sections 151-166.

1935 *Social Security Act.* Act of August 14, 1935, as amended through August 1950, U.S. Code 1946 and Supp. V, Title 42, Ch. 7, Subchs. I-V, IX-XII; Internal Revenue Code, Ch. 9, Subchs. A and C, P. L. 719, Seventy-ninth Congress, P. L. 379, P. L. 492, and P.L. 642, Eightieth Congress, P. L. 734, Eighty-first Congress. The Social Security Act provides for two Nation-wide systems of social insurance to protect wage earners and their families against loss of income due to unemployment, old age, and death:

1. Old-age and survivors insurance, an all-Federal system, operated by the United States Government through the Social Security Administration and approximately 480 field offices; and

2. Unemployment insurance, a Federal-State plan under which each State sets up its own law and State administrative agency, with the Federal Government paying all operating costs.

Supplementing these, the Social Security Act provides for public assistance on a Federal-State plan with monthly cash payments to needy old people, needy dependent children, the needy blind, and needy persons who are permanently and totally disabled.

The act also provides grants to the States for maternal and child-health services, services for crippled children, and child-welfare services, to supplement State and local funds available for such programs.

1935 *Railroad Retirement Act.* Acts of August 29, 1935, and June 24, 1937, as amended 1940, 1942, 1946, and 1948 U.S. Code 1940 and Supp. IV, Title 45, Sections 215-228r. The Railroad Retirement Act provides retirement benefits up to $144 a month to aged and disabled railroad workers and survivor benefits to their families. The act is administered by the Railroad Retirement Board, composed of three members appointed by the President, with one member recommended by the carriers and one by the railway labor organizations.

The act applies to employees of railroads, sleeping car and express companies, other companies performing services in connection with railroad transportation, and certain railway labor organizations.

1936 *Anti-Strikebreaker Law (Byrnes Act).* Act of June 24, 1936, as amended 1938, U.S. Code 1946 Supp. III, Title 18, Section 1231. The anti-strikebreaker law makes it a felony to transport in interstate commerce any person employed for the purpose of interfering by force or threats with: a. Peaceful picketing during any labor dispute affecting wages, hours, or working conditions; or b. Exercise of employee rights of self-organization or collective bargaining.

The act applies to persons who wilfully transport others or cause others to be transported, and to persons knowingly transported for these purposes. It does not apply to common carriers.

1936 *Walsh-Healey Public Contracts Act.* Act of June 30, 1936, as amended 1940 and 1942, U.S. Code 1940 and Supp. IV, Title 41, Sections 35-40, as affected by Portal-to-Portal Act of 1947, Public Law 49, Eightieth Congress. The Public Contracts Act sets basic labor standards for work done on United States Government contracts exceeding $10,000 in value for materials, articles, supplies, equipment, or naval vessels. It applies to all employees, except office and custodial, engaged in or connected with the manufacture or furnishing, including the fabrication, assembling, handling, or shipment of materials, supplies, articles, or equipment required under such contracts.

1938 *Fair Labor Standards Act (Wage and Hour Law).* Act of June 25, 1938, as amended 1939, 1940 and 1949, U.S. Code 1946, Supp. III, Sections 201-217, as affected by the Act of May 14, 1947, U.S. Code 1946, Supp. III, Title 29, Sections 251-262, and 1950 Reorganization Plan No. 6, effective May 24, 1950, 15 F.R. 3174. The Federal Wage-Hour Law is administered by the Secretary of Labor through the Administrator of the Wage and Hour Division. This law has been in effect since 1938 and sets minimum wage, overtime, and child-labor standards which apply to employees engaged in interstate commerce or in the production of goods for interstate commerce. Application does not deal in a blanket way with industries as a whole, but is determined on the basis of an employee's activities.

The basic standards set by this Act (which was amended in many respects, effective January 25, 1950) provide:

A minimum wage of 75 cents an hour (except for industries in Puerto Rico and the Virgin Islands, where lower rates may be set by administrative wage orders, based upon recommendation of an industry committee equally representing labor, management, and the general public);

Time and one-half pay for overtime after 40 hours worked in a workweek (except as otherwise specifically provided);

A minimum age of 16 for general employment (except for occupations declared hazardous by the Secretary of Labor, where a minimum age of 18 applies, and certain occupations outside of school hours, where the minimum age is 14).

1938 *Railroad Unemployment Insurance Act.* Act of June 25, 1938, as amended 1939, 1940, 1942, 1946, and 1948, U.S. Code 1940 and Supp. IV, Title 45, Sections 351-367. The Railroad Unemployment Insurance Act provides for the payment of unemployment and sickness benefits (including maternity benefits) to qualified railroad workers under a uniform nation-wide system. This act also authorizes the operation of free employment offices in which the activities are primarily directed toward the reemployment of claimants for unemployment benefits. The act is administered by the Railroad Retirement Board.

    The act applies to employees of railroads, sleeping car and express companies, other companies performing services in connection with railroad transportation, and certain railway labor organizations.

1941 *Defense Bases Act.* Act of August 16, 1941, as amended, 42 U.S.C. 1651. Extends the Longshoremen's and Harbor Workers' Compensation Act to employees of private employers engaged in public work outside the continental United States under contract with the Federal Government.

1946 *Unlawful Practices in Radio Broadcasting (Lea Act).* Act of April 16, 1946, U.S. Code 1946, Title 47, Section 506. This act prohibits certain types of coercive labor practices in the radio industry. These practices usually consist of attempts to compel a radio station to employ more persons than are needed or to restrict the use of recorded or other types of programs. The act makes it a criminal offense for any person to use or threaten to use force, violence, intimidation, duress, or other means to compel any radio station to employ or agree to employ more employees than are needed, or to make any extra payment in place of hiring additional employees.

    It is also made unlawful to use similar pressures to compel a radio station to pay or agree to pay more than once for services performed or to pay for services which were not performed, or to refrain from broadcasting noncompensated, noncommercial, education and cultural programs or programs of foreign origin. In addition, the act prohibits similar pressure upon any person to exact payment for using recordings, transcriptions, reproductions, or other materials used for broadcasting, to restrict the manufacture and use of recordings and transcriptions, or to exact payment for using transcription of programs previously broadcast and paid for.

1947 *Labor Management Relations Act (Taft-Hartley).* Act of June 23, 1947, Public Law 101, Eightieth Congress, U.S. Code 1946, Supp. III, Title 29, Sections 141-167.

1947   *Federal Mediation and Conciliation Service.* Labor Management
       Relations Act of 1947, Title II, Sections 201-205, U.S. Code 1946,
       Supp. III, Title 29, Sections 171-175. The Federal Mediation and
       Conciliation Service was established to assist labor and management
       in arriving at peaceful settlements of labor disputes. Generally, the
       Service attempts to mediate and conciliate if the dispute threatens
       a substantial interruption of interstate commerce. When a dispute
       would have only a minor effect upon interstate commerce and a
       State or local agency is available, the Federal Service usually does
       not offer its mediation and conciliation facilities.

                                                                   M.F.N.

Appendix IV

THE SAMPLE—FOR *Leaders of the Unions* (pp. 24-47)

[*Leaders of the Unions* is Report No. 2 of a research project on the characteristics of American labor leaders, started in 1941. Report No. 1, developed with the assistance of Mildred Atkinson of the University of Maryland, was published in the *Public Opinion Quarterly* (Summer 1945); the third report, *The New Men of Power* (New York: Harcourt, Brace & Co., Inc., 1948) embodies most of the statistics presented here. For further references, see that volume.]

In Appendix Table 1 we have mapped out the population of labor leaders from which our sample is drawn. The table was constructed from lists provided by the AFL and the CIO. These lists varied about eighteen months in dates, but in general our reference date is the late spring and early summer of 1946.

APPENDIX TABLE 1

WHO IS INCLUDED—A MAP OF AFL AND CIO LEADERSHIP

Position	AFL	CIO	Total
National			
Presidents	99	38	137
Secretaries	85	38	123
State			
Presidents	50	36	86
Secretaries	48	32	80
City Heads	756	222	978
Total	1,038	366	1,404

Three waves of questionnaires were sent out. A questionnaire went to each of the CIO leaders represented in Appendix Table 1. Questionnaires were also sent to every national and state officer of the AFL.[1] Since there were so many AFL city heads, we addressed a questionnaire to every other leader in this group. We sent out a total of 1,026 questionnaires. The first wave was put into the mails on May 8, 1946; the second, mailed on May 24, was sent to all those who had not responded to the first mailing; the third, mailed on July 3, was sent only to certain categories of personnel. In accompanying letters, anonymity was guaranteed the individuals who responded. In the end we obtained a sample of 410 usable returns from these categories, or 40 per cent of the number we had attempted to poll.

The response was larger among the CIO leaders than among those of the AFL. It is therefore technically difficult to combine the returns from these two union blocs. We could, of course, do so by weighting our sample, but we do not think that is wise. It is more convenient, and just as interesting for our purposes, to treat our data as two samples: one of the AFL and one of the CIO. In Appendix Table 2 we compare the samples and the populations in the AFL and the CIO by the various positions involved. This comparison shows rather clearly that the sample obtained does not differ significantly from the population as a whole in any single category of personnel.

APPENDIX TABLE 2

THE POPULATION AND THE SAMPLE OF LABOR LEADERS BY POSITIONS

Position	AFL		CIO	
	Population	Sample	Population	Sample
National				
Presidents	15%	13%	10%	12%
Secretaries	13	14	10	9
State				
Presidents	8	6	10	15
Secretaries	7	12	9	10
City Heads	57	55	61	54
Total cases (100%)	(660)	(232)	(366)	(178)

If we knew even a few facts about the labor leader population as a whole, we could then compare our sample with these facts about the population. But all we know, apart from the position, is the region of the country in which the leaders reside. In Appendix Table 3, we compare our sample with the population of leaders in terms of the four major regions

[1] The Independent unions were also polled, but our sample was too small for exact study. See, however, pp. 46-47.

of the country. It will be seen that the two distributions do not differ in any significant way.

APPENDIX TABLE 3

THE POPULATION AND THE SAMPLE OF LABOR LEADERS BY REGIONS

Region	AFL		CIO	
	Population	Sample	Population	Sample
North East	23%	25%	37%	31%
North Central	40	41	36	38
South	24	20	16	17
West	13	14	11	14
Total cases (100%)	(660)	(230) *	(366)	(177) *

* Two of the AFL men and one CIO man are from outside the U.S. proper: Canada and Alaska.

Even when we break down the geographical distribution into finer units, we find that the sample is a very close regional approximation to the population that it represents.

There is another way we can check our sample. Our sample might be biased by the fact that the labor leaders who refused to respond to our questionnaire are in some significant way different from those who did answer. How can we find out if this is so, when we know nothing about the universe we are interested in?

One technique is frequently used in mail surveys: one can assume that the investigator had been satisfied with the replies he had received as a result of his first attempt. In that case all who had not answered in the first wave would be nonresponders. We have some information about some of these nonresponders, however, for some of them answered waves two and three. We shall therefore compare those who replied to wave one with those who replied in waves two and three. If they are different, we have reason to believe that our sample is not a representative one.

Mail polls often tend to be biased by education: the more educated people respond more frequently than those who are less educated. On this point we have no definitive check; we cannot check the educational composition of *all* labor leaders with the educational composition of the labor leaders in our sample, for nobody knows the educational composition of all labor leaders. Yet the range of education within our sample is quite wide, and there are very great differences between the AFL and CIO leaders with respect to education. Should any educational bias exist, it would, of course, affect the absolute levels of our leaders. But the relative standing between the AFL and the CIO with respect to education might still be valid. And we do have the check provided by the data obtained in the different waves. We can compare the educational level of those who responded to our first mailing with the educational level of those who responded to the later waves.

APPENDIX TABLE 4

COMPARISON OF WAVES OF RESPONSE OF AFL AND CIO LEADERS BY EDUCATION

Education	AFL		CIO	
	Wave 1	Waves 2 & 3	Wave 1	Waves 2 & 3
Some High School or less	56%	62%	43%	42%
High School Graduate or more	41	35	54	54
No answer	3	3	3	4
Total cases (100%)	(127)	(105)	(130)	(48)

In Appendix Table 4, comparison is made by educational levels. Dividing the respondents into two groups—low education consisting of those with some high school or less, and higher education, those who are high school graduates or more—very little difference is found between the two waves. In the AFL, a slightly higher proportion of the less educated responded in the second wave (62 per cent as against 56), but this difference is not statistically significant. In the CIO, there is also no significant difference.

We have followed this same procedure of comparing the answers to the first wave with those to the later waves in connection with a number of the opinion questions that we asked the labor leaders. In no case do the answers differ significantly between the first and the later waves.

It is known that mail polls tend to be biased in terms of amount of interest in the subject and knowledge of the topic.[2] In the present case, however, the questions concern the labor leader's career and personal opinions. It is therefore a sample of interested people. Speculatively, we do not know why some of them should be any more interested in such topics than others. Such evidence as is available and especially the fact that there are no significant differences between those who answered an initial request and those who answered only after additional prodding gives us a fair degree of confidence in our sample of labor leaders.

[2] See E. A. Suchman and B. McCandless, "Who Answers Questionnaires," *Journal of Applied Psychology*, December 1940, pp. 753 ff.

C.W.M.

Index of names and organizations

No reference is made here to authors listed in bibliography (pp. 111-112); to political party candidates in tables on pp. 110-111; or to persons mentioned in the Beaumont letter and footnotes on pp. 135-141.